The Presidency of Andrew Jackson

AMERICAN PERSPECTIVES

EDITED BY BERNARD WISHY AND
WILLIAM E. LEUCHTENBURG

ARNOLD, MATTHEW: *Civilisation in the United States and other writings, edited by Warren Susman

BAKER, RAY STANNARD: Following the Color Line: *American Negro Citizenship in the Progressive Era,* edited by Dewey W. Grantham, Jr. TB/3053

BANCROFT, GEORGE: *The Origin of the American Revolution, from "The History of the United States," edited by Edmund S. Morgan

BERMAN, HYMAN (ed.): *The Rise of American Labor: *A Reader*

BOURNE, RANDOLPH S.: War and the Intellectuals: *Collected Essays, 1915–1919,* edited by Carl Resek. TB/3043

BRANDEIS, LOUIS D.: *Other People's Money, edited by Richard M. Abrams

BROOKS, VAN WYCK: *The Wine of the Puritans and other early writings, edited by Claire Sacks

BURKE, EDMUND: On the American Revolution: *Selected Speeches and Letters,* edited by Elliott Robert Barkan. TB/3068

CAIRNES, J. E.: *The Slave Power, edited by Harold Woodman

FOX, DIXON RYAN: The Decline of Aristocracy in the Politics of New York, 1801–1840, edited by Robert V. Remini. TB/3064

FREEHLING, WILLIAM W., (ed.): The Nullification Era: *A Documentary Record* TB/3079

GILMAN, CHARLOTTE PERKINS: Women and Economics: *A Study of the Economic Relation Between Men and Women as a Factor in Social Evolution,* edited by Carl N. Degler. TB/3073

HAMILTON, ALEXANDER: The Reports of Alexander Hamilton, edited by Jacob E. Cooke. TB/3060

HUNDLEY, DANIEL R.: *Social Relations in our Southern States, edited by William R. Taylor

HUNTER, ROBERT: Poverty: *Social Conscience in the Progressive Era,* edited by Peter d'A. Jones. TB/3065

HUTCHISON, WILLIAM R. (ed.): *Protestant Liberalism and American Culture since the Civil War: *A Reader*

JACKSON, HELEN HUNT: A Century of Dishonor: *The Early Crusade for Indian Reform,* edited by Andrew F. Rolle. TB/3063

JEFFERSON, THOMAS: Notes on the State of Virginia, edited by Thomas P. Abernethy. TB/3052

LANKFORD, JOHN (ed.): Captain John Smith's America: *Selections from His Writings* TB/3078

LIBBY, O. G.: *The Geographical Distribution of the Vote of the Thirteen States on the Federal Constitution: 1787–1788, edited by Lee Benson

MACLAY, WILLIAM: *The Journal of William Maclay, United States Senator from Pennsylvania, 1789–1791, edited by Bernard Mason

MCLOUGHLIN, WILLIAM G. (ed.): *The American Evangelicals: *A Reader*

OSOFSKY, GILBERT (ed.): *Three Slave Narratives

PARTON, JAMES: *The Presidency of Andrew Jackson, from the "Life of Jackson," edited by Robert V. Remini

PIKE, JAMES S.: *The Prostrate State: *South Carolina under Negro Government,* edited by Robert F. Durden

RAUSCHENBUSCH, WALTER: Christianity and the Social Crisis, edited by Robert D. Cross. TB/3059

REID, WHITELAW: After the War: *A Tour of the Southern States, 1865–1866,* edited by C. Vann Woodward. TB/3066

RHODES, JAMES FORD: *The Coming of the Civil War (Vol. I); The Civil War (Vol. II): an abridgment of "The History of the United States from the Compromise of 1850," edited by Grady McWhiney

RIIS, JACOB: The Making of an American, edited by Roy Lubove. TB/3070

SCHUYLER, ROBERT L.: *The Constitution of the United States: *An Historical Survey of Its Formation*

SHINN, CHARLES HOWARD: Mining Camps: *A Study in American Frontier Government,* edited by Rodman Paul. TB/3062

STEFFENS, LINCOLN: *The Struggle for Self-Government, edited by Joel A. Tarr

TARBELL, IDA M.: The History of the Standard Oil Company: *Briefer Version,* edited by David M. Chalmers. TB/3071

TINDALL, GEORGE B. (ed.): A Populist Reader. TB/3069

TOURGÉE, ALBION W.: A Fool's Errand: *A Novel of the South during Reconstruction,* edited by George M. Fredrickson. TB/3074

WEYL, WALTER E.: The New Democracy: *An Essay on Certain Political and Economic Tendencies in the United States,* edited by Charles B. Forcey. TB/3042

* *in preparation*

JAMES PARTON

The Presidency of Andrew Jackson

Edited with an Introduction
and Notes by
ROBERT V. REMINI

Harper Torchbooks
Harper & Row, Publishers
NEW YORK, EVANSTON, AND LONDON

THE PRESIDENCY OF ANDREW JACKSON

Printed in the United States of America.

This book was originally published as the major part of Volume III of *The Life of Andrew Jackson* by Mason Brothers, New York, 1860.

First HARPER TORCHBOOK edition published 1967 by Harper & Row, Publishers, Incorporated, 49 East 33rd Street, New York, N.Y. 10016.

Library of Congress Catalog Card Number: 67-21559.

CONTENTS

NOTE

Numbers in the margin refer to the editor's notes to the Torchbook edition, which are to be found in a group starting on page 462.

INTRODUCTION TO THE TORCHBOOK EDITION

BY ROBERT V. REMINI

JAMES PARTON, the distinguished nineteenth-century American biographer, was that *rara avis* among professional historians: a financially successful author. He enjoyed such popularity during his own lifetime that he was able to support himself and family quite comfortably from book royalties and the fees from his magazine and newspaper articles. At the top of his form he earned somewhere between six and eight thousand dollars a year,[1] a rather impressive sum for a writer at any time and especially during the last century. His rise to this giddy height came rapidly once he found his true literary direction, but like many other writers he first sampled a variety of careers before deciding on the one that eventually brought him fame and money.

Parton was born in Canterbury, England, on February 9, 1822 to James and Ann (Dearling) and brought to the United States by his widowed mother in 1827, along with two younger sisters and an older brother. The family settled in New York City, and within a year after their arrival Mrs. Parton married William Henry Pillow, also from Canterbury and the proprietor of a straw-hat pressing business. For several years young James attended a public school in the city, after which he transferred to an academy

[1] Milton E. Flower, *James Parton, the Father of Modern Biography* (Durham, North Carolina, 1951), p. 4.

in White Plains. He could not afford to go to college, but an appointment as librarian and instructor at another academy in White Plains enabled him to continue his study and reading. At twenty-three he became an American citizen. Not much later he moved to Philadelphia where, with his sister's brother-in-law, he opened an English Classical School. Unfortunately, after a respectable beginning, the school suddenly folded, the consequence of resentment against Parton's religious views. Disenchanted with formal religion, Parton had absorbed strong agnostic sympathies. Since he was a man of the strictest intellectual integrity he would not hide his beliefs, and when parents learned of his "aberration" they hurried their children from his school.

Upon his return to New York City where he found another teaching position, Parton began to divert himself by writing short essays. Shy and slightly embarrassed by his pretension, he signed the pseudonym "Kent," to his first article which he submitted to the *Home Journal,* a weekly magazine devoted to fashion, manners and taste. The essay, a rather ingenious trifle, argued from internal evidence that the recently published novel, *Jane Eyre,* bore the unmistakable stamp of a female author, a question hotly debated at the time. Since the article was just the sort of thing to delight subscribers of the *Journal,* it was published the first week of January, 1850. One of the editors, Nathaniel Parker Willis, immediately spotted Parton's journalistic talent and invited the young man to submit additional material. Pleased with this reception and anxious to indulge his writing interest still further, Parton promptly turned out an eleven-part series on "Education in New York," after which he produced a long list of articles, ranging from literature and the theatre to abolition and urban problems. So lively were his topics and so engagingly written that Willis asked Parton to join the staff as an editorial assistant at the salary of $10 per week. Without hesitation Parton resigned his teaching post and accepted the offer. For the next several years he kept the *Journal* amply stocked with sleek articles on subjects of current interest. Gradually he came to assume greater responsibility for the production of the magazine as Willis, ill and involved in a protracted lawsuit with Edwin Forrest, the actor, steadily withdrew from his editorial duties. But during the period of their close association and collaboration, Parton learned one lesson from Willis: to take infinite pains with every article he wrote or edited, no matter how inconsequential, so that the final version was tightly constructed, highly polished and smoothly flowing.

The years Parton spent grinding out essays for the *Journal* and serving as an editorial assistant were invaluable to him in shaping his literary career. But they ended abruptly. Again his sterling integrity got him into trouble. The immediate cause was a female, not an attractive female with whom he had fallen desperately in love, but a literary female, one Fanny Fern, a lady columnist, the first of that remarkable breed of women, whose right to be published in the *Journal* Parton stoutly defended. It began when the young assistant printed a few articles by Fanny, only to discover later that she was none other than the twice-wed Sara Willis Eldredge Farrington, the sister of Nathaniel P. Willis. When Willis learned of his sister's impropriety he ordered his assistant not to publish her work in the magazine. Parton refused, whereupon Willis sacked him.

So, thanks to his principles, Parton landed on the streets. Yet as any Victorian knew, such virtue would not go unrewarded. Sure enough, a short time later while dining out, a chance encounter dramatically altered his career. Lowell and Daniel Mason, two brothers in the book publishing business whom Parton had previously met through Willis, entered the restaurant and stopped to talk to the jobless writer. Naturally the talk turned to books. During the conversation Parton mentioned reading an article on Horace Greeley, editor of the New York *Tribune,* and with his unerring instinct for such things told the brothers that a book about the editor's life was certain to find a large public. A few days later the Masons ran into Parton on the street and immediately proposed that he undertake the Greeley biography himself. After some hesitation, the young writer agreed to the proposal provided that Greeley approved the venture and the Masons advanced him $750. Since a bachelor could live comfortably in New York in 1854 on $500 a year, the advance would cover the usual expenses and leave a little extra for travel and other research purposes.

Working full time and at top speed, Parton delivered a final manuscript in the autumn of 1854, barely more than six months after signing a contract. Published in December, *The Life of Horace Greeley* received generous praise from critics as an honest and eminently readable account of the famed editor. Even Greeley was pleased. More important, the book sold at a phenomenal rate, something like 28,000 copies during the first six months of publication, and its success propelled Parton further along the road of his new-found career.

A year later, on January 5, 1856, Parton married Fanny Fern and spent the next sixteen years tied in an unhappy union to a neurotic and complaining woman. At the time of the wedding the groom was thirty-four and Fanny eleven years his senior and the mother of two daughters by her first marriage. Their years together were punctuated by so many furious quarrels that Parton turned to his step-daughters for affection and to his writing for repose. He churned out articles at great speed which newspapers and magazines were delighted to publish, most of them little more than potboilers written to provide the funds he needed to research his next biography.

Under the circumstances the next biography was not long in coming. This was the celebrated *Life of Aaron Burr,* published in 1858. Critics were not as enthusiastic as they had been over the *Greeley,* faulting what they termed Parton's poor judgment about Burr and his journalistic style; nevertheless, the book proved so popular that within five years it raced through sixteen editions. But what was unique and important about the *Burr* was its highly interpretive approach to men and events. Hitherto, most biographies produced in the United States had been campaign documents of scant worth and fleeting interest.[2] Parton broke with this tradition to write a scholarly yet popular life which was sympathetic to its subject but which did not hesitate to criticize Burr whenever the author felt it was merited. The *Burr* was a significant advance in the writing of American biography.

The immediate popularity which Parton's initial books achieved was due principally to three factors. The first and most important was the felicity of his writing. His style was smooth, his narrative vigorous and swiftly moving, and his characters so excellently portrayed that they came sweeping off the pages in full dimension, all pulsing with life. Many years later when asked to explain his success, he responded almost without thinking: "Toil! Toil! Toil!" An author, he said, must have a "devouring rage" to write, enough to discipline himself for the endless hours of work and countless revisions necessary to shape a style "interesting enough to be read."[3] And Parton's style was so uncommonly "free and easy going," so apparently artless that literary critics airily dismissed it as journalistic and inelegant.

The second factor explaining Parton's popularity was his instinct for selecting topics attractive to the largest audience. Most of his biographies treat fascinating men. Besides Greeley and Burr, there were Andrew Jackson, Benjamin Franklin, Thomas Jefferson and Voltaire—men whose lives automatically generated wide reader interest.

[2] Only Washington Irving's *George Washington* and Henry S. Randall's *Thomas Jefferson* were in any way comparable to the *Burr*. Jared Sparks had attempted several biographical studies, most of which proved "justly ephemeral." Harvey Wish, *The American Historian* (New York, 1960), p. 50.

[3] Flower, *Parton,* p. 199; *McClure's Magazine,* I (June, 1893), 60.

Even his newspaper and magazine articles dealt with lively subjects. Although he frequently used these pieces to lecture his audience about corruption in government, greed in business, the evils of smoking and drinking, or the wisdom of Herbert Spencer, he carefully manipulated them to avoid losing the interest of his audience. Indeed, Parton pontificated with appalling regularity, and several of his biographies reflect his overbearing need to harangue his reader about his pet ideas; yet even at his worst he gave his ideas an ambience of appealing themes, thus shielding himself from criticism as a sermonizing crank.

The thoroughness of Parton's research was the third factor explaining his popular success. The biographies offered readers a great mass of information about their subjects, much of it anecdotal and personal. Years later, when he enumerated his six "great rules" for writing biography, he said the first rule required the author "to know the subject thoroughly."[4] Although historical studies in the middle of the nineteenth century were just beginning to acquire present-day professional form and method, Parton was extraordinarily skillful in discovering documents and books and in locating witnesses who could give him the information he required. Since extended segments of his books contain verbatim reports by eyewitnesses which are un-

[4] In a series of letters to Alfred R. Conkling written in 1888 and published in *McClure's Magazine* of June, 1893, Parton listed these six rules: "1, to know the subject thoroughly myself; 2, to index fully all the knowledge in existence relating to it; 3, to determine beforehand where I will be brief, where expand, and how much space I can afford to each part; 4, to work slowly and finish as I go; 5, to avoid eulogy and apology and let the facts have their natural weight; 6, to hold back nothing which the reader has a right to know." In the same letter Parton went on to say that he had "the great advantage of loving my subjects warmly," for he did not believe it was possible to "do justice to any human creature unless we love him." The most important quality of writing, he continued, is to be interesting. "The art is to be short where the interest is small, and long where the interest is great." Also, "it is a good *rule,*" he said, "not to have breaks in the continuity. . . . Readers are apt to skip them, however good they may be in themselves." *McClure's Magazine,* I (June, 1893), 59–62.

available in any other form, most of his biographies are important source books for their subjects.

But Parton did not routinely reprint every scrap of testimony gathered in research. He exercised sharp critical judgment in his handling of evidence and in evaluating the persons who provided it, which is one reason why his books have held up so well over the years. He himself believed a biography "should make great and free use" of letters and speeches, particularly for the individual "whose vocation it was to express himself in words. . . ."[5] Consequently, Parton's books freight substantial quotations by his subjects, sometimes to the point of excess.

Of the many biographies Parton wrote over a period of forty years the one work that demonstrates the best qualities of his literary art and his historical technique was the study that followed the *Burr*. The massive, three-volume *Life of Andrew Jackson,* published in 1859 and 1860 and running to over 2,000 pages, is such a remarkable fusion of scholarly perception and narrative skill that more than a century later it still maintains its place in the front rank of Jackson biographies. It is the single, most impressive support to the claim advanced by some historians that James Parton is the father of modern American biography.

Even before completing the *Burr,* Parton had started thinking about a life of Andrew Jackson. The political climate of the time quickened his interest. In the late 1850's the North and South were quarreling over the nature of the Union and the right of Congress to prohibit the extension of slavery into the territories. Worried men predicted a savage civil conflict and, as the danger loomed closer, some of them wondered aloud what Andrew Jackson might have done were he alive and President. Because Old Hickory had faced a similarly dangerous situation in the 1830's when South Carolina nullified the tariff laws and threatened secession, and because he had defeated the nullifiers and saved the Union, many Americans were certain

[5] *Ibid.,* 60.

Jackson could have resolved their present problems with one wave of an uplifted sword.

Andrew Jackson! The name itself still trumpeted like some great call to battle. The controversies that raged around Old Hickory when he was alive had not yet lost their power to provoke dispute. There were men in the 1850's, most of them old Whigs, who regarded all the evils in the government as Jackson's sole contribution to American politics. The rise of the ignorant, the vicious and the greedy to political influence and the displacement of educated men in office by politicians who knew only the art of massing bodies at the polls, these, it was said, were the General's gifts to his country, these the consequences of Jacksonian Democracy. Obviously, a life of Old Hickory published at this time would generate keen interest.

His own curiosity aroused, Parton began making preparations to write a full-scale biography by setting money aside to finance the necessary research. As he turned to the essential task of collecting books, documents and information, he encountered a series of problems. First of all, a number of men who had been very close to Jackson were still living, including former President Martin Van Buren, Chief Justice Roger B. Taney, Major William B. Lewis, Amos Kendall and Francis P. Blair. Although they could furnish valuable information if they chose, many of them proved to be suspicious, uncooperative and deliberately misleading. Some of them were supposedly writing their own histories of the period and were therefore unwilling to share their information or documents. In fact Van Buren was not only reluctant to tell what he knew but he was actively engaged in gathering documents from his friends, some of which he may have destroyed.[6] Using the

[6] In his biography of Van Buren, Holmes Alexander suggests that Van Buren burned all documents, including those loaned him by Jackson, that in any way substantiated his reputation as an intriguer. Holmes Alexander, *The American Talleyrand* (New York, 1935), p. 422. James S. Bassett in his *The Life of Andrew Jackson* (New York, 1910), p. x, agrees that Van Buren "doubtlessly destroyed" the letters

excuse that he was writing his autobiography, Van Buren asked his many correspondents to return his letters to them. Before his death Jackson had handed over a sizable packet of letters with the request that they be returned after they were copied, a request Van Buren apparently ignored.

Another problem was the availability of Jackson's own correspondence. The General, when alive, had repeatedly expressed a wish that an authoritative biography of his career be written, and there was some hope that George Bancroft, the famed politician-historian, might undertake the task. But this never materialized. Eventually Amos Kendall, the fourth auditor and postmaster general under Jackson, assumed the responsibility. To assist him in his work, Jackson loaned Kendall a large number of his private papers, and later asked him to deposit the papers with Francis P. Blair when he was finished with them. After publishing seven of a projected fifteen volumes and bringing the biography down to the end of the Creek War in 1814, Kendall lost interest in the project;[7] but instead of turning the manuscripts over to Blair, he retained some in his home and packed the rest in two large trunks which he

---

that Jackson returned to him. In working through the Van Buren Papers, now deposited in the Library of Congress, it is clear that the collection was winnowed and that a number of documents were removed. Whether those eliminated from the collection were incriminating, and whether Van Buren or his sons did the sifting is impossible to say. My own guess is that both Van Buren and his family had a hand in thinning the collection, but I do not think they systematically destroyed everything that could be judged unfavorable. What they regarded as historically important was preserved. It is interesting to note that when Van Buren's papers were presented to the Library of Congress by his heirs there were 131 letters written by Van Buren to Jackson and at least 155 letters from Jackson to Van Buren. Obviously few, if any, Jackson letters were destroyed by Van Buren.

[7] In writing his biography, Kendall made very little use of the papers Jackson had loaned him. Jackson's copy of Kendall's work is in the rare book room of the Library of Congress, the second volume of which contains a number of corrections in Jackson's own handwriting.

subsequently stored in "Jackson Hall," the old Congressional *Globe* office in Washington. Meanwhile, Jackson willed the bulk of his papers to Blair, who was supposed to use them in defense of Jackson's reputation, if and when that became necessary. Thus, when Parton prepared to research his biography of Old Hickory, a large collection of manuscripts was held by Blair and Kendall who, for one reason or another,[8] refused to show them to Parton.[9]

Still another problem of research was the lack of adequate library facilities. Consequently Parton was obliged to rely on second-hand bookstore owners to alert him to available materials. In his search for books he was aided by William Gowans of New York City, "the king of the second-hand book trade in the United States," as Parton called him.[10] Gowan turned up something like two hundred books treating various aspects of Jackson's career. Few relevant works in print were overlooked. Many of these

[8] Blair probably refused to show the papers because of his desire to have George Bancroft write the biography.

[9] The dispersion and subsequent reuniting of the Jackson manuscripts makes an unusual story. Kendall's son-in-law, William Stickney, and a man named William Terrell, a Washington newspaper man, discovered the two trunks in Jackson Hall and turned them over to the Blair family. Terrell kept approximately 100 letters which he published in the Cincinnati *Commercial* in February, 1879. Most of these have since been purchased by the Library of Congress. The bulk of the Jackson Papers was inherited by Francis Blair's son, Montgomery, and later by Montgomery's children. In 1903 the manuscripts were presented by the Blair family to the Library of Congress and now constitute the major collection of Jackson Papers. Then, in 1931, the Library of Congress purchased a sizable body of Jackson's letters (usually cited as Jackson Papers, second series) from a New York dealer. These are presumed to be the letters Kendall retained in his home, but just how they came into the hands of the dealer is not known. Previously, it had been believed that they were destroyed in a warehouse fire in 1894. The Library of Congress now owns over 22,000 Jackson manuscripts, which is rather amazing considering the number of times the integrity of the collection was violated. A full account of how the manuscripts were obtained can be read in John McDonough's *The Papers of Andrew Jackson* (Washington, D.C., 1967).

[10] James Parton, *Life of Andrew Jackson* (New York, 1859), I, p. xxv.

books, naturally, were campaign horrors, hardly worth perusing, but Parton also uncovered memoirs, reminiscences, official documents, published correspondence, newspapers and magazines which furnished important first-hand information.

In his haphazard listing of these books in the first volume of his Jackson biography Parton appraised each work as he set it down. And his annotations testify to his critical approach and powers of discrimination. Campaign literature he termed "dreadful stuff, particularly when it is cold. It can not be trusted at all." A work on the lives of Madison and Monroe by John Quincy Adams merited this comment: "Mr. Adams's statements are too general and too guarded for the work to be of much biographical value. His object was rather to tell us as little as possible than as much as possible. His success was complete." Parton had one word for a book entitled *A History of the Present Cabinet.* "Nothing." David Crockett's *Life of Martin Van Buren* was aptly described as "a burlesque biography, containing truth, error, wit, sense and nonsense in about equal proportions." And, although John H. Eaton's *Life of Andrew Jackson* was properly acknowledged as the basis of all subsequent biographies, Parton singled out its major flaw: "Not designedly false, but necessarily so because written on the principle of omitting to mention every act and trait of its subject not calculated to win general approval."[11]

The publication of this annotated bibliography[12] was something new for Parton. No doubt, in part, it was a sign of his developing professionalism; in part it was also meant to publicize the thoroughness of his research. Indeed, he read so many books and pamphlets and studied so much conflicting testimony that he ended in complete confusion about his subject. At that point, he remarked in the intro-

[11] *Ibid.*, pp. vi, xviii, xix, xx, xiii.

[12] This bibliography, minus the annotations, is reprinted in this edition.

duction of the biography, if anyone had asked him about his hero he had only one response.

> Andrew Jackson, I am given to understand, was a patriot and a traitor. He was one of the greatest of generals, and wholly ignorant of the art of war. A writer brilliant, elegant, eloquent, and without being able to compose a correct sentence, or spell words of four syllables. The first of statesmen, he never devised, he never framed a measure. He was the most candid of men, and was capable of the profoundest dissimulation. A most law-defying, law-obeying citizen. A stickler for discipline, he never hesitated to disobey his superior. A democratic autocrat. An urbane savage. An atrocious saint.[13]

This string of contradictions was not Parton's final judgment on Jackson, although to some extent he never completely shook the confusion from his mind. Unfortunately, this paragraph has been reprinted over and over and made to stand as Parton's last word on Jackson.[14] As the author himself explained in the introduction to the biography it was on account of these contradictions, resulting from his reading a bewildering array of conflicting opinions, that he understood he must travel south to meet the people with whom Jackson had lived and worked in order to decide himself what kind of man he was treating.

Early in January, 1859, Parton set out on a tour in search of the real Andrew Jackson. He headed first to Washington where he interviewed a number of people, most notably Sam Houston who gave him considerable information about Rachel Jackson[15] and about the General's famous duel with Charles Dickinson. While Houston talked, Parton took notes in a brown-backed notebook, usually in the form of brief phrases, which he later transcribed

[13] Parton, *Jackson,* I, p. vii.

[14] This distortion can be found in any number of books, including my own *Andrew Jackson* (New York, 1966), p. 14.

[15] Most of the correspondence between Jackson and his wife was destroyed in a fire at the Hermitage, Jackson's home outside Nashville, Tennessee, in 1834. Jackson to Harriet Butler, June 24, 1837, C. Norton Owen Collection, Glencoe, Illinois. Because of this loss, Parton's biography is an indispensable source for Rachel's life.

into full verbatim statements. He also conversed at length with Henry R. Schoolcraft, Indian Commissioner under Jackson. Others were less cordial. The Chief Justice of the United States, Roger B. Taney, who had been Jackson's adviser, Attorney General and Secretary of the Treasury, refused all help, saying he was much too old and too busy to bother himself with Parton's project. Outwardly more cooperative was Francis P. Blair, once a member of the so-called Kitchen Cabinet and the former editor of the Washington *Globe,* who was now living in Silver Spring, Maryyand. He expressed great enthusiasm for Parton's book and promised to do everything possible to make it accurate, but he spoke of Jackson in such exaggerated terms that Parton could scarcely believe what he said. And, although he showed the author a few letters, Blair pretended to know nothing of the great mass of letters and documents he had stored away in his house. When Parton asked him to write a chapter of reminiscences to be inserted in the book, Blair found this too much trouble and by his silence signified refusal.

After a week of intensive interviewing in Washington, Parton journeyed south to the Waxhaws area on the border of the Carolinas where Jackson was born and raised.[16] He spoke with many people who claimed to remember the President as a boy and as a young law student in Salisbury, North Carolina. They regaled Parton with countless stories which, as recorded by him, constitute the most detailed information extant on Jackson's early life. From here, Parton headed west to Nashville, where he met an entire community ready to assist him wholeheartedly with his biography. Each man in town retained a small pocket of memory about Jackson and each was more than willing to empty it into Parton's book. Of great significance was the

[16] There is a minor but continuing dispute about whether Jackson was born in North or South Carolina. Parton opted for North Carolina; Jackson himself believed it was South Carolina, and this is what most historians now accept.

information he obtained from Major William B. Lewis, one of the General's oldest and most intimate advisers. Unlike Van Buren, Blair, Taney and others, Lewis cooperated unstintingly with the author, dredging his memory for facts and producing letters and documents which he obligingly loaned to Parton. Later, at the author's request, he wrote extended statements about Jackson's quarrel with Calhoun, the Eaton affair and the Bank War. Predictably his testimony emphasized his own importance in Jackson's life; and, in view of political conditions in 1859, it is not surprising that he also emphasized Jackson's nationalism and his statesmanship in facing down the South Carolina nullifiers.

Parton later visited Alabama, the scene of Jackson's Indian wars, and he probably made a quick trip to New Orleans to inspect the site of the famous battle. But nowhere else was he treated as warmly and as enthusiastically as in Nashville. The people of that city had thrust at him "manuscript letters of the General's in great numbers," he wrote, had recovered old newspapers from trunks and insisted he take them, and had voted themselves into a sort of "Committee of the Whole" which overwhelmed him with "papers, reminiscences and hospitality." As a result of the information he gathered on this trip, the confusion in his mind about Jackson disappeared, or so he said. "And thus it was that contradictions were reconciled, that mysteries were revealed, and that the truth was made apparent."[17]

Hurrying back to New York in the spring of 1859 he spilled the truth over six hundred pages, narrating Jackson's life from birth to the eve of the Battle of New Orleans. Working under the strictest discipline, he finished the first volume in the autumn of 1859. Two months later the book was released in time for the Christmas trade. According to the contract Parton signed with the Mason Brothers, he was to deliver three separate manuscripts,

[17] Parton, *Jackson,* I, pp. viii, ix.

each over six hundred pages in length and, as recompense, he would receive thirty cents per volume on the edition sold in three volumes and ten per cent on the retail price of any edition of the book in a different form.

As the year 1860 opened, a year which was to record the election of Abraham Lincoln to the presidency and the secession of South Carolina from the Union, Parton stepped up the pace of his work, anxious to complete the remaining volumes before the year ended. He appealed again to Van Buren, Blair and Lewis for help. To Van Buren, he wrote: "I do not desire to penetrate forbidden mysteries, nor publish what obligation ought to be permitted to retain. A little general conversation with you on the policies of New York, and any pleasant reminiscences of the General that you might relate at your fireside are all I desire."[18] But the seventy-seven year-old Van Buren doused him with icy silence. Lewis, naturally, was only too happy to oblige but he was flabbergasted to hear that Parton was about to publish. He could never have his account of the Jackson-Calhoun quarrel written out in time, he said; however, he was reassured by Parton that only the first volume was coming out and that with diligence he could complete the task long before the final volume was required by the printer.

Both Volume Two, which described the Battle of New Orleans and the Florida expedition and contains some of the most thrilling pages of the entire biography, and Volume Three, which begins with Jackson's first nomination for the presidency in 1823 and concludes with the General's death in 1845, were published in 1860. It was a stunning performance, an heroic writing feat in which three massive volumes were produced in little more than one year. To be sure, each volume reprints long passages of documents and letters, but Parton's accomplishment is, nonetheless, remarkable.

Publication brought immediate recognition as "the best

[18] Parton to Van Buren, November 4, 1859, Van Buren Papers, Library of Congress.

life yet written of any one of our public men.'"[19] From the start it was justly popular, but because of the Civil War it did not sell as quickly as the author and publisher anticipated. Over the years, however, it continued to find an ever-widening audience and it still commands the highest respect from scholars of the middle period of American history.

And what of the Andrew Jackson compressed within these hefty volumes? What kind of man did Parton find? The author begins by describing a rollicking, roaring, fun-loving boy of the Waxhaws country whose wild spirits resulted from his Scotch-Irish background[20] and from the fact that he was raised without a father. Later, as a frontiersman in Tennessee, Jackson was described as a man of innate dignity and bearing, pugnacious, fiery, often angry, "but most prudent when most furious," and withal a gentleman of impeccable manners. As to Jackson's military prowess, Parton was unstinting in his praise, remarking that the General and his men, "in the darkest hour this republic has ever known, enabled it to believe again in its invincibility, by closing a war of disaster in a blaze of triumph." The invasion of Florida also merited applause, but the General's administration as governor of the Florida Territory was denounced as "violent, arrogant, and disgraceful to the civilization of his country." Those who witnessed Jackson's actions in Florida in 1821, the author wrote, "beheld them with mingled wonder and disgust. All his worst qualities were inflamed by disease and disappointment. He laid about him like a madman.'"[21]

The presidential years, which this edition reprints in

[19] *Atlantic Monthly,* vii (March, 1861), 382.

[20] Parton believed strongly in the importance of a national background. "The first questions to be asked of a man are: Where, and of whom, was he born? For example: If you know fully what a *Corsican* is, you have the key to the understanding of Bonaparte. He was a Corsican above all things else, and not in the least a Frenchman. So of Andrew Jackson: He was a Scotch-Irishman." *McClure's Magazine,* I (June, 1893), 60.

[21] Parton, *Jackson,* III, pp. 685–6, 689–90.

their entirety, underwent the same critical scrutiny. At the time he was researching the biography, Parton explained: "My book will contain no *whitewash.* I am resolved to paint the general as he was, with all his faults, errors, and sins—but all told in charity.[22] And, true to his intention, Parton did parade the General's sins before the public, but he did it with kindness and a large measure of affection.[23] However, there was one sin he could not forgive. The spoils system was the single fall from grace that was absolutely abhorrent to him and for which there was no acceptable reparation. Rotation in office, said Parton, "I consider an evil so great and so difficult to remedy, that if all his other public acts had been perfectly wise and right, this single feature of his administration would suffice to render it deplorable rather than admirable." An intellectual, a liberal and a reformer who was acutely sensitive to the stupidities and wickedness of government, Parton believed the evils of his own day were traceable to the spoils system, and since Jackson was responsible for advancing the system he lashed the old General unmercifully. This animus unfortunately distorts the final volume of the work. Parton was not able to think sensibly when it came to spoils. Said he: "Rotation necessitates corruption, organizes corruption, appears almost to justify corruption."

To other aspects of the Jackson administration Parton was much more sympathetic, although he fingered through each one making certain none had been contaminated by the spoils system. The removal of the Indians west of the Mississippi River and the selling of public lands to actual settlers at bare cost were recorded with approval. Because

[22] Parton to Mrs. Van Cleve, April 20, 1858, quoted in Flower, *Parton,* p. 51.

[23] Bassett in his *Life of Andrew Jackson* said that Parton was accustomed to the ridicule which educated men cast at Jackson, that he accepted their charges as facts and then "disposed of them with a smile." p. viii. Not quite. Parton was not amused, nor would he dismiss with a smile, Jackson's insistence upon the principle of rotation in office. He agreed with his contemporaries that it was a "deplorable" innovation in government.

Parton was intellectually committed to the doctrine of laissez-faire, he pronounced the Bank War commendable. "Every one is glad the bank was destroyed," he said, "but no one can admire the manner or the spirit in which the war was waged." The manner, he declared, was "arrogant, ferocious, and mean." Nevertheless, he claimed that any other kind of warfare would have been ineffectual against an institution so powerful and so well entrenched. But again, Parton found that old devil spoils at work and concluded that the politicians closest to Jackson had as their real object, "not to rid the country of a monstrous monopoly, but to add to the sum, already prodigious and alarming, of government patronage."[24]

Somewhat regretfully, Parton concluded that despite the good accomplished by Jackson "his elevation to power was a mistake on the part of the people of the United States," a mistake because the good evaporated and the evil grew more formidable and "has now attained such dimensions that the prevailing feeling of the country, with regard to the corruptions and inefficiency of the government, is despair." The trouble seemed to be that Jackson was not a "man of culture" who understood his own limitations and could listen to honest advice. "It must be admitted," Parton sighed, "that General Jackson, when his purpose was formed, when his feelings were roused was not capable of being convinced. His will tyrannized over him, over his friends, over Congress, over the Country." Put simply, Jackson was a "fighting man, and little more than a fighting man" who was never really roused to battle until a controversy became personal. "He was a thorough-going human fighting-cock—very kind to the hens of his own farm-yard, giving them many a nice kernel of corn, but bristling up at the faintest crow of chanticleer on the other side of the road."

Yet, despite these strictures, Parton freely admitted that a rare and wonderful phenomenon had taken place

[24] Parton, *Jackson,* III, pp. 692, 694, 397, 517.

during the Jacksonian era. The distance between the people and the chief executive was suddenly narrowed. Small wonder. The General, wrote Parton, "loved the people, the common people, the sons and daughters of toil, as truly as they loved him, and believed in them as they believed in him." He would have "laid down his hoary head on the block for them, and counted it gain and glory." Surely, then, the "instinctive preferences of the people must be right," Parton declared. "That is to say, the man preferred by the people must have more in him of what the people most want than any other of his generation."

Because he was so much in accord with his own generation, Jackson acknowledged that government must serve as an honest broker among men, said Parton, and that the rich were rightfully rich only when they aided the poor "as to make labor more profitable to the laborer." If the General did not grasp these ideas in an intellectual way, he had "an intuitive and instinctive perception of them." Unhappily, Jackson, who always meant well, was so ignorant of law, history, politics, science, "of everything which he who governs a country ought to know," that he was imprisoned in a cage of ignorance against which he periodically raged like a wild beast. Nevertheless, Parton cautioned, it should always be remembered that "a man whose ignorance, whose good intentions, and whose passions combined to render him, of all conceivable human beings, the most unfit for the office, was in fact elected President." Those who "concur in the opinion that the administration of Andrew Jackson did more harm than good to the country . . . should never for a moment forget that it was the people of the United States who elected him to the presidency."[25]

Although Parton later went on to write distinguished biographies of Jefferson, Franklin and Voltaire, the *Jackson* remained his finest work. The writing is uniformly spirited and vigorous. More important, Parton got his

[25] *Ibid.*, pp. 694, 695, 614, 696, 698–9, 700.

fingers around the elusive Jackson and held him long enough to take a good look. What he saw had substance, and he faithfully reconstructed his observation in his biography. The book, in other words, vividly recaptured the personality and character of Jackson in several moods and colors and displayed them to the reader against a background of high adventure and exciting history.

Parton had earnestly sought to write a "critical" biography, one that would examine all sides of its subject, both "the commendable and the deplorable." He did not always succeed in his objective because of his own preconceptions about the ideal of government, but where he managed to hold his balance he offered some remarkable insights into Jackson and the men around him, and he shrewdly analyzed many of the complicated motives behind major decisions.

Yet the biography contains serious flaws. First of all it is uneven, with the final volume weaker (although more important) than the preceding two, principally because Parton was himself in a quandary over the merits of Jacksonian Democracy. In addition the author reprints long documents which constitute tiresome digressions that halt the narrative dead in its tracks. The ponderous statements of William B. Lewis, written in 1859, should have been shortened or paraphrased or interpolated into the book. When Parton stepped aside to allow a biased witness to assume control of his story, he abdicated his responsibility as an historian.

But the worst fault of the book was Parton's relentless criticism of rotation and his insistence that this single aberration rendered the entire administration deplorable. Not only is this judgment too severe but it condemns Jackson for something he did not do. Granted the General was committed to the principle of rotation as a more democratic method of running the government, in practice his removals were by no means unusual or extraordinary. In the first eighteen months of his administration the President removed only 919 persons out of 10,093 in the federal service. For the entire eight years of his presidency he replaced little more than ten per cent of all office holders, approximately one in ten. When these figures are considered in the light of normal replacements due to death and resignation plus those dismissed for incompetence and dishonesty, the record is not that of a spoilsman. Moreover, as Parton knew quite well, Jackson did not inaugurate the system. The trouble is that Parton was not independent or original enough to break away from one of the most accepted clichés of his time. Although the General had long been saddled with the reputation of a spoilsman, Parton, as an historian, should have separated fact from fiction, especially since rotation was central to his overall interpretation of Jackson's administration.

And there are other faults in the book. Factual errors mar the entire work, which was almost inevitable in a study of this size written in such haste; fortunately, none of these errors is significant enough to mislead the reader or distort the events described. Also, Parton's affection for Henry Clay and some of the other Whigs blinds him to Jackson's superb political skills. Too often Old Hickory appears as an irascible old man, slamming around the White House and threatening to shoot or hang those who crossed him, a picture since reproduced in countless other books. Unfortunately diminished is the more meaningful portrait of Jackson as a cautious politician who did indeed personalize many quarrels but who frequently did so in order to generate popular support.

Parton, a recent student of the Jacksonian age has suggested, was (along with such other early historians as Herman von Holst, William Graham Sumner and James Schouler) a member of a "liberal patrician" or "Whig" school of history. These men, it is argued, came from European middle or upper-middle class families with backgrounds of education and public service; because their class had been ousted from political leadership by Jacksonian-style politics these patrician historians were biased against the crass democracy which had produced that leadership.[26] Whatever the merits of this interpretation with respect to von Holst, Sumner and Schouler, it has no validity when applied to Parton. For Parton's view of democracy was essentially ambivalent, and that ambivalence also affected his interpretation of Jackson. Like many intellectuals, Parton will, at one moment, excoriate the masses for their ignorance and for vulgarizing American life; but at the next moment he will turn around and extol democracy as the mark of an enlightened society. Periodically in the *Jackson,* Parton will rail against the vicious mob who "could feel, but not think; listen to stump orations, but not read . . . who could be wheedled, and flattered, and drilled by any man who was quite devoid of public spirit, principle, and shame, but could be influenced by no man of honor, unless he was also a man of genius." Then, a little later, he will announce that the "instinctive preferences of the people must be right" and that the "truly helpful men and women of this Republic have oftenest sprung from the cabin . . . and worked their way up to their rightful places as leaders of the people, by the strength of their own arm, brain, and resolution." This ambivalence which repeatedly surfaces in the text reveals that Parton was never completely free from uncertainty about Jackson or the democracy he symbolized.[27]

When the full three-volume study was finally published in 1860 men like Lewis, Blair and many other Jackson hands were grievously disappointed by what they read. Wrote Amos Kendall: "I have been reading Parton's Life of Jackson. It is a caricature of the noble old hero, and a libel upon his friends. It causes me to reproach myself for not finishing my work. . . . The honest old giant opposed the Bank of the United States from principle purely, not

[26] Charles G. Sellers, Jr., "Andrew Jackson versus the Historians," *Mississippi Valley Historical Review,* XLIV (March, 1958), 618.

[27] Parton, *Jackson,* III, pp. 119, 696, 150.

on account of some little quarrel with a branch bank in Virginia, as stated by Parton. This author has written a *caricature* of the old General, giving him occasionally a little praise for things that every one praised him for, but generally slurring it over afterwards.''[28] Naturally, these old cronies of the General wanted a biography that transformed Jackson's vices into virtues, one in which his statesmanship was accorded a merit unparalleled in the history of the nation. So uncritical were they about their friend that Amos Kendall could write at this time, ''General Jackson was as gentle as a lamb. I was very intimate with him, and never saw him in a passion, or heard him use a profane word.''[29] For his part, Francis P. Blair continued to hope that George Bancroft would take up the assignment and write a ''proper'' account of Jackson's life, but the success and lasting popularity of Parton's study probably discouraged Bancroft from engaging in any kind of competition.

Indeed, in the more than a century since the publication of Parton's *Jackson* only two biographies have been written which in any way compare to it: *The Life of Andrew Jackson* by John Spencer Bassett, published in 1910; and *The Life of Andrew Jackson* by Marquis James, a two-volume study issued as one volume in 1938. However, neither of these subsequent books, valuable as they are, match Parton's total performance as a critical historian and readable biographer. Bassett's study is an example of probing analysis, sound judgment and judicious handling of delicate pieces of evidence; but the writing is ghastly. Jackson was one of the most exciting men in American history and the Bassett book engulfed him in a torrent of turgid, lifeless, academic prose. Marquis James, on the other hand, wrote an immensely readable study in which each page shimmers with narrative power. Unfor-

[28] William Stickney, ed., *Autobiography of Amos Kendall* (New York, 1949), pp. 685–686.
[29] *Ibid.*, p. 686.

tunately, despite impressive research, James produced a one-dimensional Jackson that is highly partisan; it is a study of an intense nationalist ready to battle in defense of honor, wife, country and the rights of the American people. Unlike Parton, he does not begin to suggest the deep subtleties, the strange nuances and dark unease within Old Hickory.

Although Parton cannot rival Bassett's scholarship, he did cut deeply into his subject, sinking several layers below the surface and striking the hard bone of Jackson's personality. Much of his success was due to his determined effort to approach the General "critically," knowing that the value of his work depended on his ability "to present fairly" Jackson's "less favorable side." In recent years few historians have been so conscientiously objective in their intentions toward Old Hickory with the result that their writings tend to excessive partisanship or open hostility. Controversy still buffets the old Hero.

The absence of a critical, scholarly biography since the publication of Bassett's book in 1910 has fostered disagreement among historians about the character of Jackson and about the democracy he represented. Obviously, as long as the General himself remains elusive, Jacksonian Democracy will also be controversial.

A modern study of Andrew Jackson is badly needed. And when some future biographer finally takes up the assignment, he will discover he owes a tremendous debt to James Parton, the self-taught historian. Although Parton was overly cranky about the spoils system and indecisive about democracy, nevertheless, he tried, as he said, to tell the "truth" about Jackson, "simply, directly, boldly, charitably."[30] Despite many faults in his study, he succeeded better than most.

[30] *McClure's Magazine,* I (June, 1893), 59.

BIBLIOGRAPHY

James Parton inserted the following bibliography at the beginning of Volume I of his *The Life of Andrew Jackson.* It is reproduced here in its entirety although the individual titles have been completely rearranged to conform to modern standards of bibliographical listing. It should be noted, however, that in preparing his bibliography Parton did not include references to the manuscript letters or documents he utilized, nor to the narrative accounts by eyewitnesses prepared at his request and reprinted at appropriate places in the biography.

I. General Historical Literature

A. Histories

American Annual Register. Boston.

Caruthers, E. W., *Interesting Revolutionary Incidents.* . . . Philadelphia, 1856.

Drake, Samuel G., *Biography and History of the Indians.* . . . Boston, 1851.

Griswold, Rufus W., *The Republican Court.* New York, 1853.

Marshall, James V., *The United States Manual of Biography and History.* Philadelphia, 1856.

Monette, John W., *History of the Discovery and Settlement of the Valley of the Mississippi.* . . . 2 vols., New York, 1846.

New and Popular History of Ireland. London, 1851.

Thirty-Seven and Fifty-Seven: a brief Popular Account of all the Financial Panics. . . . New York, 1857.

Trumbull, Henry, *History of the Discovery of America.* . . . Boston, 1831.

Williams, E., and B. J. Lossing, *The Statesman's Manual.* 4 vols., New York.

Willis, N. Parker, *Famous Persons and Places.* New York, 1854.

B. Local Histories

Burnett, Jacob, *Notes on the Early Settlement of the Northwestern Territory.* Cincinnati, 1847.

Georgia Scenes. New York, 1858.

Hall, James, *Sketches of History, Life, and Manners in the West.* 2 vols., Philadelphia, 1835.

McConnel, T. L., *Western Characters.* New York, 1853.

McSkimin, Samuel, *The History and Antiquities of the County of the Town of Carrickfergus.* Belfast, 1829.

Pickett, Arthur James, *History of Alabama.* 2 vols., Charleston, 1851.

Putnam, A. W., *History of Middle Tennessee.* Nashville, 1859.

Ramsey, J. G. M., *The Annals of Tennessee. . . .* Philadelphia, 1853.

Sewall, R. K., *Sketches of St. Augustine.* New York, 1848.

Short Description of the State of Tennessee. Philadelphia, 1796.

Wheeler, John H., *Historical Sketches of North Carolina.* Philadelphia, 1851.

Williams, John Lee, *The Territory of Florida.* New York, 1837.

C. Accounts of the War of 1812

Brackenridge, H. M., *History of the late War between the United States and Great Britain.* Philadelphia, 1846.

Brown, Samuel R., *An Authentic History of the Second War for Independence.* 2 vols., Auburn, 1815.

Claiborne, Nathaniel Herbert, *Notes on the War in the South.* Richmond, 1819.

Headley, J. T., *The Second War with England.* 2 vols., New York, 1854.

Ingersoll, Charles J., *History of the Second War between the United States of America and Great Britain.* 4 vols., Philadelphia, 1852.

James, William, *A Full and Correct Account of the Military Occurrences of the Late War. . . .* 2 vols., London, 1818.

Latour, A. Lacarriere, *Historical Memoir of the War in*

the West Florida and Louisiana. . . . Philadelphia, 1816.
Walker, Alexander, *Jackson and New Orleans.* New York, 1856.

D. Travels

Baily, Francis, *Journal of a Tour in the Unsettled Parts of North America.* London, 1854.
Butler, Francis Anne, *Journal.* Philadelphia, 1835.
Chevalier, Michael, *Society, Manners and Politics in the United States.* Boston, 1839.
Martineau, Harriet, *Society in America.* 2 vols., New York, 1837.
Thackeray, William M., *The Irish Sketch-Book.* New York, 1847.

E. Collected Writings and Speeches

Brackenridge, H. M., *Letters.* Washington, 1832.
Calhoun, John C., *Works.* 6 vols., New York, 1854.
Colton, Calvin, ed., *The Private Correspondence of Henry Clay.* New York, 1855.
Correspondence between General Andrew Jackson and John C. Calhoun. . . . Washington, 1831.
Letters of General Adair and General Jackson. . . . Lexington, Kentucky, 1817.
Mallory, Daniel, ed., *Speeches of the Honorable Henry Clay.* 2 vols., New York, 1844.
Messages of General Jackson. Concord, New Hampshire, 1837,
Sedgwick, Theodore, Jr., ed., *A Collection of the Political Writings of William Leggett.* 2 vols., New York, 1840.
Webster, Daniel, *Works.* 6 vols., Boston, 1853.
Webster, Fletcher, ed., *Private Correspondence of Daniel Webster.* 2 vols., Boston, 1857.

II. Biographical Literature

A. Biographies of Jackson

Civil and Military History of Andrew Jackson. New York, 1825.
Cobbett, William, *Life of Andrew Jackson.* New York, 1834.
Dusenbery, B. M., ed., *Monument to the Memory of General Andrew Jackson.* Philadelphia, 1846.

Eaton, John Henry, *The Life of Andrew Jackson. . . .* Philadelphia, 1824.

Eaton, John Henry, *The Life of Major General Andrew Jackson.* Philadelphia, 1828.

Frost, John, *Pictorial Life of Andrew Jackson.* Philadelphia, 1847.

Goodwin, Philo A., *Biography of Andrew Jackson.* Hartford, 1832.

Jenkins, John S., *Jackson and the Generals of the War of 1812.* Philadelphia, 1854.

Jenkins, John S., *Life and Public Services of General Andrew Jackson.* New York, 1857.

Kendall, Amos, *Life of Andrew Jackson.* New York, 1844.

Lossing, B. J., "Life of General Andrew Jackson," *Harpers' New Monthly Magazine* (January, 1855).

Memoirs of Andrew Jackson. (Compiled by a Citizen of Massachusetts), Boston, 1828.

Memoirs of General Andrew Jackson. . . . (Compiled by a Citizen of Western New York), Auburn, 1845.

Sketch of the Life of General Andrew Jackson. New York, 1845.

B. Biographies of Others

Adams, John Quincy, *The Lives of James Madison and James Monroe.* Buffalo, 1851.

Authentic Biography of Colonel Richard M. Johnson. Boston, 1834.

Biography of Isaac Hill. Concord, New Hampshire, 1835.

Colton, Calvin, *Life and Times of Henry Clay.* 2 vols., New York, 1846.

Crockett, David, *The Life of Martin Van Buren.* Philadelphia, 1835.

Danvers, John Thierry, *A Picture of a Republican Magistrate of the New School . . . Thomas Jefferson.* New York, 1808.

Davis, Matthew L., *Memoirs of Aaron Burr.* 2 vols., New York, 1837.

Drake, Benjamin, *Life of Tecumseh and of his Brother, the Prophet.* Cincinnati, 1850.

Emmonds, William, *Biography of Martin Van Buren.* Washington, 1835.

Herring, James, and James B. Longacre, *The National Portrait Gallery of Distinguished Americans.* 2 vols., New York, 1834.

Horton, R. G., *The Life and public Services of James Buchanan.* New York, 1856.
Jenkins, John S., *The Life of James K. Polk.* Hudson, 1850.
Jenkins, John S., *The Life of John Caldwell Calhoun.* Auburn, 1850.
Life of Sam Houston. New York, 1855.
Mackenzie, William L., *The Life and Times of Martin Van Buren.* Boston, 1846.
Mackenzie, William L., *The Lives and Opinions of Benjamin Franklin Butler and Jesse Hoyt.* Boston, 1845.
Montgomery, H., *The Life of Major General William H. Harrison.* Cleveland, 1852.
Parton, J., *The Life and Times of Aaron Burr.* New York, 1858.
Quincy, Josiah, *Memoir of the Life of John Quincy Adams.* Boston, 1858.
Randall, Henry S., *Life of Thomas Jefferson.* 3 vols., New York, 1858.
Scott, Nancy N., *A Memoir of Hugh Lawson White.* Philadelphia, 1856.
Seward, William H., *Life and Public Services of John Quincy Adams.* Auburn, 1849.
Sketches and Eccentricities of Colonel David Crockett. New York, 1847.
Story, William W. *Life and Letters of Joseph Story.* 2 vols., Boston, 1851.
Young, William T., *Sketch of the Life and Public Services of General Lewis Cass.* Detroit, 1852.

III. Memoirs and Autobiographical Literature

Bennett, James Gordon, *Memoirs.* New York, 1855.
Benton, Thomas H., *Thirty Years' View.* 2 vols., New York, 1854.
Binns, John, *Recollections.* Philadelphia, 1854.
Bonaparte, Napoleon Louis, *Napoleonic Ideals.* New York, 1859.
Campaign of the British Army at Washington and New Orleans. By the author of the Subaltern. London, 1837.
Channing, William Ellery, *Memoirs.* 3 vols., Boston, 1848.
Cobb, Joseph B., *Leisure Labors; or, Miscellanies, historical, literary and political.* New York, 1858.
Cooke, John Henry, *A Narrative of Events . . . of the Attack on New Orleans. . . .* London, 1835.

Crockett, David, *An Account of Colonel Crockett's Tour. . . .* Philadelphia, 1835.

Darnell, Elias, *A Journal . . . 1812 and 1813.* Philadelphia, 1854.

De Oris, D. Luis, *Memoir upon the Negotiations between Spain and the United States. . . .* Baltimore, 1821.

Earle, Benson, *Recollections of an Artillery Officer.* 2 vols., London, a. 1830.

Elmwood, Elnathan, *A Yankee among the Nullifiers: an Autobiography.* New York, 1833.

Goodrich, S. G., *Recollections of a Lifetime.* 2 vols., New York and Auburn, 1856.

Hall, A. Oakey, *The Manhattaner in New Orleans.* New York, 1851.

McKinney, Thomas L., *Memoirs, Official and Personal.* New York, 1846.

Mayo, Robert, *Political Sketches of Eight Years in Washington.* Baltimore, 1839.

Memoirs of a Nullifier. Columbia, South Carolina, 1832.

Milburn, William Henry, *Ten Years of Preacher Life: Chapters from an Autobiography.* New York, 1859.

Nolte, Vincent, *Fifty Years in both Hemispheres.* New York, 1854.

Rush, Richard, *Residence at the Court of London.* Philadelphia, 1838.

Strickland, W. P., ed., *Autobiography of Peter Cartwright, the Backwoods Preacher.* New York, 1856.

IV. The Literature of Contemporary Politics

A. Speeches

Address to the Citizens of Middlesex. New Brunswick, New Jersey, 1837.

Benton, Thomas H., *Address on the Presentation of the Sword of General Andrew Jackson to the Congress. . . .* Washington, 1855.

Ewing, Andrew, *An Oration delivered on the Occasion of the Inauguration of the Bust erected to the Memory of General Andrew Jackson.* Nashville, 1859.

Forrest, Edwin, *Oration delivered at the Democratic Republican Celebration of the Fourth of July, 1838.* New York, 1838.

Holmes, John, *Speech . . . in the Senate [on removals from office].* Washington, 1830.

Ingersoll, C. J., . . . *Speech on the Loan Bills . . . 1814.* n.p., n.d.

Porter, Alexander, *Speech . . . in opposition to . . . Mr. Benton . . . 1836.* n.p., n.d.

Speeches on the passage of the Bill for the removal of the Indians, delivered in the Congress . . . 1830. Boston, 1830.

Tallmadge, James, Jr., *Speech . . . in the House of Representatives . . . on the Seminole War.* New York, 1819.

Tallmadge, Nathaniel P., *Speech . . . on the Subject of the Removal of the Deposits from the Bank of the United States.* Washington, 1834.

Van Buren, Martin, *Speech . . . on the Act . . . for the Settlement of the late Governor's Accounts.* Albany, 1820.

B. Pamphlets

Address of Members of the House of Representatives . . . on . . . the War with Great Britain. Raleigh, North Carolina, 1812.

Address to the People of the United States. By Touchstone. 1812.

Barney, Mrs., *Letter to President Jackson.* Baltimore, 1829.

Blair, Francis P., *General Jackson and James Buchanan.* Washington, 1856.

The Calhoun Text-Book. New York, 1843.

Cary, M., *Desultory Reflections upon the Ruinous Consequences of a non-renewal of the Charter of the Bank.* . . . Philadelphia, 1810.

Choate, Rufus, *Speech . . . on the Question of the Removal of the Deposits.* Washington, 1834.

Clay, Henry, *An Address . . . to the Public.* New Brunswick, 1828.

Crisis on the Origin and Consequences of our political Dissensions. Albany, 1815.

Defense of the Whigs. New York, 1844.

Dissolution of the Union. Philadelphia, 1832.

Duane, W. J., *Narrative and Correspondence concerning the Removal of the Deposits.* Philadelphia, 1838.

Eaton, John H., *Candid Appeal to the American Public.* Washington, 1831.

Essay on the Spirit of Jacksonism. By Aristides. Philadelphia, 1835.

The Presidency of Andrew Jackson

I.

INAUGURATION.

"No one who was at Washington at the time of General Jackson's inauguration is likely to forget that period to the [1] day of his death. To us, who had witnessed the quiet and orderly period of the Adams' administration, it seemed as if [2] half the nation had rushed at once into the Capital. It was like the inundation of the northern barbarians into Rome, save that the tumultuous tide came in from a different point of the compass. The West and the South seemed to have precipitated themselves upon the North and overwhelmed it. On that memorable occasion you might tell a 'Jackson man' almost as far as you could see him. Their every motion seemed to cry out 'victory!' Strange faces filled every public place, and every face seemed to bear defiance on its brow. It appeared to me that every Jackson editor in the country was on the spot. They swarmed, especially in the lobbies of the House, an expectant host, a sort of Prætorian band, which, having borne in upon their shields their idolized leader, claimed the reward of the hard-fought contest. His quarters were assailed, surrounded, hemmed in, so that it was an achievement to get into his presence. On the morning of the inauguration, the vicinity of the Capitol was like a great agitated sea; every avenue to the fateful spot was blocked up with people, in so much that the legitimate procession which accompanied the President-elect could scarce make its way to the eastern portico, where the ceremony was to be performed. To repress the crowd in front, a ship's cable was stretched across about two-thirds of the way up the long flight of steps by which the Capitol is approached on that side, but it seemed, at times, as if even this would scarce prove sufficient to restrain the eagerness of the multitude, every man of whom seemed bent on the glory of shaking the President's hand. Never can I forget the spectacle which presented itself on every side, nor the electrifying moment when the eager, expectant eyes of that vast and motley multitude caught sight of the tall and imposing form of their adored leader, as he came forth between the columns of the portico, the color of the whole mass changed, as if by miracle; all hats were off at once, and the dark tint which usually pervades a mixed map of men was turned, as by a magic wand, into the bright hue of ten thousand upturned and exultant human faces, radiant with sudden joy. The peal of shouting that arose rent the air, and seemed to shake the very ground. But when the Chief Justice took his place and commenced the brief ceremony of administering the oath of office, it quickly sank into comparative silence; and as the new President proceeded to read his inaugural address, the stillness gradually increased; but all efforts to hear him, beyond a brief space immediately around, were utterly vain."*

Mr. Webster, in his serio-comic manner, remarks: "I never saw such a crowd here before. Persons have come five hundred miles to see General Jackson, *and they really seem to think that the country is rescued from some dreadful danger!*"

The ceremony over, the President drove from the Capitol to the White House, followed soon by a great part of the crowd who had witnessed the inauguration. Judge Story, a strenuous Adams man, did not enjoy the scene which the apartments of the "palace," as he styles it, presented on this occasion. "After the ceremony was over," he wrote, "the President went to the palace to receive company, and there he was visited by immense crowds of all sorts of people, from the highest and most polished, down to the most vulgar and gross in the nation. I never saw such a mixture. The reign of King Mob seemed triumphant. I was glad to escape from the scene as soon as possible." A letter writer said: "A profusion of refreshments had been provided. Orange punch by barrels full was made, but as the waiters opened the door to bring it out, a rush would be made, the glasses broken, the pails of liquor upset, and the most painful confusion pre-

* Arthur J. Stansbury, in Arthur's Home Gazette, May, 1851.

vailed. To such a painful degree was this carried, that wine and ice-creams could not be brought out to the ladies, and tubs of punch were taken from the lower story into the garden, to lead off the crowd from the rooms. On such an occasion it was certainly difficult to keep any thing like order, but it was mortifying to see men, with boots heavy with mud, standing on the damask satin covered chairs, from their eagerness to get a sight of the President."

The inaugural address of the new President, which has been characterized as vague and meaningless, seems to me to be as plain and straightforward as his peculiar and difficult position admitted. On the one hand, General Jackson, by his writings and his votes, was committed to a protective tariff and internal improvement policy. On the other, he had been elected to the presidency by the strict constructionist party. His inaugural was a clear enough *acceptance of the leadership of the party which had elected him.* The entire subject of internal improvements was disposed of in one short sentence, which is, considering the circumstances, almost comic. "Internal improvements," said the President, "and the diffusion of knowledge, so far as they can be promoted by the constitutional acts of the federal government, are of high importance." Not another word. Henry Lee, I imagine, was not the author of that sentence.

6

7

The tariff men were favored with the following: "With regard to a proper selection of the subjects of impost, with a view to revenue, it would seem to me that the spirit of equity, caution, and compromise in which the constitution was formed, requires that the great interests of agriculture, commerce, and manufactures, should be equally favored; and that, perhaps, the only exception to this rule should consist in the peculiar encouragement of any products of either of them that may be found essential to our national independence.

For those who might chance to remember General Jackson's farewell address to the army, a long paragraph was inserted, which declared standing armies "dangerous to free governments in time of peace," and entitled a patriotic militia "the bulwark of our defense," and "the impenetrable ægis" of our liberties.

For the illumination of any who might have been recently looking over the Monroe correspondence, a few sentences were added, which made half the office-holders in the country quake in their slippers: "The recent demonstration of public sentiment inscribes on the list of executive duties, in characters too legible to be overlooked, the task of reform, which will require, particularly, the correction of those abuses that have brought the patronage of the federal government into conflict with the freedom of elections, and the counteraction of those causes which have disturbed the rightful course of appointment, and have placed or continued power in unfaithful or incompetent hands."

It was in this passage that the slight alteration, before alluded to, was made after the General reached Washington. Mr. McLean, who was expected to continue in the office of Postmaster-General, objected to the policy dimly shadowed forth in these remarks, and they were, in consequence, so changed as to make the President himself responsible for the acts contemplated. The phrase "executive duties" was substituted for one which was supposed to throw the responsibility more upon the members of the Cabinet. As Mr. McLean was still intractable, he was comfortably shelved on the bench of the Supreme Court, which he has since adorned.

Mr. Clay left Washington a few days after the inauguration. A public dinner was given before his departure, at which he spoke of the new President in language and temper highly honorable to himself:

"That citizen," said he, "has done me much injustice—wanton, unprovoked, and unatoned injustice. It was inflicted as I must ever believe, for the double purpose of gratifying private resentment, and promoting personal ambition.

"When, during the late canvass, he came forward in the public prints, under his proper name, with his charge against me, and summoned before the public tribunal his friend and his only witness to establish it, the anxious attention of the whole American people was directed to the testimony which that witness might render. He promptly obeyed the call, and testified to what he knew. He could say nothing, and he said nothing which cast the slightest shade upon my honor or integrity. What he did say, was the reverse of any implication of me. Then, all just and impartial men, and all who had faith in the magnanimity of my accuser, believed that he would voluntarily make a public acknowledgment of his error. How far this reasonable expectation has been fulfilled let his persevering and stubborn silence attest.

"But my relations to that citizen by a recent event are now changed. He is the Chief Magistrate of my country, invested with large and extensive powers, the administration of which may conduce to its prosperity, or occasion its adversity. Patriotism enjoins as a duty, that while he is in that exalted station, he should be treated with decorum, and his official acts be judged of in a spirit of candor. Suppressing, as far as I can, a sense of my personal wrong, willing even to forgive him, if his own conscience and our common God can acquit him; and entertaining for the majority which has elected him, and for the office which he fills, all the deference which is due from a private citizen, I most anxiously hope, that under his guidance, the great interests of our country, foreign and domestic, may be upheld, our free institutions be unimpaired, and the happiness of the nation, be continued and increased."

II.

THE CABINET AND THE KITCHEN CABINET.

It is not so well known to the public, as it is to society in Washington, that there is an imaginary difference of rank between the members of the cabinet. The Secretary of State, every one knows, is at the head of the cabinet, and sits at the President's right hand in cabinet councils, and takes precedence of every one except the President and the Vice-President. Next to him is the Secretary of the Treasury, who also has more valuable offices in his gift than any other cabinet minister ; the entire custom-house system of the country being under his control. The Secretary of War ranks third, and the Secretary of the Navy fourth. The Attorney-General formerly closed the list, as the Post-Master General was not, technically speaking, a member of the cabinet. Early in the administration of the new President, however, that officer was formally created a cabinet minister.

So little was known of General Jackson's intentions with regard to cabinet appointments that some of the members of the cabinet of Mr. Adams were actually in doubt whether [10] they ought to resign or not. Mr. Wirt, the Attorney-General, wrote to Mr. Monroe, asking his opinion on the point. Mr. Monroe advised him to resign, but added, that, in all probability, the new President would desire to retain the services of an officer who, for twelve years, had discharged the duties of his place to universal acceptance. So well did General Jackson keep his secret, that no man in or out of Washington, except the chosen few, know who would compose the new administration, until the General, with his own hands, [11] gave to the editor of the *Telegraph* the list for publication. It appeared in the official newspaper on the 26th of February. It would not even then have seen the light but for the secret opposition made to one of the appointments.

Soon after General Jackson arrived at the seat of government, he informed Edward Livingston of Louisiana, that Mr. [12] Van Buren was the foreordained Secretary of State of the incoming administration, and offered him the choice of the seats remaining. Mr. Livingston, just then elected to the Senate, preferred his Senatorship to any office in the government except the one already appropriated.

In distributing the six great offices, General Jackson assigned two to the north, two to the west, and two to the south.

Mr. Van Buren accepted the first place without hesitation, resigned the governorship of New York after holding it seventy days, and entered upon his duties at Washington three weeks after the inauguration.

Samuel D. Ingham, of Pennsylvania, was appointed to the second place in the cabinet, that of Secretary of the Treasury. Mr. Ingham came of a sturdy Bucks county

Quaker family, a thriving, industrious race, settled there for four generations. His father, a physician, farmer, and clothier, was also a devotee of classical learning, and a dissenter from the tenets of the broad-brimmed sect. His son, Samuel, showing no great inclination for classical knowledge, was apprenticed to a paper-maker, and, in due time, set up a paper-mill on the paternal farm, which proved a successful venture. From the peaceful pursuits of business he was drawn away gradually into the whirl of politics, presiding at town and county meetings of the democratic party; serving in such offices as justice of the peace, member of the Assembly, and Secretary of the commonwealth, until, in 1813, he took his seat in the House of Representatives; a position which, with one short interval, he held until his transfer to the cabinet of General Jackson. He was not a speaking member, nor did he ever acquire any general celebrity; but, as a business man, his services upon important committees were valued. His successful management of his private business, in circumstances of more than usual difficulty, constructing his mill in a region where not a mechanic whom he employed had ever seen one, and starting it with far more credit than capital, proves him to have been a man of executive ability. His conduct with regard to the bargain and corruption cry stamps him a false or a narrow soul. In Pennsylvania, during the late canvass, he had aided poor Kremer with all his talents [13] and all his influence in deluding the voters of his native State into the belief that Mr. Adams had obtained the presidency through a corrupt understanding with Mr. Clay. He wrote [14] an electioneering pamphlet against Mr. Adams, which that gentleman characterized as a gross misrepresentation of his conduct and opinions. Mr. Ingham, as we have before stated, was one of the original Calhoun men of Pennsylvania. He was still a friend and ally of Mr. Calhoun, and it was thought [15] at the time that he owed his place in the cabinet to Mr. Calhoun's influence. This was probably not the case. Ingham had done enough during the late campaign to give him a first place in the regard of the new President; and the

Jackson members of Congress from Pennsylvania, on being consulted by General Jackson, united in naming Ingham as Pennsylvania's elect and precious.

John H. Eaton, Senator from Tennessee, was appointed Secretary of War. General Jackson was, from the first, determined to have in his cabinet one of his own Tennessee circle of friends. The choice lay between the two Senators, 16 Eaton and White. Feb. 23d, Major Eaton wrote the following note to Judge White: "A letter, received some time ago from General Jackson, stated he desired you or me to be near him. In a recent conversation with him, he remarked that he had had a full and free conversation with you; and at the close remarked that he desired to have me with him. I presumed, without inquiring, that he had probably talked with you on the subject, and that you had declined accepting any situation, as you before had told me would be your feelings. Nothing definite has taken place on this matter between General Jackson and myself, and I hope you know me well enough, and my regard and friendship for you, to know this, that I should never permit myself to stand in competition with any desire you may entertain. If you have any desire, say so to me in confidence, and it shall so be received. If you have none, then in reference to every and all considerations I should consent to any such appointment. Think of this, and give me your opinion frankly."*

Every one acquainted with Judge White knew well what reply he would make to such a communication. Major Eaton was appointed.

17 Major Lewis favors the reader with a brief account of Eaton's career. "He lived," writes Major Lewis, "at Franklin, a small town eighteen miles south of Nashville. It is the county seat of Williamson county, one of the finest counties in the State, and is situated on the road leading from Nashville to Columbia, the town in which President Polk lived. Major Eaton, however, during the whole time he was in the Senate (a period of eleven years) spent the

* Memoirs of Hugh L. White, p. 266.

greater part of his time in Washington. He was a native of North Carolina, and came to Tennessee in 1808, or 1809, then being about twenty-two years of age. Having lost his father, the duty of taking care of his mother and his younger brother and sister devolved upon him, he being the eldest son. He purchased a comfortable residence in town for the family, and a tract of land in the neighborhood to place their negroes upon; and, after having made these arrangements, he returned to North Carolina, and, in due time, moved the whole family to Tennessee, and located them in Franklin, where his mother resided as long as she lived.

"Mr. Eaton was a man of education, having graduated, I think, at Chapel Hill, and was a lawyer by profession. Although a young man, and comparatively a stranger, and without family connections, he soon acquired a very respectable standing at the bar. He practiced not only in Franklin, where he lived, but in the adjacent counties, and, in the course of a few years, he became, by his pleasant and agreeable manners, and fine conversational talent, quite a favorite both of the bar and the bench. He was also a pleasant and interesting speaker, and, by his finely modulated voice, never failed to command the attention of the auditory. In 1818, he was appointed a Senator in Congress, by Governor McMinn, to fill a vacancy occasioned by the resignation of the Hon. George W. Campbell, who had been sent to Russia as Minister, by President Monroe. Among those most active in getting up a recommendation to the Governor for his appointment to the Senate, was our distinguished fellow-citizen, John Bell. He was afterward elected three times to the Senate by the legislature of his State, but he had served only two years, I think, of his last term when General Jackson offered him a seat in his cabinet, which was accepted. After this, having lost his mother, brother, and sister, he never returned to Tennessee to live."

For the moment this narrative must content us. We shall have to return to this gentleman ere long, and complete Major Lewis' story.

The Navy Department was assigned to John Branch, for many years a Senator from North Carolina. Mr. Branch was not one of those who achieve greatness, nor one of those who have greatness thrust upon them. He was born to it. Inheriting an ample estate, he lived for many years upon his plantations and employed himself in superintending their culture. A man of respectable talents, good presence, and high social position, he was naturally enough chosen to represent his State in the Senate, afterward to be its Governor, and again to the Senate. In his public career I find one act recorded which was peculiarly calculated to secure him the favorable consideration of General Jackson. He voted against the confirmation of Henry Clay, as Secretary of State, in 1825. For the rest, Governor Branch was a gentleman of the strict constructionist persuasion, a friend of Mr. Calhoun, an entirely respectable, but not a brilliant nor even a well-known character.

John McPherson Berrien, of Georgia, was appointed Attorney-General. Mr. Berrien was born and educated in New Jersey, graduating at Nassau Hall, but was admitted to the bar in Georgia, where he rose to great and merited eminence as a lawyer, Judge, and legislator. Appearing as a Senator in 1824, he exhibited talents more than respectable, and was noted for somewhat extreme opinions on those questions which were destined to create painful differences between North and South. A warm, even passionate lover of the Union, he yet opposed most vigorously the tariff bill, for which General Jackson had voted, and was among the foremost in his opposition to the revived heterodoxy of Mr. Adams' messages. He, too, like Governor Branch, voted against Mr. Clay's confirmation in 1825; and, like Governor Branch, looked up to Mr. Calhoun as the South's peculiar champion.

William T. Barry, of Kentucky, was appointed Postmaster General. Elected to Congress at the age of twenty-seven, Mr. Barry had been in public life for twenty years; chiefly, however, in State offices. He fought in the war of 1812 with great credit, under General Harrison, and was afterward the conspicuous friend of Henry Clay, supporting him for the presidency in 1824. But Mr. Clay's conduct in giving the presidency to and accepting office under Mr. Adams, Major Barry could not stomach; and there was first a coolness and then a bitterness between the old friends. To aid in defeating the administration and to bring in General Jackson, he had consented to run for the governorship of Kentucky against the Clay candidate, an office which he had more than once declined, and did not then desire. He just lost his election, but the canvass powerfully aided the Jackson party, and gave them confident hopes of carrying the State at the presidential election, which hopes, we know, were realized. How could General Jackson feel otherwise than grateful to the man who had put upon Henry Clay the exquisite mortification of losing the support of his own Kentucky? Major Barry was an agreeable and amiable man, but not a man of business—not the man for the most perplexing post in the administration. Nor was he generally known, even by name, beyond the borders of his own State.

The Cabinet, taken as a whole, and compared with those which had preceded it, could not be called splendid. There was some show of justice in a common remark of the time: "This is the millennium of the minnows." Leaving Mr. Van Buren out of view, the only cohesive element in it, common to all, was an aversion to Mr. Clay. Eaton was a Jackson man; Ingham, Branch, and Berrien, were Calhoun men; but all were anti-Clay men. The reader will not have to read many pages more before imbibing an impression that the anti-Clayism of these gentlemen was that which particularly endeared them to the new President. The appointment to the Russian Mission of John Randolph, who had fought a duel with Henry Clay three years before, strengthens this conjecture.

I should mention, perhaps, in justice to General Jackson, that Henry Clay had himself taken the stump during the late campaign in Kentucky, and denounced the General in terms of unmeasured, and, sometimes, indecent severity. Gentlemen who heard Mr. Clay on these occasions, inform me that his printed speeches are moderate and tame compared with those which he delivered in the open air, to the "hunters of Kentucky," during the campaign. He could not speak of the bargain and corruption calumny without boiling over with fury, and pouring forth a torrent of fierce Kentuckian invective. No doubt there were obliging individuals among the crowd, who took care that Mr. Clay's wrathful phrases should be reported to General Jackson. It was, moreover, a fixed idea in the General's mind, that the secret originator of the calumnies against Mrs. Jackson was no other than Mr. Clay. Mr. Clay solemnly denied and completely disproved the charge, but he could never remove that fixed idea from the soul of General Jackson.

Such, then, was the first Cabinet of the new President. With the exception of Mr. Van Buren, its members had no great influence over the measures of their chief, and play no great part in the general history of the times. There were other individuals who stood nearer to the President than they did, and exerted over him a far more potent influence.

A few days after the inauguration, Major Lewis, who had his quarters in the White House, informed the President that he was about to return to Tennessee, as it was the planting season and his plantation required his attention. "Why, Major," said the President, "you are not going to leave me here *alone*, after doing more than any other man to bring me here ?" The General clung to his Tennessee friends, ever lonely, always mourning for his dead wife. Major Lewis relented. It was agreed that he should accept an auditorship of the treasury, and remain a member of the President's family. Major Lewis, I must remind the reader, was a brother-in-law of Major Eaton. It seems a trifling fact to mention twice. The reader will discover soon that it was one of those little facts which influence great affairs.

General Duff Green, editor of the *United States Telegraph,* was much about the person of the President during the first month of his administration, and was supposed to have more influence over him than perhaps, he really possesssed. He had been the editor of a newspaper at St. Louis, and had come to Washington, some months before, a poor man, to effect an exchange of his paper for one published in Washington. He succeeded in his object; supported General Jackson with all the ardor and ability of which he was master; obtained in the spring of 1829, before the inauguration, a share of the public printing; was then a prosperous gentleman; and his paper became the confidential organ of the new administration. He was fierce for the removal from office of those who were not devotees of the new administration. General Green was and is a jovial soul, a capital story-teller, a pleasant host, liberal in expenditure, formed to go gaily with the tide, not to buffet the billows of opposition.

Editor Isaac Hill from New Hampshire, was in high favor at the White House from the very beginning of the new administration. The early life of this man was so curiously like that of Horace Greeley, that the narration of it would answer as well for the one as the other. A poor, little, lame New Hampshire boy. Consumed with a passion for reading. Scouring the country for books. Reading every thing, from "Law's Call to the Unconverted" to a penny almanac. Tramping miles for a newspaper. Learning the printer's trade because he so loved to read. Serving his time in the office of that very *Farmer's Cabinet*, at Amherst, New Hampshire, which the youthful Greeley lay in wait for by the roadside and devoured in secret. Setting up a newspaper with immense difficulty, and struggling for years for a circulation in a State that was a stronghold of federalism, until he made it democratic. A prosperous man, at length. He published books, and kept a thriving book-store, and had other irons in the fire, which he contrived to keep hot. A keen party man, and made the more so by many years of active but unsuccessful warfare with a party that despised more than they hated the name of democrat. During the strife of 1828, he had written, and spoken, and schemed, and traveled for Jackson, incurring rancorous hostility and suffering personal violence. Unable to carry the State for his candidate, he had fought such a fight for him as excited General Jackson's admiration and gratitude. The indomitable Isaac went to Washington to console himself with the triumph of the inauguration, and the new President gave him more than a friendly welcome. Before the month of March closed, Isaac Hill found himself appointed to the second Comptrollership of the Treasury, at a salary of three thousand dollars a year, and ten clerkships in his gift. Like Duff Green, he was urgent for the removal of those who had opposed the election of General Jackson.

"Every State in New England," said he in the *New Hampshire Patriot*, in November, 1828, "is now governed by the same aristocracy that ruled in 1798—that ruled during the late war. The republicans here are in a minority; but the late election show them to be a glorious majority of the whole Union. A band of New England democrats have encountered the dominant party at vast odds—they have suffered every species of persecution and contumely. Shall these men not be protected by the administration of the people under General Jackson? If that administration fail to extend this protection, then indeed it will fail of one of the principal objects for which the people placed them in power by at least two to one of the votes of the Union."

Was there ever a pair of ears so prepared to listen favorably to such sentiments as those of General Jackson in 1829? Will he be able to carry out the doctrines avowed in certain letters to Mr. Monroe in 1816 and 1817?

Amos Kendall, late the editor of a Jackson paper in Kentucky, a native of Massachusetts, was present at the inauguration, was taken into the President's confidence, was appointed fourth Auditor of the Treasury. He began his long official career with the most virtuous resolutions. "The interest of the country," he wrote to a friend, March 24th, 1829, "demands that the Fourth Auditor's office shall be filled with men of business, and not with babbling politicians. Partisan feelings shall not enter here, if I can keep them out. To others belong the whole business of electioneering. To me and my clerks other duties are assigned. Them I shall endeavor to discharge in the spirit of reform, which has made

General Jackson President. Vain I may be, proud I am, that the President has given me an opportunity to aid him in proving that reform is not an empty sound, and is not to apply merely to a change of men. Henceforth, assiduously devoted to my official duties, I shall leave my enemies and his, to their freedom of speech and the press, resting my claims to public confidence on my acts."

Man proposes : the System disposes. Never was there a busier electioneering office-holder than Mr. Kendall. He was, however, a man of indefatigable industry, and performed both his in-door and out-door duties with zeal.

These were the gentlemen—Lewis, Green, Hill and Kendall—who, at the beginning of the new administration, were supposed to have most of the President's ear and confidence, and were stigmatized by the opposition as the Kitchen Cabinet. Major Donelson, as the private secretary of the President, was also a personage of importance in the White House and in the society of Washington. General Call, formerly the General's aid, now the delegate from the Territory of Florida, was much the President's friend and often his companion.

22

23

Colonel James Watson Webb, it is evident from the columns of the *Courier and Enquirer*, was kept better advised of the secrets of the White House than any other editor out of Washington. Colonel Webb, as it chanced, had particular relations both with Mr. Van Buren and with Mr. Calhoun. He was a native of the same county as Mr. Van Buren, and had long been his friend and supporter. Mr. Calhoun, on the other hand, had given Colonel Webb his commission in the army, and given it to him in such circumstances, and in such a manner, as secured him the friendship and gratitude of the young soldier for life.

In after times, when the course of political events placed the *Courier* in opposition to Mr. Calhoun, no word disrespectful to him personally was admitted into its editorial columns; nor did Colonel Webb ever visit Washington, even at that mad period, without calling upon his early benefactor.

III.

MRS. EATON.

William O'Neal kept at Washington for many years a large old-fashioned tavern, where members of Congress, in considerable numbers, boarded during the sessions of the national legislature. William O'Neal had a daughter, sprightly and beautiful, who aided him and his wife in entertaining his boarders. It is not good for a girl to grow up in a large tavern. Peg O'Neal as she was called, was so lively in her deportment, so free in her conversation, that, had she been born twenty years later, she would have been called one of the "fast" girls of Washington. A witty, pretty, saucy, active tavern-keeper's daughter, who makes free with the inmates of her father's house, and is made free with by them, may escape contamination, but not calumny.

When Major Eaton first came to Washington as a Senator of the United States in the year 1818, he took board at Mr. O'Neal's tavern, and continued to reside there every winter for ten years. He became acquainted, of course, with the family, including the vivacious and attractive Peg. When General Jackson came to the city as Senator in 1823, he also went to live with the O'Neals, whom he had known in Washington before it had become the seat of government. For Mrs. O'Neal, who was a remarkably efficient woman, he had a particular respect. Even during his presidency, when he was supposed to visit no one, it was one of his favorite relaxations, when worn out with business, to stroll with Major Lewis across the "old fields" near Washington to the cottage where Mrs. O'Neal lived in retirement, and enjoy an hour's chat with the old lady. Mrs. Jackson, also, during her residence in Washington in 1825, became attached to the good Mrs. O'Neal and to her daughter.

In the course of time Miss O'Neal became the wife of purser Timberlake of the United States Navy, and the mother of two children. In 1828 came news that Mr. Timberlake, then on duty in the Mediterranean, had cut his throat in a fit of melancholy, induced, it was said, by previous intoxication. On hearing this intelligence, Major Eaton, then a widower, felt an inclination to marry Mrs. Timberlake, for whom he had entertained an attachment quite as tender as a man could lawfully indulge for the wife of a friend and brother-mason. He took the precaution to consult General Jackson on the subject. "Why, yes, Major," said the General, "if you love the woman, and she will have you, marry her by all means." Major Eaton mentioned, what the General well knew, that Mrs. Timberlake's reputation in Washington had not escaped reproach, and that Major Eaton himself was supposed to have been too intimate with her. "Well," said the General, "your marrying her will disprove these charges, and restore Peg's good name." And so, perhaps, it might, if Major Eaton had not been taken into the Cabinet.

Eaton and Mrs. Timberlake were married in January, 1829, a few weeks before General Jackson arrived at the seat of government. As soon as it was whispered about Washington that Major Eaton was to be a member of the new Cabinet, it occurred with great force to the minds of certain ladies, who supposed themselves to be at the head of society at the Capital, that, in that case, Peg O'Neal would be the wife of a cabinet minister, and, as such, entitled to admission into their own sacred circle. Horrible to contemplate! Forbid it, morality! Forbid it, decency! Forbid it, General Jackson!

Among those who were scandalized at the appointment of Major Eaton was the Rev. J. N. Campbell, pastor of the Presbyterian church in Washington, which the General and Mrs. Jackson had both attended, and which, it was supposed, President Jackson would attend. Not caring to speak with the General himself on the subject, Mr. Campbell communicated the ill things he had heard of Mrs. Eaton to the Rev. E. S. Ely, of Philadelphia, who had known General Jackson in his mercantile days, and had come to Washington to witness the inauguration of his old friend. Dr. Ely desired to converse with General Jackson on the subject, but finding no opportunity to do so in Washington, wrote to the General, after his return to Philadelphia, a very long letter, in which he detailed all the charges he had heard against Mrs. Eaton. He informed the President that she had borne a bad reputation in Washington from her girlhood; that the ladies of Washington would not speak to her; that a gentleman, at the table of Gadsby's Hotel, was said to have declared that he personally knew her to be a dissolute woman; that Mrs. Eaton had told her servants to call her children Eaton, not Timberlake, for Eaton was their rightful name; that a clergyman of Washington had told Dr. Ely, that a deceased physician had told him, that Mrs. Timberlake had had a miscarriage when her husband had been absent a year; that the friends of Major Eaton had persuaded him to board elsewhere, for the sake of getting him away from Mrs. Timberlake; that Mrs. Jackson herself had entertained the worst opinion of Mrs. Timberlake; that Major Eaton and Mrs. Timberlake had traveled together, and recorded their names on hotel registers as man and wife, in New York and elsewhere.

For your own sake, said the reverend doctor, for your dead wife's sake, for the sake of your administration, for the credit of the government and the country, you should not countenance a woman like this.

This letter was dated March 18th, 1829. General Jackson replied to it immediately, and in a manner peculiarly characteristic. Indeed, all his most peculiar traits were exhibited in the course of this affair.

GENERAL JACKSON TO REV. DR. ELY.

"WASHINGTON, March 23, 1829.

"DEAR SIR: Your confidential letter of the 18th instant has been received in the same spirit of kindness and friendship with which it was written.

"I must here be permitted to remark that I sincerely regret you did not personally name this subject to me before you left Washington, as I could, in that event, have apprised you of the great exertions made by Clay and his partisans, here and elsewhere, to destroy the character of Mrs. Eaton by the foulest and basest means, so that a deep and lasting wrong might be inflicted on her husband. I could have given you information that would at least have put you on your guard with respect to anonymous letters, containing slanderous insinuations against female character. If such evidence as this is to be received, I ask where is the guarantee for female character, however moral—however *virtuous?*

"To show you how much you have been imposed upon, and how much Mrs. E. has been slandered, I am warranted in the positive contradiction of the very first charge made against her—'that she was in ill-fame before Mr. Eaton ever saw her'—from the united testimony of the Hon. John Rhea, Dr. Hogg, and others who boarded with Mr. O'Neal, long before Mr. Eaton was a member of Congress. If you feel yourself at liberty to give the names of those secret traducers of female reputation, I entertain no doubt but they will be exposed and consigned to public odium, which should ever be the lot of those whose morbid appetite delights in defamation and slander.

"As to the information of Mr. ——, of Baltimore, I will barely remark that he may be a respectable man; but surely you will agree with me, that a charge so malignant in its character, unless accompanied with indubitable evidence of the criminality of the act, should not have been made, and shows him at once to be destitute of those just, manly, and charitable feelings, which should be characteristic of every good and virtuous man. In contradiction of Mr. ——'s information to you, I have many letters from Baltimore, Pennsylvania, Ohio, and other States, congratulating me and the nation on the selection of Mr. Eaton as one of my Cabinet. Besides these, many members of Congress, and among them the leading members of the New York delegation, expressed personally their high gratification at his appointment. You were assuredly justified in stating to my friends that I have no information, nor ever had, on which any reliance ought to be placed, of any infamous conduct of Mrs. Eaton.

"One observation on the bank conversation. The place where the remark was made is sufficient evidence, to my mind, that it emanated from Clay or his satellites, with a view of completing what he had *here* begun. I am fully warranted in charging Mr. Clay with circulating these slanderous reports, from information derived from a very intelligent lady, who met Mr. Clay and his wife on her way to this city. This lady says Mr. and Mrs. Clay spoke in the strongest and most unmeasured terms of Mrs. Eaton. She inquired of them to know upon what grounds these charges rested. '*Rumor, mere rumor,*' was the answer. So far from this attempt to injure Mrs. Eaton on the part of these personages having the effect intended, the lady, as soon as she arrived, sought to become acquainted with her and Mr. Eaton. Now, my dear sir, justice to female character, justice to me, and justice to Mr. Eaton, require that these secret agents in propagating slander should be made known to Mr. Eaton, that he may be enabled to defend the character of his wife against such vile and unprincipled attacks. Would you, my worthy friend, desire me to add the weight and influence of my name, whatever it may be, to assist in crushing Mrs. Eaton, who, I do believe, and have a right to believe, is a much injured woman, and more virtuous than some of her enemies?

"It is due to me to be made acquainted with the names of those bank directors who have dared to throw an imputation on the memory of my departed wife. Men who can be base enough to speak thus of the dead, are not too good *secretly* to slander the living; and they deserve, and no doubt will receive, the scorn of all good men. Mr. Eaton has been known to me for twenty years. His character heretofore, for honesty and morality, has been unblemished; and am I now, for the first time, to change my opinion of him, because of the slanders of this city? We know, *here*, that that none are spared. Even Mrs. Madison was assailed by these fiends in human shape. Mrs. Commodore —— has also been singled out as a victim to be sacrificed on the altar of defamation, because she left this city and traveled precisely in the way agreed on by Commodore ——, but did not promulgate to the gossips here. I speak advisedly in relation to this matter, for I have seen a letter from Commodore ——, giving an exposé of this whole transaction, justifying his wife's conduct and vindicating her innocence. He expresses a determination, when he returns to this country, to investigate the affair, and punish the defamers of his wife's character; and I sincerely hope he may live to do it, for I am disgusted even to loathing at the licentious and depraved state of society. It needs purifying.

"You were badly advised, my dear sir, when informed 'that Mrs. Jackson, while in Washington, did not fear to put the seal of reprobation on such a character as Mrs. Eaton.' Mrs. Jackson, to the last moment of her life, believed Mrs. Eaton to be an innocent and much injured woman, so far as relates to the tales about her and Mr. Eaton, and none other ever reached her or me. As Mrs. J. has been introduced into this affair, and as she loved truth while living, and she and myself have taken the (illegible) Psalm for our guide, to which I refer you, I will give you a concise history of the information which I and Mrs. Jackson possessed upon this subject. First, let me remark that Major O'Neal is a mason, Mr. Timberlake was a mason, and Mr. Eaton is a mason; therefore, every person who is acquainted with the obligations of masons, must know that Mr. Eaton, as a mason, could not have criminal intercourse with another mason's wife, without being one of the most abandoned of men. The high standing of Mr. Eaton, as a man of moral worth and a mason, gives the lie direct, in my estimation, to such a charge, and ought to do it, unless the facts of his alleged guilt shall be clearly and unequivocally established, when, should that be the case, he ought and would be spurned with indignation.

"I became acquainted with Major O'Neal in this city before Congress ever sat in it. I never saw him again until 1819, when I visited his house to pay my respects to Mr. Eaton, who in December preceding took his seat in the Senate for the first time. In 1823 I again visited the city in the character of Senator from Tennessee, and took lodging with Mr. Eaton at Major O'Neal's, when and where I became acquainted with Mr. and Mrs. Timberlake. I was there when Mr. Timberlake left this country for the Mediterranean, and was present when he took leave of his wife, children, and family. He parted with them in the most affectionate manner, as he did also with myself and Mr. Eaton. Between him and the latter gentleman there appeared to be nothing but friendship and confidence from the first time I saw them at Major O'Neal's, until the day of his departure. From the situation and proximity of the rooms we occupied, there could not have been any illicit intercourse between Mr. Eaton and Mrs. Timberlake without my having some knowledge of it; and I assure you, sir, that I saw nothing, heard nothing which was calculated to excite even the slightest suspicion. Shortly after Mr. Timberlake left Washington for the Mediterranean, I was told in great confidence that it was rumored in the city that Mr. Eaton and Mrs. Timberlake were too intimate. I met it, as I meet all slanders, with a prompt denial, and inquired from what source this rumor came, and found it originated with a female, against whom there was as much said as is now said against Mrs. Eaton. This report came to the ear of Mrs. Jackson through the same channel; but to the day of her death she believed it to be a base slander, as I do at this day. As to what servants may have said about her telling them not to call her children Timberlake, but Eaton, it is matter of regret to me that you have named it. My dear sir, if the tales of servants, who become offended by being dismissed, are to be believed, what security has your dear wife for her virtuous character, or that of any other lady?

"It is reported that Mr. Timberlake declared he would never again return to this country, in consequence of Mr. Eaton having seduced his wife. How can such a tale as this be reconciled with the following facts? While now writing, I turn my eyes to the mantel-piece, where I behold a present sent me by Mr. Timberlake of a Turkish pipe, about three weeks before his death, and presented through Mr. Eaton, whom in his letter he calls 'his friend.' Now, sir, could this be so, if he did really believe Mr. Eaton had injured him, or wronged him? No, I am sure you will say it is impossible.

"I have not the least doubt but that every secret rumor is circulated by the minions of Mr. Clay, for the purpose of injuring Mrs. Eaton, and through her, Mr. Eaton; but I assure you that such conduct shall never have my aid.

"When Mrs. E. visits me (she has not done so since the 4th), I shall treat her with as much politeness as I have ever done, believing her virtuous, at least as much so as the female who first gave rise to the foul tale, and as are many of those who traduce her. As to the determination of the ladies in Washington, I have nothing, nor will I ever have any thing to do with it. I will not persuade or dissuade any of them from visiting Mrs. Eaton, leaving Mrs. Eaton and them to settle the matter in their own way; but I am told that many of the ladies here have waited on her.

"The villain who could have used such an expression at a public table, as has been related to you by Mr. ——, of New York, ought to have been instantly kicked from the table, and that Mr. —— did not thus treat him, instead of telling you of it, does not elevate him much in my estimation. A man who could be so base and wanton in his conduct would not hesitate to slander the most virtuous female in the country, nay, even the Saviour, were He on earth. With regard to the tale of the clergyman, it seems to me to be so inconsistent with the charities of the Christian religion, and so opposed to the character of an embassador of Christ, that it gives me pain to read it. Now, my dear friend, why did not this clergyman come himself and tell me this tale, instead of asking you to do it? His not having done so, convinces me that he did not believe it, but was willing, through other sources, to spread the vile slander. If he had been told this by the attending physician himself, he had nothing to fear from giving his name, provided he was a person of responsibility; if he derived it from any other source than the doctor, he himself became a slanderer. The New Testament contains no such uncharitable examples as given by our Saviour while a sojourner on earth. I pray you write this clergyman, and remind him of the precepts contained in the good old book. If he reads it, he will know where to find them.

"I am authorized to say it is untrue that Mr. Eaton ever changed his lodgings, from the first time he went to Major O'Neal's to the present day, except for a few weeks, which was in consequence of his being on several committees much pressed with business, and making it necessary for him, a short time, to be near the Capitol. I should like to know the names of the members of Congress who saw the names of Mr. Eaton and Mrs. Timberlake entered on the tavern register as man and wife, and the date of those entries. If my memory serves me correctly, Mr. Eaton never traveled in company with Mrs. Timberlake but once, and then her husband went along, nor do I believe they went as far as New York; but in this I may be mistaken. But, suppose it to be true, are we to infer guilt from that circumstance? If the owner of the house, or his barkeeper, were to place upon their register the names of Mr. and Mrs. Eaton, what would that prove? Why, only that they supposed the lady with him, on his arrival at the inn, was his wife—a mistake, I will venture to say, that often occurs. There is, I expect, about as much truth in this story as the one that informed you, on your arrival at Philadelphia, that Mrs. Eaton was to preside at the President's house, or the one that represented her as intending to visit your city, in company with Major Lewis, to assist in purchasing furniture for the presidential mansion. Now, my dear sir, when such a bare-faced and unfounded misrepresentation as this can meet you in the teeth, I set down all that has been told you as unworthy entirely of credit.

"Major Lewis will go on shortly to see his daughter, at school in Philadelphia, and Mrs. Eaton, for aught I know, may go with him, to purchase furniture for her own house, as I am told she and Mr. Eaton intend keeping house. I suppose she has a right to travel, as well as any other person, if she chooses to do so; and if she desires to go under the protection of Major Lewis, if he nor her husband object, I do not think any other person has a right; but I do not know that she designs going at all—I am inclined to think she does not. Mrs. Eaton has not been in my house since I moved into it, but should she do so, the same attention and respect will be shown to her that are shown to others. On my nieces I lay no restriction. I only enjoin it on them to treat *all* well who may call to see them; they are required to visit none but those they may think proper.

"Permit me now, my dear and highly esteemed friend, to conclude this hasty, and I fear unintelligible scrawl. Whilst on the one hand we should shun base women as a pestilence of the worst and most dangerous kind to society, we ought, on the other, to guard virtuous female character with vestal vigilance. Female virtue is like a tender and delicate flower; let but the breath of suspicion rest upon it, and it withers and perhaps perishes forever. When it shall be assailed by envy and malice, the good and the pious will maintain its purity and innocence, until guilt is made manifest—not by *rumors* and *suspicions*, but by facts and proofs brought forth and sustained by respectable and fearless witnesses in the face of day. Truth shuns not the light; but falsehood deals in sly and dark insinuations, and prefers *darkness*, because its deeds are evil. The Psalmist says, 'The liar's tongue we ever hate, and banish from our sight.'

"Your friend, ANDREW JACKSON."

Dr. Ely promptly replied to this formidable letter. He was glad to learn, he said, that the President was so sure of Mrs. Eaton's innocence, and expressed a hope, that if she had done wrong in past times, she would now be restored by repentance to the esteem of the virtuous. Dr. Ely was, evidently, not quite convinced of Mrs. Eaton's immaculate purity. The President hastened to renew his efforts in her defense. He wrote again to his reverend friend.

GENERAL JACKSON TO REV. DR. ELY.

"WASHINGTON CITY, April 10, 1829.

"MY DEAR SIR: I have just received your friendly and frank letter of the 4th instant; and finding that you have been badly advised as to some matters on the subject under consideration, I am induced once more to write you. And first I must remark, that I have always thought *repentance* presupposes the existence of *crime*, and should have been gratified had you pointed to the proof of Mrs. Eaton's criminality before you recommended repentance.

"In your letter you say you had been assured by a gallant man that the rumors of which you speak, had been communicated to Mrs. Eaton and myself. This is not true, unless in *confidence*, or the information having been given by a lady, as stated to you in my last letter. If I am right in my conjectures as to the gallant man alluded to, he never did see any thing criminal in Mrs. Eaton, as he has always positively assured me; and the rebuff this *gallant gentleman* would have met with, if he had related it, would have convinced you that Mrs. Timberlake was not of such easy virtue. From that time to the present period they have been unfriendly. I think I well know the gentleman alluded to, and if I am not mistaken, although I entertain a high opinion of him, yet I do know there is no man whose prejudices run higher.

"I will relate a circumstance which has lately occurred, and then you can judge whether attempts have not been made to destroy Mrs. Eaton's character upon mere rumor, *unfounded* and under *secrecy*. Soon after General Call returned from Philadelphia he communicated to me that he had received, *confidentially*, from a *high-minded, honorable man*, 'information of a correspondence in writing between Mr. Eaton and Mr. Timberlake, which fixed on Mr. and Mrs. Eaton positive criminality—and that he had seen it.' I replied, as I always had done to the General, that this was a positive and unfounded slander, and that he ought to give up the name of such a *villain;* for, said I, pointing to the tobacco-pouch, '*that*, with the note which accompanied it, is my evidence that Mr. Timberlake had the utmost confidence in Mr. Eaton to the day of his death.' I insisted that it was due to Mr. Eaton to give him the name of this man, as he was determined to have justice done himself and lady. But, as has always been the case, the name of this man could not be had, *it was in confidence.* It is thus, my dear sir, this and all other slanders are circulated and promoted.

"I have since obtained a power of attorney (from Timberlake to Eaton), a copy of which I enclose you. Besides this, there are letters of a more recent date, expressive of the highest confidence in Mrs. Eaton and of the most friendly feeling. Yet it has been stated, and *confidently circulated*, that the conduct of Mr. Eaton was the cause of Mr. Timberlake's cutting his throat! Can any man, disposed to do justice and support truth, believe such tales, after reading the enclosed power of attorney and the letters referred to? They afford to my mind the most satisfactory evidence of the entire confidence reposed in Mr. Eaton by Mr. Timberlake up to the period of his death. Instead of communicating these slanderous tales to Mr. Eaton, they are concealed under the *pledges of confidence* by those who *profess* friendship for him. I do not wish to be understood as saying that these reports have never reached his ear, but I *do say*, that no one, so far as I am advised, has ever said to him, that *such a gentleman of high standing* has taken upon himself the responsibility of charging either Mr. or Mrs. Eaton with any act of *criminality* or even *impropriety*. I am sure our friend General Call has not, but to me he has *said* such rumors were in circulation, and when investigated were traced to the female alluded to in my last letter. In all General Call's conversations with me, and they have been frequent and *confidential*, he never did intimate any knowledge of Mrs. Eaton which was calculated, in my opinion, to cast even a shade of suspicion on her virtue. The very act which gave rise to his suspicions was one which, in my judgment, should have given him a more exalted opinion of her chastity.

"Mr. Eaton has very recently understood that the wives of two gentlemen in this city, have been speaking disrespectfully of himself and Mrs. Eaton, and he has, as it has been intimated to me, with promptness attended to the matter, and I doubt not that their lips will be hermetically sealed for the future. I have often reflected upon myself with some severity for ever having received, confidentially, any communication prejudicial to the character and standing of Mr. Eaton. I have known him for twenty years, without a speck upon his moral character, and my friend General Call has always united with me, in expressions of his great moral worth. I would then ask you, if such confidence existed between Mr. Eaton and Mr. Timberlake, to the day of the death of the latter, as is conclusively shown by the enclosed power of attorney, and the other evidence referred to, would not Mr. Eaton have been the basest man on earth, to have violated his confidence, and severed the ties that exist between masons? His general character forbids the idea, and his having taken her as his wife, is conclusive to my mind that he knew her to be virtuous. If he had been base enough to violate the confidence reposed in him by her husband, and to burst the bonds of masonry, he would have left her in disgrace and misery, instead of taking an object so *vile* and so *loathsome* to his bosom. Permit me now to say to you, in the language of sincerity, that I do not believe there is a being, worthy of belief, that can or will dare to state *a single fact*, going to show criminality or a want of virtue in her. Why, then, will not these secret slanderers, if they believe what they propagate, and have the proof—why not come out boldly, and like men armed with truth, be responsible for what they are daily in the habit of *secretly* and *confidentially* circulating? Truth fears not the open day, but falsehood and *vile slander* delight in darkness, and under the garb of friendship and in the name of *confidence*, circulate their poison.

"I question very much if any one ever told Mr. Eaton more than that rumors were afloat injurious to his character, until lately. No individuals were ever pointed out as speaking disrespectfully of Mr. Eaton and his wife, except the two ladies mentioned above; and from my knowledge of the man, I feel confident, that so soon as he can trace these slanders to any *responsible* source, he will make the individual responsible to him, be he who he may. I know he has been most cruelly treated by two men, who, to his face, have been always most friendly; and yet by innuendoes behind his back, have added to these slanders.

"The opinion I had of Mrs. Commodore —— when I last wrote you, I still entertain. After reading Commodore ——'s letter to Mr. Skinner of Baltimore, I could not give credence to the reports which had been circulated about her, and my belief of her innocence has since been strengthened by corroborating statements made to me here. If her father is really wealthy, as is stated to be the case by you, he is unworthy of confidence; for in an application which he has made to me for office, he assures me it is made in consequence of his poverty! Again you say, 'if the Commodore would furnish the authors of the rumors against his wife he must begin with her own father,' etc. Now, permit me to say that unless you have it from Mr. ——'s own lips, you ought not to believe *he* has been instrumental in circulating these rumors about his daughter. I have received a letter from him, in his own hand writing, in which he speaks in the most indignant manner of the authors of the slanders against his child, and solemnly declares his firm conviction of her innocence.

"I have been thus explicit, my dear sir, knowing that you love the truth, but believing that you have opened your ear to tales which, if I judge rightly of the high character you allude to, should never have been repeated to you; for he has either acted treacherously to me, or told you of things which have no existence. In short, he has told me himself that he never did see any act of Mrs. Eaton which was improper, though he believed her a thoughtless, volatile woman. I have written to the gentleman, informing him of the power of attorney, the letters, etc., etc., referred to above. From this evidence of confidence on the part of Mr. Timberlake in Mr. Eaton, I ask, can you believe such tales, without some direct and positive proof of criminality, and that, too, from the lips of individuals whose standing in society entitled them to credit? Where is the witness who has thus come forth in substantiation of these slanderous charges? None has yet done so, nor do I believe any will; for I believe the reports are entirely destitute of foundation.

"It puts me in mind (if I may be permitted to refer to the circumstance by way of illustration) of a tale circulated here the other day, to wit, 'that I was seized with spasms in the stomach, which would have occasioned my *instant death*, but for the immediate assistance of Dr. Henderson, who was at hand and saved me.' This was asserted to be an indubitable fact, and from the lips of Dr. Henderson himself. Now, my worthy friend, the truth is, I had no spasms, nor had I ever seen or heard of Dr. Henderson before, to the best of my recollection. But still the tale was told, and confidently believed to be true. It was repeated in the presence and hearing of my friend, Mrs. Love, who promptly contradicted it; but she was met with the reply, 'I have it from the mouth of Dr. Henderson himself; it must be true.' Thus it is with most of the tales, rumors, and surmises, which are put in circulation by the gossips of the world. Unless I am greatly mistaken, when all the facts and circumstances connected with this attempt to destroy Mr. Eaton, and blast the reputation of his wife, are brought to light, it will be found, in point of malignity and wickedness, to have few parallel cases.

"Please present me most kindly to your amiable wife, and believe me to be sincerely your friend, ANDREW JACKSON."

These letters convey but a faint idea of the interest felt by General Jackson in the vindication of the lady. He sent a gentleman to New York to investigate the hotel-register story. He wrote so many letters and statements in relation to this business that Major Lewis was worn out with the nightly toil of copying. The entire mass of the secret and confidential writings relating to Mrs. Eaton, all dated in the summer and autumn of 1829, and most of them originally in General Jackson's hand, would fill about eighty-five of these pages. And besides these, there was a large number of papers and documents not deemed important enough for preservation. To show the zeal and energy of General Jackson in the defense of a friend, I will append a catalogue of the papers preserved:

1. Letter of Dr. Ely to the President, stating the rumors. 2. The President's reply, given above. 3. Dr. Ely to the

President. 4. The President's second letter to Dr. Ely, given above. 5. Copy of purser Timberlake's power of attorney to Major Eaton. 6. A large batch of certificates by Timberlake's shipmates, showing that the purser had always spoken most affectionately of his wife and children, and had cut his throat in a fit of gloom, caused by dissipation on shore. 7. Dr. Ely to the President; says he is going to New York to inquire into the conduct of the lady there. 8. Dr. Ely to the President; says he has been to New York, and there is no truth in the stories. 9. Rev. J. N. Campbell to the President; begs him not to throw the weight of his great influence against him in his difference with Major Eaton. 10. The President to Rev. J. N. Campbell; says he will not. 11. Rev. J. N. Campbell to the President; he is glad to hear it. 12. A narrative by the President, duly signed and attested, of an interview between himself and the Rev. J. N. Campbell, which narrative the reader shall have the pleasure of perusing. 13. A finishing letter from the President to the Rev. J. N. Campbell. 16. Fifteen certificates of Mrs. Eaton's good character, addressed to the President, in reply to inquiries by him. 17. A correspondence between Major Eaton and the Rev. J. N. Campbell.

All this, and much more, in the first months of a new administration! General Jackson, indeed, made the cause his own, and brought to the defense of Mrs. Eaton all the fire and resolution with which, forty years before, he had silenced every whisper against Mrs. Jackson. He considered the cases of the two ladies parallel. His zeal in behalf of Mrs. Eaton was a manifestation or consequence of his wrath against the calumniators of his wife.

The General was so urgent in demanding of Dr. Ely the names of the persons who had spoken ill of Mrs. Eaton, that the doctor wrote, at length, to Mr. Campbell, advising him to call upon the President, and tell him all he knew. Mr. Campbell, in consequence, sought an interview with General Jackson. What transpired on this occasion the General deemed so important, that he wrote out for preservation a statement of it, with an account of the proceedings to which the interview led.

NARRATIVE BY GENERAL JACKSON.

"BE IT REMEMBERED, that on Tuesday evening, the 1st of September, 1829, I was in my parlor, when the door-keeper came to, and informed me, that the Reverend Mr. Campbell wanted an interview with me in my office. I went immediately up to my office, where I found Mr. Campbell and Major Donelson. Major Donelson having retired, Mr. Campbell observed, he supposed I knew his business, or the object of his business with me. I assured him that I did not. He then said that he had received a letter from Dr. Ely, which made it proper for him to inform me that he was the Presbyterian preacher or clergyman alluded to in Dr. Ely's letter to me, as having given the information relative to the *tale* of the deceased doctor, upon the subject of the miscarriage of Mrs. Timberlake, now Mrs. Eaton, in the absence of her husband, under circumstances which made it manifest that the child could not be his, as related to me in a letter from Dr. Ely. I was much astonished at this avowal, and replied that it was the first intimation I ever had that he was the Presbyterian clergyman who gave currency, through Dr. Ely, to this *vile tale*, and assured him that I never had the least suspicion of his being the author, and that in passing the subject through my mind, I had done injustice to another, for which I was sorry, although I had never named him to any one.

"Mr. Campbell then read to me part of Dr. Ely's letter, and entered into an explanation of his motives for not having made his communication directly to me. He said he knew Dr. Ely was my friend, and he wished me to be informed of those charges against Mrs. Eaton before I appointed Major Eaton a member of my Cabinet; that he had enjoined on Mr. Ely secrecy; that he considered it confidential, and charged him, that if he did not give it to my own ear, not to lisp it to any one. It was upon this condition alone that Mr. Ely was authorized to give up his name to me. He complained that Dr. Ely had not treated him well in communicating the information to others, and particularly to Mrs. Eaton.

To which I replied, I regretted that either he or Dr. Ely had not come directly to me with the *tale*, before Dr. Ely left Washington. If they had done so, I told him, I could easily have shown them the falsehood of some of the charges contained in Dr. Ely's letter to me, and would have pointed out to them some of the unhappy consequences that must now inevitably take place. I told him that I never had heard of this *tale*, circulated as coming from a dead doctor, before I read it in Dr. Ely's letter; that I was surprised Dr. Ely had not told him he had advised me in a confidential note, the Saturday before he left Washington, not to be drawn from my determination of appointing Mr. Eaton a member of my Cabinet, as his talents and my confidence in him made it necessary for me to have him near me. This I had determined on, and when next I saw him, told him that I could not be shaken in my purpose; that Major Eaton came into my Cabinet by my persuasion, and not from his own choice; that I knew him intimately for twenty years and upward, and believed his moral character to be without a blot.

"Mr. Campbell then detailed the information derived from this dead doctor, whom he called by the name of Craven.

"The manner of his relating the circumstances drew my particular attention, and I observed to him, as soon as he had gotten through, that this dead doctor *tale* was to me, in itself, incredible. As related by Mr. Campbell it is substantially as follows:—'The doctor told him that he had been called to Mrs. Timberlake as a physician, in consequence of her having been thrown from her carriage and much hurt; that when he entered the room where Mrs. Timberlake and an old woman were, they broke out into a loud laugh, and told him he was too late—that Mrs. Timberlake had miscarried, and he had lost his job; that Mr. Timberlake had been so long absent from home, that it was well known that the infant could not have been his.'

"I drew Mr. Campbell's attention to the absurdity of this story as related, and asked him if he had ever thought of the dilemma in which the dead doctor would be placed for *telling* such a *tale*, and he for believing and reporting it. I asked him if he did not know that doctors were prohibited by law from revealing the secrets of a sick bed, and if he did not suppose this doctor would be considered a base man and unworthy of credit, the moment this story was presented to the public. I told him the honorable, moral, and religious part of the community would have no confidence in the representations of such a man, and that he would be held responsible for it, inasmuch as he had avowed himself the author of its circulation.

"Mr. Campbell then observed, he believed that he (the doctor) had stated that he accidentally happened in, and had not been sent for as a physician.

"I told Mr. Campbell it was still more absurd to suppose that a married woman, so long absent from her husband that every one must know the child could not be his, would so wantonly publish her own disgrace and infamy to the world, when she had no need of a physician in her private chamber. This version of the story, I observed to him, was too absurd and ridiculous, as well as inconsistent with every principle and feeling of human nature, to be believed even by the most *credulous;* and that I was astonished a man of his good sense could, for one moment, give credence to it, and particularly as it involved the character of a lady.

I then inquired of Mr. Campbell what date the dead doctor had given to this transaction—the date being important.

"He replied, in 1821.

"I asked him if he was aware of the situation he would be placed in if, on inquiry, it should appear that Mr. Timberlake was in this country, and never out of it in 1821. I told him I was under the impression that it would so appear, whenever examined into; that I was induced to believe he had not been absent from the United States from the close of the war until 1824; that I had understood he was detained here prosecuting a claim against the government for property thrown overboard by Commodore Decatur previous to the capture of the frigate *President.* Having lost his vouchers, he was unable to settle his accounts, and, therefore, being considered a defaulter, could not get public employment.

"Mr. Campbell replied that Mr. Timberlake, from the information of the Doctor, must have been absent in that year.

"I answered it was my opinion he would find himself mistaken, and it would be well for him to make inquiry, and as a Christian and preacher of the Gospel, it would be his duty, if he found he had been mistaken in this information, to repair the injury he had done female character by saying to Mrs. Eaton, and to the world, that on inquiry he found there was no truth in the tale of his dead Doctor. Justice and Christianity, I told him, demanded this of him.

"After some further conversation on the subject of Mrs. Timberlake visiting his family, and the visit being returned, and that a friendly intercourse was kept up between the two families, until Dr. Craven gave him the information relative to the abortion, when all intercourse ceased, I asked Mr. Campbell why he did not, when he received this information, and before he terminated the friendly relation which had subsisted between his family and Mrs. Timberlake, go to her and inform her of this *vile tale*, and the name of the person from whom he had received it, and say to her that she must remove this stain upon her character, or all intercourse between them must cease. This, I told him, was what I thought he, as a Christian, ought to have done, pursuing the golden rule of doing to others as we would they should do unto us. This would have given her an opportunity of showing her innocence, or, if she failed, then, with a clear conscience, he and his family could have withdrawn from her society.

"The date having been given by Mr. Campbell, as stated by the dead doctor, it being an important fact by which to judge of the truth or falsehood of this *story*, I at once determined to have inquiry made as to where Mr. Timberlake was in all the year 1821; and while ruminating on this subject, Major W. B. Lewis came into my office and inquired relative to Mr. Campbell's business with me (he having been in the parlor below when the doorkeeper told me the Rev. Mr. Campbell wished to have a private interview with me). I told him Mr. Campbell came to avow himself to be the clergyman alluded to in Dr. Ely's letter to me, who had informed him (Ely) of the reported miscarriage of Mrs. Timberlake, when it was well known the child could not be her husband's, in consequence of his long absence from the country; and that Mr. Campbell had affixed to this transaction a date—1821. This, I observed, was tangible, and by it the truth or falsehood of the tale might be tested. I requested Major Lewis to ascertain, if it was practicable to do so, where Mr. Timberlake was in all that year, assuring him that I was convinced, in my own mind, and had so said to Mr. Campbell, that Mr. Timberlake was here during the whole year 1821; that I had never heard of his leaving the United States until the spring of 1824; that I had seen him at Mr. O'Neal's in the winter of 1823 and 1824, and was there when he took leave of his family, preparatory to a cruise up the Mediterranean.

"On the evening of the 2nd of September, instant, Major Lewis informed me that he had made the inquiry, as requested by me, and had learned that Mr. Timberlake was a merchant in this city about that time, and that his books were now in the possession of Mrs. Eaton, which, if looked into, would in all probability show where he was during the year 1821. I resolved to go and examine the books myself, and on the same evening—2nd September—I accordingly went up to Major Eaton's.

"On entering the parlor, I found no one there but John Henderson, Major Eaton's nephew, who informed me that his uncle was up stairs with his aunt, who was very sick. I desired him to go up and request his uncle to come below, as I wanted to see him. Major Eaton came down and invited me to walk up and see Mrs. Eaton. I did so, and found her very ill and in bed. After a short conversation with her, and being informed of an interview had with Mr. Campbell on that day, I asked Mrs. Eaton if she had the mercantile books of Mr. Timberlake in her possession. She said she had. I desired to know if she would permit me to see them. She said not only me, but any one. I then went down stairs to the parlor, were the books were brought to me, and I examined them. I soon found from entries—said to be in the handwriting of Mr. Timberlake—that he was in this country and in this city throughout the year 1821. Before leaving Major Eaton's, I took extracts from the books of Dr. Sim's and Major O'Neal's accounts, to show Mr. Campbell, and to prove to him that Mr. Timberlake must have been here in that year, and as late as February, 1822, as the entries were made in his own handwriting.

"I was convinced in my own mind that on exhibiting this proof to Mr. Campbell, he wolud at once see the cruelty of this charge, as made by his dead doctor, and the injustice done Mrs. Eaton, and would so declare to Mrs. Eaton and all others. I, therefore, on my return home, requested Major Donelson to wait upon Mr. Campbell, and having heard that Col.

Towson, by request of Mr. Campbell, was present at the interview between the latter gentleman and Major Eaton and his lady, on the 2d instant, I desired Major Donelson to request the Colonel to accompany Mr. Campbell and be present at the interview I wished to have with him.

"Agreeably to my request, the Rev. Mr. Campbell called at my office on the morning of the 3d inst., when an interview was had in the presence of Col. Towson and Major Donelson. After stating to Mr. Campbell and Col. Towson the reason which had induced me to request this meeting, it being in consequence of a conversation had with Mr. Campbell, at his own request, on the 1st inst., I stated the result of my inquiry as to the fact where Mr. Timberlake was in the year 1821, and having the proof in my hand, observed that it evidenced, beyond all contradiction, that the tale of the dead doctor could not be true. I further observed that if any doubts existed as to the entries being in the handwriting of Mr. Timberlake, the books could be seen, and that fact clearly ascertained.

"Mr. Campbell then said, I must have misunderstood him as to the date.

"I replied, I could not; he must recollect, at the time he made the statement, how earnestly I brought to his view the dilemma in which he would be placed if, at the date given to this transaction, Mr. Timberlake should be proved to be in this country. Notwithstanding this, he (then) still persisted in the declaration of Mr. Timberlake's absence in that year.

"He, however, now maintained that I had mistaken him as to the date.

"I again told him as positively *I had not.* I then asked him to give a date to the transaction, if it was not in 1821. He refused. I replied, that the date being all important, for on this depended the innocence or guilt of the lady, I requested that he would give to it a date. He did not and would not. After taking out some papers, and looking over them, he said Mr. Timberlake was absent, from his memoranda, in the autumn of 1822.

"I observed to him that there was neither justice nor Christianity in making a charge which goes to the destruction of female character, without affixing to it a date, by which truth or falsehood could be tested. Still, however, Mr. Campbell, in his last interview, positively refused to give a date, although in his first he had given 1821, and insisted that Mr. Timberlake must have been absent. Col. Towson and Major Donelson being present, their written statement is referred to as explanatory of what was further said at this interview—being on the 3d instant.

"I will barely add, in conclusion, that Mr. Campbell stated he had employed Mr. Key as counsel, who had told him his proof was sufficient. He further said his statement would be corroborated by the evidence of the mother and wife of Dr. Craven. I cautioned him not to be too sanguine with regard to his proofs. He said that he and Col. Towson had seen the mother and wife of Dr. Craven that morning, etc., etc.

"This statement is made from memoranda in writing, taken immediately after the conversation took place, from day to day; and although the very words may not be given, I am certain the whole, as far as I have attempted to state the conversation, is substantially correct.

"Andrew Jackson."

"September 3d, 1829."

"P. S.—I requested Mr. Campbell to explain his motives in coming to me to avow himself as the author of this secret slander against Mrs. Eaton; but this he failed satisfactorily to do. It was well known that I had been long and intimately acquainted with Major Eaton, knew his worth, and was satisfied that a blemish did not rest upon his moral character. Why he did not go to Mr. Eaton with it, who was here, I can not tell. He was the person who should have been informed of this slander, and especially as both Mr. Campbell and Dr. Ely acknowledged to me in the presence of my cabinet, Mr. Van Buren, Mr. Ingham, Mr. Branch, Mr. Barry, and Mr. Berrian, and also Major Lewis and Major Donelson, that they entirely acquitted Major Eaton of the charge of improper or criminal conduct.

"Why this persecution of Mrs. Eaton—the motives which induced to such conduct—I leave to the decision of the moral and Christian world. Mrs. Eaton is the wife of Major Eaton, which is the strongest evidence he can give in her virtue. Does Mr. Campbell wish to separate man and wife by his false tales? Surely this is not the doctrine taught by our Saviour, and which, if he reads his Bible, he may find in every page of that sacred book.

"Andrew Jackson."

The postscript to General Jackson's statement was evidently added some days after the date affixed to the body of the narrative, because the postscript alludes to a cabinet council held on the 10th of September. This council the President invited Mr. Campbell to attend in the following letter:

GENERAL JACKSON TO REV. J. N. CAMPBELL.

"Washington, September 10th, 1829.

"Dear Sir: After our interview in the presence of Colonel Towson and Major Donelson, Mr. Key sought one with me, in which he submitted certain propositions as the basis of an accommodation of the existing difficulty between yourself and Major Eaton, the result of which was nothing more than an agreement to suspend any further action upon the subject until the arrival of Mr. Ely, who was to be requested to visit this place immediately.

"Mr. Ely has since arrived, but I do not perceive, notwithstanding your failure as far as I am informed, to sustain the charge against Mrs. Eaton's character, that you are disposed to make those acknowledgments which, it occurs to me, an ambassador of Christ ought, on such an occasion, to make. This being the fact, and judging from your letter of the 5th, and from insinuations made to me by Mr. Ely in regard to the supposed reluctance of certain clerks to testify in the case, that my relation to it has been or may be misconceived, I have determined to call my Cabinet together this evening at 7 o'clock, when I have asked Mr. Ely to attend, and will be happy also if you will, for the purpose of disclosing to them what has happened; so that whatever may be the course of the affair hereafter, no misunderstanding of my motives and agency in it, therefore, may exist.

"Having ever entertained the highest regard for the moral character of Mr. Eaton, I brought him into my Cabinet, with the fullest persuasion that the cause of virtue and religion, which it has been my pride through life to support, would be benefited by it. I wanted no information to satisfy me of the purity of his character. As my friend, years of intimacy and experience with him, supplied the most abundant evidence of it; but a different sentiment, entertained by others, has been obtruded upon me, in a manner which, I must say, invariably excited my distrust of its sincerity. In this I may be wrong, but the golden rule which requires us to do to others what we would have others do to us, seems to me so plainly to have required that the cause of such a sentiment should have first been communicated to Mr. Eaton, that I can not yet give up this distrust.

"It can only be removed by the complete establishment of the fact upon which they have been supposed to rest their belief of his criminal intercourse with Mrs. Timberlake, and until this is done, justice to her, to myself, and the country, requires that after the proposed council with my Cabinet, I should hold no future conversation with yourself or any one else, in relation to this subject. Your obedient servant,

"ANDREW JACKSON."*

What occurred at the meeting of the Cabinet in the evening, General Jackson did not think proper to have recorded. From other sources I learn some particulars.

The members of the Cabinet, Dr. Ely, and Mr. Campbell being assembled, the President opened the proceedings with

* All these documents are from the MSS. of Major Wm. B. Lewis.

an address upon the meanness of calumny, and concluded by giving an account of the late investigations. The dispute between himself and Mr. Campbell upon the date of the alleged miscarriage was renewed with much acrimony. Mr. Campbell declared that he had not intended to give the year 1821 as the precise date of Dr. Craven's story. He had seen, that very morning, the widow and the daughter of Dr. Craven, who both confirmed his previous statement, and agreed that 1826 was the year when the damning event occurred. The President still insisted that Mr. Campbell had irrevocably committed himself to the year 1821. He further declared that Dr. Craven's wife and daughter had given two versions of the "dead-doctor tale," which were irreconcilable. The President would not hear Mr. Campbell further on that point. He had originally said 1821, and by 1821 he must abide.

The President then turned to the other charges. "As to the allegation," said he, "that Mrs. Jackson had an unfavorable opinion of Mrs. Timberlake, I declare of my own knowledge that it is false." The charge that Major Eaton and Mrs. Timberlake passed the night together in a New York hotel dwindled first, said the President, into a story that they had been seen on a bed together, and, afterward, that they had been seen sitting on a bed together. He called upon Dr. Ely to state the result of his inquiries in New York.

The reverend gentleman told his story, and concluded by saying that there was no evidence to convict Major Eaton of improper conduct.

"Nor Mrs. Eaton either," broke in the President.

"On that point," said the Doctor, "I would rather not give an opinion."

"She is as chaste as a virgin!" exclaimed the President.

When Dr. Ely had finished his narrative, Mr. Campbell asked to be allowed to say a few words in his own justification. He declared that, in all that he had done, his object had been to save the administration of General Jackson from reproach, and the morals of the country from contamination. He had communicated nothing to the opponents of the administration. He conceived that the evidence which had been elicited justified him in the course he had deemed it right to pursue.

As he was proceeding to remark upon the evidence, General Jackson interrupted him with marked asperity of manner, saying that he had been summoned thither to *give* evidence, not discuss it.

Mr. Campbell then said: "I perceive that I have mistaken the object of the invitation to come here; that it was not to give me an opportunity of saying any thing in my justification. I have therefore only to say, that I stand ready to prove, in a court of justice, all I have said, and more than I have said, or would have dared to say three days ago."

He then bowed to the council and retired. The council broke up soon after, and the President deemed Mrs. Eaton a vindicated woman. It is needless to say, that the church over which the Rev. Mr. Campbell presided was no longer favored with the attendance of the President of the United States.

Whether the efforts of the President had or had not the effect of convincing the ladies of Washington that Mrs. Eaton was worthy of admission into their circle, shall in due time be related. Upon a point of that nature ladies are not convinced easily. Meanwhile, the suitors for presidential favor are advised to make themselves visible at the lady's receptions. A card in Mrs. Eaton's card basket, is not unlikely to be a winning card.

IV.

TERROR AMONG THE OFFICE-HOLDERS.

CONSTITUTION makers do all they can to support the weakness of human virtue when subjected to the temptations of power and place. But virtue can not be dispensed with in this world. No system of "checks and balances" can be made so perfect but that much must be left, after all, to the honor of governing persons.

Among the powers entrusted to the honor of presidents of the United States was the dread power of removing from office, without trial or notice, the civil employés of the government. In the army and navy, no officer can be cashiered, no private dismissed, without trial—without being heard in his defense. In the civil service of the country, every man holds his place at the will of the head of government.

This fearful power over the fortunes of individuals and the happiness of families, is held, necessarily, in our present imperfect civilization, by a large number of persons in private life; and it is one of the ten thousand proofs of the inherent loving-kindness of human nature, that this power is generally exercised with a considerable regard for the feelings, the necessities, and the rights of the employed. The claim of old servants to indulgence and protection is almost universally recognized. The right of a person about to be dismissed from an employment to as long a notice of dismission beforehand as can be conveniently given, few persons are unfeeling enough to deny. The good policy of holding out to the faithful employée the prospect of a permanent retention of his place, and his promotion, by and by, to a better, no one but a politician has been foolish enough to question.

It does not appear to have occurred to the gentlemen who formed the Constitution under which we live, that there could ever be a President of the United States who would abuse the power of removal. His own responsibility for the conduct of those whom he appointed was supposed to be sufficient to make him careful to appoint the right men to the right places ; and his feelings, as a man and a gentleman, were deemed an adequate protection to those right men in their right places.

It is delightful to observe with what a scrupulous conscientiousness the early Presidents of this republic disposed of the places in their gift. Washington set a noble example. He demanded to be satisfied on three points with regard to an applicant for office : Is he honest ? Is he capable ? Has he the confidence of his fellow-citizens ? Not till these questions were satisfactorily answered did he deign to inquire respecting the political opinions of a candidate. Private friendship between the President and an applicant was absolutely an obstacle to his appointment, so fearful was the President of being swayed by private motives. "My friend," he says, in one of his letters, "I receive with cordial welcome. He is welcome to my house, and welcome to my heart ; but with all his good qualities he is not a man of business. His opponent, with all his politics so hostile to me, *is* a man of business. My private feelings have nothing to do in the case. I am not George Washington, but President of the United States. As George Washington, I would do this man any kindness in my power—as President of the United States, I can do nothing."

There spoke the man who was a GENTLEMAN to the core of his heart.

If General Washington would not appoint a friend because he was a friend, nor a partisan because he was a partisan, still less was he capable of removing an enemy because he was an enemy, or an opponent because he was an opponent. During his administration of eight years, he removed nine persons from office ; namely, six unimportant collectors, one district surveyor, one vice-consul, and one foreign minister. We all know that he recalled Mr. Pinckney from Paris because that conservative gentleman was offensive to the

French Directory. The other dismissals were all "for cause." Politics had nothing to do with one of them.

The example of General Washington was followed by his successors. John Adams doubted, even, whether it was strictly proper for him to retain his son in a foreign employment to which President Washington had appointed him. He removed nine subordinate officers during his presidency; but none for political opinion's sake. Jefferson, owing to peculiar circumstances well known to readers of history, removed thirty-nine persons; but he himself repeatedly and solemnly declared, that not one of them was removed because he belonged to the party opposed to his own. The contrary imputation he regarded in the light of a calumny, and refuted it as such. In one respect Mr. Jefferson was even over scrupulous. He would not appoint any man to office, however meritorious, who was a relative of his own. Mr. Madison made five removals; Mr. Monroe, nine; Mr. John Quincy Adams, two. Mr. Calhoun tells us,* that during the seven years that he held the office of Secretary of War only two of his civil subordinates were removed, both for improper conduct. In both cases, he adds, the charges were investigated in the presence of the accused, and "the officers were not dismissed until after full investigation, and the reason of dismission reduced to writing and communicated to them."†
24 Colonel McKenney mentions, in his "Memoirs," that when a vacancy occurred in one of the departments, the chief of that department would inquire among his friends for "a qualified" person to fill it.

Nor was this scrupulousness due to any lack of aspirants for governmental employment. Mr. John Quincy Adams says, in one of his letters, that he was tormented with ceaseless, with daily applications for office. In the last year of

* Works of John C. Calhoun, ii., 439.

† "Napoleon was a despot, it is said; yet he never dismissed any one from public office without an inquiry and report of facts, and rarely ever without hearing the accused functionary: never when the questions involved were civil or administrative."—*Napoleonic Ideas. By Louis Napoleon.*

Mr. Monroe's presidency, when the fourth auditorship of the treasury fell vacant, there were, among the army of applicants for the place, five United States Senators and thirty members of the House of Representatives ![*]

Up to the hour of the delivery of General Jackson's inaugural address, it was supposed that the new President would act upon the principles of his predecessors. In his Monroe letters he had taken strong ground against partisan appointments, and when he resigned his seat in the Senate he had advocated two amendments to the constitution designed to limit and purify the exercise of the appointing power. One of these proposed amendments forbade the reëlection of a President, and the other the appointment of members of Congress to any office not judicial.

The sun had not gone down upon the day of his inauguration before it was known in all official circles in Washington that the "reform" alluded to in the inaugural address meant a removal from office of all who had conspicuously opposed, and an appointment to office of those who had conspicuously aided the election of the new President. The work was promptly begun. Figures are not important here, and the figures relating to this matter have been disputed. Some have declared that during the first year of the presidency of General Jackson two thousand persons in the civil employment of the government were removed from office, and two thousand partisans of the President appointed in their stead. This statement has been denied. It can not be denied that in the first month of this administration more removals were made than had occurred from the foundation of the government to that time. It can not be denied that the principle was now acted upon that partisan services should be rewarded by public office, though it involved the removal from office of competent and faithful incumbents. Col. Benton will not be suspected of overstating the facts respecting the removals, but he admits that their number,

[*] N. Y. American, April 3, 1824.

during this year, 1829, was six hundred and ninety. He expresses himself on this subject with less than his usual directness. His estimate of six hundred and ninety does not include the little army of clerks and others who were at the disposal of some of the six hundred and ninety. The estimate of two thousand includes all who lost their places in consequence of General Jackson's accession to power; and, though the exact number can not be ascertained, I presume it was not less than two thousand. Col. Benton says that of the eight thousand postmasters, only four hundred and ninety-one were removed; but he does not add, as he might have added, that the four hundred and ninety-one vacated places comprised nearly all in the department that were worth having. Nor does he mention that the removal of the postmasters of half a dozen great cities was equivalent to the removal of many hundreds of clerks, book-keepers, and carriers.

General Harrison, who had courteously censured General Jackson's course in the Seminole war, who had warmly defended his friend, Henry Clay, against the charge of bargain and corruption, was recalled from Colombia just four days after General Jackson had acquired the power to recall him. General Harrison had only resided in Colombia a few weeks when he received the news of his recall. A Kentuckian, who was particularly inimical to Mr. Clay, was sent out to take his place.

The appointment of a soldier so distinguished as General Harrison to represent the United States in the infant republic of Colombia was regarded by the Colombians as a great honor done them, and an emphatic recognition of their disputed claim to a place among the nations. A purer patriot, a worthier gentleman, than General William Henry Harrison, has not adorned the public service of his country. His singular merits as a scholar, as a man of honor, as a soldier, and as a statesman, were only obscured by the calumny and eulogium incident to a presidential campaign. My studies of the Indian affairs of the country have given me the highest idea of his valor, skill, and humanity.

Samuel Swartwout was among the expectants at Washington—an easy, good-natured man; most inexact and even reckless in the management of business; the last man in the whole world to be intrusted with millions. He had hopes of the collectorship of New York. On the fourteenth of March he wrote from Washington to his friend, Jesse Hoyt, to let him know how he was getting on, and to give Hoyt the benefit of his observations—Hoyt himself being a seeker. "I hold to your doctrine fully," wrote Swartwout, "that no d——d rascal who made use of his office or its profits for the purpose of keeping Mr. Adams in, and General Jackson out of power, is entitled to the least lenity or mercy, save that of hanging. So we think both alike on that head. Whether or not I shall get any thing in the general scramble for plunder, remains to be proven; but I rather guess I shall. What it will be is not yet so certain; perhaps keeper of the Bergen lighthouse. I rather think Massa Pomp stands a smart chance of going somewhere, perhaps to the place you have named, or to the devil. Your man, if you want a place, is Col. Hamilton*—he being now the second officer in the government of the Union, and in all probability our next President. Make your suit to him, then, and you will get what you want. I know Mr. Ingham slightly, and would recommend you to push like a devil if you expect any thing from that quarter. I can do you no good in any quarter of the world, having mighty little influence beyond Hoboken. The great goers are the new men; the old troopers being all spavined and ring-boned from previous hard travel. I've got the bots, the fet-lock, hip-joint, gravel, halt, and founders; and I assure you if I can only keep my own legs, I shall do well; but I'm darned if I can carry any weight with me. When I left home, I thought my nag sound and strong, but the beast is rather broken down here. I'll tell you more

* Acting Secretary of State until the arrival of Mr. Van Buren.

about it when I see you in New York. In seriousness, my dear sir, your support must come from Mr. Van Buren and Mr. Col. Hamilton; I could not help you any more than your clerk."*

The President, distracted with the number of applications for the New York collectorship, and extremely fond of the man who had 'pushed like a devil,' a quarter of a century before at Richmond, gave Swartwout the place. Upon his return to New York, his proverbial good nature was put to a severe test; for the applicants for posts in the custom-house met him at every turn, crowded his office, invaded his house, and stuffed his letter-box. There was a general dismission of Adams men from the New York Custom House, and the new appointments were made solely on the ground that the applicants had aided the election of General Jackson.

Henry Lee was appointed to a remote foreign consulship, a place which he deemed beneath his talents and an inadequate reward for his services. He would have probably obtained a better place but for the fear that the Senate would reject the nomination. The Senate did reject his nomination even to the consulship, and by such a decided majority that nothing could be done for him. Even Colonel Benton voted against him. Lee, I may add, died soon after in Paris, where he wrote part of a history of the emperor Napoleon.

Terror, meanwhile, reigned in Washington. No man knew what the rule was upon which removals were made. No man knew what offenses were reckoned causes of removal, nor whether he had or had not committed the unpardonable sin. The great body of officials awaited their fate in silent horror, glad when the office hours expired at having escaped another day. "The gloom of suspicion," says Mr. Stansbury, himself an office-holder, "pervaded the face of society. No man deemed it safe and prudent to trust his neighbor, and the interior of the department presented a fearful scene of guarded silence, secret intrigue, espionage, and tale-bearing.

* Mackenzie's Van Buren, p 197.

A casual remark, dropped in the street, would within an hour, be repeated at head quarters; and many a man received unceremonious dismission who could not, for his life, conceive or conjecture wherein he had offended."

At that period, it must be remembered, to be removed from office in the city of Washington was like being driven from the solitary spring in a wide expanse of desert. The public treasury was almost the sole source of emolument. Salaries were small, the expenses of living high, and few of the officials had made provision for engaging in private business or even for removing their families to another city. No one had anticipated a necessity of removal. Clerks, appointed by the early presidents, had grown gray in the service of the government, and were so habituated to the routine of their places, that, if removed, they were beggared and helpless.

An old friend of General Jackson's was in Washington this summer. He wrote on the 4th of July to a friend: "I have seen the President, and have dined with him, but have had no free communication, or conversation with him. The reign of this administration, I wish an other word could be used, is in very strong contrast with the mild and lenient sway of Madison, Monroe, and Adams. To me it feels harsh —it seems to have had an unhappy effect on the free thoughts, and unrestrained speech, which has heretofore prevailed. I question whether the ferreting out treasury rats, and the correction of abuses, are sufficient to compensate for the reign of terror which appears to have commenced. It would be well enough if it were confined to evil-doers, but it spreads abroad like a contagion: spies, informers, denunciations—the fecula of despotism. Where there are listeners there will be tale-bearers. A stranger is warned by his friend on his first arrival to be careful how he expresses himself in relation to any one, or any thing which touches the administration. I had hoped that this would be a national administration—but it is not even an administration of a party. Our republic henceforth, will be governed by factions, and the struggle will be who shall get the offices and their emoluments—a struggle embittered by the most base and sordid passions of the human heart."

So numerous were the removals in the city of Washington that the business of the place seem paralyzed. In July, a Washington paper said:

"Thirty-three houses which were to have been built this year have, we learn, been stopped, in consequence of the unsettled and uncertain state of things now existing here; and the merchant can not sell his goods or collect his debts from the same cause. We have never known the city to be in a state like this before, though we have known it for many years. The individual distress, too, produced, in many cases, by the removal of the destitute officers, is harrowing and painful to all who possess the ordinary sympathies of our nature, without regard to party feeling. No man, not absolutely brutal, can be pleased to see his personal friend or neighbor suddenly stripped of the means of support, and cast upon the cold charity of the world without a shelter or a home. Frigid and insensible must be the heart of that man who could witness some of the scenes that have lately been exhibited here, without a tear of compassion or a throb of sympathy. But what is still more to be regretted is, that this system, having been once introduced, must necessarily be kept up at the commencement of every presidential term; and he who goes into office knowing its limited and uncertain tenure, feels no disposition to make permanent improvements or to form for himself a permanent residence. He, therefore, takes care to lay up what he can, during his brief official existence, to carry off to some more congenial spot, where he means to spend his life, or reënter into business. All, therefore, that he might have expended in city improvements is withdrawn, and the revenue of the corporation, as well as the trade of the city, is so far lessened and decreased. It is obviously a most injurious policy as it respects the interests of our city. Many of the oldest and most respectable citizens of Washington, those who have adhered to its fortunes through all their vicissitudes, who have 'grown with its growth and strengthened with its strength,' have been cast off to make room for strangers who feel no interest in the prosperity of our infant metropolis, and who care not whether it advances or retrogrades."

As an illustration of the state of things in Washington at this time, I will here transcribe the story of Colonel T. L. McKenney, for many years the honest and capable superintendent of Indian affairs, appointed to that office by Mr. Monroe:

"Some time after General Jackson had been inaugurated, the Secretary of War, Major Eaton, inquired of me *if I had been to see the President?* I said I had not. 'Had you not better go over?' 'Why, sir?' I asked—'I have had no official business to call me there, nor have I now; why should I go?' 'You know, in these times,' replied the Secretary, 'it is well to cultivate those personal relations, which will go far toward securing the good will of one in power'—and he wound up by more than intimating that the President had heard some things in disparagement of me; when I determined forthwith to go and see him, and ascertain what they were. On arriving at the door of the President's house, I was answered by the door-keeper that the President was in, and having gone to report me, returned, saying the President would see me. On arriving at the door, it having been thrown open by the door-keeper, I saw the President very busily engaged writing, and with great earnestness; so much so, indeed, that I stood for some time before he took his eyes off the paper, fearing to interrupt him, and not wishing to seem intrusive. Presently he raised his eyes from the paper, and at the same time his spectacles from his nose, and looking at me, said, 'Come in sir, come in.' 'You are engaged, sir?' 'No more so than I always am, and always expect to be,' drawing a long breath, and giving signs of great uneasiness.

"I had just said, 'I am here, sir, at the instance of the Secretary of War,' when the door was thrown open, and three members of Congress entered. They were received with great courtesy. I rose, saying, 'You are engaged, sir: I will call when you are more at leisure;' and bowed myself out. On returning to my office, I addressed a note to the President of the following import: 'Colonel McKenney's respects to the President of the United States, and requests to be informed when it will suit his convenience to see him?' to which Major Donelson replied, 'The President will see Colonel McKenney to-day, at twelve o'clock.' I was punctual, and found the President alone. I commenced by repeating what I had said at my first visit, that I was there at the instance of the Secretary of War, who had more than intimated to me that impressions of an unfavorable sort had been made upon him with regard to me; and that I was desirous of knowing what the circumstances were that had produced them. 'It is true, sir,' said the President, 'I have been told things that are highly discreditable to you, and which have come to me from such sources as to satisfy me of their truth.' 'Very well, sir, will you do me the justice to let me know what these things are that you have heard from such respectable sources?' 'You know, Colonel McKenney, I am a candid man— 'I beg pardon, sir,' I remarked, interrupting him, 'but I am not here to question that, but to hear charges, which it appears have been made to you, affecting my character, either as an officer of the government or a man.' 'Well, sir,' he resumed, 'I will frankly tell you what these charges are, and, sir, they are of a character which I can never respect.' 'No doubt of that, sir; but what are they?' 'Why, sir, I am told, and on the best authority, that you were one of the principal promoters of that vile paper, *We the People*, as a contributor toward establishing it, and as a writer afterward, in which my wife Rachel was so shamefully abused. I am told, further, on authority no less respectable, that you took an active 28 part in distributing, under the frank of your office, the "*coffin hand-bills*," and that in your recent travels, you largely and widely circulated the militia pamphlet.' Here he paused, crossed his legs, shook his foot, and clasped his hands around the upper knee, and looked at me as though he had actually convicted and prostrated me; when, after a moment's pause, I asked, 'Well, sir, what else?' 'Why, sir,' he answered, 'I think such conduct highly unbecoming in one who fills a place in the government such as you fill, and very derogatory to you, as it would be in any one who should be guilty of such practices.' 'All this,' I replied, 'may be well enough; but I request to know if this is all you have heard, and whether there are any more charges?' 'Why, yes, sir, there is one more; I am told your office is not in the condition in which it should be.' 'Well, sir, what more?' 'Nothing, sir; but these are all serious charges, sir.' 'Then, sir, these comprise all?' 'They do, sir.' 'Well, General,' I answered, 'I am not going to reply to all this, or to any part of it, with any view to retaining my office, nor do I intend to reply to it at all, *except under the solemnity of an oath*,' when I threw up my hand toward heaven, saying, '*the answers I am about to give to these allegations, I solemnly swear, shall be the truth, the whole truth, and nothing but the truth.* My oath, sir, is taken, and is no doubt recorded—' He interrupted me, by saying, 'You are making quite a serious affair of it.' 'It is, sir, what I mean to do' I answered.

"Now, sir, in regard to the paper called "*We the People*," I never did, directly or indirectly, either by my money, or by my pen, contribute toward its establishment, or its continuance. I never circulated one copy of it, more or less, nor did I subscribe for a copy of it, more or less; nor have I ever, to the best of my knowledge and belief, handled a copy of it, nor have I ever seen but two copies, and these were on the table of a friend, among other newspapers. So much for that charge. In regard to the "*coffin hand-bills*," I never circulated any, either under the frank of my office or otherwise, and never saw but two; and am not certain that I ever saw but one, and that some fool sent me, under cover, from Richmond, in Virginia, and which I found on my desk among other papers, on going to my office; and which, on seeing what it was, I tore up and threw aside among the waste paper, to be swept out by my messenger. The other, which I took to be one of these bills, but which might have been an account of the hanging of some convict, I saw some time ago, pendent from a man's finger and thumb, he having a roll under his arm, as he crossed Broadway, in New York. So much for the coffin hand-bills. As to the "militia pamphlet," I have seen reference made to it in the newspapers, it is true, but I have never handled it—have never read it, or circulated a copy or copies of it, directly or indirectly. And now, sir, as to my office. That is my monument; its records are its inscriptions. Let it be examined, and I invite a commission for that purpose; nor will I return to it to put a paper in its place, should it be out of place, or in any other way prepare it for the ordeal; and, if there is a single flaw in it, or any just grounds for complaint, either on the part of the white or the red man, implicating my capacity—my diligence, or want of due regard to the interests of all having business with it, including the government, then, sir, you shall have my free consent to put any mark upon me you may think proper, or subject me to as much opprobrium as shall gratify those who have thus abused your confidence by their secret attempts to injure me.'

"'Colonel McKenney,' said the General, who had kept his eyes upon me during the whole of my reply, 'I believe every word you have said, and am satisfied that those who communicated to me those allegations were mistaken.' 'I thank you, sir,' I replied, 'for your confidence, but I am not satisfied. I request to have my accusers brought up, and that I may be allowed to confront them in your presence.' 'No—no, sir,' he answered, 'I am satisfied; why then push the matter farther?' when, rising from his chair, he took my arm, and said, 'Come, sir, come down, and allow me to introduce you to my family.' I accompanied him, and was introduced to Mrs. Donaldson, Major Donaldson, and some others who were present, partook of the offering of a glass of wine, and retired.

"The next morning I believe it was—or if not the next, some morning not far off—a Mr. R-b-s-n, a very worthy, gentlemanly fellow, and well known to me, came into my office. 'You are busy, Colonel?' he said, as he entered. 'No, sir, not very,' I replied; 'come in—I have learned to write and talk too, at the same time. Come in; sit down; I am glad to see you.' Looking round the office, the entire walls of which I had covered with portraits of Indians, he asked, pointing to the one that hung over my desk, 'Who is that?' '*Red-Jacket*,' I answered. 'And that?' '*Shin-guab-O' Wassin*,' I replied; and so he continued. He then asked, 'Who wrote the treaties with the Indians, and gave instructions to commissions, and, in general, carried on the correspondence of the office?' 'These are within the circle of my duties, the whole being under a general supervision of the Secretary of War,' I answered. 'Well, then,' after a pause, he said, 'the office will not suit me.' 'What office,' I asked. 'This,' he replied; 'General Jackson told me, this morning, it was at my service; but before seeing the Secretary of War, I thought I would come and have a little chat with you first.'

"I rose from my chair, saying—'Take it, my dear sir, take it. The sword of Damocles has been hanging over my head long enough.' 'No,' said he, 'it is not the sort of place for me. I prefer an auditor's office, where forms are established.' This worthy citizen had, in the fullness of his heart, doubtless, and out of pure affection for General Jackson, made that distinguished personage a present of the pair of pistols which General Washington had carried during the war of the Revolution."*

Colonel McKenney retained his office some time longer, because the Secretary of War assured the President that its duties were complex and numerous, and could not be discharged by a person inexperienced in Indian affairs. He tells us, however, that he was kept in constant suspense, and had, occasionally, an ominous warning: "My chief clerk, Mr. Hambleton, came into my room one morning, soon after I had taken my seat at my table, and putting his hands upon it, leaned over. I looked up, and saw his eyes were full of tears! To my question—'Is any thing the matter, Mr. Hambleton?' 'Yes, sir—I am pained to inform you, that you are to be displaced to-day! We all feel it. Our connection has been one of unbroken harmony; and we are grieved at the thought of a separation. The President has appointed General Thompson, a member of Congress, of Georgia—he boards at my mother's, and I have it from himself. He says I shall remain, but the rest of the clerks he shall dismiss, to make room for some of the President's friends.' 'Well, Mr. H.,' I replied, 'it is what I have been constantly looking for. Your annunciation does not at all surprise me; indeed, it puts an end to my suspense; and, apart from the pain of leaving you all, and the thought that others are to be cut adrift, as well as myself, I feel relieved.' He walked a few times across my room, and then retired to his, which joined mine. Two hours after, I heard walking and earnest talking in the passage. They continued for half an hour. When they ceased, Mr. Hambleton came into my room, his face all dressed in smiles, saying, '*It is not to be!*' 'What is not to be?' 'You are not to go out. When

* McKenney's Memoirs, p. 200.

General Thompson came to the secretary this morning, with the President's reference to him, to assign him to your place, he was told, before he could act, he (the secretary) must see the President. The result of the secretary's interview with the President was, you were to be retained, and General Thompson is referred back to the President for explanation. Thompson is in a rage about it.'"

Another illustrative anecdote, which, though it may not be wholly true, is so like others that are known to be so, that I venture to think it is, at least, founded in fact. A member of Congress, appointed to a foreign mission, consulted the President as to the choice of a secretary of legation. "The President declined all interference, and remarked to the minister that the United States government would hold him responsible for the manner in which he discharged his duties, and that he would consequently be at liberty to choose his own secretary. The minister returned his acknowledgment; but before taking leave, sought his advice in regard to a young gentleman then in the State Department, and who was highly recommended by the secretary. General Jackson promptly said, 'I advise you, sir, not to take the man. He is not a good judge of preaching.' The minister observed that the objection needed explanation. 'I am able to give it,' said the General, and he thus continued: 'On last Sabbath morning I attended divine service in the Methodist Episcopal church in this city. There I listened to a soul-inspiring sermon by Professor Durbin of Carlisle, one of the ablest pulpit orators in America. Seated in a pew near me I observed this identical young man, apparently an attentive listener. On the day following he came into this chamber on business, when I had the curiosity to ask his opinion of the sermon and the preacher. And what think you, sir? The young upstart, with consummate assurance, pronounced that sermon all froth, and Professor Durbin a humbug! I took the liberty of saying to him: My young man, you are a humbug yourself, and don't know it! And now,' continued the old man, 'rest assured, my dear sir, that a man who is not a better judge of preaching than that, is unfit to be your companion. And besides,' he added, 'if he were the prodigy the Secretary of State represents him to be, he would be less anxious to confer his services upon you—he would rather be anxious to retain them himself.'"

As a general rule, the dismission of officers was sudden and unexplained. Occasionally, however, some reason was assigned. Major Eaton, for example, dismissed the chief clerk of the War Department in the terms following: "Major ——: The chief clerk of the Department should to his principal stand in the relation of a confidential friend. Under this belief, I have appointed Doctor Randolph, of Virginia. I take leave to say, that since I have been in this Department, nothing in relation to you has transpired to which I would take the slightest objection, nor have I any to suggest."

These facts will suffice to show that the old system of appointments and removals was changed, upon the accession of General Jackson, to the one in vogue ever since, which 29 Governor Marcy completely and aptly described when he said that to the victors belong the spoils. Some of the consequences of this change are the following:

I. The government, formerly served by the *elite* of the nation, is now served, to a very considerable extent, by its refuse. That, at least, is the tendency of the new system, because men of intelligence, ability, and virtue, universally desire to fix their affairs on a basis of permanence. It is the nature of such men to make each year do something for all the years to come. It is their nature to abhor the arts by which office is now obtained and retained. In the year of our Lord 1859, the fact of a man's holding office under the government is presumptive evidence that he is one of three characters, namely, an adventurer, an incompetent person, or a scoundrel. From this remark must be excepted those who hold offices that have never been subjected to the spoils system, or offices which have been "taken out of politics."

II. The new system places at the disposal of any government, however corrupt, a horde of creatures in every town and county, bound, body and soul, to its defense and continuance.

III. It places at the disposal of any candidate for the presidency, who has a slight prospect of success, another horde of creatures in every town and county, bound to support his pretensions. I once knew an apple-woman in Wall Street who had a personal interest in the election of a President. If *her* candidate gained the day, her "old man" would get the place of porter in a public warehouse. The circle of corruption embraces hundreds of thousands.

IV. The spoils system takes from the government employée those motives to fidelity which, in private life, are found universally necessary to secure it. As no degree of merit whatever can secure him in his place, he must be a man of heroic virtue who does not act upon the principle of getting the most out of it while he holds it. Whatever fidelity may be found in office-holders must be set down to the credit of unassisted human virtue.

In a word, the spoils system renders pure, decent, orderly, and democratic government impossible. Nor has any government of modern times given such a wonderful proof of inherent strength as is afforded by the fact that this government, after thirty years of rotation, still exists.

At whose door is to be laid the blame of thus debauching the government of the United States? It may, perhaps, be justly divided into three parts. First, Andrew Jackson, impelled by his ruling passions, resentment, and gratitude, *did* the deed. No other man of his day had audacity enough. Secondly, The example and the politicians of New York furnished him with an excuse for doing it. Thirdly, The original imperfection of the governmental machinery seemed to necessitate it. As soon as King Caucus was overthrown, the spoils system became almost inevitable, and, perhaps, General Jackson only precipitated a change, which, sooner or later, must have come.

While the congressional caucus system lasted, confining

the sphere of intrigue to the city of Washington, politicians did not much want the aid of the remote subordinate employées of the government. But when the area of president making was extended so as to embrace the whole nation, every tide-waiter, constable, porter, and postmaster could lend a hand. Well, then, do not burst with virtuous rage, until you have duly reflected upon the fact, too well known, that the average disinterested voter can only with difficulty be induced even to take the trouble to go to the polls and deposit his vote. Without the stimulus of interested expectation, how is the work of a presidential campaign to be got done? Who will paint the flags, and pay for the Roman candles, and print the documents, and supply the stump! The patriotic citizen, do you answer? Why does he not do it then?

The spoils system, we may hope, however, has nearly run its course. It is already well understood, that every service in which efficiency is indispensable must be *taken out of politics;* and this process, happily begun in some departments of municipal government, will assuredly continue. The first century of the existence of a nation, which is to last thirty centuries or more, should be regarded merely in the light of the "Great Republic's" experimental trip. A leak has developed itself. It will be stopped.

The course of the administration with regard to removals excited a clamor so loud and general as to inspire the opposition with new hopes. The old federalists who had aided to elect General Jackson were especially shocked. Occasionally, too, the officers removed did not submit to decapitation in silence. The most remarkable protest published at the time was from the wife of one of the removed, Mrs. Barney, a daughter of the celebrated Judge Chase. Her husband's case was one of peculiar hardship, and she narrated it with the eloquence of sorrow and indignation:

"My husband, sir, never was your enemy. In the overflowing patriotism of his heart, he gave you the full measure of his love for your military services. He preferred Mr. Adams for the presidency, because he thought him qualified, and you unqualified, for the station. He would have been a traitor to his country, he would have had even my scorn, and have deserved yours, had he supported you under such circumstances. He used no means to oppose you. He did a patriot's duty in a patriot's way. For this he is proscribed—*punished!* Oh! how punished! My heart bleeds as I write. Cruel sir! Did he commit any offense worthy of punishment against God, or against his country, or even against you? Blush while you read this question; speak not, but let the crimson negative mantle on your cheek! No, sir—on the contrary, it was one of the best acts of his life. When he bared his bosom to the hostile bayonets of his enemies, he was not more in the *line of his duty*, than when he voted against you; and had he fallen a martyr on the field of fight, he would not more have deserved a monument, than he now deserves for having been worse than martyred in support of the dearest privilege and chartered right of American freemen. Careless as you are about the effects of your conduct, it would be idle to inform you of the depth and quality of that misery which you have worked in the bosom of my family. Else would I tell a tale that would provoke sympathy in any thing that had a heart, or gentle drops of pity from every eye not accustomed to look upon scenes of human cruelty 'with composure.' Besides, you were apprised of our poverty; you knew the dependence of eight little children for food and raiment upon my husband's salary. You knew that, advanced in years as he was, without the means to prosecute any regular business, and without friends able to assist him, the world would be to him a barren heath, an inhospitable wild. You were able, therefore, to anticipate the heart-rending scene which you may now realize as the sole work of your hand. The sickness and debility of my husband now calls upon me to vindicate his and his children's wrongs. The natural timidity of my sex vanishes before the necessity of my situation; and a spirit, sir, as proud as yours, although in a female bosom, demands justice. At your hands I ask it. Return to him what you have rudely torn from his possession; give back to his children their former means of securing their food and raiment; show that you can relent, and that your rule has had at least one exception. The severity practiced by you in this instance is heightened, because accompanied by a breach of your faith, solemnly pledged to my husband. He called upon you, told you frankly that he had not voted for you. What was your reply? It was, in substance, this, 'that every citizen of the United States had a right to express his political sentiments by his vote; that no charges had been made against Major Barney; if any should be made, he should have justice done; he should not be condemned unheard.' Then, holding him by the hand with apparent warmth, you concluded—'Be assured, sir, I shall be particularly cautious how I listen to assertions of applicants for office.' With these assurances from you, sir, the President of the United States, my husband returned to the bosom of his family. With these rehearsed, he wiped away the tears of apprehension. The President was not the monster he had been represented. They would not be reduced to beggary—haggard want would not be permitted to enter the mansion where he had always been a stranger. The husband and the father had done nothing in violation of his duty as an officer. If any malicious slanderer should arise to pour his poisonous breath into the ears of the President, the accused would not be condemned unheard, and his innocence would be triumphant—they would still be happy. It was presumable also, that, possessing the confidence of three successive administrations (whose testimony in his favor I presented to you), he was not unworthy the office he held; besides, the signatures of a hundred of our first mercantile houses established the fact of his having given perfect satisfaction in the manner he transacted the business of his office. In this state of calm security, without a moment's warning—like a clap of thunder in a clear sky—your dismissal came, and, in a moment, the house of joy was converted into one of mourning. Sir, was not this the refinement of cruelty? But this was not all. The wife whom you thus agonized, drew her being from the illustrious Chase, whose voice of thunder early broke the spell of British allegiance, when in the American Senate, he swore by Heaven that he owed no allegiance to the British Crown—one, too, whose signature was broadly before your eyes, affixed to the Charter of our Independence. The husband and the father whom you have thus wronged, was the first-born son of a hero, whose naval and military renown brightens the pages of your country's history, from '76 to 1815, with whose achievements posterity will not condescend to compare yours; for he fought amidst greater dangers, and he fought for Independence. By the side of that father, in the second British war, fought the son; and the glorious 12th of September bears testimony to his unshaken intrepidity. A wife, a husband, thus derived; a family of children drawing their existence from this double revolutionary fountain, you have recklessly, causelessly, perfidiously, and therefore inhumanly, cast helpless and destitute upon the icy bosom of the world; and the children and the grandchildren of Judge Chase and Commodore Barney are poverty stricken upon the soil which owes its freedom and fertility, in part, to their heroic patriotism."

The reader ought to be informed, I think, that his friend and benefactor, Major Lewis, opposed this fatal removal policy from the beginning to the end. "In relation to the principle of rotation," he once wrote to General Jackson, "I embrace this occasion to enter my solemn protest against it; not on account of my office, but because I hold it to be fraught with the greatest mischief to the country. If ever it should be carried out *in extenso*, the days of this republic will, in my opinion, have been numbered; for whenever the impression shall become general that the government is only valuable on account of its *offices*, the great and paramount interest of the country will be lost sight of, and the government itself ultimately destroyed. This, at least, is the honest conviction of my mind with regard to these novel doctrines of rotation in office."

Gen. Jackson's private letters this summer, to friends in Tennessee, show that he was a sick, unhappy, perplexed old man. On the 7th of June, he wrote thus to an old friend:

GENERAL JACKSON TO CAPTAIN JOHN DONELSON, SEN.

"WASHINGTON, June 7, 1829.

"MY DEAR SIR: Your letter of the 19th ultimo is just received. What satisfaction to me to be informed that you and Mr. Hume had visited the Hermitage and tomb of my dear departed wife. How distressing it has been to me to have been drawn by public duty from that interesting spot where my thoughts delight to dwell, so soon after this heavy bereavement to mingle with all the bustle, labor, and care of public life, when my age, my enfeebled health and constitution, forewarned me that my time can not be long upon earth, and admonished me that it was time I should place my earthly house in order, and prepare for another, and, I hope, a better world.

"My dear wife had your future state much at heart. She often spoke to me on this interesting subject in the dead hours of the night, and has shed many tears on the occasion. Your reflections upon the sincere interest your dear sister took in your future happiness are such as sound reason dictates. Yes, my friend, it is time that you should withdraw from the turmoils of this world, and prepare for another and better. You have well provided for your household. You have educated your children, and furnished them with an outfit into life sufficient, with good management and economy, to build an independence upon. You have sufficient around you to make you and your old lady independent and comfortable during life; and, when gone hence, perhaps as much as will be prudently managed; and if it should be imprudently managed, then it will be a curse rather than a blessing to your children. I therefore join in the sentiments of my deceased and beloved wife, in admonishing you to withdraw from the busy scenes of this world, and put your house in order for the next, by laying hold of 'the one thing needful.' Go, read the Scriptures. The joyful promises it contains will be a balsam to all your troubles, and create for you a kind of heaven here on earth, a consolation to your troubled mind that is not to be found in the hurry and bustle of this world.

"Could I but withdraw from the scenes that surround me to the private walks of the Hermitage, how soon would I be found in the solitary shades of my garden, at the tomb of my dear wife, there to spend my days in silent sorrow, and in peace from the toils and strife of this life, with which I have been long since satisfied. But this is denied me. I can not retire with propriety. When my friends dragged me before the public, contrary to my wishes, and that of my dear wife, I foresaw all this evil, but I was obliged to bend to the wishes of my friends, as it was believed it was necessary to perpetuate the blessings of liberty to our country and to put down misrule. My political creed compelled me to yield to the call, and I consoled myself with the idea of having the counsel and society of my dear wife; and one term would soon run round, when we would retire to the Hermitage, and spend our days in the service of our God.

"But oh! how fluctuating are all earthly things! At the time I least expected it, and could least spare her, she was snatched from me, and I left here a solitary monument of grief, without the least hope of any happiness here below, surrounded with all the turmoils of public life, and no time for recreation or for friendship. From this busy scene I would to God I could retire and live in solitude.

"How much the conduct of —— —— corrodes my feelings! I have just received a letter from him to ——, in which he says there is a vacancy at the Franklin Academy, and promises to write me. If he does not go to school, I will withdraw from him all supplies that may indulge extravagance, and confine him to such means as, with economy, will keep him decent. We are all in tolerable health. —— is in the family way. Little Jackson growing finely, and all join in our best wishes to you and your amiable lady, and all our connections and good neighbors. Your friend, ANDREW JACKSON.

"CAPTAIN JOHN DONELSON, SEN."

"P. S.—Mr. Steel (overseer) has written me but one letter. Say to him to write me how much crop he has in, how many colts, lambs, and calves, and how my last year's colts are, and of the health of my negroes.

"I learn old Ned and Jack are both dead. Jack was a fine boy, but if he was well attended to, I lament not. He has gone the way of all the earth. A. J."

In a similar strain the President, later in the year, wrote to Judge Hugh L. White: "Both of us, I do suppose, would be more contented and happy in private life ; but the Lord hath willed it, and we must submit. How grateful I feel to you for your kind and friendly visit to the Hermitage, where lies all that made life desirable to me, and whose loss I can never cease to mourn, and over whose tomb I would like to spend the remnant of my days in solitude, preparing to meet her in a happier and a better world."

Before proceeding to the important affairs of General Jackson's administration, I will give a still nearer view of the President's office. The perusal of the following narrative will greatly aid the reader to comprehend that peculiar and intense personality which was able to accomplish so much, —at once, the weakest and the strongest then incarnate.

V.

A SUCCESSFUL POLITICIAN'S STORY.

(TAKEN DOWN AFTER INTERVIEWS.)

No matter for my name. Call me X. Clark. X may signify that I am an unknown quantity. Clark will indicate my early vocation. "My whole" will convey a hint that I am not what I was.

Our family is one of the oldest of the old New York families. Our portraits show it. We appear in brocade and diamonds, in ruffles and pig-tail, on canvas that was woven long before the revolution. We were tories then, high tories, staunch for church and king. In later days we went over to the popular side. We were republicans in Jefferson's time ; buck-tails in Van Buren's ; democrats in Jackson's. 30
Our family stood high in the party. My great uncle was supposed to know as much of the proceedings of the Albany Regency as the Albany Regency itself ; and Mr. Van Buren, 31
our political chief, the great buck of the buck-tails. New

York's favorite son, was my great uncle's friend. We deemed the fact stupendous, for Mr. Van Buren filled a great space in the public mind in the days when I was young. To my boyish fancy he was the very chief of men, foremost among the foremost, orator, statesman, magician, victor!

I was bred to the mercantile business. At fourteen, I swept the store and carried the keys. At twenty, I was a clerk in full communion. At twenty-two, a book-keeper. At twenty-six, I rejoiced in the title of secretary to a company. A more unsophisticated young man than I was at that age did not exist. Brought up to mind my own business, accustomed to deal with merchants of the old school, who said little, and meant all they said, acquainted only with the politics of a quiet mercantile ward, in which none but men of substance and respectability took a leading part, I had in me as little of the politician as can be imagined. So unacquainted was I with the world, that when a man said to me, "Mr. Clark, I am glad to see you," or, "I shall be glad to serve you," I believed him. Indeed, the member of our old firm, whose ways I chiefly relished, was a man of such a nice sense of truth, that if he had said he was glad to see a person whom he was not glad to see, he would have felt that he had told a lie. I supposed, in my innocence, that it was so with all great men.

In the spring of 1829, two events occurred of the first importance in my history. General Jackson became President of the United States, and the company of which I was the secretary ceased to exist. I said to myself, "I have lived in New York long enough; it is time I saw something of the world. Our party is in power, and our party is a party that rewards its friends. I'll go to Washington, and get a clerkship in one of the departments." My uncle approved my determination, and gave me a letter of introduction to Mr. Van Buren. My honored friend of the old firm, who was also a member of Congress, gave me a handsome recommendation as a correct and skillful accountant, and this also was in the form of a letter of introduction to Mr Van Buren. "Governor Van Buren" we called him in those days, for we had elected him Governor in the previous autumn. When I obtained my letters of introduction, his appointment as Secretary of State and his resignation of the governorship had just been announced, and the great man was daily expected to pass through New York on his way to Washington.

He came. I had read in the morning papers that he was to arrive by the day boat from Albany, and I went down to the dock to get a sight of him. Having never seen him, I felt extremely curious to behold the man of whom I had heard so much, and who, I hoped, was about to do something great for me. Two gentlemen were walking up and down the hurricane deck, arm in arm, while the boat was getting into her berth. One was a short gentleman, of middle age; the other a very young man. The crowd on the wharf were cheering.

"The Governor must have come," I said to a bystander, "but why don't he show himself? He ought to be up there on the hurricane deck."

"There he is," said the person I had addressed; "that little fellow in the surtout, and that's his son walking with him."

What a surprise! What a disenchantment! It had been a fixed idea with me that Governor Van Buren was a man of the same magnificent physical proportions as Governor Clinton. I expected him to be even more imposing and superb than Clinton. I had also a general notion that all governors were vast, which was owing, I suppose, to the circumstance that the only Governor I had ever seen seemed so to my wondering young eyes. It is impossible for this generation to conceive what a great man a Governor was thirty or forty years ago.

I saw the father and son drive away in a carriage. They were going, as I knew, to the City Hotel, the great hotel of that day, situated in the lower part of Broadway, a region long since given up to business. I followed them leisurely on foot, and on reaching the hotel, found the bar-room crowded with politicians, anxious to "pay their respects" to the new premier. In a few minutes the doors of the great dining-room were thrown open, and the clerk of the house, mounted on a chair, cried out:

"Gentlemen who desire to see Mr. Van Buren will please walk into the dining-room."

We thundered in—fifty or sixty of us; politicians in and out of place; these wanting to get in, those to stay in. We were all hail fellows well met, and there was a roar of jovial talk and banter. Politicians, you know, are friendly to every body; for no man knows who can or who can not forward his views, nor how soon a man now powerless may be in a position to help. After waiting a while, all expecting the great man to present himself, a waiter appeared, and said:

"Gentlemen, Mr. Van Buren requests your cards."

The old stagers laughed. There was a general fumbling in pockets.

"Cards?" said I. "What does he want our cards for? I have no card with me. I shall write a note to the Governor."

Amid the merriment of the group nearest me, I wrote my note in something like these words:

"SIR—I am the bearer of two letters of introduction to you: one from my uncle, Mr. —— ——, and the other from my friend, the Hon. —— ——. I have called for the purpose of delivering them to you, and shall be glad if you will name an hour when it will be convenient for you to receive them. I am, etc. "X. CLARK."

I folded my note, and placed it on the tray with the cards. The waiter vanished, reappeared, and delivered himself as follows:

"Gentlemen, Mr. Van Buren sends his compliments, and says he is fatigued with his journey, and requests the honor of your company this evening, at eight o'clock, one and all. Mr. Clark will please to wait!"

I became instantly the lion of the room. I was severely bantered.

"Clark," said one, "you are a made man. You'll get the best office in the gift of the government. Not a doubt of it."

The crowd oozed away into the congenial bar-room again, the great doors were shut, and I was left alone seated by the fire. I sat some minutes, waiting and wondering, and thinking what I should say to the Coming Man. Without having heard any one enter, I looked up at length, and lo! there, on the opposite side of the fire-place, sat the Magician! We rose and exchanged the usual salutations. I presented my letters, which Mr. Van Buren courteously took and read deliberately. He re-folded them, and said, as he did so:

"I highly esteem your uncle, and also your friend Mr. ——. No men in the State stand higher in my regard than they. If I can do any thing to oblige them or forward your views, it will give me great pleasure."

Here the interview, as I afterward knew, would have properly ended. But such was my utter inexperience of the great world, that I took these words of simple civility in their literal acceptation. I felt that I was a "made man." There was no doubt that the Secretary of State *could* forward my views if he wished to do so, and he had just informed me that he *did* wish it. What more could a young man desire? How often, in later times, have I wondered at this incredible simplicity in a boy of twenty-six.

The Governor sat silent, expecting and desiring me to take my leave. Not perceiving his intent, I asked, with the assurance of perfect verdancy:

"When do you *go* to Washington, Mr. Van Buren?"

"When do I go to Washington?" he said, with a bland stare, which mildly intimated, "What is that to *you*, young man?"

"Yes, sir," I continued; "I wish to know when you are going to Washington. It is important to me that I should know."

"Well," said he, "I can't say exactly. In a few days, I presume."

"A few days, sir!" said I; "not sooner?"

"Why," said he, "won't that suit you?"

"Well, no, Mr. Van Buren," I replied, "I can't say it does, exactly."

"Indeed!" he continued, "I am sorry you are not suited. When do you propose to go yourself?"

"I thought of going to-morrow morning."

"So soon?"

"Why, yes, sir. That is, if you have no objection. Have you any?"

"I? Oh, by no means. I think you can't do better than go to-morrow morning."

"I thought not, sir," said I, all unconscious of the absurdity of my proceedings, and of his astonishment.

Again there was an awkward pause. Again the great man waited for me to take my hat and leave. I did nothing of the kind.

"Mr. Van Buren," I resumed, "I don't know a soul in Washington. I should be obliged to you if you would give me a letter or two of introduction to your friends there."

This request, as I afterward understood, was almost too much even for his invincible politeness. He stared outright.

"A letter of introduction?" said he, musingly. "Let me see. Who is there in Washington just now? The Attorney-General is absent, I think, and so is the Secretary of the Treasury. Governor Branch is there, I believe, and Mr. Eaton."

I fancied, afterward, that he tried to overawe me by an array of distinguished names. I was deaf and blind to all hints, however, and said,

"Oh, Mr. Van Buren, it's no matter about those other gentlemen. A letter to Mr. Eaton or to Governor Branch will answer."

"Oh, they will do, will they?"

"Perfectly," said I.

As he made no movement toward writing, I ventured to place the writing materials that I had just used nearer to where he was sitting, and waited for him to indite the letters.

"Oh," said he, "you wish me to write *now*, do you?"

"Well, sir," I replied, "I *should* like it; but if it's inconvenient, I'll call again in the course of the day."

"No," said he; and he turned to the table and began to write.

He produced the following epistle:—"Messrs. Eaton and Branch: This will be handed to you by my young friend, Mr. Clark, who precedes me to Washington. Any attentions you may show him will be highly estimated by yours, etc.

"M. VAN BUREN."

With this passport to fortune in my pocket, I left the presence; and very glad, I think, must Mr. Van Buren have been to get rid of his innocent "young friend."

On the third morning after this interview, I awoke in the City of Washington. After a stroll about its wide and dreary expanses, I proceeded, with my precious letter in my pocket, to the office of the Secretary of the Navy. The antechamber into which I was shown was crowded with people waiting their turn to be admitted to the new dispenser of places. Verdant as I was, my three day's experience as an office-seeker seemed to have made me free of the craft, and I knew at a glance that every man in that room had come to ask an appointment. I waited, and waited, and waited. Two hours must have passed before it came my turn to see the Secretary. I was shown in, at length, and, advancing awkwardly and slowly to Mr. Branch, who sat at a table, wearing the air of a man who had been bored to within an inch of his life, and had almost lost the power of paying attention, I said:

"I have a letter here, sir, from Mr. Van Buren."

He took the letter, without seeming to comprehend what I had said, and was proceeding languidly to open it. He looked up at me. I suppose I was abashed at the coldness of his reception, and probably did not cut a very promising figure. In a loud, off-hand, and, as I thought, most impertinent and insulting manner, he said,

"Well, young man, and what do *you* want?"

I was no longer abashed. A sudden fury seized me, and I cried,

"What do I *want*, sir? I want nothing, sir. Nothing whatever. Yes, sir, I do want something. I want that letter! It is from MR. VAN BUREN, but I'll not trouble you with it, sir. I request that you will hand it back to me."

He did so. I seized the letter from his hand, turned upon my heel, and stalked away, boiling. "By heaven," said I to myself, as I went fuming down the steps, "if this is the way of doing business in Washington, the quicker I get back to Wall-street the better."

The cool air of Pennsylvania Avenue restored me to some degree of composure. I had half concluded to start homeward the next morning, when it occurred to me that my letter of introduction was addressed to Mr. Eaton as well as to Mr. Branch, and that it would be an absurd proceeding to give up the game with a card in my hands. To the War Department building I accordingly directed my steps, and was admitted at once to the presence of the chief. As it was late in the afternoon, the business of the day was nearly concluded, and the Secretary was at leisure and in excellent humor. Major Eaton was a stout, good-humored, agreeable man, extremely easy and cordial in his manners. He rose at my entrance, read my letter with attention, shook hands with me heartily, and invited me to be seated, and make known my desires.

Like Mr. Van Buren, he said he would be glad to promote my wishes in any way that might be in his power. We chatted a quarter of an hour in a friendly manner upon the affairs of our party in New York, when Mr. Eaton observed,

"This letter, I perceive, is addressed to Governor Branch as well as to myself. You will see the Governor, I presume."

"No, sir," said I, with tremendous emphasis, "I am NOT going to see Governor Branch. I have called upon Governor Branch, and shall not repeat the visit, I can assure you."

"No! Why, has anything unpleasant occurred?"

I then told him my story as I have told it to you, beginning with my interview with Mr. Van Buren in New York, and ending with my abrupt departure from the office of the Secretary of the Navy. Seldom have I seen any one so convulsed with laughter as Major Eaton was during the recital of my adventures. He lay back in his chair and shouted with laughter. He stood up and laughed. He walked up and down and laughed. He lay on the lounge and laughed. I laughed, too, and saw, for the first time, how ludicrous some of my performances had been. When I had finished the jolly secretary said,

"Now, Mr. Clark, will you have the goodness to tell me that story all over again?"

I repeated it, *verbatim*, and with the same result as before. Then said Eaton,

"One more favor I have to ask of you. I want you to come to my house, this evening, and tell that story to Mrs. Eaton, exactly as you have told it to me."

I went to his house in the evening, and found assembled there a large company of gentlemen, who paid assiduous court to the lady. Mrs. Eaton was not then the celebrated character she was destined, ere long, to be made, and I knew nothing of the peculiar position she held in the society of the capital. To me she seemed a strikingly beautiful and fascinating woman, all graciousness and vivacity; the life of the company. Her rooms, as I soon found, were the resort of the extreme Jackson men, and her favor was supposed to be the indispensable preliminary to preferment. Ignorant of all this, I told my story, to the lady's great amusement, and that of all her guests. I thought that I had made rather a brilliant *début* into the society of Washington; and went to my hotel well pleased with my prospects and myself.

Mr. Van Buren arrived shortly after, and I waited upon him, of course. What influences, besides those already mentioned, were brought to bear in my favor, I know not; but, in a few days, I had the gratification of learning that I was appointed to a clerkship in the Department of State, and that my attendance was required on the following morning at 10 o'clock. The place to which I was appointed was not conspicuous, but confidential; and, as I then thought, munificently remunerated. I had in charge the finances of the department, and was the usual confidential messenger from the Secretary of State to the President. It was the very place of all others, that I would have chosen, and the very place I felt myself fitted to fill with credit. My gratitude to the Secretary was boundless, and so was my desire to stand high in his regard.

At ten in the morning, I presented myself at the office of the Secretary of State. My predecessor, as I learnt afterward, had received no intimation that he was to be removed up to that moment. He was a *protégé* of the late President, Mr. Adams, and supposed that, according to previous usage, he would be retained, whoever might be displaced. He had a young family dependent solely upon his salary, and was himself an exceedingly amiable and worthy gentleman. Mr. Van Buren, upon seeing me enter his apartment rang for a messenger, to whom he said,

"Inform Mr. Jones* that I wish to speak with him for a moment."

Mr. Jones appeared. Mr. Van Buren addressed him in these words,

"Mr. Jones, I beg to make you acquainted with Mr. Clark of New York. The government, Mr. Jones, has no further occasion for your services in this department. Mr. Clark is appointed your successor. Have the goodness to take him to your room, and give him what information he requires respecting his duties."

The blow was so sudden and so unexpected, that poor Jones could scarcely conceal his feelings. He stood, for a moment, paralyzed and speechless, and then left the room without a word. I followed him to his office, upon reaching which, he said, in a tremulous voice, and a wild, absent manner,

* Fictitious name.

"Excuse me a moment, Mr. Clark, this is rather sudden. I will rejoin you in a moment."

He staggered out of the room, and remained absent about ten minutes. When he returned, all traces of emotion had vanished, both from his countenance and his manner, and he proceeded, with perfect courtesy and much patience, to explain to me the nature and routine of my future duties. I pitied him from my soul. I would not dismiss a scullion from my kitchen so. Nor would Mr. Van Buren. It was the System that beggared poor Jones, and made me a "made man." A System, like a Corporation, has no soul. (But it ought to be damned, nevertheless.—REPORTER.)

On rejoining Mr. Van Buren, he said to me,

"I know nothing about this place of yours. Find out the law and govern yourself by it."

He said to me, afterward, that he hated patronage. He preferred an office that had none.

"No matter how you dispense it, you make enemies. The man you remove is your enemy. His friends are offended. The man you appoint is not likely to be satisfied, and all the unsuccessful applicants feel themselves injured."

"I am an exception to your remark, Mr. Van Buren," said I, "for I am perfectly satisfied with my place. I would not change it for any in the department. I could wish nothing better."

As I had charge of some of the Secret Service funds, the disbursements from which required the President's special authorization, the course of my duties led me often to the White House. My first interview with the President displayed my faculty of honest blundering to fine advantage. Charged as I was, on that interesting occasion, with a packet of papers from my chief, I marched up to the door of the presidential mansion, big with a sense of the grandeur of my mission. I had also an extreme desire to see General Jackson, whom I had been accustomed from childhood to revere. An Irish porter answered my ring.

"I wish to see the President," said I, perhaps not with the condescension which becomes a great man.

The man replied, in a tone of the most irritating nonchalance,

"The President is engaged, and can't be seen."

"But I *must* see the President," said I, in a very decided manner. "I have business with the President."

He said he would take up a card. So I hastily wrote on one the name of Mr. VAN BUREN, meaning that I was there by that gentleman's orders, and was his representative. I added some indistinct words to that effect, which, as I soon learned, were either illegible or not observed. The porter became obsequious enough when he had caught the name I had written, and invited me to take a seat in the vestibule. He took up my card, and instantly returned with a request for me to "walk up."

I walked up. I entered the President's office, where half a dozen gentlemen were seated in conversation. On my presenting myself at the door, the whole group, including the President, rose, and, after eyeing me a moment, burst into laughter. I stood astonished and abashed. The President, however, immediately explained the cause of this sudden merriment.

"Mr. Clark, I presume," said he, very politely.

"The same, sir," said I.

"Excuse our laughing, Mr. Clark," he continued. "I just glanced at your card, and seeing the name of Mr. Van Buren, concluded that we were about to see that gentleman."

I explained how the error arose, and, in doing so, happened to use a phrase, the selection of which would have done honor to the most adroit of politicians.

"I brought no card of my own, Mr. President," said I, "as it did not occur to me that a messenger from Mr. Van Buren could be refused admittance. And when your porter, sir, said that you were engaged and could not be seen, I thought *I would take the responsibility* of sending up the name of Mr. Van Buren."

Upon this, the General gave a most energetic pull at the bell-rope. The offending porter appeared.

"This gentleman," said the President, "is to be admitted at all times. Mark my words—at all times. Mr. Clark, be seated. In a few moments I shall be at your service."

He spoke in a peculiarly frank and cordial, yet authoritative manner. There was the MASTER in his every tone, but a master whom it would be a delight to serve. I loved him from that hour. In his presence I always felt entirely at home, but in Mr. Van Buren's, though I saw him every day, I never felt so. My business with the President, at that time, was merely formal. He examined the statement I had brought with me, signed it, and I took my leave. I noticed that the pen with which he wrote was a steel one of remarkable size. Some one asked him, one day, when he complained of his pen, if he should take it to the blacksmith's for repair. It was a great pen, and he wrote with a furious rapidity, sometimes, that I have never seen equaled.

A few days after this interview, Mr. Van Buren, who had been for a day or two employed upon an important foreign dispatch, requested me to make a fair copy of the same, and take it to the President, and ask him if it correctly expressed his views. The Secretary of State, I may add, devoted himself most laboriously to the duties of his department, and took great pains with his official letters. He used to write on paper ruled very wide, so that he could add to or alter them the more conveniently. This particular dispatch came to my hands, I remember, black with erasures and interlineations. I copied it and took it up to the President, who read it over with great deliberation, and sat brooding over it for some minutes after he had finished it. He broke silence at length :

"Well, Mr. Clark, I don't see the use of beating round the bush in this way, when you can say what you mean in a straightforward manner. What do *you* think of it ?"

"I, Mr. President ? I am incapable of judging of such an affair. My opinion is worth nothing."

"That's for me to say," rejoined the General; "I want your opinion."

"Well, sir," said I, "since you ask me, I must say that the straightforward way of saying a thing has always seemed to me the best. In fact, I know no other. But really, General, I am very inexperienced, and perhaps—"

"I think just so," broke in the General, energetically. "Leave the paper with me, Mr. Clark, and I'll see Mr. Van Buren myself about it. Ask him to step up and see me."

I obeyed. The next morning I fancied that the manner of my chief was somewhat more reserved toward me than usual. He dropped a remark in the course of the day, which led me to infer that he did not approve of my observation to the President, non-committal though it had been. I then narrated to him the interview just as it occurred. I told him I had shrunk from expressing an opinion, but the President had demanded it peremptorily, and I was compelled to give it, such as it was. He seemed satisfied with my explanation, and never alluded to the circumstance again. He may have remembered it, however. I know I thought so ten years afterward.

Before many days elapsed, I was again in the President's private office, on an errand of the same nature, when he again asked my opinion of the paper I had brought him to read. I was not going to be caught a second time. Indeed, I had made up my mind beforehand that I would venture no more opinions on any subject in that apartment. So I said, in my blunt way:

"Mr. President, I really wish you would n't ask me what I think. The truth is, sir, Mr. Van Buren did n't seem pleased that I gave you my opinion the other day about the dispatch."

I then told him what Mr. Van Buren had said, and how I had explained the matter. The General laughed heartily.

"Why, he was n't offended, was he?" he asked. "He could n't be."

"No," said I, "he was n't offended. Still he did n't

like it, and I would decidedly prefer not to give any more opinions."

The General was exceedingly merry at this reply. At length he said:

"Come, my young friend, tell me honestly what you think of this passage, and I'll promise not to tell Van Buren any thing about it."

I then gave him my opinion. Always after that he asked me what I thought of the papers which I submitted to his perusal, and often prefaced his question by assuring me, in a jocular manner, that he would not tell Van Buren.

I soon became quite familiar with the General. Never was there a man so beset with importunate applicants for favors as he. One day, when I had had to wait long for an opportunity to transact business with him, I chanced to make a remark which, I think, had an important effect upon my whole subsequent career. He had got rid of his visitors one after another, and at last we two sat alone in the office. He had signed my accounts with his great pen, and we were conversing on some topic of the day. He seemed tired and melancholy, and I was moved to say something kind to him. I saw not before me the conquering general nor the illustrious President, but a tired, sad old man, far from his home and friends, farthest of all from his wife, and approached chiefly by flatterers, beggars, and sycophants. What to say to him I knew not, but I contrived, at last, to blunder out this:

"General, I should think you'd feel lonely here."

"Lonely?" he exclaimed. "How can you think so? Most people would think I had plenty of company. What makes you think I am lonely?"

"Well, General," I replied, "I don't mean lonely exactly. But it is not here as it was at the Hermitage, where your friends could come in and chat with you in a social way."

"No," said the President, "it is not here as it was at the Hermitage. There you're right, my young friend."

"I'll tell you, General," I continued, "exactly what I mean. Every one that comes here has an ax to grind. At least it seems so to me, and, in fact, they say so themselves."

"Yes," said the General, "I suppose that's so. Now, let me ask you, what ax have you to grind?"

"My ax is ground," said I.

"It is, is it?" said the General, laughing.

"Yes, sir, my ax is ground. I have the pleasantest place in the department, and I am perfectly satisfied with it."

"You are perfectly satisfied, are you?"

"Perfectly."

"You have reached the summit of your ambition, then?"

"Certainly, General. I ask nothing better. I wish nothing better."

"You have no ax to grind at all?"

"None, General, none whatever."

"Neither for yourself nor for any body else?"

"Neither for myself nor for any body else."

Upon this the old man rose, took my hand, and said with much tenderness:

"My young friend, come often to see me, and we'll have many a good chat together, just as if we *were* at the Hermitage."

From that time forward I can not be mistaken in supposing I was a favorite with General Jackson. He treated me with the most marked cordiality, and appeared to give me all his confidence. The time came when I put his favor to the test, and it stood the test, as I will relate by and by.

Mr. Van Buren well knew my intimacy with the President, but it made no difference in his own demeanor toward me. Mr. Van Buren never employed the arts of personal conciliation of which he has been accused. To me he was always perfectly polite, but cold and reserved. I tried hard to win his regard, but never felt that I had made the slightest progress toward it. Even when I had rendered him a personal service, out of the line of my official duty, I could not lessen the distance between us by a hair's breadth. He had a singular aversion to accounts, and an inaptitude for keeping them that was strange in a man who was so careful to discharge his pecuniary obligations. Soon after he arrived in Washington he came to me, with a puzzled expression of countenance, and said that his bank account was all in confusion, and that he would be very much obliged to me if I would look it over, and tell him positively whether he had any money in the bank or not. I told him I would do it with much pleasure, and asked him for his check-book.

"Check-book! check-book!" said he, "what is that?"

He actually did not know what a check-book was; and, indeed, they were not commonly used, thirty years ago, except by business men. When I had straightened out his account, I procured him a check-book, and explained to him the mode of using it. He manifested the same delight as a child does in a new toy, and I saw him show it as a great curiosity to one of his Southern friends.

I remember a curious incident of my intercourse with the Secretary of State. I had occasion to call upon him at his own house one morning, when I found him writing.

"Read that letter, Mr. Clark," said he, when he had finished, "and tell me what you think of it."

I read the letter, and said:

"I will tell you what I think of it with a great deal of pleasure, Mr. Van Buren, if you will tell me what it's about."

"That will do," he replied; "I think it will answer."

He then folded the letter, and immediately turned to the business upon which I had come. The letter was so worded that no one unacquainted with its subject could have attached the slightest meaning to any part of it.

This extraordinary man, cold and cautious as he seemed to me and to the world, was exceedingly amiable, and even jovial, in his own home. I caught him once lying on a sofa, engaged in a downright romp with his boys, which he finished by throwing a sofa-cushion at one of them. He was also, at times, very frank in avowing both his opinions and his expedients. One day, after he had astonished a company of Virginians with a display of what seemed to them almost a miraculous familiarity with the local politics of Virginia, I asked him how he had acquired his information, adding that the Virginians, upon going out, had expressed boundless wonder at the extent of his knowledge. He answered that he had gathered most of it from those very Virginians with whom he had conversed. He had allowed them to talk *ad libitum*, and by adding what they let fall to what he knew before, he was able to *appear* to know more than they did.

The terror of Mr. Van Buren's public life was this : *to be thought an intriguer*. The very pains which he took to avoid the appearance of intrigue was often the means of fastening the charge upon him.

But to return to General Jackson. The General was a striking illustration of the doctrine of compensation. His will, if directly resisted, was not to be shaken by mortal power ; but, if artfully managed, he was more easily swayed and imposed upon than any man of his day. There was a certain member of Congress who had set his heart upon a foreign mission, and had long tried to compass his aim, without effect. He obtained a clue, in some way, to one of the General's weaknesses, and changed his tactics in consequence. He cultivated my acquaintance assiduously, and accompanied me sometimes to the White House, where he gradually established himself upon a footing of office familiarity. I saw him one afternoon perform the following scene in the General's private office, myself being the only spectator thereof. The President was smoking his pipe.

"General Jackson," began the member, "I am about to ask you a favor—a favor, sir, that will cost you nothing, and the government nothing, but will gratify me exceedingly."

"It's granted, sir," said the President. "What is it?"

"Well, General, I have an old father at home who has as great an esteem for your character as one man can have for another. Before I left home, he charged me to get for him, if possible, one of General Jackson's pipes, and that is the favor I now ask of you."

"Oh, certainly," said the General, laughing and ringing the bell.

When the servant came, he told him to bring two or three clean pipes.

"Excuse me, General," said the member, "but may I ask you for that very pipe you have just been smoking?"

"This one?" asked the General. "By all means, if you prefer it."

The President was proceeding to empty it of the ashes, when the member once more interrupted him.

"No, General, don't empty out the tobacco. I want that pipe just as it is, just as it left your lips."

The member took the pipe to the table, folded it carefully and reverently in a piece of paper, thanked the General for the precious gift with the utmost warmth, and left the room with the air of a man whose highest flight of ambition had just been more than gratified.

In a little less than three weeks after, that man departed on a mission to one of the South American States, and it was that pipe that did the business for him. At least I thought so; and if there is any meaning in a wink, he thought so too. It was also a fact, as he in confidence assured me, that his old father *did* revere General Jackson, and *would* be much gratified to possess one of his pipes. I once heard a pill-vender say to one who had laughed at his extravagant advertisements:

"Well, these pills of mine, to my certain knowledge, *have* cured some people."

Speaking of office-seeking, I will relate to you the singular process by which a clerk in the War Department was transformed into a Senator of the United States. If I had not been an eye-witness of this man's extraordinary proceedings, I could not believe the story. He was a loud, blustering, fluent, idle politician from the north, a *protégé* or friend of one of the Burrites. He was sitting on the piazza of a hotel, one afternoon (an employment he was much addicted to), when a young man from the south began to declaim against the administration, and to denounce with particular warmth the Burrite just referred to.

"Sir," said the war-clerk, "if you feel it necessary to speak in that way, I will thank you to speak in a lower tone. The gentleman whom you are abusing is a friend of mine."

"I don't care a —— who's your friend. I shall say what I please of the scoundrel, and as loud as I please."

The clerk flew at the young southerner; but the bystanders interfered before much damage was done. In a few minutes, an officer of the army presented to the clerk a challenge from the young gentleman, which the clerk accepted. He asked me to be his second. I knew just as much of the dueling science as he did, which was nothing at all; nor did I think it proper for an employée of the government to bring discredit upon it by engaging in an affair of that kind. I declined peremptorily; and advised him to procure the assistance of a military man who understood such things. He started in pursuit of the only officer with whom he had exchanged a syllable in Washington, a captain to whom he had been casually introduced the evening before in a bar-room. He found his man and induced him to serve.

"What are your weapons?" asked the second. "You have the choice, you know."

"Have I?" exclaimed the clerk. "By Heaven, then, I have him on the hip. I choose small swords. Time, to morrow morning at sunrise."

The second remonstrated. The principal insisted. The second of the Southerner protested. The clerk was inflexible. A postponement was asked, that weapons might be procured, and the young gentleman instructed in their use. But, no; the next morning at the rising of the sun was the only time the clerk would hear of. Late in the evening, after many hours of negotiation and the interchange of notes innumerable, the second of the Southerner formally declined the meeting. The next morning the clerk posted the young man as a coward on all the walls of Washington. In the course of the day I met the victorious clerk and asked him where he had learned the use of the small sword.

"Small sword?" said he. "I never had one in my hand. I don't know what it is. And I knew *he* didn't."

He gained great eclat by this proceeding. He was regarded as a champion of the administration; and the President, who could no more help sympathizing with a fight than a duck can help liking water, was intensely gratified. The same day news came that an important vacancy had occurred in a remote Territory, and my fighting friend saw that his hour had come. He immediately wrote a resignation of his clerkship, dating it on the day of the challenge, and presented it to the chief of his department with these words,

"Of course, sir, before accepting the challenge yesterday, I resigned my place in the department. I am not the man to connect the administration with a duel. Here it is, sir, dated as you will perceive, yesterday."

The Secretary was delighted. The President was completely won. Rather than not reward a partisan who had fought for him, or who had shown a willingness to fight, he would almost have resigned his own office in favor of the champion. He gave the ex-clerk the vacant place. He gave him nine letters of introduction to personal friends in the Territory. Shortly after, that Territory was admitted into the Union as a sovereign State, and my fighting friend came back to Washington as one of its Senators. He served out his whole term without once revisiting the State he represented, and then retired to private life.

This incident reminds me of a conversation I once had with the President upon the subject of party appointments. I said,

"I want to ask you, General, about your advice to Mr. Monroe, that politics should not influence appointments. How do you reconcile that doctrine with the conduct of your administration?"

His countenance assumed a knowing, slightly waggish expression, as he replied,

"Young man, we are never too old to learn."

On another occasion he said,

"I am no politician. But if I were a politician, I would be a New York politician."

I had not held my clerkship long before I discovered that the accounts of all the departments were kept in the most antiquated and awkward manner. Custom and tradition ruled supreme. Some accounts in the treasury department were kept just as they were in the days of Alexander Hamilton, and according to modes devised and established by him. I did all I could for years to get the system of book-keeping by double entry introduced, but I met with insuperable difficulty. Not a man in high place knew what double entry was, or could be made to know. After a long struggle, I succeeded so far as to induce a certain Secretary of the Treasury to promise to examine a treatise on the art of book-keeping by double entry. I sent him one instantly, and hoped much from his well-known zeal and supposed intelligence. Some days after I received a message from the Secretary, asking me to call at his office, as he had made up his mind upon the subject of double entry, and wished me to learn his conclusions. I waited upon him.

"Ah, Mr. Clark, walk in. I am now prepared to show you, sir, that double entry is no better than single."

He took down a volume of English parliamentary reports, turned to the evidence given by the inventor of a new system of book-keeping before a committee, and pointed to these words: "Double entry itself is no safeguard against omissions and false entries."

"There!" said the Secretary, triumphantly. "You see? High authority, sir. A professor of book-keeping! No safeguard against omissions and false entries!"

"Why, Mr. Secretary," said I, utterly confounded at the man's simplicity, "*no* system can prevent omissions and false entries. If your clerk sells five hundred barrels of flour, and enters four hundred, or omits to enter them at all, how *can* any system of book-keeping prevent it? The same dishonesty can make the book balance, no matter how false the entries may be. All book-keeping presupposes a desire on the part of the book-keeper to make an honest record, and all we claim for double entry is, that it enables him to do so with greater convenience, certainty, and expedition. Double entry is a self-corrector. Your book-keeper knows, to a certainty, whether he has or has not made an exact record."

The Secretary scratched his wise noddle with the end of his pen for a minute or two, and then delivered himself thus:

"Mr. Clark, I will frankly admit that you have explained away that difficulty with a great deal of ingenuity. I grant the force of your reasoning. But, sir, there *is* a difficulty in the way that is perfectly insurmountable. You can not argue it down. It excludes argument."

"Indeed, sir!" said I. "What is that?"

"Well, sir," he rejoined, "this is an economical government, and *no Congress will ever consent to double the number of clerks in this department!*"

I am well aware that in telling this story I draw largely upon the credulity of the listener. Nevertheless, it is true. And this very Secretary held his office longer, I believe, than it has ever been held by any other incumbent since the foundation of the government. I gave up double entry after that, and I presume they are keeping accounts in Washington in the good old way to this hour.

It is not an entirely pleasant thing to be a member of the Cabinet. All feel the pressure from above. All feel that a breath unmakes them, as a breath hath made. Men feel alike whose place and preferment depend upon the will of another man. Whether they be Cabinet ministers or Cabinet porters, the moral effect of the position is the same.

I will relate one more of my interviews with General Jackson, which left an indelible impression upon my mind, and, I think, had an effect upon my fortunes. It was a trifling affair, but it is trifles that show character.

In the Northeast boundary dispute, the king of the Netherlands offered his arbitration. The offer was accepted, and we of the State Department were much occupied in preparing the necessary documents for transmission to Europe. One day, in the course of these preparations, a gentleman connected with the commission, a rather pompous individual, a son of a foreign consul, born and educated abroad, came into my office and requested me to have one set of the documents printed on the finest tinted drawing-paper, and bound in the most gorgeous and costly manner possible. This set, he said, was for the king's own use. The documents, he further remarked, ought to be bound in Paris, for the work could not be done in America as it ought to be. Nevertheless, I must have them done as well as the state of the arts in the United States admitted, regardless of expense.

Nettled both by the manner and the matter of this gentleman's discourse, and not perceiving any necessity for such a lavish expenditure of the public money, I told him that, the Secretary of State being absent from the city, I did not feel authorized to comply with his wishes. Nothing of the kind had ever been done before in the department, and any thing so unusual could only be warranted by the Secretary's special order. The documents were numerous, and would form several large volumes.

"But, sir," said he, with much hauteur, "you forget that these volumes are designed, not for ambassadors and secretaries, but for the king of a country."

"Well," said I, "without the express orders of the Secretary of State or of the President, I must decline doing any thing in the matter."

"I will assume the entire responsibility," he replied, "and hold you blameless. If the Secretary of State disapproves, I will take the consequences."

"Very well," said I, "if you shoulder the responsibility I will proceed."

After he had taken his departure, however, I looked into the law and the precedents, and became satisfied that there was neither law nor precedent for the work proposed. I also calculated the expense of the printing and binding, and found it would amount to several hundred dollars. The more I thought over the matter the greater was my repugnance to ordering the work, and the result of my cogitations was, that I went to the White House to consult the President on the subject. I found the President alone, and soon told my story.

As I proceeded, the General left his seat and began to walk up and down the room, quickening his pace as I went on. At length he broke into a loud and vehement harangue, still pacing the floor.

"Go on, Mr. Clark," he exclaimed; "you are perfectly correct, sir. Tell this gentleman from me, that Benjamin Franklin, in his woolen stockings, was no disgrace to his country. This government will never sanction what these gentlemen wish. The same habits brought reflections upon the last administration—those beautiful portfolios, those treaty boxes, and other things of that kind. It shall not be done, sir. I say again, sir, and I wish those gentlemen to know it, that no man ever did such honor to his country abroad as old Ben. Franklin, who wore his homespun blue woolen stockings, and all Paris loved him for it. Go on, sir, as you have begun. Have these things done—not meanly—but plain and simple, conformable to our republican principles. This Mr. ——, I believe, is a Frenchman. He has foreign notions. He has got his appointment; but if he had not got it, I do not say he would. A king, indeed! What's a king, that he should receive things in this splendid style? We ought to have things done in the best, plain, unpretending manner, and no other; and so, sir, have them done. Now, sir, you know my views, and the Secretary of State's also, for his views are mine in these things. Therefore go on as you deem right, religiously, and fear not. Say to the commissioner that I do not approve these extravagances. When he arrives in Europe he may have them fixed according to his notions, at his own expense, not the government's. Heaven and earth may come together, but Andrew Jackson will never swerve from principle."

"I am proud, General," said I, "to have your approbation of my course. There is just one other remark that I would like to make, with your permission."

"Proceed, sir," said the President, with the air of a man ordering a charge of cavalry.

"This commissioner," said I, "is a man of power and reputation. I am, as you are aware, in a position very different from his. It seems to me that, like a cockboat encountering a seventy-four, I shall be swamped. He is, besides, a friend of the Secretary of State. I never knew an instance of a subordinate getting on in any other way than by deferring to the wishes of his chief."

"No exception to that rule?" he asked, with one of his knowing looks.

"I have never known one," I replied.

"I think there *are* exceptions, Mr. Clark. I *think* there are. I *believe* you will not be swamped on this occasion, Mr. Cockboat. Any communication you may receive from the Secretary of State, during his absence, bring to me."

I took leave, returned to my office, and immediately wrote to the commissioner the following letter:

"SIR—The President, in a conversation with me this morning, directed me to inform you that he did not authorize, but expressly forbade, that the port-folio books relating to the Northeast Boundary for the arbitrator, the King of the Netherlands, should be done in any other manner than that of plain, republican simplicity; remarking, at the same time, that no difference should exist between those destined for the King and any others that emanate from the government. He happily illustrated his ideas on this subject, by the expression that, in his opinion, Benjamin Franklin, in his blue stockings, was no disgrace to his country. During the conversation I had with him, he directed me to say to you, that he wished every thing of the kind done in the best plain and substantial manner, and not according to foreign ideas of such things, and expressly directed me in this case to have them done in that manner. Understanding from you that these documents must be completed with dispatch, they will be done in the manner described in the shortest time possible. I am, etc.,

"X. CLARK."

I luckily kept a copy of this epistle. I say luckily, for a

day or two after, upon going to the President upon other business, I found him cool and reserved toward me. I asked him the reason.

"You have written an abusive letter to the commissioner," said he.

"No, General, I have not. I wrote him just such a letter as you directed, and here is a copy of it."

He read the letter and said it expressed his ideas exactly, and he was perfectly satisfied with it. His good humor was restored, and he again told me to bring to him any letter I might receive from the Secretary of State. It happened that I received from the Secretary a note the very next day, which read as follows: "Dear sir—Please tell my housekeeper that I shall be at home on Tuesday." Having occasion to visit the President that afternoon, I informed him that I had received from the Secretary of State a communication. He read it.

"Why," said he, "this has nothing to do with the matter in hand."

"No, General; but your words were, 'Bring me any letter you may receive from the Secretary;' you made no exception."

"Right, right, sir," said the President; "I see you are a military man."

The time came, at length, when I, too, was a suitor for presidential favor, and I venture to say that no one has ever obtained a lucrative office more easily and unexpectedly than I did. By accident I heard of the vacancy one mail before any one else in Washington. It was an office that secured to a prudent incumbent not income merely, but competence; one of those city places the fees of which had been fixed when the city was a small town. The mere growth of the city had rendered this office one of the best things in the gift of the federal government. In twenty-four hours there would have been fifty applicants for it—in a week, two hundred.

I went straightway to the President's office, and addressed him in words like these:

"General, the no-matter-what-ship of New York is vacant. You will be notified of the fact to-morrow morning. It was long ago understood between you and myself, that the straightforward way of doing business was the best, and I will proceed in that way upon the present occasion. I will ask you two questions. Do you consider me competent to discharge the duties of that office?"

"I do," said the President.

"Will you give me the appointment?"

"I will," was his instantaneous reply.

And he did. My name was sent to the Senate immediately. The nomination was confirmed, and I was soon at my new post, to the great astonishment of several worthy gentlemen who were striving, with might and main, by night and day, to secure the place for themselves. At the expiration of my term of four years, I went to Washington and asked a reappointment in precisely the same manner, and received for answer the same emphatic and instantaneous "I will," as before. On this occasion, the private secretary being busy, he requested me to write my own nomination. I did so, but as it was deemed best that the document should go to the Senate in the usual hand-writing, Major Donelson copied it, and sent it to the capitol.

The General invited me to dinner. I had sent him some months before, a barrel of hickory nuts, and after dinner he said to a servant,

"Bring some of Mr. Clark's hickory nuts."

"I am flattered, General," said I, "that you should remember it."

"Oh," said he, "I never forget my friends."

At the table, I observed, every guest was provided with two forks, one of steel, the other of silver. The President adhered to the primitive metal.

Mr. Forsyth was then Secretary of State. I called upon him, and informed him of my reappointment, and that my name was then before the Senate.

"Have you called upon your Senators?" he asked.

"I have not," was my innocent reply; "I did not suppose it necessary."

"Oh, no," said he, "it is not *necessary*. If General Jackson says so, that 's enough. There 's no Secretary of State, no Senate, no any body—if General Jackson has made up his mind."

Mr. Van Buren, who was sitting near, laughed. Mr. Forsyth laughed, I laughed, we performed a laughing trio; in the midst of which I took my leave, well assured in my own mind, that I had the best of the joke.

Four years later, however, Mr. Van Buren being President, I took a slightly different view of the matter. As the expiration of my second term drew near, I employed all the usual arts, and some of the unusual ones, to secure a reappointment, and entertained confident hopes of success. Indeed, I felt assured of it, and had reason to do so, though from the President himself I had heard nothing. My second term expired, and still I had learnt nothing of the fate of my application. The next morning, at 10 o'clock precisely, a gentleman entered my office, and, presenting his commission, informed me, with the utmost politeness, that I was no longer in the service of the government, and that I saw before me that dread being—terror of all office-holders—A SUCCESSOR!

I have seen many heads taken off in my time, but never one quite so neatly as my own.

VI.

FIRST BLOW AT THE BANK.

THE people of the United States came naturally enough by their old distrust of paper-money and banks. As early as 1690, we read in the old *News-Letters*, it required, in the village of New York, two paper dollars to buy one silver one. The colonists had been disastrously fighting the French in

Canada, and paying expenses in paper. In 1745, the great and famous expedition against Louisburgh, in Cape Breton, was paid for partly in the same unsubstantial coin, which had so depreciated in 1748 that to get one hundred pounds in gold it was necessary to give—

In Massachusetts'	paper,	1,100	pounds.
" New York	"	190	"
" East Jersey	"	190	"
" West Jersey	"	180	"
" Pennsylvania	"	180	"
" Maryland	"	200	"
" Virginia	"	125	"
" North Carolina	"	1,000	"
" South Carolina	"	700	"

The torrents of paper-money issued during the revolutionary war, which sunk in value to nothing, converted the old prejudice against paper promises-to-pay into an aversion that had the force of an instinct. To this instinctive aversion, as much as to the constitutional objections urged by Mr. Jefferson and his disciples, was owing the difficulty experienced by Alexander Hamilton in getting his first United States bank chartered. Hence, also, the refusal of Congress to recharter that bank in 1811. Hence the unwillingness of Mr. Madison to sanction the charter of the second bank of the United States in 1816. But the bank was chartered in 1816, and went into existence with the approval of all the great republican leaders, opposed only by the extreme Jeffersonians and by the few federalists who were in public life. Yes, the federalists, among whom was Daniel Webster. They opposed it ostensibly because of some of the provisions of the charter which they deemed unwise ; the real ground of opposition being that it was a republican measure, designed to relieve the country from some of the financial evils aggravated by the late war.

But, long before General Jackson came into power, the bank appeared to have lived down all opposition. In the presidential campaign of 1824 it was not so much as mentioned, nor was it mentioned in that of 1828. In all the political pamphlets, volumes, newspapers, campaign papers, burlesques, and caricatures of those years, there is not the most distant allusion to the bank as a political issue. The bank had become a universally accepted fact. General Jackson himself, though naturally averse to paper money—an opponent of Hamilton's bank in 1797, and not an advocate for that of 1816—had yet advised the establishment of a branch at Pensacola, and had signed a certificate in 1828, recommending certain persons for president and cashier of the branch at Nashville.*

At the beginning of the administration of General Jackson, the bank of the United States was a truly imposing institution. Its capital was thirty-five millions. The public money deposited in its vaults averaged six or seven millions; its private deposits, six millions more; its circulation, twelve millions; its discounts, more than forty millions a year; its annual profits, more than three millions. Besides the parent bank at Philadelphia, with its marble palace and hundred clerks, there were twenty-five branches in the towns and cities of the Union, each of which had its president, cashier, and board of directors. The employées of the bank were more than five hundred in number, all men of standing and influence, all liberally salaried. In every county of the Union, in every nation on the globe, were stockholders of the bank of the United States. One-fifth of its stock was owned by foreigners. One-fourth of its stock was held by women, orphans, and the trustees of charity funds—so high, so unquestioned was its credit. Its bank-notes were as good as gold in every part of the country. From Maine to Georgia, from Georgia to Astoria, a man could travel and pass these notes at every point without discount. Nay, in London, Paris, Rome, Cairo, Calcutta, St. Petersburgh, the notes of the bank of the United States were worth a fraction more or a fraction less than their value at home, according to the current rate of exchange. They could usually be sold at a

* Memoirs of Hugh L. White.

premium at the remotest commercial centers. It was not uncommon for the stock of the bank to be sold at a premium of forty per cent. The directors of this bank were twenty-five in number, of whom five were appointed by the President of the United States. The bank and its branches received and disbursed the entire revenue of the nation.

At the head of this great establishment was the once renowned Nicholas Biddle. To his pen Mr. Biddle owed his conspicuous position. A graduate of Princeton—a student of law in Philadelphia—secretary of legation at Paris, first under General Armstrong, then under Mr. Monroe—afterward Philadelphia lawyer and editor of a literary magazine—author of the "Commercial Digest," prepared at the request of President Monroe—unsuccessful candidate for Congress. In 1819 Mr. Monroe appointed him Government Director of the Bank of the United States, in which office he exhibited so much vivacity and intelligence, that, in 1823, he was elected president of the institution by a unanimous vote. It was a pity. Mr. Biddle was a man of the pen—quick, graceful, fluent, honorable, generous, but not practically able ; not a man for a stormy sea and a lee shore. The practically able man is not fluent of tongue or pen. The man who can not, to save his soul, sell a cargo of cotton at a profit, is your man to write brilliant articles on the cotton trade. In ordinary times, Mr. Biddle would have doubtless been able to retain his title of the Emperor Nicholas, of which he was a little vain, and to conduct his bank along the easy path with general applause. But he fell upon evil days, and the pen that made him ruined him.

He was one of those charioteers with whose magnificent driving no fault can be found, except that, at last, *it upsets the coach.* How many such charioteers there are in this world !

There is a tradition in Washington to this day, that General Jackson came up from Tennessee to Washington, in 1829, resolved on the destruction of the Bank of the United States, and that he was only dissuaded from aiming a paragraph at it in his inaugural address by the prudence of Mr. Van Buren. No less distinguished a person than Mr. Bancroft has fallen into this error.*

General Jackson had no thought of the bank until he had been President two months. He came to Washington expecting to serve but a single term, during which the question of re-chartering the bank was not expected to come up. The bank was chartered in 1816 for twenty years, which would not expire until 1836, three years after General Jackson hoped to be at the Hermitage once more, never to leave it. The first intercourse, too, between the bank and the new administration was in the highest degree courteous and agreeable. A large payment was to be made of the public debt early in the summer, and the manner in which the bank managed that affair, at some loss and much inconvenience to itself, but greatly to the advantage of the public and to the credit of the government, won from the Secretary of the Treasury a warm eulogium. "I am fully sensible," wrote Mr. Ingham to Mr. Biddle, on the 6th of June, "of the disposition of the bank to afford all practicable facility to the fiscal operations of the government, and the offers contained in your letters with that view are duly appreciated. As you have expressed the willingness of the bank to make the funds of the Treasury immediately available at the various points where they may be required for the approaching payment of the debt, the drafts for effecting the transfers for that object will be made to suit the convenience of the bank as far as the demands of other branches of the service will permit." And, on the 19th of June, when the business had been nearly done, he added: "I can not close this communication without ex-

* In his eulogy of General Jackson, pronounced at Washington, in June, 1845, Mr. Bancroft said: "He came to the presidency of the United States resolved to deliver the government from the Bank of the United States, and to restore the regulation of exchanges to the rightful depository of that power—the commerce of the country. He had designed to declare his views on this subject in his inaugural address, but was persuaded to relinquish that purpose, on the ground that it belonged rather to a legislative message."

pressing the satisfaction of the department at the arrangements which the bank has made for effecting these payments in a manner so accommodating to the Treasury, and so little embarrassing to the community." And when all was over, the Secretary again expressed his gratitude and admiration.

But while this affair was going on so pleasantly, trouble was brewing in another quarter. Isaac Hill, from New Hampshire, then second Comptroller of the Treasury, was a great man at the White House. He had a grievance. Jeremiah Mason, one of the three great lawyers of New England, a Federalist, a friend of Daniel Webster and of Mr. Adams, had been appointed to the presidency of the branch of the United States Bank at Portsmouth, New Hampshire—much to the disgust of Isaac Hill and other Jackson men of that little State. Isaac Hill desired the removal of Mr. Mason and the appointment in his place of a gentleman who was a friend of the new administration.

That the reader may see the movements of this gentleman as they appeared to General Jackson, and that he may fully understand the process by which the administration were brought into collision with the parent bank, I will present here a brief condensation of the papers and letters relating to the "Portsmouth affair," in the order in which they were produced. The correspondence began in June and ended in October. I believe myself warranted in the positive assertion, that this correspondence relating to the desired removal of Jeremiah Mason was the direct and real cause of the destruction of the bank. If the bank had been complaisant enough to remove a faithful servant, General Jackson, I am convinced, would never have opposed the rechartering of the institution.

June 27. A petition, signed by fifty-eight citizens of Portsmouth, New Hampshire, was addressed to the Directors of the Bank of the United States. It states that the Portsmouth branch has been conducted in a manner "partial, harsh, novel, and injurious to the interest of the bank;" and that the president of the branch is the guilty person. Asks his removal, and the appointment of a president and board of directors acquainted with the business necessities of Portsmouth, and disposed to dispense the favors of the bank impartially.

June 29. A similar petition from Portsmouth, signed by fifty-six members of the New Hampshire legislature. It states that small, safe loans have been refused to business men in Portsmouth, while, at the same time, large sums were loaned out of the State at greater risk; and that the course pursued by the President was "destructive to the business of Portsmouth and offensive to the whole community." Asks the removal of the president and directors, and the appointment of others named in the petition.

June 27. Levi Woodbury, of New Hampshire, United States Senator, to Mr. Ingham, Secretary of the Treasury. Marked "Confidential." Repeats the complaints of the petitions. Adds that Jeremiah Mason is *a particular friend of Mr. Webster*, who was supposed to have had much to do with procuring his appointment; that the appointment, unpopular at first, has now become odious through Mr. Mason's ungracious manners and partial, vacillating conduct. Advises the prompt removal of the president and directors, if it can be effected. P. S. "I understand the board is selected for this branch early in July"—next month.

July 11. S. D. Ingham to Nicholas Biddle. Encloses Mr. Woodbury's letter, and says that similiar complaints have been received from Kentucky and Louisiana. Adds, that the administration would learn with extreme regret that political relationship had any influence upon the granting or withholding of bank facilities. Compliments the parent bank highly upon the manner in which it has discharged its trust "in all its immediate relations to the government."

July 17. Isaac Hill to J. N. Barker and John Pemberton of Philadelphia. Encloses the two New Hampshire petitions and asks Messrs. Barker and Pemberton to hand them to the president of the bank. Admits that the movement originated in a suggestion of his own. Endorses all the statements of the petitions. Concludes by saying, that the "friends of General Jackson have had but too much reason to complain of the branch bank at Portsmouth;" that all they now want is, that it "may not continue to be an engine of political oppression;" and that, of the ten persons proposed in the legislative petition for directors, six are Jackson men and four Adams men. Mr. Hill quotes a private letter from Portsmouth, which accuses Mr. Mason of being "unaccommodating to pensioners," of making large loans to his brother-in-law at Boston, while "refusing to accommodate our merchants with two or three thousand dollars, and this, too, on the very best paper."

July 18. Nicholas Biddle to S. D. Ingham. "Confidential." Acknowledges the receipt of the secretary's letter enclosing that of Senator Woodbury. States that the letter has been submitted to the directors of the parent bank, who will investigate Mr. Woodbury's allegations, and, if they are substantiated, apply "an appropriate corrective." Meanwhile, in justice to Mr. Mason, he will say, of his own knowledge, that neither politics nor Mr. Webster suggested the selection of Mr. Mason. Mr. Webster did not even know of the nomination of Mr. Mason, until after it was made. Quotes a recent letter of Mr. Woodbury to himself, in which Mr. Woodbury says: "It is notorious that the charges against Mr. Mason in his present office *originated exclusively with his political friends*, and it was not till they created a personal rancor and inflamed condition of the public mind, seldom if ever before witnessed in this region, that others interposed from a supposed danger to the interests of both the town and the bank." Mr. Biddle gave a short history of Mr. Mason's appointment:

"The office at Portsmouth had originally the misfortune to have at its head a Mr. Cutts, who ended by defrauding the United States of upward of $20,000 of the pension fund, which the bank was obliged to replace, and last year the office was nearly prostrated in the general ruin which spread over that country. Out of $460,000 of loans, $148,000 was thrown under protest; still further protests were expected, and the actual loss sustained there will not be less than $112,000. At this period, the late president, a worthy man, but not calculated for such a state of things, resigned his place, and it became necessary at once to adopt the most energetic measures to save the property of the bank. A confidential officer was dispatched to Portsmouth, who found the affairs of the office in great jeopardy, covered with the wrecks which bad management and the most extensive frauds had occasioned. To retrieve it, it became necessary to select a man of first rate character and abilities; such a man was Mr. Mason. Of his entire competency, especially in detecting the complicated frauds, and managing the numerous law suits which seemed inevitable, there could be no doubt. Of his political opinions, we neither knew nor inquired any thing. In order to induce him to give up so much of his valuable time to the service of the bank, an estimate was made of the probable amount which we would have to pay for the professional services of a lawyer, and, by engaging Mr. Mason in that character, we were enabled to obtain his consent to accept the appointment. Since he has been in office, he has been exceedingly useful—has saved the bank from great losses—has secured the bad debts—nor, until Mr. Woodbury's letter, was I informed of any complaint against him. What is, moreover, to be much considered, is, that while he has been gradually reducing the old accommodation loans, he has actually increased the amount of the general loans of the office."

Mr. Biddle added, that he was inclined to attribute the clamor against Mr. Mason to his vigor in enforcing the payment of the old protested notes. He appended a long statement, showing that the bank had never been influenced in the bestowal of its favors by political considerations, and declaring that it never should be.

July 23d. S. D. Ingham to Nicholas Biddle. A well-written and ingenious letter in reply to Mr. Biddle's last. The secretary remarked that he was not prepared for such a sweeping assertion as that of Mr. Biddle, when he said that since the founding of the bank, no loan was ever granted or withheld through political partiality or hostility. Human nature being what it is, it was not credible that five hundred men, not selected by Omniscience, had been wholly exempt in all cases from the bias of party feelings. Mr. Biddle's assertion he therefore received "rather as evidence of Mr. Biddle's own feelings than as conclusive proof of the fact so confidently vouched for." The secretary would not assume the truth of the Portsmouth charges, but he *did* object "to a course of action which either resists inquiry, or, what is of the same tendency, *enters upon it with a full persuasion that it is not called for.*"

July 31. Jeremiah Mason to Nicholas Biddle. Informs Mr. Biddle that Isaac Hill is endeavoring to remove the pension agency from the branch bank at Portsmouth to Concord, Hill's object being to "benefit a small bank at Concord, of which, till his removal to Washington, he was the president." Says that though Concord is more central, Portsmouth is more convenient to a majority of the pensioners; and that, as the disbursements to pensioners amount to eighty thousand dollars a year, the removal of the agency will be a great loss to the branch bank. Thinks it can not be done legally. Mr. Mason concluded by saying he had heard that complaints of his official conduct had been forwarded to the parent bank, and that he desired to be informed what they were. "If,' said he, "the memorial and letters contain all the absurd untruths that were made use of to obtain signers to them, they must be extraordinary productions."

August 3. John H. Eaton, Secretary of War, to Jeremiah Mason. States that "it has been found necessary" to remove the pension agency from Portsmouth to Concord, and that a pension agent has been appointed to reside at Concord. Requests Mr. Mason to deliver into the custody of that agent all the books, papers, and money belonging to the pension agency.

August 10. Jeremiah Mason to Nicholas Biddle. Encloses the order of the Secretary of War for the transfer of the pension agency books, and says that, considering the order illegal, he thinks he shall not obey it until authorized to do so by the parent bank. "The Secretary of War," he remarks, "has no control over the navy and privateer funds, and yet it seems by his letter that the order to transfer them, with the invalid and revolutionary funds, is to come from him. No intimation is given of any direction of the President of the United States for doing this."

August 13. Jeremiah Mason to Nicholas Biddle. Says that the newly appointed Concord pension agent has presented himself at the branch bank at Portsmouth, and formally demanded the books. Mr. Mason had refused to give them up, and informed the agent that he must wait for instructions from the parent bank. In consequence of this movement, the pensions, then just due, would not be paid.

August 17. T. Cadwallader, acting president of the bank of the United States, to Jeremiah Mason. (Mr. Biddle being absent from Philadelphia, and on his way to Portsmouth, where he intended to investigate personally the charges against Mr. Mason, the instructions of the parent board were communicated to Mr. Mason by the acting president.) "You are instructed," said Mr. Cadwallader, "respectfully to inform the Secretary of War that no such authority as he claims is perceived in the acts of Congress; and that, as the bank must act under legal responsibility, you must request him to have the goodness to point out whence his authority is derived, stating that, to prevent inconvenience to the government, as well as to individuals, the payments to the pensioners will be continued as heretofore, until a further communication shall have been received from him, and submitted to the parent board."

August 25. James L. Edwards, pension clerk in the War Department, to Jeremiah Mason. States that the Secretary of War was absent from Washington, not anticipating any difficulty in the transfer of the pension agency. Requests Mr. Mason to go on paying the pensions as usual, and when Major Eaton returns the affair will be disposed of by him.

September 15. Nicholas Biddle to S. D. Ingham. This was the letter which finally and fatally embroiled the bank of the United States with General Jackson's administration. It was an honest, able, right, imprudent letter. Mr. Biddle had spent six days at Portsmouth, and had satisfied himself and satisfied the directors that the charges against Mr. Mason were "entirely groundless." "The most zealous of Mr.

Mason's enemies did not venture to assert that he had ever, on any occasion, been influenced by political feelings, and this public opinion, so imposing in the mist of distance, degenerated into the personal hostility of a very limited, and, for the most part, very prejudiced circle. *Mr. Mason was, therefore, immediately re-elected.*"

Having stated this result of the investigation, the president of the bank proceeded to declare the judgment of the bank upon the principles involved in the pending dispute. The bank, in effect, defied the administration.

"Presuming," said Mr. Biddle, "that we have rightly apprehended your views, and fearful that the silence of the bank might be hereafter misconstrued into an acquiescence in them, I deem it my duty to state to you in a manner perfectly respectful to your official and personal character, yet so clear as to leave no possibility of misconception, that the board of directors of the Bank of the United States, and the boards of directors of the branches of the Bank of the United States, acknowledge not the slightest responsibility of any description whatsoever to the Secretary of the Treasury touching the political opinions and conduct of their officers, that being a subject on which they never consult, and never desire to know, the views of any administration. It is with much reluctance the board of directors feel themselves constrained to make this declaration. But charged as they are by Congress with duties of great importance to the country, which they can hope to execute only while they are exempted from all influences not authorized by the laws, they deem it most becoming to themselves, as well as to the Executive, to state with perfect frankness their opinion of any interference in the concerns of the institution confided to their care." . .

October 8. S. D. Ingham to Nicholas Biddle. Mr. Ingham's reply is as long as a president's message. He expends pages in endeavoring to show that Mr. Biddle had misstated some of his previous positions, and other pages in saying how good and pleasant a thing it is to see a Secretary of the Treasury and a president of the United States Bank dwelling together in unity. The substantial meaning of his letter is this: "Mr. Biddle, you are altogether too touchy; instead of resenting suggestions from the Secretary of the Treasury, you ought to welcome them."

One paragraph of Mr. Ingham's letter contains a threat, to which subsequent events gave significance, though at the time it made but a slight impression: "The administration is empowered to *act* upon the bank in various ways: in the appointment or removal of five of the directors; *in the withdrawing of the public deposits;* in the exaction of weekly statements, and the inspection of its general accounts; and in all the modes incident to the management of the pecuniary collections and disbursements of the government. That these opportunities of action might be perverted and abused is conceivable, but, subjected to the principle on which we early and cordially agreed, they become causes of security and benefit; and before I dismiss this branch of the subject, I take the occasion to say, if it should ever appear to the satisfaction of the Secretary of the Treasury that the bank used its pecuniary power for purposes of injustice and oppression, he would be faithless to his trust if he hesitated to lessen its capacity for such injury, by withdrawing from its vaults the public deposits."

The conclusion of Mr. Ingham's long letter was as follows: "No one can more fervently desire than I do, that the bank shall, in all its ramifications, be absolutely independent of party; that it shall so conduct its affairs as to accomplish every purpose for which it was intended, and stand above the reach of the least plausible suspicion. No one can see with more unalloyed satisfaction its flourishing condition, or has borne more cheerful testimony to the character of its present management. Having labored ardently to create it, I may not be supposed the first to contaminate or decry it; but, however imposing its attitude, if once satisfied that the powers of its charter and the resources of its wealth are debased and perverted to practices at war with the liberties of the country, and the rights and interests of my fellow-citizens, no consideration of a personal nature will curb me in exercising the legal power with which I may be invested, to check its tendencies and reform its abuses; and it will be my care not less than my duty, never to surrender any of the rights vested in the government for this purpose."

October 9. Nicholas Biddle to S. D. Ingham. In this letter, which concluded the correspondence, Mr. Biddle explained some passages of his former letters, and heartily responded to the Secretary's desire that the bank should be totally independent of party.

So the Bank of the United States triumphed over Isaac Hill, Mr. Woodbury, and the administration. It was a dear victory.

The reader has perused the previous pages of this work to little purpose if he does not know what effect upon the mind of the President the bank's calm defiance was certain to produce. Before the next month closed, the editors of the *New York Courier and Enquirer* received a confidential hint from Washington, that the forthcoming Presidential Message would take ground against the Bank of the United States. So says Mr. James Gordon Bennett, who was then the active, working man of that great newspaper.

"For a considerable time," says Mr. Bennett, "after I joined the *Courier and Enquirer* in 1829, and the greater portion of which journal I then wrote with my own hand—and up to the year 1830, it presented no particular hostility to the United States Bank. I think it was in the month of November, 1829, when M. M. Noah was Surveyor of the Port, that in going to his office one day, I found him reading a letter which he had just received from Amos Kendall, and which informed him that ground would be taken against the Bank by General Jackson in the message to be delivered the next month on the opening of Congress. On the same day, a portion of Amos Kendall's letter, with a head and tail put to it, was sent over to the *Courier* office, and published as an editorial next morning. This was the first savage attack on the United States Bank in the columns of the *Courier and Enquirer*."

VII.

CONGRESS MEETS.

GENERAL JACKSON prepared his Messages very much as the editor of a metropolitan journal "gets up" his thundering leaders; only not quite so expeditiously. He used to begin to think about his Message three or four months before the meeting of Congress. Whenever he had "an idea," he would make a brief memorandum of it on any stray piece of paper that presented itself, and put it into his capacious white hat for safe keeping. By the time it became necessary to put the document into shape, he would have a large accumulation of these memoranda, some of them consisting of a few words on the margin of a newspaper, and some of a page or two of foolscap. These were all confided to the hands of Major Donelson, the President's faithful and diligent private secretary, whose duty it was to write them out into orderly and correct English. Thus was formed the basis of the Message, to which the members of the Cabinet added each his proportion. It is not difficult, in reading over the volume of General Jackson's Messages, to detect the traces of the General's own large steel pen.

Congress met on the seventh of December. Such was the strength of the administration in the House of Representatives, that Andrew Stephenson was re-elected to the Speakership by one hundred and fifty-two votes out of one hundred and ninety-one. This Congress, however, came in with the administration, and had been elected when General Jackson was elected.

The Message, eagerly looked for, as a first Message always

is, was delivered on the day following that of the organization of the House. A calm deliberateness of tone marked this important paper. If any where the hand of the chief was particularly apparent, it was where, on opening the subject of the foreign relations, in the midst of friendly declarations and confident hopes of a peaceful settlement of all points in dispute, the President observed that, the country being blessed with every thing which constitutes national strength, he should ask nothing of foreign governments that was not right, and submit to nothing that was wrong; flattering himself, he said, that, aided by the intelligence and patriotism of the people, we shall be able to cause all our just rights to be respected. After this Jacksonian ripple, the Message flowed on with Van Buren placidity to its close.

But who would have thought to find, in a first Message of Andrew Jackson, Great Britain singled out for compliment? "With Great Britain," said the Message, "alike distinguished in peace and war, we may look forward to years of peaceful, honorable, and elevated competition. Every thing in the condition and history of the two nations is calculated to inspire sentiments of mutual respect, and to carry conviction to the minds of both, that it is their policy to preserve the most cordial relations. Such are my own views; and it is not to be doubted that such are also the prevailing sentiments of our constituents." What does this mean? We shall see ere long.

The Message recommended that all "intermediate agency" in the election of the President and Vice-President shall be abolished, and the service of the President limited to a single term of four or six years. One passage in this part of the Message was, doubtless, designed to be particularly interesting to Mr. Clay and his friends. In case the election, through the number of candidates, devolves upon the House of Representatives, remarked the President, the will of the people may not be always ascertained, or, if ascertained, may not be regarded. Circumstances may give the power of deciding the election to a single individual. "*May he not be tempted to name his reward?"* In any case, thought the President, it is worthy of consideration, whether representatives should not be disqualified from holding office under a President of their own electing.

In two brief, pregnant paragraphs, every sentence a distinct proposition, and every proposition an error, the message defended the course of the government in its removals and appointments. The leading ideas of this passage were, that a long tenure of office is almost necessarily corrupting; that an office-holder has no more right to his office than the office-seeker; and that if any one had a right to complain of a removal from office it was *not* the luckless individual who had been suddenly deprived of the means of subsistence without cause.

The tariff was referred to with the vagueness unavoidable by a writer who was a protectionist in principle and a free-trader from necessity. The late tariff, said the message, had neither injured agriculture and commerce, nor benefited manufacturers, as much as had been anticipated; but "some modifications" were desirable, which should be considered and discussed not as party or sectional questions. The time was near at hand when the public debt would be all discharged. The gradual reduction and speedy abolition of the duties on tea and coffee were, therefore, recommended.

The finances of the country were in a satisfactory condition. Nearly six millions in the treasury; receipts for the year 1830 estimated at twenty-four millions six hundred thousand dollars; expenditures to be little more than twenty-six millions. Nearly twelve and a half millions of the public debt had been paid during the year, leaving only forty-eight and a half millions. When this debt shall have been discharged, the President continued, *then* will arise the great question, whether the surplus revenue should not be apportioned among the several States for works of public utility, and thus put to rest for ever the long-vexed question of internal improvements. In connection with this subject there was an emphatic declaration: "Nothing is clearer, in my view, than that we are chiefly indebted for the success of the constitution under which we are now acting to the watchful and auxiliary operation of the State authorities. This is not the reflection of a day, but belongs to the most deeply rooted convictions of my mind. I can not, therefore, too strongly or too earnestly for my own sense of its importance, warn you against all encroachments upon the legitimate sphere of State sovereignty."

The message suggested the formation of a Home Department to relieve the pressure on the Department of State.

The policy of the government on the Cherokee question was clearly foreshadowed. The Cherokees were given to understand that an independent sovereignty within the bounds of a sovereign State could not, in any circumstances whatever, be tolerated, and Congress was advised to set apart an ample district west of the Mississippi for the permanent occupancy of such tribes as could be induced to emigrate thither. "But," added the President, "this emigration should be voluntary; for it would be as cruel as unjust to compel the aborigines to abandon the graves of their fathers, and seek a home in a distant land."

Near the close of the message were the famous little paragraphs which sounded the first note of war against the United States Bank:

"The charter of the Bank of the United States expires in 1836, and its stockholders will most probably apply for a renewal of their privileges. In order to avoid the evils resulting from precipitancy in a measure involving such important principles, and such deep pecuniary interests, I feel that I can not, in justice to the parties interested, too soon present it to the deliberate consideration of the legislature and the people. Both the constitutionality and the expediency of the law creating this bank are well questioned by a large portion of our fellow-citizens; and it must be admitted by all, that it has failed in the great end of establishing a uniform and sound currency. Under these circumstances, if such an institution is deemed essential to the fiscal operations of the goverement, I submit to the wisdom of the legislature whether a national one, founded, upon the credit of the government and its revenues, might not be devised, which would avoid all constitutional difficulties; and, at the same time, secure all the advantages to the government and country that were expected to result from the present bank."

The President did not enumerate among the advantages of the bank which he suggested, that it would add to the patronage of a democratic administration. Such a bank as he proposed would be merely an appendage to the Treasury Department, and all its employées would be as much at the mercy of the government as a treasury-clerk.

Such was the message; in which the *fortiter in re* was so happily veiled by the *suaviter in modo.* It was, upon the whole, a candid and straightforward document. It gave no uncertain sound. The glove was fairly thrown down, though thrown with a certain grace, and the glove of finer kid than usual. What was thus plainly announced as the policy of the administration was carried out with a consistency and resolution rarely paralleled.

The debates began. No president ever watched the proceedings of Congress with more attention than President Jackson. Nothing escaped him. No matter to how late an hour of the night the debates were protracted, he never went to sleep till Major Lewis or Major Donelson came from the capitol and told him what had been said and done there. We must note such events of the session as were of particular interest to him.

VIII.

INCIDENTS OF THE SESSION.

THE proceedings of the Senate were the first to kindle the President's ire. The Senate was not so disposed to confirm as the President had been to appoint. The executive sessions, that had previously been so short and so harmonious, were now protracted and exciting. Sometimes the Senate was engaged for several days (once five days) in succession in the single business of confirming the nominations that were sent in from the presidential mansion. Some of the nominations were in the Senate for several months without being reached.

Although the proceedings in executive session are secret, many of the Senate's executive acts during this session were such as could not be concealed. A large number of the nominations were opposed, and several, upon which the President had set his heart, were rejected. No less than twenty-one Senators voted against the confirmation of Henry Lee, among whom were six of General Jackson's most intimate friends and most decided partisans. Edward Livingston, Thomas H. Benton, Felix Grundy, R. Y. Hayne, Levi Woodbury, and Hugh L. White, voted against him. Seven others of the President's nominations were rejected by majorities less decided ; and several more escaped rejection only by a vote or two.

The most remarkable case of rejection was that of Isaac Hill. It was also the one that gave the President the deepest offense, and which he avenged most promptly and most strikingly. The pretext for Mr. Hill's rejection was, that in the course of the late campaign he had libeled Mrs. Adams. He denied the charge, averring that, in his capacity of publisher, he had merely published a book of European travel that contained the aspersions complained of.

It was not unreasonable for General Jackson to conclude, and it is not unfair for us to conjecture, that it was Isaac Hill's conduct in the Portsmouth affair against the bank of the United States that caused a majority of the Senate to vote against his confirmation to the second comptrollership of the treasury. Mr. Hill, moreover, was a man of inferior presence, small and slight, lame and awkward. He was not the "style" of person whom Senators had been accustomed to see in high and responsible positions under the government.

The President set about righting the wrong which he

felt his friend had received with a tact and vigor all his own. A long communication was prepared at Washington for publication in the *New Hampshire Patriot*, calculated to make every Jackson man in the State regard the rejection of Isaac Hill as a personal affront. If Mr. Amos Kendall was not the author of this artful and forcible production, then I am sure Mr. Amos Kendall can tell us who was. "I assure you sir," said this anonymous writer, "*on my own personal knowledge*, that the President has entire confidence in Mr. Hill, and looks upon his rejection as a blow aimed at himself. He can not protect those whom he honors with appointments from combinations of designing men operating on the approving power ; but the people can. Enjoying the confidence and esteem of the President and his whole cabinet, Mr. Hill returns to you with pure hands and an honest heart. Those who have been defeated in their ambitious designs by his perseverance ; those who find the abuses by which they profited corrected by his vigilance; those who wish to destroy General Jackson, defeat all reform, and plunge our government into the sea of corruptions from which it has been redeemed, exult in Mr. Hill's rejection. But the real friends of the President and his principles look to the people and legislature of New Hampshire to wipe away the stigma cast upon this just and true man, by the unjust and cruel vote of the Senate. Let them say, by an act so signal that it can not be misunderstood, whether the President did wrong in the appointment of Mr. Hill, and whether a man so distinguished for his virtues, his talents, and his services, is unworthy of public station."*

Precisely so. The term of Mr. Senator Woodbury was about to expire. Waiving a reëlection for reasons better known to himself than to the public, Mr. Woodbury lent his great influence in New Hampshire to the support of Isaac Hill for the seat in the Senate about to be vacated. Hill was taken up by the Jackson men in the State with prompt enthusiasm, and a large number of the other party joined in

* Biography of Isaac Hill, p. 100.

the support of a man who was supposed to have been the victim of aristocratic pride and bank influence. He was elected by an unusual majority, and came back to Washington a member of the body that had deemed him unworthy of a far less elevated post. "Were we in the place of Isaac Hill," said the *Courier and Enquirer*, "we would reject the presidency of the United States, if attainable, to enjoy the supreme triumph, the pure, the unalloyed, the legitimate victory of stalking into that very Senate and taking our seat —of looking our enemies in the very eye—of saying to the men who violated their oaths by attempting to disfranchise citizens, "Give me room—stand back—do you know me? I am that Isaac Hill, of New Hampshire, who, in this very spot, you slandered, vilified, and stripped of his rights; the people, your *masters*, have sent me here to take my seat in this very chamber, as your equal and your peer."

By this election of Isaac Hill to the Senate several things were effected, some of which were peculiarly pleasing to General Jackson. Isaac Hill was more than reinstated. A restive Senate, a haughty bank, a hated Henry Clay, were rebuked and warned. New Hampshire was gratified, and *won*. Levi Woodbury was put in reserve for that place in the Cabinet which he had the rare fortune to retain for so many years. And all this was as purely the effect of Andrew Jackson's volition as though he had been autocrat instead of President.

35 The confirmation of Amos Kendall and Major Noah, two strong anti-bank men, was powerfully opposed in the Senate. The session was nearly at an end before their cases were decided. Daniel Webster, on the 9th of May, wrote to his friend Dutton: "On Monday we propose to take up Kendall and Noah. My expectation is that they will both be confirmed by the casting vote of the Vice-President, if the Senate should be full, as I think it will be. A week ago I was confident of their rejection, but one man who was relied on, will yield, I am fearful, to the importunities of friends and the dragooning of party. We have had a good deal of debate in closed session on these subjects, and sometimes pretty warm.

Some of the speeches, I suppose, will be hereafter published; none of mine, however. Were it not for the fear of the outdoor popularity of General Jackson, the Senate would have negatived more than half his nominations. There is a burning fire of discontent, that must, I think, some day break out. When men go so far as to speak warmly against things which they yet feel bound to vote for, we may hope they will soon go a little further. No more of politics."

Mr. Noah was rejected by a vote of 25 to 23. Mr. Kendall was confirmed by the casting vote of the Vice-President.

The disgust and anger of the President at the conduct of the Senate in rejecting so many of his friends were extreme. General Duff Green afterward reported a conversation which he had with the President on the subject in the early part of this session:

President.—"I have sent for you that we may converse on the subject of my nominations before the Senate. It is time that you should let the people know that, instead of supporting me and my measures, Congress is engaged in President making."

Editor.—"I trust that you know that I would not hesitate to say so if I believed the public interest required it; but excuse me for saying that, before I can censure Congress for not supporting your measures, I should be possessed of the views of the administration, that I may be enabled to reply to those who ask to be informed what those measures are."

President (much excited).—"Look at my message, sir; you will find them there—in the message, sir."

Editor.—"Some of your best friends complain that your message is so general in its terms, that no special measure is recommended; and I believe that the want of concert among your friends is attributed to the fact that there is no concert in your Cabinet. There being no Cabinet councils, there is no one who feels authorized to recommend any measure upon the authority of the administration, because it is understood that no measures are considered and adopted as such. Your friends in Congress complain that you do not hold Cabinet councils."

The President (more excited).—"Let Congress go home, and the people will teach them the consequence of neglecting my measures and opposing my nominations. How did you obtain your popularity, sir, as an editor? Was it not by opposing Congress? Speak out to the people, sir, and tell them that Congress are engaged in intrigues for the presidency, instead of supporting my measures, and the people will support you as they have done."

Editor.—"You complain that the Senate have not approved of your nominations. Will it not be unwise to anticipate the objections of that body? Your nominations may yet be approved; and if any should be rejected there may be reasons which would justify the Senate. If I were to assail the Senate, it would be attributed to your influence, and thus array against you the body itself, and those who deem it essential to preserve its independence. I can not know what impediments lie in the way of your nominations, and can not condemn until my judgment disapproves."

President.—"The people, sir, the people will put these things to rights, and teach them what it is to oppose my nominations!"*

The removal-and-appointment question was ably discussed in both houses during the session, and many plans were suggested for limiting the dread power of removal. But against so powerful an administrative majority in the house, nothing could be done on a question which was made a strictly party one, and by the proper adjustment of which the party in power could not but be a loser. Mr. Webster, it appears from his correspondence, had doubts whether the constitution gave the President the power to remove without the consent

36 of the Senate. He consulted Chancellor Kent on the point, and the Chancellor's reply strengthened his doubt.

The bank of the United States enjoyed two triumphs during this session of Congress. The Committee of Ways and Means, to which was referred that part of the President's message that related to the bank, a committee headed by the

37 distinguished Mr. McDuffie, of South Carolina, reported strongly in favor of the existing bank, and as strongly against the bank proposed by the President.

38 Later in the session, Mr. Potter, of North Carolina, introduced into the house four resolutions adverse to the bank. First, that the constitution conferred no power to create a bank; secondly, that if it had, the establishment of the bank was inexpedient; third, that paper-money and banks are in-

* United States Telegraph.

jurious to the interests of labor, and dangerous to liberty; fourth, that the house will not consent to the re-charter of the bank. These resolutions were immediately laid upon the table by the decisive and significant vote of eighty-nine to sixty-six. The President must proceed cautiously, therefore. He did proceed cautiously, but not the less resolutely. The bank exulted, and exulted openly; but the bank was a doomed bank, notwithstanding.

The removal of all the southern Indians to a territory west of the Mississippi was a measure which General Jackson entirely approved, and upon which, indeed, he was resolved. It was much debated this winter, and most strenuously opposed. The philanthropic feelings of the country were aroused. The letter of many treaties was shown to be against the measure. The peaceful Society of Friends opposed it. A volume of the leading speeches in opposition to the removal was widely circulated. The opinions of great lawyers were adverse to it. It was, indeed, one of those wise and humane measures by which great good is done and great evil prevented, but which cause much immediate individual misery, and much grievous individual wrong. It was painful to contemplate the sad remnant of tribes that had been the original proprietors of the soil, leaving the narrow residue of their heritage, and taking up a long and weary march for strange and distant hunting-grounds. More painful it would have been to see those unfortunate tribes hemmed in on every side by hostile settlers, preyed upon by the white man's cupidity, the white man's vices, and the white man's diseases, until they perished from the face of the earth. Doomed to perish they are. But no one, I presume, has now any doubt that General Jackson's policy of removal, which he carried out cautiously, but unrelentingly, and not always without stratagem and management, has caused the inevitable process of extinction to go on with less anguish and less demoralization to the whites than if the Indians had been suffered to remain in the States of Georgia, Alabama, and Mississippi. To this part of the policy of General Jackson, praise little qualified can be justly awarded. The "irrevocable logic of events" first decreed and then justified the removal of the Indians. Nor need we, at this late day, revive the sad details of a measure which, hard and cruel as it was then thought, is now universally felt to have been as kind as it was necessary.

I have had the advantage of conversing upon the Indian policy of General Jackson with the first authority in the land upon all subjects relating to the red man's mournful history —Mr. Henry R. Schoolcraft, of Washington. Mr. Schoolcraft did much service, under the General, as Indian Commissioner, in negotiating treaties. It was he who bought from the Indians, after a long winter of most tedious negotiation, a great part of what is now the State of Michigan. Said Mr. Schoolcraft:

"General Jackson was direct and explicit in giving instructions. He knew the white man, and he knew the red man, and he knew how each was accustomed to treat the other. When the United States bought the Michigan lands, crowds of white men came on to Washington with claims against the Indians for the United States to pay.

"'Don't pay them one dollar,' said the General. 'Pay the Indians honorably for their lands, their full value, in silver—not blankets, not rifles, not powder, but hard cash; and let their creditors collect their own debts. Don't you pay one of them, neither now nor at any future time. When white men deal with Indians, the Indians are sure to get into debt to the white men; at least, the white men are sure to say so. I won't hear of paying any of their "claims." The rascals are here now, I suppose. The town will be full of them, but I won't pay a dollar, and you may tell them so.'

"In fact," added Mr. Schoolcraft, "every boarding-house in Washington contained some of these claimants; a state of things which General Jackson only inferred from his own experience in Indian treaty-making. It was one of his canny guesses."

This was the session of Congress signalized by the great

debate between Mr. Hayne and Mr. Webster, the first of many debates upon nullification. The future readers of this discussion will be at a loss to discover, either in Mr. Foot's resolution that gave rise to it, or in Mr. Hayne's first speech upon that resolution, an adequate cause for Mr. Webster's magnificent explosions of eloquence. The source of his inspiration is to be sought in the unrecorded feeling of the hour. That tariff bill for which General Jackson had voted, followed as it was by a depression in the market for Southern produce had created in the Southern States an extreme and general discontent. Georgia, in the spring of 1829, had sent to Washington a solemn protest against the existing tariff, which Mr. Berrien presented to the Senate in an impressive speech. Both the protest and the speech, however, expressed the warmest devotion to the Union. But in South Carolina other language had been used. A distinguished citizen of that State had publicly said, that it was time for the South to begin to calculate the value of the Union ; and the remark had been hailed with what seemed, at a distance, to be general applause. In the chair of the Senate sat Mr. Calhoun, who was already regarded by Southern extremists as their predestined chief. There was a small, loud party in Washington who were already in the habit of giving utterance to sentiments with regard to the Union which, familiar as they are to us in 1859, thrilled with horror the patriotic spirits of thirty years ago.

In these circumstances, Mr. Samuel A. Foot, of Connecticut, introduced his harmless resolution to inquire into the expediency of suspending for a time the sale of the public lands. The debate upon this resolution, which has made it so memorable, was a brilliant accident, which surprised no one more than it surprised the eminent men who took the leading part in it. "The whole debate," wrote Mr. Webster to one of his friends, "was a matter of accident. I had left the court pretty late in the day, and went into the Senate with my court papers under my arm, just to see what was passing. It so happened that Mr. Hayne very soon rose in his first speech. I did not like it, and my friends liked it less."

The entire offense of Mr. Hayne's speech is contained in one of its sentences, if not in a single phrase. "I am one of those," said Mr. Hayne, "who believe that the very life of our system is the independence of the States, and that there is no evil more to be deprecated than *the consolidation of this government.*" This was the little matter that kindled so great a fire.

General Jackson, not yet believing that the doctrine of nullification was destined to become formidable, and being very friendly to Mr. Hayne, the brother of his old aid-de-camp and Inspector-General, was disposed, at the moment, to sympathize with the champion of South Carolina. Major Lewis, upon returning from the capitol after hearing the first day's portion of Mr. Webster's principal speech, found the General up, as usual, and waiting for intelligence.

"Been to the capitol, Major?" asked the President.

"Yes, General."

"Well, and how is Webster getting on?"

"He is delivering a most powerful speech," was the reply. "I am afraid he's demolishing our friend Hayne."

"I expected it," said the General.

The President was not long in discovering that there was possible danger in the new doctrine. His own position with regard to it was peculiar, inasmuch as he had been elected to the presidency by the aid of the extreme southern or states-rights party. It is evident that the nullifiers at this stage of their operations, expected from the President some show of acquiescence and support. They were quickly undeceived.

It had been a custom in Washington, for twenty years, to celebrate the birth-day (April 13th) of Thomas Jefferson, the apostle of democracy. As General Jackson was regarded by his party as the great restorer and exemplifier of Jeffersonian principles, it was natural that they should desire to celebrate the festival, this year, with more than usual eclat. It was so resolved. A banquet was the mode selected; to which the President, the Vice-President, the Cabinet, many leading members of Congress, and other distinguished persons were invited. Colonel Benton, who attended the banquet, narrates the part played in it by the President and Mr. Calhoun:

"There was a full assemblage when I arrived, and I observed gentlemen standing about in clusters in the ante-rooms, and talking with animation on something apparently serious, and which seemed to engross their thoughts. I soon discovered what it was—that it came from the promulgation of the twenty-four regular toasts, which savored of the new doctrine of nullification; and which, acting on some previous misgivings, began to spread the feeling, that the dinner was got up to inaugurate that doctrine, and to make Mr. Jefferson its father. Many persons broke off, and refused to attend further; but the company was still numerous, and ardent, as was proved by the number of volunteer toasts given—above eighty—in addition to the twenty-four regulars; and the numerous and animated speeches delivered—the report of the whole proceedings filling eleven newspaper columns. When the regular toasts were over, the President was called upon for a volunteer, and gave it—the one which electrified the country, and has become historical:

"'OUR FEDERAL UNION: IT MUST BE PRESERVED.'

"This brief and simple sentiment, receiving emphasis and interpretation from all the attendant circumstances, and from the feeling which had been spreading from the time of Mr. Webster's speech, was received by the public as a proclamation from the President, to announce a plot against the Union, and to summon the people to its defense. Mr. Calhoun gave the next toast; and it did not at all allay the suspicions which were crowding every bosom. It was this:

"'The Union: Next to our Liberty the most dear: may we all remember that it can only be preserved by respecting the rights of the States, and distributing equally the benefit and burden of the Union.'

"This toast touched all the tender parts of the new question—liberty *before* union—*only* to be preserved—*State-rights*—inequality of *burdens* and *benefits*. These phrases, connecting themselves with Mr. Hayne's speech, and with proceedings and publications in South Carolina, unvailed NULLIFICATION, as a new and distinct doctrine in the United States, with Mr. Calhoun for its apostle, and a new party in the field of which he was the leader. The proceedings of the day put an end to all doubt about the justice of Mr. Webster's grand peroration, and revealed to the public mind the fact of an actual design tending to dissolve the Union."*

* Thirty Years' View, i. 148.

It was supposed, at the time, that the toast offered by the President was an impromptu. On the contrary, the toast was prepared with singular deliberation, and was designed to produce the precise effect it did produce. Major Lewis favors the reader with the following interesting reminiscence: "This celebrated toast 'The Federal Union—It must be preserved,' was a cool, deliberate act. The *United States Telegraph*, General Duff Green's paper, published a programme of the proceedings for the celebration the day before, to which the General's attention had been drawn by a friend, with the suggestion that he had better read it. This he did in the course of the evening, and came to the conclusion that the celebration was to be a *nullification affair altogether*. With this impression on his mind he prepared early the next morning (the day of the celebration) three toasts which he brought with him when he came into his office, where he found Major Donelson and myself reading the morning papers. After taking his seat he handed them to me and asked me to read them, and tell him which I preferred—I ran my eye over them and then handed him the one I liked best. He handed them to Major Donelson also with the same request, who, on reading them, agreed with me. He said he preferred that one himself for the reason that it was shorter and more expressive. He then put that one into his pocket and threw the others into the fire. That is the true history of the toast the General gave on the Jefferson birth-day celebration in 1830, which fell among the nullifiers like an exploded bomb!

"I believe I related to you, when at my house, the anecdote that occurred in the General's office between him and a South Carolina member of Congress, who called to take leave of him. The General received him with great kindness, offering his hand, and begging him to be seated. After a few minutes of conversation, the member rose, and remarked to the General that he was about to return to South Carolina, and desired to know if he had any commands for his friends in that quarter. The General said, 'No, I believe not,' but immediately recalling what he had said, remarked, 'Yes, I have; please give my compliments to my friends in your State, and say to them, that if a single drop of blood shall be shed there in opposition to the laws of the United States, I will hang the first man I can lay my hand on engaged in such treasonable conduct, upon the first tree I can reach.'"

If the nullifying faction of the States Rights party were offended by the President's toast, the patriotic majority of that party were gratified, a month later, by his veto of the Maysville and Lexington road bill. No more internal improvements, said the President in his veto message, until two things are done, namely, the national debt paid, and the constitution revised so as to distinctly authorize appropriations for the construction of public works.

Though this celebrated veto message was not marked by the clearness of statement which characterized the President's first message to Congress, yet his real objections to the measure were sufficiently conspicuous. With the instinct of solvency strong within him, General Jackson had so set his heart upon the early extinction of the national debt, that any proposition involving an expenditure of the public money that could be safely avoided or deferred would have been unwelcome to him. In four years, he remarked, if no unusual diversion of the public funds be permitted, the debt will be extinguished; and "how gratifying the effect of presenting to the world the sublime spectacle of a republic, of more than twelve millions of happy people, in the fifty-fourth year of her existence—after having passed through two protracted wars, the one for the acquisition and the other for the maintenance of liberty—free from debt, and with all her immense resources unfettered!"

Congress, he added, was, on the one hand, diminishing the public revenue, by reducing the duties on tea, coffee, and cocoa, and, on the other, favoring appropriations for public works, which, in this very year, threatened to make the expenditures exceed the revenue by ten millions of dollars. He conld not consent to such an untimely liberality, and the less as he had emphatically declared his sentiments upon the subject in his annual message. Appropriations for internal improvements had always been the occasion of bitter contentions in Congress. The power of the federal government to appropriate money for such purposes was, at least, ill defined, and before any general system of using even the future surplus revenue for national works should be inaugurated, it would be best so to amend the constitution as to define its powers with the utmost exactness. The Cumberland road was an instructive admonition on this point. "Year after year contests are witnessed, growing out of efforts to obtain the necessary appropriations for completing and repairing this useful work. While one Congress may claim and exercise the power, a succeeding one may deny it; and this fluctuation of opinion must be unavoidably fatal to any scheme, which, from its extent, would promote the interests and elevate the character of the country."

This veto, the first of a long series, excited a prodigious clamor among the opposition. The opposition, however, could not command a two-thirds vote in either house. So the bill was lost. It is questionable if, from the volume of presidential messages, an argument more unanswerable can be selected than this Maysville veto message. Would that the principles it unfolds had been permanently adopted! It did vast good, however, in checking the torrent of unwise appropriation, and in throwing upon the people themselves the task of making the country more habitable and accessible.

I am sure it did not diminish the zest of General Jackson's opposition to the Kentucky turnpike to know, as he did well know, that Mr. Clay, in 1826, at the close of an after-dinner speech to some of his constituents, a speech severely denunciatory and sharply satirical of General Jackson, had given this toast: "The continuation of the turnpike road which passes through Lewisburg, and success to the cause of internal improvement, under every auspice." Nor was it it unknown to General Jackson that the managers of the road, to testify their gratitude for past services, had erected, at a conspicuous point in the road, a momument in honor of Henry Clay; which, I believe, still stands.

Three other internal improvement bills were passed during the last days of the session. Two of these the President retained until after the adjournment of Congress, which was equivalent to vetoing them. The other he disposed of in the following brief message:—"To the Senate of the United States: Gentlemen, I have considered the bill proposing to authorize a subscription of stock in the 'Washington Turnpike Road Company,' and now return the same to the Senate in which it originated. I am unable to approve this bill; and would respectfully refer the Senate to my Message to the House of Representatives on returning to that House the bill to authorize a subscription of stock in the Maysville, Washington, Paris, and Lexington Turnpike Road Company, for a statement of my objections to the bill herewith returned. The Message bears date on the 27th instant, and a printed copy of the same is herewith transmitted."

A quiet but effective defiance. The Senate voted again upon the bill, and came within five of carrying it by the requisite two-thirds. Colonel Benton and Edward Livingston voted for it. This was the last act of the session. Congress adjourned on the thirty-first of May.

IX.

MR. VAN BUREN CALLS ON MRS. EATON.

THESE may seem trivial words with which to head a chapter that treats of dynasties, successions to the presidency, and other high matters. Believing, however, that the political history of the United States, for the last thirty years, dates from the moment when the soft hand of Mr. Van Buren touched Mrs. Eaton's knocker, I think the heading appropriate.

General Jackson succeeded in showing that the charges against Mrs. Eaton were not supported by testimony, but he did not succeed in convincing the ladies who led the society of Washington that Mrs. Eaton was a proper person to be admitted into their circle. They would not receive her. Mrs. Calhoun would not, although she had called upon the lady soon after her marriage, in company with the Vice-President, her husband. Mrs. Berrien would not, although Mr. Berrien, ignorant, as he afterward said, of the lady's standing at the capital, had been one of the guests at her wedding. Mrs. Branch would not, although Mr. Branch had been taken into the Cabinet upon Major Eaton's suggestion. Mrs. Ingham would not, although the false gossip of the hour had not wholly spared her own fair fame. The wives of the foreign ministers would not. Mrs. Donelson, the mistress of the White House, though compelled to receive her, would not visit her. "Any thing else, uncle," said she, "I will do for you, but I can not call upon Mrs. Eaton." The General's reply, in effect, was this: "Then, go back to Tennessee, my dear." And she went to Tennessee. Her husband, who was also of the anti-Eaton party, threw up his post of private secretary, and went with her; and Mr. Nicholas P. Trist, of the State Department, was appointed private secretary in his stead. Six months after, however, by the interposition of friends, Major Donelson and his wife were induced to return and assume their former positions in the mansion of the President.

The two strongest things in the world were in collision—the will of Andrew Jackson and the will of lovely woman; of which latter the poet saith or singeth:

> "If she will, she will, you may depend on 't,
> If she won't, she won't, and there 's an end on 't."

Three weeks after the inauguration, when the President was in the midst of his correspondence with Dr. Ely, and when his feelings upon the subject of that correspondence were keenest, Mr. Van Buren arrived in Washington to enter upon his duties as Secretary of State.

Mr. Van Buren was a widower. He had no daughters. Apprised of the state of things in Washington, he did what was proper, natural, and right. He called upon Mrs. Eaton —received Mrs. Eaton—made parties for Mrs. Eaton ; and, on all occasions, treated Mrs. Eaton with the marked respect with which a gentleman always treats a lady whom he believes to have been the victim of unjust aspersion. A man does not get much credit for an act of virtue which is, also, of all the acts possible in his circumstances, the most politic. Many men have the weakness to refrain from doing right, because their doing so will be seen to signally promote their cherished objects. We have nothing to do with Mr. Van Buren's motives. I believe them to have been honest. I believe that he faithfully endeavored to perform the office of oil upon the troubled waters. The course he adopted was the right course, whatever may have been its motive.

The letter-writers of that day were in the habit of amusing their readers with the gossip of the capital, as letter-writers are now. But not a whisper of these scandals escaped into print until society had been rent by them into hostile "sets" for more than two years. After the explosion, one of the Washington correspondents gave an exaggerated and prejudiced, but not wholly incorrect account of certain scenes in which "Bellona" (the nickname of Mrs. Eaton) and the Secretary of State had figured. It was among the diplomatic corps, with whom Mr. Van Buren had an official as well as personal intimacy, that he strove to make converts to the Eatonian cause. It chanced that Mr. Vaughan, the British minister, and Baron Krudener, the Russian minister, were both bachelors, and both entered good-naturedly into the plans of the Secretary of State.

"A ball and supper," says the writer just referred to, "were got up by his excellency, the British minister, Mr. Vaughan, a particular friend of Mr. Van Buren. After various stratagems to keep Bellona afloat during the evening, in which almost every cotillon in which she made her appearance was instantly dissolved into its original elements, she was at length conducted by the British minister to the head of his table, where, in pursuance of that instinctive power of inattention to whatever it seems improper to notice, the ladies seemed not to know that she was at the table. This ball and supper were followed by another given by the Russian minister (another old bachelor). To guard against the repetition of the mortification in the spontaneous dissolution of the cotillons, and the neglect of the ladies at supper (where, you must observe, none but ladies sat down), Mr. Van Buren made a direct and earnest appeal to the lady of the minister of Holland, Mrs. Huygens, whom he entreated in her own language to consent to be introduced to the 'accomplished and lovely Mrs. Eaton.'

"The ball scene arrived, and Mrs. Huygens, with uncommon dignity, maintained her ground, avoiding the advances of Bellona and her associates, until supper was announced, when Mrs. Huygens was informed by Baron Krudener that Mr. Eaton would conduct her to the table. She declined and remonstrated, but in the meantime Mr. Eaton advanced to offer his arm. She at first objected, but to relieve him from his embarrassment, walked with him to the table, where she found Mrs. Eaton seated at the head, beside an empty chair for herself. Mrs. Huygens had no alternative but to become an instrument of the intrigue, or decline taking supper; she chose the latter, and taking hold of her husband's arm, withdrew from the room. This was the offense for which General Jackson afterward threatened to send her husband home.

"The next scene in the drama was a grand dinner, given in the east room of the palace, where it was arranged that Mr. Vaughan was to conduct Mrs. Eaton to the table, and place her at the side of the President, who took care, by his marked attentions, to admonish all present (about eighty, including the principal officers of the government and their ladies) that Mrs. Eaton was one of his favorites, and that he expected her to be treated as such in all places. Dinner being over, the company retired to the coffee-room, to indulge in the exhilarating conversation which wine and good company usually excite. But all would not do—nothing could move the inflexible ladies."

How exquisitely gratifying to General Jackson Mr. Van Buren's emphatic public recognition of Mrs. Eaton must have been, every reader will perceive. General Jackson had thrown his whole soul into her cause, as has been abundantly shown in previous pages of this volume. But it was not General Jackson alone whom Mr. Van Buren's conduct penetrated with delight and gratitude. It completely won the four persons who enjoyed more of General Jackson's confidence and esteem than any others in Washington. First, Major Eaton, the President's old friend and most confidential cabinet-adviser. Secondly, Mrs. Eaton. Thirdly, Mrs. O'Neal, the mother of Mrs. Eaton, the friend of the President and of his lamented wife. Lastly, but not least in importance, Major William B. Lewis, an inmate of the White House, the President's most intimate and most constant companion, and formerly the brother-in-law of Major Eaton. The preference and friendship of these four persons included the preference and support of Amos Kendall, Isaac Hill, Dr. Randolph, and all the peculiar adherents of General Jackson.

Mr. Van Buren was, moreover, just the man to "get along with" General Jackson. No one could ever quarrel with a gentleman who never gave and never took offense. Even with Mr. Clay he remained always on terms of jocularity. Mr. Clay writes in 1834: "Mr. Van Buren yesterday offered to bet me a suit of clothes upon each of the elections in the city of New York and in your State. . . . I told him yesterday, that if the people entertained the administration in its late measures, I should begin to fear that our experiment of free government had failed; that he would probably be elected the successor of Jackson; that he would introduce a system of intrigue and corruption that would enable him to designate his successor; and that, after a few years of lingering and fretful existence, we should end in dissolution of the Union, or in despotism. *He laughed, and remarked that I entertained morbid feelings.* I replied with good nature, that what I had said, I deliberately and sincerely believed."

And Jesse Hoyt, in recommending a valet to the Secretary of State, mentioned that the man's only fault was bad temper, which, he added, was of no consequence in the servant of a man who could never provoke it. It has, also, been frequently remarked, that a constitutionally irascible man finds his delightful counterpart in one who is constitutionally cool and good tempered. Accordingly, we find Mr. Van Buren writing home to his friend Hoyt, when he had been only a month in Washington: "The story you tell about the President's great confidence in Mr. Berrien, and little in me, is the veriest stuff that could be conceived. The repetition of such idle gossip constrains me to say, what I am almost ashamed to do, that I have found the President affectionate, confidential, and kind to the last degree; and that I am entirely satisfied that there is no degree of good feeling or confidence which he does not entertain for me. He has, however, his own wishes and favorite views upon points which it is not my province to attempt to control. Upon every matter he wishes to have the truth and respects it; and will in the end satisfy all of the purity of his views and intentions."

The public events of the summer of 1829, and those of the succeeding session of Congress, being known to the reader, I now invite attention to certain occurrences that took place this year in the private apartments of the President's house, of the highest importance, though never before made known.

The year 1829 had not closed before General Jackson was resolved to do all that in him lay to secure the election of Mr. Van Buren as his successor to the presidency. Nor did that year come to an end before he began to act in furtherance of the project. Before me is a letter from Andrew Jackson to his old friend Judge Overton of Tennessee, dated December 31st, 1829, which contains proof of this assertion.

41

To this letter is appended a Note by Major Lewis, explanatory of its secret purpose. For the convenience of the reader, the Note shall be submitted to his perusal first.

NOTE BY MAJOR LEWIS UPON A LETTER OF PRESIDENT JACKSON.

"The following letter was written under circumstances and for the purposes stated in the following remarks. All through the summer and fall of 1829, General Jackson was in very feeble health, and in December of the same year his friends became seriously alarmed for his safety. Indeed, his physical system seemed to be totally changed. His feet and legs particularly had been much swollen for several months, and continued to get worse every day, until his extreme debility appeared to be rapidly assuming the character of a confirmed dropsy. The General himself was fully aware of his critical and alarming situation, and frequently conversed with me upon the subject. The conversations occasionally led to another subject, in which I took a deep interest, to wit, the election of Mr. Van Buren as his successor. This I thought highly important, for the purpose of carrying out the principles upon which the General intended to administer the government. But if he were to die so soon after his advent to power, I greatly feared this object would be defeated. However, even in that event, I did not entirely despair of success. It occurred to me that General Jackson's name, though he might be dead, would prove a powerful lever, if judiciously used, in raising Mr. Van Buren to the presidency. I therefore determined to get the General, if possible, to write a letter to some friend, to be used at the next succeeding presidential election (in case of his death), expressive of the confidence he reposed in Mr. Van Buren's abilities, patriotism, and qualifications for any station, even the highest within the gift of the people. Having come to this resolution, I embraced the first favorable opportunity of broaching the subject to him, and was happy to find that he was not disposed to interpose the slightest objection to the proposition. He accordingly wrote a letter to his old friend, Judge Overton, of which the preceding is a duplicate, and handed it to me to copy, with authority to make such alterations as I might think proper. After copying it (having made only a few verbal alterations), I requested him to read it, and if satisfied with it, to sign it. He read it, and said it would do, and then put his name to it, remarking, as he returned it to me:

"'If I die, you have my permission to make such use of it as you may think most desirable.'

"I will barely add, that the General wrote this letter to his old and confidential friend, Judge Overton, at my particular request, and with a full knowledge of the object for which I wished it written. He has, fortunately for the country, however, recovered his health, and there will now, I hope, be no necessity for using it. In conclusion, I will further remark, that both the signature and indorsement, as will be perceived, are in General Jackson's own proper hand-writing."

(THE LETTER.)

GENERAL JACKSON TO JUDGE OVERTON.

"WASHINGTON, Dec. 31st, 1830.

"MY DEAR SIR: I have been anxiously awaiting the acknowledgment of my message to Congress forwarded to you, with such remarks as its subject-matter might suggest. But, as yet, I have not heard from you. As far as I have seen it commented on in the public journals, it has been well received, except in the Abbeville district, South Carolina, where it has been severely attacked. It is an old adage that 'straws show which way the wind blows.' I assure you this has somewhat astonished, though I can not say it has suprised me, because I had hints that some of my old friends had changed, and the case of Major Eaton was thought to present a fair opportunity of destroying him and injuring me, by circulating secretly foul and insidious slanders against him and his family. Be it so; I shall pursue the even tenor of my way, consulting only the public good—not the popularity of any individual.

"Congress is progressing with its labors, and I think I see in the commencement a little new leaven trying to mix itself with the old lump; but I believe the old will be hard to mix with the new. I regret also to say there is some little feeling still existing in a part of my cabinet. I am in hopes, however, that harmony will be restored, and that union of feeling and action which so happily prevailed when this administration was first organized, will be again revived. I do not think I have been well treated by those members who have been instrumental in introducing discord into my cabinet. They knew as well before as they did after their appointments who were to compose my cabinet. If they had any objection to associating upon terms of equality with any of the other members, they should have had candor enough to say so, before they accepted the offer of a seat in the cabinet. I still hope, however, that I shall not be driven to extremities; but should action become necessary on my part, you may rest assured I shall not hesitate when the public interest requires it.

"It gives me pleasure to inform you that the most cordial good feeling exists between Mr. Van Buren, Major Barry, and Major Eaton. These gentlemen I have always found true, harmonious, and faithful. They not only most cheerfully coöperate with me in promoting the public weal, but do every thing in their power to render my situation personally as pleasant and comfortable as the nature of my public duties will admit. Permit me here to say of Mr. Van Buren that I have found him every thing that I could desire him to be, and believe him not only deserving my confidence, but the confidence of the nation. Instead of his being selfish and intriguing, as has been represented by some of his opponents, I have ever found him frank, open, candid, and manly. As a councilor, he is able and prudent—republican in his principles, and one of the most pleasant men to do business with I ever saw. He, my dear friend, is well qualified to fill the highest office in the gift of the people, who in him will find a true friend and safe depository of their rights and liberty.

"I wish I could say as much for Mr. Calhoun and some of his friends. You know the confidence I once had in that gentleman. I, however, of him desire not to speak; but I have a right to believe that most of the troubles, vexations, and difficulties I have had to encounter, since my arrival in this city, have been occasioned by his friends. But for the present let this suffice. I find Mr. Calhoun objects to the apportionment of the surplus revenues among the several States, after the public debt is paid. He is, also, silent on the bank question, and is believed to have encouraged the introduction and adoption of the resolutions in the South Carolina Legislature relative to the tariff. I wish you to have a few numbers written on the subject of the apportionment of the surplus revenue, after the national debt is paid. It is the only thing that can allay the jealousies arising between the different sections of the Union, and prevent that flagitious *log-rolling-legislation*, which must, in the end, destroy every thing like harmony, if not the Union itself. The moment the people see that the surplus revenue is to be divided among the States (when there shall be a surplus), and applied to internal improvement and education, they instruct their members to husband the revenue for the payment of the national debt, so that the surplus, afterward, may be distributed in an *equal ratio* among the several States. If this meets your view, by giving it an impulse before the people, in a few written numbers, you will confer on your country a blessing that will be hailed as no ordinary boon by posterity, who must feel its benefits. I feel the more anxious about this, because I have reason to believe a decided stand will be taken by the friends of Mr. Calhoun, in Congress, against the policy, if not the constitutionality, of such a measure. Let me hear from you on the receipt of this. Present me affectionately to your amiable family, and believe me to be,

"Your friend, ANDREW JACKSON."

Judge Overton, I believe, never knew the purpose for which this letter was written. The copy retained was signed by General Jackson and placed among the secret papers of

Major Lewis, where it reposed until copied for the readers of these pages in 1858.

General Jackson and Major Lewis knew how to keep a secret; and this secret was confided, at first, to no one. Yet I find, from the correspondence of Mr. Webster and others, that some inkling of the truth with regard to General Jackson's preference of Mr. Van Buren for the succession, escaped the inner offices of the White House almost immediately. Sixteen days after the letter to Judge Overton had been written, Mr. Webster wrote to his friend, Dutton: "Mr. Van Buren has evidently, at this moment, quite the lead in influence and importance. He controls all the pages on the back stairs, and flatters what seems to be at present the Aaron's serpent among the President's desires, a settled purpose of making out the lady, of whom so much has been said, a person of reputation. It is odd enough, but too evident to be doubted, that the consequence of this dispute in the social and fashionable world, is producing great political effects, and *may very probably determine who shall be successor to the present chief magistrate.* Such great events," etc., etc., etc.

A month later (February 27th, 1830) Mr. Webster wrote to Jeremiah Mason: "Calhoun is forming a party against Van Buren, and as the President is supposed to be Van Buren's man, the Vice-President has great difficulty to separate his opposition to Van Buren from opposition to the President. Our idea is to let them pretty much alone; by no means to act a secondary part to either. We never can and never must support either. While they are thus arranging themselves for battle, that is, Calhoun and Van Buren, there are two considerations which are likely to be overlooked or disregarded by them, and which are material to be considered. 1. The probability that General Jackson will run again; that that is his present purpose I am quite sure. 2. The extraordinary power of this anti-Masonic party, especially in Pennsylvania."

Mr. Webster was correct in his opinion that General Jackson was likely to "run again," but he was exceedingly mistaken in supposing that the fact was "overlooked" by Mr. Van Buren. Mr. Van Buren was far too acute a politician not to be aware that there was only one man in the country, and he Andrew Jackson, who, in 1832, could defeat the combined opposition of Calhoun and the South, Clay and the West, Webster and the North. Mr. Van Buren, from the first, insisted upon General Jackson's running a second time. It was an essential part of the programme. It was that which alone could make the rest of the programme possible.

Then there *was* a programme? Most assuredly. The "Jackson party" came into power against the "Secretary dynasty;" but that party had not been in power a year before it had arranged a programme of succession so long, that it would have required twenty-four years to play it out. It was divided into three parts of eight years each: Andrew Jackson, eight years; Martin Van Buren, eight years; Thomas H. Benton, eight years. It will be safe for any one to deny this, because such programmes are never put into writing, and can seldom be proved. But I am assured it is a fact. The intelligent reader will find evidence of it in the political history of the time.

Among the invaluable papers of Major Lewis we must look to discover the mode by which General Jackson was brought before the people for reëlection. The first steps were taken when the President had served just one year. Read attentively the following letter, which was written in the presidential mansion:

MAJOR LEWIS TO COL. L. C. STANBAUGH OF PENNSYLVANIA. 42

"WASHINGTON, March 11th, 1830.

"DEAR SIR: Yours of the 15th has been received, and, as stated, the nomination of Major Lee has been rejected by the Senate. Though very much to be regretted, yet it is no evidence of the President's want of popularity in that body. Major Lee's own connections were the cause of his rejection.

"You have, no doubt, heard of the unfortunate affair relative to his domestic relations; which, however, on account of deep and sincere repentance, all the good and liberal minded were disposed to forgive.

Not so with his connections. They pressed the subject upon the Senate in such a manner as to compel Lee's own friends to vote against him. It does not in any manner affect the administration, as the responsibility of the nomination must rest upon those who recommended him; but it must deeply wound *his* feelings, and prove, I fear, greatly injurious to his future prospects in life.

"With regard to General Jackson's serving another term, it would be improper for me, perhaps, situated as I am, to say any thing; but, my dear sir, almost every friend he has, I mean *real friends*, thinks with you, that there is no other way by which the great Republican party, who brought him into power, can be preserved. Clay's friends are beginning to hold up their heads again; their countenances are brightening, not on account of Chilton's letter, for he is of too little consequence, but because of the anticipated splits between the friends of those who aspire to succeed the present chief magistrate. It is certainly necessary, as you suggest, that some steps should be taken to quiet the public mind; but perhaps I may differ with you as to *what* should be done, and *how* it should be done. I do not tnink it would be proper for General Jackson to avow at this time, his determination to serve another term; nor do I think it would be prudent for his friends *here*, to take the lead in placing his name before the nation for reëlection. According to the General's *own* principles (always practiced on by him), he can not decline serving again if called on by the people.

"I am not authorized to say that he would permit his name to be used again, but knowing him as I do, I feel *confident* that if he believed the interest of the country required it, and that it was the wish of the people he should serve another term, he would not hesitate one moment. If, then, it is the desire of your State that he should serve another term *let the members of her legislature express the sentiments of the people upon that subject.* But let it be done in such a way as not to make it necessary for him to *speak* in relation to the matter. Such an expression of public sentiment, would come with better grace from Pennsylvania than from any other quarter, and would have a more powerful effect—because of her well-known democratic principles, and because she has always been the General's strongest friend. *If any thing be done in the business the sooner the better.*

43 "You will have seen in the papers that Commodore Porter has been nominated to succeed Major Lee. Every one here rejoices at it.

"Yours sincerely, W. B. LEWIS."

In this letter was inclosed another—for Major Lewis never did these things by halves—the nature and object of which he himself explains in one of his precious Notes.

ANOTHER NOTE BY MAJOR LEWIS.

"The inclosed letter was prepared and sent by me to Harrisburg, for the members of the legislature to sign and forward to the President of the United States, provided a majority of them concurred in the views therein taken. Col. Stanbaugh, to whom it was inclosed, consulted with them upon the subject, and after making a few verbal alterations, a majority of the members signed and transmitted it to the President. This was the first movement made toward bringing out General Jackson for a second term. It was afterward followed up by the legislatures of New York and Ohio, principally upon my suggestions and advice to the friends of the administration in those two States. Indeed, I wrote several letters to my friends in Ohio also (of which I kept no copies), and procured others to be written, urging the absolute necessity of such a step at the next meeting of their legislature, as the most effectual, if not the only means of defeating the machinations of Mr. Calhoun and his friends, who were resolved on forcing General Jackson from the presidential chair after one term. The peculiar situation of the Vice-President, it was believed, made this necessary. He was then serving out his second term, and as none of his predecessors had ever served more than eight years, his friends thought it might be objected to, and perhaps would be injurious to him, to be presented to the nation for a third term. Under this view of the subject, they did not seem disposed to hazard the experiment. But what was to be done? It would not do for him to retire to the shades of private life for four long years. He could not run for a third term, and they dare not run him in opposition to General Jackson. Seeing no other way by which these perplexing difficulties could be surmounted, and believing there would be danger in further postponing his pretensions, his friends boldly resolved to get rid of the General, upon the ground that it was understood, during the canvass, that he was to serve four years only in case of his election. It was to defeat this project of the Vice-President and his friends that I opened a correspondence with Col. Stanbaugh, and suggested to him the necessity of bringing out General Jackson again, and the manner of doing it. The scheme succeeded admirably, and in a few months the hopes of Mr. Calhoun and his partisans were completely withered, and the idea of driving General Jackson from the field abandoned altogether."

THE INCLOSED LETTER.

"HARRISBURG, March 20, 1830.

To His Excellency Andrew Jackson, President of the United States.

"DEAR SIR: The undersigned, members of the legislature of Pennsylvania, before closing the duties assigned them by their constituents, beg leave to tender to you their best wishes for your health and happiness, and to express to you the confidence reposed by them in the sound republican principles which mark the course of your administration. The second political revolution effected in the year 1829 is progressing in a way to attain those great results which were fondly anticipated, and which, in the end, we ardently hope will tend to cement in stronger bonds the republican feelings of the country. In a free government like ours, parties must and will exist; it should be so, inasmuch as it serves to make those who are dominant vigilant and active in the discharge of the important duties which give life, health, and activity to the great principles by which, as a free people, we should be governed. If the voice of Pennsylvania, which has recently been prominently and effectively exerted in the election of our present distinguished chief magistrate, can have influence, it will, as heretofore, be exerted in inducing you to permit your name and distinguished services again to be presented to the American people. We deem it of importance to the maintenance of correct republican principles that the country should not thus early be again drawn into a warm and virulent contest as to who shall be your successor.

"If the people can indulge a hope that, in acceding to their wishes as heretofore, the warmth of former contests may be spared, they will be able to repose in peace and quiet, and before the end of your second term, will expect with confidence that the great principle of governmental reform will be so harmonized and arranged that the affairs of the nation for the future will move on certainly, peacefully, and happily. Expressing what we feel and believe to be the language of our constituents, we claim to indulge the expectation that your avowed principle 'neither to seek nor to decline to serve your country in public office,' will still be adhered to, that thereby the people may obtain repose, and toward the termination of your second term be better prepared to look around and ascertain into whose hands can be best confided the care and guardianship of our dearest rights, our happiness, and independence.

"This communication is not made with the intention of obtaining from you any declaration at this time upon this subject. We are aware that persons would be found to call such a declaration premature, before some general expression of satisfaction in relation to the course you have pursued had been exhibited, and time afforded for it to be evinced. Pennsylvania, heretofore first to express her attachment upon this subject, seeks only to maintain the position she has assumed, and to express through her representatives her continued confidence in your stern political integrity, and the wise, judicious, republican measures of your administration, and to cherish the hope that the country may again be afforded the opportunity of having those services, the benefit of which she is now so happily enjoying. On this subject, sir, we speak not only our own sentiments and opinions, but feel that the people will accord to the suggestion, and every where respond to what we have declared.

"Wishing you long life, health, and happiness, we remain your friends and fellow citizens."

To this address sixty-eight names were finally appended. Colonel Stanbaugh, in a letter to Major Lewis, narrates how those names were obtained:

"I can not tell you," he wrote, March 31, "how much I feel rejoiced that *you* see the *necessity* of placing General Jackson's name before the American people without delay as a candidate for reëlection. Two modes presented themselves to me as well calculated to afford our friends at Washington a pretext for announcing the General's name as a candidate. One was a letter, to be addressed to him, approving the measures of his administration, etc., by the General Committee of Correspondence of this State, of which I am a member; and the other way that suggested itself was a call from the different presses in the State which supported him at the last election. I had prepared letters to carry both these plans into execution, and although some of our presses, you are aware, are under the control of a *certain influence*, I believe I could get them all to come out on the subject. No matter what the private views and feelings of politicians may be who claim to belong to the democratic party, they will hesitate before they give their *own opinions and wishes*, when the question is put to them, either to support or reject the old hero.

"Pennsylvania is still sound, depend upon it, no matter what time-serving politicians, *high in power*, may say to the contrary; but just as certain it is, that the salvation of the democratic party, as well here as in other States, depends upon General Jackson's being again a candidate.

"Your letter convinced me at once that this subject can no where 'originate with better grace than in the Pennsylvania Legislature,' and there it shall originate if God spares my life till to-morrow. The views you sent me could not, in my opinion, be altered for the better, and I drew up a letter from them, with but a trifling variation, or rather addition. There were fifteen members at my house yesterday afternoon, every one of whom signed the letter, and at once came into the spirit of the subject. Two more—Senators—were here this morning and signed it. On Tuesday I hope we will be enabled to send it to the Patriot Chief. Would it not, my dear sir, be good policy for other States friendly to General Jackson to follow Pennsylvania immediately with similar declarations? It might all be done before Congress adjourns. Write to me, if you please, by return mail, and give me your opinion as to the place the letter had better make its first appearance. I think the *Pennsylvania Reporter* would be the proper place. It would have the appearance of being the act of the members, and state that they were in good earnest on the subject. The sooner it is published, I think, the better. If you write by return mail I will get your letter on Wednesday, and I can have the other published in Friday's paper. Remember me to the President, to Major Eaton, and Mrs. Eaton."

Major Lewis promptly replied. The address was published in the paper named by Colonel Stanbaugh, preceded by these words: "We are pleased to lay before our readers the following letter, signed by sixty-eight members of the Legislature, expressing their approbation of the wise, judicious, republican measures of General Jackson's administration, and respectfully urging him again to become a candidate for the presidency."

X.

AN UNHARMONIOUS CABINET.

COULD the Cabinet be other than an unharmonious one? It was divided into two parties upon the all-absorbing question of Mrs. Eaton's character. For Mrs. Eaton were Mr. Van Buren, Major Eaton, Mr. Barry, and the President. Against Mrs. Eaton were Mr. Ingham, Mr. Branch, Mr. Berrien, and the Vice-President. The situation of poor Eaton was most embarrassing and painful; for the opposition to his wife being feminine, it could neither be resisted nor avenged. He was the most miserable of men, and the more the fiery President strove to right the wrongs under which he groaned, the worse his position became. The show of civility kept up between himself and the three married men in the Cabinet was, at last, only maintained on occasions that were strictly official. Months passed during which he did not exchange a word with Mr. Branch except in the presence of the President.

To add to his disgust, charges were trumped up against himself of having, in settling the accounts of the late purser, Timberlake, connived at a fraud upon the government. An anonymous letter was sent him of a truly fiendish character. "Revenge is sweet," said this nameless devil, "and I have you in my power, and I will roast you, and boil you, and bake you; and I hope you may long live to prolong my pleasure. Lay not the flattering unction to your soul, that you can escape me. I would not that death, or any evil thing, should take you from my grasp for half the world." Never was a Cabinet minister so tormented before his time.

After enduring this unhappy state of things for nearly a year, the President's patience was completely exhausted, and he was determined that his Cabinet should either be harmonized or dissolved. Mr. Ingham afterward placed on record the manner in which the difficulty was, for a time, disposed of. His statement, which accords with the narratives of Mr. Branch and Mr. Berrien, is correct in its material particulars.

"On Wednesday, the 27th of January, 1830," wrote Mr. Ingham, "Colonel R. M. Johnson, of Kentucky, waited on me in the Treasury Department, and after some preliminary conversation, in which he expressed his regret that my family and that of Mr. Branch and Mr. Berrien did not visit Mrs. Eaton, he said that it had been a subject of great excitement with the President, who had come to the determination of having harmony in his Cabinet by some accommodation of this matter. He, Colonel Johnson, was the friend of us all, and had now come at the request of the President to see whether any thing could be done: who thought that, when our ladies gave parties, they ought to invite Mrs. Eaton; and as they had never returned her call, if they would leave the first card and open a formal intercourse in that way, the President would be satisfied; but unless something was done of this nature, he had no doubt, indeed he knew that the President was resolved to have harmony, and would probably remove Mr. Branch, Mr. Berrien, and myself. I replied to Colonel Johnson, that in all matters of official business, or having any connection therewith, I considered myself bound to maintain an open, frank, and harmonious intercourse with the gentlemen I was associated with. That the President had a right to expect the exertion of my best faculties, and the employment of my time, in the public service. As to the family of Mr. Eaton, I felt an obligation on me not to say any thing to aggravate the difficulties which he labored under, but to observe a total silence and neutrality in relation to the reports about his wife, and to inculcate the same course as to my family, and if any other representations had been made to the President, they were false. Having prescribed to myself this rule, and always acted upon it, I had done all that the President had a right to expect. That the society of Washington was liberally organized; there was but one circle, into which every person of respectable character, disposed to be social, was readily admitted, without reference to the circumstance of birth, fortune, or station, which operated in many other places. That we had no right to exert official power to regulate its social intercourse. That Mrs. Eaton had never been received by the society here, and it did not become us to force her upon it; that my family had, therefore, not associated with her, and had done so with my approbation; and that the President ought not, for the sake of his own character, to interfere in such matters. But if he chose to exert his power to force my family to visit any body they did not choose to visit, he was interfering with what belonged to me, and no human power should regulate the social intercourse of my family, by means of official or any other power which I could resist. If I could submit to such control, I should be unworthy of my station, and would despise myself. That it was eminently due to the character of the President to have it known that he did not interfere in such matters; and that the course we had pursued was preservative of his honor and political standing. I had taken my ground on mature reflection as to what was due to my family, my friends, and the administration, without any prejudice to Major Eaton or his wife, and had fully determined not to change it, whatever might be the consequence.

"Col. Johnson said that he had been requested by the President to have a conversation with the Secretary of the Navy and the Attorney-General also; but, from what I had said, he supposed it would be of no avail. The President expressed a hope that our families would have been willing to invite Mrs. Eaton to their large parties, to give the appearance of an ostensible intercourse, adding that he was so much excited that he was like a roaring lion. He had heard that the lady of a foreign minister had joined in the conspiracy against Mrs. Eaton, and he had sworn that he would send her and her husband home if he could not put an end to such doings. I replied, that it could hardly be possible that the President contemplated such a step. Col. Johnson replied that he certainly did; and again remarked that it seemed to be useless for him to see Mr. Branch and Mr. Berrien. I told him that each of us had taken our course upon our own views of the propriety without concert; and that he ought not to consider me as answering for any but myself. He then proposed that I should meet him at Mr. Branch's, and invite Mr. Berrien, that evening at seven o'clock, which was agreed to. Col. Johnson came to my house about six, and we went up to Mr. Berrien's, having first sent for Mr. Branch. On our way to Mr. Berrien's, Col. Johnson remarked that the President had informed him that he would invite Mr. Branch, Mr. Berrien, and myself, to meet him on the next Friday, when he would inform us, in the presence of Dr. Ely, of his determination; and if we did not agree to comply with his wishes, he would expect us to send in our resignations.

"Upon our arrival at Mr. Berrien's, Col. Johnson renewed the subject in presence of him and Governor Branch, and repeated substantially, though I thought rather more qualifiedly, what he had said to me. He did not go so much into detail, nor do I recollect whether he mentioned the President's remarks as to the lady above mentioned and Dr. Ely; those gentlemen will better recollect. Mr. Branch and Mr. Berrien replied, as unequivocally as I had done, that they would never consent to have the social relations of their families controlled by any power whatever but their own. Mr. Branch, Mr. Berrien, and myself went the same evening to a party at Col. Towson's, where a report was current that we were to be removed forthwith, of which I had no doubt at the time.

"The next morning, Col. J. came to my house and said that he ought, perhaps, to have been more frank last evening, and told us positively that the President had finally determined on our removal from office, unless we agreed at once that our families should visit Mrs. Eaton, and invite her to their large parties; and that he had made up his mind to designate Mr. Dickins to take charge of the Treasury Department, and Mr. Kendall to take charge of the Navy Department, and would find an Attorney-General somewhere. I observed that my course was fixed, and could not be changed for all the offices in the President's gift; and it made no more difference to me than to any other person whom the President designated to take my place. In the evening of the same day, Col. J. called again, and informed me that he had just been with the President, who had drawn up a paper explanatory of what he had intended and expected of us; that some of his Tennessee friends had been with him for several hours; that his passions had subsided, and he had entirely changed his ground. He would not insist on our families visiting Mrs. Eaton; he only wished us to assist in putting down the slanders against her; that he believed her innocent, and he thought our families ought to do what they could to sustain her, if they could not visit her; and that he wished to see me the next day. Col. Johnson added that the President had been exceedingly excited for several days, but was now perfectly calm and mild. The next day I waited on the President, and opened the subject by stating that Col. Johnson had informed me that he wished to see me, to which he assented, and went into a long argument to show how innocent a woman Mrs. Eaton was, and how much she had been persecuted, and mentioned the names of a number of ladies who had been active in this persecution, and that the lady of a foreign minister was also one of the conspirators; adding that he would send her and her husband home, and teach him and his master that a wife of a member of his cabinet was not to be thus treated; that Mrs. Eaton was as pure and chaste as Mrs. Donelson's infant daughter, but there was a combination here among a number of ladies, not those of the heads of departments, to drive her out of society, and to drive her husband out of office; but he would be cut into inch pieces on the rack before he would suffer him or his wife to be injured by their vile calumnies; that he was resolved to have harmony in his cabinet, and he wished us to join in putting down the slanders against Mrs. Eaton. I observed to the President that I had never considered it incumbent on me to investigate the character of Mrs. Eaton; such a service did not, in my judgment, come within the scope of my duties to the government; it belonged to society alone to determine such matters. The power of the administration could not change the opinion of the community, even if it could be properly used to control the relations of domestic life in any case. The society of Washington must be the best judges of whom it ought to receive. I regretted the difficulties which Major Eaton labored under, and had felt it to be my duty not to aggravate them. I had intended at an early day to have had a conversation with him on the subject, with a view to have our social relations defined; but no opportunity had offered without volunteering one, and it had not been done in that way. The course I had taken was, however, adopted with great care, to save his feelings as much as possible, consistent with what was due to my family, and the community with which we were associated. I consider the charge of my family to be a sacred trust, belonging exclusively to myself as a member of society. The administration had nothing to do with it, more than with that of any other individual, and political power could not be properly exerted over their social intercourse, and it was important to his reputation to have it understood that he did not interfere in such matters. That I was not aware of any want of harmony in the cabinet; I had not seen the slightest symptom of such a feeling in its deliberations, and I was perfectly certain that my official conduct had never been influenced in the slightest degree by a feeling of that nature. I saw no ground, therefore, for the least change on my part in this respect.

"To which the President replied in a changed tone, that he had the most entire confidence in my integrity and capacity in executing the duties of the department, and expressed his perfect satisfaction, in that respect, with my whole conduct; he had never supposed for a moment that my official acts had been influenced in the least degree by any unkind feeling toward Major Eaton; and he did not mean to insist on our families visiting Mrs. Eaton. He had been much excited for some time past by the combination against her, and he wished us to aid him in putting down their slanders, adding that she was excluded from most of the invitations to parties; and when invited, she was insulted; that the lady of a foreign minister, before referred to, had insulted her at Baron Krudener's party.

"I remarked, that some injustice might be done to that lady on that occasion; although she might not choose to associate with Mrs. Eaton, I did not think she intended to insult her; she might have supposed that there was some design, not altogether respectful to herself in the offer of the attendance to supper of the Secretary of War, whose wife she did not visit; instead of that of the Secretary of State, which, according to the usual practice, she probably considered herself entitled to. I was present, and saw most of what had happened. She evidently thought herself aggrieved at something, but acted with much dignity on the occasion. I saw no appearance of insult offered to Mrs. Eaton. He replied that he had been fully informed, and knew all about it; and but for certain reasons which he mentioned, he would have sent the foreign minister before referred to and his wife home immediately.

"After some further conversation on this and other matters, in which I consider the President as having entirely waived the demand made through Col. Johnson, that my family must visit Mrs. Eaton, as the condition of my remaining in office, and in which he expressed himself in terms of personal kindness toward me, I took my leave. He did not show me, or read any paper on the subject."

Col. Johnson explained, on reading this statement, that, in his extreme desire to restore peace, he had gone further in his communications with the Secretaries, than the President authorized him to go. The suggestion with regard to their inviting Mrs. Eaton to their "large parties," he said, was his own, not the President's. "The complaint made by General Jackson against Messrs. Ingham, Branch and Berrien was that they were using their influence to have Major Eaton and his family excluded from all respectable circles, for the purpose of degrading him, and thus drive him from office; and that the attempt had been made even upon the foreign ministers, and in one case had produced the desired effect. He proposed no mode of accommodation or satisfaction, but declared expressly that if such was the fact, he would dismiss them from office. He then read to me a paper containing the principles upon which he intended to act, which disclaimed the right to interfere with the social relations of his cabinet. . . . When the President mentioned this charge of conspiracy, I vindicated you against it. I gave it as my opinion that he was misinformed. To prevent a rupture, I requested the President to postpone calling upon those members of his cabinet till Saturday, that I might have the opportunity of two days to converse with them. When I made my report to the President, I informed him that I was confirmed in my opinion previously expressed, that he had been misinformed as to the combination and conspiracy. I informed him of your unequivocal and positive denial of the fact, and communicated every thing which transpired between us calculated to satisfy his mind on the subject. It was this report of mine that gave him satisfaction, and changed his feelings and determination—not his ground as you have supposed; with me he had no ground to change. He had assumed none except that which I have stated; nor did I ever make use of such an expression to you that he had changed his ground. It is true that I informed you that the President was very much excited, but I do not now recollect the precise language used to convey my idea of that excitement. I presume you had the advantage of your private memoranda, when you say I compared him to a roaring lion."

A day or two after, the President offered his personal mediation for the purpose of restoring harmony between Major Eaton and Mr. Branch. Mr. Branch accepted the President's offer. "I have received," he wrote to the President, January 29th, "your note of yesterday's date, and do most cheerfully accept your friendly mediation; more, however, from a desire to give you an additional evidence of the friendly feelings which have actuated my bosom toward yourself, than from a consciousness of having given to Major Eaton just cause for the withdrawal of his friendship. As a further manifestation of the frankness which I trust will ever characterize my conduct, I agree to meet him this day at two o'clock, in the presence of Major Barry, at Mr. Van Buren's, and in his presence also."

The hostile secretaries met at the house of the Attorney-General, in the presence of that functionary and of Mr. Barry. "Here," says Eaton, "Mr. Branch expressed friendship for me, and in the strongest terms declared, that he did not entertain an unkind feeling toward me, and wished he had a glass in his bosom, through which his every thought could be read. He spoke of the non-intercourse between our families, and said, he had not the slightest objection to a free association; but that he could not control his. I promptly answered, that I did not desire his or any other family to visit mine, except with their own free consent; and that it was my desire our families should, in that respect, pursue such a course as they thought fit and proper. We shook hands and parted as friends. Mr. Berrien affected much satisfaction at this reconciliation, and pretended to hail it as the harbinger of future harmony and good will."

And so this affair was temporarily adjusted. For the next fifteen months there was the semblance of harmony among the members of this ill-assorted Cabinet. The President, however, did not often consult the three gentlemen who had families. The time-honored Cabinet councils were seldom held, and were at length discontinued. Mr. Van Buren maintained and strengthened his position as the President's chief counselor and friend. The President spoke of the Secretary of State, among his familiars, by the name of "Van," and called him "Matty" to his face.

XI.

THE PRESIDENT BREAKS WITH THE VICE-PRESIDENT.

Scarcely had the Cabinet been pacificated, when the suppressed feud between General Jackson and Mr. Calhoun was changed, so far as the President was concerned, into avowed and irreconcilable hostility.

Mr. Van Buren has long rested under the imputation of having precipitated this quarrel for purposes of his own. The reader, however, is aware that General Jackson's antipathy to Mr. Calhoun was strong as early as December, 1829, and that Mr. Van Buren had no need, for purposes of his own, to inflame the President's ire against his Southern competitor for the succession. The incident which filled up the measure of the President's wrath against the Vice-President, it can now be shown, was one with which Mr. Van Buren had nothing to do. He was as innocent of this quarrel as the humblest clerk in his department, as Mr. Calhoun himself came at last to know.

Major Lewis, the innocent cause of the explosion, and a participant in all the events that led to it, has had the goodness to write out, for the reader's edification and entertainment, a complete history of the affair. His narrative, which is circumstantial and exact, puts to rest forever all the disputed questions respecting a feud which has produced, and is producing, effects upon the course of political events.

NARRATIVE BY MAJOR WILLIAM B. LEWIS.

"DEAR SIR: I have taken up the pen, in accordance with your request, with the view of relating to you the circumstances which led to the quarrel between General Jackson and Mr. Calhoun. In doing this, I will be as brief as the nature of the affair will admit; but, at the same time, I feel disposed to communicate every thing in connection with it that may be deemed necessary to a full and perfect understanding of the subject. I have for a long time intended to perform this task, but have neglected it, and, perhaps, should never have undertaken it, if you had not made the request. It is many years since the circumstances that I now intend to relate transpired, but all the leading and most essential portions of them are still fresh upon my mind.

"The Seminole campaign, which was commenced by General Jackson in December, 1817, and was brought to a close by him the following spring, was undoubtedly the main cause of the quarrel, but there were other circumstances that had also something to do with it, which I will relate before I get through with my narrative.

"That his proceedings in conducting that campaign should have been the cause or occasion of a rupture between them, was a thing, I am sure, the General could not possibly have anticipated, as he had been led to believe that Mr. Calhoun approved all that he had done. Perhaps there was no one connected with the government, with the exception of Mr. Monroe, in whom he had greater confidence than Mr. Calhoun, or for whom he had a stronger attachment. This was owing, in part, to the zeal, the ability, and the efficiency with which he supported, as a member of the House of Representatives, the war of 1812, but perhaps more particularly on account of one of the first acts he performed after receiving the appointment of Secretary of War. At the time of his appointment a serious misunderstanding existed between the General and the acting Secretary of War, Mr. George Graham. It seems that General Jackson, apprehending difficulty with the Indians in the Northwest, bordering upon Canada, stationed an officer in whom he had great confidence, with a suitable command, in that quarter, for the purpose of watching the Indians and British traders, but more especially, I suspect, the Earl of Selkirk, who was moving through that section of country about that time, with no good intentions, as the General believed, toward the United States.* Well, without giving the General any notice of his intention, the acting Secretary ordered this officer upon other duty, taking him away entirely from the post where the General had stationed him. Against this he protested most energetically, denying that he had any right to interfere with the arrangement of his troops without consulting him, and forthwith issued a general order to the officers under his command, and within his military district, that in future they were to obey no order emanating from the War Department unless it passed through the general in command! It was on account of this general order that he and General Scott became involved in an angry and bitter personal correspondence.

"Mr. Calhoun, very soon after he entered upon the duties of his office as Secretary of War, in order to put a stop to such personal controversies, and to satisfy General Jackson, as it was alleged, wrote him an official letter, assuring him that, in future, all orders for his military district should pass through him.† This was granting all that the General contended for, and was exceedingly gratifying to him, and no doubt added greatly to his personal regard for the Secretary.

"It was not long after this that he was ordered on the celebrated Seminole campaign, and doubtless it was commenced with the best and kindest feelings for Mr. Calhoun, on whom he counted fully as a friend that he

* If the General had got hold of the Earl, and been able to prove that he had been exciting the Indians against our frontier settlements, he would in all probability have made his a *precedent* for the cases of Arbuthnot and Ambrister.

† See a copy of Mr. Calhoun's letter of December 29, 1819, herewith inclosed.—Vol. ii., p. 375.

could at all times and under all circumstances rely to do him justice, at least; and more than this he neither expected nor desired, of course.

"After the campaign had been brought to a close, the General returned to Tennessee in exceedingly bad health, and worn almost to a skeleton; but he had scarcely got home when a portion of the newspaper press, aided by politicians and demagogues, commenced assailing him with great violence and bitterness, which was kept up until Congress met, in November, 1818. This body had scarcely taken their seats, when strong indications were given by its members that the attacks were soon to be transferred from the columns of the newspapers and the stump to the halls of Congress. The General was kept well advised of what was going on both in and out of Congress by his Washington friends. About the latter part of December or the first of January, it was reported that the military committee of the House was investigating the General's conduct in relation to the Seminole campaign, and it was believed they would report to the House a resolution in favor of censuring him. He received this information in Nashville, on the morning of the 7th of January, and determined at once to leave for Washington without a moment's delay. After having dispatched some business he came down to attend to, he returned to the Hermitage in the evening, and the next morning early he set out for Washington on horseback, accompanied by two of his staff. Traveling rapidly on to Kingston, a distance of 160 miles, he fell in with the Washington mail stage, and concluding to leave their horses at Kingston, he and his companions took passage in the stage and proceeded on to Washington in that. On his route he passed through Knoxville, Abingdon, and Winchester, Virginia, but having reached the last named place too late to make a connection with the Washington stage, he and his companions were necessarily detained for a short time.

"When the citizens of the village heard of his arrival and detention, they flocked in great numbers to see and pay their respects to him; but some of the most ardent of his admirers, not satisfied with this manifestation of respect, proceeded to get up, on the spur of the occasion, a small supper party, and invited him and his traveling companions to join them. The invitation was accepted, and in the course of the evening, being called on for a sentiment, the General gave the following toast—'John C. Calhoun; an honest man is the noblest work of God'—showing in the strongest and most emphatic language he could use, the great confidence he reposed in his honor and integrity! But this is not the only occasion in which his confidence had been manifested, as I shall presently show. An arrangement having been effected for the continuance of the General's journey to Washington, distant seventy-five or eighty miles, he and his friends left, and reached that city on the morning of the 23d of January, 1819, a little before sunrise. The second letter he wrote me after his arrival is dated 30th January, and is in relation to certain injurious imputations which had been published in the *Philadelphia Aurora* newspaper, against Mr. Calhoun, by a Nashville correspondent, which, if in my power, he wished me to have corrected. The General, in his letter, says—'I find Mr. Calhoun is sore from the remarks made by B. B. in the *Philadelphia Aurora.* He has professed to be my friend, approves my conduct and that of the President. Mr. Monroe has told the members, if an opportunity offers, to declare on the floor of Congress, in addition to what Mr. Adams has said, that he fully and warmly approves every act of mine, from first to last, of the Seminole campaign.' In a P. S. to his letter, the General adds, 'If you know B. B., tell him to exonerate Mr. Calhoun from a coalition with Mr. Crawford.'

"Those communications, addressed to the *Aurora*, were written by me, and the passage complained of by Mr. Calhoun is in the following words—'I regret that I am under the necessity of admitting that your suspicions, as regards the Secretary of War, are not altogether groundless. Late information from Washington City assures us here that he is playing a double game. This may be so, but for the honor of human nature, I hope it is not. I can not abandon altogether the good opinion I once entertained of him, at least not until I have other evidence of his duplicity than that which rests upon mere suspicion. I still flatter myself that my correspondent there, as well as you, may be mistaken.'

"After the receipt of the General's letter referred to above, in my next communication to the *Aurora*, dated the 20th February, 1819, I state that, 'In my letter to you of the 9th, and published in the *Aurora* of the 28th ultimo, I remarked that it was with regret that I was under the necessity of admitting that your suspicions, as it regarded the Secretary of State, were not altogether groundless—that late intelligence from Washington City assured us here he was playing a double game, etc. I had been informed, previous to writing that letter, that Mr. Calhoun had, at the same time he was professing the warmest friendship for General Jackson, joined the standard of his enemies, who had combined for the laudable purpose, not only of undermining his military reputation, but also to drive him from the army. It affords me great pleasure to find that my correspondent had been led into an error, in attributing to Mr. Calhoun a course of conduct so dishonorable. In justice to him, therefore, I feel it my duty to state that I am entirely satisfied *now* his conduct has been honorable and correct, and that he is, as he has always professed to be, the sincere friend of General Jackson,' etc.

"This, then, was a full and complete withdrawal of the alleged unjust imputation made against Mr. Calhoun, in the letter to the *Aurora* of the 9th January, 1819, and of course left no cause of complaint, whether just or unjust, against General Jackson or his friends. The General acted, on this occasion, as a true and sincere friend, by promptly doing all that was in his power to have the alleged unjust imputations withdrawn. But this is not all. I have additional evidence to show that the General's friendship for Mr. Calhoun continued for years after the date of the letter referred to above. On the 11th January, 1825, in a letter addressed to me, he says—'It was stated to me yesterday, that if I was elected, it would 46 be against the whole Cabinet influence, combined with that of the Speaker. If this be true, and success should be mine, it will be the greater triumph of principle over intrigue and management. Whether there is any truth in this rumor I know not, and if there is, I would suppose that Mr. Calhoun is not in the combination. Let things terminate as they may, nothing will induce me to depart from the course I have adopted. If I go into the office, it shall be by the unsolicited will of the people, and I shall not envy the man who gets there in any other way.' Even this is not all. I received another letter from him after the election of Mr. Adams, in which he says, 'I am satisfied that Mr. Calhoun was the only friend I had in the Cabinet.'

This letter has, unfortunately, been mislaid, and not being able to lay my hands on it just now, I am not able to give the exact date of it. I have a distinct recollection, however, of the expression quoted above.

"I have adverted to the foregoing facts and circumstances as evidences going to show conclusively that General Jackson looked upon Mr. Calhoun as one of his best friends, so late as the winter and spring of 1825. Indeed I might say to the day of his inauguration on the 4th of March, 1829, as there is not a particle of evidence in existence, as I believe, to prove the slightest change in their personal relations to that time. In February, 1825, at a time of great political excitement, when every bosom was filled with suspicion and distrust, we find the General declaring that he considered Mr. Calhoun the only friend he had in Mr. Monroe's Cabinet on that important and eventful occasion. Strong proof this, I should say, of his confidence in him, as well as his own sincerity and fidelity. But was this confidence and devotion on the part of the General reciprocated by Mr. Calhoun? I doubt it, and I think I have good reason for doubting it. If any one will attentively read a certain part of Mr. Webster's great speech in reply to Colonel Hayne of South Carolina, in February, 1830, I think he will be induced to doubt whether Mr. Calhoun was the only friend that the General had in Mr. Monroe's Cabinet, pending the contest in the House for the presidency; or, indeed, whether he was his friend at all. I allude to that portion of Mr. Webster's speech which is in reply to Colonel Hayne's Shakesperian quotations in which he made allusion to Banquo's Ghost. I did not see the point and force of the remarks at the time the speech was delivered, because I had never heard it intimated, or suggested by any one that Mr. Calhoun was really in favor of Mr. Adams being chosen by the House, in preference to General Jackson; nor did I understand it until I was told by a gentleman, whom I met at a dining party at the house of the illustrious Charles Carroll of Carrollton, on the 20th September, 1831 (Mr. Carroll's birth-day), that Mr. Calhoun had *actually pledged himself to support Mr. Adams.* I do not recollect his name, but he was said to be a gentleman of high character, and lived in the neighborhood of Carrollton. He did not speak of it as a rumor, but as a 'fixed fact,' as General Cushing would say. This was perfectly new to me, but when I connected with it Webster's splendid reply to Hayne, and his pointing and shaking his finger, at the same time, at Calhoun (who was in the chair), and exclaiming with great significancy, 'Is it not so, sir?' I must confess that I do not feel myself at liberty to doubt it. If I have not misconstrued the meaning of Mr. Webster's remarks, there can be no doubt that Mr. Calhoun secretly favored the election of Mr. Adams, and promised him his support; but finding, afterward, that Mr. Clay was to be brought within the line of 'safe precedents,' and looked to for the succession, he deserted Mr. Adams and sought shelter beneath the folds of the broad and patriotic banner of Old Hickory. It did not, however, afford him protection long. You know how the General dealt with deserters, whether regulars or militia!

"I will now proceed to relate the circumstances which led to the breach and final separation of those distinguished men. At the session of 1827 the legislature of Louisiana adopted a resolution inviting General Jackson to unite with his friends of that State, on the 8th of February, 1828, in celebrating the anniversary of the great victory achieved over the British forces on the 8th January, 1815. The invitation was accepted by the General and, during the Christmas holidays, the 27th December, 1827, I think it was, he left Nashville for New Orleans on board the steamboat *Pocahontas*, commanded by Captain Barnes, which had been tendered to him by the owners, free of all charges, for the conveyance of himself and friends to New Orleans, and back again to Nashville. Among the friends of the General, who took passage on board the *Pocahontas* was Colonel James A. Hamilton, son of the distinguished General Alexander Hamilton of the Revolution. The Colonel was a member of a committee that had been appointed by the General's friends of the city of New York, to meet him at New Orleans and unite with his other friends there, in celebrating the 8th January, and proposed, with the consent of the other members of the committee (Thaddeus Phelps and Preserved Fish, I believe) to come by the way of Nashville and pass down the river with the General and his Tennessee friends. The party consisted of the General, Mrs. Jackson and Major Donelson of his family; General Houston and staff, Judge Overton, Dr. and Mrs. Shelly, myself and a few others whose names are not now recollected. Having time to spare, the *Pocahontas* leisurely descended the river, stopping at a few places only until she reached Natchez, where, by previous engagement, the General was to partake of a public dinner given to him by his friends and old comrades-in-arms. Here we were detained until late in the evening, when the *Pocahontas* was again got under way, and dropped slowly down the river, on her way to the great emporium of the Southwestern States. About this time, and on this portion of our journey it was, I had an interesting conversation with Colonel Hamilton which led, ultimately, to very important results. On several previous occasions we had conversed about the pending presidential election, and of the General's prospects generally; but on this occasion he inquired of me particularly with regard to the vote of Georgia. I told him the General's friends at Nashville were of the opinion that the probabilities were in favor of his getting it, unless Mr. Crawford's friends should unite in opposition to him, and possibly in that event he might lose it.

"'But we count much, Colonel,' I said, 'upon the general Southern feeling which is undoubtedly in favor of the General.'

"He inquired of me if I did not think Mr. Crawford and his friends might be conciliated.

"'If that can be done,' he added, 'Georgia would undoubtedly give her vote to the General.'

"He thought it was an object deserving the attention of his friends, and expressed a willingness to assist, if desired, in removing all doubts and difficulties in relation to the vote of that important Southern State. Colonel Hamilton then inquired if I was acquainted with the original cause of quarrel between the General and Mr. Crawford.

"'Yes,' I told him, 'I knew all about it from the beginning to that time.'

"'I should like very much,' he said, 'to be made acquainted with all the circumstances in relation to it.'

"'The original cause,' I remarked, 'grew out of a treaty Mr. Crawford made, in the spring of 1816, with the Cherokee Indians, when he was Secretary of War, against the advice and remonstrance of the General. In this treaty Mr. Crawford allowed them a large body of land to which they had no claim whatever, and which had been previously ceded to the United States by the Creek Indians. In the summer of 1814 the General made a treaty at Fort Jackson with the Creeks, after their surrender and submission to the authorities of the United States, and in that treaty the whole of the country from the settlements on the Bay of Mobile to the Tennessee line, a distance of some two hundred or two hundred and fifty miles, including nearly all the State of Alabama, and which he considered of great importance to the whole country, and vitally so as regarded the growth and prosperity of the southwestern portion of it, was ceded to the United States.

"'The Cherokee chiefs were present at that treaty, and claimed a large portion of the land, the best and most important portion, but from a full investigation of the matter it was clearly shown that they had no right to it whatever. They endeavored to get the Creeks to say it belonged to them, alleging, as a reason, they would have to give it up at any rate. Weatherford, the principal chief of the Creek nation, refused. He said it did not belong to them, and he would make no such admission. Yet, in opposition to the advice of the General, Mr. Crawford recognized the claim of the Cherokees to it, at the risk of sacrificing the great advantages which were secured to us by the Treaty of Fort Jackson.* 47

"'The General had two important objects in view, in requiring the Creeks to cede to the United States the whole of that vast tract of land as an indemnity for the expenses of the war. First, to separate the Creeks and Cherokees, on the east, from the Choctaws and Chickasaws, on the west, by planting a dense and strong population of whites between them, who, in future, would hold them in check. Secondly, by opening and settling that region of country, to strengthen and give protection to Mobile and the settlements upon the bay. Every body now must see the wisdom and foresight of his views, who has any knowledge of the immense population and wealth embraced within the limits of the country ceded by the Fort Jackson Treaty. Under all the circumstances, it is not at all surprising, it seems to me, that the General should have felt indignant at the unaccountable conduct of the Secretary of War.

"'But,' I remarked to Colonel Hamilton, 'this is not the only thing the General complains of, and concerning which he was exceedingly sensitive. He was induced to believe that Mr. Crawford had a principal agency in getting up the movement in Congress against him in January, 1819, upon the subject of the Seminole campaign. This he inferred from the active part his personal friends were taking against him in Congress, and more especially Mr. Cobb, who represented Mr. Crawford's district in Congress, and was a confidential and devoted friend of his, and all of whom zealously supported the resolution of censure, reported to the House of Representatives by the Military Committee. However, I have not heard the General say much about Mr. Crawford of late,' I observed; 'indeed, I may say, nothing, since Mr. Adams was chosen President over both of them, by the House, in 1825! Nor do I know what are his feelings now in relation to those old disputes. His mind, of late, has been too much occupied, I presume, with matters of higher import than to dwell upon things that have become obsolete.' 48

---

* This is *called* the "Treaty of Fort Jackson;" but, more properly speaking, it was a *capitulation*; an act of surrendering to an enemy, upon stipulated terms or conditions. A sufficient quantity of their land was demanded by the government of the United States to indemnify them for the expenses of the war. —W. B. L.

"Colonel Hamilton said that he was very desirous that a reconciliation should be effected, if possible, between them, and asked me if I would be willing to speak to the General upon the subject. He intended, he said, in returning to New York, to pass through the Southern States, and expected to see Mr. Crawford, and nothing would give him more pleasure than to be the medium of a reconciliation between them. I told him if he desired it I would, with great pleasure, speak to the General upon the subject, and let him know what he thought of it. I accordingly sought an opportunity of having a conversation with the General in relation to the matter. After informing him what Colonel Hamilton had said, and the strong desire he felt that a reconciliation should take place between him and Mr. Crawford, he remarked to me that formerly his feelings toward Mr. Crawford had been pretty bitter, and he thought he had sufficient grounds for them, but the causes which gave birth to them had all passed away, and that he had no longer any such feelings.

"'Mr. Crawford,' he added, 'is truly an unfortunate man, and is more deserving sympathy than the enmity of any one, and especially on account of his physical prostration.'

49

"'Am I at liberty, then,' I asked, 'to say to Colonel Hamilton that you are willing that every thing heretofore of an unpleasant nature shall be buried in oblivion?'

"'Perfectly so,' was his answer.

"I related this to the Colonel, who was exceedingly gratified at it, and said he had no doubt it would be cordially responded to by Mr. Crawford.

"We were now rapidly approaching the great center of attraction. Many steamboats had passed us crowded with passengers. It looked as if all the boats that belonged to the great father of rivers, and its numerous tributaries, had so managed and regulated their affairs as to be at Orleans on the 8th of January, and taking with them immense crowds from the great West and Southwest.

"It was now the 7th, and we were but a few miles above Orleans, and our noble boat *Pocahontas* was rounded to, and we landed about an hour before sunset, where we remained until about eleven o'clock the next day. The weather was clear, warm, and bright, promising a beautiful day for the celebration of the ever memorable and glorious eighth. But promises are not always to be relied on, and in this case they were completely falsified. The following morning was dark and gloomy. In the south was to be seen a heavy cloud, giving unmistakable indications of an approaching thunder storm, which were realized about nine or ten o'clock, when the rain commenced falling in torrents, accompanied by thunder and lightning. It did not last long, however, and was followed by a most magnificent rainbow, which seemed to span the entire city, and was considered by the people a most auspicious omen. I am not going to bore you with an account of the celebration. If so disposed, I am not competent to do it justice. It was undoubtedly the most magnificent pageant I ever saw of the kind, and I have seen many. Besides, it would be out of place here. Suffice it to say that the General was feasted and caressed by his friends some five or six days, and he then left for Nashville on board the *Pocahontas*, under the command of his true and trusty friend, Capt. Barnes. Before she was permitted to leave the landing, however, she was literally crammed with all sorts of good things, such as wines, brandy, fruits, sweetmeats, etc., by his kind and grateful friends, whose city he had saved from murder, pillage, rapine, and other crimes of a still more revolting character, if what was averred at the time can be relied on as true.

"Col. Hamilton left about the same time, but he, as he said he should do on our trip down, returned through Georgia, Virginia, etc. The General and his party reached Nashville without the occurrence of a single accident from the time we left home. I heard nothing of Col. Hamilton from the time we parted in New Orleans.

"Soon after I returned to Nashville I received a letter from Mr. Eaton, one of our Senators in Congress, informing me that my daughter, who was at school in Philadelphia, was quite ill, and had been so for some time, and added he thought I had better come on to see her without delay.

"The day after I got his letter, the 3d April, 1828, I left for Philadelphia, taking Washington in my route, and on reaching that city, I learned from Mr. Eaton that he had just got a letter from the lady who had charge of my daughter, informing him that she was much better.

"This was very gratifying news, and made it unnecessary for me to hasten my departure from Washington. While there I was made acquainted with Mr. Van Buren, it being the first time I had ever met with him. I found the General's friends were all in high spirits, and counting with great certainty upon his being elected. Indeed, I found the same confidence existing among his friends everywhere, from the time I left home until I reached the city. After remaining a few days, I left for Philadelphia, and was happy to find, on my arrival, that my daughter's health, under the skillful treatment of that eminent physician, Dr. Physic, had been entirely restored. I did not remain long, however, in that city; and, as I was anxious to get back home, I hurried on to New York, which, never having visited, I desired to see. The morning after my arrival there I called upon Col. Hamilton, and had a long conversation with him in relation to his trip through the Southern States. Every thing in that quarter, he assured me, looked bright and promising. Our friends, he added, were confident of carrying every State for the General. I inquired of him if he saw Mr. Crawford as he passed through Milledgeville. He said he did not, unfortunately, in consequence of his being out on his circuit holding court, and was not expected to return for a week or two. He regretted it, but it was impossible for him to wait, and had, therefore, concluded to mention the subject he desired to speak to Mr. Crawford about to Governor Forsyth. He related to the Governor fully the conversation we had on board of the boat as we passed down the river, and also what passed between the General and myself upon the subject of an amicable settlement of the differences which had so long existed between him and Mr. Crawford, and desired the Governor to communicate it to Mr. Crawford when he returned to Milledgeville. This he promised to do, and advise me of the reply that Mr. Crawford might make to it. I inquired of him if he had heard from the Governor in relation to the matter since. He said that he had, and he was greatly surprised at what Mr. Crawford had authorized him to say. He (Mr. Crawford) remarked that he had been charged with having proposed, in cabinet council, to have the General arrested, etc., which he said was false. No such proposition was ever made by him; but that Mr. Calhoun did propose his arrest and punishment in some way, showing on various occasions a hostility to his proceedings in his Seminole campaign. Col. Hamilton handed me Governor Forsyth's letter to read, and I confess I was not less surprised than the Colonel seemed to be, knowing, as I did, the pains Mr. Calhoun had taken to impress upon the General's mind that he had stood firmly by him, and sustained him in relation to his proceedings in that celebrated campaign. In January, 1819, I received information from Washington which induced me to doubt the sincerity of Mr. Calhoun's friendship for the General, and so stated in a communication I sent to the *Philadelphia Aurora:* but on receiving a letter from General Jackson, assuring me he had no doubt of the sincerity of his friendship, and requesting me to have the statement alluded to above contradicted, I had, from that time until I saw Governor Forsyth's letter, looked upon him as a sincere friend of the General. I do not recollect the exact words of Mr. Crawford, as reported by Governor Forsyth, but what is stated above is substantially correct.

"I did not remain long in New York, and on returning home, I proposed to avail myself of the opportunity of running up the Hudson to Albany, and thence along the entire line of New York's great and magnificent canal, which had not then been long finished. I found the route rather tedious and uncomfortable, but the opportunity it afforded me of seeing such a work and the fine country through which it ran, was a sufficient compensation for the want of comfort. I got back to Nashville about the 1st of June, fully convinced that the coalition of Adams and Clay was doomed to experience a most humiliating defeat at the approaching election, and I sought an early opportunity of so stating to the General. But I did not think it advisable to say any thing to him about Governor Forsyth's letter to Colonel Hamilton, from an apprehension that it might produce an explosion, as he had been kept under a constant excitement for the last twelve or eighteen months by the attacks of his enemies on himself and Mrs. Jackson; and to be made acquainted with 'this unkindest cut of all' by the hand of one whom he had considered a true friend, I was afraid would be more than he could bear; and as I was not particularly desirous of witnessing such an exhibition just at that time, I thought it best not to mention it to him.

"Well, the election took place in November, and, as every intelligent man in the country, not blinded by passion, or partisan feelings, supposed would be the case months before it occurred, the General was elected by an overwhelming majority. That was the verdict which the people rendered upon the charges of bargain, intrigue, and corruption, made against Adams and Clay, and which has never been revised, though three efforts have been made without effect, one in the person of Mr. Adams, and two in the person of Mr. Clay.

"The General left home in the latter part of January, 1829, for Washington, and reached that city on the 9th or 10th, I think, of February.

"We found the town crowded with strangers even at that early day, and the number rapidly increased from that time until the inauguration. Great anxiety was felt by the politicians in relation to the organization of the new Cabinet. Jealousy, distrust, and dissatisfaction soon became manifest to the most casual observer. All wanted a friend in the Cabinet, but as the number was limited to six, all could not, of course, be gratified. The friends of Mr. Calhoun were the most dissatisfied, when it was understood who were to compose the Cabinet. Although *one half* the members were expected to be his friends, still they were not satisfied, because they were not *exactly* the friends they wanted in the Cabinet. There was no one from South Carolina. The General proposed to appoint Mr. Eaton, a personal friend of his from Tennessee, but the friends of Mr. Calhoun made great efforts to prevent it, and to have either Colonel Hayne or General Hamilton of South Carolina substituted for him. Having failed in this, nothing daunted, they still kept up their efforts with the hope of being able to drive him (Eaton) the personal friend of the General out of the Cabinet. This the President considered very unkind, to say the least of it. He did not know that Mr. Calhoun encouraged this proceeding on the part of his friends, *still he thought he could have put a stop to it, if so disposed.* The truth is, that many of General Jackson's friends believed that the support of him by the friends of Mr. Calhoun was, from the first, a secondary consideration with them. That they were using his popularity and strength with which to break down Adams and Clay; and then at the close of the General's first term, to set him aside (Adams and Clay having been previously put out of the way), and elevate Mr. Calhoun to the presidency.

51

And really, it seems to me, that their conduct after the election would justify such a conclusion.

"This state of things continued without much change or variation, until the following November. Mr. Monroe, ex-president, had been in Richmond attending a State convention, as one of its delegates, and after it adjourned, on his way home he passed through Washington, and remained a day or two with the view of seeing his old friends and acquaintances. While there, as a matter of course, he called to see General Jackson. The General invited him to dine with him, and, on this occasion he also invited the members of the cabinet, and Mr. Finch Ringold, Marshal of the District of Columbia, and a warm, personal, and confidential friend of Mr. Monroe's. The dinner party consisted of the President, ex-President Monroe, members of the Cabinet, Mr. Ringold, Major Donelson, and myself. Mr. Monroe sat on the right hand of the President, Mr. Eaton on the left, Mr. Ringold next to Mr. Eaton, and I sat at the end of the table, having Mr. Ringold between me and Mr. Eaton. The other members of the Cabinet sat on the opposite side of the table, the Secretary of State fronting the President, and Major Donelson at the other end of the table fronting me. This was the exact arrangement with regard to the position of each member of the party.

"Some short time after the company was seated, Mr. Ringold remarked to me that he was glad to see the General and Mr. Monroe together, and enjoying themselves so well. Mr. Monroe, he said, was a great friend of his upon the subject of his Seminole campaign, and stood by him with great firmness in opposition to every member of his Cabinet. I remarked I always understood Mr. Monroe approved the General's proceedings in that campaign, and was decidedly his friend; but I was not aware that he was the only one of his Cabinet.

"'Yes, sir,' he said, 'he was the *only one*.'

"'Well, then, if that be so, the General has been laboring under a very great mistake,' I replied, 'for he has always been under the impression that Mr. Calhoun was also decidedly his friend.'

"Mr. Ringold insisted that he was not. Believing that Mr. Ringold possessed as fully the confidence of Mr. Monroe as any man in Washington during his administration, I was desirous of drawing him out fully upon this, at one time, very exciting subject, and therefore continued the conversation.

"'Well, then,' I asked, 'what will you do with Mr. Adams? Do you not recollect that he wrote a long and very able letter to our minister, justifying the course of the General in that campaign, and vindicating the government in its approval of all his acts?'

"'Yes,' he said, 'I remember it very well. It is true, he did write a very able letter to our minister in Madrid; but,' said he, 'the General is under no obligations to *him* for it, for Mr. Monroe made him do it.'

"'Well, really Mr. Ringold, you surprise me more than ever. With most of the General's Tennessee friends, Mr. Adams would have been their choice for the presidency, had the General not been a candidate.'

"'Well, sir,' said he, 'they were under no obligations to Mr. Adams for writing that letter.'

"And he repeated that Mr. Monroe was the *only member* of his Cabinet that was in favor of sustaining the General in every thing he did. After this I spoke to Mr. Eaton, and asked him if he had heard the conversation between Mr. Ringold and myself? He said he had not; that he had been conversing with the gentleman on the opposite side of the table. He inquired what we had been talking about. I told him that Mr. Ringold had assured me there was not a single member of Mr. Monroe's Cabinet who approved of General Jackson's course in Florida, when prosecuting his Seminole campaign, but Mr. Monroe himself. Mr. Eaton said he must be mistaken, as both Mr. Adams and Mr. Calhoun were considered very decided friends of the General in relation to his proceedings on that occasion. Mr. Ringold repeated they were not, and that Mr. Monroe stood alone upon that subject in his Cabinet. Here the conversation ended.

"After dinner was over the company retired to the parlor, but did not remain long before they all left, with the exception of Mr. Eaton. The General rang for a servant, and ordered his pipe to be brought to him, as was his usual habit, after the company had withdrawn.

"His pipe was brought, and he seemed to be in deep meditation while smoking, and, as I supposed, was paying no attention to the conversation between Mr. Eaton and myself. He heard me, however, inquire of Mr. Eaton if the remarks of Mr. Ringold about the Seminole war and Mr. Monroe's cabinet did not surprise him; and, starting up from his apparent reverie, demanded to know what we were talking about. Mr. Eaton repeated to him what Mr. Ringold had said at the dinner-table, in relation to the Seminole campaign, and the opposition of Mr. Monroe's entire cabinet to the General's course. He seemed, however, to be incredulous, and remarked that Mr. Ringold must be mistaken.

"I replied, 'I am not sure of that.'

"'Why are you not?' inquired the General.

"'Because I have seen a letter, written eighteen months ago, in which Mr. Crawford is represented as saying that you charged him with having taken strong ground against you in Mr. Monroe's cabinet, but in that you had done him injustice, for it was not he, but Mr. Calhoun, who was in favor of your being arrested, or punished in some other way.'

"'You saw such a letter as *that?*' he inquired.

"Yes, I told him I had, and read it too.

"'Where is that letter?'

"'In New York,' I replied.

"'In whose hands, and by whom written?'

"'It is in the hands of Col. Hamilton, and written by Governor Forsyth, of Georgia,' I answered.

"'Then,' said he, 'I want to see it, and you must go to New York to-morrow.'

"'Very well; if you desire it, I have not the least objection.'

"In the morning, the General still insisting on my going to New York, I left in the early stage, and reached that city in the evening of the second day.

"After supper, I called upon Col. Hamilton, and informed him of the object of my visit to him. He said, as regarded himself, he would have no objection to send Governor Forsyth's letter to the General, but he thought it would be more respectful to the Governor to see him first and ask his consent. He remarked that Congress would meet in a few days, and as the Governor had just been elected to the United States Senate, he would soon be in Washington, and 'I will meet him there and speak to him on the subject.'

"'If that arrangement will be satisfactory to the General,' he said, 'I would prefer it; but if he should not be willing to wait until then, write me, and I will come to Washington, and bring the letter with me.'

"I told him, as the proposition was a reasonable one, I thought the General would be perfectly willing to wait until the Governor got to Washington. On my return, I saw the General, and related to him the arrangements the Colonel and myself had made, and he expressed himself entirely satisfied with it. The meeting of Congress, which took place a few days after, brought Governor Forsyth and Col. Hamilton together, as was expected; and, on talking over the matter, the Governor said he would prefer that Mr. Crawford should be written to upon the subject, that he might speak for himself over his own signature, which, no doubt, he would do without the least hesitation. He preferred that course, he added, because his remarks to him, as stated in his letter to Col. Hamilton, possibly might not be altogether correct. With this understanding they came to my office, and informed me of the course it was thought most advisable to take.

"I agreed with them entirely, and told Col. Hamilton I had no doubt the General himself would prefer that Mr. Crawford should be written to, and his statement obtained over his own signature. He then proposed that we should go and see the President, and inform him of the proposed arrangement. We started immediately for the President's house, but the Governor, according to my recollection, did not accompany us, alleging that it was necessary for him to return to the Capitol.

"Col. Hamilton, however, informed the General what it was proposed to do, and if it met his approbation, Governor Forsyth would immediately write to Mr. Crawford upon the subject. The General said all he wanted was Mr. Crawford's statement, and if it was proposed to have it in his own hand-writing, so much the better. Governor Forsyth accordingly wrote to Mr. Crawford, and in due time a letter was received from him confirming what had been stated in the letter to Col. Hamilton, with a few explanations and modifications. The General was then furnished with a copy of it, which he inclosed in a letter to Mr. Calhoun, dated May 13, 1830, which was the commencement of the celebrated correspondence between those distinguished men that led to an open rupture and final separation.

"Mr. Calhoun, in his correspondence with the General, says, 'I should be blind not to see that this whole affair is a political maneuver, in which the design is that you should be the instrument and myself the victim, but in which the real actors are carefully concealed by an artful movement.' Again he says, 'Your character is of too high and generous a cast to resort to such means, either for your own advantage or that of others. This the *contrivers* of the *plot* well knew,' etc. Who the contrivers, plotters, and actors in these political designs against him were, can only be conjectured, as he does not name them. If he intended to include me as one of them, I know he labored under a great mistake; and I think he is equally mistaken with regard to others who, probably, are alluded to. Indeed, I think he was mistaken in supposing that there was any plot at all, of any kind, got up for the purpose of making a political victim of him. The Crawford developments which led to the correspondence between the General and himself originated, undoubtedly, in the conversation between Col. Hamilton and myself, on board the steamboat, on our way to New Orleans, in relation to a reconciliation between the General and Mr. Crawford. In that conversation not one word was said about Mr. Calhoun or Mr. Van Buren, who, no doubt, was one of the persons to whom Mr. Calhoun alludes in the extracts I have quoted above. In proposing a reconciliation, Col. Hamilton seemed to be actuated alone by a desire to place the vote of Georgia for the General beyond the possibility of a doubt. If he had any other motive or desire, he did not disclose it to me. However, knowing the warmth of the Colonel's friendship for Mr. Crawford, I thought it possible he might have another object in view, but of a very different character from what Mr. Calhoun supposed. Mr. Crawford was said to be a man of very slender means, and I thought it possible Colonel Hamilton desired that he and the General should be on good terms, with the hope, in case the General should be elected, of having him provided for under the federal government with a situation that would be more acceptable than the small office he at that time held under the State of

Georgia. But this is mere conjecture on my part, for Colonel Hamilton did not make the slightest intimation of the kind in his conversation with me.

"With regard to Governor Forsyth's letter to Colonel Hamilton, I have no recollection of having ever spoken of it to any one, and probably should not have done so, if it had not been for the remarks of Mr. Ringold at the President's dinner-table. The whole affair was, as I verily believe, the result of accident.

"It has been said, I know, that Mr. Van Buren was instrumental, indeed the *principal* agent, in getting up this quarrel; but, so far as my knowledge extends, I am bound, in justice to him, to say, that I think there is not the slightest grounds for such an imputation. When the General received Mr. Calhoun's long letter of the 29th May, 1830, in answer to his of the 13th of that month, inclosing a copy of Mr. Crawford's, it was on a Sunday morning, and just as he was about to step into his carriage to go to church. On ascertaining it was from Mr. Calhoun, he came up to my room and requested me to look over it in his absence, and note such portions of it as would require his particular attention. On his return he inquired if I had read it.

"'I have,' I replied.

"'Have you made any notes?'

"'I have made no notes, General, for the reason that I think it is necessary you should read the whole letter before you make any reply to it.'

"I then handed it to him, and he retired to his own room to read it; but he had time to read a small portion of it only before dinner was announced. When he came down he appeared to be excited, but said nothing, and as soon as dinner was over he returned to his own room and finished reading it. After having got through with the letter he sent for me, and, I must say, I never saw him more excited under any circumstances in my life than he was on this occasion. He said he had never been so much deceived in any man as he had been in Mr. Calhoun—a man for whom he had the warmest friendship, and in whom he had reposed the most unbounded confidence.

"'In this letter (holding Mr. Calhoun's letter in his hand) he has acknowledged every thing with which he is charged by Mr. Crawford, and which is in direct contradiction of all his previous assurances made to me in relation to the Seminole campaign.'

"Pausing for a moment, and seeming to suppress his feelings, he handed me the letter, and requested me to take it to Mr. Van Buren and ask him to read it, and let him know what he (Mr. Van Buren) thought of it. I stepped over with it to Mr. Van Buren's, and directed the servant at the door to say to him I wished to see him in his office for a few moments.

When he came down I remarked that the General had received a letter that morning from Mr. Calhoun, in reply to his of the 13th, and had directed me to hand it to him, with the request that 'you will read it and let him know what you think of it.' He took the letter out of my hand, opened it, and commenced reading; but when he got to the bottom of the first page, he stopped and very deliberately folded it up again, and said:

"'Major, I prefer not to read Mr. Calhoun's letter, for I see it is to end in an open rupture between him and the General, and I have no doubt but an attempt will be made to hold me responsible for it. Under these circumstances it may become necessary for me to make a public statement, and as I have have had nothing whatever to do with it, in fact know nothing about it, I want to have it in my power to say so with a clear conscience.'

"He then handed the letter back to me, and begged that I would explain to the General his reason for not reading it. When I returned to the President, he inquired if I had seen Mr. Van Buren. I told him I had.

"'What does he think of Mr. Calhoun's letter?'

"'Mr. Van Buren thinks it is best for him that he should not read it,' and I gave him his reasons for declining to do so. He smiled, and remarked,

"'I reckon Van is right. I dare say they will attempt to throw the whole blame upon him.'

"He requested me to hand him the letter, and said 'its receipt must be acknowledged this evening, as Mr. Calhoun will leave in the Richmond boat to-night, or very early in the morning, and I want him to receive my reply before he gets off.' He then stepped into his office, acknowledged, in a short note, his letter of the day before, asked me to copy it, which being done, he dispatched his messenger with it immediately.

"It has been frequently stated that this quarrel had its origin in the Eaton affair. This is a mistake. That the latter was the occasion of much excitement, as well as great bitterness of feeling, there is no doubt, but of *itself* it would not have caused a separation between the General and Mr. Calhoun. It is also true that nearly all those who exerted themselves, *first* to prevent Mr. Eaton's appointment as a member of the Cabinet, and afterward, having failed in that, to drive him out of it, were the friends of Mr. Calhoun. The General, however, did not seem disposed to hold him accountable for the acts of his friends, though he did think he could have controlled them if he had been so disposed; yet, according to Mr. Calhoun's own logic, the General would have been justified in doing so. In his long letter to him (May 29, 1830), speaking of the course of Mr. Crawford's friends in both houses of Congress, upon the subject of the Seminole campaign, he says, '*Why, then, did he* (Mr. Crawford) *not interpose with his friends on the Committee to do you justice?*' If it were the duty of Mr. Crawford, the sworn enemy, at that time, of the General, to interfere with his friends to do him justice, how much more so was it the duty of Mr. Calhoun, his avowed friend, to interfere with *his* friends, who were trying to break up his Cabinet at the very commencement of his administration!

"You must have a pretty correct idea of the extent of those efforts, as I showed you, when here, a manuscript book containing the correspondence between the General and the Rev. Dr. Ely, and others, having reference to the same subject. In order to put a stop to such impertinent interference with his public duties, he wrote down on a blank piece of paper, several days before his inauguration, the names of those he intended to bring into his Cabinet, and handed it to me, with the request that I would take it down to the *Telegraph* office, the Jackson organ, and hand it to General Green, the editor and proprietor, and say to him, 'I want it published in the *Telegraph of to-morrow morning.*' General Green, in looking over the list, was evidently disconcerted. He remarked to me that he regretted to see Mr. Eaton's name on it.

"'Why so,' I asked.

"'Because,' he said, 'if Mr. Eaton is taken into the Cabinet, I think it will cause both him and the General a great deal of trouble, which I should exceedingly regret.'

"As General Green was a devoted friend of Mr. Calhoun, and perfectly conversant with the feelings and views of his friends generally, I thought the remark presaged no good to the incoming administration. I will do General Green, however, the justice to say, that I do not believe he had the least hostility to Mr. Eaton. On the contrary, I believe he had kind and friendly feelings for him at that time at least. I simply remarked, in reply to his objection to Mr. Eaton's being brought into the Cabinet, that the General had made up his mind on that subject, and I did not think it could be now changed. The names of the gentlemen who were to compose the new Cabinet were published in the *Telegraph* the next morning.

"But did this put an end to annoyance to the President upon that subject? Not at all! On the following evening he received a call from Colonel Towson, a gallant and distinguished military officer, and at that time the Paymaster-General of the United States army. The parlor, as usual, was crowded, and the Colonel finding there was no chance of speaking to the General privately, asked if there was any room in which he could have a private interview with him for a few minutes?

"'Certainly,' the General said, and invited him to his bed chamber.

"He opened the door and begged the Colonel to walk in, but when he got to the door, and saw me seated at a table writing, he drew back.

"'Come in,' the General repeated, 'there is no one here but Major Lewis, and between him and me there are no secrets.'

"The Colonel then came in, and he and the General seated themselves near the fire-place. I had no wish to listen to their conversation, but as the room was small, and they spoke in their usual tone of voice, I could not help hearing every word they said; and as the General did not propose I should leave the room I continued to write on, as I knew he was anxious that the writing upon which I was engaged should be finished in time for that night's mail. After being seated, the Colonel remarked that he saw published in the *Telegraph* of that morning 'a list of the names of the persons that you propose, General, it is said, to bring into your Cabinet.'

"'Yes, sir,' he replied, 'those gentlemen will compose my Cabinet.'

"'There is no objection, I believe, personally, to any of them,' said the Colonel, 'but there is one of them your friends think it would be advisable to substitute with the name of some other person.'

"'Which of the names do you refer to, Colonel?' he inquired.

"'I mean that of Mr. Eaton,' he said.

"'Mr. Eaton is an old personal friend of mine,' the General remarked. 'He is a man of talents and experience, and one in whom his State, as well as myself, have every confidence. I can not see, therefore,' he added, 'why there should be any objection to him.'

"'There is none, I believe, personally to *him*,' the Colonel said, 'but there are great objections made to his wife.'

"'And pray, Colonel, what will his wife have to do with the duties of the War Department?' asked the General.

"'Not much, perhaps,' said the Colonel, 'but she is a person with whom the ladies of this city do not associate. She is not, and, probably, never will be received into society here, and if Mr. Eaton shall be made a member of the Cabinet, it may become a source of annoyance to both you and him.'

"'That may possibly be so,' he said, 'but Colonel, do you suppose that I have been sent here by the people to consult the ladies of Washington as to the proper persons to compose my Cabinet? In the selection of its members I shall consult my own judgment, looking to the great and paramount interests of the whole country, and not to the accommodation of the society and drawing-rooms of this or any other city. Mr. Eaton will certainly be one of my constitutional advisers, unless he declines to become a member of my Cabinet.'

"The Colonel, discovering it would be useless to say any thing more upon the subject, rose, made his bow, and left. But he did not ground his arms at this rebuff of the General. As he could not prevent Mr. Eaton from getting *in*, he seemed resolved, at all hazards, to drive him *out* of the Cabinet, and he therefore continued his opposition to him until it assumed the character of disrespect both to the Secretary of War and the

President. Taking this view of his conduct, the General had made up his mind to have his name struck from the Army Register, and would undoubtedly have done so, if Mr. Eaton had not interposed to prevent it.

"NOTE.—In relating the conversation which took place in the General's bed chamber, between him and Colonel Towson, I do not wish to be understood as intending any disrespect, either to the gallant colonel or the society of Washington, among whom I had many warm and esteemed friends when I lived in that city, as well as at this time, who would be ornaments to any society. In the foregoing narrative, I have been desirous of representing every occurrence correctly, and, I believe, in most instances, I have used the very words spoken, and particularly as relates to General Jackson. "WM. B. LEWIS.

"NASHVILLE, October 25, 1859."

To complete our knowledge of this affair, it is necessary to glance for a moment at the correspondence between the President and Vice-President.

As soon as General Jackson had obtained the letter from Mr. Crawford to Governor Forsyth, which declares that it was Calhoun, not Crawford, who had proposed the arrest or punishment of General Jackson in 1818, General Jackson sent that letter to Mr. Calhoun with a brief epistle of his own.

GENERAL JACKSON TO MR. CALHOUN.

"May 13, 1830.

"SIR: The frankness, which, I trust, has always characterized me through life, toward those with whom I have been in the habits of friendship, induces me to lay before you the inclosed copy of a letter from William H. Crawford, Esq., which was placed in my hands on yesterday. The submission, you will perceive, is authorized by the writer. The statements and facts it presents being so different from what I had heretofore understood to be correct, requires that it should be brought to your consideration. They are different from your letter to Governor Bibb, of Alabama, of the 13th May, 1818, where you state, 'General Jackson is vested with full power to conduct the war in the manner he may judge best,' and different, too, from your letters to me at that time, which breathe throughout a spirit of approbation and friendship, and particularly the one in which you say, 'I have the honor to acknowledge the receipt of your letter of the 20th ultimo, and to acquaint you with the entire approbation of the President of all the measures you have adopted to terminate the rupture with the Indians.' My object in making this communication is to announce to you the great surprise which is felt, and to learn of you whether it be possible that the information given is correct; whether it can be, under all the circumstances of which you and I are both informed, that any attempt seriously to affect me was moved and sustained by you in the cabinet council, when, as is known to you, I was but executing the *wishes* of the government, and clothed with the authority to 'conduct the war in the manner I might judge best.'

"You can, if you please, take a copy: the one inclosed you will please return to me. I am, sir, very respectfully, your humble servant,

"ANDREW JACKSON."

Mr. Calhoun was betrayed by his extreme desire to stand well with the President, and to defeat the supposed machinations of his rival, into the weakness of replying to this letter at prodigious length. Instead of taking the proper and dignified ground of declining to reveal the proceedings of a cabinet council, he avowed that, in the belief that General Jackson had transcended his orders in 1818, he *did* express that opinion in the cabinet council, and proposed the investigation of General Jackson's conduct by a court of inquiry. He justified his course, and inveighed against Mr. Crawford for betraying the secret. He reminded General Jackson that the approbatory sentence quoted by him in his letter was written before the news of the seizure of the Spanish ports and of the execution of Arbuthnot and Ambrister had reached Washington. He adduced many proofs of Crawford's hostility to General Jackson and to himself, and denounced this whole proceeding as a plot to effect his own political extinction and the exaltation of his enemies. He declared that his conduct toward General Jackson, from the beginning of their acquaintance, had been that of a true friend and faithful public servant. General Jackson's reply was the following:

52

GENERAL JACKSON TO MR. CALHOUN.

"May 30th, 1830.

"SIR: Your communication of the 29th instant was handed me this morning just as I was going to church, and of course was not read until I returned.

"I regret to find that you have entirely mistaken my note of the 13th instant. There is no part of it which calls in question either your conduct or your motives in the case alluded to. Motives are to be inferred from actions, and judged by our God. It had been intimated to me many years ago, that it was you, and not Mr. Crawford, who had been secretly endeavoring to destroy my reputation. These insinuations I indignantly repelled, upon the ground that you, in all your letters to me, professed to be my personal friend, and approved *entirely* my conduct in relation to the Seminole campaign. I had too exalted an opinion of your honor and frankness, to believe for one moment that you could be capable of such deception. Under the influence of these friendly feelings (which I always entertained for you), when I was presented with a copy of Mr. Crawford's letter, with that frankness which ever has, and I hope ever will, characterize my conduct, I considered it due to you, and the friendly relations which had always existed between us, to lay it forthwith before you, and ask if the statements contained in that letter could be true. I repeat, I had a right to believe that you were my sincere friend, and, until now, never expected to have occasion to say of you, in the language of Cæsar, *Et tu Brute?* The evidence which has brought me to this conclusion is abundantly contained in your letter now before me. In your and Mr. Crawford's dispute I have no interest whatever; but it may become necessary for me hereafter, when I shall have more leisure, and the documents at hand, to place the subject in its proper light, to notice the historical facts and references in your communication, which will give a very different view of this subject.

"It is due to myself, however, to state that the knowledge of the executive documents and orders in my possession will show conclusively that I had authority for all I did, and that your explanation of my powers, as declared to Governor Bibb, shows your own understanding of them. Your letter to me of the 29th, handed to-day, and now before me, is the first intimation to me that *you* ever entertained any opinion or view of them. Your conduct, words, actions, and letters, I have ever thought, show this. Understanding you now, no further communication with you on this subject is necessary. I have the honor to be, very respectfully, your obedient servant, ANDREW JACKSON."

Mr. Calhoun persisted in continuing the correspondence. He added, however, nothing of importance to what he had stated in his first communication, and General Jackson again declared that he desired to hear no more upon the subject. He gave Mr. Calhoun plainly to understand that friendly relations between them were for ever out of the question.

In reviewing this affair, at once so trivial and so important, I find no evidence whatever that Mr. Calhoun was guilty of duplicity toward General Jackson. Not only was he not bound to communicate to General Jackson the transactions of the Cabinet council, but he was bound *not* to reveal them. Nor does it appear that he ever professed, publicly or privately, to General Jackson or to any one else, that he approved *all* of the General's proceedings in Florida. Nor was it any just cause of reproach that he did not approve those proceedings. He admitted and believed that General Jackson's motives had been patriotic, and if he disapproved some of his acts, the General had no right to make that disapproval a ground of offense. Mr. Calhoun's only fault in this business was in his deigning to make any reply to the General's first letter, except civilly to decline giving the information sought. He should have taken high ground at first, and kept it. He should have disdained to fight Mr. Crawford with his own weapons, and not followed his bad example of revealing Cabinet secrets. If he had done so, General Jackson might have hated him, but could never have despised him. A manly defiance General Jackson liked next to complete submission.

The truth is, that before this affair began, the President was, in his heart, totally estranged from Mr. Calhoun, and would have been glad of any pretext for breaking with him.

XII.

THE "GLOBE" ESTABLISHED.

THE feud between the President and the Vice-President, which was not known to the public for nearly a year after their correspondence closed, began to produce serious effects almost immediately. Among those who most lamented the estrangement, and had most reason to lament it, was General

Duff Green, editor of the *United States Telegraph*, and printer to Congress. "We endeavored," he said afterward, in his paper, "to postpone the crisis by direct appeals to the President and to Mr. Calhoun. We refused to read the correspondence between them, because we had hoped, although almost against hope, even up to the last moment, that the eyes of the President would be opened, and that a reconciliation would take place. When the question came in this shape there was less difficulty. It was not a desertion of our friends or of our principles. We were compelled to choose, and we took the weaker side; not because we preferred Mr. Calhoun, but because his was the side of truth and honor."

There is reason to believe that the inner circle of Jacksonians were, in some degree, dissatisfied with the organ of the administration before the quarrel between General Jackson and Mr. Calhoun occurred. The destruction of the Bank of the United States being one of their fixed and most cherished purposes, they must have desired an organ that could be relied upon to aid them in the long contest which they saw impending. Mr. Kendall, in fact, in one of his letters to Duff Green, in 1830, held this language: "Had I been rejected by the Senate, I should at once have started a newspaper in Washington. It appeared to be the readiest way by which I could provide the means of comfort for a destitute family, and vindicate the principles of equal rights, violated in the proscription of printers as a class. Besides, I had some ambition to promote, at this point, the great cause of reform."

Mr. Kendall, however, was not rejected by the Senate, and the *Telegraph* remained the sole organ of the party at the seat of government.

Soon after the difference between the first officers of the government was known by their friends to be irreconcilable, the *Telegraph* began, gradually and cautiously, to change its tone. For a considerable time General Jackson would not perceive the change, for he was attached to the paper and to its editor, and had many agreeable recollections connected with both. The *Telegraph* had supported him, both before and after his election, with that daring unscrupulousness which was congenial with the feelings of this man of war. Mr. Kendall, however, and Major Lewis saw the coming defection of General Green very plainly, and advised the President to provide in time for the establishment of another organ.

"No," said the General, "you are mistaken. Give Duff time. He will come out right after a little reflection."

Major Lewis felt so confident of the correctness of his surmises that he wrote confidentially, and without consulting the President, to Mr. Gooch, of the *Richmond Inquirer*, asking him if he would come to Washington and establish an organ, in case the President should, at any future time, desire it. Mr. Gooch declined. Mr. Kendall had his eye upon another gentleman, his old friend and voluntary contributor, Francis P. Blair, of Kentucky.

Col. Benton, in his "Thirty Years' View," gives a striking, but not quite correct account of the manner in which the President procured the services of Mr. Blair. "In the summer of 1830," says Col. Benton, "a gentleman in one of the public offices showed the President a paper, the *Frankfort* (Kentucky) *Argus*, containing a powerful and spirited review of a certain nullification speech in Congress. He inquired for the author, ascertained him to be Mr. Francis P. Blair—not the editor, but an occasional contributor to the *Argus*—and had him written to on the subject of taking charge of a paper in Washington. The application took Mr. Blair by surprise. He was not thinking of changing his residence and pursuits. He was well occupied where he was—clerk of the lucrative office of the State Circuit Court at the capital of the State, salaried president of the Commonwealth Bank (by the election of the legislature), and proprietor of a farm and slaves in that rich State."

It is true that General Jackson was struck with the article referred to by Col. Benton; but it was only after much subsequent persuasion and repeated proofs of Duff

Green's defection that the President gave a reluctant consent that Mr. Blair should be summoned to the rescue. Nor was Mr. Blair in the pleasant pecuniary circumstances detailed by Col. Benton. He was a man of broken fortune, forty thousand dollars in debt, living upon the slender emoluments of his two offices. It is surprising that the author of the "Thirty Years' View" should have been unacquainted with facts which Mr. Blair often amuses his friends by relating.

If the country had been searched for the express purpose of selecting the man best fitted for the editorship of the proposed organ, no one could have been found whose history, opinions, antipathies, and cast of character so adapted him for the post as Francis P. Blair, of Kentucky. Descended from the Scotch family of whom the famous Hugh Blair was a member, born in Virginia, reared and educated in Kentucky, he had been from his youth up an ardent but disinterested politician. For ten years he had taken part in the discussion of the question whether the branches of the bank of the United States were, or were not, subject to State taxation, a question that was nowhere argued with such heat and pertinacity as in Kentucky. Mr. Blair was against the bank. The ten years' agitation had made him acquainted with all the vulnerable points of the institution, and familiar with the weapons of attack. He was among the most decided opponents of the bank in the Union. Another of his special antipathies was nullification ; and yet another was John Quincy Adams and the high federalism of his messages. Master of an easy and vigorous style, which could become slashing and fierce upon occasion, his whole training as a writer and a politician had been belligerent. He was only a warrior upon paper, however. In person slender and unimposing, in demeanor retiring and quiet, in character amiable, affectionate, and grateful, the man and the editor were two beings as dissimilar as can be imagined. Jackson men who called at the office of the *Globe*, expecting to find the thunderer of their party a man of Kentuckian proportions, with pistols peeping from his breast-pocket, and a bowie-knife stiffening his back, were amazed upon being told that the little man sitting in a corner, writing on his knee, was the great editor they had come to get a sight of.

The summons to Washington, though unexpected, Mr. Blair obeyed without hesitation and without delay. He reached the capital in sorry plight; almost penniless, with a single presentable coat, and that a frock-coat; with a great gash in the side of his head from an overset near Washington. When he entered the President's office, Major Lewis could hardly conceal his disappointment. For weeks, Mr. Blair had been the coming man to all the *habitués* of that apartment. Whenever General Duff had ventured to come out a little bolder than usual against the administration or its friends, they had said to one another, in effect, "Never mind. Wait till Blair comes. *He* will talk to him." And this was he—this little man attired in frock-coat and court-plaster! Said Major Lewis, with a sly glance at the black patch, "Mr. Blair, we want stout hearts and sound heads here."

The General took to him at once, and he to the General. At the very first interview, the President revealed to him the situation of affairs without any reserve whatever. The difficulties he had had in his own household, the alleged machinations of the nullifiers, the supposed atrocities of the bank, the imaginary devices of that arch-devil, Henry Clay, the cabinet combination against poor Major Eaton—all were unfolded. "There 's my nephew, Donelson," said the General; "he seems to be leaning toward the nullifiers. But he 's my nephew. I raised him. I love him. Let him do what he will, I love him. I can't help it. Treat him kindly, but if he wants to write for your paper, you must look out for him." The President invited Mr. Blair to dinner. When the hour came, the editor was horrified to find a great company of ambassadors and other high personages assembled in the East Room, all in costume superb. The tails of his uncomfortable frock coat hung heavily upon the soul of the stranger, who shrunk into a corner abashed and miserable. The President, as soon as he entered the room, sought him out, placed him at the table in the seat of honor at his own right hand, and completed the conquest of his heart. In Francis P. Blair, General Jackson gained a lover as well as a champion.

Like Jonah's gourd, the *Globe* appeared to spring into existence in a night—without capital, without a press, without types, without subscribers, without advertisements. Amos Kendall made a contract for the printing. Major Lewis, Mr. Kendall, and all the confidants of the administration exerted themselves to obtain subscribers. The office-holders were given to understand that to subscribe for the *Globe* was the thing they were expected to do, and the Jackson presses throughout the country, announced that the *Globe* was, and the *Telegraph* was not, the confidential organ of the administration. Subscribers came in by hundreds in a day, and the *Globe* became a paying enterprise in a few weeks. Partly by subscription, and partly by papers paid for in advance, a press and materials were soon purchased. A known friend of the bank advanced two hundred dollars for this purpose. The next morning, Mr. Blair, having in the meantime learned the probable object of this donation, returned the money.

To swell the profits of the *Globe* office, the President desired to obtain for it the printing of the departments, or, at least, a share of that profitable business. As some of the secretaries showed no alacrity to make the transfer desired, the fertile brain of Major Lewis devised a very simple but quite effectual expedient for compelling them to do so. He induced the President to issue an order to each member of the cabinet, requiring him to present to the President a quarterly account of the sums paid, and to whom paid, in his department for printing. Major Lewis drew up the order. Major Donelson, as usual, copied it. The President signed it. Such an order, in the peculiar posture of affairs at the time, was equivalent to a command to give the *Globe* office a share of the department printing; and the command was obeyed.

In due time, came the election of Messrs. Blair and Rives as printers to Congress, which added fortune to the fame and power given them by the *Globe*. Mr. John C. Rives, the well-known partner of Mr. Blair, was a gentleman who added to respectable literary attainments an extraordinary efficiency in the management of business.

The *Telegraph* waged an active warfare against General Jackson for several years, supporting Henry Clay for the presidency in 1832, with hopes for Mr. Calhoun in 1836 or 1840. The campaign of 1832 gave it a temporary inflation, which the result of that campaign changed into partial collapse. The editor still lives in Washington, a prosperous gentleman, delighting to tell over, to after-dinner circles, the story of his short and turbulent career as Jacksonian organ.

XIII.

CONGRESS IN SESSION.

The administration of General Jackson, however distracted by internal broils, whatever motives of a partisan or personal character influenced it, always came before the public with an imposing air of calm dignity and single-eyed patriotism. No one could ever suppose, from its public papers, that, from the beginning to the end of its existence, it scarcely knew a month of internal peace and real coöperative harmony.

Congress met again on the 6th of December, and on the day following Major Donelson was at the Capitol with the message, one of the most carefully elaborated documents ever presented to Congress.

It opened with jubilation. Plenty and peace had crowned the year. "With a population unparalleled in its increase, and possessing a character which combines the hardihood of enterprise with the considerateness of wisdom," every where was seen a steady improvement. A glowing paragraph expressed the congratulations of the nation upon the success of the late revolution in France, which had enabled Lafayette to place upon the throne the prince Louis Philippe, a man who, the President hoped, would deserve the proud appellation of PATRIOT KING. The recent diplomatic triumph of 53 Mr. McLane, which placed our trade with the West Indies on its present footing, after six previous negotiations had resulted in failure, was explained, and the negotiators on both sides duly complimented, Mr. McLane being mentioned by name. The Sultan had opened to us the Black Sea, and placed our commerce, in all respects, on the footing of the most favored nations. With Mexico, Russia, France, Spain, Portugal, negotiations were pending with every prospect of issues advantageous to the United States. Denmark had at length appropriated the sum of six hundred and fifty thousand dollars, the whole amount claimed, to indemnify American merchants for the spoliations of 1808 to 1811, and it now only remained for Congress to effect a just distribution of the money among the claimants.

These administrative triumphs having been detailed, the authors of the message grappled with the serious business of the occasion, which was to defend the course of the President in his veto of the Maysville road, and in his withholding his assent from the light-house bill, and the bill authorizing a subscription to the Louisville and Portland Canal Company, both of which had been passed at the close of the last session of Congress. That the expense of constructing light-houses properly devolved upon the general government, the President did not doubt; but there were some features of the light-house bill in question of which he could not approve. To the number of light-house keepers, already very large, the bill proposed to add the extraordinary number of fifty-one. The expenditures of the government for the protection of commerce were immense, and, as he had been led to conclude, unreasonable, and he looked rather to their diminution than their increase. Moreover, the present bill contained the entirely fatal objection of authorizing certain surveys which were clearly of a local character, and designed for the promotion of local interests.

With regard to the bill proposing a subscription of the public money to the stock of a private company, he was utterly and for ever opposed to that mode of assisting public works. He thought it unconstitutional, impolitic, injurious, and demoralizing. With his consent it should never be done.

The message proceeded to vindicate the Maysville veto, the use of the veto power generally, and the proposed apportionment of the surplus revenue among the States. Amid all the clamor and controversy to which his measures had given rise, the President said he had been consoled by the reflection that if he had really mistaken the interests and wishes of the people, an opportunity would soon be afforded them of placing in the presidential chair one who would interpret their desires more correctly. Meanwhile, the money saved by the vetos would be rigidly applied to the extinguishment of the public debt.

The President repeated his recommendations for the removal of "all intermediate agency" in the election of the chief magistrate, and for limiting his period of service to one term.

He artfully defended the policy of removing the Indians, denying that the removal was either unjust or inhuman. "Doubtless," he remarked, "it will be painful to leave the graves of their fathers; but what do they more than our ancestors did, or than our children are now doing? To better their condition in an unknown land, our forefathers left all that was dear in earthly objects. Our children, by thousands, yearly leave the land of their birth, to seek new homes in distant regions."

The tariff was a topic, of course, and it was touched with an uncertain hand, of course. The people were implored not to regard the tariff as a sectional matter, and to approach it in a spirit of conciliation. The revenue of the year had been $24,161,018; the expenditures, exclusive of the public debt, $13,742,311; the payment on account of the public debt had been $11,354,630; balance in the treasury, $4,819,781.

The message concluded with a second and louder warning to the United States bank. "Nothing has occurred," said the President, "to lessen, in any degree, the dangers which many of our citizens apprehend from that institution, as at present organized. In the spirit of improvement and compromise which distinguishes our country and its institutions, it becomes us to inquire, whether it be not possible to secure the advantages afforded by the present bank, through the agency of a bank of the United States, so modified in its principles and structure as to obviate constitutional and other objections. It is thought practicable to organize such a bank, with the necessary officers, as a branch of the Treasury Department, based on the public and individual deposits, without power to make loans or purchase property, which shall remit the funds of the government, and the expense of which may be paid, if thought advisable, by allowing its officers to sell bills of exchange to private individuals at a moderate premium. Not being a corporate body, having no stockholders, debtors, or property, and but few officers, it would not be obnoxious to the constitutional objections which are urged against the present bank; and having no means to operate on the hopes, fears, or interests of large masses of the community, it would be shorn of the influence which makes that bank formidable."

This message was one of the longest ever presented to Congress. The care and elaboration of the argumentative portions of it show how deeply its leading topics were agitating the public mind, and how resolutely the administration was marching toward the objects it had prescribed to itself.

One event only of this session of Congress need detain us —Colonel Benton's first formal attack upon the Bank of the

United States. "The current," says the author of the "Thirty Years' View," "was all setting one way. I determined to raise a voice against it in the Senate, and made several efforts before I succeeded—the thick array of the Bank friends throwing every obstacle in my way, and even friends holding me back for the regular course, which was to wait until the application for the renewed charter should be presented ; and then to oppose it. I foresaw that, if this course was followed, the Bank would triumph without a contest—that she would wait until a majority was installed in both Houses of Congress—then present her application—hear a few barren speeches in opposition ;—and then gallop the renewed charter through."

The speech of Mr. Benton, on this occasion, was one of the ablest and most effective of his whole senatorial career of thirty years. It emptied the Senate chamber, but it roused the people. We shall have, in a future page, to give the substance of his arguments against the Bank, and, therefore, pass over this truly Bentonian fulmination.

"This speech," continues Colonel Benton, "was not answered. Confident in its strength, and insolent in its nature, the great moneyed power had adopted a system in which she persevered until hard knocks drove her out of it : it was to have an anti-Bank speech treated with the contempt of silence in the House, and caricatured and belittled in the newspapers ; and according to this system my speech was treated. The instant it was delivered, Mr. Webster called for the vote, and to be taken by yeas and nays, which was done ; and resulted differently from what was expected—a strong vote against the Bank—twenty to twenty-three ; enough to excite uneasiness, but not enough to pass the resolution and legitimate a debate on the subject. The debate stopped with the single speech ; but it was a speech to be read by the people—the masses—the millions ; and was conceived and delivered for that purpose ; and was read by them ; and has been complimented since as having crippled the Bank, and given it the wound of which it afterward died ; but not within the year and a day which would make the slayer responsible for the homicide. The list of yeas and nays was also favorable to the effect of the speech. Though not a party vote, it was sufficiently so to show how it stood—the mass of the democracy against the Bank—the mass of the anti-democrats for it."

This being the "short session," Congress adjourned on the third of March, when the Twenty-first Congress ceased to exist.

XIV.

DISSOLUTION OF THE CABINET.

TOWARD the close of this brief and uneventful session of Congress, Mr. Calhoun published his "Book," as it was sneeringly called at the time; a pamphlet of fifty pages octavo, containing his late correspondence with the President, and a mass of letters, statements, and certificates illustrative thereof. In a prefatory address to the people of the United States, Mr. Calhoun explained his reasons for making a publication so unusual and unexpected.

"Previous to my arrival at Washington" (in December, 1830), said he, "I had confined the knowledge of the existence of the correspondence to a few confidential friends, who were politically attached both to General Jackson and myself; not that I had any thing to apprehend from its disclosure, but because I was unwilling to increase the existing excitement in the present highly critical state of our public affairs. But when I arrived here, late in December, I found my caution had been of no avail, and that the correspondence was a subject of conversation in every circle, and soon became a topic of free comment in most of the public journals. The accounts of the affair, as is usually the case on such occasions, were, for the most part, grossly distorted, and were, in many instances, highly injurious to my character. Still I deemed it my duty to take no hasty step, being determined to afford time for justice to be done me without appeal to you ; and, if it should be, to remain silent, as my only object was the vindication of my conduct and character. Believing that further delay would be useless, I can see no adequate motive to postpone, any longer, the submission of all the facts of the case to your deliberate and final decision."

The pamphlet was discussed in a strictly partisan spirit ; all the Jackson papers condemning it, all the opposition papers applauding it. A few weeks after its appearance, the New York *Courier and Enquirer* gave extracts from nearly two hundred democratic papers, vindicating the President and condemning the course of Mr. Calhoun. "Every republican paper in the Middle and Northern States," said the *Courier*, "friendly to Andrew Jackson's reëlection, has unequivocally condemned the publication made by Mr. Calhoun of his attack on the President. In the South, out of South Carolina, it is nearly the same ; and even in South Carolina, a strong party is forming against him, and in favor of Jackson."

"Mr. Calhoun's *attack* on the President !" "Condemns unequivocally Mr. Calhoun *and* the nullifiers !" Artful conjunction ! Were the politicians far astray when they said, that "General Jackson's popularity could stand any thing ?"

The President's retort was prompt, adroit, audacious, and overwhelming. By a series of skillful movements, he shelved the three members of his cabinet—Messrs. Ingham, Branch, and Berrien—who were Mr. Calhoun's friends and political allies. This was done about a month after the adjournment of Congress, and the moment was admirably chosen. It was long enough after the publication of Mr. Calhoun's pamphlet for it to have been well ridiculed in the administration papers, and to have ceased to be an exciting topic. It was in the lull preceding the excitement of the coming presidential election. It was nine months before there could be any trouble with the Senate respecting confirmations. Indeed, we may truly say of this disruption of the cabinet in 1831, that of all known political management it was the consummate stroke. Jacksonian boldness united with Van Buren tact could alone have achieved it.

A dissolution of the cabinet was the expedient hit upon. Mr. Van Buren and Major Eaton were to resign and to be provided for. Mr. Barry, the Postmaster-General, should retain his place awhile. The obnoxious Three were expected to take a hint and leave ; if not, the President was prepared to ask their resignations. Go they should.

Every thing was considered, and, as far as possible, provided for before the first step was taken. Mr. Edward Livingston, Senator from Louisiana, was notified of coming events, and offered the post of Secretary of State, which he agreed to accept. He had recently paid off, principal and interest, the sum due from him to the government, on account of the misconduct of his clerks in 1803. Thus, a possible objection to his appointment was removed. Mr. Louis McLane, Minister to England, was recalled ; which provided a place for Mr. Van Buren and a new Secretary of the Treasury for General Jackson. Judge Hugh L. White, Senator from Tennessee, was the gentleman designed to fill the place about to be vacated by Major Eaton. If Judge White accepted, of which there was then no doubt, there would be a vacant seat in the Senate for Major Eaton, to which, it was thought, he could be appointed. Mr. Levi Woodbury was ready to take the place of Secretary of the Navy.

By the bold and artful measures contemplated a great many desirable objects were expected to be gained. A united cabinet, devoted to General Jackson and to the furtherance of his schemes, was one object. The removal of Mr. Van Buren from the scene of strife to a safe and commanding position abroad was thought to be a proceeding well calculated to promote his interests. Moreover, the President had made known to many persons, at the beginning of his administration, his resolve that no member of his cabinet should be his successor. A minor object was, to retrieve the unhappy

Eaton from his painfully embarrassing situation, and restore him to the place he preferred, a seat in the Senate.

The following is the correspondence between the President and the members of the Cabinet relative to the resignations. The reader will observe the dates:

MR. EATON TO THE PRESIDENT.

"WASHINGTON CITY, April 7, 1831.

"DEAR SIR: Four days ago I communicated to you my desire to relinquish the duties of the War Department, and I now take occasion to repeat the request which was then made. I am not disposed, by any sudden withdrawal, to interrupt or retard the business of the office. A short time will be sufficient, I hope, to enable you to direct your attention toward some person in whose capacity, industry, and friendly disposition you may have confidence, to assist in the complicated and laborious duties of your administration. Two or three weeks—perhaps less—may be sufficient for the purpose.

"In coming to this conclusion, candor demands of me to say, that it arises from no dissatisfaction entertained toward you—from no misunderstanding between us, on any subject; nor from any diminution, on my part, of that friendship and confidence which has ever been reposed in you.

"I entered your Cabinet, as is well known to you, contrary to my own wishes; and having nothing to desire, either as it regards myself or friends, have ever since cherished a determination to avail myself of the first favorable moment, after your administration should be in successful operation, to retire. It occurs to me that the time is now at hand when I may do so with propriety. Looking to the present state of things—to the course of your administration, which, being fairly developed, is before the people for approval or condemnation, I can not consider the step I am taking objectionable, or that it is one the tendency of which can be to affect or injure a course of policy by you already advantageously commenced, and which I hope will be carried out to the benefit and advancement of the people.

"Tendering my sincere wishes for your prosperity and happiness, and for your successful efforts in the cause of your country, I am, very truly, your friend,

"J. H. EATON.

"To ANDREW JACKSON, President of the United States."

THE PRESIDENT TO MR. EATON.

"WASHINGTON CITY, April 8, 1831.

"DEAR SIR: Your letter of yesterday was received, and I have carefully considered it. When you conversed with me the other day on the subject of your withdrawing from the Cabinet, I expressed to you a sincere desire that you would well consider of it; for however reluctant I am to be deprived of your services, I can not consent to retain you contrary to your wishes and inclination to remain, particularly as I well know that in 1829, when I invited you to become a member of my Cabinet, you objected and expressed a desire to be excused, and only gave up your objections at my pressing solicitation.

"An acquaintance with you of twenty years' standing, assured me that in your honesty, prudence, capacity, discretion, and judgment, I could safely rely and confide. I have not been disappointed. With the performance of your duties, since you have been with me, I have been fully satisfied, and, go where you will, be your destiny what it may, my best wishes will always attend you.

"I will avail myself of the earliest opportunity to obtain some qualified friend to succeed you; and until then, I must solicit that the acceptance of your resignation be deferred. I am, very sincerely and respectfully, your friend, "ANDREW JACKSON.

"Major J. H. EATON, Secretary of War."

MR. VAN BUREN TO THE PRESIDENT.

"WASHINGTON, April 11, 1831.

"DEAR SIR: I feel it to be my duty to retire from the office to which your confidence and partiality called me. The delicacy of this step, under the circumstances in which it is taken, will, I trust, be deemed an ample apology for stating more at large than might otherwise have been necessary, the reasons by which I am influenced.

"From the moment of taking my seat in your Cabinet, it has been my anxious wish and zealous endeavor to prevent a premature agitation of the question of your successor, and, at all events to discountenance and, if possible, repress the disposition, at an early day manifested, to connect my name with that disturbing topic. Of the sincerity and constancy of this disposition, no one has had a better opportunity to judge than yourself. It has, however, been unavailing. Circumstances not of my creation, and altogether beyond my control, have given to this subject a turn which can not now be remedied, except by a self-disfranchisement which, even if dictated by my individual wishes, could hardly be reconcilable with propriety or self-respect.

"Concerning the injurious effects which the circumstance of a member of the Cabinet's occupying the relation toward the country to which I have adverted, is calculated to have upon the conduct of public affairs, there can not, I think, at this time, be room for two opinions. Diversities of ulterior preference among the friends of an administration are unavoidable, and even if the respective advocates of those thus placed in rivalship be patriotic enough to resist the temptation of creating obstacles to the advancement of him to whose elevation they are opposed, by embarrassing the branch of public service committed to his charge, they are, nevertheless, by their position, exposed to the suspicion of entertaining and encouraging such views—a suspicion which can seldom fail, in the end, to aggravate into present alienation and hostility the prospective differences which first gave rise to it. Thus, under the least unfavorable consequences, individual injustice is suffered, and the administration embarrassed and weakened.

"Whatever may have been the course of things under the peculiar circumstances of the earlier stage of the republic, my experience has fully satisfied me that at this day, when the field of selection has become so extended, the circumstance referred to, by augmenting the motives and sources of opposition to the measures of the Executive, must unavoidably prove the cause of injury to the public service, for a counterpoise to which we may in vain look to the peculiar qualifications of any individual; and even if I should in this be mistaken, still I can not so far deceive myself as to believe for a moment that I am included in the exceptions.

"These obstructions to the successful prosecution of public affairs, when superadded to that opposition which is inseparable from our free institutions, and which every administration must expect, present a mass to which the operations of the government should at no time be voluntarily exposed. The more especially should this be avoided at so eventful a period in the affairs of the world, when our country may particularly need the utmost harmony in her councils.

"Such being my impressions, the path of duty is plain, and I not only submit with cheerfulness to whatever personal sacrifices may be involved in the surrender of the station I occupy, but I make it my ambition to set an example which, should it in the progress of the government be deemed, notwithstanding the humility of its origin, worthy of respect and observance, can not, I think, fail to prove essentially and permanently beneficial.

"Allow me, sir, to present one more view of the subject. You have consented to stand before your constituents for reëlection. Of their decision, resting as it does upon the unbought suffrages of a free, numerous, and widely-extended people, it becomes no man to speak with certainty. Judging, however, from the past, and making a reasonable allowance for the fair exercise of the intelligence and public spirit of your fellow-citizens, I can not hesitate in adopting the belief that the confidence, as well in your capacity for civil duties as in your civic virtues, already so spontaneously and strikingly displayed, will be manifested with increased energy, now that all candid observers must admit their utmost expectations to have been more than realized.

"If this promise, so auspicious to the best interests of our common country, be fulfilled, the concluding term of your administration will, in the absence of any prominent cause of discord among its supporters, afford a most favorable opportunity for the full accomplishment of those important public objects, in the prosecution of which I have witnessed on your part such steady vigilance and untiring devotion. To the unfavorable influence which my continuance in your Cabinet, under existing circumstances, may exercise upon this flattering prospect, I can not, sir, without a total disregard of the lights of experience, and without shutting my eyes to the obvious tendency of things for the future, be insensible. Having, moreover, from a deep conviction of its importance to the country, been among the most urgent of your advisers to yield yourself to the obvious wishes of the people, and knowing the sacrifice of personal feeling which was involved in your acquiescence, I can not reconcile it to myself to be in any degree the cause of embarrassment to you during the period which, as it certainly will be of deep interest to your country, is moreover destined to bring to its close, your patriotic, toilsome, and eventful public life.

"From these considerations I feel it to be doubly my duty to resign a post the retention of which is so calculated to attract assaults upon your administration, to which there might otherwise be no inducement—assaults of which, whatever be their aim, the most important as well as most injurious effect is upon those public interests which deserve and should command the support of all good citizens. This duty I should have discharged at an earlier period, but for considerations, partly of a public, partly of a personal nature, connected with circumstances which were calculated to expose its performance then to misconstruction and misrepresentation.

"Having explained the motives which govern me in thus severing, and with seeming abruptness, the official ties by which we have been associated, there remains but one duty for me to perform. It is to make my profound and sincere acknowledgments for that steady support and cheering confidence which, in the discharge of my duties, I have, under all circumstances, received at your hands: as well as for the personal kindness at all times extended to me.

"Rest assured, sir, that the success of your administration, and the happiness of your private life, will ever constitute objects of the deepest solicitude with your sincere friend and obedient servant,

"M. Van Buren.

"The President."

THE PRESIDENT TO MR. VAN BUREN.

"Washington, April 12, 1831.

"Dear Sir: Your letter resigning the office of Secretary of State was received last evening. I could indeed wish that no circumstance had arisen to interrupt the relations which have, for two years, subsisted between us, and that they might have continued through the period during which it may be my lot to remain charged with the duties which the partiality of my countrymen has imposed upon me. But the reasons you present are so strong that, with a proper regard for them, I can not ask you, on my own account, to remain in the Cabinet.

"I am aware of the difficulties you have had to contend with, and of the benefits which have resulted to the affairs of your country, from your continued zeal in the arduous tasks to which you have been subjected. To say that I deeply regret to lose you, is but feebly to express my feelings on the occasion.

"When called by my country to the station which I occupy, it was not without a deep sense of its arduous responsibilities, and a strong distrust of myself, that I obeyed the call; but cheered by the consciousness that no other motive actuated me than a desire to guard her interests, and to place her upon the firm ground of those great principles which, by the wisest and purest of our patriots, have been deemed essential to her prosperity, I ventured upon the trust assigned me. I did this in the confident hope of finding the support of advisers able and true; who, laying aside every thing but a desire to give new vigor to the vital principles of our Union, would look with a single eye to the best means of effecting this paramount object. In you, this hope has been realized to the utmost. In the most difficult and trying moments of my administration, I have always found you sincere, able, and efficient—anxious at all times to afford me every aid.

"If, however, from circumstances in your judgment sufficient to make it necessary, the official ties subsisting between us must be severed, I can only say that this necessity is deeply lamented by me. I part with you only because you yourself have requested me to do so, and have sustained that request by reasons strong enough to command my assent. I can not, however, allow the separation to take place, without expressing the hope, that this retirement from public affairs is but temporary; and that if in any other station the government should have occasion for your services, the value of which has been so sensibly felt by me, your consent will not be wanting.

"Of the state of things to which you advert, I can not but be fully aware. I look upon it with sorrow, and regret the more, because one of its first effects is to disturb the harmony of my Cabinet. It is, however, but an instance of one of the evils to which free governments must ever be liable. The only remedy for these evils, as they arise, lies in the intelligence and public spirit of our common constituents. They will correct them—and in this there is abundant consolation. I can not quit this subject without adding that, with the best opportunities for observing and judging, I have seen in you no other desire than to move quietly on in the path of your duties, and to promote the harmonious conduct of public affairs. If, on this point, you have had to encounter detraction, it is but another proof of the utter insufficiency of innocence and worth to shield from such assaults.

"Be assured that the interest you express in my happiness is most heartily reciprocated—that my most cordial feelings accompany you, and that I am, very sincerely, your friend,

"ANDREW JACKSON.

"P. S. It is understood that you are to continue in your office until your successor is appointed.

"MARTIN VAN BUREN, Secretary of State."

MR. INGHAM TO THE PRESIDENT.

"WASHINGTON, April 18, 1831.

"SIR: In communicating to me, this morning, the information of the resignations of the Secretary of State and Secretary of War, together with the reasons which had induced the former to take this step, you were pleased to observe that this proceeding was made known to me as one of those whom you had associated with you in the administration of the government, and you suggested that I would, after a few days' reflection, have a further conversation with you on this subject. But, in recurring to the brief remarks made at the time, as well as to the letter of resignation of the Secretary of State, which you were good enough to submit for my perusal, I have not been able to ascertain what particular matter was intended to be proposed for my reflection, as connected with this event. Under these circumstances, and being desirous of avoiding the possibility of misapprehension as to your views, I would respectfully inquire whether the measure adopted by the Secretaries of State and of War, is deemed to involve considerations on which you expect a particular communication from me, and, if so, of what nature.

"I have the honor to be, respectfully, your obedient servant,

"S. D. INGHAM.

"To the President of the United States."

MR. INGHAM TO THE PRESIDENT.

"WASHINGTON, April 19, 1831.

"SIR: I am gratified to find myself entirely relieved, by the distinct explanations at the interview to which you invited me to-day, from the uncertainty as to the object of your communication yesterday, which I had referred to in my note of last evening; and have to make my acknowledgments for the kindness with which you have expressed your satisfaction with the manner in which I have discharged the duties of the station to which you had thought proper to invite me, and your conviction of the public confidence in my administration of the Treasury Department. I beg leave, however, to add, in my own justification, for not following the example of the Secretary of State and Secretary of War, in making a voluntary tender of the resignation of my office, as soon as I was acquainted with theirs, that I was wholly unconscious of the application, to myself, of any of the reasons, so far as I was apprised of them, which had induced them to withdraw from the public service. It, therefore, seemed to be due to my own character, which might otherwise have been exposed to unfavorable imputations, that I should find a reason for resigning, in a distinct expression of your wish to that effect; this wish has now been frankly announced, and has enabled me to place my retirement on its true ground.

"I have, therefore, the honor of tendering to you my resignation of the office of Secretary of the Treasury of the United States, which you will be pleased to accept, to take effect as soon as my services may be dispensed with consistently with your views of the public interest.

"I seize the occasion to offer you my thanks for the many testimonials I have received of your kindness and confidence during our official connection, and especially for the renewed assurance, this day, of the same sentiment. "S. D. INGHAM.

"His Excellency, ANDREW JACKSON, President of the United States."

THE PRESIDENT TO MR. INGHAM.

"WASHINGTON, April 20, 1831.

"SIR: Late last evening I had the honor to receive your letter of that date, tendering your resignation of the office of Secretary of the Treasury. When the resignations of the Secretary of State and Secretary of War were tendered, I considered fully the reasons offered, and all the circumstances connected with the subject. After mature deliberation, I concluded to accept those resignations. But when this conclusion was come to, it was accompanied with a conviction that I must entirely renew my Cabinet. Its members had been invited by me to the stations they occupied; it had come together in great harmony, and as a unit. Under the circumstances in which I found myself, I could not but perceive the propriety of selecting a Cabinet composed of entirely new materials, as being calculated, in this respect at least, to command public confidence and satisfy public opinion. Neither could I be insensible to the fact, that to permit two only to retire, would be to afford room for unjust misconceptions and malignant misrepresentations concerning the influence of their particular presence upon the conduct of public affairs. Justice to the individuals whose public spirit had impelled them to tender their resignations, also required, then, in my opinion, the decision which I have stated. However painful to my own feelings, it became necessary that I should frankly make known to you the whole subject.

"In accepting of your resignation, it is with great pleasure that I bear testimony to the integrity and zeal with which you have managed the fiscal concerns of the nation. In your discharge of all the duties of your office, over which I have any control, I have been fully satisfied; and in your retirement you carry with you my best wishes for your prosperity and happiness.

"It is expected that you will continue to discharge the duties of your office until a successor is appointed.

"I have the honor to be, with great respect, your most obedient servant,

"ANDREW JACKSON.

"SAMUEL D. INGHAM, Secretary of the Treasury."

MR. BRANCH TO THE PRESIDENT.

"WASHINGTON, April 19th, 1831.

"SIR: In the interview which I had the honor to hold with you this morning, I understood it to be your fixed purpose to reorganize your cabinet, and that as to myself it was your wish that I should retire from the administration of the Navy Department.

"Under these circumstances, I take pleasure in tendering to you the commission, which, unsolicited on my part, you were pleased to confer on me.

"I have the honor to be, with great respect, yours, etc.,

"JOHN BRANCH.

"To the President of the United States."

THE PRESIDENT TO MR. BRANCH.

"WASHINGTON, April 19th, 1831.

"SIR: Your letter of this date, by your son, is just received—accompanying it is your commission. The sending of the latter was not necessary; it is your own private property, and by no means to be considered part of the archives of the government. Accordingly I return it.

"There is one expression in your letter to which I take leave to except. I did not, as to *yourself*, express a wish that you should retire. The Secretaries of State and of War having tendered their resignations, I remarked to you that I felt it to be indispensable to reorganize my cabinet proper; that it had come in harmoniously, and as a unit; and as a part was about to leave me, which on to-morrow would be announced, a reorganization was necessary to guard against misrepresentation. These were my remarks, made to you in candor and sincerity. Your letter gives a different import to my words.

"Your letter contains no remarks as to your performing the duties of the office until a successor can be selected. On this subject I should be glad to know your views. I am, very respectfully, yours,

"ANDREW JACKSON.

"The Hon. JOHN BRANCH, Secretary of the Navy."

MR. BRANCH TO THE PRESIDENT.

"WASHINGTON, April 19th, 1831.

"SIR: I have the honor to acknowledge the receipt of yours of this date, in answer to mine of the same.

"In reply to your remark that there is one expression in my letter to which you must except, I would respectfully answer that I gave what I understood to be the substance of your conversation. I did not pretend to quote your language.

"I regret that I misunderstood you in the slightest degree; I, however, stand corrected, and cheerfully accept the interpretation which you have given to your own expression.

"I shall freely continue my best exertions to discharge the duties of the department, until you provide a successor.

"I have the honor to be, with the greatest respect, your obedient servant, "JOHN BRANCH.

"To the President of the United States."

THE PRESIDENT TO MR. BRANCH.

"WASHINGTON, April 20, 1831.

"SIR: Late last evening, I had the honor to receive your letter of that date, tendering your resignation of the office of Secretary of the Navy.

"When the resignations of the Secretary of State and Secretary of War were tendered, I considered fully the reasons offered, and all the circumstances connected with the subject. After mature deliberation, I concluded to accept those resignations. But when this conclusion was come to, it was accompanied with a conviction that I must entirely renew my cabinet. Its members had been invited by me to the stations they occupied; it had come together in great harmony, and as a unit. Under the circumstances in which I found myself, I could not but perceive the propriety of selecting a cabinet composed of entirely new materials, as being calculated, in this respect at least, to command public confidence and satisfy public opinion. Neither could I be insensible to the fact, that to permit two only to retire would be to afford room for unjust misconceptions and malignant representations concerning the influence of their particular presence upon the conduct of public affairs. Justice to the individuals whose public spirit had impelled them to tender their resignations, also required then, in my opinion, the decision which I have stated. However painful to my own feelings, it became necessary that I should frankly make known to you my view of the whole subject.

"In accepting your resignation, it is with great pleasure that I bear testimony to the integrity and zeal with which you have managed the concerns of the navy. In your discharge of all the duties of your office over which I have any control, I have been fully satisfied; and in your retirement you carry with you my best wishes for your prosperity and happiness. It is expected that you will continue to discharge the duties of your office until a successor is appointed.

"I have the honor to be, with great respect, your most obedient servant, "ANDREW JACKSON.

"JOHN BRANCH, Secretary of the Navy."

MR. BERRIEN TO THE PRESIDENT.

"WASHINGTON, 15th June, 1831.

"SIR: I herewith tender to you my resignation of the office of Attorney-General of the United States. Two considerations restrained me from taking this step at the moment when your communication to the Secretary of the Treasury, announcing your determination to reorganize your cabinet, first met my eye. There was nothing in the retirement of the Secretaries of State and of War, or in the distinct and personal considerations which they had assigned for this measure, which made it obligatory upon, or even proper for me to adopt a similar course. Such a step, with any reference to that occurrence, could only become so, on my part, as an act of conformity to your will. You had felt this, and had announced your wishes to the Secretaries of the Treasury and of the Navy, respectively. I had a right to expect a similar communication of them, and conformed to the wishes and opinions of my fellow-citizens of Georgia, when I determined to await it. An additional consideration was presented by the fact that I had been charged, at the moment of my departure from this place, with the performance of certain public duties which were yet unfinished, and my report concerning which you did not expect to receive until my return. I was gratified to learn from yourself that you had taken the same view of this subject, having postponed the communication of your wishes to me until my arrival at this place, without expecting in the mean time any communication from me. It is due to myself further to state, that from the moment when I saw the communication referred to, I have considered my official relation to you as terminated, or as subsisting only until my return to the city should enable me to conform to your wishes by the formal surrender of my office, which it is the purpose of this note to make.

"I retire, then, sir, with cheerfulness from the station to which your confidence had called me, because I have the consciousness of having endeavored to discharge its duties with fidelity to yourself and the country. Uninfluenced by those considerations which have been avowed by that portion of my colleagues who have voluntarily separated themselves from you—totally ignorant of any want of harmony in your cabinet, which either has, or ought to have impeded the operations of your administration, I perform this act simply in obedience to your will. I have not the slightest disposition to discuss the question of its propriety. It is true that in a government like ours, power is but a trust to be used for the benefit of those who have delegated it; and that circumstances might exist in which the necessity of self-vindication would justify such an inquiry. The first consideration belongs to those to whom we are both and equally accountable. From the influence of the second you have relieved me by your own explicit declaration that no complaint affecting either my official or individual conduct has at any time reached you. You have assured me that the confidence which induced you originally to confer the appointments upon me remains unshaken and undiminished, and have been pleased to express the regret which you feel at the separation which circumstances have, in your view of the subject, rendered unavoidable. You have kindly added the assurance of your continued good wishes for my welfare. You will not, therefore, refuse to me the gratification of expressing my earnest hope that, under the influence of better counsels, your own and the interests of our common country may receive all the benefits which you have anticipated from the change of your confidential advisers. A very few days will suffice to enable me to put my office in a condition for the reception of my successor, and I will advise you of the fact as soon as its arrangement is complete.

"I am, respectfully, sir, your obedient servant,

"JNO. MACPHERSON BERRIEN.

"To the President of the United States."

THE PRESIDENT TO MR. BERRIEN.

"WASHINGTON, June 15, 1831.

"SIR: I have received your letter resigning the office of Attorney-General.

"In the conversation which I held with you, the day before yesterday, upon this subject, it was my desire to present to you the considerations upon which I acted in accepting the resignation of the other members of the cabinet, and to assure you, in regard to yourself, as well as to them, that they imply no dissatisfaction with the manner in which the duties of the respective departments have been performed. It affords me great pleasure to find that you have not misconceived the character of those considerations, and that you do justice to the personal feelings with which they are unconnected.

"I will only add that the determination to change my cabinet was dictated by an imperious sense of public duty, and a thorough, though painful conviction, that the stewardship of power with which I am clothed called for it as a measure of justice to those who had been alike invited to maintain near me the relation of confidential advisers. Perceiving that the harmony in feeling so necessary to an efficient administration had failed, in a considerable degree, to mark the course of this, and having assented, on this account, to the voluntary retirement of the Secretaries of State and War, no alternative was left me but to give this assent a latitude coextensive with the embarrassments which it recognized, and the duty which I owed to each member of the cabinet.

"In accepting your resignation as Attorney-General, I take pleasure in expressing my approbation of the zeal and efficiency with which its duties have been performed, and in assuring you that you carry with you my best wishes for your prosperity and happiness.

"I am, very respectfully, your obedient servant,

"ANDREW JACKSON.

"JOHN M. BERRIEN, Esq."

"P. S.—You will please to continue to discharge the duties of the office of Attorney-General until you make all those arrangements which you may deem necessary, on which, when completed, and I am notified thereof by you, a successor will be appointed. A. J."

MR. BERRIEN TO THE PRESIDENT.

"WASHINGTON, June 22, 1831.

"SIR: In conformity to the suggestion contained in my note of the 15th instant, I have to inform you that the arrangements necessary to put the office of Attorney-General in a condition for the reception of my successor are now complete.

"The misrepresentations which are circulated in the newspapers on the subject of my retirement from office, make it proper that this correspondence should be submitted to the public, as an act of justice both to you and to myself. I am, respectfully, sir, your obedient servant,

"JNO. MACPHERSON BERRIEN.

"To the President of the United States."

THE PRESIDENT TO MR. BERRIEN.

"WASHINGTON, June 22, 1831.

"SIR: Your note of this day is received, advising me, in 'conformity to the suggestions contained in my (your) note of the 15th instant. I (you) have to inform you (me) that the arrangements necessary to put the office of the Attorney-General in a condition for the reception of my successor are now complete.'

"For reasons assigned in your note, you further observe, 'make it proper that this correspondence should be submitted to the public, as an act of justice both to you and myself.' I am sure I can have no objection to your submitting them as you propose, as you believe this to be necessary. I am, respectfully, your obedient servant, ANDREW JACKSON.

"JOHN M. BERRIEN, Esq."

A dissolution of the cabinet except at the end of a presidential term, had never before occurred in the United States, and has occurred but once since. So unexpected was this event (the general public having received no intimation of the Eatonian scandals, and not immediately discerning the connection between the cabinet explosion and Mr. Calhoun's pamphlet) that a slight rumor of some approaching change was ridiculed in the Jackson papers within three days of the announcement of Mr. Van Buren's resignation. It produced a prodigious sensation. At that day, all official distinctions were more valued than they now are, and a cabinet minister was regarded as an exceedingly great man. It seemed as if the Republic itself was shaken when the great city of Washington was agitated, as all the hive is wild when the queen-bee is missing. It added to the effect of the dissolution, that the leading editors would not, and the editors-in-ordinary could not give any sufficient explanation of the event. Some vague allusions to 'Madame Pompadour' found their way into print, but the Jackson papers hurled fierce anathemas at those who gave them currency.

The journals in the confidence of the administration had evidently received their cue, however, and strove to make the dissolution redound to the glory of Mr. Van Buren. The comments of the *Courier and Enquirer* will amuse the reader, I think. When the following remarks were written, the resignation of Mr. Berrien, owing to his absence from Washington, had not occurred:

"What has Mr. Calhoun gained by the firebrand he has thrown into the democratic ranks? Mr. Van Buren it is true has retired from office, but he returns to a State where his political knowledge and consistency are invaluable—a State that can and will support him for the highest office when the proper time arrives. Mr. Calhoun has strengthened Mr. Van Buren by his violent opposition—he has returned from the cabinet and is thrown back on the people with a higher reputation for disinterested zeal and upright principles. In this movement, however, Mr. Calhoun has sacrificed Mr. Ingham and Mr. Branch, his two friends; and the members of the new cabinet are not assailable on any point. How stands the case, then? General Jackson has lost two friends in his cabinet and gained four. Mr. Van Buren becomes a private citizen, and mingles again with his political friends in an energetic support of the President. On all sides General Jackson is strengthened and his enemies discomfited; well indeed, may Mr. Van Buren be called the 'great Magician,' for he raises his wand and the whole cabinet vanishes.

"What will Mr. Calhoun now say to this new order of things? His friends will not venture to declare that Mr. Van Buren rules General Jackson—they can not say that Mr. Van Buren at Albany manages the affairs of the administration at Washington. All motives for assailing Mr. Van Buren are at an end; trouble and difficulty have been produced, but on whom does it fall—who suffers, who almost staggers under the blow? Mr. Calhoun and his imprudent advisers."

This view of the case commended itself to the judgment of a majority of the people, who are apt to relish a bold measure, whatever its moral quality. The comments of the opposition seemed rather to injure than to benefit their cause. One paper in Cincinnati said: "Let John C. Calhoun shake off all affectation of respect for the presumptuous and ignorant dotard, who enjoys the salary and subscribes his name as President." Such language merely enraged and disgusted the friends of the President, and offended some of his opponents. The *New York American* published the following:

"*To the Hero—Touching his 'Unit.'*
Your rats united might have been,
But, should we judge from actions,
We 'd say, although a 'Unit' then,
They now are *Vulgar* fractions."

Mr. Van Buren returned to New York, where his friends received him triumphantly. Early in August, Mr. McLane arrived from London, and Mr. Van Buren, soon after, went abroad as American Minister to the Court of St. James. Mr. Livingston reigned over the State Department in his stead. Mr. Woodbury was duly appointed Secretary of the Navy.

On one point only did the scheme of the President fail of

success. Judge White refused, point blank, to accept the place of Secretary of War, and thus create a vacancy in the Senate for Major Eaton. He had been, for some time, jealous of Mr. Van Buren's ascendency in the councils of the President, an ascendency to which he had himself aspired, and which, for a short period, he had been thought to enjoy. Perhaps he had indulged hopes of being adopted as the successor of General Jackson; for General Jackson had shown him his list of rules for the guidance of his administration, one of which was that no member of the cabinet should succeed him. The General, too, had written to him, in October, 1828, as soon as his election to the presidency was felt to be certain, in terms which appeared to justify such an expectation. "I thank you kindly," wrote the General, "for the suggestions you have made, and will always thank you for your friendly counsel. We have grown up together, have passed to the top and over the hill of life together, and permit me to assure you there is *no one* in whom I have greater confidence, in their honor, integrity, and judgment than in yours." Again, in December: "It will give me pleasure at all times to receive your views upon all and every subject; you have my confidence and friendship, and to you and Major Eaton I look as my confidential friends." Again, in the autumn of 1829, the President had written to him in the most affectionate terms, almost imploring him not to resign his seat in the Senate, where his services had been so efficient, and were still so much desired.

Gradually, however, the President seemed to be estranged from his old friend. So, at least, thought some of the associates of Judge White. Mr. Tazewell, a friend of both, recorded his observations. "Judge White," he says, "was one, and, I believe, the most confidential of all the President's advisers, as well before as after his inauguration, while the Senate continued in session. When the Senate adjourned in 1829, Judge White went home and did not return until the commencement of the next session. I was prevented from taking my place in that body until February, 1830.

54

Very soon after I took my seat, I saw very plainly that new relations had sprung up between the President and some of his former friends. Judge White did not seem to have observed this; and his feelings toward General Jackson remained unchanged, although it was evident to all others, that he no longer occupied the same place in the estimation of the President which he had done. I never knew the cause of this apparent estrangement, but thought it might be easily conjectured."

Was it in human nature, that Judge White should not detest Mr. Van Buren? Knowing well that one object of this dissolution of the cabinet was Mr. Van Buren's elevation, he would not be prevailed upon to lend a helping hand. It is asserted by Colonel Benton, but denied by the biographer of Judge White, that the aspirations of his wife were the spur to his own ambition.

When it was known that Judge White had declined a place in the cabinet, the most extraordinary exertions were made by the President and his friends to induce him to change his purpose. Mr. J. K. Polk, General Coffee, Mr. 55 Grundy, Mr. Catron, General Armstrong, and other Tennessee friends wrote to him, entreating him to accept. General Armstrong's letter was familiar and fervent. "I have just parted from the President," he wrote on the 1st of May. "He informs me, confidentially, that you have declined the office of Secretary of War. The old man said he wrote you yesterday, urging you still to accept. I know your friendship for the President, and I know, too, Judge, the sacrifices you have ever been willing to make for the love of your country. I write this at the request of the old General, because he says I have been present here, and can describe plainly to you the situation of things as they are. The old man says, that *all his plans will be defeated unless you agree to come*, should it be but for a period short of the continuance of his administration. The public have settled down on you, Judge, as the man. The wishes and confidence of every one seem to require your acceptance. Nothing that you can offer will satisfy your friends; because, as the old man says—this is a crisis in which he wishes his best friends to be with him—and you well know that you are the nearest; so he declares, Judge. Now for my own views. The good of the country—the honor of your best friend—the character of the State—and, lastly, it must not be said that aid is refused the old chief from Tennessee, and that, too, by Judge White. Judge, pardon me for attempting to influence you. I write because I know you will do one thing, and that is, believe what I say. Could you but witness the anxiety of the General, and the distress that follows, under the supposition that you will not join him, I know you would yield."

But, no. He did not yield. The *Courier and Enquirer* informed the public that Judge White, of Tennessee, on account of severe domestic afflictions, had declined the office of Secretary of War, which the President had offered him. From that time to the end of his life, Judge White was *taboo* among the extreme Jacksonians. No more were his public labors extolled in the *Globe;* no more was his advice asked upon important measures. He went into opposition, at length; was feebly run for President against Mr. Van Buren; and was driven, finally, into retirement.

A new man was summoned to the councils of the President, Lewis Cass, Governor of the Territory of Michigan, who was installed as head of the Department of War in July. Though little known, at that day, to the country at large, Governor Cass had been for nearly a quarter of a century in the service of the government. It was he who, as member of the Ohio Legislature in 1806, originated the measures against Aaron Burr which caused the explosion of that individual's Mexican projects. Born in New Hampshire to a revolutionary father, Lewis Cass trudged on foot across the Alleghanies, when he was but seventeen, to seek his fortune in the western wilderness. He studied law, and became a leading man in Ohio; won the notice and favor of President Jefferson by his zeal against Burr, and received the appointment of marshal. He served with ability and distinction through the war of 1812, fighting at the battle of the Thames by the side of General Harrison, as his volunteer aid-de-camp. President Madison appointed him, in 1813, Governor of Michigan, a post which he held for the unusual period of nineteen years, until he was invited by General Jackson to the Cabinet in 1831.

The vacant Attorney-Generalship was conferred upon Mr. Roger B. Taney, then Attorney-General of Maryland, now the Chief Justice of the Supreme Court of the United States. Mr. Taney was a lawyer of the first distinction in his native State. He was one of the Federalists who had given a zealous support to General Jackson in 1828.

Louis McLane, who came from England to take the office of Secretary of the Treasury, was a native of Delaware, where he studied law under James A. Bayard, known in political history as the friend and correspondent of Alexander Hamilton. Mr. McLane, also, was a gentleman of the Federalist persuasion, and a friend to the Bank of the United States. He had distinguished himself, in London, by the zeal and ability with which he conducted important negotiations, and was supposed to be one of the numerous gentlemen then living who indulged hopes of attaining the presidency.

As the disruption of the Cabinet occurred in April, and Mr. McLane did not return to the United States until August, there was an interregnum in the Treasury Department of more than three months, during which disgraceful events occurred. A few weeks after the dissolution, the scandalous stories respecting Mrs. Eaton began to circulate in the newspapers, and, at length, the various narratives of Messrs. Ingham, Branch, and Berrien appeared. Poor Eaton, stung to madness by the exposure, was betrayed into writing one of the absurdest notes to Mr. Ingham ever penned by an angry man. A hostile correspondence was the first result.

MR. EATON TO MR. INGHAM.

"FRIDAY NIGHT, June 17, 1831.

"SIR: I have studied to disregard the abusive slanders which have arisen through so debased a source as the columns of the *U. S. Telegraph.*

I have been content to wait for the full development of what he had to say, and until persons of responsible character should be brought forth to endorse his vile abuse of me and my family. In that paper of this evening is contained the following remark of my wife: 'It is proved that the Secretaries of the Treasury, and of the Navy, and of the Attorney-General refused to associate with her.' This publication appears in a paper which professes to be friendly to you, and is brought forth under your immediate eye. I desire to know of you, whether or not you sanction, or will disavow it.

"The relation we have sustained toward each other, authorizes me to demand an immediate answer. Very respectfully,

"J. H. EATON.

"S. D. INGHAM, Esq."

MR. INGHAM TO MR. EATON.

"WASHINGTON, June 18, 1831.

"SIR: I have not been able to ascertain, from your note of last evening, whether it is the publication referred to by you, or the fact stated in the *Telegraph*, which you desire to know whether I have sanctioned or will disavow. If it be the first you demand, it is too absurd to merit an answer. If it be the last, you may find authority for the same fact in a Philadelphia paper, about the first of April last, which is deemed to be quite as friendly to you as the *Telegraph* may be to me. When you have settled such accounts with your particular friends, it will be time enough to make demands of others. In the meantime, I take the occasion to say, that you must be a little deranged, to imagine that any blustering of yours could induce me to disavow what all the inhabitants of this city know, and perhaps half the people of the United States believe to be true.

"I am, sir, respectfully yours, S. D. INGHAM.

"JOHN H. EATON, Esq."

MR. EATON TO MR. INGHAM.

"June 18, 1831.

"SIR: I have received your letter of to-day, and regret to find that to a frank and candid inquiry brought before you, an answer impudent and insolent is returned. To injury unprovoked, you are pleased to add insult. What is the remedy! It is to indulge the expectation that, though a man may be mean enough to slander, or base enough to encourage it, he yet may have bravery sufficient to repair the wrong. In that spirit I demand of you *satisfaction* for the wrong and injury you have done me.

"Your answer must determine whether you are so far entitled to the name and character of a gentleman as to be able to act like one.

"Very respectfully, J. H. EATON.

"SAMUEL D. INGHAM, Esq."

MR. INGHAM TO MR. EATON.

"WASHINGTON, June 20, 1831.

"SIR: Your note of Saturday, purporting to be a demand of satisfaction for injury done to you, was received on that day; company prevented me from sending an immediate answer. Yesterday morning your brother-in-law, Dr. Randolph, intruded himself into my room with a threat of personal violence. I perfectly understand the part you are made to play in the farce now acting before the American people. I am not to be intimidated by threats, or provoked by abuse, to any act inconsistent with the pity and contempt which your condition and conduct inspire.

"Yours, sir, respectfully, S. D. INGHAM.

"JOHN H. EATON, Esq."

MR. EATON TO MR. INGHAM.

"June 20, 1831.

"SIR: Your note of this morning is received. It proves to me that you are quite brave enough to do a mean action, but too great a coward to repair it. Your contempt I heed not; your pity I despise. It is such contemptible fellows as yourself that have set forth rumors of their own creation, and taken them as a ground of imputation against me. If that be good cause, then should you have pity of yourself, for your wife has not escaped them, and you must know it. But no more; here our correspondence closes. Nothing more will be received short of an acceptance of my demand of Saturday, and nothing more be said to me until face to face we meet. It is not in my nature to brook your insults, nor will they be submitted to. J. H. EATON.

"S. D. INGHAM, Esq."

The next day Eaton attempted to carry his threat into execution. In a letter to the President, Mr. Ingham gave a version of the events of that day: "It is not necessary for me now to detail the circumstances which have convinced me of the existence of vindictive personal hostility to me among some of the officers of the government near your person, and supposed to be in your special confidence, which has been particularly developed within the last two weeks, and has finally displayed itself in an attempt to waylay me on my way to my office yesterday, as I have reason to believe, for the purpose of assassination. If you have not already been apprised of these movements, you may perhaps be surprised to learn that the persons concerned in them are the late Secretary of War and the acting Secretary of War; and that the Second Auditor of the Treasury, Register of the Treasury, and the Treasurer of the United States, were in their company; and that the Treasurer's and Register's rooms, in the lower part of the building of the Treasury Department, and also a grocery store between my lodgings and the office, were alternately occupied as their rendezvous while lying in wait—the former affording the best opportunity for observing my approach. Apprised of these movements, on my return from taking leave of some of my friends, I found myself obliged to arm, and, accompanied by my son and some other friends, I repaired to the office to finish the business of the day, after which I returned to my lodgings in the same company. It is proper to state, that the principal persons who had been thus employed for several hours, retired from the Department soon after I entered my room, and that I received no molestation from them, either at my ingress or egress. But having recruited an additional force in the evening, they paraded until a late hour on the streets near my lodgings, heavily armed, threatening an assault on the dwelling I reside in."

The President immediately addressed a letter to each of the officials charged with waylaying Mr. Ingham, enclosed to each a copy of Mr. Ingham's letter, and asked to be informed whether "you, or either of you, have had any agency or participation, and if any, to what extent, in the alleged misconduct imputed in his letter herewith enclosed." Every man of them denied in toto the accusations of Mr. Ingham. They were also exculpated by Major Eaton, in a card published in the *Globe.* "From the moment" said Eaton, "that I perceived Mr. Ingham was incapable of acting as became a man, I resolved to pursue that course which was suited to the character of one who had sought difficulties and shunned all honorable accountability. I harbored no design upon the heart of one who had shown himself so heartless. Having ascertained that his sensibilities were to be found only upon the surface, I meant to make the proper application. On the

19th I notified him that unless the *call* I had made upon him was promptly and properly answered, he might expect such treatment as I thought his conduct deserved. My note of the 20th also advised him of my intention. Accordingly it appeared matter of duty for me to dissolve all connection with the administration of the government. How, then, can Mr. Ingham suppose that I would involve those gentlemen in a disgraceful conspiracy against him; one in which, as public officers, they could not engage even if inclination had sanctioned. Their own characters are a sufficient answer to the accusation, unaided by their positive denial of its truth. I did endeavor to meet Mr. Ingham, and to settle our difference. Unattended by any one, I sought after and awaited his appearance during the accustomed hours for business, openly and at places where he daily passed to his office. He was not to be found! I passed by, but at no time stopped at or attempted to enter his house, nor to beseige it by day or by night."

The next day Mr. Ingham, finding the city of Washington neither a safe nor a comfortable dwelling-place, left it in disgust, and, the *Globe* said, in terror. He took the "whole of the four o'clock stage," said the *Globe*, and induced the driver to make excellent time to Baltimore. The President, soon after, gave Eaton the appointment of Governor of Florida, where he had lands and lots supposed to be valuable. At a later day, the President sent him to represent the United States at the court of Spain. Upon his return home, Eaton quarreled with his old chief, and remained unreconciled until the day of his death. Mrs. Eaton, in 1859, is still living in the city of Washington.

The dissolution, its causes, and its consequences, were the newspaper topic of the whole summer. The entire correspondence relating to it, beginning with the Calhoun pamphlet, and ending with Eaton's final statement, would form a volume as large as that which the reader is now holding in his hands. Among the documents is a labored, long, and tedious address by Mr. Crawford, justifying himself for betraying the proceedings of Mr. Monroe's Cabinet. Eaton's statement asserts many things, but proves nothing. He labors hard, but labors in vain, to show that the alleged irregularities of his wife were a mere pretext, and that the secret of the opposition to himself was, that he was not the friend of Mr. Calhoun.

The dissolution inspired the opposition with new, with extravagant hopes. "Who could have imagined," wrote Mr. Clay from his retirement, "such a cleansing of the Augean stable at Washington? a change, almost total, of the cabinet. Did you ever read such a letter as Mr. Van Buren's? It is perfectly characteristic of the man—a labored effort to conceal the true motives, and to assign assumed ones, for his resignation, under the evident hope of profiting by the latter. The 'delicate step,' I apprehend, has been taken, because, foreseeing the gathering storm, he wished early to secure a safe refuge. Whether that will be on his farm, or at London, we shall see. Meantime, our cause can not fail to be benefited by the measure. It is a broad confession of the incompetency of the President's chosen advisers, no matter from what cause, to carry on the business of the government."

This was written when the news of the explosion first reached Kentucky. Six weeks later, he wrote: "I think we are authorized, from all that is now before us, to anticipate confidently General Jackson's defeat. The question of who will be the successor, may be more doubtful. The probabilities are strongly with us. It seems to me that nothing can disappoint the hopes of our friends, but anti-Masonry." 56

Mr. Webster took a more serious view of the "prospect before us." He wrote to Mr. Clay, in October, urging his return to the Senate: "We are to have an interesting and an arduous session. Every thing is to be attacked. An array is preparing, much more formidable than has ever yet assaulted what we think the leading and important public interests. Not only the Tariff, but the Constitution itself, in its elementary and fundamental provisions, will be assailed with talent, vigor, and union. Every thing is to be debated, as if nothing had ever been settled."

True. Nullification hung like a dark cloud over the southern horizon. South Carolina was in a ferment. Unless the Tariff were rectified at the next session, South Carolina would do such things as then she knew not of. Mr. Calhoun, in the course of the summer, in an address that darkened all the first page of the largest newspaper then existing, avowed himself a believer in the doctrine of nullification. Perhaps, this address was a retort to the President's "Charleston letter," so famous in its day, which had delighted the country two months before. That Charleston letter has an interest for us still.

GENERAL JACKSON TO A COMMITTEE OF THE CITIZENS OF CHARLESTON.

"WASHINGTON CITY, June 14th, 1831.

"GENTLEMEN: It would afford me much pleasure, could I at the same time accept your invitation of the 5th instant, and that with which I was before honored by the municipal authorities of Charleston. A necessary attention to the duties of my office, must deprive me of the gratification I should have had in paying, under such circumstances, a visit to the State of which I feel a pride in calling myself a citizen by birth.

"Could I accept your invitation, it would be with the hope that all parties—all the men of talent, exalted patriotism, and private worth, who have been divided in the manner you describe, might be found united before the altar of their country on the day set apart for the solemn celebration of its independence—independence which can not exist without Union, and with it is eternal.

"Every enlightened citizen must know that a separation, could it be effected, would begin with civil discord, and end in colonial dependence on a foreign power, and obliteration from the list of nations. But he should also see that high and sacred duties which must and will, at all hazards, be performed, present an insurmountable barrier to the success of any plan of disorganization, by whatever patriotic name it may be decorated, or whatever high feelings may be arrayed for its support. The force of these evident truths, the effect they must ultimately have upon the minds of those who seem for a moment to have disregarded them, make me cherish the belief I have expressed, that could I have been present at your celebration, I should have found all parties concurring to promote the object of your association. You have distinctly expressed that object—'to revive in its full force the benign spirit of the Union, and to renew the mutual confidence in each other's good will and patriotism.' Such endeavors, calmly and firmly persevered in, can not fail of success. Such sentiments are appropriate to the celebration of that high festival, which commemorates the simultaneous declaration of Union and Independence—and when on the return of that day, we annually renew the pledge that our heroic fathers made, of life, of fortune, and of sacred honor, let us never forget that it was given to sustain us as a *United* not less than an *Independent* people.

"Knowing, as I do, the private worth and public virtues of distinguished citizens to whom declarations inconsistent with an attachment to the Union have been ascribed, I can not but hope, that if accurately reported, they were the effect of momentary excitement, not deliberate design; and that such men can never have formed the project of pursuing a course of redress through any other than constitutional means; but if I am mistaken in this charitable hope, then, in the language of the Father of our country, I would conjure them to estimate properly 'the immense value of your national Union to your collective and individual happiness;' to cherish 'a cordial, habitual, and immovable attachment to it; accustoming yourselves to think and speak of it as of the palladium of your political safety and prosperity, watching for its preservation with jealous anxiety: discountenancing whatever may suggest even a suspicion that it can, in any event, be abandoned; and indignantly frowning upon the first dawning of every attempt to alienate any portion of our country from the rest, or to enfeeble the sacred ties which now link together the various parts.'

"Your patriotic endeavors, gentlemen, to lessen the violence of party dissension, can not be forwarded more effectually than by inculcating a reliance on the justice of our National Councils, and pointing to the fast approaching extinction of the public debt, as an event which must necessarily produce modification in the revenue system, by which all interests, under a spirit of mutual accommodation and concession, will be probably protected.

"The grave subjects introduced in your letter of invitation, have drawn from me the frank exposition of opinions, which I have neither interest nor inclination to conceal.

"Grateful for the kindness you have personally expressed, I renew my expressions of regret that it is not in my power to accept your kind invitation; and have the honor to be, with great respect,

"Your obedient and humble servant, ANDREW JACKSON."

That dread disease, the cholera, was first heard of in the United States this year. It was ravaging some portions of Europe, and making startling advances northward. Long the hope was cherished that the Atlantic ocean would arrest the progress of the scourge. The country escaped it in 1831.

XV.

THE BANK-VETO SESSION.

THIS was the great session of Jackson's administration. The session of Congress preceding a presidential campaign is always exciting, and generally important; but none since the earliest years of the republic has been so exciting or so important as this. Illustrious names, great debates, extraordinary incidents, momentous measures, combine to render it memorable.

Strengthened by Mr. Clay's return to the Senate, and supposed to be strengthened by Mr. Calhoun's defection, magnificently endowed with talent, and supplied with every motive to exertion which can inflame ambition or stimulate patriotism, the opposition did all its utmost to lessen the public confidence in an administration which they believed to be, not the most corrupt one ever known in the United States, but the only one that had been corrupt. The "Old Man" of the White House was the strength and inspiration of the party in power. He watched the transactions at the capitol with the eye of a lynx, and the patient resolution of a man who only knows the two alternatives, to carry his point or perish. On the great question of the session he was almost alone. Not one man in his cabinet entirely sympathized with him. It was only in Col. Benton and some members of the kitchen cabinet that he found the complete acquiescence that was so dear, but, at the same time, so unnecessary to him. "Of all the men I have known," said Mr. Blair to me, "Andrew Jackson was the one most entirely sufficient for himself." Not only had he no such word as *fail*, but no belief, not the slightest, that he could fail in any thing seriously undertaken by him. And he never did.

In the Senate of this Congress were Daniel Webster, Henry Clay, William Marcy, Theodore Frelinghuysen, Geo. M. Dallas, John M. Clayton, John Tyler, Robert Y. Hayne,

John Forsyth, Felix Grundy, Hugh L. White, George Poindexter, William R. King, Thomas H. Benton, Isaac Hill. In the house—John Quincy Adams, Rufus Choate, Edward Everett, C. C. Cambreleng, Erastus Root, Gulian C. Verplanck, John Branch, George McDuffie, John Adair, Richard M. Johnson, John Bell, James K. Polk, Thomas Corwin, C. C. Clay.

Curiously enough, the message was one of the quietest and shortest ever presented to Congress by General Jackson. The previous practice of defending the measures of the administration by elaborate argument, and preventing attack by anticipating it, was abandoned in the concoction of this document. It showed everywhere the touch of another hand. The diplomatic successes of the government, which had been numerous during the year, though not of striking importance, were set forth at length. The President concluded this portion of the message with a passage which, besides doing brave duty upon banners and in campaign papers, was quoted with applause in foreign countries. "I have great satisfaction in making this statement of our affairs, because the course of our national policy enables me to do it without any indiscreet exposure of what in other governments is usually concealed from the people. Having none but a straightforward, open course to pursue—guided by a single principle that will bear the strongest light—we have happily no political combinations to form, no alliances to entangle us, no complicated interests to consult; and in subjecting all we have done to the consideration of our citizens, and to the inspection of the world, we give no advantage to other nations, and lay ourselves open to no injury." Edward Livingston had occasion to remember the latter part of this passage a year or two later.

Railroads, then a leading topic, and beginning to assume national importance, were mentioned with felicitations. "We have a reasonable prospect," said the President, "that the extreme parts of our country will be so much approximated, and those most isolated by the obstacles of nature rendered so accessible, as to remove an apprehension, sometimes entertained, that the great extent of the Union would endanger its permanent existence."

The financial condition of the country was extremely satisfactory. The revenue of the year had reached the unprecedented amount of $27,700,000. The expenditures, exclusive of the public debt, would not exceed $14,700,000. Not less than sixteen and a half millions of the public debt had been paid off during the year. The President did not conceal his exultation at this pleasant state of things. "The amount," he added, "which will have been applied to the public debt from the fourth of March, 1829, to the first of January next, which is less than three years since the administration has been placed in my hands, will exceed forty millions of dollars."

In view of the speedy extinction of the debt, Congress was notified that the chief business of the session must be to adjust the tariff to the new state of affairs; but the subject was disposed of in a single paragraph, and nothing further was said of dividing the surplus revenue among the States.

Again, the recommendation respecting the election of President and Vice-President by a direct vote of the people was repeated. Again the message closed with a warning to the United States bank. "Entertaining," said the President, "the opinions heretofore expressed in relation to the bank of the United States, as at present organized, I felt it my duty in my former messages frankly to disclose them, in order that the attention of the legislature and the people should be seasonably directed to that important subject, and that it might be considered and finally disposed of in a manner best calculated to promote the ends of the constitution and subserve the public interests. Having thus conscientiously discharged a constitutional duty, I deem it proper, on this occasion, without a more particular reference to the views of the subject then expressed, to leave it for the present to the investigation of an enlightened people and their representatives."

Of the transactions of this session, we need concern ourselves only with those that grew directly out the President's own course, and those which directly influenced his subsequent conduct.

Without delay, and, I believe, without debate, the Senate confirmed the nominations of Edward Livingston, Louis McLane, Levi Woodbury, Lewis Cass, and Roger M. Taney to their respective places in the cabinet. Not so the nomination of Mr. Van Buren to the post of British ambassador. Mr. Calhoun, at that time, in common with most of the opposition, attributed to the machinations of Mr. Van Buren his rupture with the President, and the dissolution of the cabinet. Mr. Clay and Mr. Webster were of opinion that it was Mr. Van Buren who had induced the President to adopt the New York system of party removals. Mr. Clay ought to have known the President and Mr. Van Buren better than to cherish an opinion so erroneous. But it seems he did not. And, certainly, Mr. Van Buren, by supporting the President in that bad system, and supplying him with plausible arguments to justify it, must ever be held to share in the responsibility of having debauched the public service. I believe, however, that so far from urging the new policy upon the President, his influence tended to lessen the number of removals.

The leaders of the Senate had resolved upon the rejection of Mr. Van Buren. They knew, before Congress came together, that this could be done, and they had discovered an available pretext for doing it. That pretext was found in the very transaction upon which the late Secretary of State plumed himself most, and which General Jackson esteemed the first and one of the most valuable triumphs of his administration.

We noticed, with surprise, that the first Message of General Jackson contained a compliment to Great Britain, a nation which the General, in 1814 and 1815, had characterized by a variety of uncomplimentary epithets, and concerning whose red-coated sons he had revolutionary recollections of a disagreeable character. The complimentary paragraph was inserted to aid Mr. McLane in a negotiation with the British ministry for regaining the privilege of trading with the British West Indies in American vessels. The negotiation, as we all know, was successful, and the great trade we now enjoy with those islands is chiefly the result of the treaty then concluded. Yet the pretext for rejecting Mr. Van Buren was found in a passage of one of his despatches to Mr. McLane in relation to the negotiation of that treaty—a passage which the President claimed as his own, and authorized a Senator to claim publicly for him. The following was the paragraph complained of:

"The opportunities which you have derived from a participation in our public councils, as well as other sources of information, will enable you to speak with confidence (as far as you may deem it proper and useful so to do) of the respective part taken by those to whom the administration of this government is now committed, in relation to the course heretofore pursued upon the subject of the colonial trade. *Their views upon that point have been submitted to the people of the United States; and the counsels by which your conduct is now directed are the result of the judgment expressed by the only earthly tribunal to which the late administration was amenable for its acts.* It should be sufficient that the claims set up by them, and which caused the interruption of the trade in question, have been explicitly abandoned by those who first asserted them, and are not revived by their successors. If Great Britain deems it adverse to her interests to allow us to participate in the trade with her colonies, and finds nothing in the extension of it to others to induce her to apply the same rule to us, she will, we hope, be sensible of the propriety of placing her refusal on those grounds. *To set up the acts of the late administration as the cause of forfeiture of privileges which would otherwise be extended to the people of the United States, would, under existing circumstances, be unjust in itself, and could not fail to excite their deepest sensibility.* The tone of feeling which a course so unwise and untenable is calculated to produce would, doubtless, be greatly aggravated by the consciousness that Great Britain has, by order in Council, opened her colonial ports to Russia and France, notwithstanding a similar omission on their part to accept the terms offered by the act of July, 1825.

"You can not press this view of the subject too earnestly upon the consideration of the British ministry. It has bearings and relations that reach beyond the immediate question under discussion."

"Now," said Mr. Webster, "this is neither more nor less than saying to Mr. McLane: 'You will be able to tell the British minister, whenever you think proper, that you, and I, and the leading persons in this administration, have opposed the course heretofore pursued by the government and the country, on the subject of the colonial trade. Be sure to let him know that, on that subject, *we* have held with *England*, and *not* with *our own government*.'" Mr. Webster added: "Sir, I submit to you, and to the candor of all just men, if I am not right in saying that the pervading topic throughout the whole is, not American rights, not American interests, not American defense, but denunciation of past *pretensions* of our own country, reflections on the past administrations, and exultation, and a loud claim of merit for the administration now in power. Sir, I would forgive mistakes; I would pardon the want of information; I would pardon almost any thing, where I saw true patriotism and sound American feeling; but I can not forgive the sacrifice of this feeling to mere Party. I can not concur in sending abroad a public agent who has not conceptions so large and liberal, as to feel that in the presence of foreign courts, amidst the monarchies of Europe, he is to stand up for his country, and his whole country; that no jot nor tittle of her honor is to come to harm in his hands; that he is not to suffer others to reproach either his government or his country, and far less is he himself to reproach either; that he is to have no objects in his eye but American objects, and no heart in his bosom but an American heart; and that he is to forget self, to forget party, to forget every sinister and narrow feeling, in his proud and lofty attachment to the Republic whose commission he bears."

The debate was animated but brief. Fifty-one days, Colonel Benton informs us, were consumed in the preliminary maneuvers, but the debates lasted but two. It was in the course of this discussion that Governor Marcy let fall an expression which he acknowledged, when he was writing out his speech, that he would have willingly recalled. He had the honesty to place it upon record, and it has since become famous. It occurred at the end of the following passage: "I know, sir, that it is the habit of some gentlemen to speak with censure or reproach of the politics of New York. Like other States, we have contests, and, as a necessary consequence, triumphs and defeats. The State is large, with great and diversified interests; in some parts of it, commerce is the object of general pursuit; in others, manufacture and agriculture are the chief concerns of its citizens. We have men of enterprise and talents, who aspire to public distinction. It is natural to expect from these circumstances and others that might be alluded to, that her politics should excite more interest at home, and attract more attention abroad, than those of many other States in the Confederacy. It may be, sir, that the politicians of New York are not so fastidious as some gentlemen are as to disclosing the principles on which they act. They boldly preach what they practice. When they are contending for victory, they avow their intention of enjoying the fruits of it. If they are defeated, they expect to retire from office; if they are successful, they claim, as a matter of right, the advantages of success. They see nothing wrong in the rule, that to the victor belongs the spoils of the enemy."

Mr. Van Buren found an able defender in Governor Forsyth of Georgia. "Long known to me," said Mr. Forsyth, "as a politician and as a man, acting together in the hour of political adversity, when we had lost all but our honor—a witness of his movements when elevated to power, and in the possession of the confidence of the chief magistrate, and of the great majority of the people, I have never witnessed aught in Mr. Van Buren which requires concealment, palliation, or coloring—never any thing to lessen his character as a patriot and as a man—nothing which he might not desire to see exposed to the scrutiny of every member of this body, with the calm confidence of unsullied integrity. He is called an artful man—a giant of artifice—a wily magician. Those ignorant of his unrivaled knowledge of human character, his power of penetrating into the designs, and defeating the purposes of his adversaries, seeing his rapid advance to public honors, and popular confidence, impute to art what is the natural result of those simple causes. Extraordinary talent, untiring industry, incessant vigilance, the happiest temper, which success can not corrupt nor disappointment sour; these are the sources of his unexampled success—the magic arts—the artifices of intrigue, to which only he has resorted in his eventful life. Those who envy his success, may learn wisdom from his example."

The nomination of Mr. Van Buren was rejected. Colonel Benton in his "Thirty Years, View," gives us some rare glimpses into the Senate chamber while the deed was in progress: "It was Mr. Gabriel Moore, of Alabama, who sat near me, and to whom I said, when the vote was declared, 'You have broken a minister, and elected a vice-president.' He asked me how? and I told him the people would see nothing in it but a combination of rivals against a competitor, and would pull them all down, and set him up. 'Good God!' said he, 'why didn't you tell me that before I voted, and I would have voted the other way.'"

. . . .

"On the evening of the day, on the morning of which all the London newspapers heralded the rejection of the American minister, there was a great party at Prince Talleyrand's —then the representative at the British court, of the new King of the French, Louis Philippe. Mr. Van Buren, always master of himself, and of all the proprieties of his position, was there, as if nothing had happened; and received distinguished attention, and complimentary allusions. Lord Aukland, grandson to the Mr. Eden who was one of the Commissioners of Conciliation sent to us at the beginning of the revolutionary troubles, said to him, 'It is an advantage of a public man to be the subject of an outrage'—a remark, wise in itself, and prophetic in its application to the person to whom it was addressed. He came home—apparently gave himself no trouble about what had happened—was taken up by the people—elected, successively, Vice-President and President—while none of those combined against him ever attained either position.

"There was, at the time, some doubt among their friends as to the policy of the rejection, but the three chiefs were positive in their belief that a senatorial condemnation would be political death. I heard Mr. Calhoun say to one of his doubting friends, 'It will kill him, sir, kill him dead. He will never kick, sir, never kick;' and the alacrity with which he gave the casting votes, on the two occasions, both vital, on which they were put into his hands, attested the sincerity of his belief, and his readiness for the work. How those tie-votes, for there were two of them, came to happen twice, 'hand-running,' and in a case so important, was matter of marvel and speculation to the public on the outside of the locked-up senatorial door. It was no marvel to those on the inside, who saw how it was done. The combination had a superfluity of votes, and, as Mr. Van Buren's friends were every one known, and would sit fast, it only required the superfluous votes on one side to go out; and thus an equilibrium between the two lines was established. When all was finished, the injunction of secrecy was taken off the proceedings, and the dozen set speeches delivered in secret session immediately published—which shows that they were delivered for effect, not upon the Senate, but upon the public mind."

The rejection secured Mr. Van Buren's political fortune. His elevation to the presidency, long before desired and intended by General Jackson, became, from that hour, one of his darling objects. The "party," also, took him up with a unanimity and enthusiasm that left the wire-pullers of the White House little to do. Letters of remonstrance and approbation, signed by influential members of the party, were sent over the sea to Mr. Van Buren, who soon found that his rejection was one of the most fortunate events of his public life. To one of these encouraging letters he forwarded a reply which did him no harm either with the party or the President. "In testifying to my public conduct," he wrote, "the Committee are pleased to speak with eulogium of me, as contributing while in the cabinet to the success of the present administration; that signal success, I feel called upon to declare, is preëminently due to the political sagacity, unwearying industry, and upright, straight forward course of our present venerated chief. All the humble merit I can claim is, that of having exerted myself to the utmost to execute his patriotic and single hearted views, and of having sacrificed all personal considerations to insure their success, when threatened with extraneous embarrassments. That my exertions were ardous, painful, and incessant, I may without vanity, assert: whether my sacrifices have not been repaid with unmerited detraction and reproach, I leave to my countrymen to determine. Still I shall ever regard my situation in that cabinet as one of the most fortunate events of my life, placing me as it did in close and familiar relation with one who has well been described by Mr. Jefferson as, 'possessing more of the Roman in his character than any man living,' and whose administration will be looked to, in future times, as a golden era in our history. To have served under such a chief, at such a time, and to have won his confidence and esteem, is a sufficient glory, and of that, thank God, my enemies can not deprive me."

It is generally supposed that it was the rejection of Mr. Van Buren by the Senate in 1832 that caused him to be adopted by the democratic party as their candidate for the vice-presidency in that year. Col. Benton appears to have been of that opinion. An attentive perusal of the *Globe* and *Courier and Enquirer* for 1831 will convince any one, I think, that before Mr. Van Buren sailed for England, he was the predestined candidate of the party for the second office. I have a curious letter on the subject, addressed in 1831 by Major Lewis to Amos Kendall, which contains an italicized word of much significance. In this letter was suggested, for the first time, the plan of nominating President and Vice-President by national convention—an idea borrowed from the politics of New York. The following gives an insight into the ways of politicians that the reader ought to prize highly:

MAJOR WM. B. LEWIS TO MR. AMOS KENDALL.

"WASHINGTON, 25th May, 1831.

"MY DEAR SIR: Yours of the 17th inst., written from Mr. Isaac Hill's, has been received. I am much gratified to learn that our friends in New Hampshire, and particularly Mr. Hill, are pleased with the appointment of Governor Woodbury. It is important that our friends everywhere should harmonize and act in concert, and particularly in the New England States, where it is by union alone they can expect to succeed.

"Your information with regard to our Boston friends accords with that which I have received from others. I have lately received several letters from Boston, and among them one from my friend D——, who gives a circumstantial account of Duff's visit to that place. If you see Mr. Derby, please present my respects to him, and say to him I have received his letter. I fear the offices in that place were injudiciously disposed of, as, from all accounts, the gentlemen who hold them look more to themselves than the individual who bestowed them. I am not so sure but it would have been better had they been given to the anti-Statesman party.

"I feel confident, however, that every reliance may be placed in the good feeling and fidelity of Parker, McNiel, and Derby. The postmaster, 57 N. Green, is with us, but I have not yet been favored with a visit from him. I have no doubt his trip to Washington is for the purpose of ascertaining how the land lies. If that be his object, I incline to the belief that he will not be much gratified at the information he will receive.

"I have had a conversation with several of our friends here upon the subject of the vice-presidency, and the universal opinion is that it is premature to *nominate* a candidate. There will be great difficulty in selecting an individual who will be satisfactory to the different local interests of the 58 Union. Mr. Barbour, it is feared, will not be acceptable to Pennsylvania 59 and New York; nor is it believed Dickinson would be willingly supported by the Southern anti-tariff States.

"Mr. McLane, I am inclined to think, would be the strongest man that could be run by the republican party; but there are almost insurmountable objections to him. Surrounded by so many difficulties as the case is, and taking every thing into consideration, many of our friends (and the most judicious of them) think it would be best for the republican members of the respective legislatures to propose to the people to elect delegates to a national convention, to be holden for that purpose, at Harrisburg, or some other place, about the middle of next May. That point is preferred to prevent an improper interference by members of Congress, who about that time will leave this city for their respective homes. If the friends of the administration, when brought together from every part of the Union, in convention, can not harmonize, I know of no other plan by which it can be done. If the legislature of New Hampshire will propose this, I think it will be followed up by others, and have the effect, no doubt, of putting a stop to partial nominations. You had better reflect upon this proposition, and, if you think with me, make the suggestion to our friend Hill.

"In your letter you say, 'Duff said Mr. Calhoun must be run for Vice-President again.' That this is their intention I have no doubt.

"You will see from the *Globe* that we had an unusually large meeting here last evening, friendly to the administration. It is said by those who were present to have been twice as large as the Clay meeting that preceded it. At this meeting it was proposed by one of Duff's partisans to add a preamble and resolutions approving Calhoun's conduct, and nominating him for reëlection as Vice-President. The General (Green) had his myrmidons judiciously arranged through the company for effect, and when the question for their adoption was proposed, they vociferated in their favor with prolonged voices. But it would not do; the resolutions were voted down by an overwhelming majority. Mr. Rives, your clerk, who was present, told me that out of a company of about seven hundred, he did not believe there were more than twenty or thirty in favor of the resolutions. Green, I am told, was very much mortified, and looked 'excessively cowed.' Dr. and Mrs. Sharpe have been with us. They left here yesterday. The Doctor, you know, was a strong Calhoun man; continued so until he saw Green; but Blair says he left cured of Calhounism. The General is rather an unfortunate agent for the Vice-President.

"Livingston and Woodbury have entered upon the duties of their respective departments. Judge White has again declined. I do not know who will be selected to fill the War Department, but am rather of the opinion that Col. Drayton will be the man. If so, it is not improbable but the President may offer the appointment of Attorney-General to John Bell, of Nashville. Those appointments, however, are not positively determined on. Every thing here looks well. The President is in good health, and looks well. Mr. Van Buren will leave, probably, the first week in June, and Mr. Eaton about the first of July. Please present my respects to Mrs. Kendall, and believe me to be sincerely yours,

"W. B. Lewis."

The suggestion with regard to holding a National Convention found favor in the eyes of Mr. Amos Kendall and

Mr. Isaac Hill, though they thought Baltimore a better place for the purpose than Harrisburg. Accordingly, we observe in the *Globe* of July 6th, 1831, one of those mysterious "Extracts from the Letter of a Gentleman" (in Concord, New Hampshire), which are so useful in political management. "The Republican members of the New Hampshire Legislature," said the Extract from the Letter of a Gentleman in Concord, Amos Kendall by name, "to the number of about 169 (whole number of members say 235) met last evening. An address and resolutions approving of the principles and measures of the present administration, the veto of the President on the Maysville Road bill, disavowing the doctrine of nullification, disapproving Clay's American system, but recommending a judicious reduction of the duties, disapproving of the United States Bank, passed the Convention unanimously. The Convention also recommended a General Convention of Republicans friendly to the election of General Jackson, to consist of delegates equal to the number of electors of President in each State, to be holden at Baltimore on the third Monday of May, 1832, to nominate a candidate for Vice-President, and take such other measures in support of the reëlection of Andrew Jackson as may be deemed expedient. The Republican party was never more harmonious and united in this State than at the present time. It is completely identified in the support of General Jackson; and it is entirely out of the power of the coalition to shake his popularity in this State. There is no point in which we are better agreed than in decided opposition to re-chartering the United States Bank."

The *Globe* seconded the motion of Major Lewis by appending a few "Remarks" to the Extract from the Letter of a Gentleman in Concord. "It is gratifying to perceive," said the editor of the *Globe*, "that the Bank Extras sent to the members of the New Hampshire Legislature, have only aroused them to the danger of giving prolonged existence to that institution. The recommendation of a Convention at Baltimore to nominate a candidate for the Vice-Presidency deserves a serious consideration. It is probably the best plan which can be adopted to produce entire unanimity in the Republican party, and secure its lasting ascendency."

Thus was prepared, beforehand, the machinery by which Mr. Van Buren was nominated, first for the vice-presidency, and, secondly, for the presidency; by which, too, he was afterward overthrown; by which all presidents and vice-presidents, since 1832, have been nominated. With the preparation of this machinery, which he has been accused of originating, he had nothing to do. Nor was he the inventor of it as employed in the politics of his native State.

Returning to the proceedings of Congress, we are compelled to notice a painful and disgraceful affair, in which General Houston, of Texas, was the principal actor. When we last parted with this distinguished man, he had just leaped over the breastwork of the Horseshoe Bend of the Tallapoosa, and had fallen wounded, all but mortally, in doing his duty as ensign of the thirty-ninth infantry. Since that day of terror and of glory, he had run a bright career, and had had various fortune. He had been Governor of Tennessee. He had represented Tennessee in the House of Representatives. But in 1830 he had come to Washington, broken in fortune, unhappy in his domestic circumstances, a suitor for governmental favor. He applied for a contract for supplying rations to the Indians that were about to be removed, at the public expense, beyond the Mississippi. The President was extremely desirous that he should have the contract—so desirous, that he seemed inclined to give it to him, contrary to the spirit of the law, which obliged it to be awarded to the lowest bidder. Colonel McKenney, the Superintendent of Indian Affairs, was of opinion that the rations could be supplied, at a profit, for less than seven cents per day for each Indian. Houston's bid was eighteen cents, which, McKenney thought, would afford a profit of thousands of dollars a week, and, indeed, was equivalent to the bestowal of a large fortune. He also contended that time should be allowed, after advertising for proposals, for bids to come in from the section of

60

country where the rations were to be furnished. Time was not allowed. The affair was hurried on toward consummation, and it looked, at one time, as though Houston would get the contract at his own price.

At this stage of the proceedings, Duff Green, then the friend, confidential editor, and adviser of the President, heard of the scheme, and, foreseeing the clamor that would arise in case the contract were so bestowed, went to the President to remonstrate against it. "I apologized for calling," he testified afterward before a Committee of the House, "by referring immediately to the contract; said that I was confident that it could be furnished for much less than I understood the department was about to give. The President said that they had ascertained that the ration had cost twenty-two cents; General Houston had gone on to New York, and had brought with him (or obtained) a wealthy partner (or security), and that the contract would be given to him at eighteen cents. I then referred to the price of beef, corn, etc., in the west, and said I was confident the rations could be furnished at six cents. He replied, quickly, 'Will *you* take it at *ten?*' I said, 'No, sir.' He then said, 'Will *you* take it at twelve cents? if you will, you shall have it at that.' I told him that I was not a bidder for the contract; that, although I was satisfied I could realize an immense sum upon such a contract, I was influenced to call upon him by a desire to serve him and the administration, and not by a wish to speculate; and left him."

Not satisfied with this interview, General Green addressed a letter, on the same day, to the Secretary of War on the subject. "After leaving you last evening," he wrote (March, 1830), "I examined, for the first time, your proposals for rations. From my knowledge of the prices of beef and corn in the Western States, I am confident that the proposed ration ought not to cost ten cents, yet I understand you to say that you expect to give from eighteen to twenty cents, and that the issue, at these prices, will amount to twelve thousand dollars per day. That a contract of such amount should be made without giving notice to the Western States, where the provisions must be purchased, will be a cause of attack; but when I read the advertisement, and see that it is so worded as not to convey an idea of the speculation it affords, and connect it with the fact, which is within my own knowledge, that it was prepared under the special advisement of General Houston, who has gone on to New York, and has brought on from there a wealthy partner to join him in the contract, I should be unfaithful to the administration, to General Jackson, and to myself, if I did not bring the subject before you in such a shape as to guard against the consequences which I foresee will follow any such contract as the one he contemplates. Such a contract may enrich a few who are concerned in it, but will destroy the confidence of the public, I fear, in the administration, and impair the fair fame of the President, which it is your duty and mine to guard. Will it not be well to extend the time, so as to enable the people of Missouri and Arkansas to bid?"

Upon further reflection, the President was so far convinced of his error as to give up the plan of furnishing the rations by contract. General Houston was disappointed and thrown upon Texas. And, perhaps, the United States owes the possession of that State to the failure of General Houston to obtain the contract for supplying the Indians.

Some of the facts here related having gained publicity, General Houston and his contract became the subject of many newspaper articles, satirical and vituperative. In the summer of 1831, Houston published a Proclamation of a comical nature, intended to neutralize those attacks:

"A PROCLAMATION!!!

"Whereas, I have recently seen a publication, originating in the Cherokee Nation, east of the Mississippi, dated '18th May, 1831,' and signed 'I. S.,' which said publication, or letter, has been republished in several newspapers, such as the *Kentucky Reporter*, *United States Telegraph*, etc., and as I presume it will find a general circulation, notwithstanding the absurd personalities which it contains; and as it is not the first which has found its way into the public prints, containing ridiculous and unfounded abuse of me:—Now know all men by these presents, that I, Sam. Houston, 'late Governor of the State of Tennessee,' do hereby declare to all scoundrels whomsoever, that they are authorized to accuse, defame, calumniate, traduce, slander, vilify, and libel me, to any extent, in personal or private abuse. And I do further proclaim, to whomsoever it may concern, that they are hereby permitted and authorized to write, indite, print, publish, and circulate the same, and that I will in nowise hold them responsible to me in law, nor honor, for either the use of the 'raw material,' or the fabrication of any, or all of the above named articles connected with the 'American System?' nor will I have recourse to nullification, in any case whatsoever, where a conviction would secure to the culprit the dignity of a penitentiary residence. And as some ingenuity has been already displayed in the exhibition of specimens, and others may be induced to invest a small capital in the business, from feelings of emulation and an itching after experiment, Be it known, for the especial encouragement of all scoundrels hereafter, as well as those who have already been engaged, that I do solemnly propose on the first day of April next, to give to the author of the most elegant, refined, and ingenious lie or calumny, a handsome gilt copy (bound in sheep) of the *Kentucky Reporter*, or a snug, plain copy of the *United States Telegraph* (bound in dog), since its commencement.

"Given under my hand and private seal (having no seal of office) at Nashville, in the State of Tennessee, 13th July, 1831.

"SAM. HOUSTON. [L. S.]"

In the spring of 1832 he was in Washington again, where he forgot his Proclamation. Before leaving the capital to enter upon his new and marvelous career in the Southwest, he was betrayed by his passions into the commission of an act which subjected him to the censure of the House of Representatives, and which he himself must, long ago, have learned to deplore. He committed a most atrocious and unprovoked assault upon a member of the House of Representatives, Mr. William Stanberry, of Ohio. The following correspondence explains itself:

GENERAL HOUSTON TO MR. WILLIAM STANBERRY.

"WASHINGTON CITY, April 3d, 1832.

"SIR: I have seen some remarks in the *National Intelligencer* of the 2d instant, in which you are represented to have said, 'Was the late Secretary of War removed in consequence of his attempt fraudulently to give to Governor Houston the contract for Indian Rations?'

"The object of this note is to ascertain whether my name was used by you in debate, and, if so, whether your remarks have been correctly quoted.

"As the remarks were inserted in anticipation of their regular place, I hope you will find it convenient to reply without delay. I am, your most obedient servant, SAM. HOUSTON."

WILLIAM STANBERRY TO CAVE JOHNSON.

"HOUSE OF REPRESENTATIVES, April 4th, 1832.

"SIR: I received this morning by your hands a note, signed Sam. Houston, quoting from the *National Intelligencer* of the 2d instant, a remark made by me in the House. The object of the note is to ascertain whether Mr. Houston's name was used by me in debate, and whether my remarks were correctly quoted.

"I can not recognize the right of Mr. Houston to make this request.

"Very respectfully yours, etc.,

"WILLIAM STANBERRY."

Exasperated by this reply, Houston made no secret of his intention to assault Mr. Stanberry, who, from that time, went armed to and from the capitol. Ten days elapsed, however, before the bad design of the irate Tennesseean was executed, and it was executed then with peculiar circumstances of atrocity. Senator Buckner, of Missouri, stood by and saw it done, and afterward testified without a blush, that he made no attempt to prevent the shameful deed. Houston, he said, was standing near a fence in one of the avenues, when Mr. Stanberry came along. "It occurred to me immediately, that there would be a difficulty between them. 'Are you Mr. Stanberry?' asked Houston. Stanberry replied very politely, bowing at the same time, 'Yes, sir.' 'Then,' said Houston, 'you are the damned rascal;' and with that, struck him with a stick which he had held in his hand. Stanberry threw up his hands over his head and staggered back. His hat fell off, and he exclaimed, 'Oh, don't!' Houston continued to follow him up, and continued to strike him. After receiving several severe blows, Stanberry turned, as I thought, to run off. Houston, at that moment, sprang upon him in the rear, Stanberry's arms hanging down, apparently defenceless. He seized him and attempted to throw him, but was

61

not able to do so. Stanberry carried him about on the pavement some little time. Whether he extricated himself, or Houston thrust him from him, I am not able to determine. I thought he thrust him from him. As Houston passed him, he struck him and gave him a trip—Stanberry fell. When he fell, he continued to halloo; indeed, he hallooed all the time pretty much, except when they were scuffling. I saw Stanberry, after receiving several blows, put out both hands, he then lying on his back. I did not discover what was in his hands, or if any thing was, but I heard a sound like the snapping of a gun-lock, and I saw particles of fire. Houston appeared to take hold of Stanberry's hands and took something from them which I could not see. After that, Houston stood up more erect, still beating Stanberry with a stick over the head, arms, and sides, Stanberry still keeping his arms spread out. After Houston had given him several more blows, he lay on his back and put up his feet. Houston then struck him *elsewhere*. Mr. Stanberry, after he had received several blows, ceased to halloo, and lay, as I thought, perfectly still. All this time I had not spoken to either of the parties, or interfered in any manner whatever. I now thought Stanberry was badly hurt, or, perhaps, killed, from the manner in which he lay. I stepped up to Houston to tell him to desist, but, without being spoken to, he quit of his own accord. Mr. Stanberry then got up on his feet, and I saw the pistol in the right hand of Gov. Houston for the first time."

On the day following, the Speaker of the House of Representatives received a note from Mr. Stanberry: "Sir, I was waylaid in the street, near to my boarding-house, last night about eight o'clock, and attacked, knocked down by a bludgeon, and severely bruised and wounded by Samuel Houston, late of Tennessee, for words spoken in my place in the House of Representatives, by reason of which I am confined to my bed, and unable to discharge my duties in the house, and attend to the interests of my constituents. I communicate this information to you, and request that you will lay it before the house."

The Speaker laid it before the house, and the house spent exactly one calendar month in debating the subject, hearing testimony, and the defense of the accused. James K. Polk, of Tennessee, distinguished himself by his zeal in endeavoring to prevent an investigation. The end of the matter in the house was that Houston was condemned to be reprimanded by the Speaker; and reprimanded he was, but in such a manner as to leave the house in no doubt that the Speaker (Andrew Stephenson) sympathized with the assailant rather than with the assailed—with General Houston rather than with the insulted house over which he presided.

General Jackson, I regret to be obliged to record, sustained his friend Houston in this bad deed. He said to a friend, in substance, that "after a few more examples of the same kind, members of Congress would learn to keep civil tongues in their heads." Perhaps the people of the United States will learn, after a few more examples of the same kind, that the man who replies to a word by a blow confesses by that blow the justice of that word. At a later day, when Houston was tried for this assault in a court of the District of Columbia, and was sentenced to pay a fine of five hundred dollars, the President nullified the proceeding by the little document annexed:

"I, Andrew Jackson, President of the United States of America, to the Marshal of the District of Columbia, greeting:

"Whereas, at a session of the Circuit Court of the United States, held in and for the county of Washington and District of Columbia, in the year 1832, a certain Samuel Houston was convicted of an assault and battery, and sentenced to pay a fine of five hundred dollars and costs of prosecution:

"Now be it known that I, Andrew Jackson, President of the United States of America, in consideration of the premises, divers good and sufficient reasons me thereunto moving, have remitted, and do hereby remit unto him, the said Samuel Houston, the fine aforesaid, in order that he be discharged from imprisonment.

"In testimony whereof I have hereunto subscribed my name, and caused the seal of the United States to be affixed to these presents.

Done at the city of Washington, this third day of July, A. D. 1834, and of the Independence of the United States the fifty-eighth.

"ANDREW JACKSON."

"By the President.

"JOHN FORSYTH, Secretary of State."

While the Houston affair was still the talk of the country, another member of Congress, Thomas D. Arnold, of Tennessee, was most grossly assaulted, and that, too, upon the very threshold of the house, and in the presence of a hundred members. A certain Major Heard thought proper to take offense at the zeal with which Mr. Arnold had denounced the conduct of Houston in the House of Representatives. Meeting Arnold in the streets, he attempted to assault him there, but was deterred by the member's resolute defiance. "I was accosted," said Mr. Arnold, in a card published in the *Telegraph*, "by a man of ruffian appearance, who required me to stop. I did so. He approached pretty near. I discovered he was very much agitated; his lip quivered, and he turned pale. He asked if my name was Arnold; I told him it was. He said, 'Then you are the man who abused my friend Houston so severely.' He was going to say something else, but the instant I saw the subject he had broached, I demanded to know his name. He replied his name was Heard, and added, Major Heard. I told him I knew nothing of him, and intended to have nothing to do with him. I fortunately had a walking-cane in my hand, and kept it in such a position that he saw I could strike as soon as he could. He wore a cap, and had a large stick in his hand; I think it was an orange limb, headed and feruled. I turned my back upon him as soon as I could do it in safety. As I walked off, he said he 'intended to whip me, *and that he would do it yet, by God*.' He did not pursue me, as I discovered. I do not wish to be protected by my constitutional privilege, but I think it due to the American people that they should know the state of things at this place."

A few days after, Heard accomplished his purpose. Just after the adjournment of the house, the ruffian fell upon Mr.

Arnold with a club, and failing to bring him to the ground with that weapon, fired a pistol at him. The ball grazed Arnold's arm and tore his coat, and passing over his shoulder, came within an ace of entering the body of Mr. Tazewell. Arnold felled the assailant to the ground with his cane, and was about to stab him with the sword thereof, when his arm was caught by a bystander, and Heard was taken to prison.

Having disposed of these personal matters, we may now proceed to affairs more important. The two great topics of the session were the tariff and the bank. The tariff bill passed at this session having been the direct cause of the nullification explosion, it will be convenient to defer our account of it until we come to speak of nullification. As the long session wore on, all other subjects were swallowed up in the discussion of the question, Shall the bank of the United States be re-chartered, or shall it not? Congress, the press, the President, the people, politicians, business men, all men, were drawn into the maelstrom of this great debate. We, too, for our sins, must skirt its borders, if not plunge headlong in, never to emerge.

XVI.

THE BANK VETO.

There was division in the Bank councils. A large number of the Bank's wisest friends desired, above all things, to keep the question of re-chartering out of the coming presidential campaign. Others said: "It is now or never with us. We have a majority in both Houses in favor of re-chartering. Let us seize the opportunity while we have it, for it may never return." "No," said the opposite party, "the President will most assuredly veto the bill; and we can not carry it over the veto. Then, if the President is reëlected, which, alas ! is only too possible, the Bank is lost irrecover ably. Precipitation gives us but one chance ; delay may afford us many."

Mr. Clay's powerful will decided this controversy. Said he, in substance, " We have the President in a dilemma, upon one of the horns of which we can certainly transfix him. The legislature of his favorite State, his own devoted Pennsylvania, has unanimously pronounced in favor of re-chartering the Bank. The Bank is *in* Pennsylvania. Pennsylvania is proud of it, and thinks her prosperity identified with it. If the President vetoes the bill, he loses Pennsylvania, the bulwark of his power and popularity. If he does not veto the bill, he loses fatally in the South and West. Now is our time." This reasoning may not have quite convinced the leading friends of the Bank ; but the commanding influence of Henry Clay, then in the very zenith of his power and of his fame, caused it to be adopted as the policy of the institution.

How little he knew Pennsylvania, the State that, for forty years, has generally controlled politics ! " Go, my son, study Pennsylvania," should be the advice of a parent launching his offspring into the sea of American politics. Pennsylvania, large, solid, heavy, and central, is the ballast State of the Union. Pennsylvania represents the " general average" of sense and feeling. An event that thrills Ohio, drives New England mad, and New York frantic, only ruffles, and that but for a moment, Pennsylvania's ample and placid countenance. Can you move Pennsylvania ? Then you are master of the situation.

Early in December, when Congress had been less than two weeks in session, a convention of National Republicans (soon to be styled Whigs) assembled at Baltimore to nominate opposition candidates for the presidency and the vice-presidency. So soon did Major Lewis's suggestion bear fruit. Henry Clay and John Sergeant were the candidates selected, both devoted to the Bank, one a citizen of Pennsylvania. In the Address issued by the Convention the Bank question was made a leading issue of the contest. The Bank was eulogized as a "great and beneficent institution," which, "by facilitating exchanges between different parts of the Union, and maintaining a sound, ample, and healthy state of the currency, may be said to supply the body politic, economically viewed, with a continual stream of life-blood, without which it must inevitably languish and sink into exhaustion."

Three times, the address continued, the President had gone out of his way to denounce this blessed fountain of national life, as "a sort of nuisance, and consign it, as far as his influence extends, to immediate destruction." If, therefore, the President be reëlected, it is all over with the Bank of the United States. "Are the people of the United States prepared for this? Are they ready to destroy one of their most valuable establishments to gratify the caprice of a chief magistrate who reasons and advises upon a subject, with the details of which he is evidently unacquainted, in direct contradiction to the opinion of his own official counselors?"

If any such there be, they will vote for Andrew Jackson. But no, fellow-citizens, we have a higher opinion of your good sense and patriotism. Clay and Sergeant, the great defenders of the sacred Bank, are, unquestionably, the men for whom you will cast your votes.

So the issue between the opposition and the administration was joined. The administration, there is good reason to believe, would have gladly avoided the issue at this session. Mr. Clay wrote to a friend, a few days after the publication of the address: "The Executive is playing a deep game to avoid, at this session, the responsibility of any decision on the bank question. It is not yet ascertained whether the bank, by forbearing to apply for a renewal of their charter, will or will not conform to the wishes of the President. I think they will act very unwisely if they do not apply." I am likewise assured, upon authority no less distinguished than Mr. Edward Livingston, that, at this stage of the contest, the President was really disposed to cease the war upon the bank. It was Mr. Livingston's opinion that if, at the beginning of this session, the bank had shown a little complaisance to the President, had consulted him, had consented to certain modifications of its charter, the President could have been induced to sign the re-chartering bill. Mr. Biddle and Mr. Clay determined otherwise. They seized the earliest moment to taunt and defy the President, who accepted the issue.

On the 9th of January, Mr. George M. Dallas, of Pennsylvania, presented to the Senate a memorial from the president and directors of the bank, asking a renewal of their charter. The memorial, which was chiefly an apology for what might seem a premature agitation of the subject, was couched in language most modest and respectful. It was not for them, said the directors, to speak of the value to the public of an institution established with so much difficulty and conducted with so much toil. But the bank was connected in so many ways with the business of the country, that it was highly desirable the country should learn, as soon as possible, whether the present financial system was to cease on the 4th of March, 1836, or endure for many years to come. If Congress, in its wisdom, should decree the extinction of the bank, the directors would do all in their power to aid the community to devise new financial facilities, and would endeavor to close the bank with as little detriment to the business of the country as their experience in the management of financial affairs would enable them.

In presenting this gentlemanlike memorial, Mr. Dallas, a friend of the bank, admitted that he thought its presentation, just then, unwise. He feared that the bank "might be drawn into real or imagined conflict with some higher, some more favorite, some more immediate wish or purpose of the American people." Observe the senator's descending scale of adjectives: "Some higher, some more favorite, some more immediate." Hard lot, to be a statesman in a country where all politics necessarily resolve themselves into a contest for the first office—a contest renewed as soon as the wretched incumbent has taken his seat! Not what is best, but what will tell in the presidential campaign, is always the question.

The memorial, presented thus early in the session, was a prominent subject of debate during all the winter and spring of 1832. January, February, March, April, May, and June, passed away before the final passage of the bank bill was voted upon. And never was there exhibited so striking an illustration of the maxim, that WILL, not talent, governs the world. The will of one man, Andrew Jackson, operating upon the will of one other man, Thomas H. Benton, carried the day against the assembled talent and the interested capital of the country. The bank, as we all now believe, ought to have fallen ; but the mode in which the war against it was conducted, was arrogant, ferocious, and mean. Instead of opposing it on broad Jeffersonian principles, Benton kept assailing it with charges of misconduct, most of which were frivolous, and all of any importance were proved to be false. Never were the affairs of an institution so microscopically investigated. Never was one shown to be more free from intentional or unintentional blame. I boldly affirm, that in the huge volume containing the results of the official investigation, published in the spring of 1832, not one accusation involving the integrity of the directors is sustained. The bank was proved to have been conducted with honesty and skill. Nor had the conduct or misconduct of the bank any thing to do with the question whether or not the bank had a right to exist. The mode adopted of assailing the institution could not have much effect upon Congress, and was not expected to have. The people, the voters at the next presidential election, were the individuals sought to be influenced by it.

Col. Benton confesses as much in his "Thirty Years' View." "Seeing," he says, "that there was a majority in each house for the institution, and no intention to lose time in arguing for it, our course of action became obvious, which was, to attack incessantly, assail at all points, display the evil of the institution, rouse the people, and prepare them to sustain the veto. It was seen to be the policy of the bank leaders to carry the charter first, and quietly, through the Senate ; and afterward, in the same way in the House. We determined to have a contest in both places, and to force the bank into defenses which would engage it in a general combat, and lay it open to side-blows, as well as direct attacks. With this view a great many amendments and inquiries were prepared to be offered in the Senate, all of them proper or plausible, recommendable in themselves, and supported by acceptable reasons, which the friends of the bank must either answer, or reject without answer; and so incur odium. In the House it was determined to make a move, which, whether resisted or admitted by the bank majority, would be certain to have an effect against the institution—namely, an investigation by a committee of the house, as provided for in the charter. If the investigation was denied, it would be guilt shrinking from detection; if admitted, it was well known that misconduct would be found. I conceived this movement, and had charge of its direction. I preferred the House for the theater of investigation, as most appropriate, being the grand inquest of the nation; and, besides, wished a contest to be going on there while the Senate was engaged in passing the charter; and the right to raise the committee was complete in either house. Besides the right reserved in the charter, there was a natural right, when the corporation was asked for a renewed lease, to inquire how it had acted under the previous one. I got Mr. Clayton, a new member from Georgia (who had written a pamphlet against the bank in his own State), to take charge of the movement, and gave him a memorandum of seven alleged breaches of the charter, and fifteen instances of imputed misconduct to inquire into, if he got his committee; or to allege on the floor if he encountered resistance."

Mr. Clayton did encounter resistance. "All these charges," continues Col. Benton, "he read to the house, one by one, from a narrow slip of paper, which he continued rolling round his finger all the time. The memorandum was mine—in my hand-writing—given to him to copy and amplify, as they were brief memoranda. He had not copied them; and having to justify suddenly, he used the slip I had given him, rolling it on his finger, as on a cylinder, to prevent my handwriting from being seen: so he afterward told me himself. The reading of these twenty-two heads of accusation, like so many counts in an indictment, sprung the friends of the bank to their feet—and its foes also—each finding in it something to rouse them—one to the defense, the other to the attack."

The committee of investigation was appointed, and appointed, of course, by an anti-bank speaker. It consisted of seven members—Mr. Clayton, of Georgia, (chairman), Richard M. Johnson, Francis Thomas, C. C. Cambreleng, George McDuffie, John Quincy Adams, and Mr. Watmough. The first four of these gentlemen were opposed to re-chartering the bank; the last three were in favor of it. On the 23d of March, the committee had reached Philadelphia, and begun their investigations. Fifty days elapsed before the committee were ready to report, and then they were unable to agree. Three separate reports were accordingly presented to the House, one by the majority, one by the minority, and one by Mr. Adams. The last two exonerated the bank from all the important charges, and the report of Mr. Adams declared that the bank had been conducted with as near an approach to perfect wisdom as the imperfection of human nature permitted. These three reports, with the documents appended, form an octavo volume of five hundred and seventy-two pages.

Believing that the mode in which the bank had been conducted had nothing to do with the question of re-chartering, which ought to have been debated, and was decided on other grounds, I shall pass lightly over these formidable reports. Two or three points, however, are interesting in themselves, and may worthily detain us a moment.

One of the Bentonian accusations against the Bank was, that it had issued notes not signed by the president and cashier. The directors showed that this was owing to the physical impossibility of those officers signing the number of notes required by the parent Bank and its twenty-five branches. Consequently, after taking the opinion of the three great lawyers of the day, Horace Binney, Daniel Webster, and William Wirt, the directors had authorized the presidents and cashiers of the twenty-five branches to issue *checks*, which closely resembled the notes of the Bank in general appearance, and were not usually distinguished from them.

Another of the charges urged by Colonel Benton was, that the Bank was criminally profuse in its accommodation to editors who favored the re-chartering. Two cases were investigated—a loan to Duff Green, of the *Telegraph*, and loans to the proprietors of the *New York Courier and Enquirer*. It was shown, first, that the loan to General Green was a safe and legitimate business transaction; secondly, that at the time the loan was made, the *Telegraph* had led the opposition against the Bank; thirdly, that when applying for the loan, Green had expressly stated that "no accommodation given by the Bank will induce me to alter, in any respect, the course which my paper has pursued in relation to it;" fourthly, that Mr. Biddle had replied in the following terms: "The Bank is glad to have friends from conviction; but seeks none from interest. For myself, I love the freedom of the press too much to complain of its occasional injustice to me; and if the loan be made, it shall be with a perfect understanding—to be put into the note, if necessary—that the borrower is to speak his mind about the Bank just as freely as he did before, which I take to be 'ample room and verge enough.'"

The case of Colonel Webb and the *Courier* received an extraordinary share of attention. The readers of a New York newspaper were daily reminded, for about ten years, and are not yet permitted to forget, that the amount of the accommodation afforded by the Bank to the *Courier and Enquirer*, at different times, was $52,975. There were three editors of that important newspaper in 1830, James Watson Webb, M. M. Noah, and James Gordon Bennett; the two latter opposed to the re-charter in toto; the first, opposed to certain features of the Bank, but in favor of re-chartering it with modifications. The anti-Bank articles, which were a specialty of the paper in 1830, were written by Messrs. Noah and Bennett; most of them by Bennett, who had an aversion to all banks, and who knew, and knows, how important it is to a daily paper to have an imposing and powerful object to attack. Colonel Webb was not the author of one of these articles, though he permitted their insertion, and approved them as a part of the party tactics of the hour. Nor was he aware, at that time, that the President was prepared to carry his hostility to the Bank to the point of its total extinction.

"The first article," said Colonel Webb, in a letter to Mr. Cambreleng, "which ever appeared in our columns, was written in Washington about a month previous to the Message of 1829. It was inserted in our columns during my absence from the city, or without my examination. I disapproved of it, its arguments, and conclusions. I never, in my life, wrote a line against the Bank, but I permitted and sanctioned articles against it because we had become committed; because the President had assailed it, and because I was under the erroneous impression that it was prostituted to the advancement of Henry Clay to the presidency. I became convinced that this was not the case, and I eagerly seized upon the expression of a Jackson legislature in Pennsylvania, upon the danger of embroiling the two States (the folly of which Mr. Van Buren now suffers under), and the going out of Tylee* and coming in of Noah, to take the course which I was persuaded would best subserve the interests of the people, and, at the same time, accord fully with my own opinions."

The first consequence to the paper of its espousal of the cause of the bank was a refusal on the part of the New York banks to afford it pecuniary accommodation. "I can prove," said Colonel Webb, in the same letter to Mr. Cambreleng, "that at the time of our espousing the re-charter of the United States' Bank, we had $13,500 of accommodation in

* A former proprietor.

the City Bank alone, on the endorsement of Mr. A. L. Stewart; that we had a large similar accommodation for nearly two years from this one institution; that in consequence of our favorable opinions of the United States' Bank, they made us pay up every penny of our accommodation, and threw out our note with Mr. Stewart's endorsement; that the Manhattan and National Banks pursued the same course; and that, in consequence, we were cut off from our usual resources of obtaining those accommodations to which the amount of our capital employed, and the extent of our business entitled us, and which we surely did not sacrifice by publishing a newspaper. We were literally proscribed by our local institutions. I went to Philadelphia, and gave to Mr. Biddle a full and perfect history of our paper, and asked for a loan of $20,000. It was granted."

The statement forwarded by Colonel Webb of the business of his establishment, the first of the kind then existing in the country, proved that the loans granted by the bank were safe, proper, and usual. Some of the items will interest gentlemen connected with the press: 3300 daily subscribers at ten dollars; 2300 weekly or semi-weekly subscribers, at an average of four dollars and fifty cents; 275 advertising subscribers, at thirty dollars; daily income from advertising, fifty-five dollars; daily cash receipts for advertising, ten dollars; gross annual income, $60,750; expenses, $35,000; profit, $25,750; annual cost of paper, $22,000. Colonel Webb considered the establishment worth $150,000.

The most signal triumph of the bank and its president, during this investigation, occurred in connection with the testimony of Reuben M. Whitney. Whitney had formerly been a merchant of Philadelphia and a director of the Bank of the United States. At this time, he was a bankrupt, and one of the bank's most rancorous enemies, and the chief source of Colonel Benton's catalogue of charges. When testifying before the committee he gave such evidence as must have blasted for ever the good name of the president of the bank, if it had not been demonstrated to be the foulest perjury. Observe the circumstantial manner in which this individual told his scandalous tale :

Question by Mr. Clayton. Did Mr. Thomas Wilson, the former cashier, ever acquaint you with any circumstance relating to the accounts of Mr. Thomas Biddle in the bank? if yea, state fully what it was.

Answer. Some time in 1823, Mr. Wilson and Mr. Andrews mentioned to me that some transactions had taken place in the bank in which T. and J. G. Biddle* were concerned, which they were not willing should exist without some member of the board being informed of them. I asked what they were. They replied that T. and J. G. Biddle had been in the habit of coming to the bank, and getting money, and leaving certificates of stock which represented it, in the first teller's drawer, without paying interest. They also stated, that the Messrs. Biddle had had notes discounted for them by the president, which were entered on the books of the preceding discount day. I asked them what sums there were of the kind in existence at that time. They went with me to the first teller's drawer, and we found one sum of $45,000, dated 25th May, and one for $24,000, dated 26th May. We then went to the discount clerk's desk, and found one note at fifteen days, dated 13th May, for $20,000 of T. Biddle's, and one note of Charles Biddle's, dated 21st May, at sixteen days, for $38,319. The two former sums represented cash, and the two latter new notes, which they stated to me had been discounted by order of the president. Of all these I made a memorandum (now produced) at the time, which corresponds with the entries now in the books now shown to me.

Question by Mr. Thomas. Did you communicate these matters to the president? if yea, state when and where.

Answer. Immediately after examining the books I came into the president's room and communicated to him what had been communicated to me, and what I had learned by examining the books. After stating this, I desired that nothing of a similar nature should occur while I was a director of the bank. *He told me there should not.*

Question by Mr. Clayton. Did you not direct the officers to enter what you discovered on the books, and was it done?

Answer. I directed the officers to enter on the books the money that had been loaned from the teller's drawer, and which was represented by stock certificates. It was done; I did not see it done, but I know it was done. Subsequently I saw this entry of "bills receivable," which I knew was the entry made for that purpose. In the entry in the semi-weekly statement, or state of the bank, under date of 27th May, under head of bills receivable, the sum of $69,000 is entered, which is the exact amount

* Extensive Brokers of Philadelphia, second cousins of Nicholas Biddle.

of the two sums of $45,000, and $24,000, represented by stock certificates in the teller's drawer.

Question by Mr. Adams. Did you in your communication, immediately after directing the entries to be made in the books, inform the president that you had directed those entries to be made?

Answer. I can not say that I did.

Question by Mr. McDuffie. The memorandum you have produced is the one before referred to by you; when was it made?

Answer. I made it at the time the communication was made to me by Mr. Wilson and Mr. Andrews, and this memorandum now produced is the one.

Question by Mr. Adams. Have you ever had any communication, written or verbal, on this subject, with any member of the committee?

Answer. I have, verbally, with Mr. Clayton, and in the presence of Mr. Cambreleng. I have also told different individuals of it immediately after it occurred, as well as at various times since.

Question by Mr. Adams. Did you go to Mr. Clayton without any previous solicitation?

Answer. I had received a letter from Colonel Benton, informing me he had recommended Judge Clayton to me.

Question by Mr. Biddle, the President of the Bank. Where did the alleged conversation between you, Mr. Wilson, and Mr. Andrews, take place?

Answer. In the area of the banking room, not far from the first teller's desk. These gentlemen, one or both of them, went with me to the teller's desk. I made the memorandum of the cash there, and my memorandum of the notes I made at the discount clerk's desk; one or both of them went with me to the discount clerk's desk, and there I made my memorandum of the notes. Mr. Burtis was, I think, the discount clerk. I can not say whether I directed the entries on the books of the loans before I went to the discount clerk. I gave the direction to both Mr. Wilson and Mr. Andrews, if both were present, or to but one, if only one was present. I stated to you the particulars I had learned, as stated in the memorandum. You did not deny them. *You colored up a good deal.* I can not say whether there was any person who could have overheard this conversation, but I presume not. I can not say whether or not I have had any conversation with them since; I think it probable I have, as I do not know how else I learned that the item of bills receivable related to these transactions.

At the moment, Mr. Biddle, astounded at this damning testimony, could only deny that it contained one syllable of truth. Shortly after, however, he proved to the committee, by evidence the most incontestible, that (to use his own language), "on the very day when R. M. Whitney swears that he conversed with me in this room at Philadelphia, where we are now sitting—for many days before that day, and for many days after that day—*I was actually in the city of Washington.* The first evidence is the original minutes of the bank, by which it will be seen, that, from the 22d day of May to the 1st of June, I was absent from the bank, and that R. M. Whitney himself attended the meetings of the Board, when the fact of my absence was recorded." He produced a large bundle of letters, written by him, and addressed to him, at Washington, which established the fact of his presence there beyond all possibility of doubt. He also showed, by the testimony of many witnesses, that no transaction of the kind described so minutely by the wretched Whitney had ever occurred. "Thus," said the Minority Report, "was this artfully devised story, which was intended to blast the reputation of a high-minded and honorable man, through one of those extraordinary interpositions by which Providence sometimes confounds the contrivances of the wicked, made to recoil upon the head of its inventor, who must for ever stand forth as a blasted monument of the speedy and retributive justice of Heaven."

So blinded, however, was General Jackson to all moral distinctions by his intense hostility to the bank, that he continued to countenance this Whitney; welcomed him to the presidential mansion, and lent a greedy ear to his tales of bank corruption, which were then the surest passport to presidential favor.

Mr. Adams intimates, at the conclusion of his report, that, so completely had the investigation vindicated the bank, Colonel Richard M. Johnson, one of General Jackson's special adherents and associates, rose and declared that he "had seen nothing in the conduct of the president and directors inconsistent with the purest honor and integrity." Colonel Johnson, however, was an easy, good-natured man, and was persuaded to sign the report of the majority. He never would have been Vice-President if he had not. Mr. Adams concluded his report with these words: "Had that same candid and explicit declaration, due, as the subscriber believes, to the most rigorous justice, been made by the other members who sanctioned the majority report, many a painful remark in the paper now submitted, perhaps the whole paper itself, would have been suppressed. But to vindicate the honor of injured worth is, in his opinion, among the first of moral obligations; and, in concluding these observations, he would say to every individual of the House, and to every fellow-citizen of the nation, inquisitive of the cause of any over-anxious sensibility to imputations upon the good name of other men which they may here find—

> "When truth and virtue an affront endures,
> The offense is mine, my friend, and should be yours."

The bill re-chartering the Bank of the United States passed the Senate on the eleventh of June, by a vote of twenty-eight to twenty, and the house on the third of July, by a vote of one hundred and nine to seventy-six. It was presented to the President on the fourth of July, and by him returned to Congress, VETOED, on the tenth of the same month. The message accompanying the vetoed bill was one of the longest and one of the most adroit ever sent to Congress by a President. It shows that the President, when he gave to Mr. Amos Kendall an appointment in the treasury, knew well what he was doing.

The objections of the administration to the renewal of the bank charter, as expressed in this famous message, may be summed up in one ugly word, and that word is MONOPOLY.

Here, said the President (in effect), is a certain small body of men and women, the stockholders of the bank of the United States, upon whom the federal government has bestowed, and by the renewal bill proposes to continue, exclusive privileges of immense pecuniary value; and, by doing so, restricts the liberty of all other citizens. This is a monopoly. The granting of it, in the first place, inasmuch as the effect of the measure could not have been foreseen, may be excused; but for its continuance there is not the shadow of an excuse. The following odious features of the monopoly were enumerated in the message:

1. Eight millions of the stock of the bank was held by foreigners. The renewal of the charter would raise the market value of that stock at least twenty or thirty per cent. Renew the charter, and the American republic will make a present to foreign stockholders of some millions of dollars, without deriving the slightest advantage from the munificent gift.

2. Let it be granted that the government should bestow this monopoly. Then a fair price should be paid for it. The actual value of the privileges conferred by the bill is computed to be seventeen millions of dollars, and the act proposes to sell those privileges for the annual sum of two hundred thousand dollars; or, in other words, for three millions of dollars, payable in fifteen annual installments of two hundred thousand dollars each.

3. The act excludes competition. Persons of wealth and respectability had offered to take a charter on terms more favorable to the government than those proposed by the bill.

4. The bill concedes to banks dealing with the bank of the United States what it denies to individuals. If a State bank in Philadelphia owes money to the bank of the United States, and has notes issued by the St. Louis branch, it can pay its debt with those notes; but a merchant must either sell his St. Louis notes at a discount, or send them to St. Louis to be cashed. This boon to banks operates as a bond of union among the banking institutions of the whole country, "erecting them into an interest separate from that of the people."

5. The stock held by foreigners can not be taxed, a fact which gives such stock a value ten or fifteen per cent. greater than that held by citizens.

6. As each State can tax only the amount of stock held

by its citizens, and not the amount employed in the State, the tax will operate unequally and unjustly.

7. Though nearly a third of the stock of the Bank is held by foreigners, foreigners have no voice or vote in the election of the officers of the Bank. Of the twenty-five directors, five are appointed by the government, and twenty by the citizen stockholders. Stock is continually going abroad, and the renewal of the charter will greatly accelerate its departure. The consequence will inevitably be, to throw the control of the Bank into the hands of a few resident stockholders, who will be able to reëlect themselves from year to year, and who will wield a power dangerous to the institutions of the country.

8. Should the stock ever pass principally into the hands of the subjects of a foreign country, and we should become involved in a war with that country, the interests and feelings of the directors will be opposed to those of their countrymen. "All the operations of the Bank within would be in aid of the hostile fleets and armies without. Controlling our currency, receiving our public moneys, and holding thousands of our citizens in dependence, it would be more formidable and dangerous than the naval and military power of the enemy." If we must have a Bank, every consideration of sound policy, and every impulse of American feeling, admonishes that it should be purely American. And this the more, as domestic capital was so abundant, that competition in subscribing to a local bank had recently almost led to a riot.

From this enumeration, the Message proceeded to discuss the question of the constitutionality of the bill. A preliminary remark excited great clamor at the time. "Each public officer," said the President, "who takes an oath to support the Constitution, swears that he will support it *as he understands it*, and not as it is understood by others:" even though those "others" be the Judges of the Supreme Court of the United States. "The opinion of the Judges has no more authority over Congress than the opinion of Congress has over the Judges; and, on that point, the President is independent of both." The Judges, it was true, had decided the law incorporating the Bank to be constitutional, but only on the general ground that Congress had power "to make all laws which shall be necessary and proper" for carrying the powers of the general government into execution. Necessary and proper! The question, then, resolved itself into an inquiry whether such an institution as this bill proposed was necessary and proper. To that inquiry the author of the Message addressed himself; arriving, of course, at the conclusion that the act contained many provisions most unnecessary and most improper; and, therefore, unconstitutional.

The Message, which displayed throughout the marks both of ability and earnest conviction, concluded with the following admirable words—words that Edward Livingston learned to use in the old days when Thomas Jefferson was the republican leader, and himself a young convert to his immortal principles:

"Distinctions in society will always exist under every just government. Equality of talents, of education, or of wealth, can not be produced by human institutions. In the full enjoyment of the gifts of heaven and the fruits of superior industry, economy, and virtue, every man is equally entitled to protection by law. But when the laws undertake to add to these natural and just advantages, artificial distinctions, to grant titles, gratuities, and exclusive privileges, to make the rich richer and the potent more powerful, the humble members of society, the farmers, mechanics, and laborers, who have neither the time nor the means of securing like favors to themselves, have a right to complain of the injustice of their government. There are no necessary evils in government. Its evils exist only in its abuses. If it would confine itself to equal protection, and, as heaven does its rains, shower its favors alike on the high and the low, the rich and the poor, it would be an unqualified blessing. In the act before me, there seems to be a wide and unnecessary departure from these just principles.

"Nor is our government to be maintained, or our Union preserved, by invasion of the rights and powers of the several States. In thus attempting to make our general government strong, we make it weak. Its true strength consists in leaving individuals and States, as much as possible, to themselves; in making itself felt, not in its power, but in its beneficence, not in its control, but in its protection, not in binding the States more closely to the center, but leaving each to move unobstructed in its proper orbit.

"Experience should teach us wisdom. Most of the difficulties our government now encounters, and most of the dangers which impend over our Union, have sprung from an abandonment of the legitimate objects of government by our national legislation, and the adoption of such principles as are enbodied in this act. Many of our rich men have not been content with equal protection and equal benefits, but have besought us to make them richer by act of Congress. By attempting to gratify their desires, we have, in the results of our legislation, arrayed section against section, interest against interest, and man against man, in a fearful commotion which threatens to shake the foundations of our Union. It is time to pause in our career, to review our principles, and, if possible, revive that devoted patriotism and spirit of compromise which distinguished the sages of the revolution, and the fathers of our Union. If we can not at once, in justice to the interests vested under improvident legislation, make our government what it ought to be, we can, at least, take a stand against all new grants of monopolies and exclusive privileges, against any prostitution of our government to the advancement of the few at the expense of the many, and in favor of compromise and gradual reform in our code of laws and system of political economy.

"I have now done my duty to my country. If sustained by my fellow-citizens, I shall be grateful and happy; if not, I shall find, in the motives which impel me, ample grounds for contentment and peace. In the difficulties which surround us, and the dangers which threaten our institutions, there is cause for neither dismay nor alarm. For relief and deliverance let us firmly rely on that kind Providence which, I am sure, watches with peculiar care over the destinies of our Republic and on the intelligence and wisdom of our countrymen. Through *His* abundant goodness, and *their* patriotic devotion, our liberty and Union will be preserved."

Concerning the financial and legal principles laid down in this important document, financiers and lawyers differ in opinion. The humbler office of the present chronicler is to state that the bank-veto message of President Jackson came with convincing power upon a majority of the people of the United States. It settled the question. And it may be safely predicted that while that message endures, and the Union, as it is now constituted, endures, a bank of the United States can never exist. If ever it should be seriously proposed to establish one again, that message will rise from its grave in the volume of presidential messages, where it sleeps forgotten, to crush the proposition.

It was the singular fortune of the bank-veto message to delight equally the friends and the foes of the bank. The opposition circulated it as a campaign document! Duff Green published it in his extra *Telegraph*, calling upon all the opponents of the administration to give it the widest publicity, since it would damn the administration wherever it was read. The *New York American* characterized it thus: "It is indeed and verily beneath contempt. It is an appeal of ignorance to ignorance, of prejudice to prejudice, of the most unblushing partisan hostility to the obsequiousness of partisan servility. No man in the cabinet proper will be willing to share the ignominy of preparing or approving such a paper."

Nicholas Biddle himself was enchanted with it, for he thought it had saved the bank by destroying the bank's great enemy. "You ask," he wrote to Henry Clay, "what is the effect of the veto? My impression is, that it is working as well as the friends of the bank and of the country could desire. I have always deplored making the bank a party question, but since the President will have it so, he must pay the penalty of his own rashness. As to the veto message, I am delighted with it. It has all the fury of a chained panther, biting the bars of his cage. It is really a manifesto of anarchy, such as Marat or Robespierre might have issued to the mob of the Faubourg St. Antoine; and my hope is, that it will contribute to relieve the country from the dominion of these miserable people. You are destined to be the instrument of that deliverance, and at no period of your life has the country ever had a deeper stake in you. I wish you success most cordially, because I believe the institutions of the Union are involved in it."

So little did Mr. Biddle, and such as he, know the country in which they lived! As little do such now know it!

There was rare speaking in the Senate after the reception of the veto. Mr. Webster opened the debate upon it in a ponderous speech, which foretold the direst consequences to the country unless the people, at the approaching election, reversed the President's decision. Mr. Clay followed in one of his most energetic harangues, which brought him into personal collision with Col. Benton. Benton, it must be owned, made some telling hits in replying to Mr. Clay. The veto, said the Kentuckian, has grown obsolete in England; and even in France, its frequent exercise by Louis XVI. caused the gay Parisians to dub him with the derisive name of Monsieur Veto. True, said Benton. But what was the nature of the laws which that unfortunate king had annulled by his veto? "One was the decree against the emigrants, dooming to death and confiscation of estate every man, woman, and child who should attempt to save their lives by flying from the pike, the guillotine, and the lamp-post. The other was a decree exposing to death the ministers of religion who could not take an oath which their consciences repulsed. To save tottering age, trembling mothers, and affrighted children from massacre—to save the temples and altars of God from being stained by the blood of his ministers—were the sacred objects of those vetoes; and was there anything to justify a light or reproachful allusion to them in the American Senate? The king put his constitutional vetoes to these decrees; and the *canaille* of Saint Antoine and Marceau—not the gay and laughing Parisians, but the bloody *canaille*, instigated by leaders more ferocious than themselves—began to salute the king as Monsieur Veto, and demand his head for the guillotine. And the queen, when seen at the windows of her prison, her locks pale with premature white, the effect of an agonized mind at the ruin she witnessed, the *poissardes* saluted her also as Madame Veto; and the Dauphin came in for the epithet of the Little Veto. And now, why this allusion? What application of its moral? Surely it is not pointless; not devoid of meaning and practical application. We have no bloody guillotines here, but we have political ones: sharp axes falling from high, and cutting off political heads! Is the service of that ax invoked here upon 'General Andrew Veto?' If so, and the invocation should be successful, then Andrew Jackson, like Louis XVI., will cease to be in any body's way in their march to power."

Mr. Clay said that the veto had placed the friends of the President in an agonizing dilemma. "Their condition," said he, "reminds me of the fable invented by Dr. Franklin, of the eagle and the cat. The eagle pounced from his lofty flight in the air, upon a cat, taking it to be a pig. Having borne off his prize, he quickly felt most painfully the claws of the cat thrust deeply into his sides and body. While flying, he held a parley with the supposed pig, and proposed to let go his hold if the other would let him alone. No, says puss, you brought me from yonder earth below, and I will hold fast to you until you carry me back; a condition to which the eagle readily assented."

"Well," said Benton, "and what is the application of the fable?" "General Jackson is the eagle; the bank is the cat; the parley is the proposition of the bank to the President to sign its charter, and it will support him for the presidency—if not, will keep its claws stuck in his sides. But, Jackson, different from the eagle with his cat, will have no compromise, or bargain with the bank. One or the other shall fall! and be dashed to atoms!!"

Col. Benton complained of Mr. Clay's indecorous mode of speaking of the President, which, he said, was the more improper, as Mr. Clay was a rival candidate for the suffrages of the people. This remark led to a most pointed and angry colloquy between the two Senators.

Mr. Clay said: "There are some peculiar reasons why I should not go to that Senator for my views of decorum, in regard to my bearing toward the chief magistrate, and why he is not a fit instructor. I never had any personal encounter with the President of the United States. I never complained of any outrages on my person committed by him. I never published any bulletins respecting his private brawls. The gentleman will understand my allusions. I never complained, that while a brother of mine was down on the ground, senseless or dead, he received another blow. I have never made any declarations like these relative to the individual who is President. There is also a singular prophecy as to the consequences of the election of this individual, which far surpasses, in evil foreboding, whatever I may have ever said in regard to his election. I never made any prediction so sinister, nor made any declaration so harsh, as that which is contained in the prediction to which I allude. I never declared my apprehension and belief, that if he were elected, we should be obliged to legislate with pistols and dirks by our side."*

Col. Benton replied: "It is true, sir, that I had an affray with General Jackson, and that I did complain of his conduct. We fought, sir; and we fought, I hope, like men. When the explosion was over, there remained no ill will, on either side. No vituperation or system of petty persecution was kept up between us. Yes, sir, it is true, that I had the personal difficulty which the Senator from Kentucky has had the delicacy to bring before the Senate. But let me tell the Senator from Kentucky there is no 'adjourned question of veracity' between me and General Jackson. All difficulty between us ended with the conflict; and a few months after it, I believe that either party would cheerfully have relieved the other from any peril; and now we shake hands and are friendly when we meet. I repeat, sir, that there is no 'adjourned question of veracity' between me and General Jackson, standing over for settlement. If there had been, a gulf would have separated us as deep as hell." Col. Benton declared he had never made the dirk-and-pistol prophecy quoted by Mr. Clay.

Mr. Clay denied that there was any adjourned question of veracity between himself and General Jackson. "He made," said Mr. Clay, "a certain charge (of bargain) against

* Mr. Clay alluded to the following words attributed to Mr. Benton: "If General Jackson shall be elected, he will surround himself with a pack of political bull dogs, to bark at all who dare to oppose his measures. For myself, as I can not think of legislating with a brace of pistols in my belt, I shall, in the event of the election of General Jackson, resign my seat in the Senate, as every independent man will have to do, or risk his life and honor."

me, and he referred to witnesses to prove it. I denied the truth of the charge. He called upon his witness to prove it. I leave it to the country to say whether that witness sustained the truth of the President's allegation. The witness (Mr. Buchanan) is now on his passage to St. Petersburg, with a commission in his pocket." Mr. Clay reverted to the dirk-and-pistol remark attributed to Col. Benton. "Can you, sir," he asked, turning toward Col. Benton, "can you look me in the face, and say that you never used that language out of the State of Missouri?"

"I look, sir," replied Benton, "and repeat that it is an atrocious calumny; and I will pin it to him who repeats it here."

"Then," said Mr. Clay, "I declare before the Senate that you said to me the very words."

"False, false, false," roared Benton.

"I fling back," cried Clay, "the charge of atrocious calumny upon the Senator from Missouri."

The infuriated Senators were here called to order on all sides, and the chair compelled them to desist. Colonel Benton then said: "I apologize to the Senate for the manner in which I have spoken: but not to the Senator from Kentucky."

Mr. Clay apologized: "To the Senate I also offer an apology. To the Senator from Missouri none."

It was quite a curious coincidence, that on one of these fine mornings, when Colonel Benton was so fiercely battling for the President in the Senate chamber, the President had to submit to a surgical operation for the extraction of the bullet which he had carried in his left arm ever since the time of the Benton affray, in Nashville, twenty years before. The General laid bare his arm, grasped his well known walking stick, and told the doctor (Dr. Harris, of Philadelphia) to "go ahead." The doctor made a bold incision into the flesh, gave the arm a squeeze, and out jumped the ball upon the floor. It was all over and the arm bandaged in one minute. My informant does not state whether the General restored the ball to its rightful owner or his representative, nor whether Colonel Benton was able to look the President comfortably in the face that evening.

On the 16th of July, at six o'clock in the morning, Congress adjourned. The opposition members went home to join their allies of the press in the attempt to convince the people of the United States that the veto was ruining the country, and would completely ruin it, unless they elected Messrs. Clay and Sergeant to the first offices of the government in the following November.

The opposition press told the people that the veto had caused the stock of the great bank to decline four per cent.; that bricks had fallen from five dollars per thousand to three; that wild consternation pervaded the great cities; that real estate had lost a fourth of its value; that western men were contracting to deliver pork, next season, at two dollars and a half if Clay was elected, and at one dollar and a half if Jackson was elected; that mechanics were thrown out of employment by thousands, and were going supperless to bed; that no more steamboats were to be built on the western rivers until there was a change of rulers; that the old friends of General Jackson were falling away from him in every direction; that mass-meetings were held in every State denouncing the veto; that the Irish voters were seceding from General Jackson, thousands of them at one meeting; and that the defeat of the tyrant was as certain to occur as the sun was certain to rise on the morning of election day.

XVII.

RE-ELECTION OF GENERAL JACKSON.

A STRANGE, sad, exciting, eventful summer was that of 1832.

It opened gayly enough. The country had never been under such headway before. In looking over the newspapers for May of that year, the eye is arrested by the incident of Washington Irving's triumphal return home after an absence from his native land of seventeen years. He had gone away an unknown youth, or little known beyond his own circle, and came back a renowned author who had won as much honor for his country as for himself. The little speech which he delivered at the banquet given him in the city of New York, delightfully reveals the innocent astonishment which the young Republic, once so fearful of its future, felt at the mighty pace at which it seemed to be going toward greatness. The modest Irving, unused to speak in public, spoke with faltering voice of his warm and unexpected welcome. But when he came to describe the changes he observed in his native city, the marvelous prosperity that every where met his eyes, his tongue was loosened, and he burst into momentary eloquence.

"From the time," said he, "that I approached the coast, I saw indications of the growing greatness of my native city. We had scarce descried the land, when a thousand sails of all descriptions gleaming along the horizon, and all standing to or from one point, showed that we were in the neighborhood of a vast commercial emporium. As I sailed up our beautiful bay, with a heart swelling with old recollections and delightful associations, I was astonished to see its once wild features brightening with populous villages and noble piles, and a teeming city extending itself over heights which I had left covered with groves and forests. But how shall I describe my emotion when our city itself rose to sight, seated in the midst of its watery domain, stretching away to a vast extent; when I beheld a glorious sunshine brightening up the spires and domes, some familiar to memory, others new and unknown, and beaming on a forest of masts of every nation, extending as far as the eye could reach. I have gazed with admiration upon many a fair city and stately harbor, but my admiration was cold and ineffectual, for I was a stranger, and had no property in the soil. Here, however, my heart throbbed with pride and joy as I admired. I had birthright in the brilliant scene before me—

'This was my own, my native land.'

"It has been asked, 'Can I be content to live in this country?' Whoever asks that question must have but an inadequate idea of its blessings and delights. What sacrifice of enjoyments have I to reconcile myself to? I come from gloomier climates to one of brilliant sunshine and inspiring purity. I come from countries lowering with doubt and danger, where the rich man trembles and the poor man frowns—where all repine at the present and dread the future. I come from these, to a country where all is life and animation; where I hear on every side the sound of exultation; where every one speaks of the past with triumph, the present with delight, the future with growing and confident anticipation. Is this not a community in which one may rejoice to live? Is this not a city by which one may be proud to be received as a son? Is this not a land in which every one may be happy to fix his destiny and ambition, if possible to found a name? I am asked how long I mean to remain here. They know but little of my heart or my feelings who can ask me this question!—As long as I live."

Just so the country felt as it read Mr. Irving's glowing sentences in the month of May, 1832.

Before the next month had run its course, a great terror pervaded the continent. The cholera, that had ravaged Europe last year, and spread over America a vague alarm, broke out in Quebec on the ninth of June. An emigrant ship lost forty-two of her passengers from the disease while crossing the ocean, and seemed to communicate it to the city as soon as she arrived. Swiftly the disease made its southward progress—swiftly, but capriciously—leaping here a region, diverging there, sparing some unhealthful localities, and desolating others supposed to be peculiarly salubrious. It reached New York fifteen days after its appearance in Quebec. There was no parade on the fourth of July. Hospitals were hastily prepared in every ward. The cases increased in number for just one month ; at the expiration of which three hundred persons daily sickened, and nearly one hundred died, of cholera alone. Grass grew in some of the thoroughfares usually thronged, and whole blocks of stores were closed. By the middle of August, when 2,565 persons had died of the disease, it had so far subsided that the people who had fled began to return, and the city to regain its wonted aspect.*

As the epidemic subsided in New York, it gained further South. It raged in Philadelphia, terrified Baltimore, threatened Washington, and darted malignant influences into the far West. Cincinnati was attacked, and the troops stationed at unknown Chicago did not escape. New Orleans had it, instead of the yellow fever.

As a vulture, brooding in the air, invisible, discerns its prey afar off, and swooping downward seizes it in its horrid talons, unexpected, irresistible, and then, having torn the blood out of its heart, ascends again to the upper air, and surveying once more the outspread land, espies another help-

* The following paragraph is from the *New York Journal of Commerce* of July 26th, 1832 : "There never was a more delightful exhibition of Christian benevolence than is now witnessed in this city. The generous donations which have been recorded, and which still continue to flow in, form but an item in the general aggregate. Numbers of our most accomplished ladies are engaged, day after day, in making garments for the poor and distressed, while committees of gentlemen, who at home sit on elegant sofas and walk on Brussels carpets, are searching out the abode of poverty, filth, and disease, and administering personally to the wants of the wretched inmates. There is no telling the misery which they often meet with and relieve."

less victim, and rushes down upon it, so did this wayward and terrible cholera seem to select, from day to day, for no reasons that science could penetrate, a fresh town to suddenly affright and desolate.

About the middle of August, the President, accompanied by Mr. Blair and other friends, left Washington for a visit to the Hermitage, and did not return until the nineteenth of October. On this journey it was remarked the President paid his expenses in gold. "No more paper-money, you see, fellow-citizens, if I can only put down this Nicholas Biddle and his monster bank." A telling maneuver in a country of doubtful banks and counterfeit-detectors, distressing to all women, and puzzling to most men. "Ninety-five counterfeits of the bills of the bank of the United States alone," Col. Benton had kept the country in mind of during the late debates. Gold, long since gone out of circulation, was held up to the people as the currency which the administration of General Jackson was struggling to restore. A golden piece of money, as most of us remember, was a curiosity at that time. It was a distinction in country places to possess one. Clay and eternal rag-money, Jackson and speedy gold, was diligently represented to be the issue between the two candidates. Storekeepers responded by announcing themselves as anti-bank hatters, and hard-money bakers. The administration had given the politicians a "good cry" to go before the country with, and it was not allowed to fall to the ground.

Amid the terrors of the cholera, one would have expected to find the presidential campaign carried on with less than the usual spirit. There was a lull in midsummer. But, upon the whole, no contest of the kind was ever conducted with so much energy and so much labor. The pamphlets of the campaign still astonish collectors by their number, their ability, and their size. Against the administration seem to have been arrayed the talent of the country, the great capitalists, the leading men of business, and even the smaller banks, making common cause with the great bank, doomed to quick extinction if General Jackson were reëlected. Let us note briefly a few instructive incidents of the contest.

At the last moment, it appears, there was some reason to fear that the machinery devised to secure the nomination of Mr. Van Buren would fail to effect its purpose. Among those who objected to place him upon the ticket with General Jackson was that very Major Eaton for whom he had done and risked so much. Eaton was a delegate from Tennessee to the nominating convention. Major Lewis writes to me: "Mr. Eaton objected to the nomination of Mr. Van Buren, alleging that it would endanger the election of General Jackson. I had not seen Mr. Eaton for five or six months; but learning, only the day before the convention was to meet, that he would oppose the nomination of Mr. Van Buren, I immediately wrote him in strong and decided terms, warning him of the danger of such a course, *unless he was prepared to quarrel with the General!* He was sent as a delegate from Tennessee, and went directly to Baltimore, where the convention was to sit, the evening before it was to meet, without passing through Washington as was expected; but fortunately he received my letter in time to save both himself and Mr. Van Buren, perhaps."

The convention met, as Messrs. Lewis, Hill, Blair, and Kendall had decreed it should meet, at Baltimore on the 21st of May. Three hundred and twenty-six delegates were present. The General's old friend, Judge Overton, of Tennessee, was to have presided over the assembly, but was prevented from doing so by sickness. The convention soon came to a vote upon the candidates for the second office. Mr. Van Buren received two hundred and sixty votes; Mr. P. P. Barbour, of Virginia, forty; Col. Richard M. Johnston, twenty-six. The opposition noticed, with comment, that this convention adjourned without deigning to issue the usual address to the people.

The plan of the Calhoun wing of the democratic party, if wing it could be called, and if it had a plan, was explained, at the time, by General Duff Green to one of the friends of

Mr. Clay, and by Mr. Clay to his nearest friend, Judge Brooke, of Maryland. It was a wild scheme, or seems such to us who coolly scan it at this distance of time. "Duff explained fully the views and wishes of the Calhoun party. These are, that his name shall, in the course of the ensuing summer (say August), be presented as a candidate; that, if no ticket is run in Virginia by our friends, and if they will coöperate with his, he can obtain the vote of that State; that, with a fair prospect of receiving the vote of Virginia, he will obtain those also of North Carolina, Georgia, and South Carolina, and probably of Alabama and Mississippi; that the result would be to defeat the reëlection of General Jackson, and to devolve the election on the House; that there they suppose I would be elected; and that they would be satisfied with my election. I have neither said nor done any thing in reply to all this, to commit my friends or myself. I could not, without dishonor, have ventured upon any sort of commitment of them. They are, in fact, free, and so I wish them to remain, to act according to their own sense of propriety."

A coalition between the leader of the nullifying free-traders and the champion of the protective system would have been an astonishing conjunction, indeed. And Mr. Clay does not appear to object to it on the ground of its incongruity. He proceeds to ask Judge Brooke whether the thing could be done, and if done, whether it would achieve the end desired of ousting Jackson and finishing the public career of Van Buren. The two factions, so irreconcilably opposed in principle, had already coalesced to reject the nomination of Mr. Van Buren; and the well-informed Dr. Hammond, in his "Political History of New York," intimates that, at the same time, the subsequent compromise between nullification and protection was substantially agreed upon. Let us not, however, get beyond our depth. Suffice it here to say that the scheme of running Mr. Calhoun, so as to throw the election into the House, was not attempted, and that the forces of the opposition, except the anti-masonry party, were concentrated upon Messrs. Clay and Sergeant.

The anti-masonry party, which had nominated Mr. Wirt for the presidency, and Mr. William Ellnaker, of Pennsylvania, for the vice-presidency, was a noisy and earnest party, but proved to have little power except in two localities, western New York and Vermont.

The grounds upon which the opposition rested their case against the administration need not be repeated here. Most of them will occur to the reader.

We support General Jackson, said the friends of the administration, because he has restored the government to the principles of Jefferson ; because he has stayed the corrupt and unconstitutional expenditure of the public money for internal improvements designed for the benefit of localities ; because he has waged war upon that gigantic and overshadowing monopoly, the bank of the United States ; because on the tariff he stands between the two dangerous extremes of free trade and prohibition, and counsels moderation and compromise ; because, in less than two years from the beginning of his administration, the trade to the West Indies, which had been lost by the mismanagement of that which preceded it, was again opened to the United States, on terms of reciprocity ; because, within the same period, treaties of the utmost importance and difficulty have been negotiated with Denmark, Turkey, and France ; because the dispute on the subject of boundaries on our eastern frontier has been brought to an issue by an award advantageous to the United States ; because our relations with every portion of the world are harmonious, and the United States never stood higher in the respect of the world than at this moment ; because Andrew Jackson, himself sprung from the people, and in heart-felt sympathy with them, is the champion and defender of the people against monopolies, bank aristocrats, gambling stockholders, and all others who prey upon the earnings of the farmer and mechanic.

The opposition, in waging this important contest, relied chiefly upon banquets, speeches, pamphlets, newspapers, and caricatures. Caricatures, poorly designed and worse executed, were published in great numbers in the course of the season. A favorite idea of the caricaturists was to depict Mr. Van Buren as an infant in the arms of General Jackson, receiving sustenance from a spoon in the hand of the General. One popular picture represented the President receiving a crown from Mr. Van Buren and a scepter from the devil. Another showed the President raving at a delegation. Another gave Clay and Jackson in the guise of jockeys, riding a race toward the White House—Clay half a length a head. Another represented Jackson, Van Buren, Benton, Blair, Kendall, and others, attired as burglars, aiming a huge battering-ram at the bank's impregnable front door. Another portrayed General Jackson as Don Quixote, tilting at one of the huge pillars of the same marble edifice, and breaking his puny lance against it.

The other party made great use of transparencies, processions, and hickory poles. M. Chevalier, a French gentleman then traveling in the United States, gives an amusing account of the Jackson processions. They were so frequent that the traveler was led to suppose them one of the institutions of the country. "Besides the camp-meetings," he says, "the political processions are the only things in this country which bear any resemblance to festivals. The party dinners, with their speeches and deluge of toasts, are frigid, if not repulsive ; and I have never seen a more miserable affair than the dinner given by the Opposition ; that is to say, by the middle class, at Powelton, in the neighborhood of Philadelphia. But I stopped involuntarily at the sight of the gigantic hickory poles which made their solemn entry on eight wheels, for the purpose of being planted by the democracy on the eve of the election. I remember one of these poles, with its top still crowned with green foliage, which came on to the sound of fifes and drums, and was preceded by ranks of democrats, bearing no other badge than a twig of the sacred tree in their hats. It was drawn by eight horses, decorated with ribbons and mottoes. Astride on the tree itself were a dozen Jackson men of the first water, waving flags with an air of anticipated triumph, and shouting '*Hurra for Jackson!*'

"But this entry of the hickory was but a by-matter compared with the procession I witnessed in New York. It was nearly a mile long. The democrats marched in good order, to the glare of torches; the banners were more numerous than I had ever seen them in any religious festival; all were in transparency, on account of the darkness. On some were inscribed the names of the democratic societies or sections: *Democratic young men of the ninth* or *eleventh ward;* others bore imprecations against the Bank of the United States; *Nick Biddle* and *Old Nick* here figured largely. Then came portraits of General Jackson afoot and on horseback; there was one in the uniform of a general, and another in the person of the Tennessee farmer, with the famous hickory cane in his hand. Those of Washington and Jefferson, surrounded with democratic mottoes, were mingled with emblems in all tastes and of all colors. Among these figured an eagle, not a painting, but a real, live eagle, tied by the legs, surrounded by a wreath of leaves, and hoisted upon a pole, after the manner of the Roman standards. The imperial bird was carried by a stout sailor, more pleased than ever was a sergeant permitted to hold one of the strings of the canopy, in a Catholic ceremony. From further than the eye could reach, came marching on the democrats. I was struck with the resemblance of their air to the train that escorts the *viaticum* in Mexico or Puebla. The American standard-bearers were as grave as the Mexican Indians who bore the sacred tapers. The democratic procession, also, like the Catholic procession, had its halting-places; it stopped before the houses of the Jackson men to fill the air with cheers, and halted at the doors of the leaders of the Opposition, to give three, six, or nine groans. If these scenes were to find a painter, they would be admired at a distance, not less than the triumphs and sacrificial pomps which the ancients have left us delineated in marble and brass; for they are not mere grotesques after the manner of Rembrandt—they belong to history, they partake of the grand; they are the episodes of a wondrous epic which will bequeath a lasting memory to posterity, that of the coming of democracy."*

Betting upon the result of the elections was in great vogue this year, and for several years after. We have seen Mr. Clay and Mr. Van Buren amicably betting a suit of

* The following may seem, and is, a very nonsensical anecdote. Those who can remember the excitement of 1832, will not consider it altogether misplaced here. It is, moreover, an illustration of "universal suffrage:" "During General Jackson's second presidential campaign there flourished at the Quarantine Ground, Staten Island, an honest old fellow, a baker by trade, and a stanch democrat withal. One evening a political meeting was held at a small tavern which then stood on the shore road, a short distance east of the present Pavilion at New Brighton. Our good friend, and several other residents at the Quarantine, attended the meeting. Among them was old Dr. H., who was a noted wag, and it occurred to him that if a speech could be got out of the old baker it would be exceedingly amusing. Accordingly, he called on him for an address.

"'No, no,' said the baker; 'I can make bread, but I can't make speeches.'

"The suggestion, however, had excited the audience, and the old man was at length compelled to make the effort. So, rising in his seat, he said:

"'Feller-citizens: it is well known to you all that when John Quincy Adams was President, the Emperor of Brazil seized several of our ships, and wouldn't let 'em come home. So President Adams wrote him a letter, and a very *purty* letter it was, too—for to give him his due, he knew how to write, if he didn't know any thing else. So the Emperor he got the letter, and, after he had read it, he asked who this Adams was? and his head men told him he was President of the United States. "Well, well," says the Emperor, "he wants me to send them ships home, but I won't do it; for it is quite plain to me that a man who can write so beautiful, don't know any thing about fighting; so the ships must stay where they are." Well,' continued the baker, 'by-and-by Ginral Jackson got to be President, and he wrote a letter to the Emperor, and it was something lik this:

"'"You Emperor, send them ships home right away.

"'"ANDREW JACKSON."

"'Well, the Emperor got that letter too, and after he had read it, he laughed, and said, "This is a mighty queer letter! Who is this Jackson? 'Pears to me I've heerd of him before." "We'll tell you," said his head men, "who he is. He is the New Orleans Jackson." "What!" said the Emperor, "the New Orleans Jackson: That's quite another matter. If this man don't write so beautiful, he knows how to fight; so send them ships home right away." And it was done.'

"This was regarded as a very effective political speech, and was received with thunders of applause."—*Harper's Magazine.*

clothes upon an election. Members of Congress were generally given to the practice. The minor office-holders sought to show their confidence in the success of their party, and to intimidate the opposition, by the extravagance of their bets. Isaac Hill writes to Jesse Hoyt in October: "To meet the braggarts of the opposition I advise my friends that any sum will be safe on the electoral vote of Pennsylvania and New York." Mr. William L. Mackenzie computed, from the evidence of letters, that Jesse Hoyt's election bets amounted in nine years to one hundred and twenty thousand dollars. The letters of Mr. John Van Buren, published a few years ago by Mr. Mackenzie, give us a curious insight into the mysteries of election betting. Note these sentences:

"Can you get any bets on Governor, even? We shall lick the dogs so in this State that the 'Great West' will hear the howling." . . . "Can you get bets on three, four, and five thousand majority for Marcy, two hundred dollars on each?—if not, I will bet five hundred dollars on four thousand—perhaps, if we lose New Jersey, you can get this. If you can't do better, I should like a bet of three hundred dollars on five thousand majority for Marcy—unless we lose New Jersey: in that event I will wait to get better terms." . . . "I should be most particularly obliged to you, if you can get me an even bet against Marcy to any amount less than five thousand dollars. I think I would bet one hundred dollars on each one thousand majority up to five thousand. I would bet fifteen hundred dollars against one thousand dollars on an even election. I consider Marcy's election, by from seven thousand five hundred to fifteen thousand majority, as sure as God." . . . "P. S. I don't care to bet on five thousand majority for Marcy just now: if it is not too late to back out." . . . "In this State our majority will range from fifteen thousand to twenty-five thousand. Bets on fifteen are perfectly safe." . . . "By the looks of Webb's paper (although it is intended no doubt to operate on New Jersey) the opposition gain confidence. Can you tempt them with a wager on three, four, and five thousand majorities—two hundred dollars on each—or five hundred dollars on four thousand? If neither of these can be got to-morrow, bet them five hundred dollars on five thousand majority. There will be no betting after to-morrow." . . "They say 'the blood of the martyrs is the seed of the Church,' and heaven knows I have been freely tapped in the good cause."

One other feature of this campaign remains to be noticed.

Both parties were confident of victory; but if one party was more confident than the other, it was the opposition. The reason of this was, that the printed matter relating to the controversy, with which the country was inundated, was mostly on the side of the opposition. Reading people, themselves under the domination of the printing press, could not but attach great importance to this circumstance. Reading people are not now all aware that not more than one half of the voters of this Union can be reached by print, and that no party that chiefly relies upon the press can carry a general election. A striking pamphlet can influence voters, and so does a well-conducted newspaper; but a hickory pole, a taking cry, a transparency, a burst of sky rockets and Roman candles (alas! that it should be so!) have a potency over a large third of our voters that printed eloquence can not exert.

An event occurred at the close of the month of August that served to complete the infatuation of the party opposed to General Jackson. The *Courier and Enquirer*, so long the sturdy and influential champion of the administration, turned against it, removed the names of Jackson and Van Buren from the head of its editorial columns, and openly joined the opposition. "Since 1823," said Col. Webb, in the course of an explanatory article of three columns, "I have been the firm, undeviating friend of Andrew Jackson, through good and through evil report. I have defended his reputation and advocated his cause; and for the last five years my exertions in his behalf, as the conductor of a public journal, have been known to this community. But the time has now arrived when I owe it to the people, to the institutions of the country, and to myself, to declare my deliberate conviction that he has not realized the high hopes which his reputation and previously written and declared opinions promised, nor redeemed the sacred pledges which he voluntarily gave on his elevation to the first station in the world. Let me not be misunderstood. I do not—I never will—impeach his patriotism or his integrity; but as a sentinel at my post, true to the duty which I voluntarily assumed when I became the editor of a public journal, I feel called upon to proclaim to the people that Andrew Jackson is not their president; that, enfeebled by age, and the toils, cares, and anxieties of an active and laborious life, he no longer possesses his former energy of character or independence of mind; but confiding in those who have wormed themselves into his confidence, he has intrusted the affairs of this great nation, and the happiness of thirteen millions of freemen, to the hands of political gamblers, money-changing, time-serving politicians, who, in the pursuit of their unhallowed purposes, threaten ruin to the country and to that sacred charter of our liberties which was matured by the wisdom of our fathers, after having been purchased with their blood, and the sacrifice of every selfish motive on the altar of public good. The events of the past three years, the occurrences which are almost daily transpiring, the high-handed infringements of the Constitution, and the tone of the official paper at Washington, all but too clearly prove that a few mercenary and unprincipled officers of government, possessing the confidence of the Executive, and leagued with a band of reckless money-changers at Albany, are bringing disgrace and distress upon the country, and destroying the fairest fabric of liberty which an all-wise and beneficent Providence ever bestowed upon man."

Colonel Webb soon had an opportunity of learning whether or not General Jackson possessed his "former energy of character." He was mistaken in attributing General Jackson's late anti-bank measures to the influence of others. General Jackson's animosity to the bank had supplanted in his mind, for the time, all his other animosities. Only four of his confidential counselors, Messrs. Benton, Taney, Blair, and Kendall, were prepared to sustain him in all the measures he had taken, and all the measures he contemplated, against it. Major Lewis held back. A majority of the Cabinet gave him but a cold and hesitating support, and one important member thereof was known to be a friend of the bank. The President needed no stimulant in his warfare against an institution, to destroy which was as much his ruling passion in 1832, as it had been, in 1815, his ruling passion to drive the British army into the sea. The bank had defied him in 1829. The bank had ignored him in 1831. Perish the bank! The United States was not a country large enough to contain two such presidents as Andrew Jackson and Nicholas Biddle.

The defection of the great newspaper had its influence upon the press. Eight papers, if we may believe the opposition editors, soon followed its example.

A few weeks later, the *American* dolorously exclaimed: "The city is lost! The returns from the country come in all one way! There is no doubt that Jackson and Van Buren are elected!"

The result of the election astonished every body. Not the wildest Jackson man in his wildest moment had anticipated a victory quite so overwhelming. Two hundred and eighty-eight was the whole number of electoral votes in 1832. General Jackson received two hundred and nineteen—seventy-four more than a majority. Mr. Van Buren, for the vice-presidency, received one hundred and eighty-nine electoral votes—forty-four more than a majority. Clay and Sergeant obtained FORTY-NINE! William Wirt, of Maryland, and William Ellnaker, of Pennsylvania, the candidates of the anti-masonry party, received the electoral vote of one State, Vermont—a result to which the vehement denunciations of a printer's boy, named Horace Greeley, may have contributed a few votes. South Carolina threw her vote away upon John Floyd, of Virginia, and Henry Lee, of Massachusetts, neither of whom were nullifiers.

The States that voted for General Jackson were these: Maine, New Hampshire, New York, New Jersey, Pennsylvania, Virginia, North Carolina, Georgia, Tennessee, Ohio, Louisiana, Mississippi, Indiana, Illinois, Alabama, and Missouri—sixteen. All of these States but one gave their electoral vote to Mr. Van Buren for the vice-presidency. Pennsylvania preferred William Wilkins for that office, one of her own citizens, who received accordingly thirty votes, and caused Mr. Van Buren to fall thirty votes behind his chief. The States that gave a majority for Clay and Sergeant were: Massachusetts, Rhode Island, Connecticut, Delaware, Maryland, and Kentucky—six.

How can we explain a result so unexpected? First, General Jackson, in his leading public measures (always excepting his appointment-and-removal policy) was RIGHT. Secondly, Society, in all countries and all ages, by the nature of things, is divided into three classes, Top, Bottom, and Middle—kings, lords, and commons—the three estates—Office-Holders, Capitalists, and Workingmen—call them what you will. Any two of these is more than a match for any one of them. In Europe, the despot unites with the masses, and sways the scepter in safety. Or, he unites with the nobles, and the people must submit. The nobles and the people together can put down the despot. In the election of 1832, the President of the United States supported by the masses of the people, repeated, on this republican theater, a triumph supposed to belong only to the history of the Old World.

The Bank of the United States was doomed. The *Globe* had the audacity to say, soon after the election, that members of the defeated party were prompting the "minions of the bank" to save the institution by the only expedient that could save it—the assassination of the President! It further stated, that two members of the Opposition had been overheard to declare, that the man who should do the deed would render his country a signal service, which the bank would gladly reward with a gift of fifty thousand dollars. There was one man then living in the United States who believed that there was truth in these stories. Andrew Jackson was his name. When, a little later, a lunatic aimed a pistol at him, he thought for days that the "minions of the bank" had set him on.

The present Emperor of France witnessed part of this contest between the President of the Republic and the President of the Bank. From an allusion to it in the "Idées Napoléoniennes," we must infer that Napoleon III. was a Jackson man at that day. "The United States," observes the imperial author, "offer us a striking example of the inconveniences which attend the weakness of a civil authority. Although, in that country, there are none of the fermentations of discord, which for a long time yet will trouble Europe, the central power, being weak, is alarmed at every independent organization; for every independent organization threatens it. It is not military power alone which is feared; but money power—the bank: hence a division of parties. The president of the bank might have more power than the President of the country; for a much stronger reason, a successful general would eclipse the civil power."

Well, the clamor of the election, the shouts of triumph, the groans of the defeated, died away in the month of November, and were forgotten. The President, it will be admitted, was a very popular man just then. But who could have foreseen that, within one little month, he was to win over to his side, the very class and the only class that had opposed his reëlection, and attain a popularity more fervid and universal than has been incurred by a citizen of the United States since the first term of General Washington's presidency? Who could have expected to see all New England, headed by New England's favorite, Daniel Webster, joining with all the North and most of the South, in one burst of enthusiastic praise of Andrew Jackson?

Indeed, some of the newspapers went so far as to nominate General Jackson for a third term. "My opinion is," wrote Mr. Wirt, "that he may be President for life if he chooses."

XVIII.

NULLIFICATION AS AN IDEA.

"A RENDERING void and of no effect, or of no legal effect," is the definition given by Noah Webster of this word, nullification. It was introduced into American politics as early as 1798, when the passage of the odious Alien and Sedition laws prompted the Legislatures of Virginia and Kentucky to adopt certain resolutions known to history as the Resolutions of '98, of which Mr. Madison and Mr. Jefferson were the chief authors. One of these resolutions declared that when the general government assumed powers not delegated by the States, "a nullification of the act was the rightful remedy." The resolutions declared, however, that the act nullified must be "so palpably against the constitution as to amount to an undisguised declaration that the compact is not meant to be the measure of the powers of the general government, but that it will proceed to exercise over the States all powers whatsoever, by seizing the rights of the States, and consolidating them in the hands of the general government." The authors of the resolutions contemplated a concurrence with the act of nullification by other States, or by all the States. Their object, evidently, was to provide for a united protest against usurpation, and, if necessary, for united action against it. The resolutions were drawn and passed by men who loved the union of these States. They were drawn and passed in the interest of the Union, for the sake of the Union, to cement the Union, to avert danger from the Union, to provide a way of restoring the Union if it should ever be threatened with dissolution.

The interpretation put upon the Resolutions of '98 by the Nullifiers of 1832 was this: Any single State may nullify any act of Congress which it deems unconstitutional. Mr. Calhoun contended that such nullification was not an act tending to dissolve the Union, but, on the contrary, to strengthen it. Every thing else could go on as before. The nullifying State merely refused obedience to *one* objectionable act, and would wait patiently for Congress to repeal it. The extreme nullifiers, the men of that party who had honest minds, boldly avowed that the resolutions of 1798 meant that *any State of this Union may secede from the Union whenever it likes!* And this is the real meaning of the nullification doctrines of 1832. The language of Mr. Calhoun, guarded and labored as it is, amounts to that, and nothing short of that. He proposed the nullification of a revenue law, and a revenue law *must* be universal in its operation or it can not any where be obeyed. He contemplated a posture of affairs which rendered it necessary for the Union to obey South Carolina, or for South Carolina to give laws to the Union.

What, then, of the Supreme Court, the appointed arbiter between State and State, between a State and the United States? Why, said Mr. Calhoun, the Supreme Court is as much the creature of a Majority as Congress itself; and the very object of nullification is to resist the encroachments of tyrant Majority. The Supreme Court is *already committed to the side of the stronger*, to which stronger the judges owe their offices; and, therefore, can not justly be allowed a voice in the matter. Lest any one should find it impossible to believe, without the evidence, that a man of Mr. Calhoun's force and ability could deliberately utter such sentiments, I will insert here the curious paragraph from his first formal utterance upon nullification, which disposes of the Supreme Court. The italics are Mr. Calhoun's:

"It is an universal and fundamental political principle, that the power to protect can safely be confided only to those interested in protecting, or their responsible agents, a maxim not less true in private than in public affairs. The danger in our system is, that the General Government, which represents the interests of the whole, may encroach on the States, which represent the peculiar and local interests, or that the latter may encroach on the former. In examining this point, we ought not to forget that the government, through all its departments, judicial as well as others, is administered by delegated and responsible agents; and that *the power which really controls ultimately all the movements is not in the agents, but those who elect or appoint them.* To understand, then, its real character, and what would be the action of the system in any supposable case, we must raise our view from the mere agents to this high controlling power which finally impels every movement of the machine. By doing so, we shall find all under the control of the will of a majority, compounded of the will of the majority of the people of the States estimated in federal numbers. These united constitute the real and final power, which impels and directs the movements of the General Government. The majority of the States elect the majority of the Senate; of the people of the States, that of the House of Representatives; the two united, the President; and the President and a majority of the Senate appoint the Judges; a majority of whom, and a majority of the Senate and the House with the President, really exercise all of the powers of the government, with the exception of the cases where the Constitution requires a greater number than a majority. The Judges are, in fact, as truly the Judicial Representatives of this united majority, as the majority of Congress itself, or the President is its legislative or executive representative; and to confide the power to the Judiciary to determine, finally and conclusively, what powers are delegated and what reserved, would be in reality to confide it to the majority, whose agents they are, and by whom they can be controlled in various ways; and, of course, to subject (against the fundamental principle of our system and all sound political reasoning) the reserved powers of the States, with all of the local and peculiar interests they were intended to protect, to the will of the very majority against which the pretection was intended. Nor will the tenure by which the Judges hold their office, however valuable the provision in many other respects, materially vary the case. Its highest possible effect would be to *retard* and not *finally* to *resist*, the will of a dominant majority."

Of course it would. And the belief is, and has always been prevalent in the United States, that the majority *ought* to be the ruling power in the republic.

The comment of General Jackson upon this reasoning is about the best which the discussion elicited. "If this thing goes on," he exclaimed to his old courier, General Sam. Dale, of Mississippi, "our country will be like a bag of meal with both ends open. Pick it up in the middle or endwise, it will run out." A homely and forcible summing up of the Websterian argument.

It behoves every citizen of the United States to understand this subject of nullification. And never was there more need that it should be generally understood than in the year 1860. So much of it as relates to General Jackson and his administration, I will now proceed to elucidate as clearly as I can.

Every Southerner who has visited the North, and every Northerner who has traveled in the South, has been struck with the contrast exhibited in the general aspect of the two sections. The Northerner who finds himself, for the first time, in the heart of a Southern State, surveys the scene around him with astonishment. He is told that the country upon which he looks has been settled for a hundred or a hundred and fifty years ; but he beholds all the signs which, in his own section, denote a new settlement. He is amazed at the apparent fewness of the people, at the vast quantities of wild or worn out lands, at the dilapidated tenements, at the air of desolation which pervades the scene. The villages are few and far between, and present a contrast the most complete to the trim, tidy, clean, well-shaded, delightful villages of his northern home. If he alights and mingles among the people, and, particularly, if he resides for a while upon a plantation, he discovers that his first impressions were not altogether correct. He learns that there *is* at the South a certain substantial prosperity, not indicated by the general appearance of the country. But he also perceives that such prosperity as there is, is shared by a comparatively small portion of the people. Young men without capital or influential friends do not find there that variety of employments, those chances to rise, which gives to every kind of northern talent such a stimulus to exertion. The stranger finds himself regarding the amiable young men whom he meets with a kind of compassionate curiosity. He wonders what they are going to do in life. Between those colossal estates there does not seem any room for a young fellow to edge in and make his way. The professions, too, offer less inducement there than elsewhere, owing to the general smallness of the towns and the thinness of the country population.

A fine old Virginia gentleman, one of the olden time, who has inherited a fine estate, finds life at the South sufficiently pleasant, no doubt. But to unfriended, uncapitaled, aspiring young men, the class whose energy and ambition make the North what it is, the South does not offer a tempting sphere of exertion.

The contrast between the slow and limited prosperity of the South, and the swift, noisy, marvelous progress of the North, was never so striking as it was during the administration of General Jackson. The North was rushing on like a western high-pressure steamboat, with rosin in the furnace and a man on the safety-valve. All through western New York, Ohio, Indiana, Illinois, the primeval wilderness was vanishing like a mist, and towns were springing into existence with a rapidity that rendered necessary a new map every month, and spoiled the gazetteers as fast as they were printed. The city of New York, as Mr. Irving has beautifully told us, began already to feel itself the London of the New World, and to calculate how many years must elapse before it would be the London of the universe.

The South, meanwhile, was depressed and anxious. Cotton was down. Tobacco was down. Corn, wheat, and pork were down. For several years the chief products of the South had either been inclining downward, or else had risen in price too slowly to make up for the (alleged) increased price of the commodities which the South was compelled to buy. Few new towns changed the Southern map. Charleston languished, or seemed to languish ; certainly did not keep pace with New York, Boston, and Philadelphia. No Cincinnati of the South became the world's talk by the startling rapidity of its growth. No Southern river exhibited, at every bend and coyne of vantage, a rising village. No Southern mind, distracted with the impossibility of devising suitable names for a thousand new places per annum, fell back in despair upon the map of the old world, and selected at random any convenient name that presented itself, bestowing upon clusters of log-huts such titles as Utica, Rome, Palermo, Naples, Russia, Egypt, Madrid, Paris, Elba, and Berlin. No Southern commissioner, compelled to find names for a hundred streets at once, had seized upon the letters of the alphabet and the figures of arithmetic, and called his avenues A, B, C, and D, and instead of naming his cross streets, numbered them.

Upon the fact of this contrast between the North and South, all the earlier nullification debates turned. Mr. Clay struck the key-note when he began his three days' speech upon the tariff in 1832, with a glowing picture of the prosperity of the country. Southern gentlemen replied, particularly Mr. John Tyler, of Virginia, that Mr. Clay's eloquent periods applied only to one section of the Union. The North, it was true, was bounding forward on a bright career, but the South was paralyzed and desolate. Northern members could not deny the essential truth of the Southerners' lamentation. It was respecting the CAUSE of the contrast that the debaters differed.

The cause, the cause, ye most chaste stars ! How could any man, at that day, look upon the South and not see the cause ? The Southern system, be it wrong or be it right, be it wise or be it unwise, is one that does not attract emigrants ; and the Northern system does ! That is the great cause.

From the hour when Columbus sprang exulting upon these western shores, the great interest of America has been emigration. That country of the new world has prospered most which has attracted the greatest number of the best emigrants, by affording them the best chance to attain the sole object of emigration, the improvement of their condition ; and that portion of that country has out-stripped the rest which offered to emigrants the most promising field of labor. For, a MAN, view him in what light you may, is the most precious thing in the world. He is wealth in its most concentrated form. A stalwart, virtuous, skillful, thoughtful man, progenitor of an endless line of such, planted in our western wilds, to hew out home and fortune with his own glorious and beautiful right hand and heart, is worth to the State that wins him a thousand times his weight in Koh-i-nor. Such have poured into the northern States, in an abounding flood, these fifty years. Behold what they have wrought!

Such emigrants go to the South in inconsiderable numbers. Partly, because from infancy they learn to loathe the very name of slavery. They sicken at the thought of it. They shrink from contact with it. They take Wesley's characterization of it in the most literal acceptation of the words, and esteem it the SUM of all villainies—that solely possible crime which includes, in its single self, all the wrong that man can wreak on man. Whether they are right, or whether they are wrong, in so thinking, is not a question here. They think so. And if they did not, they would not go in great numbers to the South, because it does not afford to a man with six children and a hundred dollars the immediate opportunities for profitable and congenial labor which the North affords. On the prairies, in the forests of the North, the struggling emigrant finds himself surrounded by neighbors whose condition, antecedents, prospects, social standing, are all similar to his own. There is no great proprietor to overtop him. There is no slave with whom he has to compete. He forgets that there is any such thing as a graduated social scale, and feels that by virtue of his manhood alone, he stands on a level with the best.

To this great cause of the contrast between the South and the North is to be added the unskillful labor of slaves. In the debate of 1832, no one dwelt more forcibly upon this than Mr. George M. Dallas, of the Senate. "The lights of science," said he, "and the improvements of art, which vivify and accelerate elsewhere, can not penetrate, or, if they do, penetrate with dilatory inefficiency among the operatives of the South. They are merely instinctive and passive. While the intellectual industry of other parts of this country springs elastically forward at every fresh impulse, and manual labor is propelled and redoubled by countless inventions, machines, and contrivances, instantly understood and at once exercised, the South remains stationary, inaccessible to such encouraging and invigorating aids. Nor is it possible to be wholly blind to the moral effect of this species of labor upon those freemen among whom it exists. A disrelish for humble and hardy occupation ; a pride adverse to drudgery and toil ; a dread that to partake in the employments allotted to color may be accompanied also by its degradation, are natural and inevitable. The high and lofty qualities which, in other scenes, and for other purposes, characterize and adorn our Southern brethren, are fatal to the enduring patience, the corporeal exertion, and the painstaking simplicity, by which only a successful yeomanry can be formed. When, in fact, the Senator from South Carolina asserts that 'slaves are too improvident, too incapable of that minute, constant, delicate attention, and that persevering industry which is essential to the success of manufacturing establishments,' he himself admits the defect in the condition of southern labor, by which the progress of his favorite section must be retarded. He admits an inability to keep pace with the rest of the world. He admits an inherent weakness ; a weakness neither engendered nor aggravated by the tariff, which, as societies are now constituted and directed, must drag in the rear, and be distanced in the common race."

These explanations, and explanations such as these, though they were received by southern gentlemen then, as they are by southern gentlemen now, with respect and courtesy, were not satisfactory to them then any more than they are now. No, said Mr. Tyler, the protective tariff is the cause of our calamities and our decay. "We buy dear and sell cheap"—that is the simple secret. The tariff raises the price of all we buy, and diminishes the demands for our products abroad, by diminishing the power of foreign nations to buy them. To this assertion the protectionists replied then, as they reply now, by the broad statement that every article of manufacture, adequately protected, soon becomes cheaper than it ever was before. Mr. Clay appealed to his own experience, as a hemp-grower, when he said that the cottton bagging supplied by the Kentucky planters had fallen in price since it was protected by a high duty. As soon, he maintained, as it is made possible in the United States to manufacture an article of general utility, two forces, constantly operating, unite to cheapen it, namely, Competition and Ingenuity.

This is not the place for a discussion of the tariff question, nor is the present chronicler the individual to undertake that question any where. The object here is merely to show the state of feeling at the time, which emboldened Mr. Calhoun to take the course he did. The North and the South were divided in opinion as to the effects of protective duties upon the prosperity of the country ; the North believing that such duties were beneficial to the whole country ; the South being of opinion, that they were stimulating to northern industry, but paralyzing to southern.

It is also to be noted, that from a very early period in the history of the United States, there has been some degree of antipathy between the two sections, an antipathy engendered by ignorance and fostered by misrepresentation. It can be truly said, that, at this moment, neither section understands the other, because neither section sympathizes with the other. And there is no true knowledge without love. I see indications of ill feeling in the newspapers as early as 1796, when slavery was not a sectional institution. In the *Connecticut Courant* of 1796, a communication appeared, signed Pelham, copied into the *Philadelphia New World*, which anticipates much that is current in 1860. This article is valuable as a mere historical curiosity :

"We have reached," says Pelham, "a critical period in our political existence. The question must soon be decided, whether we will continue a nation, at the expense even of our Union, or sink encumbered with the present mass of difficulty into confusion and slavery. On a subject so interesting as this, it is hazardous to speak. But it is still more hazardous to remain silent.

"I think it will not be an easy task to discover any thing like an equivalent gained by the Northern States, for the admission of the negroes into the mass of inhabitants in the Southern States, in order to swell the size of the representation into the general Congress. The importance of this point to the Southern States, will strikingly appear by a very slight examination. Negroes are in all respects, except in regard to life and death, the cattle of the citizens of the Southern States. If they were good for food, the probability is, that even the power of destroying their lives would be enjoyed by their owners, as fully as it is over the lives of their cattle. It can not be, that their laws prohibit the owners from killing their slaves, because those slaves are human beings, or because it is regarded as a mortal evil to destroy them. If that were the case, how can they justify their being treated in all other respects like brutes? For it is in this point of view alone that negroes in the Southern States are considered, in fact, as different from cattle. They are bought and sold; they are fed or kept hungry; they are clothed or reduced to nakedness; they are beaten, turned out to the fury of the tempest, and torn from their dearest connections, with as little remorse as if they were beasts of the field. On what principle, then, were they noticed among their masters in the scale of representation? They have no interests to protect; no happiness to advance; the laws afford them no security except for their lives; and the government furnishes them with no advantages. If, to balance this claim, the Northern States had demanded, that three-fifths of the whole number of their horses and cattle should be added to the amount of free persons, the claim, doubtless, would have been rejected with indignation. But it was thought expedient that the Southern States should be indulged in a claim equally absurd and unfounded. Where the equivalent rests, I am ignorant.

"When it becomes a serious question, whether we shall give up our government, or part with the States south of the Potomac, no man north of that river, whose heart is not thoroughly democratic, can hesitate what decision to make. That this question is nearly ripe for decision, there can be but little doubt. It is therefore time that the public mind should be employed in examining it attentively, in order that, when the period arrives, the decision may be made coolly and with firmness."

That the feeling disclosed in these paragraphs was not confined to the North, can be easily shown. Col. Crockett, a Tennesseean of the olden time, told the people of Boston, at the public dinner given him at that city in 1832, that he and thousands more of the Southern people had been brought up to despise the inhabitants of New England. "We have always been taught," he said, "to look upon the people of New England as a selfish, cunning set of fellows, that were fed on fox ears and thistle tops; that cut their wisdom-teeth as soon as they were born; that made money by their wits, and held on to it by nature; that called cheatery mother-wit; that hung on to political power because they had numbers; that raised up manufactures to keep down the South and West; and, in fact, had so much of the devil in all their machinery, that they would neither lead nor drive, unless the load was going into their own cribs. But I assure you, gentlemen, I begin to think differently of you, and I think I see a good many good reasons for so doing. I don't mean that because I eat your bread and drink your liquor, that I feel so. No; that don't make me see clearer than I did. It is your habits, and manners, and customs; your industry; your proud, independent spirits; your hanging on to the eternal principles of right and wrong; your liberality in prosperity, and your patience when you are ground down by legislation, which, instead of crushing you, whets your invention to strike a path without a blaze on a tree to guide you; and above all, your never-dying, deathless grip to our glorious constitution. These are the things that make me think that you are a mighty good people."

The caricatures and burlesques of Jackson's day are full of this mutual antipathy. They show us that the feeling between the two sections was similar to that which exists between a country gentleman of the proud old school, with an estate heavily mortgaged, and a rich manufacturer living in his neighborhood, sprung from nothing, and carrying the country all before him with his showy mansion and bursting purse. One of these burlesques, the "Memoirs of a Nullifier," corroborates Col. Crockett with tolerable humor. The author conducts his readers into the judgment hall of Rhadamanthus, and reports the examination of the spirit of a departed Yankee:

"Soon we heard one of the constables call out, 'Virgil Hoskins! Virgil Hoskins!' 'Here,' answered our companion the Yankee peddler, quaking up to the bar. Rhadamanthus was seated with a great number of huge account-books before him. 'Virgil Hoskins is your name, is it?'

said he. 'Here it is among the H's, page 49,358. Ah, Virgil! there's a terribly long account against you. Let's see a few of the charges.' (*Reads.*)

"VIRGIL HOSKINS. DR.

"June 27, 18—. To selling, in the course of one peddling expedition, 497,368 wooden nutmegs, 281,532 Spanish segars made of oak leaves, and 647 wooden clocks.

"'What do you say to that charge, Hoskins?'

"*Hoskins.* 'Why, that was counted in our place about the greatest peddling trip that ever was made over the Potomac.'

"*Rhadamanthus reads:* June 29, 18—. To stealing an old grindstone, smearing it over with butter, and then selling it as a cheese.

"*Hoskins, in great surprise.* 'Jimminny! Surely you wouldn't punish a man for that, would you?'

"*Rhadamanthus reads:* December 13, 1780. To making a counterfeit dollar of pewter, when you were six years old, and cheating your own father with it.

"*Hoskins.* 'Daddy was mighty glad when he found it out. He said it showed I had a genius.'

"*Rhadamanthus reads:* July 2, 18—. To taking a worn-out pair of shoes, which you found in the road, and selling them to a pious old lady as being actually the shoes of Saint Paul.

"*Hoskins, with exultation.* 'I made four dollars and twelve and a half cents by that.'

"*Rhadamanthus reads:* July 2, 18—. To taking an empty old watch-case, putting a live cricket into it, and then selling it as a patent lever in full motion.

"*Hoskins.* 'He, he, he; that was one of the 'cutest tricks I ever played in all my life.'

"*Rhadamanthus:* 'It would occupy me a week, Hoskins, to go through all the charges against you. These few are sufficient. I really am getting entirely out of patience with New England, for it gives me more trouble than all the rest of the world put together. You are sentenced to be thrown into a lake of boiling molasses, where nearly all your countrymen already are, with that same old grindstone tied to your neck, and to remain there for ever.'"

The same writer represents a Yankee orator promulgating from the stump:

"1. That two and two do not make four, but something else, I have not yet exactly ascertained what.

"2. That the higher the tax upon articles of merchandise, the lower will be the price; the imagination can fix no limit to the cheapness to be thus obtained.

"3. That the higher the price of Northern manufactures, the better for us, as it will make us rich.

"4. That the lower the price of cotton, and other Southern products, the better for those who raise them, as it will force them to be economical, and economy is one of the chief of the virtues."

The burlesque concludes by a chemical analysis of a Yankee's soul:

"The devil is a wonderfully skillful chemist, and knows how to analyze all substances, whether material or spiritual. In a few minutes he erected a furnace, seized one of the Yankees, and disengaged from the body that which in these animals supplies the place of a soul. It stood up before us, a thing utterly strange and indescribable. He put it into a large crucible, reduced it to a fluid mass, and then separated the component parts.

"It consisted of—

	Parts in a thousand.
Cunning,	125
Hypocrisy,	125
Avarice,	125
Falsehood,	125
Sneakingness,	125
Nameless and numberless small vices,	140
Essence of onions, New England rum, molasses, and cod-fish,	235
	1000

A retort appeared at the North, which was more than equal in humor and point to the "Memoirs of a Nullifier." It was entitled, "A Yankee among the Nullifiers." The following amusing passage is full of the feeling of the hour:

"As I was one evening in company with sundry Nullifiers, one of them related the following:

"'I am very particular,' said he, 'never to use an article of American manufacture on any consideration whatever. It costs me a great deal more, to be sure, to obtain those of foreign production. But I am determined not to encourage the advocates of protection; and would sooner go fifty miles, and pay a hundred per cent. more than a thing is worth, if it be only imported, than have a similar article of American manufacture brought to my very door and sold at a fair price.

"'But in spite of all my care, I sometimes get confoundedly taken in.

Why, it was only last week that I discovered a monstrous cheat that had been put upon me. Falling into conversation with a Yankee, I launched out as usual against the Tariff, and swore that I would go bareheaded and barebacked till the end of time, sooner than I would wear a coat made of American cloth, or a hat manufactured in an American shop.

" 'With that the fellow poked out his hand and desired, if it was no offense, to examine the quality of my coat. "You may examine it as much as you please," said I; "but you 'll find it 's none of your Yankee manufacture?"

" ' "There 's where your mistaken, Mister," said he. "I helped make that cloth myself at the Pontoosuc Factory, in old Barkshire, Massachusetts."

" ' "The devil you did!" said I. "Why, I purchased this cloth of a merchant who assured me positively that it was of British manufacture. But what makes you think it is American cloth, and especially that it was made at the Pon——, what do you call it, Factory?"

" ' "Why, I know by the feel of it. Any fool might know that."

" 'He then made a like request—provided always it was no offense—to examine my hat. "You are devilish afraid of giving offense," said I, at the same time handing him my hat; "but at all events you 'll not find that of American manufacture. It 's real London made. I paid ten dollars for it to the importer."

" ' "The more fool you, then," said he; "why, I made that hat with my own hands, in the town of Danbury, Connecticut; and I can buy as many jest like it as you can shake a stick at, for four dollars apiece."

" ' "Confound you, for a lying Yankee!" said I, beginning to get angry at the fellow's impertinence—"do you pretend to be a hatter and cloth manufacturer too? But here 's sufficient evidence, inside of the hat, to convict you of an untruth; here 's the name of the manufacturer, Bond-street, London."

" ' "Ha! ha! ha!" said he, laughing in my face—"I printed that label in Hartford, Connecticut."

" ' "You Yankee scoundrel!" said I, "what hav'nt you done?"

" ' "I never did so foolish a thing," replied he, "as to pay twice as much for British manufactures as I have to give for American ones; and after all, find the goods had been made in the workshops of our own country."

" 'This capped the climax of the fellow's impertinence; and I kicked him out doors for his pains.' "

Here, then, was material upon which the great nullifier could work—the discontent of the South with the protective system, and the popular antipathy between the two sections of the Union. It proved an explosive material in his hands.

XIX.

NULLIFICATION AS AN EVENT.

CALHOUN began it. Calhoun continued it. Calhoun stopped it.

So much is known. But the means are not accessible, and are not likely to be, of forming a certain judgment respecting the character of this celebrated person. We can not positively determine whether he was a selfish, or merely a mistaken man ; or, in other words, whether it was the love of the presidency, or of justice and South Carolina, that impelled him.

The old Jackson men of the inner set still speak of Mr. Calhoun in terms which show that they consider him at once the most wicked and the most despicable of American statesmen. He was a coward, conspirator, hypocrite, traitor, and fool, say they. He strove, schemed, dreamed, lived, only for the presidency ; and when he despaired of reaching that office by honorable means, he sought to rise upon the ruins of his country—thinking it better to reign in South Carolina than to serve in the United States. General Jackson lived and died in this opinion. In his last sickness he declared that, in reflecting upon his administration, he chiefly regretted that he had not had John C. Calhoun executed for treason. "My country," said the General, "would have sustained me in the act, and his fate would have been a warning to traitors in all time to come."

It is painful to be compelled to think ill of a character beloved by the people of one State, admired by the people of many States, generally respected in all the States. Bulwer and others have maintained that we can not learn a man's character from his writings. Perhaps not, when his writings are imaginative and emotional, because such effusions do not tell the secret of secrets—whether the good feelings of the author have power to control his conduct. A man of the right stamp lives better than he writes: a man of the wrong stamp writes better than he lives. The writings of Mr. Calhoun, voluminous, argumentative, difficult to read, seem to reveal to us an honest, earnest nature. We should naturally infer from them that, soured in some degree by his disappointment with regard to the presidency, he had fallen under the domination of one idea, which he spent his last years in promulgating, and of which he seemed to die. We also learn from those who associated familiarly with him that he was personally the most amiable, gracious, and even fascinating of men. The pages of the Senate-chamber liked to serve him. The reporters of the Washington press were fond of him. His neighbors in South Carolina loved him. It was only his equals and rivals, Clay, Jackson, Crawford, and the rest, who hated him; and they *did* hate him most cordially. And I am bound to state that, after long holding out against their view of his character, a close survey of his political career has compelled me to doubt both his patriotism and his sincerity. I can not reconcile some of his important actions with the usual theory that he was a pure, but mistaken man. I can not resist the conclusion that it was the mania for the presidency (which has led so many promising spirits to their damnation) that inspired all his later efforts. It does really seem that from the hour when public men feel themselves to be on the road to the presidential mansion—that whited sepulchre of all that is best in human nature—they all, in some degree, cease to be worthy of themselves. They take on board, as it were, and stow away in the hold of their souls a huge magnet, which pulls the needle of conscience all awry. If only those candidates for the presidency who have passed that tremendous ordeal without just reproach throw stones at Mr. Calhoun's memory, his good name is safe.

But let us come to the facts. The war of 1812 left the country burthened with a debt of one hundred and thirty millions of dollars, and blessed with a great number of small manufactories. The debt and the manufactories were both results of the war. By cutting off the supply of foreign manufactured articles, the war had produced upon the home manufacturing interest the effect of a prohibitory tariff. To pay the interest of this great debt and occasional installments of the principal, it was necessary for the government to raise a far larger revenue than had ever before been collected in the United States. The new manufacturing interest asked that the duties should be so regulated as to afford some part of that complete protection which the war had given it. The peace, that had been welcomed with such wild delight in 1815, had prostrated entire branches of manufacture to which the war had given a sudden development.

Among those who advocated the claims of the manufacturers in the session of 1815–'16, and strove to have the protective principle permanently incorporated into the revenue legislation of Congress, the most active, the most zealous, was John C. Calhoun, member of the House of Representatives from South Carolina. He spoke often on the subject, and he spoke unequivocally. Mr. Clay, who was then the friend, ally, and messmate of Mr. Calhoun, admitted that the Carolinian had surpassed himself in the earnestness with which he labored in the cause of protection.

One of his arguments was drawn from the condition of Poland at the time. "The country in Europe," said he, "having the most skillful workmen, is broken up. It is to us, if wisely used, more valuable than the repeal of the Edict of Nantes was to England. She had the prudence to profit by it—let us not discover less political sagacity. Afford to ingenuity and industry immediate and AMPLE PROTECTION, and they will not fail to give a preference to this free and happy country."

The protectionists, led by Messrs. Clay and Calhoun, triumphed in 1816. In the tariff bill of 1820, the principle was carried farther, and still farther in those of 1824 and 1828. Under the protective system, manufactures flourished, and the public debt was greatly diminished. It attracted skillful workmen to the country, as Mr. Calhoun had said it would, and contributed to swell the tide of ordinary emigration.

But, about the year 1824, it began to be thought, that the advantages of the system were enjoyed chiefly by the Northern States, and the South hastened to the conclusion that the protective system was the cause of its lagging behind. There was, accordingly, a considerable southern opposition to the tariff of 1824, and a general southern opposition to that of 1828. In the latter year, however, the South elected to the presidency General Jackson, whose votes and whose writings had committed him to the principle of protection. Southern politicians felt that the General, as a southern man, was more likely to further their views than Messrs. Adams and Clay, both of whom were peculiarly devoted to protection.

As the first years of General Jackson's administration wore away without affording to the South the "relief" which they had hoped from it, the discontent of the southern people increased. Circumstances gave them a new and most telling argument. In 1831, the public debt had been so far diminished as to render it certain that in three years, the last dollar of it would be paid. The government had been collecting about twice as much revenue as its annual expenditures required. In three years, therefore, there would be an annual surplus of twelve or thirteen millions of dollars. The South demanded, with almost a united voice, that the duties should be reduced so as to make the revenue equal to the expenditure, and that, in making this reduction, the principle of protection should be, in effect, abandoned. Protection should thenceforth be "incidental" merely. The session of 1831–'2 was the one during which southern gentlemen hoped to effect this great change in the policy of the country. The President's Message, as we have seen, also announced that, in view of the speedy extinction of the public debt, it was high time that Congress should prepare for the threatened Surplus.

The case was one of real difficulty. It was a case for a

statesman. No *body* of men ever assembled could have disposed of it without doing injury to some important interest. To reduce the revenue thirteen millions, at one fell and indiscriminate swoop, would close half the workshops in the country. At the same time, for the United States to go on raising thirteen millions a year more than was necessary for carrying on the government, would have been an intolerable absurdity.

Mr. Clay, after an absence from the halls of Congress of six years, returned to the Senate in December, 1831—an illustrious figure, the leader of the opposition, its candidate for the Presidency, his old renown enhanced by his long exile from the scene of his well-remembered triumphs. The galleries filled when he was expected to speak. He was in the prime of his prime. He never spoke so well as then, nor as often, nor so long, nor with so much applause. But he either could not, or dared not, undertake the choking of the Surplus. What wise, complete, far-reaching measure *can* a candidate for the presidency link his fortunes to? He treated it as he did a certain "lion" in 1819, mentioned in a previous volume. He wounded, without killing it; and he was *compelled*, at a later day, to do what it had been glorious voluntarily to attempt in 1832. He proposed merely "that the duties upon articles imported from foreign countries, and not coming into competition with similar articles made or produced within the United States, be forthwith abolished, except the duties upon wines and silks, and that those be reduced." After a debate of months' duration, a bill in accordance with this proposition passed both Houses, and was signed by the President. It preserved the protective principle intact; it reduced the income of the government about three millions of dollars; and it inflamed the discontent of the South to such a degree, that one State, under the influence of a man of force, became capable of—Nullification.

The President signed the bill, as he told his friends, because he deemed it an approach to the measure required. His influence, during the session, had been secretly exerted in favor of compromise. Major Lewis, at the request of the President, had been much in the lobbies and committee-rooms of the capitol, urging members of both sections to make concessions. The President thought that the just course lay between the two extremes of abandoning the protective principle and of reducing the duties in total disregard of it.

"You must yield something on the tariff question," said Major Lewis to the late Governor Marcy, of New York, "or Mr. Van Buren will be sacrificed."

Said Governor Marcy in reply: "I am Mr. Van Buren's friend, but the protective system is more important to New York than Mr. Van Buren."

To return to Mr. Calhoun. His hostile correspondence with the President was published by him, as we have before stated, in the spring of 1831. The President retorted by getting rid of the three members of the cabinet who favored the succession of Mr. Calhoun to the presidency. Three months after, in the *Pendleton Messenger* of South Carolina, Mr. Calhoun continued the strife by publishing his first treatise upon nullification. As there was no obvious reason for such a publication at that moment, the Vice-President began his essay by giving a reason for it. "It is one of the peculiarities," said he, "of the station I occupy, that while it necessarily connects its incumbent with the politics of the day, it affords him no opportunity officially to express his sentiments, except accidentally on an equal division of the body over which he presides. He is thus exposed, as I have often experienced, to have his opinions erroneously and variously represented. In ordinary cases, the correct course I conceive to be to remain silent, leaving to time and circumstances the correction of misrepresentations; but there are occasions so vitally important, that a regard both to duty and character would seem to forbid such a course; and such I conceive to be the present. The frequent allusions to my sentiments will not permit me to doubt that such, also, is the public conception, and that it claims the right to know, in relation to the question referred to, the opinions of those who hold important official stations; while, on my part, desiring to receive neither unmerited praise nor blame, I feel, I trust, the solicitude which every honest and independent man ought, that my sentiments should be truly known, whether they be such as may be calculated to recommend them to public favor or not. Entertaining these impressions, I have concluded that it is my duty to make known my sentiments; and I have adopted the mode which, on reflection, seemed to be the most simple, and best calculated to effect the object in view."

The essay, which fills five columns of the *Courier and Enquirer*, is divided into two parts. First, the Vice-President endeavors to show that nullification is the natural, proper, and peaceful remedy for an intolerable grievance inflicted by Congress upon a State or upon a section; secondly, that the tariff law of 1828, unless rectified during the next session of Congress, will be such a grievance. He went all lengths against the protective principle. It was unconstitutional, unequal in its operation, oppressive to the South, an evil "inveterate and dangerous." The reduction of duties to the revenue standard could be delayed no longer "without the most distracting and dangerous consequences." "The honest and obvious course is, to prevent the accumulation of the surplus in the treasury, by a timely and judicious reduction of the imposts; and thereby to leave the money in the pockets of those who made it; and from whom it can not be honestly nor constitutionally taken, unless required by the fair and legitimate wants of the government. If, neglecting a disposition so obvious and just, the government should attempt to keep up the present high duties, when the money was no longer wanted, or to dispose of this immense surplus by enlarging the old, or devising new schemes of appropriations; or, finding that to be impossible, it should adopt the most dangerous, unconstitutional, and absurd project ever devised by any government, of dividing the surplus among the States (a project which, if carried into execution, could not fail to create an antagonist interest between the States and General Government, on all questions of appropriations, which would certainly end in reducing the latter to a mere office of collection and distribution), either of these modes would be considered by the section suffering under the present high duties, as a fixed determination to perpetuate forever what it considers the present unequal, unconstitutional, and oppressive burden ; *and, from that moment, it would cease to look to the general government for relief.*"

Nullification is distinctly announced in this passage. It seems to be again announced, as a thing inevitable, in the concluding words of the essay : "In thus placing my opinions before the public, I have not been actuated by the expectation of changing the public sentiment. Such a motive, on a question so long agitated, and so beset with feelings of prejudice and interest, would argue, on my part, an insufferable vanity, and a profound ignorance of the human heart. To avoid, as far as possible, the imputation of either, I have confined my statements on the many and important points on which I have been compelled to touch, to a simple declaration of my opinion, without advancing any other reasons to sustain them than what appeared to me to be indispensable to the full understanding of my views. With every caution on my part, I dare not hope, in taking the step I have, to escape the imputation of improper motives ; though I have without reserve freely expressed my opinions, not regarding whether they might or might not be popular. I have no reason to believe that they are such as will conciliate public favor, but the opposite ; which I greatly regret, as I have ever placed a high estimate on the good opinion of my fellow-citizens. But, be this as it may, I shall at least be sustained by feelings of conscious rectitude. I have formed my opinions after the most careful and deliberate examination, with all the aids which my reason and experience could furnish ; I have expressed them honestly and fearlessly, regardless of their effects personally ; which, however interesting to me individually, are of too little importance to be taken into the estimate where the liberty and happiness of our country are so vitally involved."

In this performance, Mr. Calhoun did not refer to his forgotten championship of the protective policy in 1816. The busy burrowers of the press, however, occasionally brought to the surface a stray memento of that championship, which the press of South Carolina denounced as slanderous. A Mr. Reynolds, of South Carolina, was moved, by his disgust at such reminders, to write to Mr. Calhoun, asking him for information respecting "the origin of a system so abhorrent to the South." Mr. Calhoun's reply to the inquiry does not read like the letter of an honest man. It certainly conveyed impressions at variance with the truth. He said that "he had always considered the tariff of 1816 as in reality a measure of revenue—as distinct from one of protection;" that it reduced duties instead of increasing them; that the protection of manufactures was regarded as a mere incidental feature of the bill; that he had regarded its protective character as temporary, to last only until the debt should be paid; that, in fact, he had not paid very particular attention to the details of the bill at the time, as he was not a member of the committee which had drafted it; that "his time and attention were much absorbed with the question of the currency," as he was chairman of the committee on that subject; that the tariff bill of 1816 was innocence itself compared with the monstrous and unconstitutional tariff of 1828, and had no principle in common with it.

These assertions may not all be quite destitute of truth, but they are essentially false, and the impression created by them is most erroneous. The reader has but to turn to the debates of 1816, to discover that the discussion of the tariff bill turned entirely on its protective character, and that Mr. Calhoun was the special defender of its protective provisions. The strict constructionist or State rights party was headed then in the House by John Randolph, who, on many occasions during the long debate, rose to refute Mr. Calhoun's protective reasoning. Calhoun was then a member of the other wing of the republican party. He was a bank man, an internal improvement man, a protectionist, a consolidationist—

in short, a republican of the Hamiltonian school, rather than the Jeffersonian. He was strenuous in asserting, among other things, that protection would benefit the planter as much as it benefited the manufacturer. In fact, there is not 65 a protective argument now employed by Mr. Carey or the New York *Tribune*, which can not be found in the speeches of Mr. Calhoun upon the tariff of 1816. Indeed, it was Mr. Calhoun's course on this question in 1816 which gave him that popularity in Pennsylvania which induced his friends in that State to start him for the presidency in 1824. His principal tariff speech had been printed upon a sheet, framed, hung up in bar-rooms and parlors along with the Farewell Address of General Washington. A member of Congress from Pennsylvania reminded Calhoun of this fact during the session of 1833.

Mr. Nicholas P. Trist, then of the State Department, in a series of articles in the *Richmond Inquirer*, fell upon Mr. Calhoun's Reynolds letter, and tore it to shreds. He found that (to use his own language) it contained more errors than it contained words. He copied from the old newspapers column after column of the debates of 1816, in which Mr. Calhoun figured as the most active and even enthusiastic of the protectionists. He showed that his name was associated with that of Henry Clay in the defense of the principle, and that both were frequently replied to at the same time by members of the other division of the party. These articles of Mr. Trist created what is now termed "a sensation." The President was greatly pleased with them, and had not the least difficulty in accepting Mr. Trist's conclusion, "that Mr. Calhoun was totally destitute of all regard for truth."

Mr. Calhoun's fulmination in the *Pendleton Messenger* was dated July 26th, 1831. Congress met in December following, and debated the tariff all the winter and spring. Late in the month of June, by a majority of thirty-two to sixteen in the Senate, by a majority of one hundred and twenty-nine to sixty-five in the House, Mr. Clay's bill, reaffirming the protective principle, and abolishing duties on articles not needing protection, was passed. A month after, Congress adjourned; the Vice-President went home to South Carolina; and that fiery little State soon prepared to execute the threats contained in the Vice-President's Pendleton manifesto.

The legislature of the State, early in the autumn, passed an act calling a convention of the citizens of South Carolina, for the purpose of taking into consideration the late action of Congress, and of suggesting the course to be pursued by South Carolina in relation to it. At Columbia, on the nineteenth of November, the convention met. It consisted of about one hundred and forty members, the élite of the State. The Hamiltons, the Haynes, the Pinckneys, the Butlers, and, indeed, nearly all the great families of a State of great families were represented in it. It was a body of men as respectable in character and ability as has ever been convened in South Carolina. Courtesy and resolution marked its proceedings, and the work undertaken by it was done with commendable thoroughness. A committee of twenty-one was appointed to draw up an address to the people of the State, or rather a programme of the proceedings best calculated to promote the end designed. The chief result of the labors of this committee was the celebrated ORDINANCE, which ordinance, signed by the entire convention, consisted of five distinct decrees, to the execution of which the members pledged themselves. It was ordained—

I. That the tariff law of 1828, and the amendment to the same of 1832, were "null, void, and no law, nor binding upon this State, its officers or citizens."

II. No duties enjoined by that law on its amendment shall be paid, or permitted to be paid, in the State of South Carolina, after the first day of February, 1833.

III. In no case involving the validity of the expected nullifying act of the legislature, shall an appeal to the Supreme Court of the United States be permitted. No copy of proceedings shall be allowed to be taken for that purpose. Any attempt to appeal to the Supreme Court "may be dealt with as for a contempt of the court," from which the appeal is taken.

IV. Every office-holder in the State, whether of the civil or the military service, and every person hereafter assuming an office, and every juror, shall take an oath to obey this Ordinance, and all acts of the legislature in accordance therewith or suggested thereby.

V. If the government of the United States shall attempt to enforce the tariff laws, now existing, by means of its army or navy, by closing the ports of the State, or preventing the egress or ingress of vessels, or shall in any way harass or obstruct the foreign commerce of the State, then South Carolina will no longer consider herself a member of the Federal Union : "the people of this State will thenceforth hold themselves absolved from all further obligation to maintain or preserve their political connection with the people of the other States, and will forthwith proceed to organize a separate government, and do all other acts and things which sovereign and independent States may of right do."

Such was the Nullifying Ordinance of November 24th, 1832—Mr. Calhoun's peaceful, constitutional, and union-cementing remedy for a federal grievance. The convention issued an address to the people of the other States of the Union, justifying its proceedings, and then adjourned.

The people of South Carolina accepted the Ordinance with remarkable unanimity. There was a union party in the State, respectable in numbers and character, but the nullifiers commanded an immense, an almost silencing majority. Robert Y. Hayne, a member of the convention, was elected governor of the State, and the legislature that assembled early in December, was chiefly composed of nullifiers. The message of the new governor endorsed the acts of the convention in the strongest language possible. "I recognize," said the governor, "no allegiance as paramount to that which the citizens of South Carolina owe to the State of their birth or their adoption. I here publicly declare, and wish it to be distinctly understood, that I shall hold myself bound, by the highest of all obligations, to carry into full effect, not only the ordinance of the convention, but every act of the legislature, and every judgment of our own courts, the enforcement of which may devolve on the executive. I claim no right to revise their acts. It will be my duty to execute them; and that duty I mean, to the utmost of my power, faithfully to perform."

He said more: "If the sacred soil of Carolina should be polluted by the footsteps of an invader, or be stained with the blood of her citizens, shed in her defense, I trust in Almighty God that no son of hers, native or adopted, who has been nourished at her bosom, or been cherished by her bounty, will be found raising a parricidal arm against our common mother. And even should she stand ALONE in this great struggle for constitutional liberty, encompassed by her enemies, that there will not be found, in the wide limits of the State, one recreant son who will not fly to the rescue, and be ready to lay down his life in her defense. South Carolina can not be drawn down from the proud eminence on which she has now placed herself, except by the hands of her own children. Give her but a fair field, and she asks no more. Should she succeed, hers will be glory enough to have led the way in the noble work of REFORM. And if, after making these efforts due to her own honor, and the greatness of the cause, she is destined utterly to fail, the bitter fruits of that failure, not to herself alone, but to the entire South, nay, to the whole Union, will attest her virtue."

The legislature instantly responded to the message by passing the acts requisite for carrying the ordinance into practical effect. The Governor was authorized to accept the services of volunteers, who were to hold themselves in readiness to march at a moment's warning. The State resounded with the noise of warlike preparation. Blue cockades, with a palmetto button in the center, appeared upon thousands of hats, bonnets, and bosoms. Medals were struck ere long, bearing this inscription: "John C. Calhoun, First President of the Southern Confederacy." The legislature proceeded soon to fill the vacancy created in the Senate of the United States by the election of Mr. Hayne to the governorship. John C. Calhoun, Vice-President of the United States, was the individual selected, and Mr. Calhoun accepted the seat. He resigned the vice-presidency, and began his journey to Washington in December, leaving his State in the wildest ferment.

Two months of the autumn of this year, as we have before mentioned, General Jackson spent in visiting his beloved Hermitage. But he had had an eye upon South Carolina. Soon after his return to Washington in October, came news that the convention of the South Carolina nullifiers was appointed to meet on the nineteenth of November. On the sixth of that month, the President sent secret orders to the collector of the port of Charleston of an energetic character :

"Upon the supposition that the measures of the convention, or the acts of the legislature may consist, in part, at least, in declaring the laws of the United States imposing duties unconstitutional, and null and void, and in forbidding their execution, and the collection of the duties within the State of South Carolina, you will, immediately after it shall be formally announced, resort to all the means provided by the laws, and particularly by the act of the 2d of March, 1799, to counteract the measures which may be adopted to give effect to that declaration.

"For this purpose you will consider yourself authorized to employ the revenue cutters which may be within your district, and provide as many boats, and employ as many inspectors, as may be necessary for the execution of the law, and for the purposes of the act already referred to. You will, moreover, cause a sufficient number of officers of cutters and inspectors to be placed on board, and in charge of every vessel arriving from a foreign port or place, with goods, wares, or merchandise, as soon as practicable after her first coming within your district, and direct them to anchor her in some safe place within the harbor, where she may be secure from any act of violence, and from any unauthorized attempt to discharge her cargo before a compliance with the laws; and they will remain on board of her at such place until the reports and entries required by law shall be made, both of vessel and cargo, and the duties paid, or secured to be paid to your satisfaction, and until the regular permit shall be granted for landing the cargo; and it will be your duty, against any forcible attempt, to retain and defend the custody of the said vessel, by the aid of the officers of the customs, inspectors, and officers of the cutters, until the requisitions of the law shall be fully complied with; and in case of any attempt to remove her or her cargo from the custody of the officers of the customs, by the form of legal process from State tribunals, you will not yield the custody to such attempt, but will consult the law officer of the district, and employ such means as, under the particular circumstances, you may legally do, to resist such process, and prevent the removal of the vessel and cargo.

"Should the entry of such vessel and cargo not be completed, and the duties paid, or secured to be paid, by bond or bonds, with sureties to your satisfaction, within the time limited by law, you will, at the expiration of that time, take possession of the cargo, and land and store the same at Castle Pinckney, or some other safe place, and in due time, if the duties are not paid, sell the same, according to the direction of the 56th section of the act of the 2d of March, 1799; and you are authorized to provide such stores as may be necessary for that purpose."

A few days after the dispatch of these orders, General Scott was quietly ordered to Charleston, for the purpose, as the President confidentially informed the collector, "of superintending the safety of the ports of the United States in that vicinity." Other changes were made in the disposition of naval and military forces, designed to enable the President to act with swift efficiency, if there should be occasion to act.

If ever a man was resolved to accomplish a purpose, General Jackson was resolved on this occasion to preserve intact the authority with which he had been entrusted. Nor can any language do justice to the fury of his contemptuous wrath against the author and fomenter of all this trouble. The recently published autobiography of Gen. Sam. Dale, of Mississippi, contains a passage which affords us a peep into the White House when nullification was the ruling topic. Dale had distinguished himself during the New Orleans campaign as a bearer of despatches, in which capacity he had rendered General Jackson much service, and won his regard.

At the height of the nullification excitement, "Big Sam" found himself at the city of Washington:

"The third day, Colonel William R. King, of the Senate, brought me word that President Jackson desired to see me. 'Tell Dale,' said he to Colonel King, 'that if I had as little to do as he has, I should have seen him before now.' The General was walking in the lawn in front of his mansion as we approached. He advanced, and grasped me warmly by the hand.

"'No introduction is needed,' said the Colonel.

"'Oh no,' said the General, shaking my hand again, 'I shall never forget Sam Dale.' We walked into his reception-room, and I was introduced to Col. Benton, and five or six other distinguished men. They were all very civil, and invited me to visit them. They were talking over '*Nullification*,' the engrossing subject at that period, and the President, turning to me, said, 'General Dale, if this thing goes on, our country will be like a bag of meal with both ends open. Pick it up in the middle or endwise, and it will run out. I must tie the bag and save the country.' The company now took leave, but when I rose to retire with Col. King, the General detained me, ordered up some whisky, and directed his servant to refuse all visitors until one o'clock. He talked over our campaigns, and then of the business that brought me to Washington. He then said, 'Sam, you have been true to your country, but you have made one mistake in life. You are now old and solitary, and without a bosom friend or family to comfort you. God called mine away. But all I have achieved—fame, power, every thing—would I exchange if she could be restored to me for a moment.'

"The iron man trembled with emotion, and for some time covered his face with his hands, and tears dropped on his knee. I was deeply affected myself. He took two or three turns across the room, and then abruptly said, 'Dale, they are trying me here; you will witness it; but, by the God of heaven, I will uphold the laws.'

"I understood him to be referring to nullification again, his mind evidently having recurred to it, and I expressed the hope that things would go right.

"'They SHALL go right, sir,' he exclaimed, passionately, shivering his pipe upon the table.

"He calmed down after this, and showed me his collection of pipes, many of a most costly and curious kind, sent to him from every quarter, his propensity for smoking being well known. 'These,' said he, 'will do to look at. I still smoke my corn-cob, Sam, as you and I have often done together: it is the sweetest and best pipe.'

"When I rose to take leave, he pressed me to accept a room there. 'I can talk to you at night; in the day I am beset.' I declined on the plea of business, but dined with him several times, always, no matter what dignitaries were present, sitting at his right hand. He ate very sparingly, only taking a single glass of wine, though his table was magnificent. When we parted for the last time, he said, 'My friend, farewell; we shall see each other no more; let us meet in heaven.'

"I could only answer him with tears, for I felt that we should meet no more on earth."

XX.

NULLIFICATION EXPLODES AND TRIUMPHS.

CONGRESS met on the third of December. Mr. Calhoun had not reached Washington, and his intention to resign the vice-presidency was not known there. Judge White, of Tennessee, was elected president of the Senate, *pro tem.*, and the President of the United States was then notified that Congress was ready to receive the annual message.

The message of 1832 reveals few traces of the loud and threatening contentions amid which it was produced. It is an unusually quiet and business-like document. The ravages and the subsidence of the cholera were briefly referred to. The recall of Mr. Van Buren from England was merely mentioned as an "unexpected" and "unfortunate" circumstance, which had interrupted sundry negotiations with the English government. The income of the year would reach twenty-eight millions of dollars; the expenditures sixteen millions and a half; the payments on the public debt eighteen millions. The President was now enabled to announce that on the 1st of January, 1833, there would remain of the public debt less than seven millions, which would be extinguished early in the course of that year. "I can not," he said, "too cordially congratulate Congress and my fellow-citizens on the near approach of that memorable and happy event, the extinction of the public debt of this great and free nation. Faithful to the wise and patriotic policy marked out by the legislation of the country for this object, the present administration has devoted to it all the means which a flourishing commerce has supplied, and a prudent economy preserved, for the public treasury. Within the four years for which the people have confided the executive power to my charge, fifty-eight millions of dollars will have been applied to the payment of the public debt."

It remained, the message continued, for Congress to revise the tariff, so as to reduce the revenue to the reduced necessities of the government. This *must* be done: but so done, if possible, as not to injure the manufacturing interest. "Large interests have grown up under the implied pledge of our national legislation, which it would seem a violation of public faith suddenly to abandon. Nothing could justify it but the public safety, which is the supreme law. But those who have vested their capital in manufacturing establishments can not expect that the people will continue permanently to pay high taxes for their benefit, when the money is not required for any legitimate purpose in the administration of the government. Is it not enough that the high duties have been paid as long as the money arising from them could be applied to the common benefit in the extinguishment of the public debt?" This was not the doctrine of the first message, which contemplated a permanent surplus revenue for division among the States. The President here recommended all, or nearly all, that the nullifiers demanded.

The troubles in South Carolina were dismissed in a single paragraph, which expressed a hope of a speedy adjustment of the difficulty.

The United States Bank was not suffered to die in peace. "I recommend," said the President, "that provision be made to dispose of all stocks now held by the general government in corporations, whether created by the general or State governments, and to place the proceeds in the treasury." But this was not all. Congress was urged to institute an inquiry "whether the public deposits in that institution may be entirely safe." Rumors were abroad, said the President, impeaching the character of the bank, which, being widely credited, seemed to call for formal investigation.

The President now brought forward his famous recommendations respecting the public lands. They should no longer, he thought, be made a source of revenue, but should be sold to actual settlers, in limited parcels, at a price barely sufficient to pay the cost of surveying and selling, and the expenses incurred in fulfilling our compacts with the Indians. "The adventurous and hardy population of the west," observed the President, "besides contributing their equal share of taxation under our impost system, have, in the progress of our government, for the lands they occupy, paid into the treasury a large proportion of forty millions of dollars, and, of the revenue received therefrom, but a small part has been expended among them. When, to the disadvantage of their situation in this respect, we add the consideration that it is their labor alone which gives real value to the lands, and that the proceeds arising from their sale are distributed chiefly among States which had not originally any claim to them, and which have enjoyed the undivided emolument arising from the sale of their own lands, it can not be expected that the new States will remain longer contented with the present policy, after the payment of the public debt."

The President was also of opinion that the federal government should relinquish the ownership of public lands to the several States within whose borders they lay. The message contained the usual recommendation for the election of President and Vice-President by the direct vote of the people, and for limiting their time of holding office to a single term; which last could not, of course, be omitted in view of the recent reëlection.

While Congress was listening to this calm and suggestive message, the President was absorbed in the preparation of another document, and one of a very different description. A pamphlet containing the proceedings of the South Carolina Convention reached him on one of the last days of November. It moved him profoundly; for this fiery spirit loved his country as few men have loved it. Though he regarded those proceedings as the fruit of John C. Calhoun's treasonable ambition and treasonable resentment, he rose, on this occasion, above personal considerations, and conducted himself with that union of daring and prudence which had given him such signal success in war. He went to his office alone, and began to dash off page after page of the memorable Proclamation which was soon to electrify the country. He wrote with that great steel pen of his, and with such rapidity, that he was obliged to scatter the written pages all over the table to let them dry. A gentleman who came in when the President had written fifteen or twenty pages, observed that three of them were glistening with wet ink at the same moment. The warmth, the glow, the passion, the eloquence of that proclamation, were produced then and there by the President's own hand.

To these pages were added many more of notes and memoranda which had been accumulating in the presidential hat for some weeks, and the whole collection was then placed in the hands of Mr. Livingston, the Secretary of State, who was requested to draw up the Proclamation in proper form. Major Lewis writes to me: "Mr. Livingston took the papers to his office, and, in the course of three or four days, brought the proclamation to the General, and left it for his examination. After reading it, he came into my room and remarked that Mr. Livingston had not correctly understood his notes—there were portions of the draft, he added, which were not in accordance with his views, and must be altered. He then sent his messenger for Mr. Livingston, and, when he came, pointed out to him the passages which did not represent his views, and requested him to take it back with him and make the alterations he had suggested. This was done, and the second draft being satisfactory, he ordered it to be published. I will add that, before the proclamation was sent to press to be published, I took the liberty of suggesting to the General whether it would not be best to leave out that portion to which, I was sure, the State-rights party would particularly object. He refused.

"Those are my views," said he with great decision of manner, "and I will not change them nor strike them out."

This celebrated paper was dated December 11th, 1832. The word proclamation does not describe it. It reads more like the last appeal of a sorrowing but resolute father to wayward, misguided sons. Argument, warning, and entreaty were blended in its composition. It began by calmly refuting, one by one, the leading positions of the nullifiers. The *right to annul*, and the *right to secede*, as claimed by them, were shown to be incompatible with the fundamental idea and main object of the constitution; which was "to form a more perfect Union." That the tariff act complained of did operate unequally was granted, but so did every revenue law that had ever been or could ever be passed.

"The wisdom of man never yet contrived a system of taxation that would operate with perfect equality. If the unequal operation of law makes it unconstitutional, and if all laws of that description may be abrogated by any State for that cause, then indeed is the Federal Constitution unworthy of the slightest effort for its preservation. We have hitherto relied on it as the perpetual bond of our Union. We have received it as the work of the assembled wisdom of the nation. We have trusted to it as to the sheet anchor of our safety, in the stormy times of conflict with a foreign or domestic foe. We have looked to it with sacred awe as the palladium of our liberties, and with all the solemnities of religion have pledged to each other our lives and fortunes here, and our hopes of happiness hereafter, in its defense and support. Were we mistaken, my countrymen, in attaching this importance to the Constitution of our country? Was our devotion paid to the wretched, inefficient, clumsy contrivance, which this new doctrine would make it? Did we pledge ourselves to the support of an airy nothing, a bubble that must be blown away by the first breath of disaffection? Was this self-destroying, visionary theory the work of the profound statesmen, the exalted patriots, to whom the task of constitutional reform was entrusted ? Did the name of Washington sanction, did the States ratify such an anomaly in the history of fundamental legislation ? No. We were not mistaken. The letter of this great instrument is free from this radical fault : its language directly contradicts the imputation : its spirit—its evident intent contradicts it."

The right of a State to secede was strongly denied. "To say that any State may at pleasure secede from the Union is to say that the United States are not a nation." The individual States are not completely sovereign, for they voluntarily resigned part of their sovereignty. "How can that State be said to be sovereign and independent whose citizens owe obedience to laws not made by it, and whose magistrates are sworn to disregard those laws, when they come in conflict with those passed by another ?"

Finally, the people of South Carolina were distinctly given to understand, that, in case any forcible resistance to the laws were attempted by them, the attempt would be resisted by the combined power and resources of the other States. For one word, however, of this kind, there were a hundred of entreaty. "Fellow-citizens of my native State !" exclaimed the President, "let me not only admonish you as the first magistrate of our common country not to incur the penalty of its laws, but use the influence that a father would over his children whom he saw rushing to certain ruin. In that paternal language, with that paternal feeling, let me tell you, my countrymen, that you are deluded by men who are either deceived themselves or wish to deceive you.

. . . .

"Contemplate the condition of that country of which you still form an important part !—consider its government uniting in one bond of common interest and general protection so many different States—giving to all their inhabitants the proud title of AMERICAN CITIZEN—protecting their commerce—securing their literature and their arts—facilitating their intercommunication—defending the frontiers—and making their name respected in the remotest parts of the earth! Consider the extent of its territory, its increasing and happy population, its advance in arts which render life agreeable, and the sciences which elevate the mind! See education spreading the lights of religion, morality, and general information into every cottage in this wide extent of our Territories and States! Behold it as the asylum where the wretched and the oppressed find a refuge and support! Look on this picture of happiness and honor, and say, WE, TOO, ARE CITIZENS OF AMERICA. Carolina is one of these proud States, her arms have defended, her best blood has cemented this happy Union! And then add, if you can, without horror and remorse, this happy Union we will dissolve—this picture of peace and prosperity we will deface—this free intercourse we will interrupt—these fertile fields we will deluge with blood—the protection of that glorious flag we renounce—the very name of Americans we discard. And for what, mistaken men! for what do you throw away these inestimable blessings—for what would you exchange your share in the advantages and honor of the Union? For the dream of a separate independence—a dream interrupted by bloody conflicts with your neighbors, and a vile dependence on a foreign power."

Such were the tone and manner of this celebrated proclamation. It was clear in statement, forcible in argument, vigorous in style, and glowing with the fire of a genuine and enlightened patriotism. It was such a blending of argument and feeling as Alexander Hamilton would have drawn up for Patrick Henry.

The proclamation was received at the North with an enthusiasm that seemed unanimous, and was nearly so. The opposition press bestowed the warmest encomiums upon it. Three days after its appearance in the newspapers of New York, an immense meeting was held in the Park, for the purpose of stamping it with metropolitan approval. Faneuil Hall in Boston was quick in responding to it, and there were Union meetings in every large town of the Northern States. In Tennessee, North Carolina, Virginia, Maryland, Delaware,

Missouri, Louisiana, and Kentucky the proclamation was generally approved as an act, though its extreme federal positions found many opponents. Mr. Clay's opinion of it was that of many of the Southern politicians. "One short week," wrote Mr. Clay on the day the document appeared, "produced the message and the proclamation—the former ultra on the side of State rights, the latter ultra on the side of consolidation. How they can be reconciled, I must leave to our Virginia friends. As to the proclamation, although there are good things in it, especially what relates to the Judiciary, there are some entirely too ultra for me, and which I can not stomach. A proclamation ought to have been issued weeks ago, but I think it should have been a very different paper from the present, which, I apprehend, will irritate instead of allaying the excited feeling."

In South Carolina, it did "irritate the excited feeling." The legislature of that State, being still in session, immediately passed the following resolution:

"Whereas, the President of the United States has issued his proclamation, denouncing the proceedings of this State, calling upon the citizens thereof to renounce their primary allegiance, and threatening them with military coercion, unwarranted by the constitution, and utterly inconsistent with the existence of a free State: Be it, therefore,

"*Resolved*, That his excellency the Governor be requested, forthwith, to issue his proclamation, warning the good people of this State against the attempt of the President of the United States to seduce them from their allegiance, exhorting them to disregard his vain menaces, and to be prepared to sustain the dignity and protect the liberty of the State against the arbitrary measures proposed by the President."

Governor Hayne issued his proclamation accordingly, and a most pugnacious document it was. He denounced the doctrines of the President's proclamation as "dangerous and pernicious;" as "specious and false;" as tending "to uproot the very foundation of our political system, annihilate the rights of the States, and utterly destroy the liberties of the citizen ; as contemplating "a great, consolidated empire, one and indivisible, the worst of all despotisms." The Governor declared that the State would maintain its sovereignty, or be buried beneath its ruins. "As unhappy Poland," said he, "fell before the power of the autocrat, so may Carolina be crushed by the power of her enemies ; but Poland was not surrounded by free and independent States, interested, like herself, in preventing the establishment of the very tyranny which they are called upon to impose upon a sister State. If, in spite of our common kindred and common interests, the glorious recollections of the past, and the proud hopes of the future, South Carolina should be coldly abandoned to her fate, and reduced to subjection by an unholy combination among her sister States—which is believed to be utterly impossible—and the doctrines promulgated by the President are to become the foundations of a new system, cemented by the blood of our citizens, it matters not what may be our lot. Under such a government, as there could be no liberty, so there could be no security either for our persons or our property."

"Fellow-citizens," said Governor Hayne, in conclusion, "in the name and behalf of the State of South Carolina, I do once more solemnly warn you against all attempts to seduce you from your primary allegiance to the State ; I charge you to be faithful to your duty as citizens of South Carolina, and earnestly exhort you to disregard those 'vain menaces' of military force, which, if the President, in violation of all his constitutional obligations, and of your most sacred rights, should be tempted to employ, it would become your solemn duty, at all hazards, to resist. I require you to be fully prepared to sustain the dignity and protect the liberties of the State, if need be, with 'your lives and fortunes.' And may that great and good Being, as a 'father careth for his children,' inspire us with that holy zeal in a good cause, which is the best safeguard of our rights and liberties."

The proclamation of the Governor of South Carolina was made public on the last day of the year 1832. The first of February, 1833, the day appointed for the nullification of the tariff laws to take effect, was drawing alarmingly near. Meanwhile the military posts in South Carolina were filling with troops of the United States, and a naval force was anchored off Charleston. The Carolinians continued their military preparations. Fair fingers were busier than ever in making palmetto cockades, and, it is said, a red flag with a black lone star in the center was adopted as the ensign of some of the volunteer regiments. Nullifying steamboats and hotels, it is also reported, exhibited the flag of the United States with the stars downward.

When the proclamation of Governor Hayne reached Washington, the President forthwith replied to it by asking Congress for an increase of powers adequate to the impending collision. The message in which he made this request, dated January 16th, 1833, gave a brief history of events in South Carolina, and of the measures hitherto adopted by the administration ; repeated the arguments of the recent proclamation, and added others ; stated the legal points involved, and asked of Congress such an increase of executive powers as would enable the government, if necessary, to close ports of entry, remove threatened custom-houses, detain vessels, and protect from State prosecution such citizens of South Carolina as should choose, or be compelled, to pay the obnoxious duties.

One of the points made in this message, amused as many of the people, at the time, as were calm enough to be amused. "Oppression" was the favorite word of the South Carolinians in discoursing upon their grievances. That the revenue system hitherto pursued, said the President, "has resulted in no such oppression upon South Carolina, needs no other proof than the solemn and official declaration of the late chief magistrate of that State in his address to the Legislature. In that he says that 'the occurrences of the past year, in connection with our domestic concerns, are to be reviewed with a sentiment of fervent gratitude to the Great Disposer of human events; that tributes of grateful acknowledgment are due for the various and multiplied blessings he has been pleased to bestow on our people; that abundant harvests in every quarter of the State have crowned the exertions of agricultural labor; that health, almost beyond former precedent, has blessed our homes; *and that there is not less reason for thankfulness in surveying our social condition.*'" This was a happy hit. It was probably the first time that the formal utterances of thanksgiving which precede state papers were ever made to do duty as rebutting evidence.

Mr. Calhoun was in his place in the Senate chamber when this message was read. He had arrived two weeks before, after a journey which one of his biographers compares to that of Luther to the Diet of Worms. He met averted faces and estranged friends every where on his route, we are told; and only now and then, some daring man found courage to whisper in his ear: "If you are sincere, and are sure of your cause, go on, in God's name, and fear nothing." Washington was curious to know, we are further assured, what the arch-nullifier would do when the oath to support the constitution of the United States was proposed to him. "The floor of the Senate chamber and the galleries were thronged with spectators. They saw him take the oath with a solemnity and dignity appropriate to the occasion, and then calmly seat himself on the right of the chair, among his old political friends, nearly all of whom were now arrayed against him."*

After the President's message had been read, Mr. Calhoun rose to vindicate himself and his State, which he did with that singular blending of subtlety and force, truth and sophistry, which characterized his later efforts. He declared himself still devoted to the Union, and said that if the government were restored to the principles of 1798, he would be the last man in the country to question its authority.

A bill conceding to the President the additional powers requested in his message of January 16th was promptly re-

* Jenkins' Calhoun, p. 247.

ported, and finally passed. It was nicknamed, at the time, the Force Bill, and was debated with the heat and acrimony which might have been expected. As other measures of Congress rendered this bill unnecessary, and it had no practical effect whatever, we need not dwell upon its provisions nor review the debates upon it. It passed by majorities unusually large, late in February.

The first of February, the dreaded day which was to be the first of a fratricidal war, had gone by, and yet no hostile and no nullifying act had been done in South Carolina. How was this? Did those warlike words mean nothing? Was South Carolina repentant? It is asserted by the old Jacksonians that one citizen of South Carolina was exceedingly frightened as the first of February drew near, namely, John C. Calhoun. The President was resolved, and avowed his resolve, that the hour which brought the news of one act of violence on the part of the nullifiers, should find Mr. Calhoun a prisoner of state upon a charge of high treason. And not Calhoun only, but every member of Congress from South Carolina who had taken part in the proceedings which had caused the conflict between South Carolina and the general government. Whether this intention of the President had any effect upon the course of events, we can not know. It came to pass, however, that, a few days before the first of February, a meeting of the leading nullifiers was held in Charleston, who passed resolutions to this effect: that, inasmuch as measures were then pending in Congress which contemplated the reduction of duties demanded by South Carolina, the nullification of the existing revenue laws should be postponed until after the adjournment of Congress; when the Convention would re-assemble, and take into consideration whatever revenue measures may have been passed by Congress. The session of 1833 being the "short" session, ending necessarily on the fourth of March, the Union was respited thirty-two days by the Charleston meeting.

It remains now to relate the events which led to the pacification of this painful and dangerous dispute.

The President, in his annual message, as we have just seen, recommended Congress to subject the tariff to a new revision, and to reduce the duties so that the revenue of the government, after the payment of the public debt, should not exceed its expenditures. He also recommended that, in regulating the reduction, the interests of the manufacturers should be duly considered. We discover, therefore, that while the President was resolved to crush nullification by force, if it opposed by force the collection of the revenue, he was also disposed to concede to nullification all that its more moderate advocates demanded. Accordingly, Mr. McLane, the Secretary of the Treasury, with the assistance of Mr. Gulian C. Verplanck, of New York, and other administration members, prepared a new tariff bill, which provided for the reduction of duties to the revenue standard, and which was deemed by its authors as favorable to the manufacturing interest as the circumstances permitted. This bill, reported by Mr. Verplanck on the 28th of December, and known as the Verplanck bill, was calculated to reduce the revenue thirteen millions of dollars, and to afford to the manufacturers about as much protection as the tariff of 1816 had given them. It put back the "American System," so to speak, seventeen years. It destroyed nearly all that Mr. Clay and the protectionists had effected in 1820, 1824, 1828, and 1832. Is it astonishing that the manufacturers were panic-stricken? Need we wonder that, during the tariff discussions of 1833, two congresses sat in Washington, one in the capitol, composed of the representatives of the people, and another outside of the capitol, consisting of representatives of the manufacturing interest? Was it not to be expected that Mr. Clay, seeing the edifice which he had constructed with so much toil and talent about to tumble into ruins, would be willing to consent to any measure which could even postpone the catastrophe?

The Verplanck bill made slow progress. The outside pressure against it was such, that there seemed no prospect of its passing. The session was within twenty days of its inevitable termination. The bill had been debated and amended, and amended and debated, and yet no apparent progress had been made toward that conciliation of conflicting interests without which no tariff bill whatever can pass. The dread of civil war, which overshadowed the capitol, seemed to lose its power as a legislative stimulant, and there was a respectable party in Congress, led by Mr. Webster, who thought that all tariff legislation was undignified and improper while South Carolina maintained her threatening attitude. The constitution, Mr. Webster maintained, was on trial. The time had come to test its reserve of self-supporting power. No compromise, no concession, said he, until the nullifying State returns to her allegiance.

No question of so much importance as this can be discussed in Congress without a constant, secret reference to its effect upon the next presidential election. "It is mortifying, inexpressibly disgusting," wrote Mr. Clay to Judge Brooke, in the midst of the debate upon his own compromise bill of this session, "to find that considerations affecting an election now four years distant, influence the fate of great questions of immediate interest more than all the reasons and arguments which intimately appertain to those questions. If, for example, the Tariff now before the House should be lost, its defeat will be owing to two causes—First, The apprehension of Mr. Van Buren's friends, that if it passes, Mr. Calhoun will rise again as the successful vindicator of Southern rights; and second, Its passage might prevent the President from exercising certain vengeful passions which he wishes to gratify in South Carolina. And if it passes, its passage may be attributed to the desire of those same friends of Mr. Van Buren to secure Southern votes."

The fact deplored by Mr. Clay is unquestionable, but the inference which is usually drawn from it may be questioned. Does not the fact reveal to us, that politicians in the United States, no matter what their unpatriotic ambition, are compelled in all their public acts, to watch their masters' eye, and, upon the whole, to carry out their masters' will? To what lengths would not some of them carry their impious domination, if there were no quadrennial Day of Judgment for them? This terror of the presidential election prevents much good it is true, but it also prevents much evil.

On the 12th of February, Mr. Clay introduced his celebrated Compromise Bill for the regulation of the tariff. It differed from the measure devised by the administration and engineered by Mr. Verplanck, chiefly in this: Mr. Verplanck proposed a sudden, and Mr. Clay a gradual, reduction of duties. The Verplanck bill tended mainly to the conciliation of the nullifiers; the Clay compromise, to the preservation of the manufacturers. Mr. Clay's bill provided that, on the last day of the year 1833, all ad valorem duties of more than twenty per cent. should be reduced one tenth; on the last day of the year 1835, there should be a second and a similar reduction; another, to the same amount, at the close of 1837; and, so on, reducing the duties every two years, until on the 31st of June, 1842, all duties should be reduced to or below the maximum of twenty per cent. The object of Mr. Clay was to save all that he could save of the protective policy, and to postpone further action upon the tariff to a more auspicious day.

Then was seen an enchanting exhibition of political principle! Which of these two bills, O reader, innocent and beloved, was most in accordance with Mr. Calhoun's new opinions? Which of them could he most consistently have supported? Not Mr. Clay's, you will certainly answer. Yet it was Mr. Clay's bill that he did support and vote for; and Mr. Clay's bill was carried by the aid of his support and vote. If this course does not prove, that Mr. Calhoun was a "coward and a conspirator," it does prove, I think, that he was not a person of that exalted and Roman-toga cast, which he set up to be, and which he enacted, for some years, with considerable applause. The nullifiers in Congress could have carried the Verplanck bill if they had given it a frank and energetic support. They would have carried it, if the ruling motive of their chief had been purely patriotic.

The most remarkable narrative left by Colonel Benton for

the entertainment of posterity, is that which he gives, in his "Thirty Years' View," of this strange coalition between Mr. Clay and Mr. Calhoun for the passage of the Compromise Bill. Mr. Clay, he tells us, had introduced the measure into the Senate, but the manufacturers could not be reconciled to some of its provisions; and, without their consent, nothing could be done. At this stage of the affair, Senator John M. Clayton, of Delaware, a protectionist, gave Mr. Clay a piece of advice, which he followed. "These South Carolinians," said Clayton to Clay, "are acting very badly, but they are fine fellows, and it is a pity to let Jackson hang them." He urged Mr. Clay to make a "new move" with his bill, get it referred to a select committee, and so modify it as to render it acceptable to a majority.

The bill was referred to a select committee, accordingly, and that select committee was appointed, of course, by Judge White, the president of the Senate. Respecting the appointment of this important committee, Judge White has left on record a little tale, which shows, among other things, how keenly the President watched the proceedings of Congress, and how resolved he was to deprive the Opposition of all the glory of pacificating the country.

"Before the members of the committee were named," writes Judge White, "I received a note from the President, requesting me to go to his house, as he wished to see me. I returned for answer, that while the Senate was in session it was out of my power to go, but that as soon as it adjourned I would call on him. I felt the high responsibility which rested on me in appointing the committee; the fate of the bill, in a good degree, depended on it; and if the bill failed, we would probably be involved in a most painful conflict. I endeavored to make the best selection I could, by taking some tariff-men, some anti-tariff, one nullifier, and Mr. Clay himself —hoping that if a majority of a committee, in which all interests and views were represented, could agree on any thing, it was likely it would pass. Taking these principles for my guide, I wrote down the names of seven members, Mr. Clayton, of Delaware, being one; and immediately before we adjourned, handed the names to the secretary, with directions to put them on the journal, and in the course of the evening waited on the President. Soon after we met, he mentioned that he had wished to see me on the subject of appointing a committee on Mr. Clay's bill, to ask that Mr.

Clayton might not be put on it; as he was hostile to the administration, and unfriendly to Mr. McLane, he feared he would use his endeavor to have a preference given to Mr. Clay's bill over that of the Secretary of the Treasury, or words to that effect. I observed, in answer, that it would always give me great pleasure to conform to the wishes of my political friends, whenever I could do so with propriety; but that the treasury bill had been so altered and mangled, and that, as I understood, in a good degree by the votes of his own party, that it had but few friends; that we seemed to be on the eve of a civil war, and that, for the sake of averting such a calamity, I would further all in my power any measure, come from whom it might, which would give peace to the country, and that any bill, having that for its object, was esteemed by me a measure *above party*, and any man who was the author of it was welcome to all the credit he could gain by it. But, at all events, it was too late to talk on the subject, as I had handed the names of the committee to the secretary before we adjourned; and that as I had a very high opinion of Mr. Clayton's talents and liberal feelings, I had put him on the committee, without knowing he was personally unkind to the Secretary of the Treasury. He then asked me if I could not see the secretary of the Senate that evening, and substitute some other name for Mr. Clayton, before the journal was made up. I told him I could not—in my judgment it would be wrong; and then the interview terminated."*

Mr. Clayton was retained on the committee, therefore, and it was directly owing to his tact and firmness, according to Colonel Benton, that the bill was passed. He began by making it a *sine qua non* that the compromise bill, with all the amendments agreed upon, should be voted for by Mr. Calhoun and the other nullifiers, so as to commit them to the principles involved in the bill, and to give the manufacturers an assurance of the perpetuity of the compact. He was equally explicit in demanding that Mr. Clay, also, should record his vote upon the bill and its amendments. The closing struggle between policy and principle let our eye-witness, Colonel Benton, describe :

"Mr. Clayton being inexorable in his claims, Mr. Clay and Mr. Calhoun agreed to the amendments, and all voted for them, one by one, as Mr. Clay offered them, until it came to the last—that revolting measure of the home valuation. As soon as it was proposed, Mr. Calhoun and his

* Memoirs of Hugh L. White, p. 299

friends met it with violent opposition, declaring it to be unconstitutional, and an insurmountable obstacle to their votes for the bill if put into it. It was then late in the day, and the last day but one of the session, and Mr. Clayton found himself in the predicament which required the execution of his threat to table the bill. He executed it, and moved to lay it on the table, with the declaration that it was to lie there. Mr. Clay went to him and besought him to withdraw the motion; but in vain. He remained inflexible; and the bill then appeared to be dead. In this extremity, the Calhoun wing retired to the colonnade behind the Vice-President's chair, and held a brief consultation among themselves; and presently Mr. Bibb, of Kentucky, came out and went to Mr. Clayton, and asked him to withdraw his motion to give him time to consider the amendment. Seeing this sign of yielding, Mr. Clayton withdrew his motion—to be renewed if the amendment was not voted for. A friend of the parties immediately moved an adjournment, which was carried; and that night's reflections brought them to the conclusion that the amendment must be passed; but still with the belief that, there being enough to pass it without him, Mr. Calhoun should be spared the humiliation of appearing on the record in its favor. This was told to Mr. Clayton, who declared it to be impossible; that Mr. Calhoun's vote was indispensable, as nothing would be considered secured by the passage of the bill unless his vote appeared for every amendment separately, and for the whole bill collectively. When the Senate met, and the bill was taken up, it was still unknown what he would do; but his friends fell in, one after the other, yielding their objections upon different grounds, and giving their assent to this most flagrant instance (and that a new one) of that protective legislation against which they were then raising troops in South Carolina! and limiting a day, and that a short one, on which she was to be, *ipso facto,* a seceder from the Union. Mr. Calhoun remained to the last, and only rose when the vote was ready to be taken, and prefaced a few remarks with the very notable declaration that he had then to 'determine' which way he would vote. He then declared in favor of the amendment, but upon conditions which he desired the reporters to note; and which being futile in themselves, only showed the desperation of his condition, and the state of impossibility to which he was reduced. Several senators let him know immediately the futility of his conditions; and without saying more, he voted on ayes and noes for the amendment, and afterward for the whole bill."

The compromise bill, which passed in the Senate by a vote of twenty-nine to sixteen, was sprung upon the House of Representatives, and carried in that body by a *coup-de-main.* The Verplanck bill, Col. Benton indignantly informs us, was afloat in the House, "upon the wordy sea of stormy debate," as late as the 25th of February. "All of a sudden," he continues, "it was arrested, knocked over, run under, and merged and lost in a new one, which expunged the old one and took its place. It was late in the afternoon when Mr. Letcher, of Kentucky, the fast friend of Mr. Clay, rose in his place, and moved to strike out the whole Verplanck bill—every word except the enacting clause—and insert, in lieu of it, a bill offered in the Senate by Mr. Clay, since called the 'compromise.' This was offered in the House without notice, without signal, without premonitory symptom, and just as the members were preparing to adjourn. Some, taken by surprise, looked about in amazement; but the majority showed consciousness, and, what was more, readiness for action. The bill, which made its first appearance in the House when members were gathering up their over-coats for a walk home to their dinners, was passed before those coats had got on the back; and the dinner which was waiting had but little time to cool before the astonished members, their work done, were at the table to eat it. A bill without precedent in the annals of our legislation, and pretending to the sanctity of a compromise, and to settle great questions for ever, went through to its consummation in the fragment of an evening session, without the compliance with any form which experience and parliamentary law have devised for the safety of legislation."

67

The bill passed in the House by a vote of one hundred and nineteen to eighty-five.

That the President disapproved this hasty, and, as the event proved, unstable compromise, is well known. The very energy with which Col. Benton denounces it shows how hateful it was to the administration. General Jackson, however, signed the bill concocted by his enemies. It would have been more like him to have vetoed it, and I do not know why he did not veto it. The time may come when the people of the United States will wish he had vetoed it, and thus brought to an issue, and settled finally, a question which, at some future day, may assume more awkward dimensions, and the country have no Jackson to meet it.

Mr. Calhoun left Washington, and journeyed homeward post-haste, after Congress adjourned. "Traveling night and day, by the most rapid public conveyances, he succeeded in reaching Columbia in time to meet the convention before they had taken any additional steps. Some of the more fiery and ardent members were disposed to complain of the compromise act, as being only a half-way, temporizing measure; but when his explanations were made, all felt satisfied, and the convention cordially approved of his course. The nullification ordinance was repealed, and the two parties in the State abandoned their organizations, and agreed to forget all their past differences."* So the storm blew over.

One remarkable result of the pacification was, that it strengthened the position of the leading men of both parties. The course was cleared for Mr. Van Buren. The popularity of the President reached its highest point. Mr. Calhoun was rescued from peril, and a degree of his former prestige was restored to him. The collectors of political pamphlets will discover that, as late as 1843, he still had hopes of reaching the presidency by uniting the South in his support, and adding to the united South Pennsylvania. With too much truth he claimed, in subsequent debates, that it was the hostile attitude of South Carolina which alone had enabled Mr. Clay to carry his compromise. "I had him down," said Calhoun, in the Senate, speaking of Mr. Clay, "I had him on his back—I was his master." "*He* my master!" retorted the Kentuckian, "I would not own him for the meanest of my slaves!"

A very few years after these events, before Mr. Van Buren was President, and before Mr. Calhoun was Mr. Van Buren's friend, the Nullifier adopted new tactics. He became the eulogist of slavery, falsely accusing the North of a desire to interfere with that institution in the Southern States. His first speech on this subject contains every argu-

* Jenkins' Calhoun, p. 314.

ment, assertion, and fact, which constitutes, at this moment, the capital of the party in power. Until he spoke, the South generally felt that slavery was only to be regarded as a choice of evils—an unfortunate inheritance, to be endured as long as it must be endured, to be abolished as soon as it could be abolished safely.* It was John C. Calhoun that effaced from the heart of the South the benign sentiments of Washington, Jefferson, Madison, and Randolph.

It was Calhoun who began all that is to be deplored in the agitation of slavery questions. It was he who strove to rob the people of the North of their right to petition, and the people of the South of their right to receive what they choose through the mail. It was he who cut the magnetic cord that connected the South with the feeling of the age, and thus made the peaceful solution of the problem difficult, and its speedy solution impossible. It was he who made slavery a maddening topic in the press. It was well said by Mr. Isaac Hill, of New Hampshire, in 1836, that "of all the vehicles tracts, pamphlets, and newspapers, printed and circulated by the abolitionists, there is no ten or twenty of them that have contributed so much to the excitement as a single newspaper printed in this city. I need not name this paper when I inform you that, for the last five years, it has been laboring to produce a Northern and a Southern party—to fan the flame of sectional prejudice, to open wider the breach, to drive harder the wedge, which shall divide the North from the South." It was the *United States Telegraph*, the confiden-

* "A hard necessity, indeed, compels us to endure the evil of slavery for a time. It was imposed upon us by another nation, while yet we were in a state of colonial vassalage. It can not be easily or suddenly removed. Yet, while it continues, it is a blot on our national character, and every real lover of freedom confidently hopes that it will be effectually, though it must be gradually, wiped away, and earnestly looks for the means by which this necessary object may be attained. And, until it shall be accomplished, until the time shall come when we can point without a blush to the language held in the Declaration of Independence, every friend of humanity will seek to lighten the galling chain of slavery, and better to the utmost of his power the wretched condition of the slave."—*Roger M. Taney in* 1818, *in defense of Rev. Mr. Gruber.*

tial organ of Mr. Calhoun, that was referred to in this passage.

Mr. Clay, as many readers may remember, won great glory at the North by his course during the session of 1833. He was received in New York and New England, this year, with that enthusiasm which his presence in the manufacturing States ever after inspired. The warmth of his reception consoled him for his late defeat at the polls, and gave new hopes to his friends.

But the Colossus of the session was Daniel Webster, well named, then, the Expounder of the Constitution. In supporting the administration in all its anti-nullification measures, he displayed his peculiar powers to the greatest advantage. The subject of debate was the one of all others the most congenial to him, and he rendered services then to his country to which his country may yet recur with gratitude. "Nullification kept me out of the Supreme Court all last winter," he says in one of his letters in 1833. He mentions, also, that the President sent his own carriage to convey him to the capitol on one important occasion. After the adjournment he visited the great West, where he was welcomed with equal warmth by the friends and the opponents of the administration. It was then, I have imagined, that he, too, took the mania for the presidency, of which he died.

Perhaps it is not extravagant to say, that the net result to the United States of the nullification of 1832, and a result worth its cost, was the four exhaustive Propositions into which Mr. Webster condensed his opinions respecting the nature of the compact which unites these States. We can not more fitly take leave of this subject than by reading them again:

"1. That the constitution of the United States is not a league, confederacy, or compact, between the people of the several States in their sovereign capacities; but a government proper, founded on the adoption of the people, and creating direct relations between itself and individuals.

"2. That no State authority has power to dissolve these

relations; that nothing can dissolve them but revolution; and that, consequently, there can be no such thing as secession without revolution.

"3. That there is a supreme law, consisting of the constitution of the United States, acts of Congress passed in pursuance of it, and treaties; and that, in cases not capable of assuming the character of a suit in law or equity, Congress must judge of, and finally interpret, this supreme law, so often as it has occasion to pass acts of legislation; and, in cases capable of assuming, and actually assuming, the character of a suit, the Supreme Court of the United States is the final interpreter.

"4. That an attempt by a State to abrogate, annul, or nullify an act of Congress, or to arrest its operation within her limits, on the ground that, in her opinion, such law is unconstitutional, is a direct usurpation on the just powers of the general government and on the equal rights of other States; a plain violation of the constitution, and a proceeding essentially revolutionary in its character and tendency."

XXI.

THE SUMMER TRAVELS OF THE PRESIDENT.

GENERAL JACKSON passed his sixty-sixth birth-day in the spring of 1833. He stood then at the highest point of his career. Opposition was, for the moment, almost silenced; and the whole country, except South Carolina, looked up to him as to a savior. He had but to go quietly on during the remaining years of his term, making no new issues, provoking no new controversies, to leave the chair of state more universally esteemed than he was when he assumed it. Going quietly on, however, was not his forte. A storm was already brewing, compared with which the excitements of his first term were summer calms.

The old friends of the old man were leaving him. I observe, in a letter of the President to the Land Commissioner, dated July 20th, 1833, that he announces the death of "that worthy and excellent man, General John Coffee." "With his dying breath," adds the President, "Coffee asked me to appoint William Weakly as his successor to the office of Surveyor-General of the District of Alabama. Weakly is a worthy man; appoint him." Robert Purdy, too, that fighting gentleman who served as Coffee's second in his duel with young McNairy, in 1805, died about this time, and left an office vacant for the President to fill.

It may be convenient just to mention here—reserving explanations for another page—that three important changes in the cabinet occurred in the month of May, this year. Mr. Livingston, the Secretary of State, left the cabinet to go out as embassador to France, in the hope of peacefully arranging the spoliation imbroglio. Mr. Louis McLane, the Secretary of the Treasury, was advanced to the Department of State. William J. Duane, a distinguished lawyer of Philadelphia, son of the President's old friend, Colonel Duane, of the far-famed *Aurora*, was appointed Secretary of the Treasury. This appointment was the President's own. Strongly attached to Colonel Duane, and having the highest opinion of his talents and integrity, General Jackson was accustomed, when speaking of his son, to exhaust compliment by saying, "He's a chip of the old block, sir." So he took him into his cabinet. Mr. Duane was a conscientious opponent of the Bank of the United States, and a democrat of the Jeffersonian school.

The greater part of this summer, so fruitful of disaster, was spent by General Jackson in traveling—in drinking deep draughts of the bewildering cup of adulation. A few amusing or characteristic incidents of his journeyings may detain us a moment from matters more important.

An event occurred on the first day's journey that was not of an adulatory nature. On the sixth of May, the President, accompanied by members of his cabinet and by Major Donelson, left the capital, in a steamboat, for Fredericksburg, Virginia, where he was to lay the corner-stone of that monument to the mother of Washington which is still unfinished. At Alexandria, where the steamer touched, there came on board a Mr. Randolph, late a lieutenant in the navy, who had been recently dismissed the service. Randolph made his way to the cabin, where he found the President sitting behind a table reading a newspaper. He approached the table, as if to salute the President.

68

"Excuse my rising, sir," said the General, who was not acquainted with Randolph. "I have a pain in my side which makes it distressing for me to rise."

Randolph made no reply to this courteous apology, but appeared to be trying to take off his glove.

"Never mind your glove, sir," said the General, holding out his hand.

At this moment, Randolph thrust his hand violently into the President's face, intending, as it appeared, to pull his nose. The captain of the boat, who was standing by, instantly seized Randolph, and drew him back. A violent scuffle ensued, during which the table was broken. The friends of Randolph clutched him, and hurried him ashore before many of the passengers knew what had occurred, and thus he effected his escape. The passengers soon crowded into the cabin to learn if the General was hurt.

"Had I known," said he, "that Randolph stood before me, I should have been prepared for him, and I could have defended myself. No villain," said he, "has ever escaped me before; and he would not, had it not been for my confined situation."

Some blood was seen on his face, and he was asked whether he had been much injured?

"No," said he, "I am not much hurt; but in endeavoring to rise I have wounded my side, which now pains me more than it did."

One of the citizens of Alexandria, who had heard of the outrage, addressed the General, and said: "Sir, if you will pardon me, in case I am tried and convicted, I will kill Randolph for this insult to you, in fifteen minutes !"

"No, sir," said the President, "I can not do that. I want no man to stand between me and my assailants, and none to take revenge on my account. Had I been prepared for this cowardly villain's approach, I can assure you all that he would never have the temerity to undertake such a thing again."

Randolph published statements in the newspapers of the "wrongs" which he said he had received at the hands of the government. The opposition papers, though condemning the outrage, did not fail to remind the President of certain passages in his own life and conversation which sanctioned a resort to violence. Randolph, I believe, was not prosecuted for the assault. His friends said that his object was merely to pull the presidential nose, which, they further declared, he did.

Returning from Fredericksburg, after performing there the pious duty assigned him, the President, early in June, accompanied by Mr. Van Buren, Governor Cass, Mr. Woodbury, Major Donelson, Mr. Earl, and others, began that famous tour which enabled the North to express its detestation of nullification, and its approval of the President's recent conduct. Baltimore, Philadelphia, New York, Newark, Elizabethtown, Boston, Salem, Lowell, Concord, Newport, Providence, each received the President with every demonstration of regard which ingenuity could devise. Every one in the United States knows how these things are done. Every one can imagine the long processions; the crowded roofs and windows; the thundering salutes of artillery; steamboats gay with a thousand flags and streamers; the erect, gray-headed old man, sitting his horse like a centaur, and bowing to the wild hurrahs of the Unterrified with matchless grace; the rushing forward of interminable crowds to shake the President's hand; the banquets, public and private; the toasts, addresses, responses; and all the other items of the price which a popular hero has to pay for his popularity.

The enthusiasm was real and almost universal. The New York *American*, however, complained that the reception in this city wore a too partisan complexion. "The mass of the citizens, the clergy, the learned professions, and the great middle class, could not approach him at all," said the *American*.

At Philadelphia, the President was induced, after much persuasion, to consult the celebrated Dr. Physick, with regard to that pain in the side and the bleeding at the lungs to which he was subject. Upon meeting the Doctor, the President explained his symptoms, concluding with these words: "Now, Doctor, I can do any thing you think proper to order, and bear as much as most men. There are only two things I can't give up: one is coffee, and the other is tobacco." Rather important exceptions, one would suppose. Mr. Trist, from whom I received this anecdote, added that Doctor Physick was completely captivated by the General's manner. The next day, Mr. Trist had occasion to consult the Doctor upon a case in which both of them were deeply interested; but, said Mr. Trist, he was so full of General Jackson, so penetrated with the gentleness, the frankness, the peculiar and indescribable charm of his demeanor, that he could talk of nothing else.

In New York, the President had a narrow escape or two. After receiving in Castle Garden the address of the corporation, he mounted his horse and passed over the long wooden bridge which formerly connected that fort with the Battery, followed by his suite and a great concourse of officials. He had just reached the land when the crowded bridge gave way, and let the multitude down among the rocks and into the shallow water below. Vice-President, Governor, Cabinet ministers, mayor, aldermen, military officers, and citizens generally, were mingled in an indiscriminate and struggling mass. The wildest confusion and alarm prevailed for several minutes. Gradually, however, the crowd emerged from the ruins, and no one was seriously hurt. Major Jack Downing 70 tells us that Governor Marcy tore his pantaloons a second time, and that Governor Cass lost his wig. But, he adds, as Governor Cass had all the Indian tribes in his department, he would have no difficulty in finding "a scalp to suit him." Again, in going up Broadway, the General's horse took fright, and would have thrown any horseman less accomplished than himself. On another occasion the wadding of a cannon came within a few inches of singeing the President's white and bristling head.

The Rev. Dr. Van Pelt, of this city, favors the reader with an interesting reminiscence of the President's excursion to Staten Island in the steamboat *Cinderella*. Returning from the Island, the President was enjoying on the upper deck of the boat the enchanting scenery of the most beautiful bay in the world.

"What a country God has given us!" exclaimed the President to Dr. Van Pelt. "How thankful we ought to be that God has given us such a country to live in."

"Yes," replied the Doctor, "and this harbor, General, *we* think the finest thing in it."

"We have the best country," continued the General, "and the best institutions in the world. No people have so much to be grateful for as we. But ah! my reverend friend, there is one thing that I fear will yet sap the foundations of our liberty—that monster institution, the bank of the United States! Its existence is incompatible with liberty. One of the two must fall—the bank or our free institutions. Next Congress, the effort to effect a re-charter will be renewed; but my consent they shall never have!"

He spoke with great energy, and continued to denounce the bank in unmeasured terms. The Doctor changed the subject, at length, by saying:

"I hear, General, that you were blessed with a Christian companion." ("Companion" is clerical for wife.)

"Yes," said the President, "my wife was a pious, Christian woman. She gave me the best advice, and I have not been unmindful of it. When the people, in their sovereign pleasure, elected me President of the United States, she said to me, 'Don't let your popularity turn your mind away from the duty you owe to God. Before Him we are all alike sinners, and to Him we must all alike give account. All these things will pass away, and you and I, and all of us must stand before God.' I have never forgotten it, Doctor, and I never shall."

Tears were in his eyes, adds Dr. Van Pelt, as he said these words.

As the boat was nearing the city, some slight confusion on board the boat occurred. To the apology of the marshal, Mr. Coventry Waddell, the General replied: "You were in action, I suppose, sir, and no apology is necessary. You are a young man, Mr. Waddell, and I see around me many who have seen fewer years than I have, and what I now say may be of some use to them. Always take all the time to reflect that circumstances will permit, but when the time for action has come, stop thinking."

Upon reaching Battery Place, an officer approached the President, and asked whether he preferred to ride in a barouche or on horseback. Turning to Mr. Van Buren, the General said,

"Matty, shall we ride in a carriage or on horseback?"

"As the President pleases," said Mr. Van Buren.

"Well, then," added the General, "let us ride on horseback."

Turning to Dr. Van Pelt, he said,

"Farewell, my friend."

"Farewell," said the doctor; "we may never meet again in this world."

"Then may we meet in a better," rejoined the President.

"You have my best wishes, General," said the doctor.

"I believe it," said the General, as he mounted and rode away.

A few days after the departure of the President for New England, the furniture used by him during his stay in the city was sold at auction, and thus divided among his admirers as mementoes of his visit.

Boston received him with extraordinary liberality and enthusiasm. One floor of the Tremont House was set apart for the entertainment of the President and his party. Carriages-and-four were kept at their disposal. Tickets to every place of amusement in the city were daily provided in profusion. All tolls and fares were intermitted to the friends of the President. Harvard University conferred upon him, in solemn form, in the chapel at Cambridge, the degree of Doctor of Laws; and one of the seniors, Francis Bowen, addressed the President, on behalf of the students, in the Latin language. These ceremonies, of course, gave the wits of the opposition an opportunity—which they improved. Major Jack Downing, whose humorous letters amused the whole country this summer, records that when the President had finished his speech at Downingville, he cried out to him, "You must give them a little Latin, *Doctor*." Whereupon the President, nothing abashed, "off hat agin," and thus resumed: "E pluribus unum, my friends, sine qua non!"

At Boston, the President, overcome by fatigue, had a dangerous attack of his malady, bleeding at the lungs, which confined him to his room for several days. The hotel was suddenly enveloped in silence. The carpets in the halls of the story occupied by the President were doubled, and the street was covered with tan. The President rallied, and continued his journey as far as Concord. At that point, he suddenly turned his course homeward, visiting Providence and Newport, steaming past New York without stopping, and making the best of his way to the seat of government. The reason assigned for this hasty return was the precarious state of the President's health. But that was not the only reason.

The veracious Downing assures us that the General was delighted with his "tower." "He is amazingly tickled with the Yankees," writes the Major, "and the more he sees on 'em, the better he likes 'em. 'No nullification here,' says he. 'No,' says I, 'General; Mr. Calhoun would stand no more chance down east here than a stumped-tail bull in fly time.'"

Later in the summer, the President, accompanied by Mr.

Blair, of the *Globe*, visited his favorite sea-shore resort, the Rip-raps of Virginia. A little circumstance that occurred on the steamboat that conveyed the party down the Chesapeake shows that Andrew Jackson had that kind of assurance of safety and success which Cæsar had in his fortunes and Napoleon in his star. The boat was a crazy old tub, and the waves were running high. An aged gentleman on board exhibited a good deal of alarm. "You are uneasy," said the General to him; "you never sailed with *me* before, I see."

XXII.

WAR UPON THE BANK RENEWED.

It is the nature of every thing that has life to try to prolong its life. So the Bank of the United States could not make up its mind to die on the 4th of March, 1836. By the aid of the press, and, possibly, by other means less legitimate, it still hoped to obtain a re-charter from Congress by a majority that would render the veto of the President powerless.

I say, *possibly*, by means less legitimate. The charge was made, and there was probably truth in the charge; but how much truth, it is impossible to ascertain. Unquestionably, the president, the directors, the employées of the great bank desired a re-charter, as much as the Jackson politicians desired a perpetuation of their power; and for the same reasons. Unquestionably, the resources and the influence of the bank were, in some degree, employed to secure a re-charter. Unquestionably, a member of Congress or an influential editor who presented a note to be discounted at the bank, was more likely to obtain the accommodation sought than any other man of equal credit. I think it highly probable that this species of favoritism was carried, in the later years of the struggle for life, to an extent that was most unwise, if not criminal. The instance related by Col. Benton must be taken with some allowance; for Col. Benton, in the height of the contest, was bank-mad, and was prepared to believe any thing ill of Nicholas Biddle. "The manner," says Benton, "in which the loans to members of Congress were made, was told me by one of these members who had gone through this process of bank accommodation; and who, voting against the bank, after getting the loan, felt himself free from shame in telling what had been done. He needed $4,000, and could not get it at home; he went to Philadelphia—to the bank—inquired for Mr. Biddle—was shown into an ante-room, supplied with newspapers and periodicals; and asked to sit, and amuse himself—the president being engaged for the moment. Presently a side door opened. He was ushered into the presence—graciously received—stated his business—was smilingly answered that he could have it, and more if he wished it; that he could leave his note with the exchange committee, and check at once for the proceeds: and if inconvenient to give an endorser before he went home, he could do it afterwards: and whoever he said was good, would be accepted. And in telling me this, the member said he could read 'bribery' in his eyes."

I have been told, twenty times, in the course of my inquiries on this subject, that Daniel Webster's checks for sums as large as five thousand dollars were paid by the bank when Mr. Webster had not a dollar in the bank. Every one must have heard similar stories, for they are still current. When, however, we look over the list of directors, and find there the names of men known to have been honest and honorable all their lives, men of even punctilious honesty in their private dealings, we find it impossible to believe such tales. In later years, when the bank had ceased to be a national institution, and was governed almost absolutely by the "emperor Nicholas," there was, indeed, a looseness in the management of its affairs that we know not whether to ascribe to corruption or to incapacity. A memoir of Nicholas Biddle, if honestly written, would be a most valuable contribution to the history of the country and of business, and would explain many things in the later career of the bank which are now lost in a chaos of figures, statements, counter-statements, and vituperation. Even when the final crash came, no man in the country seems to have been more sincerely astonished at it than Nicholas Biddle. How instructive it would be to men of business to have such an incredible mystery explained.

But it does not belong to our subject to explore in that direction. The directors of the bank made no attempt to conceal that they spent considerable sums in printing and circulating documents designed to vindicate the bank against the charges of the President of the United States. The bank, said they in their celebrated report of December, 1833, owns no press and sustains no press; does not interfere, and has not interfered with elections. In defending itself against the charges brought by the administration, it had expended in four years, the sum of fifty-eight thousand dollars; an expenditure which the directors justified as well as avowed. "The Bank," they said, "asserts its clear right to defend itself equally against those who circulate false statements, and those who circulate false notes. Its sole object, in either case, is self-defense. It can not suffer itself to be calumniated down, and the interests confided to its care sacrificed by falsehoods. A war of unexampled violence has been waged against the Bank. The institution defends itself. Its assailants are what are called politicians; and when statements which they can not answer, are presented to the country, they reproach the bank with interfering in politics. As these assaults, too, are made at the period of public elections, the answers of the bank must of course follow at the same time: and thus, because these politicians assail the bank on the eve of elections, unless the institution stands mute, it is charged with interfering in politics, and influencing elections. The bank has never interfered in the slightest degree in politics, and never influenced or sought to influence elections; but it will not be deterred by the menaces or clamors of politicians, from executing its duty in defending itself. Of the time and manner and degree and expense connected with this service, the board of directors claim to be the sole and exclusive judges."

General Jackson, as we have before mentioned, recommended Congress, in his message of December, 1832, to sell out the stock held by the United States in the bank, and to investigate again the condition of the bank, with a view to ascertain whether the public deposits were safe in its keeping. This intimation of the bank's insolvency caused a fall of six per cent. in the market price of its stock. In Congress, however, the institution was still so strong that the proposition to sell out the public stock, and the resolution implying a want of confidence in the bank's solvency, were voted down by immense majorities. Congress evidently regarded the recommendations of the message of 1832 as the offspring of an implacable enmity, which even victory had not been able to soften.

Congress had baffled the President, but could not divert him from his purpose. Three fixed ideas wholly possessed his mind: First, that the bank was insolvent; secondly, that the bank was steadily engaged in buying up members of Congress; thirdly, that the bank would certainly obtain a two-thirds majority at the very next session unless he, the President, could give the institution a crippling blow before Congress met.

The reason why the President thought the bank insolvent must be briefly explained. In March, 1832, the Secretary of the Treasury, Mr. McLane, informed Mr. Biddle of the government's intention to pay off, on the first of July, one-half of the three per cent. stock, which would amount to six millions and a half of dollars; but added, "if any objection occurs to you, either as to the amount or mode of payment, I will thank you to suggest it." An objection did occur to Mr. Biddle, and he went to Washington for the purpose of making it known to the Secretary of the Treasury. So far as the bank is concerned, said Mr. Biddle, there is no objection whatever. But, added he, the payment of so large a sum, several millions of which will immediately leave the country on account of the foreign stockholders, will certainly embarrass the business men of the commercial centers. Duties to the amount of nine millions were to be paid before the first of July, which could not be done unless merchants enjoyed rather more than less of the usual bank accommodation. Mr. Biddle advised the government to postpone the payment, therefore, and agreed to pay the interest on the amount which would thus be left in the bank. The offer was accepted. The arrangement was beneficial to the bank, as it paid but three per cent. for the use of the money; beneficial to the government, as it received as much interest as it paid the stockholders; beneficial to the country, as it prevented a large sum from going abroad at a time when it was pressingly needed at home.

It excited surprise and remark at the time that Mr. Biddle should have gone to Washington, in person, to arrange this postponement, instead of expressing his views by letter. But the truth was, as the directors explained, that "the letter of the Secretary was received so immediately before the period fixed for issuing the notice of payment, that if any thing were to be done at all, it was to be done only by personal communication with the Secretary, as there was no time for correspondence."

A second time, the extinguishment of the same stock was postponed, which the directors thus explained: "The resources of the government were threatened with the greatest danger by the appearance of the cholera, which had already begun its ravages in New York and Philadelphia, with every indication of pervading the whole country. Had it continued as it began, and all the appearances in July warranted the belief of its continuance, there can be no doubt it would have prostrated all commercial credit, and seriously endangered the public revenue, as in New York and Philadelphia alone, the demand on account of the foreign three per cents. was about five millions. The bank, therefore, made an arrangement with the foreign owners of this stock, to the amount of $4,175,373 92, to leave their money in the country for another year, the bank assuming to pay the interest instead of the government. Having settled this, the bank resumed its usual facilities of business to the community."

General Jackson, although he consented to the first postponement, drew from Mr. Biddle's conduct, particularly his coming to Washington, the inference that the bank could not pay the three per cents., and was, in fact, an insolvent institution. "I tell you, sir," he would say, "she's broke. Mr. Biddle is a proud man, and he never would have come on to Washington to ask me for a postponement if the bank had had the money. Never, sir. The bank's broke, and Biddle knows it. Her stock is not worth seventy-five cents on the dollar this minute." No argument could shake this opinion; and when, in 1842, the United States Bank of Pennsylvania went to pieces, and brought ruin upon thousands, the comment of General Jackson amounted to this: "I told you so."

Col. Benton also adduces the President's declaration of the bank's insolvency as a proof of his sagacity, and he draws a horrible picture of the disaster of 1842, to justify the President's hostility to the bank in 1833. He also denies that the hostility of the Presldent had any thing in it of the rancorous or vindictive.

If there is in existence any credible evidence that the Bank of the United States was not solvent in 1833, or any credible evidence that the bank was then endeavoring to secure a re-charter by unequivocally dishonorable means, I have not been able to discover it. Its complaisance to members of Congress may have been carried too far. It was not in human nature that it should not be. An institution such as the Bank of the United States was in 1833, giving an honorable livelihood and social distinction to five hundred persons, can no more go out of existence without a struggle, than a strong man can die without a struggle in the prime of his powers. And this is really one of the weightiest objections against the existence of such an institution. A bank with a limited charter will as certainly direct its energies to procure a renewal as an office-holder, under the rotation system, is chiefly concerned to obtain a reappointment. He would gladly serve the people, if the people, in return, would secure his children's bread; but, as the people will not do that, he serves his party, who will if they can.

But a truce to disquisition. We have now arrived at that measure—fruitful of many disasters and of great eventual good—known as the Removal of the Deposits. The caricaturists of 1833 represent the President and his friends in the act of carrying huge sacks of money from the Bank of the United States. In this sense the deposits were never removed. The measure proposed by the President, was not to remove the public money suddenly and in mass from the bank, but merely to *cease depositing* the public money in the bank, drawing out the balance remaining in its vaults as the public service required. The amount of public money in the bank had averaged nearly eight millions of dollars for some years past, which sum was so much added to the bank's available capital.

What a simple, what a harmless measure this appears! And harmless it would have been, but for one lamentable circumstance. *The government had not devised a proper place to which to transfer the public money.* The subtreasury had not yet been thought of, or only thought of. The complete and eternal divorce which that wise and simple expedient effected between bank and state, came too late to save the country from four years of most disastrous "experiment." The plan proposed in 1833 was, instead of depositing the public money in the Bank of the United States and its twenty-five branches, to deposit it in a similar number of State banks. What good could be hoped from such a partial measure? We can not wonder that every member of the Cabinet, except two, besides some important members of the kitchen cabinet, and a large majority of the President's best friends, opposed it from the beginning to the end.

The measure occurred to the President while he was conversing, one day early in the year 1833, with Mr. Blair, of the *Globe*, who hated the bank only less than the President himself did. "Biddle," said Mr. Blair, "is actually using the people's money to frustrate the people's will. He is using the money of the government for the purpose of breaking down the government. If he had not the public money he could not do it."

The President said, in his most vehement manner: "He shan't have the public money. I'll remove the deposits! Blair, talk with our friends about this, and let me know what they think of it."

Mr. Blair complied with this request. He consulted several of the President's constitutional and unconstitutional advisers—among others, Mr. Silas Wright, of New York. Every man of them opposed the removal, unless it were done by the authority of Congress. Mr. Wright was particularly decided in his opposition. He said that the withdrawal of the public money from the bank would compel it to curtail its business to such a degree, that half the merchants in the country would fail. Mr. Wright argued upon the subject as though the public money, instead of being deposited in the Bank of the United States, was about to be thrown into the sea. The real effect of the removal—which was to stimulate the business of the country to the point of explosion—did not occur to him, nor to any one.

In the course of a day or two, Mr. Blair informed the President that he had consulted the leading friends of the administration upon the measure proposed, and that they were all against it. "Oh," said the President, with a nonchalance that surprised the editor of the *Globe*, "my mind is made up on *that* matter. Biddle shan't have the public money to break down the public administration with. It's settled. My mind's made up." That was the only explanation he ever gave, in conversation, of his course with regard to the deposits. When letters of remonstrance reached him, hundreds in a day, his comment was ever the same: "Biddle shall not use the public money to break down the government." The same idea was through all his public papers on the subject.

Before proceeding to relate the manner in which the President accomplished his purpose, I will afford the reader an "inside view" of the perturbations of the cabinet caused by the announcement of his intention. The narrative annexed was written, soon after the events occurred, by Major Lewis, chiefly for his own use and entertainment. No part of it has ever been published before. The reader who is curious in cabinet-ware, will be amused and edified by its perusal. It will illustrate our motto : "Desperate courage makes One a majority."

NARRATIVE BY MAJOR WM. B. LEWIS.

"I received from General Cass, September 23d, 1833, the following note: 'My dear Major, may I ask you, as a particular favor, to postpone your journey till day after to-morrow? I have a particular reason for making this request, which I will explain to you to-morrow, and which, I am sure, you will consider satisfactory.'

"This note of Governor Cass' led to a very interesting and important conversation. Business made it necessary that I should visit Virginia, and having been already detained by request of the President, several days beyond the time I had set for my departure, I determined to leave on the morning of the 24th. Governor Cass knew this, but wishing to have some conversation with me before I left, desired, as stated in his note, that I would postpone my trip until the next day. This I could not do, but consented to see him the next morning after an early breakfast at my office, if that would answer his purpose. He consented to this arrangement, and accordingly called about half past eight o'clock.

"He commenced the conversation by remarking that his object in desiring to see me before I left, was to inform me that he had determined to resign his seat in the cabinet, and wished to converse with me upon the subject before he handed his letter of resignation to the President. I was very much surprised at this, and inquired of him the reason for this step he was about to take. He said he differed with the President with regard to the measures which were about to be adopted for the removal of the public deposits from the United States Bank, and, as his remaining in the cabinet might embarrass his operations, he owed it, he thought, both to himself and the President, to withdraw. This, he said, was the reason, and, owing to the relations which had so happily subsisted between himself and me ever since he came to Washington, he did not like to do so without first apprising me of his intentions.

"I told him I regretted exceedingly that he should think it necessary to resign. I thought he had taken a mistaken view of the subject, and expressed a wish that he would reconsider the matter.

"He said that he had already reflected much upon this subject, and that both he and Mr. McLane, Secretary of State, were fully of the opinion that they ought not to remain in the cabinet. He added that he had already prepared his letter of resignation, and intended handing it on that day to the President.

"This information rendered me very unhappy, for I foresaw that an explosion in the cabinet, at that conjuncture, might be attended with serious, if not fatal consequences to the administration. I thought it doubtful, at best, whether Congress would sustain the President in directing the deposits to be removed from the custody of the United States Bank; but if Governor Cass and Mr. McLane withdrew from the cabinet, and their friends, who were numerous and powerful in and out of Congress, should throw themselves against the measure, *I believed Congress would not sustain him.* With these apprehensions weighing upon my mind, I resolved, for the sake of the President, the success of whose administration I had greatly at heart, to make an effort to prevent, if possible, a step so fatal to it as I believed that would be. I, therefore, inquired of Governor Cass if he had spoken to the President upon the subject of his intended resignation. He said he had not. I again repeated to him that I thought there was no necessity for him and McLane to resign; that I was sure their disagreeing with the President in relation to the removal of the deposits, or the manner of doing it, would not make the slightest difference with him. I added that I knew his confidence in both of them was unimpaired, and that I felt fully warranted in saying that he would greatly prefer they should remain in the cabinet. I then begged him to go and see the President that morning, and have a conversation with him upon the subject.

"He consented to do so, and left immediately. In about half an hour he returned, and appeared to be exceedingly gratified at the interview. He said he never saw the President so kind, or more frank, than on that occasion.

"'Well,' said I, 'what did he say to you? Does he think you and McLane had better resign?'

"'Not at all,' he replied. 'He assured me that his confidence in both of us was undiminished, and that he should regret exceedingly to lose us; and, at the same time, added there was not the least necessity for our withdrawing from his cabinet.'

"'Then,' I replied, 'I hope you will not withdraw,' adding that I thought it would be treating him very badly were he and Mr. McLane to desert him in such a crisis.

He replied that if McLane would consent to remain, he would be willing to continue.

"'Well then,' said I, 'go down without delay to the State Department, and see him, and, if possible, prevail on him not to leave the cabinet,' which he did immediately.

"After dispatching some public business, which it was necessary for me to attend to before leaving for Virginia, I stepped over to the President's house to take leave of him, and at the same time to see Governor Cass, who promised, after having a conversation with Mr. McLane, to meet me there. I had scarcely entered the house before he came with a pleasant smile upon his face.

"'Well,' said I, 'do you bring me good news?'

"Nothing definite had, as yet, been agreed upon, he replied; but he had hopes of being able to get every thing arranged in such a manner as would not only be satisfactory, but obviate the necessity of their withdrawing from the cabinet. I told him I had no doubt of it, and hoped he would not cease his exertions until the arrangements were accomplished. As he was anxious to see the President and have a further conversation with him, I took my leave of him and departed for Virginia. This unpleasant affair was thus happily arranged.

"While upon this deposit question, it may not be improper nor yet unprofitable to advert to other circumstances connected with the subject. It is one that excited much feeling and involved important consequences both to the country and the party in power. It was the origin of much trouble and difficulty among the friends and supporters of General Jackson—a rock upon which the democratic party (so called) had well nigh been wrecked at the time, and from which it never afterward entirely recovered.

"With whom the idea of withdrawing the public money from the United States Bank originated, I know not, but it was started soon after President Jackson's second election, and was warmly discussed by a few of his friends in Washington, from that time until the order was given by him for their removal. I happened one evening to be at Mr. Blair's, editor of the *Globe*, in the month of February, 1833, in company with Dr. William Jones, city postmaster, when the conversation turned upon the United States Bank, and the withdrawal of the public deposits from its custody. Mr. Blair maintained most vehemently that the damned bank ought to be put down, and the only effectual way of doing it was to take from it the whole of the public money; if it were allowed to retain that, he said, it would undoubtedly be re-chartered.

"'How could the possession of the public money aid it,' I inquired, 'in obtaining a charter?'

"'Why,' said he, 'by corrupting the members of Congress; it would have the *means*,' he added, 'of buying up half the members, and would do it unless the public funds were taken from it.'

"'How very extravagantly,' I remarked to Mr. Blair, 'you talk; you must entertain a very poor opinion of the integrity and honor of the members of Congress, to believe them capable of such degrading and infamous conduct.'

"He said their conduct at the last, as well as at the present session, showed they were capable of *any thing* where the interest of the bank was concerned. He would not trust them any more than he would Biddle and the other officers of the bank, and he would not trust either further than he could throw a bull by the tail.

"'But,' said I, 'Mr. Blair, do you really think the President would order the public money to be drawn from the bank merely for the sake of crippling, or, as you say, *breaking* it?'

"Why, yes, he said, he thought he would; at any rate, he thought he ought to do it.

"'Well,' I remarked, 'I differ with you in opinion. I neither think he ought nor will do it.'

"I then inquired of him if he thought the Vice-President elect, Mr. Van Buren, would advise such a measure.

"'Yes,' he said, 'I have no doubt of it.'

"I told him I did not believe it.

"'Why do you not believe it?' said he. 'Have you ever heard him express his opinions upon the subject?'

"'No,' I replied, 'but Mr. Van Buren is too prudent and discreet a man, and, withal, has too much sense to advise such rash measures.'

"This remark excited him still more, and snatching up his hat, said he would not wait to know what he thought in relation to the matter, and started in pursuit of him. As he left the room, I remarked to him I would not leave until he returned.

"Mr. Blair was gone nearly or quite an hour before he returned; but Dr. Jones, who was present during the whole of the conversation, and myself remained until he came back. He entered the room with evidently dissatisfied as well as subdued looks.

"'Well,' said I, 'Mr. Blair, have you seen Mr. Van Buren?'

"'Yes,' was his reply.

"'Is he in favor of removing the deposits or not. Are you or myself right as regards his opinions upon this subject?'

"His reply was, that Mr. Van Buren was *opposed* to the removal. Such a step, he thought, would be both injudicious and impolitic.

"I told him I agreed with him, and that I thought he would find a large majority of the President's friends of the same way of thinking.

"Here the conversation ended, and Dr. Jones and myself left.

"Although Mr. Blair was disappointed and mortified at finding Mr. Van Buren opposed to this favorite scheme of his, yet it did not dampen his ardor in the least. It was his theme by day and by night, talking to all his friends that would listen to him, and urging it as absolutely necessary to prevent the bank from getting its charter renewed. It was useless to tell him that the President could prevent that, at any time, by the use of the veto power. The reply was that it would be carried over his veto! He let no opportunity slip of arousing the fears of the President, and exciting his feelings against the bank; and in this he was aided by Mr. Kendall and Mr. Reuben M. Whitney.

"A few weeks later, I embraced the earliest opportunity to inquire of Mr. Van Buren what had been determined upon with regard to the removal of deposits? His answer was, he thought the President had made up his mind to remove them from the United States Bank. I told him I regretted it, because I thought it would be productive of much mischief to the country, to the party in power, and to the President himself. He said the question was *settled*, and made a few remarks in justification of the course of the President, by which I saw very clearly that his opinions had undergone a change. I dropped the subject, and have never mentioned it to Mr. Van Buren since.

. . . .

"Not long after the President returned from the Rip Raps, I happened to be with him in his private chamber, and as the conversation turned upon the all engrossing topic of removing the deposits, he asked me if I had seen the correspondence between him and Colonel Duane upon that subject. I told him I had not. He then took from his private files a large package of papers, and said:

"'Here it is. Read it, and let me know what you think of it.'

"I accordingly gave it an attentive perusal, which, as it was very voluminous, took me at least two hours. As I handed back the papers, 'Well,' said he, 'don't you think Mr. Duane's letters are very weak?' 'No,' I told him, 'I thought they were very well written; in fact, that I thought the correspondence evidenced a good deal of ability on both sides. The difficulty, however,' I remarked, 'upon my mind was not as regarded the *right* to do the thing, but the necessity for doing it. It would seem to me,' I added, 'that it would be much better to wait until Congress met, and let them legislate upon the subject, unless he thought the public funds in danger of being lost if permitted to remain longer in the United States Bank.'

"'I do think so,' he quickly and energetically replied. 'Besides,' said he, 'I have no confidence in Congress.'

"'But, General,' I remarked, 'Mr. Duane would be assuming a very heavy responsibility in removing the public moneys from the custody of the bank, in the face of a resolution passed by the House of Representatives at its last session, by a very large majority, perhaps two-thirds, declaring them, in its opinion, safe.'

"'But,' said he, 'I don't want him to assume the responsibility. Have I not said that I would take the responsibility?'

"'Yes,' I told him, 'he had said so; but it was doubtful whether any person could be made responsible but the Secretary himself, because if done at all, it must be done by him, as the law gave that power to no other person.'

"I then inquired of him what he would do if Congress, when it met, should pass a joint resolution, directing the Secretary to restore the deposits to the bank?

"'Why,' said he, 'I would veto it.'

"This, I told him, would be, in my opinion, a much stronger question against the administration than the vetoing of the bill re-chartering the bank. The southern members were, I added, almost to a man, *obliged*, from the peculiar notions of their constituents, to sustain his veto upon that bill, but not as regards this measure, which involves no constitutional question. 'Besides,' said I, 'many of the members who were elected to support your administration *generally*, only wanted a *pretext* to throw themselves into the ranks of the opposition.'

"'Under such circumstances, General,' I remarked, 'suppose they should be able to carry the resolution over your veto? What then would you do? If you refuse to permit the secretary to do it, the next step, on the part of the House, would be to move an impeachment, and if Congress have the power to carry this resolution through in defiance of the veto power, they would be able to prosecute it to a successful termination.'

"'Under such circumstances,' he replied, elevating himself to his full height and assuming a firm and dignified aspect, 'then, sir, I would resign the presidency and return to the Hermitage!'

"After the General's emphatic declaration that he would resign and return to the Hermitage rather than be instrumental in restoring the deposits to the United States Bank, there was a pause in our conversation for a few minutes; but it was renewed again by my asking him what object was to be attained by a removal of the deposits from the bank at that time?

"'To prevent it from being re-chartered,' was the reply.

"'But,' said I, 'can not that object be as certainly attained, as well without as with the removal of them?'

"'No, sir,' said he, 'if the bank is permitted to have the public money, there is no power that can prevent it from obtaining a charter—it will have it if it has to buy up all Congress, and the public funds would enable it to do so!'

"'Why, General,' I remarked, 'as the bank's charter expires twelve months before you go out of office, you will at all times have it in your power to prevent it by vetoing any bill that may be sent to you for that purpose. Would it not be better, then,' I asked, 'to let it go quietly out of existence?'

"'But, sir,' said he, 'if we leave the means of corruption in its hands, the presidential veto will avail nothing.'

"This conviction had fastened itself so *firmly* on his mind, I discovered, that it was impossible to remove it by any thing I could say, and I therefore dropped the subject. The conversation was conducted on the part of the President with calmness and moderation—evincing not the least excitement as was sometimes the case when speaking about, or discussing the question of removal.

"He then asked me if I would read Mr. McLane's opinions, or arguments against removing the deposits; 'but,' said he, 'it is not written with his usual ability—owing undoubtedly, to his having taken a wrong view of the subject." I told him, as it was getting late, and as the opinion appeared to be a very long one, I would, with his leave, embrace some other opportunity of reading it. The conversation referred to above, took place a short time before the removal of Mr. Duane from the Treasury Department.

"The General was very much annoyed at the idea of having to remove him, and would gladly have avoided it if he could have done so consistently with what *he* considered his duty to the public. He had, previously to the unfortunate difficulty, entertained for him a high personal regard. Indeed, he told me apparently with great satisfaction, in the latter part of November, or early in December, 1832, that he intended to offer the Treasury Department to him, when Mr. McLane should be transferred to the State Department, which would be the following spring.

"'My cabinet appointments have been generally made upon the recommendation of my friends, but this,' said he, 'will be *my own*. I like the stock; his father was an able financier, a sound republican, a good patriot, and an honest man; and the son, in my estimation, is in every respect equal to his father.'

"He little dreamed, when pronouncing this eulogy upon father and son, that the appointment which he spoke of conferring upon the latter, in his private chamber, would occasion him so much trouble and heart-burning! But it is not given to man to dive into the secrets of futurity. When things were rapidly drawing to a crisis, with regard to Mr. Duane, and perceiving, from frequent conversations with the President, that he still had a lingering feeling of kindness for him, I asked the General if some arrangement could not be made by which *he* would be spared the pain and Mr. Duane the mortification of a removal? He said he knew of none.

"'Would not Mr. Duane,' I inquired, 'be willing to take some other situation and leave the department voluntarily?'

"He did not know, he said, but if he would he should have it. I then asked him if he would allow me to endeavor to ascertain. He said he had not the least objection, and authorized me to say that if he desired it he he should have a foreign mission. It was found impossible, however, to make any such arrangement, and the President, as things then stood, was left no alternative but to dismiss him, which he did."

It thus appears that the hearty supporters of the President in the removal of the deposits were Mr. Blair, Mr. Kendall, Mr. Taney, Mr. Barry, and Reuben M. Whitney. To these was soon added the indomitable Benton, the predestined champion of the measure in the Senate. He was in Virginia, he tells us, when he first heard of the President's intention. "I felt," he says, "an emotion of the moral sublime at beholding such an instance of civic heroism. And I repaired to Washington at the approach of the session with a full determination to stand by the President, which I believed to be standing by the country; and to do my part in justifying his conduct, and in exposing and resisting the powerful combination which it was certain would be formed against him."

XXIII.

MR. DUANE'S NARRATIVE.

It is not true, as has been a hundred times asserted, that Mr. Duane was appointed Secretary of the Treasury for the purpose of removing the deposits. The post was offered him in December, 1832, when the President had not yet conceived the idea of removing them by an act of executive authority. Mr. Duane owed his appointment to the respect and affection which General Jackson entertained for his father and for himself. There was no intrigue or mystery about it.

In 1838 Mr. Duane wrote, and printed for distribution among his friends, the story of his brief and troublous tenure of the second place in General Jackson's Cabinet. His narrative, besides giving many glimpses of General Jackson, valuable for the purposes of biography, tells the greater part of the story of the removal of the deposits, and tells it in a very entertaining manner. As this narrative was, doubtless, printed for the purpose of rescuing from oblivion the singular events recorded in it, I shall be promoting the author's purpose by presenting to the readers of these pages an abstract of its contents. The work itself is only to be found in the libraries of a few collectors, and, occasionally, on the shelves of a public institution.

In December, 1832, Mr. Duane was practicing his profession in Philadelphia, anticipating nothing so little as an invitation to enter public life. He had supported General Jackson in the campaigns of 1824 and 1828, with the ardor natural to him. "I thought," he remarks, "that his country owed him a large debt of gratitude; that it would be useful to our institutions to have in our executive chair a person unaccustomed to intrigue, too prevalent at Washington; and that he, who had given such sound advice to Mr. Monroe while President, would never contradict, in practice, what he then declared to be the only patriotic and honorable course for the chief magistrate of a free and enlightened people."

The General, on his part, had shown his confidence in Mr. Duane by appointing him, first, a government director of the United States Bank; secondly, District-Attorney; thirdly, a commissioner under the convention with Denmark; all of which offices Mr. Duane declined; but was induced to accept the Danish commissionership by the repeated and pressing solicitations of the President. In December, 1832, Mr. McLane came from Washington to Philadelphia, and sought an interview with Mr. Duane, during which the following conversation took place:

THE SECRETARY OF THE TREASURY.—"Mr. Duane, I have been particularly desired by the President to seek this interview with you, on matters of much consequence, not only to himself, but to the country. The President has, for some time past, meditated a change in his cabinet. It has been deferred until after the termination of the elections in the States;

and as they are now over, the proposed change is urged anew. The present Secretary of State is to go to France; the present Secretary of the Treasury is to take his place in the Department of State; and the question is, who is to go into the treasury? It is settled that a citizen of Pennsylvania is to be appointed, and the President and his friends have sought in that State for a person in all respects competent as an officer, and faithful as a friend. A list of names has been looked at, and, after due inquiry, the President is decidedly convinced that you, sir, present the fairest claims to official and personal consideration. You are of the old democratic party of Pennsylvania, and have grown with its growth. You are known as a mild but unvarying friend of the great political principles which Pennsylvania cherishes. Your personal reputation, too, gives you a moral influence, of the extent of which you are not, perhaps, yourself aware. You were the early and have been the steadfast friend of General Jackson, and should continue in every proper way to sustain him whom you contributed to elevate. So satisfied, indeed, is the President of your peculiar fitness for the department, and of your being just such a person as he can politically as well as personally rely upon, that I can not use too strong terms in describing his solicitude that you should not refuse the station."

Mr. Duane.—"I have listened, sir, to what you have stated with surprise and distress; so that it can not be supposed that I can give a positive reply. I can not express how gratified and proud I am at this mark of confidence. If, however, I am now to give utterance to what I feel, it is to ask the President to blot this matter from his mind. It is true that I have been and am sincerely friendly to the President; that I possess the personal and political confidence of many worthy men in Pennsylvania; and that I have a strong inclination to do all in my power to evince my principles and promote the welfare of the people. But it is also true that my abilities are overrated; that my influence in Pennsylvania is more limited than is supposed; and that no weight can be given, by my accession, to the administration. Such an occasion as the present can not be heedlessly regarded by me, but all considerations united forbid me to assent. I have through life sought the shade, and whenever I have been out of it, it has not been from choice. I have always desired to tread on the earth, lest, in ascending even a single step of the political ladder, I should be obliged to resume my former place. Perhaps this is morbid pride, but be it what it may, it has a powerful influence over me."

The Secretary of the Treasury.—"All you have said, Mr. Duane, shows you have the merit you deny yourself the possession of. You have, by declining office, on several occasions, omitted to advance yourself. I am the President's friend and yours, and am not the man to advocate anything of a doubtful nature, by which the public may be affected. Others are more competent, perhaps, to judge of your qualifications than you are yourself. Heretofore there have been some difficulties; there may be some at this time, owing to excitement in the South; but that will soon cease, and in a few months you will be perfectly *au fait* as to all general duties. As to your standing in Pennsylvania, we have information to be relied on; we believe your appointment would be pleasing there, and the President desires to do what will gratify that State. Apart from other considerations, the President's own spontaneous preference of you is a compliment not to be overlooked; you will derive credit from it, where you are not known, among all who respect the patriotism and pure intentions, as well as the natural sagacity of the President. I am persuaded that the appointment would be acceptable to many of the President's most distinguished friends. Indeed, the fact that he goes to the people, and not to Congress to select, will give weight to the choice. You will earn a high reputation in the office proposed; and the labors will be less burdensome than those to which you have been accustomed."

MR. DUANE.—"To tear up, as it were, by the roots, my business in Philadelphia, on the uncertainty of continuing in office for four years, would be very imprudent. Changes of residence, associations, and expenditure, are sound objections. Friends to me ought not to urge a proceeding of so doubtful a character."

THE SECRETARY OF THE TREASURY.—"Every man owes something to his country. Even on the question of mere interest, the change will be advantageous. You may be certain of employment for four years, at six thousand dollars per year, and the mode of living is that of a private gentleman in Philadelphia. By identifying yourself with General Jackson and his friends, and making a sacrifice, if it is one, you establish a claim for continuance in this, or appointment to some other station."

MR. DUANE.—"Out of thankfulness, and a desire to make a return for such confidence, my heart urges me to say 'yes;' but my head by no means assents. It will be rude as well as unkind to the President to decide at once, and upon so sudden an appeal on so serious a subject; therefore I will reflect."

Consultation with friends, and a month's reflection, resulted in Mr. Duane's notifying the President that he accepted the post offered him. On the thirtieth of January, 1833, he sent his letter of acceptance to Washington, which the President joyfully acknowledged on the first of February. On the first of June following Mr. Duane took the customary oath, and entered upon the performance of his duties as Secretary of the Treasury. Before he slept that night, an event occurred which led him to suspect that the place of cabinet minister is not all that the fancy of a politician paints it.

In the evening of his first day in office, Mr. Duane relates:

"Mr. Reuben M. Whitney called upon me at my lodgings, at the desire, as he said, of the President, to make known to me what had been done, and what was contemplated, in relation to the United States Bank. He stated that the President had concluded to take upon himself the responsibility of directing the Secretary of the Treasury to remove the public deposits from that bank, and to transfer them to State banks; that he had asked the members of the cabinet to give him their opinions on the subject; that the President had said, 'Mr. Taney and Mr. Barry had come out like men for the removal;' that Mr. McLane had given a long opinion against it; that Mr. Cass was supposed to be against it, but had given no written opinion; that Mr. Woodbury had given an opinion which was 'yes' and 'no;' that the President would make the act his own, by addressing a paper or order to the Secretary of the Treasury; that Mr. Amos Kendall, who was high in the President's confidence, was now preparing that paper; that there had been delay owing to the affair at Alexandria; but, no doubt, the President would soon speak to me on the subject; that the paper referred to would be put forth as the proclamation had been, and would be made a rallying point; that he (Mr. Whitney) had, at the desire of the President, drawn up a memoir or exposition, showing that the measure might be safely adopted, and that the State banks would be fully adequate to all the purposes of government. He then read the exposition to me; and, as I desired to understand matters so important and so singularly presented, I asked him to leave the paper with me, which he accordingly did. He also read to me divers letters from individuals connected with State banks. The drift of his further observations was to satisfy me that the executive arm alone could be relied on to prevent a renewal of the United States Bank charter.

"The communication thus made to me created surprise and mortification. I was surprised at the position of affairs which it revealed; and mortified at the low estimate which had been formed of the independence of my character. I listened, however, respectfully, to one who gave such evidence of the confidence reposed in him; and awaited the explanation, which he intimated the President would give. Soon after this interview, I took occasion to express my mortification at my position, to the member of the cabinet who had represented the President in asking me to accept office. On the next evening (Sunday), Mr. Whitney again called on me, in company with a stranger, whom he introduced as Mr. Amos Kendall, a gentleman in the President's confidence, who would give me any further explanations that I might desire, as to what was meditated in relation to the United States Bank, and who then called on me, because he was about to proceed forthwith to Baltimore. I did not invite nor check communication. Very little was said, and, perhaps, because I could not wholly conceal my mortification at an attempt apparently made with the sanction of the President, to reduce me to a mere cypher in the administration.

"The next morning, June 3d, I waited upon the President, and, as I had been apprised by Mr. Whitney would be the case, he soon introduced the subject of the bank. I stated that Mr. Whitney had made known to me what had been done, and what was intended, and had intimated that his communication was made at the President's desire. The President replied, in a tone of dissatisfaction, that it was true he had conferred with Mr. Whitney, and obtained information from him as to the bank, but that he did not make him his confidant, nor had he told him to call on me. I enumerated the representations which Mr. Whitney had made, and their correctness was admitted. I said I feared that I should not be able to see the subject in the light in which the President viewed it; to which he remarked, that he liked frankness, that my predecessor and himself had sometimes differed in opinion, but it had made no difference in feeling, and should not in my case; that the matter under consideration was of vast consequence to the country; that unless the bank was broken down, it would break us down; that if the last Congress had remained a week longer in session, two thirds would have been secured for the bank by corrupt means; and that the like result might be apprehended at the next Congress; that such a State bank agency must be put in operation, before the meeting of Congress, as would show that the United States Bank was not necessary, and thus some members would have no excuse for voting for it. My suggestions as to an inquiry by Congress (as in December, 1832), or a recourse to the judiciary, the President repelled, saying it would be idle to rely upon either; referring as to the judiciary to decisions already made, as indications of what would be the effect of an appeal to them in future. After mentioning that he would speak to me again, before his departure to the eastward, the President said he would take with him the opinions of the members of the cabinet, but would send them to me from New York, along with his views; and, on his return, would expect me to give him my sentiments frankly and fully.

"On the 5th of June, the day before his departure, we accordingly had another conversation, which he ended by saying, he did not wish any one to conceal his opinions, and that all he asked was, that I should reflect with a view to the public good.

"I had heard rumors of the existence of an influence at Washington, unknown to the constitution and to the country; and the conviction that they were well founded, now became irresistible. I knew that four of the six members of the last cabinet, and that four of the members of the present cabinet, opposed a removal of the deposits; and yet their exertions were nullified by individuals, whose intercourse with the President was clandestine. During his absence, several of those individuals called on me, and made many of the identical observations, in the identical language, used by himself. They represented Congress as corruptible, and the new members as in need of especial guidance. They pointed out the importance of a test question, at the opening of the new Congress, for party purposes. They argued that the exercise of the veto power must be secured; that it could be in no other way so effectually attained as by at once removing the deposits; and that, unless they were removed, the President would be thwarted by Congress. In short, I felt satisfied, from all that I saw and heard, that factious and selfish views alone guided those who had influence with the executive; and that the true welfare and honor of the country constituted no part of their objects. I was painfully impressed with these convictions, and also mortified that I should have been considered capable of entering into schemes like these; when, on the 1st of July, I received from the President, the *letter* and *views*" (which he had promised).

The package was of formidable dimensions, consisting of more than two hundred pages of manuscript. The important documents were two in number, namely, a letter from the President, giving an outline of the financial system proposed to be substituted for the one then in use, and a letter of prodigious magnitude, completely unfolding the President's views. The smaller epistle may have been the President's own; the larger one was the production of Mr. Kendall; but both were signed, Andrew Jackson. In the paper by Mr. Kendall the history of the war against the bank was related, and various reasons were given for the measure contemplated. The main reason advanced was, that the people had reëlected General Jackson distinctly on the bank issue, and that he owed it to the people to complete the work of destroying the bank which the veto had begun. The President's own letter informed Mr. Duane what the President desired him to do. It should be read with particular attention.

GENERAL JACKSON TO MR. DUANE.

"Boston, June 26th, 1833.

". . . . . It is, in my opinion, desirable that you should appoint a discreet agent to proceed forthwith, with proper credentials from your department, to the cities of Baltimore, Philadelphia, and Boston, to consult with the Presidents and Directors of State banks, in those cities, upon the practicability of making an arrangement with them, or some of them, upon something like the following terms, viz.:

"1st. That one bank be selected in Baltimore, one in Philadelphia, two in New York, and one in Boston, with a right, on the part of the government, to add one in Savannah, one in Charleston, S. C., one in the State of Alabama, one in New Orleans, and one in Norfolk, upon their acceding to the terms proposed, which shall receive the deposits in those places respectively, *and* be responsible to the government for the whole public deposits of the United States.

"2d. That these banks shall have the right, by a convention of their presidents or otherwise, to select all the banks, at other points throughout the United States, in which the public money shall be deposited, with an absolute negative by the Secretary of the Treasury.

"3d. That the Secretary of the Treasury shall have power to discontinue the deposits in any bank or banks, or break up the whole arrangement, whenever he may think proper; he giving, in such case, the longest notice of his intention to do so which the public interest may admit of.

"4th. That the primary and secondary banks shall make returns of their entire condition, to the Secretary of the Treasury, monthly, and as much oftener as he may require, and report to the Treasurer weekly the state of his deposits; and that they will also submit themselves to a critical examination of their books and transactions by the Secretary of the Treasury, or an authorized agent, whenever the Secretary may require it.

"5th. That the arrangement of the government be only with the primary banks, which shall be responsible to it, not only for the safety of the entire deposits, wherever made, but for making payments at any places in the United States, without charge to the government, in gold and silver, or its equivalent, of any sum which may be required there to be paid by the Secretary of the Treasury; that they shall also pay any expenses that may attend the removal of the deposits, as also the compensation and expenses of any agent, temporary or permanent, whom the Secretary may appoint to examine into their affairs.

"6th. That they will render, or cause to be rendered, without charge, any service which can now be lawfully required of the Bank of the United States.

"7th. It would be inconvenient to employ all the State banks in good credit, at the places designated for the location of the primary banks; but it is, nevertheless, extremely desirable to secure their good will and friendly coöperation. The importance of that object is too obvious to require elucidation. It is supposed it might be accomplished by an arrangement between the primary banks and the other institutions in their immediate vicinity, by which, in consideration of an assumption by them of a share of the responsibilities assumed by the primary banks, an equitable share, all circumstances considered, of the benefits of the public deposits, would be secured to the institutions referred to. This might be done by allowing them, respectively, a credit at the selected banks equal to their share of the deposits, taking into view the amount of capital, the trouble of the primary banks, and all other circumstances entitled to consideration. If such an arrangement could be made it would increase the actual security of the government, consolidate the entire mass of the mercantile community of the principal cities in favor of the system, and place its success and permanency beyond contingency.

"If the negotiation is, in the first instance, opened with delegations from all the banks in the cities referred to, and them candidly informed of the desire of the government to award facilities and extend equal benefits to all, but that in case of failure to make such an arrangement it would have to select, at its own pleasure, the requisite number, there is reason to hope the arrangement would be brought about. Amos Kendall, Esq., would, in my opinion, be a proper person to be employed in the proposed negotiation. These views will be regarded by you as suggestions for your consideration only, and will, if adopted, without doubt be rendered more complete and effectual by such modifications and additions as may present themselves to your own mind."

Imagine the feelings of a prudent Philadelphian upon reading the details of a scheme so novel, complicated, wild, impossible as this. What bank, well established and self-respecting, could be expected to submit to such espionage, or to assume such responsibilities?

In the same package Mr. Duane received the opinions of the other members of the cabinet upon the measure proposed, and also a brief abstract of the President's own view of the bank question generally. The opinion of the President was given in four propositions: First, the present bank charter ought not to be renewed on any conditions whatever. Secondly, there should be no Bank of the United States out of the District of Columbia. Thirdly, the President of the United States, if a new national bank were chartered, should have the appointing of its president, and a certain number of its directors. Fourthly, no bank should be recommended until the proposed State bank system had been tried and found inadequate. We are tempted to infer from these propositions, what the opposition asserted in 1832 and 1833, that the real object of the politicians who influenced General Jackson was, not to rid the country of a monstrous monopoly, but to add to the sum, already prodigious and alarming, of governmental patronage.

Mr. Duane promptly replied to the President's communications. He told the President that he was opposed to the new fiscal scheme utterly. He thought it unjust to deprive the Bank of the United States of the deposits, because the bank paid the government a stipulated sum per annum for the use of the deposits. "Their continuance is part of the contract" between the bank and the government. Their removal, he thought, would be most disrespectful to Congress, inasmuch as the House had declared the deposits safe in the keeping of the bank, by a vote of one hundred and nine to forty, and this so recently as the last session. Nor did he think that State banks of the first standing would accept the deposits on the conditions proposed; and in no others would the public money be safe. *Could not the government dispense entirely with the assistance of banks?* Perhaps it could not. But he was of opinion that a matter so important as a radical change in the fiscal policy of the country was one which Congress alone had authority to regulate. Ere long Congress would be compelled, by the near expiration of the bank charter, to deliberate on the subject. To Congress it belonged; to Congress it should be left. Moreover, if the State bank system failed, and Mr. Duane believed it would fail, the Bank of the United States would come before the country with an argument so plausible and convincing that it would probably be able to secure a renewal of its charter. In the course of his remarks, Mr. Duane alluded with some feeling to the officious, and apparently authorized visit of Reuben M. Whitney—a man not esteemed by Philadelphians.

The Secretary enforced and illustrated his opinions at great length, and with much spirit and ability. His letter was the production of a gentleman and a man of honor, modest, respectful, affectionate even, but resolute. As the President had then returned from his Northern tour, the Secretary delivered his epistle in person, and received a reply a few hours after.

General Jackson pounced like a hawk upon the cardinal defect of Mr. Duane's eloquent paper. "You object to *my* plan," said the General, in substance, "but you propose none of your own! If this affair is to be settled by Congress, I, the President of the United States, will be expected to recommend a new fiscal system for its consideration. Now, what have you to suggest? Think over the subject, my dear sir, and let me see you soon at the White House."

"I waited on the President," continues Mr. Duane, "on the 15th of July. He commenced the conversation by saying that he had read my letter of the 10th of July (then lying on the table before him), and feared we did not understand each other.

"'My object, sir,' said he, 'is to save the country; and it will be lost if we permit the bank to exist. We must prepare a substitute, or our friends in Congress will not know what to do. I do justice to your motives, but some parts of your letter gave me uneasiness. One part only I will mention: that referring to Mr. Whitney. I am sorry you put that in, for he is not in my confidence. He is an abused man, sir, and has much information of which Mr. Polk and I have availed ourselves, but he can not be called my confidant. I was sorry to see his name introduced, and don't see that your argument needed it.'

"I replied that I had been accustomed to write freely and without disguise; that, in the present instance, I had barely stated facts: that I had been unused to official correspondence; that, I confessed, I had been mortified at the approaches of Mr. Whitney, and when I felt strongly I wrote so; that I meant no disrespect to the President, however, and as its omission would not affect the rest of my letter, I would at once strike out the passage relating to Mr. Whitney. Suiting the action to the word, I took up a pen and struck out two or three lines.

"'Now,' said the President, 'we are friends, and should be so. If we differ in opinion, what of it? It is but opinion, after all; and I like you the better for telling me frankly what you think.'

"He then alluded to passages in my letter which had a reference to Congress and the judiciary, and deprecated any reliance whatever upon either. He said it would be idle to resort to a court which had decided that the very bills which Congress had prohibited were legal; that there was but one course—to use the power possessed by the executive.

"I replied that we differed upon one point only. That he had asked me, upon my responsibility to Congress, to remove the deposits; and that I could not remove them without violating what I considered my duty; that on all other points I agreed with him, and was ready to go hand in hand to provide a substitute for the United States Bank.

"'Sir,' said he, 'I addressed you as Secretary of the Treasury, and told you to use my letter as your shield.'

"'You called on me, sir,' I replied, 'to exercise a power conferred on me by law; and you said you did not mean to interfere with the independent exercise of it. You called on me to do an act for which I might be impeached; and if I comply, your letter will be no protection, for, in effect, it tells me I may do as I please. The very circumstance that you disclaim the exercise of control over me, would forbid my holding your letter up as a shield.'

"The President here remarked that I did not understand that part of his letter to which I alluded, but, instead of explaining it, he said:

"'I am preparing a reply to your communication, and ask you to read it attentively. I am disposed to confide in you, and to be your friend, and if anybody tells you otherwise, don't believe him.'

"I said I felt myself worthy of his confidence; that I had come to speak of a substitute for the present fiscal agent; that if the United States Bank were to be soon closed, I did not apprehend evil as to the public funds or operations; that the funds of the government in the former United States Bank remained there until a few days before it expired; that nearly three years must elapse ere the doors of the present bank would be shut; that, in my letter, I had suggested a relinquishment of all bank agency, but that time for inquiry and reflection, as to the plan of a substitute, was indispensable; that I doubted whether a provision for fiscal operations could or ought to be made, without inquiry into the condition of the general currency; that a regulation of commerce, and a control over bank paper, seemed to be demanded; that legislators alone could duly investigate such important subjects; that I had no confidence in the competency of State banks for fiscal purposes; and that an extension of patronage to them would only increase evils already too great.

"The President said he had already declared against delay, and why there should be none; that there might be, as I supposed, abuses, but there were other and greater abuses; that to wait for inquiry would give a triumph to the bank; that State institutions were now our only resource; that he had himself asked Congress so to organize the treasury department as to dispense with banks, but that he had not been attended to, by Congress or the people."

The interview then terminated. The President replied to Mr. Duane's elaborate argument of July 10th in a letter not less elaborate, and Mr. Duane rejoined in a masterly paper on the 19th of the same month. Neither of these letters produced the slightest effect upon the individuals to whom they were addressed. Mr. Duane firmly maintained his ground, and the President (need I say it?) firmly held to his purpose. Other interviews followed.

"I waited upon the President," says the Secretary of the Treasury, "twice on the 19th and again on the 20th of July, and at those interviews the same course of argument was pursued. I desired to bring the President to a point, and that was not easily effected. At last he said:

"I want to press no man's conscience. My wish is to meet Congress with a declaration that we have a safe substitute for the United States Bank. How can we do this without inquiry? I desire Mr. Kendall to make that inquiry. I doubt whether the State banks will come into my plan of mutual guarantee, which I consider the only safe one; but we must try. For one, I shall be for positively removing the deposits, if the three per cents. shall not be given up by the bank in October. But the law gives you the power; the act must be yours. What, however, I want is *inquiry*, not to *make* arrangement. Information ought to be got even for Congress, and it is through you it should be collected. Now, do you understand me? Until we get information, and consider it, we shall remain uncommitted."

"I supposed that I now understood the President, and even began to flatter myself that I had gained a point. I understood him, that there was to be a fair inquiry such as the importance of the object demanded; that the information needful in such a case was to be collected; and that, until such information should be collected and considered, there was to be no commitment; that my own sense of duty was not to be interfered with; and that, if the United States Bank should deliver up the three per cents. in October, a removal of the deposits would not be pressed upon me. Under these impressions, and far from suspecting that the basis on which they rested had been insincerely laid, or would be faithlessly changed, I prepared a letter of instruction" (for the guidance of Mr. Kendall in his proposed tour of inquiry).

The letter of instructions directed INQUIRY ONLY. Mr. Kendall was to visit the principal cities, converse with bankers, and ascertain whether the President's plan could be carried out—whether respectable banks would accept the deposits on the terms proposed by the President in his letter to Mr. Duane of June 26th. The closing paragraph of Mr. Duane's letter of instructions was the following: "Having thus, sir, placed before you the views of the President, and such suggestions on my own part as seemed to be called for, it becomes my duty to myself, in order to guard against expectations, on the part of the banks, that may not be realized, or misapprehension elsewhere, distinctly to say that my performance of the present act of duty, as an executive agent, is not to be understood as an indication of any intention on my part, under existing circumstances, to exercise the power vested in me by law. Whether such an emergency may not arise as may warrant the exercise of that power, it is unnecessary now to anticipate; it is sufficient to observe, that, in my opinion, *none such exists at present.*"

To these words the President strongly objected. "Why send Mr. Kendall about the country to inquire, if no necessity for action exists?" he asked. "Previously to inquiry," wrote the President, "you declare that nothing has yet occurred to render necessary the movement anticipated by it, and thus leave me to infer that should the inquiry establish the competency of the State banks to perform the agency proposed to them, you will not feel yourself at liberty to carry into effect the decision transferring the public deposits to them, which, the President, on advisement with his cabinet, may make. Please inform me whether I am correct in supposing that this is your determination. If I am, it will then be my duty, in frankness and candor, to suggest the course which will be necessary on my part."

Mr. Duane says: "I considered this leter not only a violation of the assurance given in the President's letter from Boston, that he did not mean to interfere with the independent exercise of the discretion conferred on me by law, but a palpable infringement of the agreement, admitted in the above letter itself, that there was to be no present commitment. The construction put upon the concluding paragraph of the draft of instructions was forced and unwarranted. That paragraph simply stated, in writing, what the above letter itself shows had been agreed upon orally, that there was to be no present commitment. The question of the actual removal of the deposits had been reserved; and yet, the above letter demanded a commitment at once. These, and other manifestations of bad faith, gave me much uneasiness. My inclination, therefore, was to refuse to omit the paragraph objected to. It occurred to me, however, that but one change was proposed; that the instructions still required the agent to collect information; and that, if fairly collected, such information must disabuse the President himself."

So Mr. Duane consented to the omission of the obnoxious paragraph. He gave the President distinctly to understand, however, that he held himself entirely uncommitted as to the final decision of the question. "All that I can promise," he said, "consistently with the respect due to you as well as myself, is, that, when the moment for decision, after inquiry and discussion, shall arrive, *I will concur with you, or retire.*"

Surely, *now* Mr. Kendall will be able to start upon his important journey. Not yet. The President returned the draft of instructions to Mr. Duane accompanied by the civilest of civil notes. "Your last," said the President, "manifests a spirit, which, I trust, will enable us, before the time arrives for acting upon the report of the agent, to agree as nearly as may be desirable in the decision which may be made on the subject. I return you herewith the draft of the instructions, with some notes, suggesting a few changes, which you will doubtless see no impropriety in adopting, leaving out the last paragraph."

These "changes," Mr. Duane found, were neither "few" nor unimportant. The "the material parts" of his manuscript "were erased and changed." After much reflection, though strongly tempted to resign at once, he concluded to make the changes desired by the President. "The mission of an agent to make inquiry," he says, "I had no right to resist; nor could I dictate what should or should not be the nature of his inquiry. It was only as to the removal of the deposits, that I could exercise an independent discretion." The instructions were completed, therefore, and the agent took his departure. A month elapsed before his return, during which the perplexed secretary enjoyed comparative repose.

Late in the month of August, Mr. Kendall had completed his inquiries and his report. "His mission," Mr. Duane assures us, "was abortive in the particulars which had been deemed essential. The plan of bank agency, which the President had considered the only safe one, was, I believe, unanimously rejected. The answers of some of the banks willing to act, showed that they ought not to be trusted. Several of the most substantial institutions refused to act as fiscal agents, under any circumstances. The materials from which the condition of the banks was to be ascertained, had been very imperfectly furnished. Some of the banks answered, that the proposed plans were impracticable. Others pointed out the fallacy of the means suggested for the security of the public money. Others denied that State banks could give such facilities as government required. The banks, most ready to become depositories, showed the least ability to pay their own responsibilities in coin. Yet it was into this chaos that I was asked to plunge the fiscal concerns of the country, at a moment when they were conducted by the legitimate agent with the utmost simplicity, safety, and dispatch."

Col. Benton attributes the reluctance of the State banks to their terror of the Monster. "Instead of a competition among the banks," he says, "to obtain the deposits, there was holding off, and an absolute refusal on the part of many. Local banks were shy of receiving them—shy of receiving the greatest possible apparent benefit to themselves—shy of receiving the aliment upon which they lived and grew! and why this so great apparent contradiction? It was the fear of the Bank of the United States! and of that capacity to destroy them to which Mr. Biddle had testified in his answers to the Senate's Finance Committee; and which capacity was now known to be joined to the will; for the bank placed in the same category all who should be concerned in the removal —both the government that had ordered it, and the local banks which received what it lost. *But a competent number were found;* and this first attempt to prevent a removal by preventing a reception of the deposits elsewhere, entirely failed."

After receiving Mr. Kendall's report, the President called a Cabinet council, which convened on the 10th of September. The President, on this occasion, spoke at some length and with great energy:

"Gentlemen," he began, "I have got here (holding up a paper) the report of the agent on the deposit question, and I want to call your attention to it. The first question is, whether the State banks are safe places to put the public moneys in. The next is, whether, if they are, it is not our duty to put them there—whether we are not called upon, by the late disclosures of the corrupt conduct of the United States Bank, to cast off the connection at once. This is an important business. You know I have long had it in agitation, and what took place in Congress. I deemed it my duty to ask your opinions; and, although I mentioned to Mr. Duane that the subject was under consideration, I must, in justice to myself, as well as to him, say, I did not think it proper, before his appointment, to explain to him my views. But after doing so, I did think it due to our country that we should go on. The present is a most serious state of things. How shall we answer to God, our country, or ourselves, if we permit the public money to be thus used to corrupt the people? Observe, I do not want immediate action, but I desire a day to be fixed. Nor do I want to touch a dollar of the money that is in the bank; but I do want that the money coming in may be put where it will be safe, and not used for purposes of so infamous a kind. I want harmony in my Cabinet. I am well pleased with you all. I want to go unitedly in this solemn duty. The former conduct of the bank, in its corrupt loans, in its attempts to depreciate the credit of the country, in its whole corrupt state, justified our acting; but the last disclosures leave us no excuse for further delay. The country will reproach us if we do not go on. By the last resolution of the bank, the whole of its funds may be employed for corrupt purposes; and remember, that, for a part of the sum spent, no explanation or voucher is given; that it was by accident one of the directors, Mr. Wager,* noticed this monstrous abuse. And give me leave to tell you that this is a small part, could the truth be got at. I anxiously desire, then, that we should at least do something. This report, if you put confidence in it—and I think you may—shows the readiness of the State banks to take the public money, and their ability and safety as substitutes for the present agent. Why, then, should we hesitate? Why not proceed, I say, as the country expects us to do? Here are the papers. When you have read them let us come to an understanding."

As soon as the President had concluded, Mr. Duane thanked him for explaining to the cabinet the circumstances of his appointment. The President handed to Mr. McLane the report and papers of Mr. Kendall, and the council was at an end.

* Mr. Peter Wager was one of the five government directors of the bank, nominated by the President of the United States. They kept General Jackson well supplied with information respecting the proceedings of the board of directors, and were called, therefore, by the friends of the bank, *spies.* The "last disclosures," referred to by the President, may be gathered from the following passage of a Report which had recently been furnished the President by four of the government directors: "On the 30th November, 1830, it is stated on the minutes, that 'the president submitted to the board a copy of an article on banks and currency, just published in the *American Quarterly Review*, of this city, containing a favorable notice of this institution, and suggested the expediency of making the views of the author more extensively known to the public than they can be by means of the subscription list.' Whereupon, it was, on motion, '*Resolved*, That the president be authorized to take such measures, in regard to the circulation of the contents of the said article, either in whole or in part, as he may deem most for the interests of the bank.' "

A week passed before the cabinet again convened ; during which the *Globe* and other administration papers began to assail the character and motives of Mr. Duane, as if to prepare the public mind for his dismissal. The Secretary called the attention of the President to these simultaneous attacks. "It is impossible," says Mr. Duane, "to describe the earnestness of the President's professions in reply. He declared that no one had attempted to shake his confidence ; that it remained as it ever had been ; that he regretted even a difference in opinion between us ; and that he would put all doubts at rest by conferring on me the highest appointment then at his disposal. This he mentioned twice in the course of our conversation, saying he had meditated a change from one honorable station to another, not only as an act proper in itself, but in order to do what would be satisfactory to myself and friends."

On the seventeenth of September the cabinet again assembled. "The President opened the proceedings," Mr. Duane tells us, "by saying that he trusted advantage had been taken of the time which had passed since the preceding meeting, maturely to consider what he had then said. Then, addressing himself to the Secretary of State, he asked his opinion as to the propriety of a speedy change of the place of public deposit. Mr. McLane at once proceeded to state his objections, in detail, in an emphatic and lucid manner. When the Secretary of State had closed, the President put the same question to me ; and I simply answered, that I desired to have the whole subject presented in the clearest light before Congress—that I had full confidence in their desire as well as ability to correct abuses, and avert the mischiefs referred to by the President—that I deprecated the proposed connection with State banks—and apprehended serious evils to the public in case the contemplated change should be made. The Secretary at War (Governor Cass), when appealed to, said, "You know, sir, I have always thought that the matter rests entirely with the Secretary of the Treasury." The Secretary of the Navy (Governor Woodbury) entered into an explanation of the opinion which he had given in April against a removal of the deposits prior to the summer of 1834. Although he had then considered an earlier change injudicious, he must now go with the President. The Attorney-General (Mr. Taney) barely said, that he had been from the beginning for an immediate change, and was now more than ever for it. The President then said, 'Gentlemen, I desire to meet you to-morrow, and will then make known my own views.'"

The cabinet met on the morrow. It was at this meeting that the President caused to be read the paper known to history as "the Paper read to the Cabinet on the eighteenth of September." In this document the President recapitulated the history of the war upon the bank, recounted the charges against it, repeated at great length the reasons for the removal of the deposits, and concluded by announcing that the removal was resolved upon, and that he, the President, assumed the entire responsibility of the act. The closing paragraph contained the whole paper: "The President again repeats, that he begs his cabinet to consider the proposed measure as his own, in the support of which he shall require no one of them to make a sacrifice of opinion or principle. Its responsibility has been assumed, after the most mature deliberation and reflection, as necessary to preserve the morals of the people, the freedom of the press, and the purity of the elective franchise, without which, all will unite in saying, that the blood and treasure expended by our forefathers in the establishment of our happy system of government, will have been vain and fruitless. Under these convictions, he feels that a measure so important to the American people can not be commenced too soon, and he therefore names the first day of October next as a period proper for the change of the deposits, or sooner, provided the necessary arrangements with the State banks can be made."

When this paper had been read, the members of the cabinet offered neither remonstrance nor remark, but began in silence to prepare for their departure. "As those present were retiring," continues the Secretary of the Treasury, "I approached the President, and asked him to allow me to take and read his exposition. He directed his secretary to deliver it to me. I then asked the President, whether I was to understand him as directing me to remove the deposits? He replied, that it was his desire that I should remove them, but upon *his* responsibility; adding with great emphasis, that, 'If I would stand by him it would be the happiest day of his life.'"

All the rest of that day the secretary sat brooding over the posture of affairs, questioning within himself whether it were right even to keep his promise of resigning his place in case he could not agree with the President. His resignation, he well knew, would not retard for a day the consummation of the President's unalterable purpose. Ought not the President to assume the additional responsibility of removing him?

Early the next morning, the President sent to inquire whether he had made up his mind. He answered that he would make known his decision on the day after the morrow. An hour or two later, Major Donelson called, and informed Mr. Duane that the President had determined to announce in the *Globe of the next day*, that the government would cease to deposit the public money in the Bank of the United States on the 1st of October. Astounded at this intelligence, Mr. Duane instantly wrote and dispatched to the President a remonstrance against the publication. The *Globe* of the next morning, however, contained the announcement.

Upon reading the paragraph in the *Globe*, Mr. Duane repaired to the White House, carrying in his pocket a letter, retracting his promise to resign, and positively refusing to order the change in the fiscal system announced in the official newspaper. The conversation which he had with the President on this occasion, Mr. Duane thus records:

Secretary. "I have, at length, waited upon you, sir, with this letter."
President. "What is it?"

Secretary. "It respectfully and finally makes known my decision, not to remove the deposits, or resign."

President. "Then you do not mean that we shall part as friends."

Secretary. "The reverse, sir, is my desire; but I must protect myself."

President. "But you said you would retire, if we could not finally agree."

Secretary. "I indiscreetly said so, sir; but I am now compelled to take this course."

President. "I have been under an impression that you would resign, even as an act of friendship to me."

Secretary. "Personal wishes, sir, must give way. The true question is, which must I observe, my promise to execute my duty faithfully, or my agreement to retire, when the latter conflicts with the former?"

President. "I certainly never expected that any such difficulties could arise between us; and think you ought still to consider the matter."

Secretary. "I have painfully considered it; and hope you will not ask me to make a sacrifice. All that you need is a successor, and him you may have at once."

President. "But I do not wish to dismiss you. I have too much regard for yourself, your family, and friends, to take that course."

Secretary. "Excuse me, sir, you may only do now what you said in your letter of the 22d of July, it would be your duty to do, if I then said I would not thereafter remove the deposits."

President. "It would be at any time disagreeable to do what might be injurious to you."

Secretary. "A resignation, I think, would be more injurious. And permit me to say, that the publication in yesterday's *Globe* removes all delicacy. A worm if trodden upon will turn. I am assailed in all the leading papers of the administration, and if my friend, you will not tie up my hands."

President. "Then, I suppose you mean to come out against me."

Secretary. "Nothing is further from my thoughts. I barely desire to do what is now my duty; and to defend myself if assailed hereafter."

[Here the President expatiated on the late disclosures in relation to the bank, the corruptibility of Congress, etc., and at length, taking a paper from his drawer, said:]

President. "You have been all along mistaken in your views. Here is a paper that will show you your obligations; that the executive must protect you."

Secretary. "I will read it, sir, if such is your wish; but I can not anticipate a change of opinion."

President. "A secretary, sir, is merely an executive agent, a subordinate, and you may say so in self-defense."

Secretary. "In this particular case, Congress confers a discretionary power, and requires reasons if I exercise it. Surely this contemplates responsibility on my part."

President. "This paper will show you that your doubts are wholly groundless."

Secretary. "As to the deposits, allow me, sir, to say my decision is positive. The only question is as to the mode of my retirement."

President. "My dear Mr. Duane, we must separate as friends. Far from desiring that you should sustain any injury, you know I have intended to give you the highest appointment now in my gift. You shall have the mission to Russia. I would have settled this matter before, but for the delay or difficulty" (as I understood the President) "in relation to Mr. Buchanan."

Secretary. "I am sincerely thankful to you, sir, for your kind disposition, but I beg you to serve me in a way that will be truly pleasing. I desire no new station, and barely wish to leave my present one blameless, or free from apprehension as to the future. Favor me with a written declaration of your desire that I should leave office, as I can not carry out your views as to the deposits, and I will take back this letter" (the one I had just presented).

President. "Never have I had any thing that has given me more mortification than this whole business. I had not the smallest notion that we could differ."

Secretary. "My principles and opinions, sir, are unchanged. We differ only about time. You are for acting now; I am for waiting for Congress."

President. "How often have I told you that Congress can not act until the deposits are removed."

Secretary. "I am unable, sir, to change my opinion at will upon that point."

President. "You are altogether wrong in your opinion, and I thought Mr. Taney would have convinced you that you are."

Secretary. "Mr. Taney, sir, endeavored to prevail on me to adopt his views, but failed. As to the deposits, I barely desired a delay of about ten weeks."

President. "Not a day—not an hour; recent disclosures banish all doubt, and I do not see how you can hesitate."

Secretary. "I have often stated my reasons. Surely, sir, it is enough that were I to act, I could not give reasons satisfactory to myself."

President. "My reasons, lately read in the cabinet, will release you from complaint."

Secretary. "I am sorry I can not view the subject in the same light."

Our conversation was further extended, under varying emotions on both sides, but without any change of opinion or decision. At length I retired, leaving the letter.

During the next three days various letters passed between the President and the Secretary, without producing upon either the effect desired. At length, on the twenty-third of September, the President sent a note to Mr. Duane, which concluded with the well-known words: "I feel myself constrained to notify you that your further services as Secretary of the Treasury are no longer required."

On the self-same day, Mr. Roger B. Taney, the Attorney-General, was appointed Secretary of the Treasury. Three days after, he signed the order which directed collectors and other government employés to deposit the public money in the State banks designated in the order. The deed was done.

The vacant attorney-generalship was filled by the appointment of Mr. Benjamin F. Butler, of New York, the townsman, law student, law partner, political pupil, friend and admirer of Mr. Van Buren. The paper read to the cabinet on the eighteenth of September was, soon after, published in the *Globe*, and copied thence into all the leading papers friendly to the administration.

The conduct of Mr. Duane, when the attacks of the administration press had compelled him to make known that conduct, called forth from all parts of the country expressions of approval as warm as they were just. He deserves to be held in lasting remembrance as one of that host of worthies of every age and country who have preserved their honor untarnished amid temptations that appealed with equal power to the weaknesses and to the virtues of human nature. Those are the temptations which men of honor find it hardest to resist. Such as are addressed to their meaner passions, to their ambition, their love of ease, wealth, and credit they can easily resist; but when to these are added the passionate solicitations of a friend and benefactor, the entreaties of honored associates and allies, the deliberate arguments of able and trusted chiefs in the law, the claims of a large circle who share the public honors of their relative, and do not always sympathize with the high feeling which seems to lower both him and them in the social scale—then a man must be made of sterling metal, indeed, who holds fast to his integrity. Mr. Duane had every motive, worthy and unworthy, which a public man can ever have to yield to the President's desires. In not yielding, he displayed a genuine, moral heroism.

The organ of the administration at Washington, in commenting upon Mr. Duane's dismissal, used the following language: "Mr. Duane was dismissed for faithlessness to his solemn written pledges, and for the exhibition of bad feeling, which made him totally unfit for the station to which he had been elevated. He was *not* dismissed merely for refusing to remove the deposits."*

XXIV.

THE BANK CURTAILS.

PUGILISTS begin a fight for the championship by shaking hands; but there comes a moment, in the course of the contest, when the man who is going to lose the battle loses his temper. The bank, so courteous and dignified in 1829, lost its temper for a moment, when the "Paper read to the Cabinet on the Eighteenth of September"—a paper replete with accusations against its honor—announced to all the world the removal of the government deposits. The Report published by the directors, in reply to the President's fulmination, spoke of it as "a paper signed Andrew Jackson, purporting

* Globe, November 19, 1833.

to have been read to a Cabinet." The Report proceeded, however, with moderation and dignity to reply to each of the President's charges of misconduct; and, so far as one unversed in the mysteries of finance can judge, it refuted those charges, and proved that the bank had been managed honestly, prudently, and successfully.

That it was an error of judgment on the part of the bank to spend fourteen thousand dollars a year in "self-defense," is shown by the utter failure of that expenditure to conciliate the popular mind. Whether the bank was justified in making the expenditure was a question for the stockholders to determine. The United States was a stockholder, and had a right to object. But who will tell us how much money from the treasury of the United States was employed in enabling the administration to obey the law, before laid down in these pages, that every thing in the universe, having in it the principle of life, will do all it can to perpetuate its life? Mr. Kendall, an employé of the government, was a paid writer for the *Globe* during a great part of its existence as the organ of General Jackson's administration. His salary as special contributor was eight hundred dollars a year. This was fair enough I suppose, as Messrs. Blair and Rives paid the salary. Yet I venture to estimate that the public money transmuted into public opinion during the bank war amounted to a greater sum than the bank expended for a similar purpose during its entire career of twenty years.

In the new posture of affairs the bank was obliged to do more than defend itself against paper bullets. A voice from the bank parlor informs me that, upon learning the intention of the government to remove the deposits, Mr. Biddle and the directors were undecided for some time which of two courses to adopt. To curtail, or not to curtail—that was the question. A friend of Mr. Biddle, a gentleman of note in the financial world, advised him not to curtail; but to give the country a striking proof of the strength of the bank by rather enlarging its loans than lessening them. This plan, he urged, would also render the sudden cessation of the bank in 1836 so paralyzing to the business of the country that the people would rise as one man, in the *presidential election* of that year, and hurl from power the party that would be supposed to have arrested the national progress. Mr. Biddle was convinced by this reasoning. A circular letter to the cashiers of the twenty-five branches, ordering them to continue to their customers the usual accommodation, and even, in some cases, to increase their loans, was drawn up by Mr. Biddle. The gentleman before referred to (to whom the reader is indebted for this information) prepared the requisite twenty-five copies of this letter, folded them, superscribed them, and placed them in Mr. Biddle's hands, ready for the mail.

The packet of circulars, however, was not sent to the post-office that evening. Perhaps it occurred to the president of the bank that the policy proposed would effect in 1836 a prostration of business so complete that the capital of the bank would be swallowed up in the general ruin. Whatever the reason may have been, the circulars were put into the fire instead of the mail, and a policy more prudent and obvious was adopted. The amount of public money in the bank on the first of October, 1833, was $9,891,000. The directors resolved simply to curtail the loans of the bank to the extent of the average amount of public money held by it. This was done. It was done gradually. It was done no faster than the balance of public money diminished. The bank itself tells us, in one of its publications, exactly what it did:

"On the eighth of October, 1833, the bank directed 'that the committee on the offices be authorized to direct such gradual reduction in the amount and the time of the loans, at the respective offices, as may, in their judgment, be made, without inconvenience to the customers of the bank, or the community.' This authority has been executed in such a way as to accomplish its object with the least pressure upon the community; and the bank sum up their operations in the following manner:

1st. That the bank never directed any curtailment of its loans until the actual removal of the deposits.

2d. That the only actual reduction of loans took place from the 1st of October to the 1st of December, when the loans were diminished $5,641,098 26

While at the same time the public and private deposits were reduced 5,887,864 63

3d. That from the 1st of December, 1833, to the 1st of April, 1834, the loans have not been reduced, but, on the contrary, have actually been increasing, and were greater on the 1st of April, 1834, than on the 1st of October, 1833, by 353,712 95

While, during that same period, the public deposits had decreased no less than 2,239,393 89

4th. That the total reduction of loans from the 1st of October to the 1st of April was 5,057,527 22

While the public deposits had been reduced . $6,935,568 84
Private deposits, ... 842,834 57
Making an aggregate of . . . . . ——— 7,778,403 41

Being a reduction of loans less, by nearly three millions, than the reduction of deposits.

5th. That so far from cramping the trade of the country, it has actually purchased, from the 1st of October to the 1st of April, of domestic and foreign bills of exchange, . . . 34,671,324 00

6th. That the State banks were permitted to be indebted to the bank an average amount of 3,464,956 00

This curtailment compelled a similar one on the part of many of the State banks, while the "pet banks," the new depositaries of the public money, had not yet begun to reap the advantages of their position. Hence it was that during the first six months of the operation of the new system, there was a pressure in the money market—sharp, sudden, and severe—which caused many disastrous failures, general consternation, considerable distress, and tremendous outcry. Col. Benton, in many a paragraph of rolling thunder, attributes the whole of this distress and alarm to the criminal contrivance of the monster bank. But he attributes the crash of 1837 to the same cause! He dwells long upon the fact that, as late as fifteen months after the deposits ceased to be made in the bank of the United States, there were still in its vaults three or four millions of the public money. He does not tell us that the contraction of the bank's loans ceased long before that time; nor that the bank could not safely use money subject to instantaneous call ; nor that the public money was left in the bank for purposes which could be more easily imagined than safely avowed. Can any bank lose an eighth of its available capital without curtailing its business, or running imprudent risks ?

Congress met on the second of December, when the commercial pressure was becoming severe. In his message the President again congratulated the country on the prosperous state of the public finances. Thirty-two millions had been received into the treasury. The expenditures would not exceed twenty-five millions. The public debt had been reduced to an inconsiderable sum, which would soon be discharged ; a fact which the President stated with exultation. The late removal of the deposits was again avowed to be the President's own measure, one which he had " urged upon the department" of the treasury for some months before the deed was done. So certain was it, said the President, that the bank was a corrupt and corrupting political engine, so sure was he that the present commercial panic was needlessly caused by it for the purpose of compelling a restoration of the deposits, that " in my own sphere of duty, I should feel myself called on, by the facts disclosed, to order a *scire facias* against the bank, with a view to put an end to the chartered rights it has so palpably violated, were it not that the charter itself will expire as soon as a decision would probably be obtained from the court of last resort."

The message concluded with a fifth repetition of the recommendation for the abolishment of " every intermediate agency" in the election of President and Vice-President, and that " their eligibility should be limited to one term of either four or six years." The persistent man !

XXV.

THE PANIC SESSION OF CONGRESS.

THE twenty-third Congress, from the extraordinary number of its members who have filled important stations, has been styled the Star Congress. In the Senate were Webster, Clay, Calhoun, Benton, Wright, Frelinghuysen, Southard, Clayton, Rives, Tyler, Mangum, Preston, Forsyth, Grundy, White, and Poindexter—a galaxy of stars. In the House were Franklin Pierce, Choate, John Quincy Adams, John Davis, Cambreleng, Fillmore, Horace Binney, Stephenson, Henry A. Wise, McDuffie, Richard M. Johnson, John Bell, Cave Johnson, Polk, David Crockett, Corwin, Vinton, Ewing, and C. C. Clay—all well known names. Of the members of this Congress, five have been President; five, Vice-President; eight, Secretary of State; twenty-five, Governor of a State. In the House, on a test question, the administration could rely on a majority. In the Senate, the Opposition could command a majority which was small, but safe and sufficient.

From the first week in December, 1833, to the last day of June, 1834, the ruling—almost the only—topic of debate in Congress, in the newspapers, among the people, was the removal of the deposits. With one exception, no subject has ever been discussed in the United States with so much ability, bitterness, and pertinacity. Indeed, it was the great topic from 1833 to 1842. It lived through the panic of 1834, the inflation of 1835, the madness of 1836, the crash of 1837, the depression of 1838 to 1842, and only received its final quietus in 1844. The result of the discussion was the sub-treasury—a result which might as well have been reached in 1834 as in 1838, if General Jackson had been less precipitate and his advisers more acute. Prodigious as the price was which the country had to pay for the total and final separation of the government from banks, the result was one which the country now feels was worth its price.

During the whole of this eventful session of Congress, a kind of duello was going on between the President and the bank party. Blow seemed to be given for blow, and both parties were excited and angry beyond previous example. When all was over, so many hostile and mortifying acts had been done on both sides, that it was uncertain which of the two had had the worst of the contest. To the excitement within the walls of the capitol was added a clamor without, which increased in loudness and intensity as the debates proceeded. We are now briefly to review the events of this session.

Thrice in the very first week the President provoked the ire of the opposition. First, in his annual message, which contained offensive passages against the bank. Secondly, in the report of the Secretary of the Treasury, which re-stated those reasons for the removal the deposits with which we are already familiar. Thirdly, by vetoing Mr. Clay's Land Bill, providing for a distribution among the States of the proceeds of the sales of the public lands.

The Land Bill Mr. Clay regarded as one of the conditions of the late compromise. He considered that the administration was bound in honor to accept it as such, and that its rejection amounted to a breach of faith. General Jackson, however, was utterly opposed to the principle of the bill, had repeatedly avowed his opposition to it, and was resolved, from the day of its introduction, to veto it if it passed. The bill was handed to him for his signature when the last Congress was within twenty-four hours of expiring. Instead of vetoing the measure at the time, he chose to "pocket" it, and the bill was returned to Congress on one of the first days of the present session, to the extreme mortification of Mr. Clay and his friends. The veto message was assailed with peculiar violence, but it was never answered, and is unanswerable. A main objection of the President was, that the bill created new obstacles to the reduction of the price of the public lands. By the operation of the bill, every State would have an immediate interest in keeping up the price, whereas it was the dictate of true policy to give the utmost possible encouragement to the actual settler, whose labor alone gave value to the land. "I do not doubt," said the President, "that it is the real interest of each and all the States in the Union, and particularly of the new States, that the price of these lands shall be reduced and graduated; and that, after they have been offered for a certain number of years, the refuse, remaining unsold, shall be abandoned to the States, and the machinery of our land system entirely withdrawn."

Mr. Clay, not content, as it were, with these three blows, afforded the President an opportunity to give him a fourth, by introducing the following resolution:

"*Resolved*, That the President of the United States be requested to inform the Senate whether a paper purporting to have been read by him to the heads of the several departments, relating to the deposits of the public money in the treasury of the United States, and alleged to have been published by his authority, be genuine or not; and if it be genuine, that he be also requested to cause a copy of the said paper to be laid before the Senate."

The reader will note the use of the word "treasury" in this resolution. It was Mr. Clay's position, in the subsequent debates, that the bank of the United States was the treasury of the United States. The resolution was agreed to by a vote of twenty-three to eighteen. The President, *of course*, refused compliance with both requests. "I have yet to learn," he wrote, "under what constitutional authority that branch of the legislature has a right to require of me an account of any communication, either verbally or in writing, made to the heads of departments acting as a Cabinet council."

A few days after, Mr. Horace Binney, of Philadelphia, presented to the House of Representatives a memorial from the president and directors of the Bank of the United States. This document, in language respectful and dignified, stated that the custody of the public moneys was a part of the original contract between the bank and the government. The bank paid for the privilege in money and service. Recently, the bank had been deprived of this advantage by an order from the Secretary of the Treasury. The bank had in all respects faithfully and punctually performed its part of the contract. "The board of directors, therefore, deem it their duty forthwith to apprise you of this violation of the chartered rights of the stockholders, and to ask such redress therefor as to your sense of justice may seem proper." The memorial had no results. A resolution ordering the restoration of the deposits to the bank was introduced later in the session, but was lost by the regular party vote. For the first time in many years, there was an anti-bank majority in the House of Representatives, and no considerations of justice or policy can break the spell of party discipline at such times as these.

Early in the session the President sent to the Senate the names of five gentlemen for confirmation as government directors of the Bank of the United States. Of these five, four had rendered themselves obnoxious to the bank and to the bank party by giving the President information of the proceedings of the board of directors, and copies of certain portions of its minutes. Their names were, H. D. Gilpin, John T. Sullivan, Peter Wager, and Hugh M'Eldery. Upon receiving these unwelcome names the Senate acted upon them with an alacrity and promptitude which they were not accustomed to exhibit in deciding upon General Jackson's nominations. Not satisfied with the results of their experiment in rejecting Isaac Hill and Mr. Van Buren, they rejected these names also, after voting down a proposition to inquire into their fitness. The President sent their names a second time to the Senate, accompanied with a message vindicating their conduct, and eulogizing their characters, and remonstrating against the course of the Senate. The nominations were then referred to the Committee on Finance, who reported against them, and the Senate again rejected the odious names. Later in the session the President nominated other gentlemen, who were confirmed. This was worse than a fruitless victory to the friends of the bank, for the impression was created in the minds of the people that the bank was afraid to subject its proceedings to the relentless scrutiny of honest opponents.

On the 26th of December, two weeks after the refusal of the President to give the Senate a copy of his cabinet paper, Mr. Clay introduced his famous resolutions directly censuring the President for dismissing Mr. Duane and removing the deposits:

"*Resolved,* That by dismissing the late Secretary of the Treasury, because he would not, contrary to his sense of his own duty, remove the money of the United States in deposit with the Bank of the United States and its branches, in conformity with the President's opinion, and by appointing his successor to effect such removal, which has been done, the President has assumed the exercise of a power over the treasury of the United States not granted to him by the constitution and laws, and dangerous to the liberties of the people.

"*Resolved,* That the reasons assigned by the Secretary of the Treasury for the removal of the money of the United States, deposited in the Bank of the United States and its branches, communicated to Congress on the third of December, 1833, are unsatisfactory and insufficient."

These resolutions, we may as well state at once, were eventually reduced to one, which read as follows:

"*Resolved,* That the President, in the late executive proceedings, in relation to the public revenue, has assumed upon himself authority and power not conferred by the constitution and laws, but in derogation of both."

The speech delivered by Mr. Clay, in support of his resolutions, was exasperating to General Jackson in the highest degree. He accused the President of an "open, palpable, and daring usurpation." After having assumed all the other powers of the government, executive, legislative, and judicial, he had ended by seizing the public purse, as Cæsar had seized the treasury of Rome. "For more than fifteen years," said Mr. Clay, "I have been struggling to avoid the present state of things. I thought I perceived, in some proceedings, during the conduct of the Seminole war, a spirit of defiance to the constitution and to all law. With what sincerity and truth —with what earnestness and devotion to civil liberty—I have struggled, the Searcher of all human hearts best knows. With what fortune, the bleeding constitution of my country now fatally attests."

It was after reading this speech that General Jackson exclaimed: "Oh, if I live to get these robes of office off me, I will bring the rascal to a dear account."

Mr. Calhoun, if possible, surpassed Mr. Clay in the vehemence of his denunciations. He said that the plundering of the Roman treasury by Julius Cæsar was a virtuous action, compared with the recent conduct of Andrew Jackson. "*That,*" said Mr. Calhoun, "was a case of an intrepid and bold warrior, as an open plunderer, seizing forcibly the treasury of the country, which, in that republic, as well as ours, was confined to the custody of the legislative department of the government. The actors in our case are of a different character—artful, cunning, and corrupt politicians, and not fearless warriors. They have entered the treasury, not sword in hand, as public plunderers, but, with the false keys of sophistry, as pilferers, under the silence of midnight. The motive and the object are the same, varied in like manner by circumstances and character. 'With money I will get men, and with men money,' was the maxim of the Roman plunderer. With money we will get partisans, with partisans votes, and with votes money, is the maxim of our public pilferers."

Mr. Webster opposed the removal of the deposits, and supported Mr. Clay's resolution, in terms less offensive to the President than these, but not less decided and forcible. After a debate of three months' continuance, seldom interrupted, Mr. Clay's resolution of censure was passed in the Senate by a vote of twenty-six to twenty. Another barren victory. Three weeks later, the President sent to the Senate an elaborate Protest against the resolution, and asked that it be entered upon the journal. Another month was consumed in debating the question whether or not the Senate should comply with the President's request. At length, by a vote of twenty-seven to sixteen, the protest was disposed of by the passage of four resolutions, of which the last two contain the substance:

"*Resolved,* That the aforesaid protest is a breach of the privileges of the Senate, and that it be not entered on the journal.

"*Resolved,* That the President of the United States has no right to send a protest to the Senate against any of its proceedings."

Thus nearly five months of the session were chiefly consumed in an affair which neither had any results nor could be rationally expected to have any. Even the resolution of censure, impotent and harmless as it was, was not suffered to repose in peace upon the record. It had been scarcely entered upon the journal before Colonel Benton gave notice of a resolution to expunge it; and from that hour, a leading object of his senatorial labors was to procure the passage of his expunging resolution.

The President, meanwhile, was employing his powers and his time far more effectively. The reader may remember, that as long ago as the year 1829, when the war upon the bank began, an attempt was made to deprive the branch of the Bank of the United States at Portsmouth of the pension agency. The bank refused to give up the books, and Mr. Eaton, the Secretary of War, withdrew his demand, and gave up the project. A similar attempt to remove the pension agency from the branch at Albany met with a similar failure. Since that time, the pensions, amounting to about four millions a year, had been paid by the bank and its branches without interference from the government. In January, 1834, a few days after the introduction of Mr. Clay's resolutions of censure, the President attempted to take the whole of this business from the bank. He announced the appointment of fifteen State banks as pension agents, and formally demanded from the Bank of the United States the surrender of the books and papers relating to pensions, and half a million of dollars remaining in its vaults designed for the next payments. The bank, acting under the best legal advice attainable in the country, refused to surrender either the books or the money.

On the 4th of February, the President, in a special message, communicated this refusal to Congress, accusing the bank of attempting to defeat the measures of the administration, and of assuming functions belonging only to the government. The subject had been referred to the Attorney-General, who had discovered in a supplementary pension act of 1832, a clause which gave the Secretary of War the power to appoint the time and place for the payment of certain pensions. The sum allowed by the act was "to be paid to the officer at such places and days as the secretary may direct." The inference drawn by the Attorney-General from these words is one of the most curious on record. "As the power," said he, "to appoint the *place* of payment is unlimited, the secretary may appoint a place at which there is no bank or other pension agent; in which case the *power to appoint an agent* to pay must, necessarily, exist, or the acknowledged power to appoint a *place* of payment be defeated. In this class of cases, the power to appoint a place of payment, is thus seen to include, as incidental to it, the power of appointing an agent to pay. And if that power be possessed, in any one case, it would seem to be possessed in every other; unless, indeed, it can be held, that the same word, in this law, means one thing in reference to one place, and a totally different thing in reference to another—a construction too refined to be readily adopted."

If this be not a "refined" construction of laws clearly designating the Bank of the United States as the agent for the disbursement of pensions, I know not where an example of refined construction can be found. It was remarked at the time by a friend of the administration, that Mr. Butler had not studied law at Kinderhook for nothing.

The Senate rejected Mr. Butler's reasonings. Three months later in the session, that body passed resolutions to the following effect: 1. That the Department of War is not warranted in appointing pension agents in any State or Territory where the Bank of the United States or one of its branches has been established, except when specially authorized by act of Congress. 2. That no power is conferred *by any law* upon the department, or Secretary of War, to remove the agency for the payment of pensions, and the funds, books, and papers, connected with that agency, from the Bank of the United States, and to appoint other agents to supersede the bank in the payment of such pensions." In this interpretation, a minority of the House Committee of Ways and Means concurred. The President held to his purpose, however, and carried his point, and was sustained in it by the people.

M. Chevelier, who witnessed this singular contest, mentions that the enemies of the bank "express the greatest sympathy for the illustrious relics of the revolution, whom the arrogance of the bank, as they say, is about to plunge, at the close of their career, into the most dreadful misery; they pour forth the most pathetic lamentations over those glorious defenders of the country, whom a *money-corporation* is about to strip of the provision made for their declining years by the nation's gratitude. You may imagine all the noisy arguments and patriotic harangues, that can be delivered on this text. On the 4th of February, the President sent a message to Congress in the same strain. All this is mere declamation, of the most common-place and the most hypocritical kind; for who will prevent the deliverers of America from duly receiving their pensions, except those who shall refuse them drafts on the bank, which the bank would pay at once? But a people under fascination is not influenced by reason, and it is at this moment believed by the multitude that the bank has determined to kill the noble veterans of Independence by hunger. Once more, then, anathemas against monopoly, hatred to the moneyed aristocracy! HURRA FOR JACKSON! JACKSON FOR EVER!"

As the session wore on, the pressure in the money market increased, the failures became more numerous, the panic more intense, the clamor more vociferous. The tables of Congress were loaded with petitions for and against the restoration of the deposits. A part of the morning hour for three months was absorbed in receiving these petitions. One of the New York members of the House had the curiosity to save a copy of each of the petitions presented on this subject, and had the whole of them bound into one stupendous volume of nearly two thousand pages. I had prepared, at considerable labor, a catalogue of the contents of this monotonous collection, but even this would occupy more of these pages than can be spared for the purpose. There were in all two hundred and twenty-three petitions, of which fifty-two approved the removal of the deposits, and one hundred and seventy-one asked their restoration to the Bank of the United States. The great cities sent petitions in curious variety. Philadelphia, for example, furnished the following: One from the citizens generally, to which ten thousand names were appended; one from each of the municipal divisions of Philadelphia; one from each of the banks; one from each of the trades; one from "six hundred strangers" in Philadelphia; one from the young men, and one from the women of Philadelphia; one from five thousand Philadelphia democrats; one from the city council; one from the German working men of Philadelphia; one from the Philadelphia Board of Trade; one from the Philadelphia Chamber of Commerce; and one from the Philadelphia Alms-House. New York, Boston, Baltimore, and New Orleans were only less zealous than Philadelphia in forwarding petitions. The great petition from Boston was signed by ten thousand persons; the principal one from New York by six thousand; the most important one from Baltimore by three thousand. The smallest towns contributed their mite to swell the mountain of petitions, and, indeed, the whole country appeared to abandon itself to the work.

The opposition leaders in Congress did not fail to make the most of the prevailing excitement. "The city is full of distress petitioners," wrote Mr. Clay in one of his private letters; "*the more the better!*" In seconding a motion to print one of the great petitions, Mr. Clay enacted, one morning, a remarkable scene in the Senate chamber. He suddenly ceased to address Mr. Van Buren as the president of the Senate, and broke into an apostrophe to Mr. Van Buren as the friend of Andrew Jackson:

"'To you, sir,' exclaimed the orator, addressing the Vice-President, 'to you, then, sir, in no unfriendly spirit, but with feelings softened and subdued by the deep distress which pervades every class of our countrymen, I make the appeal. By your official and personal relations with the President you maintain with him an intercourse which I neither enjoy nor covet. Go to him and tell him, without exaggeration, but in the language of truth and sincerity, the actual condition of his bleeding country. Tell him it is nearly ruined and undone by the measures which he has been induced to put in operation. Tell him that his experiment is operating on the nation like the philosopher's experiment upon a convulsed animal in an exhausted receiver, and that it must expire in agony if he does not pause, give it free and sound circulation, and suffer the energies of the people to be revived and restored. Tell him that in a single city more than sixty bankruptcies, involving a loss of upwards of fifteen millions of dollars, have occurred. Tell him of the alarming decline in the value of all property, of the depreciation of all the products of industry, of the stagnation in every branch of business, and of the close of numerous manufacturing establishments, which, a few short months ago, were in active and flourishing operation. Depict to him, if you can find language to portray, the heart-rending wretchedness of thousands of the working classes cast out of employment. Tell him of the tears of helpless widows, no longer able to earn their bread, and of unclad and unfed orphans who have been driven by his policy out of the busy pursuits in which but yesterday they were gaining an honest livelihood. Tell him that in his bosom alone, under actual circumstances, does the power abide to relieve the country; and that unless he opens it to conviction, and corrects the errors of his administration, no human imagination can conceive and no human tongue can express the awful consequences which may follow. Entreat him to pause, and to reflect that there is a point beyond which human endurance can not go; and let him not drive this brave, generous, and patriotic people to madness and despair.'"

Colonel Benton records that, "during the delivery of this apostrophe, the Vice-President maintained the utmost decorum of countenance, looking respectfully, and even innocently,

at the speaker all the while, as if treasuring up every word he said, to be faithfully repeated to the President. After it was over, and the Vice-President had called some Senator to the chair, he went up to Mr. Clay, and asked him for a pinch of his fine maccoboy snuff (as he often did), and, having re-
72 ceived it, walked away." Mr. Niles tells us, in his *Register*, that at a great meeting, held, soon after, in Philadelphia, it was "resolved" that the Vice-President would deserve the execrations of all good men, if he did not faithfully deliver to the President the message intrusted to him by the Honorable Henry Clay.

The President, during these mad months, was as immovable as the Crag of Fergus, whence he sprang. "I was accustomed," says Colonel Benton, "to see him often during that time, always in the night (for I had no time to quit my seat during the day); and never saw him appear more truly heroic and grand than at this time. He was perfectly mild in his language, cheerful in his temper, firm in his conviction; and confident in his reliance on the power in which he put his trust. I have seen him in a great many situations of peril, and even of desperation, both civil and military, and always saw him firmly relying upon the success of the right through God and the people, and never saw that confidence more firm and steady than now. After giving him an account of the day's proceedings, talking over the state of the contest, and ready to return to sleep a little and prepare much for the combats of the next day, he would usually say: 'We shall whip them yet. The people will take it up after a while.' But he also had good defenders present, and in both Houses, and men who did not confine themselves to the defensive."

Far from it. Colonel Benton informs his readers that he himself spoke thirty times, during the session, on the one topic of debate.

It became the custom, as the excitement increased, for the great petitions to be conveyed to Washington by imposing deputations of distinguished citizens, some of which sought the presence of the President, and laid their griefs before him. The adventures of one of these deputations, a friendly informant, who witnessed their interview with the President, enables me to relate. The petition of the New York merchants, bearing six thousand signatures (all obtained by the labors and money of Mr. Biddle's devoted adherents), was intrusted to the care of a deputation of great bankers and great merchants, headed by Mr. James G. King. 73 When these worthy gentlemen entered the office of the President, at the White House, they discovered him seated at a table writing, with a long pipe in his mouth, which rested on the table and revealed the intensity of the President's interest in his work, by the volumes of smoke which gushed from its blackened bowl.

"Excuse me a moment, gentlemen," said the President, half rising, and bowing to the group. "Have the goodness to be seated."

In a few minutes he pushed back his paper, rose, and said:

"Now gentlemen, what is your pleasure with me?"

The members of the deputation were introduced to the President by the gentleman whose recollections of the scene I am now recording. Mr. King then began, in his usual deliberate and dignified manner, to state the object of the interview, which was to inform the President of the embarrassments under which the merchants of New York were laboring, and to ask such relief as the Executive alone was supposed to be able to afford. Mr. King had uttered only a few sentences of the address which he had meditated, when the President interrupted him with an irrelevant question.

"Mr. King, you are the son of Rufus King, I believe?"

"I am, sir," was the reply.

Whereupon the President broke into a harangue which astonished the grave and reverend seigniors to whom it was addressed.

"Well, sir," said the President, "Rufus King was always a federalist, and I suppose you take after him. Insolvent do you say? What do you come to me for, then? Go to

Nicholas Biddle. We have no money here, gentlemen. Biddle has all the money. He has millions of specie in his vaults, at this moment, lying idle, and yet you come to *me* to save you from breaking. I tell you, gentlemen, it's all politics."

He continued to speak in a strain like this for fifteen minutes, denouncing Biddle and the bank in the manner usual with him, and gradually working himself up to a high degree of excitement. He laid down his pipe ; he gesticulated wildly ; he walked up and down the room ; and finished by declaring, in respectful but unmistakable language, that his purpose was unchangeable not to restore the deposits. He ceased, at length. The deputation, correctly surmising that their mission was a failure, rose to retire, and were dismissed by the President with the utmost politeness. The gentleman who had introduced the deputation left the apartment with them, but was overtaken by a messenger, as he was descending the stairs, who informed him that the President wished him to return. He accordingly went back to the office, where he found the President exulting over the result of the interview. "Did n't I manage them well ?" he exclaimed. The only object of the President in calling him back was to enjoy a chuckle with him over the scene that had transpired.

Upon retiring to their hotel, the deputation deliberated upon what was to be done next. They concluded to take the President's advice, and go to Mr. Biddle. Before they reached Philadelphia, however, a hint of their intention was conveyed to the president of the Bank, who retired to Andalusia, his country-seat on the Delaware. When the deputation called, therefore, Mr. Biddle was "out of town."

A few days after this interview, a delegation of the Mechanics and Artisans of New York arrived in Washington, bearing another monster petition, asking the restoration of the deposits. They, too, desired to make known their sorrows to the President. By this time the President was beginning to be heartily disgusted with this novel method of agitation, and it was only after repeated endeavors that the delegation succeeded in obtaining the interview desired. The result of their conference was unsatisfactory in the extreme.

"Feeling it to be our duty," they said in their report, "to wait on the President again, and communicate to him personally the situation and wishes of our constituents, we presented ourselves on the 13th, but finding him engaged in preparing to attend a funeral we left our card, intimating our intention to call on him the next morning at ten o'clock. We accordingly repaired to his residence on the morning of the 14th, and were admitted at once to his presence. Two gentlemen were with him at the time, who retired in a few moments. The President received us with,

"'Good morning, gentlemen; pray be seated.'

We introduced each other, and then took seats. The President also sat down by a table and signed several papers, after which he took up a letter, broke the seal, and read it very deliberately; then another letter; and was engaged with a third when company was announced. During all this time he did not seem to notice our presence, and, fearing to interrupt important business, we had patiently waited his leisure; but perceiving, at length, that we must introduce our subject without further delay, or lose the opportunity, we commenced by saying,

"'You are aware, sir, that we are a delegation from the mechanics and artisans of the city of New York, to make known to the government the pecuniary difficulties under which the citizens are laboring at the present time.'

"He answered, 'Well what do you want? what would you have me do? what do you come here for? why don't you go to the United States Bank? Go to Nicholas Biddle!'

"His manner was agitated, expressing impatience and anger. We replied that we were not authorized to make application to the bank, but to the government, for an amelioration of our sufferings, to which he replied:

"'I have been applied to by committee after committee, from New York, Philadelphia, Baltimore, and New York again—one, two, five, seven, and you are the eighth. I have dealt openly and candidly with all. You have seen the committee from your city; they could tell you my determination. I told them, and I now tell you, I never will restore the deposits; I never will re-charter the United States Bank, or sign a charter for any bank, so long as my name is Andrew Jackson.'

"His energy and his anger increased as he continued to speak. We replied that we did not come to ask the re-charter of the United States Bank, but merely to declare that our complaints did not originate in faction, and to request from the government the adoption of some system which might tend to restore mercantile confidence.

"He asked, 'How am I to do that?'

"We replied that were not instructed to dictate to the government what to do; but we looked upon the want of a good understanding between the President and the Bank as the great cause of our present embarrassment. At this he became excessively agitated, rose from his seat, and shaking his finger in an earnest and threatening manner, said:

"'In what way have I produced it?'

"To which we replied, 'You informed Congress in your official communications that you did not believe the bank was solvent—that it would not be able, on winding up, to pay all demands against it.'

"The President replied, 'I did so, and I say it now. It will not pay all; it is a corrupt and abominable institution, buying up presses and interfering with elections throughout the country. It has violated its charter repeatedly.'

"We answered that the business portion of the citizens of New York, we believed, viewed it in a different light. But if the bank has violated its charter, the law points out the proper course to be pursued. Here his excitement assumed an extraordinary shape, his whole frame trembling with agitation.

"'Well,' said he, 'have I not pursued lawful measures?'

"We answered that the charter authorized the President to issue a *scire facias*, but we believed that course had not been pursued. He answered, in a vehement manner:

"'It may be, however, before the affairs of the bank are wound up.'

"He became too angry now to hope for any good growing out of further conversation. One of our committee, with a hope of appeasing his extreme irritation, said to him, in the kindest manner:

"'May it please the President, we have been particularly instructed by those whom we represent, not only to present our memorial to both houses of Congress, but to state personally to the Executive our grievances, and ask the wisdom of the government to devise some method for our relief.'

"But the President continued, 'Why am I teased with committees? Here I am receiving two or three anonymous letters every day, threatening me with assassination if I don't restore the deposits and re-charter the bank—the abominable institution—the monster, that has grown up out of circumstances, and has attempted to control the government. I've got my foot upon it, and I'll crush it.' (The *Globe* lay before him on the table, containing some of the letters referred to.) He continued, 'Am I to violate my constitutional oath? Is it to be expected that I am to be turned from my purpose? Is Andrew Jackson to bow the knee to the golden calf, as did the Israelites of old? I tell you, if you want relief, go to Nicholas Biddle.'

"We replied, 'Nicholas Biddle will tell us that he is but following the recommendations of the Executive, in winding up the affairs of the bank by curtailing its discounts.' The rage of the President now increased, if possible, to a degree which we shall not attempt to describe. He continued:

"'Did I advise him to withdraw thirty-five millions from the purchase of inland bills of exchange in the western country? I tell you I am opposed to all banks and banking operations, from the South Sea bubble to the present time. The Israelites, during the absence of Moses to the Mount, made a golden calf, and fell down and worshiped it, and they sorely suffered for their idolatry. The people of this country may yet be punished for their idolatry. Let the United States Bank relieve the community by issuing their notes, and I pledge myself that the State banks shall not oppress it.'

"Believing that we had already said more than was well received, we now withdrew. During this interview several persons were present."

A floating paragraph of the day, which I can not trace to any responsible source, stated, that to one of the deputations the President addressed the following language: "In the name of God, sir! what do the people think to gain by sending their memorials here? If they send ten thousand of them, signed by all the men, women, and children in the land, and bearing the names of all on the grave-stones, I will not relax a particle from my position."

It was officially announced in the *Globe*, soon after the date of the interview with the artizans' delegation, that the President would receive no more deputations sent to Washington to converse with him on questions relating to the currency.

The storm of words raged on, meanwhile, within the walls of the capitol. One member of the House, in a moment of exasperation, drew up a resolution proposing the impeachment of the President; and on the same piece of paper he wrote some notes for the speech which he designed to deliver on introducing his resolution. One of these notes expressed the opinion that the story of General Jackson's having shed his youthful blood in the revolutionary war was an electioneering story, destitute of truth. The paper, left accidentally on the floor of the House, fell into the hands of the editor of the *Globe*, who described it to General Jackson. On this occasion the General was betrayed, by his ungovernable wrath, into the use of language that had seldom fallen from his lips since the death of his wife.

"The d——d, infernal scoundrel!" roared the President. "Put your finger here, Mr. Blair," he added pointing to the long dent in his head left by the sword of the officer whose boots he had refused to clean fifty years before.

Mr. Blair found that the wound had been far more serious than was supposed. He could lay a whole finger in the scar.

In the midst of the angry debates of this session, Congress was frequently called upon to consider events which, at other times, would have allayed undue excitement. Among the deaths announced during the winter and spring of 1834, were those of General Lafayette, William Wirt, John Randolph, and the last of the signers of the declaration of inde-
74 pendence, Charles Carroll, of Carrollton. Judge Bouldin, of Virginia, while in the very act of alluding to the death of John Randolph, paused in the midst of a sentence, fell to the floor, in a few moments breathed his last, and was borne from the hall a corpse. The unfinished sentence thus began: "But I can not tell the reasons why his death was not announced without telling what I told a friend that I should say in case I did——" Then the grim messenger laid an icy finger upon his heart and stilled it forever. The House, appalled at the event, hastened to adjourn. A funeral of peculiar solemnity, attended by the President, the Cabinet, and both houses of Congress, gave a brief pause to the war of words. A few
75 weeks after, General Blair, of South Carolina, the only member of the House from that State who was not a nullifier, shot himself dead, in a moment of despair, caused by a relapse into habits of intemperance against which he had vainly struggled for many years.

Although the greater part of the session was worse than wasted in angry speeches, there were not wanting efforts to conciliate the contending factions. Mr. Webster, taking the hint, perhaps, from Mr. Clay's tariff compromise of the last

Congress, strove to unite the moderate men of all parties in the support of a bill to re-charter the Bank of the United States for six years. Mr. Calhoun, who was an anti-bank man in 1830, but now acted with the Opposition, proposed to re-charter the bank for twelve years. Mr. Clay, however, would listen to nothing less than twenty years. All these propositions, and all similar ones, came to naught, and need not detain us.

On the 4th of April, the House came to a vote upon four resolutions reported by a majority of the Committee of Ways and Means, of which the chairman was Mr. Polk, of Tennessee. 1. Resolved, that the bank ought not to be re-chartered; yeas, 134, nays, 82. 2. That the deposits ought not to be restored to the bank; ayes, 118, nays, 103. 3. That the State banks, under new regulations to be ordered by Congress, ought to continue to be the custodians of the public money; ayes, 117, nays, 105. 4. That a new investigation of the conduct of the bank ought to be made, with a view to ascertain the cause of the commercial embarrassments, and whether the charter of the bank had been violated, and whether there had been in the conduct of the bank any "abuses, corruptions, or malpractices;" yeas, 175, nays, 42. In accordance with the last resolution, a select committee was appointed, consisting of seven members, Messrs. Francis Thomas, Edward Everett, Henry A. Muhlenberg, John Y. Mason, W. W. Ellsworth, Abijah Mann, and R. T. Lytle. The committee was empowered to visit the parent bank and any of its branches, to examine the books of the bank, and to send for persons and papers.

The bank succeeded in frustrating the designs of the committee. The directors appointed a committee of seven of their number to meet the House Committee and assist them in their investigations. The House Committee, accordingly, or repairing to the apartment in the bank designated for their use, found it preoccupied by the bank committee, one of whom, a member *ex officio*, was Nicholas Biddle. The House Committee objected to this proceeding, and asked the appropriation of a room in the bank to their exclusive use. The directors refused compliance with this request, and intimated to the committee that the use of a room in the bank, on any terms, was regarded by the directors as a favor to the committee. In fact, the directors politely reminded the committee that beggars must not be choosers. When, therefore, the House Committee presented themselves at the bank a second time, they found Mr. Biddle and his committee already in possession of the apartment, and disposed to treat the House Committee as distinguished guests.

The House Committee returned to their hotel, and resolved to conduct their investigation there. They notified the president and directors of the bank of their intention, and appointed a day and hour for the attendance of the president and directors, who were asked to submit certain books and papers of the bank to the inspection of the committee. The directors replied that they did not feel justified in submitting their books and papers to the secret, *ex parte* inspection of a hostile body. The committee then notified the directors that they would again repair to the bank and examine the books there, either at the counter or in an apartment. At the appointed hour, the committee entered the bank and demanded to see the books. The directors again refused to comply with the demand, and stated their reasons in writing. The committee, in writing, demanded the surrender of certain specified books, for the specified purpose of ascertaining whether the bank had employed its power in producing distress or in controlling elections. The directors replied, in writing, by pointing out the mode in which they thought the inquiry ought to be conducted; and by explaining the conditions upon which alone any books would be submitted to inspection. They required the committee "when they asked for books and papers, to state specifically in writing, the purposes for which they are proposed to be inspected; and if it be to establish a violation of the charter, then to state specifically in writing, what are the alleged or supposed violations of charter, to which the evidence is alleged to be applicable."

The committee refusing to do this, no books were shown them, and they returned to their hotel. Their next step was to demand copies of certain books, entries, and papers designated by them. The directors replied that it would require the labor of two clerks for ten months to execute the copies demanded. As a last resort, the baffled committee caused the marshal of the district to serve subpœnas upon the president and directors, with a clause (*duces tecum*) commanding them to bring with them the books required. The directors obeyed the summons so far as to attend the committee at their apartment, but disobeyed the clause of the subpœna requiring them to produce the books. Upon entering the committee room the president of the bank handed to the chairman of the committee a document, signed by himself and every member of the board. In this paper the directors stated that "they do not produce the books required, because they are not in the custody of either of us, but, as has been heretofore stated, of the board; and considering that as corporators and directors we are parties to the proceeding, we do not consider ourselves bound to testify, and, therefore, respectfully decline to do so."

The attempt to investigate having completely failed, the committee returned to Washington, reported their proceedings to the House, and concluded by moving "that the speaker of this House do issue his warrant to the sergeant-at-arms to arrest Nicholas Biddle, president, Manuel Eyre, Lawrence Lewis, Ambrose White, Daniel W. Cox, John Holmes, Chas. Chauncey, John Goddard, John R. Neff, William Platt, Matthew Newkirk, James C. Fisher, John S. Henry, and John Sergeant, directors of the Bank of the United States, and bring them to the bar of this House, to answer for the contempt of its lawful authority."

The minority of the committee, Messrs. Everett and Ellsworth, submitted a report to the House, which justified the directors in every particular. "Firmly believing," said they, "that the directors are innocent of the crimes and corruptions with which they have been charged, and that, if guilty, they ought not to be compelled to criminate themselves, we are clearly of the opinion that the directors of the bank have been guilty of no contempt of the authority of the House, in having respectfully declined to submit their books for inspection, except as required by charter." The motion of the majority was never acted upon by the House, and so the bank added one more to its long series of fruitless triumphs.

The last few days of the session were signalized by events that amounted almost to a second disruption of the cabinet. The reader is aware that Mr. McLane, the Secretary of State, had opposed the recent currency measures of the President, from their inception to their consummation. He had, for a whole year, desired to resign, and on more than one occasion had resolved to do so, and, I believe, had once actually penned a letter of resignation. He was dissuaded from resigning by the politicians surrounding the President, who remembered well the disruption of 1831, and shuddered at the possible effects of a second on the fortunes of the party. Mr. McLane, however, as we have before hinted, indulged presidential aspirations. He believed that the people would not sustain the late measures, and deemed it unjust that he should share the odium of acts which he had done his utmost to prevent. He wavered long between contending attachments and desires ; but a few days before the adjournment of Congress, he resigned his place, and retired to private life, the *Globe* declaring that though the Secretary and the President had differed in opinion, they parted friends. Mr. John Forsyth, of Georgia, the particular friend and defender of Mr. Van Buren, was appointed to the vacant place.

The new Secretary of the Treasury, Mr. Taney, had not yet been confirmed by the Senate. The President, knowing well what would happen when the nomination should be submitted to the action of a hostile Senate, held back his name until the last week of the session. June 23d, the nomination was sent in, and instantly rejected by a vote of thirty to fifteen.

The nomination of Mr. Butler to the attorney-generalship was confirmed. Mr. Woodbury was soon gratified by the promotion he had longed for, in being appointed to the place from which Mr. Taney was compelled to retire. The Navy Department was assigned to Mr. Mahlon Dickerson, once governor of New Jersey, and for sixteen years a representative of that State in the Senate of the United States.

The Senate had yet another blow to give the President before parting. The mission to England was vacant still. The President, who had long ago fixed upon a gentleman to fill that coveted post, and had, indeed, promised it to him, sent his name to the Senate near the close of the session. It was Andrew Stephenson, for many years the speaker of the House, a man most hateful to the opposition from his strict partisanship in the appointment of committees. The Senate rejected the nomination. The President adhered to his purpose, however, till a Senate was found willing to confirm the nomination.

As a part of the history of the removal of the deposits, we may add an incident or two of the subsequent career of Mr. Taney. In 1835, a vacancy occurred on the bench of the Supreme Court by the resignation of one of the associate Justices. A place upon that bench had been the dream of Mr. Taney's life, from youth to middle age. General Jackson sent his name to the Senate for confirmation to the vacant seat. The Senate, of which a majority was still hostile to the administration, did not so much as deign to notice the nomination. Before Congress again assembled, the death of Chief Justice Marshall left vacant the highest judicial place in the President's gift. The long service of Justice Story, his great ability, worth, and reputation, his early championship of the republican party in New England, the known wish of the late Chief Justice, all combined to designate him as the rightful successor to the vacant seat. The President nominated Mr. Taney, and the Senate, wherein then the administration commanded a majority, confirmed the nomination.

On the last day of June, after a session of seven wasted

months, Congress adjourned, leaving the President as completely master of the situation as he was before it convened.

As the commercial embarrassments diminished, the clamor against the administration died away, and the fall elections demonstrated that the party in power had been shaken, but not seriously weakened. There were opposition gains here and there, but the empire State this year elected Marcy governor over Seward by a majority that surprised the democrats, and utterly disheartened the whigs. A stranger would have thought the administration lost beyond redemption in April. In November, it was found that Hurrah for Jackson was still an argument against which nothing could prevail. In April, the grand jury of Rowan county, North Carolina, the county in which Andrew Jackson had studied law, "*presented*" the removal of the deposits as an act of usurpation, and the administration that had done the deed as profligate, proscriptive, and tyrannical. In April, the leaders of the opposition could not stir abroad without incurring the risk of an ovation, and Mr. Biddle's casual presence in Wall street was the sensation of the day. In November, the excitement was a thing of the past, and almost effaced from recollection by a new topic.

Upon a calm review of the consequences of transferring the public money to the State banks, no person, who is both candid and disinterested, can hesitate to admit, I think, that the act was as unwise as it was precipitate and unnecessary. The State banks, as a senator remarked, "soon began to feel their oats." The expression is homely, but not inapt. The extraordinary increase in the public revenue during the next two years, added immense sums to the available capital of those banks, and gave a new and undue importance to the business of banking. Banks sprang into existence like mushrooms in a night. The pet banks seemed compelled to extend their business, or lose the advantage of their connection with the government. The great bank felt itself obliged to expand or be submerged in the general inflation. It expanded twelve millions during the next two years. All the other banks expanded, and all men expanded, and all things expanded. It was the period of expansion. Many causes, as we all know, conspired to produce the unexampled, the disastrous, the demoralizing inflation of 1835 and 1836 ; but I do not see any escape from the conclusion, that the *inciting* cause was the vast amounts of public treasure that, during those years, were "lying about loose" in the deposit banks. General Jackson desired a currency of gold and silver. Never were such floods of paper money emitted as during the continuance of his own fiscal system. He wished to reduce the number and the importance of banks, bankers, brokers, and speculators. The years succeeding the transfer of the deposits were the golden biennium of just those classes. In a word, his system, as far as my small acquaintance with such matters enables me to judge, worked ill at every moment of its operation, and upon every interest of business and morality. To it, more than to all other causes combined, we seem to owe the inflation of 1835 and 1836, the universal ruin of 1837, the dreary and hopeless depression of the five years following.

During the summer of 1834, General Jackson paid his accustomed visit to the Hermitage, and partook of the usual banquet at Nashville, and made the usual detour on his return. In the towns through which he passed, he was greeted with, if possible, more than the old enthusiasm.

XXVI.

THE FRENCH IMBROGLIO.

THE particular complaisance of General Jackson's administration toward Great Britain has already excited our surprise. Still less could it have been foreseen, that the only country with which it was to be dangerously embroiled was the old ally of the democratic party, the favorite land of Jefferson and Jeffersonians—France.

In May, 1806, the British government issued an Order in

Council, which declared the northern coast of Europe, from Denmark to the Bay of Biscay, all of which was then under the sway of Napoleon, to be in a state of blockade.

Napoleon retorted, in November following, by the Berlin Decree, which was in these words: "The British Isles are in a state of blockade. All trade and communication with Great Britain are strictly prohibited. All letters going to or coming from England or addressed to English persons, are not to be forwarded: and all those written in English are to be suppressed. Every individual who is a subject of Great Britain is to be made prisoner of war wherever he may be found. All goods belonging to Englishmen are to be confiscated, and the amount paid to those who have suffered through the detention of ships by the English. No ships coming from Great Britain, or having been in a port of that country, are to be admitted. All trade in English goods is rigorously prohibited."

In January, 1807, the British government was provoked by the Berlin decree to issue another Order in Council, of which the following was the most important article: "No vessel shall be permitted to trade from one port to another, both which ports shall belong to or be in possession of France or her allies, or shall be so far under their control as that British vessels may not freely trade thereat; and the commanders of his Majesty's ships of war and privateers shall be, and are hereby instructed to warn every neutral vessel coming from any such port, and destined to another such port, to discontinue her voyage, and not to proceed to any such port; and any vessel, after being so warned, or any vessel coming from any such port, after a reasonable time shall have been afforded for receiving information of his Majesty's order, which shall be found proceeding to another such port, shall be captured and brought in, and, together with her cargo, shall be condemned as lawful prize."

This order, not having been found adequate to its purpose, was followed, in November of the same year, by another, which declared "that all the ports and places of France and her allies, or of any other country at war with his Majesty, and all other ports and places in Europe from which, although not at war with his Majesty, the British flag is excluded, and all ports or places in the colonies, belonging to his Majesty's enemies, shall from henceforth be subject to the same restrictions, in point of trade and navigation, with the exceptions hereinafter mentioned, as if the same were actually blockaded by his Majesty's naval forces in the most strict and rigorous manner."

Napoleon had no sooner read this order than he responded to it by issuing the famous Milan decree, which ordered that every ship, to whatever nation it may belong, which shall have submitted to be searched by an English ship, or which shall be on her voyage to England, or which shall have paid any tax whatever to the English government, shall be declared to be "denationalized." The second article of the decree notified the maritime world that "whether the ship denationalized by the arbitrary measures of the English government enter our ports or those of our allies, or whether they fall into the hands of our ships of war or privateers, they are declared to be good and lawful prizes."

Both under the British orders-in-council and under the Napoleonic decrees, spoliations upon the commerce of the United States were committed. It will devolve upon that hapless man, the Future Historian, to whom so many puzzling questions are daily referred, to explain why the spoliations committed under the orders-in-council caused a war between the United States and Great Britain, and why those perpetrated under the decrees of Napoleon did not provoke a war between the United States and France. It concerns us only to know that, while the war of 1812 was supposed to have righted the wrongs committed by Britain, the French spoliations remained unatoned until the second term of General Jackson's presidency.

Those spoliations were of a character singularly atrocious. In many well-authenticated cases, ships were confiscated only on the ground that they had been boarded by the officers of a British man-of-war. Other ships were confiscated because they had been *forced* by an armed vessel to enter an English port. In some cases, American citizens were detained in France, under the *surveillance* of the police, for months, because they were suspected of the crime, least pardonable by Napoleon, of being English.

From the time of the general peace, in 1815, until General Jackson's accession to power, the American government had sought compensation for these outrages in vain. The French government was brought to admit the justice of the claim, but disputed its amount, and exhibited that distaste for the discussion of the subject which men and governments generally manifest when the object sought of them is the payment of a stale debt. The first message of President Jackson announced his intention to press the affair to a settlement. "The claims of our citizens," said the President, "for depredations upon their property long since committed, under the authority, and, in many instances, by the express direction of the then existing government of France, remain unsatisfied, and must, therefore, continue to furnish a subject of unpleasant discussion, and possible collision, between the two governments. I cherish, however, a lively hope, founded as well on the validity of those claims, and the established policy of all enlightened governments, as on the known integrity of the French monarch, that the injurious delays of the past will find redress in the equity of the future. Our Minister has been instructed to press these demands on the French government with all the earnestness which is called for by their importance and irrefutable justice, and in a spirit that will evince the respect which is due to the feelings of those from whom the satisfaction is required."

It pleased the sapient counselors of Charles X., glad of any pretext to postpone a disagreeable subject, to pretend to regard the words "possible collision" in the light of a "menace." The American Ambassador, Mr. Rives, of Virginia, contrived to mollify their feelings, and the negotiation languidly proceeded, till the revolution of 1830 drove Charles

X. from his throne and country, and made Louis Philippe king of the French.

Louis Philippe was the cordial friend of the United States and an admirer of General Jackson. He remembered his early wanderings in the American wilderness with a delight that was enhanced by his imprisonment in the forms of a court. There was nothing about which he oftener conversed, or conversed more interestingly, than his youthful adventures among the wild woods and the wild men of the west. Under him, the negotiation for indemnity made such progress, that, on the 4th of July, 1831, a treaty was concluded in Paris, and signed by Mr. Rives, which bound the French government to pay to the United States the sum of five millions of dollars, in six annual instalments ; the first to be paid one year from the date of the ratification of the treaty. The treaty was ratified at Washington on the 2d of February, 1832. The first instalment, therefore, was due in Paris on the 2d of February, 1833.

The affair was then supposed to be settled. So little did Congress expect any further difficulty or delay, that it immediately, and as a matter of course, passed a law providing for the appointment of three commissioners to make an equitable division of the money among the various claimants. The commissioners were to meet in June, 1833, and were to continue the labor of distribution, if necessary, for three years, at salaries of three thousand dollars a year. The treaty of indemnity bound the United States to make certain reductions of the duties upon French wines, and a law in accordance with this stipulation was promptly passed by Congress. Nothing remained but for France to pay the money.

The government of France changes so frequently, that it may be necessary to remind the reader, that the government over which Louis Philippe presided was a limited, or constitutional monarchy, resembling that of Great Britain. There was a Chamber of Peers and a Chamber of Deputies ; the former an ornamental nonentity ; the latter, the governing power of the country. In the Chamber of Deputies sat the leading members of the cabinet, who held their places only so long as they could command a majority therein. The king had no more control over the public purse than the Sovereign of England or the President of the United States. All the expenditures of the government required an appropriation by the Chamber of Deputies, the immediate representatives of the people, who exhibited the reluctance to vote money which such bodies invariably do, when they are composed of two parties, one in power, the other ambitious of power. Mr. Rives and the king, when they signed the treaty of 1831, were aware that the real difficulty had yet to be encountered. Mr. Rives, however, in the flush of his diplomatic triumph, could not be expected to enlarge upon this branch of the subject in his communications to his government. He had done his duty ; let the chambers do theirs. He came home in triumph, and said nothing calculated to disturb the impression that the instalments would be paid, as a matter of course, as soon as they were due.

The 2d of February, 1833, the day on which the first instalment was due at Paris, arrived. The administration deigned to employ the services of the United States Bank on this occasion, although even then the removal of the deposits was in agitation at the White House. On the 7th of February, a draft upon the French Minister of Finance, drawn in favor of the cashier of the Bank of the United States, was signed by the Secretary of the Treasury. The American Chargé des Affaires notified the French Government, in due form, that such a draft was on its way. This draft was *purchased* by the Bank of the United States, and its proceeds were immediately placed to the credit of the government. The bank sold the draft to parties in England, who, on the 23d of March, presented it to the French Minister of Finance for payment. The Minister informed the bearer of the draft, that no money had been appropriated by the deputies for the American indemnity, and it could not be paid. The financial complication resulting from the non-payment of the draft, involving the English holders, the Bank of the United States and the American government, can be readily imagined. I spare the reader the recital of the President's new quarrel with the bank which arose when Mr. Biddle attempted to adjust the matter with the Secretary of the Treasury. I will merely say, that the dishonoring of a bill in Paris drawn by the Secretary of the Treasury of the United States, was an event not calculated to lessen the disgust felt by General Jackson at the neglect of the French government to provide for the fulfillment of the treaty.

It is not difficult to account for that neglect. The treaty of 1831, which was such a feather in the cap of Mr. Rives, which was so complacently announced in the President's message, and so highly extolled in the party newspapers, was not regarded in France as an affair of the first importance. The king was occupied in securing his always shaky throne; the ministry in battling with an active and able opposition; the Chambers in the questions of the hour and the strife for place. The news of the ratification of the treaty reached Paris in April, 1832, five days before the expiration of the session of the Chambers; and neither king, ministry, nor deputies thought of providing money to meet an instalment due in February, 1833. In November, the Chambers were again in session, and sat until April, 1833. But as there was no American minister in Paris to press the claim of the United States, the bill to provide for the first instalment was not introduced till near the close of the session; was not then made a ministerial measure; was not supported by the ministry either with unanimity or with vigor; and was not acted upon by the Chamber of Deputies.

It was a fault in the administration of General Jackson to leave the French mission vacant at such a time; but upon receiving the news that the draft of February, 1833, had been dishonored, the administration hastened to atone for its error in a striking manner. Mr. Edward Livingston, the Secretary of State, resigned his office, accepted the appointment of minister to France, and was despatched to his post in a national vessel. He was accompanied by his son-in-law,

Mr. Thomas P. Barton, who was appointed Secretary of Legation. In October, 1833, Mr. Livingston presented his credentials to the king, who received him with particular cordiality. "The king's answer to my address," wrote Mr. Livingston, "was long and earnest. I can not pretend to give you the words of it, but, in substance, it was a warm expression of his good feeling toward the United States, for the hospitality he had received there. As to the convention, he said, 'assure your government that unavoidable circumstances alone prevented its immediate execution, but it will be faithfully performed. Assure your government of this,' he repeated; 'the necessary laws will be passed at the next meeting of the Chambers. I tell you this not only as king, but as an individual whose promise will be fulfilled.'"

The king was mistaken, and Mr. Livingston was disappointed. At the next session of the Chambers, the bill appropriating the money due to the United States was lost by a majority of five—the Minister of Finance himself voting against it!* The ministry in general not only would not stake their places upon carrying the measure, but gave it a languid support that invited and justified opposition.

The king, there is every reason to believe, was sincerely desirous to pay the money. He expressed to Mr. Livingston great regret at the failure of the appropriation. He did more than that. In confidential conversations with the American minister he intimated clearly enough his opinion that the only way left to induce the Chamber to vote the money was for the President of the United States to insert a passage in his next message which should show that the American government was in earnest in the matter, and was resolved to insist upon the prompt payment of the indemnity. Mr. Livingston communicated these conversations to his government, and, accordingly, the message of 1834 con-

* It is due to the reader to state that some of the facts recorded in this chapter, not to be found in the public documents, I received from surviving members of Mr. Livingston's family. To Mr. Thomas P. Barton, of this city, the reader is under particular obligations for interesting information communicated to me in the most obliging and agreeable manner.

tained a strong passage respecting the unpaid indemnity. This message was prepared with unusual care, and was written with great ability. It gave a history, full and exact, of the late proceedings of the French legislature; and concluded the discussion of the subject with five short and quiet paragraphs, which electrified two continents.

The President said it was a principle of international law, that when one nation refused to pay a just debt, the aggrieved nation might "*seize on the property*" belonging to the citizens of the defaulting nation. If, therefore, France did not pay the money at the next session of the chambers, the United States ought to delay no longer to take by force what it could not get by negotiation. Nay, more. "Since France," said the President, "in violation of the pledges given through her minister here, has delayed her final action so long that her decision will not probably be known in time to be communicated to this Congress, I recommend that a law be passed *authorizing reprisals upon French property*, in case provisions shall not be made for the payment of the debt at the approaching session of the French Chambers. Such a measure ought not to be considered by France as a menace. Her pride and power are too well known to expect any thing from her fears, and preclude the necessity of the declaration that nothing partaking of the character of intimidation is intended by us. She ought to look upon it as the evidence only of an inflexible determination on the part of the United States to insist on their rights."

Such words as these, I need scarcely say, were not such as the King of the French expected to read in the message. His idea of "strong language" and a "high tone" differed from that of General Jackson. When he suggested to Mr. Livingston to advise the President to employ strong language in speaking of the indemnity, he used those words in a European and diplomatic sense. Nothing could be further from his thoughts than such terms as "reprisals," "seizures," "sequestration," and "taking redress into our own hands." Members of General Jackson's own cabinet deemed the paragraphs quoted above needlessly irritating and menacing, but the General would not consent to abate a word of them.

"No, gentlemen," he exclaimed, one day, during a Kitchen Cabinet discussion of the message, "I know them French. They won't pay unless they 're made to."

The French King, alive to all the importance of the subject, was so anxious to obtain the message at the earliest moment, that he sent a courier to Havre to await the arrival of the packet, and convey the document to Paris. Louis Philippe, therefore, received the message before it reached the American Ambassador, and was the first man in Paris who read it. I am enabled to state, that the king read the message with much surprise, but more amusement. He thought it a capital joke. He was amused at the interpretation put upon the advice he had given Mr. Livingston. The language of the message, which a Tennessean deemed eminently moderate and dignified, sounded in the cabinet of the Tuilleries, like a fiery declaration of war. Upon the whole, however, the king was pleased and satisfied with the message, because he thought it calculated to produce the effect upon the deputies which he desired it should produce.

The next day, the editors of Paris received their files of American newspapers. The press of France under Louis Philippe was not the tool of despotism which it must be under any man of Bonapartean lineage. With one voice, the Parisian newspapers, ministerial, opposition, and neutral, denounced the message as an insult to France, so gross, that it would be infamy not to resent it. A clamor arose, the violence of which can not be overstated. The excitement was increased when, shortly after, American newspapers arrived containing the extracts from Mr. Livingston's confidential correspondence which are alluded to above. Imagine the embarrassment of the king, the disgust of the American Minister, the exultation of the opposition, the indignation of the people, the comments of the press, upon the publication of despatches which showed the King of the French attempting to gain influence in the Chamber of Deputies by inciting the President of the United States to act upon its fears!

The French government, weak because the King was

weak, cowardly because the King was not brave, felt itself compelled to bow to the storm. The French minister resident in Washington was immediately recalled, and Mr. Livingston was informed that passports were at his disposal. The chambers were notified that diplomatic intercourse between France and the United States had been suspended. A bill was introduced in the chamber by the Minister of Finance proposing to pay the money, provided the Congress of the United States should pass no hostile act in accordance with the President's hostile message. The minister explained to the chamber that the message was nothing more than the expression of the President's individual opinion, and was not to be considered the act of the people until its recommendations had been adopted by their representatives in Congress.

Mr. Livingston, instead of asking for the passports which had been offered him, determined to await the arrival, hourly expected, of the orders of his own government. He wrote, meanwhile, an eloquent and ingenious paper, addressed to the ministry, designed to show that the French people had interpreted the message erroneously; that it was a document written to heal, not widen the breach; that it expressed a sincere and profound desire to avoid hostile measures; that no man knew better than the President how unworthy and how hopeless were the attempt to extort from the fears of a brave and high-spirited nation what could not be obtained from its justice. All this the King understood, and so did a majority of his Cabinet. The difficulty, then, was to allay the excitement of the people and silence the thunders of the press.

Mr. Livingston received his dispatches from Washington —dispatches written before General Jackson had heard of the recall of the French minister from the United States. The President ordered Mr. Livingston, in case the money was not appropriated by the Deputies at the winter session of 1835, to demand his passports and leave the country.

The action of Congress upon the message was well calculated to soothe the pride of the French people, and ought, at once, to have terminated the difficulty. On the 14th of January, the Senate, *without one dissentient voice*, passed the following resolution:

"*Resolved,* That it is inexpedient, at present, to adopt any legislative measures in regard to the state of affairs between the United States and France."

On no other occasion during the turbulent administration of General Jackson, was the vote of the Senate, upon an important question, unanimous. Resolutions of a similar character were presented in the House of Representatives. On technical grounds, only, the House objected to suspend the rules for their reception. The pacific action of Congress had its effect upon the Chamber of Deputies. In May, by a vote of 289 to 137, the chamber passed a bill appropriating a sum sufficient to pay the three instalments due upon the indemnity. Unfortunately, a condition was annexed to the payment of the money which the American government felt to be utterly inadmissable. The bill forbade the ministry to pay the instalments until the President had apologized for the language of the message of 1834! The exact apology demanded was stated by the Minister for Foreign Affairs: "We will pay the money," said he, "when the government of the United States is ready, on its part, to declare to us, by addressing its claim to us officially, in writing, that it regrets the misunderstanding which has arisen between the two countries; that this misunderstanding is founded on a mistake; that it never entered into its intention to call in question the good faith of the French government, nor to take a menacing attitude toward France." "If the government of the United States," he added elsewhere, "does not give this assurance, we shall be obliged to think that this misunderstanding is not the result of an error." Again: "The government of the United States knows that upon itself depends henceforth the execution of the treaty of July 4th, 1831."

Mr. Livingston, after the passage of this bill, asked for his passports, embarked on board the frigate *Constitution*, and returned to the United States, leaving behind him, as Chargé des Affaires, his son-in-law, Mr. Barton. I should add that before leaving Paris, he officially informed the French government that the President had approved the pacific interpretation of the message of 1834 which Mr. Livingston had given to it, on his own responsibility, soon after its arrival in France. This he considered, and General Jackson considered, was more than equivalent to the apology which the Chamber of Deputies demanded.

Congress had adjourned when Mr. Livingston reached the United States. A clause of an appropriation bill, giving the President the command of three millions of dollars, in case any thing should occur during the intermission to render an extraordinary expenditure necessary, had been fortunately lost at the last moment of the session. The President was, therefore, still obliged to rely upon the efficacy of words. Orders were immediately sent out to Mr. Barton to convey to the Minister of Finance a formal demand for the payment of the three instalments overdue. The Chargé presented the demand accordingly. The minister replied that he was not authorized to pay the money until the "formalities" enjoined by the Chamber of Deputies had been complied with on the part of the government of the United States. Mr. Barton communicated this refusal to his government. The President then directed the Chargé to demand of the French government its "final determination," and, if the instalments were not paid, to close the office of the Legation, deposit its contents with the Consul, and return to the United States.

Before the result of this last application was known to the President, Congress met, and the message had to be presented. The President recounted the history of the affair, informed Congress of the last orders sent to the Chargé, and promised another communication as soon as Mr. Barton, or a despatch from that gentleman, should arrive. Congress and the country were kept in painful suspense for six weeks awaiting the news that might forebode inevitable war.

A caricature published during this period expressed the popular feeling. General Jackson and Louis Philippe figure as pugilists in a ring. General Jackson has just dealt the king a blow on the nose, that has caused his crown to topple forward, and his portly person to reel and stagger. The President says: "General Valaré wants an apology, does he? By the Eternal! he shall have a taste of Old Virginia rip-raps, in the shape of a tough hickory whip, that will make him belch compliance, as old Bainbridge, Hull, and Decatur made your crusty neighbor, Johnny Bull!" Behind the king are frogs in uniform, one of whom says: "Vive le roi! vive la bagatelle! L'Americain generale c'est bete! Vive Valaré! General Shackson, God dame!" Behind General Jackson rises Neptune, who slaps the General upon the back, and encourages him with such elegant expressions as these: "Fowl him, Andy! Give it to him, my boy! Old Ironsides, or even the Pennsylvania, will do to make Johnny Crapeau's stomach qualmish!"

Mr. Barton received the final determination of the French government, which was, not to pay the indemnity until the President had apologized. He set sail on his return home in December, 1835, and reached New York, after a long voyage, in January, 1836. Hindrances unavoidable and exasperating delayed his arrival in Washington for two or three days, during which the impatience of the President rose to fever heat. He reached Washington at last, and went to the residence of Mr. Livingston, who accompanied him to the mansion of the President. On the way thither they were joined by Mr. Van Buren and Mr. Forsyth, both of whom were embarrassed and anxious beyond their power to conceal.

"Well, sir," asked the Secretary of State, "what are you going to tell the President?"

"I am going to tell him the whole truth, as I understand it," replied Mr. Barton.

The Chargé perceived a certain constraint and agitation in the group. He stopped near the steps of the White House, and asked,

"Gentlemen, do you want oil poured upon the flames, or water?"

"Oh, WATER, by all means!" exclaimed the company in chorus.

"That," said Mr. Barton, "will be the effect of the little that I have to say."

They entered the presidential sanctum and were soon joined by its irascible master.

"So, sir," said the General to Mr. Barton, "you have got here at last, have you!"

This seemed to the gentleman addressed an ominous beginning to an interview, a possible result of which was war with a powerful nation. He hastened to explain the causes of his detention—the negligence of a pilot and an extraordinary fall of snow. The President was mollified, and darted forthwith to the heart of the matter.

"Tell me, sir, do the French mean to pay that money?"

"General Jackson," was the reply, "I am sorry to inform you that they do not?"

The President rose from his chair, and, turning to the group of anxious officials, exclaimed,

"*There*, gentlemen! What have I told you, all along?"

He strode up and down the room several times in a state of extreme excitement. It was too evident to the gentlemen present that Mr. Barton's communication had not produced upon the President's mind the effect of water upon fire.

"What do they say about it, sir?" suddenly demanded the President. "What excuse do they give?"

"General," said Mr. Barton, "I am exceedingly desirous to make you acquainted with the state of affairs in France, as far as I myself understand it; but to do this effectually I must beg to be allowed to tell my story in my own way."

"Right, sir," said the President, seizing a chair and sitting down in it with emphasis. "Go on, sir."

"I verily believe, General," began Mr. Barton, "that down to a recent period, the French government was trifling with us."

Up sprang the President again, at these words.

"Do you hear that, gentlemen? *Trifling with us!* My very words. I have always said so."

The President resumed his seat, and Mr. Barton his explanation.

"I mean by trifling with us, that they thought the treaty a matter of no great importance, and one which was not pressing, and would not be pressed by the United States. It could be attended to this year, or next year—it was of small consequence which."

The ex-Chargé proceeded to say, that the popular opposition to the payment of the indemnity had risen to such a height in France, that any ministry that should pay it before the President had apologized would, not only lose their places, but subject themselves to impeachment. There was no man in France who would dare to encounter the odium of attempting it. The king would endanger his throne if he should give it his sanction. France was in a kind of frenzy on the subject, and no considerations addressed to its reason or its prudence had the slightest weight. The king, the ministry, the capitalists, and all reflecting persons sincerely desired to avoid a collision with the United States, from which France could gain nothing that she desired to gain. But the people were mad; and no one could predict how far the government might be compelled to yield to their fury.

This was the substance of Mr. Barton's communication to the President, and it had the effect desired of allaying the irritation of his mind. The President dismissed him with every mark of approval and friendship.

The message to Congress which announced Mr. Barton's return, and communicated the intelligence which he brought, was meant to be as pacific and conciliatory as the circumstances were supposed to permit. But it contained passages of fearful import to the lovers of peace. "The return of our Chargé des Affaires," said the President, "is attended with public notices of naval preparations on the part of France destined for our seas. Of the cause and intent of these armaments I have no authentic information, nor any other means of judging, except such as are common to yourselves and to the public ; but whatever may be their object, we are not at liberty to regard them as unconnected with the measures which hostile movements on the part of France may compel us to pursue. They at least deserve to be met by adequate preparation on our part, and I therefore strongly urge large and speedy preparations for the increase of the navy, and the completion of our coast defenses. If this array of military force be really designed to affect the action of the government and people of the United States on the questions now pending between the two nations, then indeed would it be dishonorable to pause a moment on the alternative which such a state of affairs should present to us. Come what may, the explanation which France demands can never be accorded ; and no armament, however powerful and imposing, at a distance or on our coast, will, I trust, deter us from discharging the high duties we owe to our constituents, to our national character, and to the world."

The French Chargé des Affaires was ordered home, and all intercourse between the two governments ceased. Neither government could yield without destroying itself, and the people of both countries were in the temper that precedes and provokes hostilities. Many members of Congress who had opposed General Jackson's fiscal measures, his tariff policy, his land policy, his Indian policy, his proscriptive policy, gave him the most cordial support in his attempt to compel the payment of the French indemnity. No one did so with so much effect as Mr. John Quincy Adams. "Sir," exclaimed Mr. Adams, on one occasion, in the House, "this treaty has been ratified on both sides of the ocean ; it has received the sign manual of the sovereign of France, through his Imperial Majesty's principal Minister of State ; it has been ratified by the Senate of this republic ; it has been sanctioned by Almighty God ; and still we are told, in a voice potential, in the other wing of this capitol, that the arrogance of France —nay, sir, not of France, but of her Chamber of Deputies—

the insolence of the French Chambers must be submitted to, and we must come down to the *lower* degradation of reöpening negotiations to attain that which has already been acknowledged to be our due ! Sir, is this a specimen of your boasted chivalry ? Is this an evidence of the existence of that heroic valor which has so often led our arms on to glory and immortality ? Reöpen negotiations, sir, with France ? Do it, and soon you will find your flag insulted, dishonored, and trodden in the dust by the pigmy States of Asia and Africa—by the very banditti of the earth."

Mr. Seward records that the effect produced by this speech was such, that, for some time after the orator ceased, the House was "lost" in excitement. As the aged statesman sank back exhausted into his chair, "the very walls shook with the thundering applause he had awakened."

The darkest hour is just before the morning. The message of the President, announcing Mr. Barton's return home, and vaguely alluding to the hostile movements of the French fleet, was sent to the capitol on the 18th of January. Three weeks later, February 8th, the President, in a brief but pregnant message, informed Congress that the government of Great Britain had offered its mediation, and that he had accepted the offer. He had, at the same time, notified the mediating power that the apology demanded by France was totally out of the question. He recommended Congress to suspend proceedings upon the non-intercourse act, but to continue those preparations for defense which would become immediately necessary if the mediation failed. The President said that he "highly appreciated the elevated and disinterested motives" which prompted the offer of mediation, and that he relied much upon "the great influence of Britain to restore the relations of ancient friendship between France and the United States."

The affair was settled in a very few days. February 22d the President had the pleasure of informing Congress that France had accepted the offer of mediation as soon as it was made, and that there was every reason to hope for a speedy termination of the dispute. On the 10th of May he sent the following communication to the capitol: "Information has been received at the treasury department that the FOUR INSTALMENTS UNDER OUR TREATY WITH FRANCE HAVE BEEN PAID TO THE AGENT OF THE UNITED STATES. In communicating this satisfactory termination of our controversy with France, I feel assured that both Houses of Congress will unite with me in desiring and believing that the anticipations of the restoration of the ancient cordial relations between the two countries, expressed in my former messages on this subject, will be speedily realized. No proper exertions of mine shall be wanting to efface the remembrance of those misconceptions that have temporarily interrupted the accustomed intercourse between them."

General Cass retired soon after from the War Department, and went to represent the United States at the French court. The French minister resumed his residence in Washington. Louis Philippe conceived the highest idea of General Jackson's resolution and ability. A few years later, he commissioned an artist to paint a portrait of the General for the Tuileries, which was the last portrait ever taken of General Jackson. In other ways the king gave proof of his particular esteem for the character of the General. I have been told that the Duke of Wellington applauded, in his brief, idiomatic manner, the spirit with which General Jackson had maintained the rights of his country in this affair. The people of the United States, when the danger of war was over, and the complete success of General Jackson became apparent, applauded his conduct with nearly as much unanimity as enthusiasm. In the newspapers of the opposition I find the warmest encomiums of the measures which secured the payment of the French indemnity.

XXVII.

OTHER EVENTS OF 1835 AND 1836.

The eighth of January, 1835, was the day which General Jackson esteemed the most glorious of his presidency It was the anniversary of the battle of New Orleans, which has now been for forty-five years celebrated in the United States as a party festival. In 1835, the occasion was seized by the democratic leaders to celebrate also the payment of the last instalment of the national debt. The President had looked forward to the extinguishment of that debt as he would have done to the deliverance of his own estate, if it had been heavily mortgaged, or as a western pioneer anticipates the day when his farm shall be completely his own. Financiers of the Biddle school, some of whom proclaimed the national debt a national blessing, regarded the solicitude of the President on this subject as primitive and puerile. It may be safely predicted that to a policy just as primitive and puerile all financiering will come at last. Out of debt! The honest citizen feels the magic of the words. Out of debt! The public man of the future will be contented with little less for his country.

The party made the most of this auspicious event. A banquet of extraordinary magnificence was given at Washington on the eighth of January, 1835. Col. Benton presided. Among the Vice-Presidents were James K. Polk, Silas Wright, William R. King, Henry A. Muhlenberg, Isaac Hill, John Y. Mason, and E. K. Kane. The distinguished guest of the occasion was the rising sun, Mr. Van Buren. General Jackson declined to attend, but sent a toast: "The Payment of the Public Debt. Let us commemorate it as an event which gives us increased power as a nation, and reflects luster on our federal Union, of whose justice, fidelity, and wisdom it is a glorious illustration."

Col. Benton entered into the affair with peculiar enthusiasm. Upon the removal of the cloth, he delivered an exulting little speech, which was one of his most characteristic efforts. "The national debt," he exclaimed, "is paid! This month of January, 1835, in the 58th year of the republic, Andrew Jackson being President, the national debt is paid! and the apparition, so long unseen on earth—a great nation without a national debt!—stands revealed to the astonished vision of a wondering world! Gentlemen," he concluded, "my heart is in this double celebration; and I offer you a sentiment, which, coming direct from my own bosom, will find its response in yours:

"PRESIDENT JACKSON: May the evening of his days be as tranquil and as happy for himself as their meridian has been resplendent, glorious, and beneficent for his country."

If we may believe the authorized report published in a pamphlet, and printed by the ten thousand, the number of toasts offered at this banquet was about one hundred. An impossible number. From the character of many of these sentiments, it is evident that the politicians of that day knew the weak place in the President's heart. The adulation of the President on this occasion, was shameful to human nature. There seems to have been a strife among the guests which of them could coin a sentence of the most ingenious and original flattery. Take a few specimens:

By MR. WOODBURY.—*The President of the United States.* Venerable in years—illustrious in deeds.

By MR. FORSYTH.—*The Battle of New Orleans.* Not more glorious for the valor which achieved the victory, than for the humanity displayed in alleviating the sufferings of the vanquished foe.

By MR. DICKERSON.—*The Eighth of January*, 1815. An important era in the history of America—second only to the 4th of July, 1776.

By COL. RICHARD M. JOHNSON.—*Andrew Jackson at the battle of New Orleans.* He prevented *booty*, and he protected *beauty*.

By MR. SILAS WRIGHT.—*The Citizen Soldier.* The strength and security of free governments. WASHINGTON, LAFAYETTE, and JACKSON have personified the character.

These are about *one twelfth* of the toasts printed in the report that expressly extolled the President on his favorite measures. The agency that General Jackson had in the discharge of the national debt was simply this: He vetoed bills appropriating money for internal improvements. These vetoes suspended the internal improvement system, and caused the public debt to be extinguished two or three years, perhaps, five years, sooner than it would have been if Mr. Adams had been reëlected in 1828.

There is always some one to remind the most idolized man that he is mortal. If General Jackson was unduly elevated by the glorification which he received on the eighth of January, an event occurred on the thirtieth of the same month, which excited in his mind feelings of another character. On that day, the President, the Cabinet, both Houses of Congress, and a concourse of citizens, assembled in the hall of the House of Representatives to take part in the funeral ceremonies in honor of a deceased member of the House from South Carolina. After the usual solemnities, a procession was formed to escort the body to the grave. The President, near the head of the procession, accompanied by Mr. Woodbury and Mr. Dickerson, had crossed the great rotunda of the capitol, and was about to step out upon the portico, when a man emerged from the crowd, and, placing himself before the President, at the distance of eight feet from him, leveled a pistol at his breast, and pulled the trigger. The cap exploded with a loud report without discharging the pistol. The man dropped the pistol upon the pavement, and raised a second which he had held in his left hand under his cloak. That also missed fire. The President, the instant he comprehended the purpose of the man, rushed furiously at him with uplifted cane. Before he reached him, Lieutenant Gedney of the navy had knocked the assassin down, and he was immediately secured and taken to jail. The President, boiling with rage, was hurried into a carriage by his friends and conveyed to the White House. For some days, his belief remained unshaken that the man had been set on to attempt his destruction by a clique of his political enemies.

The prisoner was proved to be a lunatic. His name was

Lawrence. He was an English house painter, who had been long out of employment. Hearing, on all sides, that the country had been ruined by the measures of General Jackson, the project of assassinating him had fastened itself in his crazy brain. The physicians who examined him reported: "He stated, that believing the President to be the source of all his difficulties, he was still fixed in his purpose to kill him, and if his successor pursued the same course, to put him out of the way also—and declared that no power in this country could punish him for having done so, because it would be resisted by the powers of Europe, as well as of this country. He also stated, that he had been long in correspondence with the powers of Europe, and that his family had been wrongfully deprived of the crown of England, and that he should yet live to regain it—and that he considered the President of the United States nothing more than his clerk. We now think proper to add, that the young man appears perfectly tranquil and unconcerned, as to the final result, and seems to anticipate no punishment for what he has done."

Lawrence was placed in an asylum; and the affair, which, at first, had assumed portentous importance, soon ceased to be a topic of remark. The insinuations of the *Globe*, that "a secret conspiracy had prompted the perpetration of the horrible deed," do not appear to have obtained more than a momentary belief even among the devotees of the party. It was a curious illustration of the changeful nature of party ties, that the gentleman whom the President most suspected of a participation in the attempt to assassinate him was that very George Poindexter, of Mississippi, who had so eloquently defended General Jackson during the Seminole War debates of 1819.

Among the great crowd who attended this funeral and witnessed part of the scene we have briefly described, was Miss Martineau, who, in her "Retrospect of Western Travel," gives some curious particulars of the subsequent excitement in Washington:

"It so happened that we were engaged to a party at Mr. Poindexter's the very evening of this attack upon the President. There was so tremendous a thunder storm that our host and hostess were disappointed of almost all their guests except ourselves, and we had difficulty in merely crossing the street, being obliged to have planks laid across the flood, which gushed between the carriage and the steps of the door. The conversation naturally turned upon the event of the morning. I knew little of the quarrel which was now to be so dreadfully aggravated; but the more I afterward heard, the more I admired the moderation with which Mr. Poindexter spoke of his foe that night, and as often as I subsequently met him.

"I had intended to visit the President the day after the funeral; but I heard so much of his determination to consider the attack a political affair, and I had so little wish to hear it so treated, against the better knowledge of all the world, that I stayed away as long as I could. Before I went, I was positively assured of Lawrence's insanity by one of the physicians who were appointed to visit him. One of the poor creature's complaints was that General Jackson deprived him of the British crown, to which he was heir. When I did go to the White House, I took the briefest possible notice to the President of the 'insane attempt' of Lawrence; but the word roused his ire. He protested, in the presence of many strangers, that there was no insanity in the case. I was silent, of course. He protested that there was a plot, and that the man was a tool, and at length quoted the Attorney-General as his authority. It was painful to hear a chief ruler publicly trying to persuade a foreigner that any of his constituents hated him to the death; and I took the liberty of changing the subject as soon as I could. The next evening I was at the Attorney-General's, and I asked him how he could let himself be quoted as saying that Lawrence was not mad. He excused himself by saying that he meant general insanity. He believed Lawrence insane in one direction; that it was a sort of Ravaillac case. I besought him to impress the President with this view of the case as soon as might be."

The summer of 1835 is memorable as the time when the agitation of the slavery question began to assume the intensity and bitterness which has characterized it since. At that period, and for some time after it, the people of the Northern States were so generally averse to the discussion of the subject that a man could not deliver an anti-slavery lecture, or publish an anti-slavery newspaper, without running an imminent risk of being mobbed and murdered. In Boston, New York, Philadelphia, and Cincinnati, violent scenes were exhibited, with the inevitable effect of inflaming the zeal of the party assailed. The attacks upon Mr. Garrison, 80 the murder of Mr. Lovejoy, the offering of twenty thousand 81 dollars for the head of Mr. Arthur Tappan, the attempt to deprive the people of the right of petition—what effect could such proceedings have but to invest the abolition leaders with the character of martyrs, and to infuse into their hearts the energy and fire that inspired the martyrs of old ?

Few were the abolitionists in number, but their activity was constant. Among the measures devised by them for the spread of their doctrines was the dissemination of pamphlets and newspapers in the Southern States. Some subscribers were obtained in the South for abolition papers, and large numbers of tracts and periodicals were sent to Southern men who were conspicuous supporters of the Southern system. Besides these, pictures representing slavery in its worst aspects were sent to the South through the mail, and otherwise. Col. Benton said in the Senate this year that "many pictures, as well as many diabolical publications on this subject, had been sent to him, the whole of which he had cast into the fire."

The circulation of these pictures and publications through the mail excited the anger and the fear of some of the Southern people. In Charleston, the public excitement was such, during the summer of 1835, that the postmaster feared for the safety of the mails. He was warned by the press and by assemblages of the people not to deliver abolition pamphlets and periodicals, no matter to whom they were directed. In these circumstances he wrote to the Postmaster-General for instructions.

A change had taken place in the Post-Office Department. Mr. Barry had resigned his place, and accepted the mission to Spain. Mr. Amos Kendall, long known to the country as a member of the kitchen cabinet, was appointed Postmaster-General. Upon receiving the letter of the postmaster of Charleston, the administration was placed in an embarrassing situation, from which it could have escaped only by an act of honest boldness, which would have jeopardized the election of Mr. Van Buren to the presidency.

In deciding upon the course to be pursued, General Jackson proved unfaithful, as I think, to the rights and the interests of the South. He receded from the positions of his nullification message. One would have expected him to say: "My fellow-citizens of the South shall be protected in their right to receive whatever they choose through the United States mail. If but one man in Charleston has subscribed to an abolition paper, it shall be delivered to him, though it require an army and a fleet to effect it. And as to those publications which have been sent without having been ordered, the persons to whom they are addressed, and they only, shall decide whether to take them from the post-office or not. It is their right to do this; and I, as the sworn protector of the individual against all who would wrong him, will employ in their protection the power and resources of the nation, intrusted to me for that purpose."

General Jackson held no such language as this. He might have taken such a position and safely maintained it. From what evils he would have saved his country and his South, if he had done so! He permitted Mr. Kendall to reply to the postmaster of Charleston in the extraordinary terms following:

THE POSTMASTER-GENERAL TO THE POSTMASTER OF CHARLESTON.

"POST OFFICE DEPARTMENT,
"August 4th, 1835.

"SIR: In your letter of the 29th ult., just received, you inform me that by the steamboat mail from New York your office had been filled with pamphlets and tracts upon slavery; that the public mind was highly excited upon the subject; that you doubted the safety of the mail itself out of your possession; that you had determined, as the wisest course, to detain these papers; and you now ask instructions from the department.

"Upon a careful examination of the law, I am satisfied that the Postmaster-General has no legal authority to exclude newspapers from the mail, nor prohibit their carriage or delivery on account of their character or tendency, real or supposed. Probably it was not thought safe to confer on the head of an executive department a power over the press, which might be perverted and abused.

" But I am not prepared to direct you to forward or deliver the papers of which you speak. The Post-Office Department was created to serve the people of *each* and *all* of the *United States*, and not to be used as the instrument of their *destruction*. None of the papers detained have been forwarded to me, and I can not judge for myself of their character and tendency; but you inform me that they are, in character, 'the most inflammatory and incendiary, and insurrectionary in the highest degree.'

" By no act or direction of mine, official or private, could I be induced to aid, knowingly, in giving circulation to papers of this description, directly or indirectly. We owe an obligation to the laws, but a higher one to the communities in which we live, and if the *former* be perverted to destroy the *latter*, it is patriotism to disregard them. Entertaining these views, I can not sanction, and will not condemn the step you have taken.

" Your justification must be looked for in the character of the papers detained, and the circumstances by which you are surrounded.

" I am, etc.,

" AMOS KENDALL."

This was a palpable shirking of the responsibility. The postmaster of Charleston was in a dilemma, and asked instructions from his chief. The chief would neither "sanction" nor "condemn," nor even advise, but left the subaltern totally without assistance. Amos Kendall's letter lost the administration the support of the most honest, disinterested, and able of its editorial allies—William Leggett, of the *New York Evening Post*. But it secured Mr. Kendall's confirmation in the Senate; it strengthened the party in the South; and took some available wind from the sails of Mr. Calhoun.

The message of 1835, the last but one of General Jackson's annual communications to Congress, demands a moment's attention from us. The country seemed to the President prosperous beyond example. The financial measures of the administration were producing their stimulating effect. "Every branch of labor," the President said, "we see crowned with the most abundant rewards; in every element of national resources and wealth, and individual comfort, we witness the most rapid and solid improvement." The national debt was paid, and there was a surplus in the treasury of eleven millions. The proceeds of the sales of the public lands, during the year, had reached the amazing amount of eleven millions of dollars; and such was the pressure of business upon the land office, that the mere manual labor of signing documents absorbed the time and exhausted the strength of the Commissioner.

The President's love of a hard currency appeared conspicuously in this message. The State banks, strengthened by the government deposits, and disposed to comply with all the reasonable requirements of the government, would gladly coöperate with Congress in the suppression of notes under twenty dollars. "The attainment of such a result will form," said the message, "an era in the history of our country which will be dwelt upon with delight by every true friend of its liberty and independence. It will lighten the great tax which our paper system has so long collected from the earnings of labor, and do more to revive and perpetuate those habits of economy and simplicity, which are so congenial to the character of republicans, than all the legislation which has yet been attempted."

In dealing with the subject of "incendiary publications," the President's message was more guarded and more right than the letter of Mr. Kendall. The President was careful to specify only such publications as were "addressed to the passions of slaves, and calculated to stimulate them to insurrection, and to produce all the horrors of a servile war." He called "the special attention of Congress to the subject," and suggested "the passage of a law to prohibit, under severe penalties, the circulation in the Southern States, through the mail, of incendiary publications intended to instigate the slaves to insurrection."

With an emphatic repetition of the President's opinion respecting the election of President and Vice-President, the message of 1835 concluded.

A bill with regard to anti-slavery publications was introduced by Mr. Calhoun, early in the session, which went far beyond the suggestions of the President's message. This bill forbade postmasters to receive *any* publication or picture touching the subject of slavery, which should be addressed to an individual residing in a slave State. The bill was lost. I allude to it for the sake of two incidents of the debate. In one of his speeches upon the bill, Mr. Calhoun again had the insolence to threaten Congress with nullification, in case the bill were not passed. "I must tell the Senate," said he, "be your decision what it may, the South will never abandon the principles of this bill. If you refuse coöperation with our laws, and conflict should ensue between your and our law, the Southern States will never yield to the superiority of yours. We have a remedy in our hands, which, in such events, we shall not fail to apply. We have high authority for asserting that, in such cases, 'State interposition is the rightful remedy'—a doctrine first announced by Jefferson, adopted by the patriotic and republican State of Kentucky, by a solemn resolution, in 1798, and finally carried out into successful practice on a recent occasion, ever to be remembered, by the gallant State which I, in part, have the honor to represent."

But the most memorable event of this debate was the contrivance of a tie in the Senate, to compel Mr. Van Buren to vote upon the bill. The object of this maneuver was to destroy Mr. Van Buren as a candidate for the presidency. It was supposed that if he voted for the measure, the North would abandon him; and if he voted against it, he was lost at the South. It was Mr. Calhoun who arranged the tie, and it was he who, at the right moment, demanded the yeas and nays. When the vote was about to be taken upon the engrossment of the bill, the Vice-President, as Col. Benton records, was out of his chair, walking behind the colonnade. "My eyes," adds Benton, "were wide open as to what was to take place. Mr. Calhoun, not seeing him, eagerly and loudly asked where was the Vice-President? and told the Sergeant-at-arms to look for him. But he needed no looking for. He was within hearing of all that passed, and ready for the contingency: and immediately stepping up to his chair, and standing up, promptly gave the casting vote in favor of the engrossment. I deemed it a political vote, that is to say, given from policy; and I deemed it justifiable under the circumstances."

These were not the only political votes given at this session. Again Congress had to grapple with an enormous and increasing surplus in the treasury. In dealing with it, the opposition displayed the same want of wisdom which seems to me to have marked their conduct from the beginning to the end of General Jackson's administration. They made no attempt to lessen or prevent the surplus, because to have done that effectually they would have been compelled to adopt General Jackson's oft-repeated suggestions with regard to the public lands. It was speculations in the public lands that created the surplus. General Jackson's three simple and grand ideas with regard to the disposal of the public domain had only to be enacted into a law, and the surplus had ceased. Sell the land, said the General, only to actual settlers; sell it in limited quantities; sell it at the bare cost of surveying and selling. A measure embodying these three principles would have laid the ax at the root of the difficulty.

Consider, for a moment, the state of things at the time. On the 1st of January, 1834, the banking capital of the country was two hundred millions; the bank notes in circulation amounted to ninety-five millions; the bank loans and discounts, to three hundred and twenty-four millions. On the 1st of January, 1836, the banking capital had increased to two hundred and fifty-one millions; the paper issues, to one hundred and forty millions! the loans and discounts to four hundred and fifty-seven millions! Result—universal expansion of business, and great increase in the price of all commodities save one. That sole exception was the public land, the price of which was fixed by law at a dollar and a quarter per acre. Hence arose that mad speculation in the public lands which, in 1835 and 1836, filled the treasury to overflowing with paper promises-to-pay.

No event of that period affords so striking an illustration of the state of things as the great New York fire of December, 1835. In a night, property to the amount of eighteen millions of dollars was destroyed; fifty-two acres of the wholesale business region of the city were covered with ruins; five hundred and twenty-eight buildings were burned. Nine months after the fire, nearly all traces of it had been obliterated; the burnt region was covered with stores larger and handsomer than those which had been destroyed; and all this, without the failure or the suspension of a single firm! Nay, many men were enriched by the catastrophe.

It was in such a state of things that Congress entered upon the discussion of the question: What shall we do with the surplus revenue?—a surplus, be it remembered, which was then deposited in the State banks, and which had stimulated the business of the country to the alarming extent indicated above. The plan proposed by Mr. Calhoun, adopted by Congress, and not vetoed by the President, amounted to this: *Let us deposit more of the public money with the States, and place it on permanent deposit, instead of temporary.*

The State deposit act of 1836 provided that the surplus above five millions, at the end of every year, should be divided among the States; that the States were to give to the federal government certificates of deposit, payable to the United States; that the Secretary of the Treasury could sell or assign these certificates whenever he needed the money to meet appropriations; that the certificates, when sold or assigned, should bear an interest of five per cent.; that the deposits not sold or assigned should bear no interest; and, finally, that deposits could be returned to the Secretary of the Treasury at the pleasure of any State holding them. This measure was well described by Col. Benton when he said: "It is, in name, a deposit; in form, a loan; in essence and design, a distribution. Names can not alter things; and it is as idle to call a gift a deposit, as it would be to call a stab of the dagger a kiss of the lips. It is a distribution of the revenues, under the name of a deposit, and under the form of a loan.

It is known to be so, and is intended to be so; and all this verbiage about a deposit is nothing but the device and contrivance of those who have been for years endeavoring to distribute the revenues, sometimes by the land bill, sometimes by direct propositions, and sometimes by proposed amendments to the constitution."

There is too much reason to believe that the passage of this bill was due to the supposed necessities of presidential candidates. It passed by extraordinary majorities, both parties desirous to share the popularity of the contemplated distribution. Col. Benton intimates that the same motive induced the President to give the measure his assent. "The bill was approved by the President," says the author of the "Thirty Years' View," "but with a repugnance of feeling and a recoil of judgment which it required great efforts of friends to overcome; and with a regret for it afterwards which he often and publicly expressed. It was *understood* that some of Mr. Van Buren's friends favored the President's approval, and recommended him to sign it—induced by the supposed effect which its rejection might have on the democratic party in the election. The opponents of the bill did not visit the President to give him their opinions, nor had he heard their arguments. If they had seen him, their opinions concurring with his own feelings and judgment, his conduct might have been different, and the approval of the act withheld."

Congress sat until the fourth of July. Before the adjournment, Col. Benton, who, almost alone among the public men of the day, saw the ruin that awaited the country if the land speculations continued, attempted to introduce a measure to compel purchasers of public lands to pay for them in specie. The proceeds of the sales of public lands had risen from four millions a year to five millions a quarter, and they were still on the increase. Col. Benton's proposition met with no encouragement in a body, a majority of whose members were interested in the very speculations which it was designed to check. One week after Congress adjourned, the President, upon his own authority, against the known will of Congress, against the advice of a majority of his cabinet, issued that famous "Specie Circular," which ordered all land commissioners, after a certain date, to reject paper money in payment of public lands, and to accept gold and silver only. Col. Benton, in his rapid, graphic manner, tells us how and why this order was issued: "The President saw the public lands fleeting away—saw that Congress would not interfere—and knew the majority of his cabinet to be against his interference. He did as he had often done in councils of war—called the council together to hear a decision. He summoned his cabinet, laid the case before them, heard the majority of adverse opinions, and directed the order to issue. His private secretary, Mr. Donelson, was directed to prepare a draught of the order. The author of this 'View' was all the while in the office of this private secretary. Mr. Donelson came to him with the President's decision, and requested him to draw up the order. It was done; the rough draft carried back to the council, put into official form, signed, issued. It was a second edition of the removal of the deposits scene, and made an immense sensation. The disappointed speculators raged. Congress was considered insulted, the cabinet defied, the banks disgraced."

The specie circular was eighteen months too late. Issued in the spring of 1835, it had saved the country. Issued in July, 1836, it could only precipitate the crash which had then become inevitable. Its chief effect was to draw gold and silver from the eastern to the western States, and the pressure in the money market, which had already begun, increased from that time. It was severe during the autumn months; severer during the winter; severest in the spring. Unrelieved for a single week, the pressure increased steadily from May, 1836, until it ended in the stupendous ruin of May, 1837.

In November, 1836, General Jackson beheld the consummation of his most cherished hopes in the election of Mr. Van Buren to the presidency.

Mr. Clay, despairing of success, despairing almost of his

country, had shrunk from the contest. "You seem to think," he wrote to Judge Brooke, "that I despond as to our public affairs. If you mean that I have less confidence than I formerly entertained in the virtue and intelligence of the people, and in the stability of our institutions, I regret to be obliged to own it. Are we not governed now, and have we not been for some time past, pretty much by the will of one man? And do not large masses of the people, perhaps a majority, seem disposed to follow him wherever he leads, through all his inconsistencies? If that single man were an enlightened philosopher, and a true patriot, the popular sanction which is given to all his acts, however inconsistent or extravagant, might find some justification. But when we consider that he is ignorant, passionate, hypocritical, corrupt, and easily swayed by the base men who surround him, what can we think of the popular approbation which he receives? One thing only was wanted to complete the public degradation, and that was that he should name his successor."

General Harrison and Francis Granger were the whig candidates; Martin Van Buren and Richard M. Johnson the democratic. If these had been the only names presented to the people, Mr. Van Buren would have been chosen by a majority only less decided than that which had reëlected General Jackson in 1832. But Judge White, of Tennessee, long the friend and supporter of General Jackson, but long the bitter enemy of Mr. Van Buren, permitted his name to be used by a democratic faction for the purpose of defeating the favorite of his old chief. Colonel Benton tells us, in one place, that Judge White was "instigated to divide the democratic party, and defeat Mr. Van Buren," by Mr. Calhoun; and, in another place, that he was induced to run by the solicitations of an ambitious wife. Strange to relate, Tennessee, from an early period of the canvass, showed a particular disinclination to support General Jackson's candidate. Tennessee and Georgia cast their votes for Judge White. South Carolina again threw her vote away upon a candidate named in no other State—Willie P. Mangum. Massachusetts wasted her vote upon Daniel Webster. Harrison and Granger received the votes of Vermont, New Jersey, Delaware, Maryland, Indiana, Kentucky, and Ohio—seventy-three. Mr. Van Buren triumphed in Maine, New Hampshire, Rhode Island, Connecticut, New York, Pennsylvania, Virginia, North Carolina, Louisiana, Mississippi, Illinois, Alabama, Missouri, Arkansas, Michigan—one hundred and seventy. There was no choice of Vice-President by the people, as the votes of four States were given to Mr. Tyler. The Senate, upon whom the election devolves in such cases, gave the office to Colonel Richard M. Johnson.

The private letters of General Jackson show that he was overjoyed at the result of the election—a result which, for seven years, he had eagerly anticipated, and to promote which he had, for seven years, schemed and labored. It was a signal triumph, for it was one which secured to him all the objects nearest his heart. Mr. Van Buren, who, in conjunction with Edward Livingston, had given to General Jackson's administration its strong Jeffersonian flavor, was not likely, thought the General, to abandon the principles which he believed to be at once right and popular; good for the country and safe for the party. The election of Mr. Van Buren dismayed the opposition, stung Calhoun, deprived the bank party of its last hope, and secured in their places the great army of Jacksonian office-holders.

Leaving the State of New York out of the canvass, the election of Mr. Van Buren to the presidency was as much the act of General Jackson, as though the constitution had conferred upon him the power to appoint his successor. Nor was Mr. Van Buren particularly active in the matter. Feeling sure of General Jackson's preference, relying on that, knowing that to be the strength of his position, he seems to have been comparatively indifferent to other means of support. The correspondence, published by Mr. McKenzie, between Mr. Van Buren and his most intimate friends, all tends to confirm this impression.

When James Gordon Bennett wrote to Jesse Hoyt imploring pecuniary aid from Mr. Van Buren, of whose cause Mr. Bennett had long been a stanch supporter, Mr. Van Buren replied: "If Mr. Bennett can not continue friendly to me on public grounds and with perfect independence, I can only regret it, but I desire no other support. Whatever course he may pursue, as long as it is an honest one, I shall wish him well. He does not understand the relation between the editors he quarrels with and myself, or he would not complain of me for their acts. They are as independent of me in in the management of their papers, as I wish him to be, and remain."

XXVIII.

WHITE HOUSE ANECDOTES.

It belongs to our task to show how General Jackson, when President of the United States, appeared to those who conversed and associated with him. The material here is superabundant and interesting, but somewhat unmanageable.

He lived always in a crowd. The city of Washington, we may premise, was the unforeseen result of an after-dinner conversation between Hamilton, Jefferson, and two or three "Potomac members" of Congress. Hamilton, finding himself in a minority upon one of his fiscal measures, implored the aid of Jefferson's influence over the Virginia delegation. "Dine with me to-morrow," said Jefferson, "and I will invite some of the opposing members to meet you." After dinner, the subject was discussed, and two members agreed to change their votes—to save the Union, of course. It was observed, by one of the gentlemen present, that the measure proposed would prove so repugnant to the Southern people, that "some concomitant measure should be adopted to sweeten it to them a little." A lump of sugar would be needful after the medicine. The lump of sugar proposed and swallowed was, the selection of a site for the permanent capital of the country in the wilderness on the banks of the Potomac. In how many ways have the fortunes and the morals of the United States been influenced by that talk over Mr. Jefferson's mahogany in the year 1790 !

The city has never lost its extempore character. It is more like a camp than a town. Not a camp in which an army rests for a night ; but a camp such as we may imagine those "winter-quarters" to have been, into which, winter after winter, Cæsar led his victorious legions. The White House has more in common with the marquee of a commander-in-chief than the home of a civilized family. As in a camp, too, every one is esteemed according to his rank in the service, so, in Washington, a man is honored for the office he holds. Shut out from all the world, like boys in a college, the honors of the place, which seem trivial at a distance, become objects of desire as intense as that which impels ambitious youths to wear out their days and nights in competing for a medal or a book.

Amid the bustle, and throng, and strife of Washington, General Jackson maintained the same easy and profuse hospitality to which he had been accustomed at the Hermitage, and every one of his thousands of guests brought away something curious to tell of him. He was one of those positive and peculiar men whose commonest action becomes an anecdote, and I have, consequently, accumulated a mass of anecdotical reminiscences of him, which I can not withhold, but know not how to compress into reasonable compass. I may add, before going further, that the liberal hospitality of the White House compelled the President to eke out his salary by drawing upon the proceeds of his farm. Before leaving Washington in 1837, he had to send for six thousand dollars of the proceeds of his cotton crop in order to pay the debts which his last year's salary failed to cover. In the spring of 1836, when the Hermitage was damaged by fire to the extent of three thousand dollars, he was really embarrassed to find the means of repairing and refurnishing it. He wrote to a friend in Philadelphia: "I have directed my son to offer for sale a piece of valuable land in Tennessee. I find this will be necessary before I can venture to incur the responsibility of another purchase. Here I have no control of my expenses, and can calculate nothing on my salary." His son Andrew was then a married man and a father; a circumstance that added greatly to the General's happiness, and considerably to his expenditures.

But to our purpose. We are to observe, first, how the President impressed those foreign visitors whom curiosity attracted to the official mansion.

An English traveler, who recorded his recollections in the "New Monthly Magazine," drew a portrait of the General that was very striking.

"General Jackson," he wrote, "is tall, bony, and thin, with an erect military bearing, and a head set within a considerable *fierté* upon his shoulders. A stranger would at once pronounce upon his profession: and his frame, features, voice, and action, have a natural and most peculiar warlikeness. He has (not to speak disrespectfully) a *game-cock look* all over him. His face is unlike any other: its prevailing expression is energy; but there is, so to speak, a lofty honorableness in its thin worn lines, combined with a penetrating and sage look of talent, that would single him out, even among extraordinary men, as a person of a more than usually superior cast. He looks like the last person in the world to be 'humbugged;' and yet a caricature of him would make an admirable Don Quixote. In the days of chivalry he would have been the mirror of tried soldiers—an old iron-gray knight invincible and lion-like, but something stiff in his courtesy. His eye is of a dangerous fixedness, deep set, and overhung by bushy gray eyebrows, his features long, with strong, ridgy lines running through his cheeks; his forehead a good deal seamed; and his white hair, stiff and wiry, brushed obstinately back, and worn quite with an expression of a *chevaux de frise* of bayonets. In his mouth there is a redeeming suavity as he speaks; but the instant his lips close, a vizor of steel would scarcely look more impenetrable. His manners are dignified, and have been called high-bred and aristocratic by travelers; but, to my mind, are the model of republican simplicity and straightforwardness. He is quite a man one would be proud to show as the exponent of the manners of his country. General Jackson would be a bad diplomatist in Europe, or any where, without power. He has but one *cheval de bataille*—he rides down and breaks through every thing that other men would think of avoiding or circumventing. He cuts all gordian knots. He is no 'head to creep into crevices.' Having made up his mind as to his aim, and trusting to his own directness of purpose, he shuts his eyes, like the monarch of the herd, and charges—generally with success. His passions are said to be tremendously violent; and a long life has but little subdued their warmth. His paroxysms are not unfrequent; and sooth to say, he has often cause: for never was man so crossed and thwarted as he has been in his administration. His stern uprightness and singleness of mind, however, bring him well through. His immediate passion is soon over, but his purpose does not evaporate with his anger; and he has shown, since he has been in power, some rather startling specimens of his inflexibility."

To this I may add that the portrait which accompanies this volume is the most successful of our attempts to furnish a correct engraving of General Jackson. It is a little triumph in its way. It gives the most exact idea of the President as he used to appear in the streets of Washington. The picture from which it was taken was painted in the White House, by Mr. Earl, for the "successful politician" whose recollections are elsewhere recorded. Some of the most characteristic and life-like portraits of the General are to be found in the caricatures of the time, of which an extraordinary number were produced during the last five years of his presidency. Even at this late day, I have been able to collect twenty, in which General Jackson is the principal figure.

Miss Kemble, who was "starring" then through the country with her father, was "presented to the President in due form," during one of her Washington engagements. She describes him in her journal as "very tall and thin, but erect and dignified; a good specimen of a fine old, well-battered soldier; his manners perfectly simple and quiet, and, therefore, very good." She adds that "he talked about South Carolina, and entered his protest against scribbling ladies, assuring us that the whole of the southern disturbances had their origin in no larger a source than the nib of the pen of a lady." The lady referred to by the President was, possibly, one of the "set" opposed to Mrs. Eaton—perhaps the wife of a colonel who figured in that affair. 83

Mr. Stuart, a Scotch traveler, whose "Three Years in North America" was a book of note twenty-five years ago, recorded his observations of the President. He saw him first at church, where the General listened with evident delight to his favorite preacher, Dr. Durbin. "Nothing," says the traveler, "struck me more than seeing him mixing in the passages of the church with the rest of the congregation, as a private individual, and conversing with such of them as he knew on going out, without the slightest official assumption. He bowed to Mr. Kennedy, in the seat where I was. The President has very little the appearance or gait of a soldier, as I have been accustomed to them. He is extremely spare in his habit of body—at first sight not altogether unlike Shakespeare's starved apothecary—but he is not an ungenteel man in manner and appearance, and there are marks of good humor, as well as of decision of character, in his countenance."

The opinion of Mr. Duane respecting the character of the President and his administration was recorded by him, in a letter to a friend, several weeks before his dismissal from the office of Secretary of the Treasury. "I consider the President," he wrote, "intoxicated with power and flattery. 'Constant dropping wears away stones.' Why, indeed, should we be surprised that he has bent under the influence of such passions as, in ancient and modern times, overcame men greater by nature and education than he is? It is the fact that men change that makes a republic preferable to a monarchy. Washington and Jefferson would not trust themselves with power longer than eight years. General Jackson was, at one time, so fearful of the influence of power and passion upon himself, that he was in favor of limiting service in the presidency to four years. But what a revolution do we behold! Now he is not only content to retain power for eight years, but desirous to transfer it to a favorite! Such is the effect of power and flattery! Are you amazed? I am not; the matter is easily explained. When he came into office, the President supposed that he would find much purity at Washington, especially among his supporters, who had been making so many professions. Instead of that, he found the leaders at the head of factions, each desiring to drive the coach of state. He found his tables groaning under the weight of petitions for offices. He saw several of the late friends of his competitor, standing with cap in hand, to catch the falling crumbs. He heard adulation from every body; plain truth from nobody. He came into office to be the friend of a whole people, but he became the mere purveyor for the hungry expectants of discordant factions. In short, all the circumstances around him were calculated to make him entertain an exalted opinion of himself, and a contemptuous one of others. His own natural passions contributed to this result. Such is my explanation—my apology, if you please. He is changed, or else we knew him not."

Among the young men who surrounded General Jackson during the early years of his presidency, there was none who enjoyed more of his affection, and none who was more worthy of it, than Mr. Nicholas P. Trist, of Virginia, the husband of one of Mr. Jefferson's grand-daughters. Mr. Trist was no politician in the partisan sense of the word, but a wise and able one in its true acceptation. He was also one of those happily constituted men who see clearly and lovingly the nobler traits of a friend, and are blind to the less worthy ones. In his intercourse with General Jackson, both as his friend and as his secretary, Mr. Trist saw him when his nature, so to speak, was in equilibrium; when he was gentle, kind, winning, and just. The picture he has drawn of him is strictly true, but it does not convey all the truth; for, as we have before remarked, Jackson in equilibrium and Jackson excited by passion, or biased by prejudice, were two very different beings.

Soon after Mr. Trist joined General Jackson's family as his private secretary, he accompanied the General to the rip-raps of Virginia:

"One evening," writes Mr. Trist, "after I parted with him for the night, revolving over the directions he had given about some letters I was to prepare, one point occurred on which I was not perfectly satisfied as to what those directions had been. As the letters were to be sent off early next morning, I returned to his chamber door, and, tapping gently, in order not to wake him if he had got to sleep, my tap was answered by 'come in.'

"He was undressed, but not yet in bed, as I had supposed he must be by that time. He was sitting at the little table, with his wife's miniature—a very large one, then for the first time seen by me—before him, propped up against some books; and between him and the picture lay an open book, which bore the marks of long use.

"This book, as I afterward learned, was *her* prayer-book. The miniature he always wore next to his heart, suspended round his neck by a strong, black cord. The last thing he did every night, before lying down to rest, was to read in that book with that picture under his eyes.

"In Washington, on going one day into the President's office, I found that I had broken in upon a *tête-à-tête* between him and Charles, his negro driver. Charles was looking the culprit to his best, that is, as well as was permitted by a lurking smile, which betrayed his consciousness that nothing very terrible was coming. As I entered, the General was saying, 'Charles, you know *why* I value that carriage. This is the second time it has happened; and, if it ever happens again, I will send you back to Tennessee.'

"This lecture and threat Charles had brought upon himself by having left his coach-box, as the natural consequence of which the horses had run away and broken the carriage.

"In this scene I was struck with the fact that the General's thoughts and feelings dwelt upon the carriage, upon the injury sustained by it, without turning at all upon the expense of the injury to the horses, noble dapple grays, his favorite color, of his own rearing, and descendants of his famous horse Truxton. I at once inferred that this 'why' had reference to his wife; and upon inquiry of Col. Earl, my conjecture was verified. Because the carriage had been *hers*, it was better than any new one; it must never be given up, but always repaired and made as good as new, though the cost might be greater than that of a new one.

. . . .

"There was more of the woman in his nature than in that of any man I ever knew—more of woman's tenderness toward children, and sympathy with them. Often has he been known, though he never had a child of his own, to walk up and down by the hour with an infant in his arms, because by so doing he relieved it from the cause of its crying; more also of woman's patience and uncomplaining, unnoticing submissiveness to trivial causes of irritation. There was in him a womanly modesty and delicacy, as respects the relation of the sexes. Scipio was not more continent—more chaste would be the right word as to him—than I feel sure he was, in thought as well as in conduct. By no man was the homage due to woman, the only true homage she can receive—faith in her—more devoutly rendered. This chaste tenderness toward the sex was constantly manifesting itself, and in a manner so unstudied, so perfectly spontaneous, as to show that it was as natural to him as to breathe. As regards patience, I have often seen his temper tried to a degree that it irritated mine to think of, by those neglects in small things that go so hard with an invalid—as he always was at the period when I knew him—and which are so apt to test one's temper. But things of this kind passed off without so much as a shade coming over his countenance.

"Of course I do not mean to say that he was not subject to anger, and, at times, to the most vehement outbursts of passion. I have no doubt that he could be, and has been, a perfect volcano. Though I never witnessed any thing of the sort, there was that about him which told that he could be so, and confirmed what you heard of the fearfulness of his wrath. I speak of what he habitually was.

"This peculiar tenderness of nature entered largely, no doubt, into the composition of that *manner* of his with which so many have been struck, and which was of the highest available stamp, as regards both dignity and grace. Mr. Jefferson was strongly impressed with this on their meeting at Lynchburg—that meeting made memorable by the toast, 'Honor to the man who has filled the measure of his country's glory.' No better judge of manners lived than Jefferson, whose own were a charm to every one who approached him, and whose associations through life had been such that it must have been no easy matter for him to receive an impression of that kind. And yet, so strong had that impression been, that many years afterward—but the year before his death—upon being visited by an old friend whom he had known amidst the most polished circles of Paris, he dwelt upon this point as the most surprising thing about Jackson. How he could have got such manners—manners which, for their polish, no less than their dignity, would have attracted the attention of every one at any court in Europe—was to him an enigma. This was related to me, many years after Mr. Jefferson's death, by the gentleman referred to.

. . . .

"Another of the numberless particulars of the undying fidelity—the truly feminine fidelity—of General Jackson's character manifesting itself in regard to his wife's memory, was the relation established by him toward Col. Earl, the portrait-painter. As a Nashville artist, Earl had been a *protégé* of Mrs. Jackson, one of the many objects on which the kindness of heart recorded in the epitaph—so different in truthfulness from most epitaphs—had found its indulgence. This was enough. By her death, this relative became sanctified for the General's heart. Earl became forthwith *his protégé.* From that time forward the painter's home was under his roof, at Washington, in Tennessee, in the President's house, as at the Hermitage, where he died before the General. And this treatment was amply repaid. His devotion was more untiring even than his brush, and its steadiness would have proved itself, at any moment the opportunity might have offered, by his cheerfully laying down his life in his service. If he had had a thousand lives, they would, I feel sure, have been so laid down, one after the other, with the same perseverance that one canvas after another was lifted to his easel, there to keep its place till it had received 'the General.'

"Of the numberless cases which might be collected, corresponding to those above related of the impression made by his manner, I will mention one now, because of the idea it affords of him under another aspect, which was quite a common one with him, namely, a dry archness in administering a gentle rebuke when he thought it called for. One would expect something of the kind in his composition on being informed that, with him, the book of books—after the Bible, of course—was the 'Vicar of Wakefield.'

84 "The incident I am about to give occurred to Mr. Buchanan, by whom I have heard it related.

"An American lady—a daughter, I think, of Charles Carroll, of Carrollton—on her return from a residence in England, during which she had associated on the most familiar footing with the highest aristocracy of the island, among the rest, *the* 'Duke'—being desirous of seeing General Jackson, an hour was appointed for him to receive her. A few minutes before the time arrived, Mr. Buchanan, who knew of the arrangement, or perhaps was a party to it, upon going into the President's office found him there, immersed in work, and, very contrary to his wont, not at all neat in his dress and personal appearance; he had not even shaved, and had a slovenly look otherwise, which he had never before seen in him. Alarmed at the effect this might have upon the expected visitor, Mr. Buchanan ventured upon a hint to the effect that the hour being come, it would be advisable to engage in making preparations for the visit.

"'Mr. Buchanan,' observed the General, 'I once heard tell of a man in Tennessee, who got along very well in the world, and finally made a fortune, by minding his own business.' Saying which, he arose and left the room. In a very few minutes afterwards he walked into the parlor, to which Mr. Buchanan had repaired, presenting as neat an appearance in every respect as if he had passed hours at his toilet.

"The lady departed, expressing the same admiration of his manners that hundreds had experienced before her.

"Mr. Buchanan being upon the carpet, I will conclude with another incident which I have heard him relate more than once.

"The time this occurred was when the American settlers in Texas were known to be in full retreat, with Sam. Houston at their head, before Santa Aña and his advancing army. At that precise juncture, a breathless suspense prevailed throughout our country as to how the thing was to end; whether the Americans would make a stand, and try their hand at a fight whilst still in Texas, or run clear across the border, and thus get under the cover of that nationality of which they had divested themselves.

"At this critical moment, which soon after terminated in the news of the battle of San Jacinto, Mr. Buchanan called to see the President, whom he found in his office, with the map of Texas before him. He had been tracing the progress of Santa Aña (forwards,) and that of his pupil (backwards,) and did not seem at all elated at the spectacle presented by these movements. As Mr. Buchanan looked over the map, the General, putting his finger upon San Jacinto, said, 'Here is the place. If Sam Houston is worth one *bawbee*, he will make a stand here, and give them a fight.'

"A few days after, the news was received at Washington of what had taken place at that very spot."*

To these pleasant recollections, contributed to the *Evening Post*, I can add others received in manuscript from Mr. Trist's own hand. Here is a little anecdote, recorded at the moment:

"'I care nothing about clamors, sir, mark me! I do precisely what I think just and right.'

"The above are the precise words just uttered in my hearing, by Andrew Jackson; and as they convey a just idea of the man, so far as I have been able to penetrate him (and I have had the best opportunities) I have determined to commit them to paper while fresh in my mind. The occasion was this: Cabinet council on the 4th of May, 1833. (Present the Secretary of State, Livingston, of the Treasury, M'Lane, of War, Cass). The Maine boundary question was under consideration. Mr. Livingston had asked me for a rule, to draw some lines upon a map. After some minutes, search, I entered the President's office with a rule in my hand. The map was on the table before the President, Mr. Livingston was at his side, looking over the map with him, and making some remarks on the measure under consideration. He had just uttered the idea, that its adoption would probably raise a clamor, when the President interrupted him with the above words. As he uttered the last, his forefinger came down perpendicularly

85

* New York *Evening Post*, July, 1853.

upon the map. To impress any one capable of reading man, with the real character of the 'Old Roman,' to have seen and heard him at this moment would have sufficed. *All* that I have seen of him (and I have seen him at all hours, and in every possible relation) is in perfect keeping with the above.

"N. P. TRIST.

"May 4th, 1833."

Mr. Trist gives the reader characteristic glimpses of the General in the following narratives:

"In the fall of 1836, on my arrival in Washington, *en route* for Virginia, I found General Jackson alone in the White House, with the exception of Colonel Earl, the other members of his household having left for Tennessee, and I was invited to remain with him until his departure for the Hermitage. I did so, and on one of the days of my stay I was his only companion in the afternoon walk, in which he was generally accompanied by Colonel Earl. Striking across the President's square in a north-west direction, and pursuing the same course towards Katorama, we came to a ravine into which our path descended, and as we crossed the rivulet at the bottom, some dilapidated houses stood before us on the brow of the hill. Those houses gave rise to the incident which I relate to you.

"A short time previously, during a visit of the General to the Rip Raps, at the mouth of Chesapeake Bay, for the benefit of sea air and bathing, some riots had occurred at Washington which had occasioned great alarm, especially among the colored population, against whom they were directed. The mob, as I learned, had manifested intense exasperation against, and had been very anxious to get hold of, a certain Augustus, a remarkably fine looking mulatto, who was one of the President's hired domestics, in the capacity of waiter on his office. As the story ran, Augustus had disappeared, and no trace of him could be found so long as the General was away; but the moment the latter had got back, there was Augustus also.

"As we crossed the rivulet, the General observed, 'Those are the houses which the mob destroyed,' adding a severe censure upon the city authorities for not having immediately suppressed the riots. He went on with the subject, mentioning that he had been waited upon by a deputation, to express the wish of those whom it represented, that Augustus should not be retained in the place he occupied (which proceeding was, of course, regarded by him as an approval of the mob's hunt after Augustus); and his reply had been to this effect: 'My servants are amenable to the law if they offend against the law, and if guilty of misconduct which the law does not take cognizance of, they are amenable to *me*. But, I would have all to understand distinctly that they are amenable to me *alone*, and to no one else. They are entitled to protection at my hands, and this they shall receive.

"I observed that I had heard of all this, and was sorry to learn it, as I knew that the effect would be to make Augustus a fixture in the office.

"'Why so, sir?' in a tone of some sharpness, showing that my remark had crossed the current of his feelings. I replied by saying that Augustus could read and write; that, from his hourly opportunities as regards papers and conversations, and even Cabinet discussions, every thing was at his mercy; and that, of course, among his (the General's) opponents there were some not above tampering with a domestic in such a position. 'They are welcome, sir, said he, to anything they can get out of my papers. They will find there, among other things, false grammar and bad spelling; but they are welcome to it all, grammar and spelling included. Let them make the most of it. Our government, sir, is founded upon the intelligence of the people; it has no other basis; upon their capacity to arrive at right conclusions in regard to measures and in regard to men; and I am not afraid of their failing to do so from any use that can be made of any thing that can be got out of my papers.'

"Of course, I made the objection that this view of the matter might do very well *if* the people could be put in possession of the *whole* truth; if they could be made fully and perfectly acquainted with a subject, in every particular and every circumstance pertinent to its merits. But this being impossible, while, on the other hand, mere fragments of truth often bear a complexion calculated to convey totally false impressions regarding the whole of which they constitute a part, such partial disclosures could not but be attended often with mischievous consequences. 'Well, if they can't know all, let them know as much as they can. The more they know of matters the better.'

"While writing the above I have been reminded of a remark made by Mr. Gallatin, at the beginning of General Jackson's administration. Speaking of Jefferson, he said that Jefferson's name had a power with the people—with the honest, unsophisticated masses—that no other name ever possessed—ever approached to. And it was because no man could come in contact with him—no man could really know him, without being penetrated with the truth that he was the sincerest and earnestest democrat living; the firmest and most unwavering in the democratic faith—in his confidence in the reliability of the people. 'This man,' added Gallatin, pointing toward the White House, 'has a popularity of the same sort. It seems to be no less strong than that of Jefferson, but he is the only one that can at all compare with Jefferson in this respect."

"(Observe that this was said at the very beginning of Jackson's administration, and before his hold upon the confidence of the people had been put to a single one of the many severe tests which the future had in store for it, and which proved the accuracy of Gallatin's insight into its nature.)

"In the treatment of the wounds received by Jackson in his encounter with the Bentons, a slug or fragment of ball was overlooked, which for years afterwards proved, on many occasions, the cause of an inflammation that threatened serious consequences. One of these occurred at Washington during the General's service in the Senate, and, in this instance, the alarm of his friends was greater than ever before. It was, also, far more extensively communicated, corresponding, in this respect, to the importance which his *life* had acquired, and the value now attaching to it under the party aspect. From these causes, the anxiety about it rose to the pitch of a wide spread consternation, and this had for its fruit an appeal to Mrs. Jackson, in the hope that through her influence the General might be prevailed upon to call in another physician. The case was in the hands of Dr. Sims, an old friend, who was always the family doctor when Jackson was at Washington. Mrs. Jackson having become thoroughly enlisted in the cause, the General's most intimate friends, knowing the tenderness of his devotion to her, and his invariable deference to her wishes, counted upon the result as certain. The entreaty was made by her, and to the amazement of all, it proved a failure. All she had to report to the confederates was an entreaty from him. He had replied to hers, "Dr. Sims is my friend—an old and valued friend. His professional reputation, his standing as a physician, his feelings as a man, as a friend, are all at stake in this matter. My dear, the thing is impossible; it can not be. *He* shall cure me, or he shall kill me. I entreat you never to speak to me again upon the subject.'

"At a very early period of General Jackson's presidential service, and while he was still 'green in office,' I was with him one day on State Department business, and upon getting through with this, he said to me, 'Here is a paper which has been sent up from your department for my approval, with Mr. Brent's signature as Acting Secretary.' I replied with a smile (the smile of superior knowledge respecting official details, which *he* was not to be presumed to be acquainted with), 'He *is* Acting Secretary, the Secretary of State being absent from the city.' I had not been long in the department, but long enough to have become imbued with this belief, which prevailed there, and was habitually practiced upon. Its correctness *I* had 'taken for granted.' Not so the General. 'If you will look into the law, sir, you will see that the chief clerk is *ex officio* Acting Secretary, only in case of vacancy in the office, and not merely from the Secretary's being absent. Please inform Mr. Brent of this, and that he must be appointed Acting Secretary before he can validly act as such, under present circumstances.' Observe that Mr. Brent was an old gentleman (and a most estimable old gentleman he was) who had grown gray in the office then held by him.

"At a later period, Col. Aspinwall, our Consul at London, having sent in his account for certain expenses incurred by him for the defense of some American sailors who had been tried there on the charge of piracy, and this account being supported by proper vouchers, and there being no doubt of its correctness, the proper paper was sent up from the department for the General's signature—the President's approval of the disbursement being requisite in all cases of expenditure of the fund to which this one would be chargeable, if approved. Col. Aspinwall was held in great respect by General Jackson, to which he was richly entitled on every score, independently of the strong title to the General's favor of his having but one arm, in consequence of the other's having been left on the battle field in the war with England; in addition to all which he was known to be poor, with a family to be supported out of his very small salary. It could not, therefore, but be decidedly painful to the General to withhold from the Colonel any thing to which he was honestly entitled; and the honesty of this claim was a matter which, independently of the vouchers, the Colonel's character placed above doubt. Nevertheless, it was withheld, though, I believe, ultimately paid. Trivial as the amount was, instead of signing his name under 'approved,' without understanding the matter, (as some years afterward, in a memorable case relating to the same fund, and for an amount not trivial, happened to a President who had passed his life in all sorts of 'civil' employments), the General determined that *he* must thoroughly understand the matter before the requisite approval could be given. It was sent back to the department, with instructions to write to Col. Aspinwall, asking for explanations that would make the case fully understood. *Piracy*, he said, being a crime which necessarily denationalizes a man, inasmuch as it subjects him to the jurisdiction of any and every government, he doubted whether persons under indictment and trial for this crime, by the tribunals of a foreign State, could be regarded as retaining their national character, and consequently whether any expenditure on their behalf was lawful and proper.

"These two instances afford a correct idea of what the 'military chieftain' habitually was as respects those matters of official routine, about which the impression so generally prevailed that he could not but be altogether incompetent, and entirely dependent upon his subordinates.

"On one occasion, upon my going into the President's office (this was in the earlier part of nullification times), Major Donelson addressed a remark to me which led to a conversation about the nullification theory, and the Virginia State-rights doctrine of 1798, with which that theory claimed to be identical—my object in the conversation being to explain the Virginia doctrine, and show the absurdity of this pretension. I spoke in an under tone, that I might not disturb the General's cogitations, as he sat smoking his pipe, facing the fire-place, several yards distant from the

Major and myself. The dinner bell rang, and the General, taking my arm as we descended the stairs, said, 'Trist, beware of your metaphysics.' Until now, I supposed that he had not heard a word of what we had been saying. I replied, 'My metaphysics, as you call them, General, have been my salvation in this case. But for them, I should inevitably have been a nullifier, as several of my friends have become; for they have enabled me to see into the fallaciousness of the reasoning by which it is pretended to identify nullification with the Virginia doctrine. Had I not seen into this, I must inevitably have been a nullifier; for, to my mind, our doctrine is founded on reasoning which is unanswerable. It is the true theory of the constitution, and the only thing that can preserve us against consolidation.' 'No doubt of that,' said he, 'but still, I say, beware of your metaphysics; there is no telling where they may lead and land you. Hair-splitting is dangerous business.'"

I am tempted to draw once more upon Mr. Trist's portfolio, although the narrative which tempts me does not relate to General Jackson's White House life. The story, however, was often told *in* the White House. It is incomparably the best illustration of General Jackson's force of character and strength of purpose that has ever seen the light of publication. Mr. Trist heard it related by Mr. Enoch Parsons, one of General Jackson's oldest Tennessee friends. He was so struck with the story that he induced Mr. Parsons to write it out, and from the original manuscript I transcribe it here. Mr. Parsons was a member of the legislature of Tennessee when the news reached that State of the dread massacre at Fort Mims, and General Jackson lay helpless in bed, slowly recovering from the wounds he had received in the affray with the Bentons:

"I arrived at Nashville," wrote Mr. Parsons, "on the Saturday before the third Monday in September, 1813. I found in the public square a very large crowd of people, and many fine speeches were making to the people, and the talking part of a war was never better performed. I was invited out to the place where the orators were holding forth, and invited to address the people. I declined the distinction; the talking ended; and resolutions were adopted, the substance of which was that the enlightened legislature would convene on the next Monday, and they would prepare for the emergency.

"The legislature was composed of twenty senators and forty representatives, some of them old, infirm men. As soon as the Houses were organized, at my table I wrote a bill, and introduced it, to call out 3,500 men, under the General entitled to command, and place them in the Indian nation, so that they might preserve the Mississippi territory from destruction, and prevent the friendly Indians from taking the enemy's side, and to render service to the United States until the United States could provide a force. The bill pledged all the revenue of the State for one hundred years to pay the expense, and authorized the Governor to borrow money from any source he could, and at the lowest rate he could, to defray the expenses of the campaign. The Secretary of State, William G. Blount, Major John Russell, a senator, and myself signed or endorsed the Governor's note for twenty thousand dollars, and the old patriotic State Bank lent the money which the note called for.

"At this time General Jackson was lying, as he had been between ten and twenty days, with the wounds received in the battle with the Bentons and others, and had not been out of his room, if out of his bed. The constitution of the State would not allow the bill to become a law until it had passed in each house three times on different days. The bill was, therefore, passed in each house on Monday, and lay in the Senate for Tuesday.

"After the adjournment of the Houses on Monday, as I passed out of the Senate chamber, I was accosted by a gentleman, and presented with General Jackson's compliments and a request that I should see him forthwith. I had not been to his room since my arrival. I complied with his request, and found he was minutely informed of the contents of the bill I had introduced, and wished to know if it would pass, and said that the news of the introduction of the bill had spread all over the city, and that it was called the War Bill or Parsons' Bill. I assured the General it would pass, and on Wednesday would be a law, and I mentioned that I regretted very much that the General entitled to command, and who all would desire should command the forces of the State, was not in a condition to take the field. To which General Jackson replied:

"'The devil in hell, he is not.'

"He gritted his teeth with anguish as he uttered these words, and groaned when he ceased to speak. I told him that I hoped I was mistaken, but that I did not believe he could just then take the field. After some time I left the General. Two hours after, I received fifty or more copies of his orders, which had been made out and printed in the mean time, and ordered the troops to rendezvous at Fayetteville, eighty miles on the way, on Thursday. At the bottom of the order was a note, stating that the health of the commanding general was *restored.*

"That evening or the next day, I saw Dr. May, General Jackson's principal physician, and inquired of him if he thought General Jackson could possibly march, Dr. May said that no other man could, and that it was uncertain whether, with his spunk and energy, *he* could; but that it was entirely uncertain what General Jackson could do in such circumstances.

"I felt much anxiety for the country and for the General; and when the General started, which was, I think, on the day before the law passed, Dr. May went with him and returned in three or four days. I called on Dr. May, upon his return, and enquired, how the General had got along. Whereupon the Doctor stated, that they had *to stop the General frequently, and wash him from head to foot in solutions of sugar of lead to keep down inflammation;* and that he was better, and he and his troops had gone on! The legislature then prefixed a supplemental bill to suspend all actions in which the volunteers were concerned in the courts until their return. These statutes may be seen by looking into the laws of Tennessee of 1813, and which I conceive were the right kind of laws. The troops were taken into the service of the United States, and with them General Jackson fought the first three Indian battles."

There, reader, you have ANDREW JACKSON—his real secret, the explanation of his character, of his success, of his celebrity. If any one inquires of you what manner of man Andrew Jackson was, answer him by telling Mr. Parsons' story.

Mr. Trist informs me, that, during his residence in the White House, he frequently saw the President exhibit the same utter defiance of bodily anguish. He would transact business with calmness and precision, when he was suffering the acutest pain, and when he was so pitiably feeble that signing his name threw him into a perspiration. He could not be kept from work; nor was it of any benefit to him if he did abstain; for, says Mr. Trist, if he did not work with his hands, he wore himself out with thinking.

Mr. John Van Buren, who was a very young man during General Jackson's administration, has only agreeable recollections of the President. All dependents and inferiors, he remarks, loved him—boys, clerks, women, and servants, as well as horses and dogs. "He was an open-air man," who had no secrets and locked nothing up. "While the fight lasted there was no tiring him out;" when the feud was at an end, he would not permit the most distant reference to it in his presence. The tie between General Jackson and his successor was one of the sincerest mutual affection and respect; each finding in the other admirable qualities wanting in himself. In the White House, as everywhere, General Jackson was the MASTER—every one's master. He could be influenced, advised and persuaded; but there were times when no man could move him a hair's breadth, when every man had to yield to his will, or stand aside.

Upon no one did General Jackson make an impression so deep or so lasting as upon Mr. Francis P. Blair, the editor of the *Globe.* A man naturally thinks well of one to whom he owes deliverance, fortune, power, and fame. But twenty years have passed since Mr. Blair ceased to be the recipient of benefits conferred through General Jackson. He has had leisure to reflect upon the scenes through which he passed during the General's administration. And if gratitude blinds our eyes to the faults of a friend, it may also be most truly said, that no man can rightly judge another who does not in some degree sympathize with him. The judgments dictated or biased by hatred, or by antipathy, are false necessarily. Love is the enlightener of the human soul. Its judgments are the only ones that approach correctness; for the good in a man is the *man;* the bad in him is temporary, accidental, and occasional. At least, I like to think so.

Mr. Blair's opinion of General Jackson—as expressed in conversation—I confess, fills me with astonishment. He deliberately concurs in Colbert's judgment, that Andrew Jackson was the greatest man that ever lived. The bravest of the brave; the wisest of the wise; the most tender, the most resolute, the most discreet, and the most eloquent of human beings. Fighting men loved him for his valor, and cowards loved him for the protection he gave them. No man, and no combination of men, could ever overcome him; he was victorious on every field. Clay, Webster, Calhoun, Preston, Biddle, the bank, the capitalists—the brightest men and the most powerful agencies—were leagued against him for eight years, without gaining over him one important advantage. He attempted nothing which he did not accomplish, (*except* compelling the ladies of Washington to associate with Mrs. Eaton). He gained constantly in Congress, and left his party in a majority in both Houses. His eloquence surpassed that of the most renowned orators. When he grew warm in conversation, and his gray bristles shook, he thrilled the listeners' nerves and souls, as no other man could thrill them. No man could resist the impetuous intensity of his speech. He was a man of absolute sincerity, incapable of guile, or artifice, or acting for effect. He loved the people with a deep, exhaustless love; believed in them; would have laid down his hoary head on the block for them, and counted it gain and glory. He was the controlling soul of his administration at every moment of its existence. He was the animating spirit of the *Globe* newspaper, the author of the best editorial suggestions, the inspirer of its most successful articles. He transferred the mantle of power to Mr. Van Buren for reasons that were wise and patriotic; because he knew that, of all the public men then living, Martin Van Buren was the most certain to adhere to the simple policy marked out by Jefferson, and to continue the war against monopolies and a loose construction of the constitution. Mr. Van Buren was no intriguer. It was the terror of his public life to be thought one. When the *Globe* was in the plentitude of its power, when politicians trembled at its frown, and stood cap in hand before it, Mr. Van Buren, neither by word nor manner nor management, ever made the slightest attempt to conciliate its favor. He never made one suggestion respecting its course or its contents. His demeanor to the editor, in their daily intercourse, was the same precisely when the opposition of the *Globe* might have kept him out of the presidency, as it had been when the paper was struggling into existence without a dozen subscribers. General Jackson's choice of a successor was among the wisest of his acts.

To these opinions, sincerely held by Mr. Blair, I will add one anecdote related by him, tending to show that, dearly as General Jackson loved a horse, he loved his friend better.

Three young horses, descended from the great Truxton, were brought from the Hermitage to Washington. On a beautiful spring day they were to be tried upon a race-course near the city. Early in the morning of that day, Mr. Blair had occasion to visit the President's office, where he found Major Donelson, booted and spurred, just about to mount and ride away to the race-course to see what the young horses could do. 88

"Come with us, Blair," said Major Donelson, "it's a fine day, and you'll enjoy it."

"No," said Mr. Blair, "I can't go to day. Besides, I've no horse."

"Well, get one from a livery stable."

"Not to-day, Major."

"The President, who was in the room, busy over some papers, cried out:

"Why, Mr. Blair, take my horse. Donelson, order my horse for Mr. Blair."

The Secretary hesitated, looked confused, and at last stammered out:

"Well, Blair, come on, then."

They walked out together, and on getting to the bottom of the steps, found the General's well known horse already saddled and bridled.

"Why, the General is going himself, then!" exclaimed Mr. Blair.

"He was going," said the Major, sorrowfully, "but he won't go now."

"But let us go back and persuade him."

"It will be of no use," said Major Donelson. "He had set his heart upon seeing those colts run to-day. But he has now set his heart upon *your* going. I know him, Blair. It will only offend him if we say another word about it. He has made up his mind that you shall go, and that he will not. So, mount."

The editorship of the *Globe* and the congressional printing were important to Mr. Blair; but it was such acts as these that won his heart. He tells you calmly that General Jackson made his fortune. When he relates stories like this, his voice falters and his eyes moisten.

A lady, who was constantly at the White House during the early part of General Jackson's administration, describes the evening scene in the President's own parlor. She desires to see it painted, and suggests the subject to artists. A large parlor, scantily furnished, lighted from above by a chandelier; a bright, blazing fire in the grate; around the fire four or five ladies sewing, say Mrs. Donelson, Mrs. Andrew Jackson, Mrs. Edward Livingston, and another or two; five or six children, from two to seven years of age, playing about the room, too regardless of documents and work-baskets. At a distant end of the apartment the President, seated in an arm-chair, wearing a long, loose coat, smoking a long, reed pipe, with a red clay bowl, exhibiting the combined dignity of a patriarch, a monarch, and an Indian chief. A little behind the President, Edward Livingston, Secretary of State, reading to him, in a low tone, a dispatch from the French Minister for Foreign Affairs. The President listens intently, yet with a certain bland assurance, as though he were saying to himself, "Say you so, Monsieur? We shall see about that." The ladies glance toward him, now and then, with fond admiration expressed in their countenances. The children are too loud occasionally in their play. The President inclines his ear closer to the Secretary, and waves his pipe, absently, but with an exquisite smiling tenderness, toward the noisy group, which, Mrs. Donelson perceiving, she lifts her finger and whispers admonition.

XXIX.

CLOSE OF THE ADMINISTRATION.

MR. VAN BUREN had been elected to succeed General Jackson. The administration commanded a majority in both Houses. Mr. Polk, a strenuous and unscrupulous partisan, was speaker of the House of Representatives. The impending session of Congress was the "short" session. The opposition was disheartened, and the President's popularity was undiminished. In these circumstances it would have been reasonable to expect that the last few months of General Jackson's tenure of power would exhibit a lull in the fierce contentions which for eight years had distracted the country.

Those who indulged an expectation of that nature, if any such there were, were disappointed ; for strife, acrimony, violence, vituperation, were as much the order of the day at Washington, during this last session of Congress, as they had been during the panic session itself.

The last annual message of General Jackson, remarkable in many respects, differs in one particular from all other papers, public or private, that bear his signature. It announced that Andrew Jackson had changed his mind ! The expansion of the business of the country had become alarming. The receipts of the treasury had reached the astounding sum of nearly forty-eight millions of dollars, of which no less than twenty-four millions had accrued from the sale of the public lands ; and the balance in the treasury would amount, on the first of January, to little less than forty-two millions. It was this terrible surplus that had awakened the President's apprehensions, and caused a revision of his opinions. He was opposed to any policy which contemplated a surplus, and regretted the passage of the deposit act, to which he had given "a reluctant assent."

The distribution of the surplus among the States, he

said, had already produced effects that threatened disaster, and Congress was accordingly advised to act at once upon the principle of collecting no more revenue than the wants of the government required.

The message proceeded to justify the specie circular, to commend the working of the State-bank system, and to condemn the United States Bank of Pennsylvania for continuing in circulation the notes of the extinct United States Bank.

For the eighth time the President repeated his recommendation with regard to the election of President and Vice-President. He complimented highly the government employés, through whose "integrity and ability" he was enabled to leave the various executive departments in "a prosperous condition."

During the first week of the session, Col. Benton made known to the Senate his intention to force to a decisive vote his proposal to expunge from the journal Mr. Clay's resolution of 1834, which censured the President for removing Mr. Duane and the deposits. For nearly three years the persistent Benton had been agitating this notable scheme, and with so much effect that the legislatures of several States, New York among the number, had instructed their Senators to vote for the expunging. It was made a party measure. In vain did the opposition contend that the constitution required the Senate to KEEP a record of its proceedings. How, asked Mr. Webster, can we be said to *keep* a record, if any part of it is expunged? Col. Benton replied to all arguments by delivering eulogiums upon the character and administration of General Jackson, so fervid, so eloquent, so admirably expressed, that, to this day, whoever reads them forgets, for the moment, every thing in the public conduct of General Jackson that was not wise, noble, and heroic. In the warmth of his enthusiasm he forgot his fears of the coming crash, which he was accustomed to predict. All Europe, he said, beheld with admiration the *success* of our efforts to supply ourselves with gold and silver, the blessed currency of the constitution. Seventy-five millions of specie in the country "are the *security* of the people against the dangers of a depreciated and inconvertible paper money!" He pronounced the administration of General Jackson to be as "brilliant, beneficent, and glorious," as his military life had been "resplendent with dazzling events." "Solitary and alone," said the orator in conclusion, "and amid the jeers and taunts of my opponents, I put this ball in motion. The people have taken it up, and rolled it forward, and I am no longer any thing but a unit in the vast mass which now propels it."

Monday, the 16th of January, was the day upon which the great deed was done. Col. Benton tells us, that "expecting a protracted session, extending through the day and night, and knowing the difficulty of keeping men steady to their work and in good humor, when tired and hungry, the mover of the proceeding took care to provide, as far as possible, against such a state of things; and gave orders that night to have an ample supply of cold hams, turkeys, rounds of beef, pickles, wines, and cups of hot coffee, ready in a certain committee room near the Senate chamber by four o'clock on the afternoon of Monday."

It was a wise precaution, for the debate was protracted until midnight. After a debate of nearly thirteen consecutive hours, members of the opposition came round to Col. Benton's desk, and said: "This question has degenerated into a trial of nerves and muscles. It has become a question of physical endurance; and we see no use in wearing ourselves out to keep off for a few hours longer what has to come before we separate. We see that you are able and determined to carry your measures: so call the vote as soon as you please. We shall say no more." Mr. Webster was the last speaker, and when he sat down there was a dead silence, which was broken at last by the single word, "Question." The yeas and nays were ordered, and the resolution to expunge was carried by a vote of twenty-five to nineteen. Thereupon, the Secretary of the Senate "produced the original manuscript journal of the Senate, and opening at the page which contained the condemnatory sentence of March 28th, 1834, proceeded in open Senate to draw a square of broad black lines around the sentence, and to write across its face in strong letters these words: 'Expunged by order of the Senate, this 16th day of March, 1837.'"

At once a storm of hisses, groans and outcries burst from the crowded galleries; which were silenced only when the apparent ringleader was seized and dragged to the bar of the chamber. "The gratification of General Jackson," adds Benton, "was extreme. He gave a grand dinner to the expungers (as they were called) and their wives; and being too weak to sit at the table, he only met the company, placed the 'head-expunger' in his chair, and withdrew to his sick chamber. That expurgation! it was the 'crowning mercy' of his civil, as New Orleans had been of his military life!"

The only result of this nonsensical affair was to fix it in the memory of the American people, that, in the year 1834, the Senate of the United States passed a vote of censure upon one of the acts of President Jackson. The page of the journal which Col. Benton caused to be disfigured in the manner which he so exultingly describes will long continue to be shown to inquisitive visitors as one of the curiosities of the capitol.

Violent scenes were passing, meanwhile, at the other end of the capitol. The passage of the message in which the President paid a parting compliment to the employés of the departments, was actually made the pretext for an investigation into the conduct of the gentlemen complimented. On motion of Mr. Henry A. Wise of Virginia, the passage was referred to a special committee, who proceeded to examine witnesses, and, among others, the notorious Reuben M. Whitney. The conduct of this witness, according to the statement of Mr. Wise, was "supercilious, self-important, contumacious, and contemptuous." Many questions he refused to answer; others he would answer only in writing; to none was his reply satisfactory. "He would write his answer," said Mr. Wise, "at the table, and, then, with an impudent air of nonchalance, would fold his arms, cock up his legs against the wall, and cast glances full of defiance and expressive of contempt at me and my friend, Mr. Bailie Peyton, of Tennessee." Conduct like this led, at last, to a collision between Mr. Peyton and the witness ; of a violent but bloodless character, in which Mr. Wise bore an energetic part.

During the last month of his presidency, General Jackson came into collision again with his old enemy, Mr. Calhoun. In the course of a speech, Mr. Calhoun had remarked upon the land speculations in which almost every man in the country who had capital or credit was then engaged. A sentence or two of his speech, as reported in the *Globe*, gave the impression that the President himself was concerned in land speculations. In a long letter, of a remarkably respectful and moderate character, the President demanded a prosecution of the charge. "If you will neither do justice yourself," said he, "nor place the matter in a position where justice may be done me by the representatives of the people, I shall be compelled to resort to the only remedy left me, and before I leave the city, give publicity to this letter, by which you will stand stigmatized as one who, protected by his constitutional privilege, is ready to stab the reputation of others, without the magnanimity to do them justice."

With this letter were enclosed two notes certifying to the correctness of the *Globe's* report : one from a spectator in the gallery of the Senate chamber, and one from the short-hand writer who reported the speech.

Mr. Calhoun spared the President the necessity of giving publicity to his letter. The morning after he had received it, the Senator from South Carolina informed the Senate, that he had received from the President of the United States a communication of such a nature that he felt it his duty to cause it to be read to them, and he handed it to the clerk for that purpose. After it had been read, Mr. Calhoun proceeded to comment upon it. "It has excited in my bosom," said the Senator, "but one feeling, that of pity for the weakness of its author, contempt for his menace, and humiliation that one occupying the office which he does, should place himself in a situation so unworthy of his exalted station. Nor do I intend to invoke the interposition of the Senate to protect the privilege attached to a Senator from one of the sovereign States of this confederation, which has been outraged in my person."

Mr. Calhoun proceeded to recapitulate his previous speech, and denied that he had used the language attributed to him by the reporter. Two Senators testified to the correctness of Mr. Calhoun's recapitulation. Mr. Calhoun then concluded his remarks by observing, that he was "gratified by this testimony, and that all might now see, from these statements, and the acquiescence of other Senators, what little cause the President had for the outrage upon his privilege, and that of the Senate, and for applying language to him which is never used in intercourse between gentlemen, and better suited to the purlieus of Billingsgate than to the mansion of the Chief Magistrate."*

The President took no further notice of the affair, nor did the Senate take any action upon it.

Signs of coming revulsion in the world of business were so numerous and so palpable, during this session, that it is wonderful so few observed them. The short crops of 1836 and the paper inflation had raised the price of the necessaries of life to a point they had never reached before, and have never reached since. Flour was sold in lots, at fifteen dollars a barrel; in single barrels, at sixteen; in smaller quantities, at eighteen. The growing scarcity of money had already compelled manufacturers to dismiss many of their workmen; and, thus, at a moment, when financiers cherished the delusion that the country was prosperous beyond all previous example, large numbers of worthy mechanics and seamstresses were suffering from downright want. It was during this winter of delirium and distress, that some vile demagogue in the city of New York, promulgated from the steps of the City Hall, the lie that the high price of flour was caused by spec-

* Calhoun's Works, *Vol. III.* p. 1 to 9.

ulators, whose stores were said to be filled with flour, kept from the market in the expectation of its realizing a famine price. A mob of infuriated men, foreigners most of them, surrounded a great flour store in the lower part of the city, battered down the doors, rolled the barrels into the street, and destroyed or carried off their contents. For two or three days the city was kept in groundless terror of a general uprising of the distressed workingmen, and a general spoliation of the provision stores.

Business men were gasping all the winter for breath, but scarcely a man of them believed that the pressure was any thing but temporary and accidental. After a day of extraordinary stringency, the newspapers, in one chorus, would declare that then the worst was over; the bottom had been touched; relief was at hand. Col. Benton, who had so extolled the state of the currency in January, tells us that, in February, he knew that the grand crash was both inevitable and near. "It was in the month of February," says he, "that I invited the president-elect into a committee room, and stated to him my opinion that we were on the eve of an explosion of the paper system and of a general suspension of the banks—intending to follow up that expression of opinion with the exposition of my reasons for thinking so; but the interview came to a sudden and unexpected termination. Hardly had I expressed my belief of this impending catastrophe than he spoke up and said, 'Your friends think you a little exalted in the head on that subject.' I said no more. I was miffed. We left the room together, talking on different matters, and I saying to myself, '*You will soon feel the thunderbolt.*'"

The last public act of President Jackson, done as the last hour of the third of March was expiring, illustrates his firmness, his audacity, and his tact.

The specie circular of July, 1836, was the ruling topic of debate in both Houses during the greater part of the session. It revived, as might have been foreseen, all the currency and bank questions which for so many years had stirred the passions of both political parties. Presuming that the reader has had enough of these heated and fruitless discussions, I will only state that, after a long and acrimonious debate, the specie circular was rescinded by great majorities. Mr. Calhoun refused to vote upon the rescinding bill, though he was in favor of it. The currency, he declared, was in a state of disorder so inextricable that nothing short of the crash and ruin which he felt to be impending could render its rectification possible.

But the specie circular was more than rescinded. The rescinding bill contained various provisions, the effect of which was *to render bank notes, under certain restrictions, a legal tender.* There is reason to believe that the astonishing majorities which passed this measure were largely composed of members who were themselves deeply involved in the very speculations which the specie circular was designed to prevent. General Jackson, as I learn from one of his letters to Mr. Trist, was puzzled and amazed at the conduct of his friends on this occasion :

GENERAL JACKSON TO NICHOLAS P. TRIST.

"WASHINGTON, March 2d, 1837.

"MY DEAR MR. TRIST : Your letter of Friday evening, Nov. 4th, 1836, found me confined to my room, indeed, I might say to my bed, and I have been only four times down stairs since the 15th of November last, although I have been obliged to labor incessantly, and now within one day of the close of the session engaged in preparing another veto message to a bill from the Senate, and, I may add, fostered by some of my friends and all the opposition, which, I trust, will be my excuse for not answering your letter sooner. I have often heard from you and your amiable family, was happy to learn you were all enjoying good health, and may that greatest of all blessings, good health, continue with you all until the end of long life, and then a happy immortality.

"The papers will give you the proceedings of Congress. I here inclose you the proof-sheets of my farewell address to my fellow-citizens of these United States. There will be some verbal amendments in the phraseology, but none in the substance or principle.

"As I will always be happy to hear from you, and as I will leave here on the 6th, I will be happy to receive a letter from you at the Hermitage, and when you visit the United States, I will be happy to see you and your family there, where I promise you a hearty welcome.

"To-morrow ends my official career for ever. On the 4th, I hope to be able to go to the capitol to witness the glorious scene of Mr. Van Buren—once rejected by the Senate—sworn into office by Chief Justice Taney, also being rejected by the factious Senate. This shows the power of public opinion, and thus, unless corrupted by a paper, banking, and gambling system, of which, from the symptoms displayed in the Senate, I have some fear, our republic will for ever endure.

"I am free to declare that the votes of some of our friends in the Senate, are perfectly unaccountable to me on this paper system. Good professed State-rights men, and professed hard money men—the constitutional currency—still they vote to pass a bill to make bank bills part of our currency.

"But I must close. I am too weak to copy this if I had time. With my kind salutations to you, and to all your family, I remain your friend,

"ANDREW JACKSON.

"N. P. TRIST, Esq., Consul, Havana."

The General, in this letter, speaks of vetoing the bill. He changed his intention, however, as the bill could have been passed over his veto. He killed the measure by not acting upon it. The following is the last paper to which General Jackson affixed his signature as President of the United States:

"REASONS OF PRESIDENT JACKSON FOR NOT ACTING DEFINITELY ON THE BILL ENTITLED 'AN ACT DESIGNATING AND LIMITING THE FUNDS RECEIVABLE FOR THE REVENUES OF THE UNITED STATES.'

"The bill from the Senate, entitled 'An act designating and limiting the funds receivable for the revenues of the United States,' came to my hands yesterday, at 2 o'clock, P. M. On perusing it, I found its provisions so complex and uncertain that I deemed it necessary to obtain the opinion of the Attorney General of the United States on several important questions touching its construction and effect, before I could decide on the disposition to be made of it. The Attorney General took up the subject immediately, and his reply was reported to me this day, at five o'clock, P. M. As this officer, after a careful and laborious examination of the bill, and a distinct expression of his opinion on the points proposed to him, still came to the conclusion that the construction of the bill, should it become a law, would be yet a subject of much perplexity and doubt (a view of the bill entirely coincident with my own), and as I can not think it proper, in a matter of such interest and of such constant application, to approve a bill so liable to diversity of interpretations, and more especially as I have not had time, amid the duties constantly pressing upon me, to give the subject that deliberate consideration which its importance demands, I am constrained to retain the bill, without acting definitely thereon; and to the end that my reasons for this step may be fully understood, I shall cause this paper, with the opinion of the Attorney General, and the bill in question, to be deposited in the Department of State."

"ANDREW JACKSON.

"WASHINGTON, March 3, 1837—one quarter before twelve, P. M."

To the last day of his residence in the presidential mansion, General Jackson continued to receive proofs that he was still the idol of the people. The eloquence of the opposition had not availed to lessen his general popularity in the least degree. We read of one enthusiastic Jacksonian conveying to Washington, from New York, with banners and bands of music, a prodigious cheese, as a present to the retiring chief. The cheese was four feet in diameter, two feet thick, and weighed fourteen hundred pounds—twice as large, said the *Globe*, as the great cheese given to Mr. Jefferson on a similar occasion. The President, after giving away large masses of his cheese to his friends, found that he had still more cheese than he could consume. At his last public reception he caused a piece of the cheese to be presented to all who chose to receive one, an operation that filled the White House with an odor that is pleasant only when there is not too much of it. Another ardent lover of the President gave him a light wagon composed entirely of hickory sticks, with the bark upon them. Another presented an elegant phaeton, made of the wood of the old frigate Constitution. The hickory wagon the General left in Washington, as a memento to his successor. The constitutional phaeton he took with him to the Hermitage, where I saw it, faded and dilapidated, in 1858.

The farewell address of the retiring President was little more than a resumé of the doctrines of his eight annual messages. The priceless value of the Union; the danger to it of sectional agitation; the evils of a splendid and powerful government; the safety and advantages of plain and inexpensive institutions; the perils of a surplus revenue; the injustice of a high tariff; the unconstitutionality of that system of internal improvements which the Maysville veto had checked; the curse of paper money; the extreme desirableness of a currency of gold and silver, were the leading topics upon which the President descanted. "My own race," said he, "is nearly run; advanced age and failing health warn me that before long I must pass beyond the reach of human events, and cease to feel the vicissitudes of human affairs. I thank God that my life has been spent in a land of liberty, and that he has given me a heart to love my country with the affection of a son. And filled with gratitude for your constant and unwavering kindness, I bid you a last and affectionate farewell."

This farewell address provoked from the opposition a comparison with another document bearing the same title. It was presumption, they said, in the President to suppose that there was any thing in his character, or in his relation to the people, which justified an imitation of a paper that ought to remain for ever unique. The *New York American* concluded its comments upon the address with these words: "Happily it is the last humbug which the mischievous popularity of this illiterate, violent, vain, and iron-willed soldier can impose upon a confiding and credulous people."

As an instructive contrast to this bitter sentence, consider the following lines, written about the same time, by John Lawson, an inhabitant of the same city, and upon the same subject:

"ANDREW JACKSON.

Come, stand the nearest to thy country's sire,
  Thou fearless man of uncorrupted heart,
  Well worthy undivided praise thou art,
And 'twill be thine when slumbers party ire.
Raised by the voice of freemen to a height
  Sublimer far than kings by birth may claim,
Thy stern, unselfish spirit dared the right,

And battled 'gainst the wrong. Thy holiest aim
Was freedom in the largest sense, despite
Misconstrued motives and unmeasured blame.
Above deceit, in purpose firm and pure,
Just to opposers and to friends sincere,
Thy worth shall with thy country's name endure,
And greener grow thy fame through every coming year."

The sun shone brilliantly on the fourth of March, the day of Mr. Van Buren's inauguration. The scene at the Capitol, to which the General had fondly looked forward for many a day, was described at the time by Mr. N. P. Willis with his own felicity:

"The republican procession, consisting of the Presidents and their families, escorted by a small volunteer corps, arrived soon after twelve. The General and Mr. Van Buren were in the 'constitution phaeton,' drawn by four grays, and as it entered the gate, they both rode uncovered. Descending from the carriage at the foot of the steps, a passage was made for them through the dense crowd, and the tall white head of the old Chieftain, still uncovered, went steadily up through the agitated mass, marked by its peculiarity from all around it. . . . . The crowd of diplomatists and senators in the rear of the columns made way, and the ex-President and Mr. Van Buren advanced with uncovered heads. A murmur of feeling rose up from the moving mass below, and the infirm old man, emerged from a sick-chamber, which his physician had thought it impossible he should leave, bowed to the people, and, still uncovered in the cold air, took his seat beneath the portico. Mr. Van Buren then advanced, and with a voice remarkably distinct, and with great dignity, read his address to the people. The air was elastic, and the day still; and it is supposed that near twenty thousand persons heard him from his elevated position distinctly. I stood myself on the outer limit of the crowd, and though I lost occasionally a sentence from the interruption near by, his words came clearly articulated to my ear."

In his inaugural address Mr. Van Buren alluded to his predecessor in becoming terms. "In receiving from the people," he said, "the sacred trust twice confided to my illustrious predecessor, and which he has discharged so faithfully and so well, I know that I can not expect to perform the arduous task with equal ability and success. But, united as I have been in his counsels, a daily witness of his exclusive and unsurpassed devotion to his country's welfare, agreeing with him in sentiments which his countrymen have warmly supported, and permitted to partake largely of his confidence, I may hope that somewhat of the same cheering approbation will be found to attend upon my path. For him, I but express with my own, the wishes of all—that he may yet long live to enjoy the brilliant evening of his well-spent life."

General Jackson began his homeward journey on the third day after Mr. Van Buren's inauguration. "I saw," says Benton, "the patriot ex-President in the car which bore him off to his desired seclusion. I saw him depart with that look of quiet enjoyment which bespoke the inward satisfaction of the soul at exchanging the cares of office for the repose of home."

NOTES

[1] Page 1, line 2: Jackson's inauguration: March 4, 1829.

[2] Page 1, line 7: Adams' administration: John Quincy Adams (1767–1848) was the sixth President of the United States and served from 1825 to 1829.

[3] Page 2, line 9, Chief Justice: John Marshall (1755–1835), Chief Justice of the United States from 1801 to 1835.

[4] Page 2, line 16, Mr. Webster: Daniel Webster (1782–1852), U.S. Representative from Massachusetts, 1823–1827, and U.S. Senator, 1827–1841.

[5] Page 2, line 23, Judge Story: Joseph Story (1779–1845), associate justice of the United States Supreme Court from 1811 to 1845.

[6] Page 3, lines 15 and 16, strict constructionist party: Partisans of this party were sometimes called the Old Republicans or Radicals and were led by Senator Martin Van Buren of New York. They supported William H. Crawford of Georgia for the presidency in 1824 but switched to Jackson in the election of 1828. They preached a states' rights philosophy, opposing a strong central government, protective tariffs and internal improvements, at the same time advocating economy in budgeting national expenditures and a narrow interpretation of the U.S. Constitution.

[7] Page 3, line 23, Henry Lee: Lee (1787–1837) was an important publicist during the presidential campaign of 1828. He helped Jackson write the inaugural address and was named counsel to Algiers, but the Senate refused to confirm his nomination.

[8] Page 4, line 18, Mr. McLean: John McLean (1785–1861) was the Postmaster General in the administrations of James Monroe and John Quincy Adams. He was continued in that position by Jackson until his appointment to the U.S. Supreme Court in 1829.

[9] Page 4, line 27, Mr. Clay: Henry Clay (1777–1852) served as Secretary of State during the administration of John Quincy Adams. He was elected to the U.S. Senate from Kentucky in 1831.

[10] Page 6, line 8, Mr. Wirt: William Wirt (1772–1834), Attorney General during the administrations of James Monroe and John Quincy Adams.

[11] Page 6, line 17, editor of the *Telegraph:* Duff Green (1791–1875) was the editor of the *Telegraph.* It was a Washington newspaper and the mouthpiece of the Democratic party until the founding of the Washington *Globe.*

[12] Page 6, line 23, Van Buren: Martin Van Buren (1782–1862), U.S. Senator from New York (1821–1828), and elected Governor of that state in November, 1828.

[13] Page 7, line 25, Kremer: George Kremer (1775–1854), U.S. Representative from Pennsylvania, 1823–1829.

[14] Page 7, line 28, corrupt understanding: The charge of a "corrupt bargain" involved an alleged deal in which Adams promised Clay the position of Secretary of State if Clay would get him enough votes to win the House election for President in 1825.

[15] Page 7, line 33, Mr. Calhoun: John C. Calhoun (1782–1850) of South Carolina served as Vice President during the administration of John Quincy Adams and during the first administration of Andrew Jackson, 1825–1833.

[16] Page 8, line 8, White: Hugh Lawson White (1773–1840), U.S. District Attorney and state judge in Tennessee before winning appointment to the U.S. Senate in 1825 to replace Jackson who had resigned. White served in the Senate until 1840.

[17] Page 8, line 29, Major Lewis: William B. Lewis (1784–1866), Jackson's close friend and confidant, a Tennessean and the brother-in-law of John H. Eaton, another close adviser of Jackson's.

[18] Page 9, lines 23–24, Governor McMinn: Joseph McMinn (1758–1824), Governor of Tennessee, 1815–1821.

[19] Page 10, line 19, Nassau Hall: Princeton.

[20] Page 10, line 36, General Harrison: William Henry Harrison (1773–1841) won the famous battle of Tippecanoe over the Shawnee Indians. He also recaptured Detroit from the British during the War of 1812.

[21] Page 12, line 30, brother-in-law of Major Eaton: The wives of Eaton and Lewis were sisters.

[22] Page 15, line 16, Major Donelson: Andrew Jackson Donelson (1799–1871), Jackson's nephew and private secretary.

[23] Page 15, line 18, General Call: Richard Keith Call (1791–1862) served in the War of 1812, practiced law in Pensacola and in 1823 was sent to Congress as the delegate from the Florida Territory.

[24] Page 40, line 25, Colonel McKenney: Thomas L. McKenney (1785–1859) served as Chief of the Bureau of Indian Affairs until his removal by Jackson. His *Memoirs* describe his travels among the northern and southern Indian tribes.

[25] Page 41, line 34, Col. Benton: Thomas Hart Benton (1782–1858) moved from Tennessee to Missouri after a gunfight with Jackson. He was elected U.S. Senator from Missouri in 1821 and served in that capacity until 1851, after which he wrote his autobiographical *Thirty Years' View*. Benton and Jackson reconciled their differences in 1824.

[26] Page 42, line 19, Seminole war: A war waged by Jackson against the Seminole Indians in 1818 which necessitated his invasion into Spanish-held Florida. The invasion eventually led to the annexation of Florida.

[27] Page 43, line 22, Col. Hamilton: James A. Hamilton (1788–1878), the son of Alexander Hamilton.

[28] Page 48, line 7, *"coffin hand bills"*: Hand bills distributed during the presidential election of 1828 showing six black coffins over which were listed the names of American militiamen Jackson allegedly executed during the war against the Creek Indians.

[29] Page 52, line 20, Governor Marcy: William Learned Marcy (1786–1857), comptroller and judge in New York before his election to the U.S. Senate in 1831. He served as Governor of New York, 1833–1839.

[30] Page 59, line 5 from the bottom, buck-tails: Bucktails was that faction of the New York Republican party supporting Van Buren. They received their name because the sachems of Tammany Hall invariably attended party meetings with a buck's tail stuck in their hats.

[31] Page 59, line 2 from the bottom, Albany Regency: The Albany Regency was a governing council set up in Albany, New York, by Martin Van Buren to run the party and state in his absence. Among others, it consisted of such distinguished men as William L. Marcy, Silas Wright, Jr., Benjamin F. Butler, Azariah C. Flagg and Edwin Croswell.

[32] Page 61, line 26, Governor Clinton: De Witt Clinton (1769–1828), Governor of New York, 1817–1821 and 1825–1828. He and Van Buren were political rivals.

[33] Page 88, line 11 from the bottom, federalists: The Federalist party emerged during the presidency of George Washington and supported the fiscal policies of Washington's Secretary of the Treasury, Alexander Hamilton. It gradually disappeared from national politics following the Hartford Convention of 1814, although it hung on for years in several northern states.

[34] Page 91, lines 2–3, Mr. Bancroft: George Bancroft (1800–1891) wrote a ten-volume *History of the United States,* published from 1834 to 1874. His usefulness as a writer for the Democratic cause helped win him an appointment as collector of the port of Boston in 1837.

[35] Page 108, line 26, Major Noah: Mordecai Manuel Noah (1785–1851), editor of the New York *Courier and Enquirer,* was appointed surveyor of the port of New York in 1829.

[36] Page 110, line 14 from the bottom, Chancellor Kent: James Kent (1763–1847) presided over the New York Court of Chancery, 1814–1823, after which he wrote his famed *Commentaries on the American Law.*

[37] Page 110, line 8 from the bottom, Mr. McDuffie: George McDuffie (1790–1851) U.S. Representative from South Carolina, 1821–1834, Governor of South Carolina 1834–1836, and U.S. Senator 1842–1846.

[38] Page 110, line 5 from the bottom, Mr. Potter: Robert Potter (c. 1800–1841) U.S. Representative from North Carolina 1829–1831; he later moved to Texas where he fought for Texas independence.

[39] Page 113, line 1, Mr. Hayne: Robert Y. Hayne (1791–1839) U.S. Senator from South Carolina 1823–1832, later Governor of South Carolina 1832–1834.

[40] Page 114, lines 12–13, his old aide-de-camp and Inspector-General: General Arthur P. Hayne (1790–1867), Jackson's aid during the Creek War and Robert Y. Hayne's older brother.

[41] Page 124, line 2 from bottom, Judge Overton: John Overton (1766–1833), judge of the Tennessee superior court, 1804–1810, and judge of the Tennessee supreme court 1811–1816. He was one of Jackson's oldest friends. With Eaton and Lewis he was an important promoter of Jackson's presidential candidacy.

[42] Page 129, line 10 from bottom, Col. L. C. Stanbaugh: Colonel Stanbaugh, a leader of the Pennsylvania state legislature.

[43] Page 130, line 6 from bottom, Commodore Porter: David Porter (1780–1843), an American naval officer appointed in 1831 *chargé d'affaires* and later minister in Constantinople, where he served until his death.

[44] Page 135, lines 19–20, Colonel R. M. Johnson: Richard M. Johnson (1781–1850) served in the U.S. Senate 1819–1829 and in the House 1829–1837. He was elected Vice President in a Senate election in 1837.

[45] Page 143, line 25, General Scott: Winfield Scott (1786–1866) began a long and distinguished military career with the War of 1812.

[46] Page 146, line 7, Speaker: Henry Clay.

[47] Page 149, line 6, Weatherford: William Weatherford (c. 1780–1824), chief of the Creek Indians and sometimes called Chief Red Eagle, was seven-eighths white.

[48] Page 149, line 30, Mr. Cobb: Thomas W. Cobb (1784–1830), U.S. Representative from Georgia 1817–1821, 1823–1824 and as U.S. Senator 1824–1828.

[49] Page 150, line 18, physical prostration: Crawford suffered a severe stroke in 1823 after which he retired from politics. He was appointed judge of the circuit court in 1827, where he served until his death in 1834.

[50] Page 152, lines 3–4, Governor Forsyth: John Forsyth (1780–1841) Governor of Georgia 1827–1829, U.S. Senator 1829–1834 and was appointed Secretary of State by Jackson in 1834.

[51] Page 153, lines 30–31, General Hamilton: James Hamilton, Jr. (1786–1857), U.S. Representative from South Carolina 1822–1829, and Governor of that state during the nullification crisis.

[52] Page 163, line 12 from the bottom, Arbuthnot and Ambrister: Alexander Arbuthnot and Robert Ambrister were two British subjects executed by Jackson for aiding the Indians during his Seminole campaign in Florida.

[53] Page 172, line 8, Mr. McLane: Louis McLane (1786–1857), U.S. Representative and Senator from Delaware, U.S. minister to England 1829–1831, after which he became Secretary of the Treasury in Jackson's cabinet.

[54] Page 193, line 8 from bottom, Mr. Tazewell: Littleton W. Taze-

well (1774–1860), U.S. Senator from Virginia 1824–1832, and Governor of the state, 1834–1836.

[55] Page 194, lines 20–21, Mr. J. K. Polk, General Coffee etc: James Knox Polk, General John Coffee, Felix Grundy, John Catron, General Robert Armstrong.

[56] Page 201, line 9 from the bottom, anti-Masonry: Masons were accused of kidnapping and murdering one William Morgan of Batavia, New York. Violence against Masons broke out in New York in 1826 and quickly spread into Pennsylvania and New England.

[57] Page 214, line 18 from bottom, N. Green: Nathaniel Greene, editor of the Boston *Statesman* and a staunch advocate of Jackson's election in 1828.

[58] Page 214, line 10 from the bottom, Mr. Barbour: Philip Barbour (1783–1841), U.S. Representative from Virginia 1827–1830, appointed by Jackson an associate justice of the U.S. Supreme Court in 1836.

[59] Page 214, line 9 from the bottom, Dickinson: Mahlon Dickerson (1770–1853), U.S. Senator from New Jersey 1817–1833, appointed Secretary of the Navy by Jackson in 1834.

[60] Page 217, line 16, Horseshoe Bend of the Tallapoosa: Site of Jackson's victory over the Creek Indians in 1814. Sam Houston distinguished himself during the battle.

[61] Page 221, line 17 from bottom, Senator Buckner of Missouri: Alexander Buckner (1785–1833), U.S. Senator 1831–1833.

[62] Page 230, line 14 from bottom, Mr. Clayton: Augustin S. Clayton (1783–1839), U.S. Representative from Georgia 1832–1835.

[63] Page 254, lines 1–2, Judge Brooke: Francis Brooke (1763–1851) elected judge of the supreme court of appeals of Virginia (not Maryland as stated by Parton) in 1811, serving until his death. He was a close friend of Henry Clay, with whom he frequently corresponded.

[64] Page 274, line 7 from bottom, Col. Crockett: Davy Crockett (1786–1836), U.S. Representative from Tennessee 1827–1831, 1833–1835, and a political opponent of Jackson.

[65] Page 288, line 5, Mr. Carey: Mathew Carey (1760–1839), an American publicist and economist, was a strong advocate of protective tariffs.

[66] Page 312, line 10, Mr. Bibb: George M. Bibb (1776–1859), U.S. Senator from Kentucky 1829–1835.

[67] Page 313, line 6, Mr. Letcher: Robert P. Letcher (1788–1861), U.S. Representative from Kentucky 1823–1833, 1834–1835.

[68] Page 319, line 5, Mr. Randolph: Robert B. Randolph.

[69] Page 320, line 21, Mr. Earl: Ralph E. W. Earl (d. 1838), a close friend of Rachel and Andrew Jackson. He painted several portraits of the General and was known as the "court painter." He became Jackson's constant traveling companion and lived at the Hermitage.

[70] Page 321, line 2 from bottom, Major Jack Downing: Major Downing was the pen name of Seba Smith (1792–1868) whose satirical letters in the Portland *Courier* were great favorites of the reading public.

[71] Page 331, lines 14–15 from bottom, sub-treasury: The sub-

treasury plan passed in the Van Buren administration required government funds to be placed in federal depositories located in various cities around the country, thus ending federal participation in private banking.

[72] Page 380, line 6, Mr. Niles: Hezekiah Niles (1777–1839), the founder and editor of the Baltimore *Niles' Weekly Register.*

[73] Page 381, line 7, Mr. James G. King: James Gore King (1791–1853), son of Rufus King and promoter and president of the Erie Railroad, later served as U.S. Representative from New Jersey, 1849–1851.

[74] Page 386, line 17, Judge Bouldin: Thomas T. Bouldin (1781–1834), U.S. Representative from Virginia 1829–1833 and an unsuccessful candidate for reelection. However, he was appointed to fill the vacancy occasioned by the death of John Randolph. He served from August 1833 until his death while addressing the House in February 1834.

[75] Page 386, line 9 from bottom, General Blair: James Blair (c. 1790–1834), U.S. Representative from South Carolina, 1821–1822, 1829–1834.

[76] Page 392, line 9, the whigs: The Whig party was the successor of the National Republican party, emerging in 1834. It was a coalition of anti-Jackson factions which opposed strong executive leadership and was led by such men as Henry Clay and Daniel Webster.

[77] Page 414, line 8 from bottom, Lieutenant Gedney: Thomas R. Gedney.

[78] Page 415, line 1, Lawrence: Richard Lawrence.

[79] Page 416, line 11 from bottom, Ravaillac: François Ravaillac (1578–1610), assassin of King Henry IV of France.

[80] Page 417, line 2, Mr. Garrison: William Lloyd Garrison (1805–1879), the noted abolitionist and editor of the *Liberator.*

[81] Page 417, line 3, Mr. Lovejoy: Elijah P. Lovejoy (1802–1837) advocated in his newspaper the immediate abolition of slavery. He was killed while guarding his presses from a rampaging mob.

[82] Page 430, line 2, my son: Andrew Jackson, Jr., adopted by Rachel and Andrew Jackson in 1810, was the son of Severn Donelson.

[83] Page 431, line 12 from bottom, Miss Kemble: Fanny Kemble (1809–1893), the distinguished English actress who toured America in 1832 and later married Pierce Butler of Philadelphia.

[84] Page 436, line 20, Mr. Buchanan: James Buchanan (1791–1868), U.S. Representative from Pennsylvania 1821–1831, minister to Russia 1832–1833, and U.S. Senator 1834–1845.

[85] Page 437, line 8 from bottom, Maine boundary question: A dispute between the United States and Great Britain resulting from the Treaty of 1783 (which ended the American Revolution) over the precise location of the boundary between Maine and Canada.

[86] Page 442, line 13 from bottom, Fort Mims: Fort Mims, Alabama, the scene of a massacre of white settlers by Creek Indians in August 1813. This action triggered the Creek War which ended with Jackson's great victory at Horseshoe Bend.

[87] Page 442, lines 11–12 from bottom, affray with the Bentons: When Jackson was summoned by the Governor of Tennessee to lead volunteers against the Creeks after the Fort Mims massacre, he was recovering from a gunfight with Thomas Hart Benton and Jesse Benton.

[88] Page 447, line 1, Truxton: Jackson's famous racehorse.

THOMAS C. COCHRAN: The American Business System: *A Historical Perspective, 1900-1955* TB/1080
ROBERT L. HEILBRONER: The Limits of American Capitalism TB/1305
FRANK H. KNIGHT: Risk, Uncertainty and Profit TB/1215
ABBA P. LERNER: Everybody's Business TB/3051
HERBERT SIMON: The Shape of Automation TB/1245

Historiography & Philosophy of History

JACOB BURCKHARDT: On History and Historians. △ *Intro. by H. R. Trevor-Roper* TB/1216
H. STUART HUGHES: History as Art and as Science: *Twin Vistas on the Past* TB/1207
ARNALDO MOMIGLIANO: Studies in Historiography TB/1288
GEORGE H. NADEL, Ed.: Studies in the Philosophy of History: *Essays from* History and Theory TB/1208
KARL R. POPPER: The Open Society and Its Enemies △ Vol. I TB/1101; Vol. II TB/1102
KARL R. POPPER: The Poverty of Historicism ° △ TB/1126
G. J. RENIER: History: Its Purpose and Method △ TB/1209
W. H. WALSH: Philosophy of History △ TB/1020

History: General

L. CARRINGTON GOODRICH: A Short History of the Chinese People. △ *Illus.* TB/3015
DAN N. JACOBS & HANS H. BAERWALD: Chinese Communism: *Selected Documents* TB/3031
BERNARD LEWIS: The Arabs in History △ TB/1029
BERNARD LEWIS: Middle East and West ° △ TB/1274

History: Ancient and Medieval

HELEN CAM: England before Elizabeth △ TB/1026
NORMAN COHN: The Pursuit of the Millennium △ TB/1037
CHRISTOPHER DAWSON, Ed.: Mission to Asia △ TB/315
ADOLF ERMAN, Ed.: The Ancient Egyptians TB/1233
GALBERT OF BRUGES: The Murder of Charles the Good. *Trans. and ed. by J. B. Ross* TB/1311
F. L. GANSHOF: Feudalism △ TB/1058
DENO GEANAKOPLOS: Byzantine East and Latin West △ TB/1265
DENYS HAY: Europe: Emergence of an Idea TB/1275
DENYS HAY: The Medieval Centuries ° △ TB/1192
SAMUEL NOAH KRAMER: Sumerian Mythology TB/1055
NAPHTALI LEWIS & MEYER REINHOLD, Eds.: Roman Civilization Vol. I TB/1231; Vol. II TB/1232
MARSILIUS OF PADUA: The Defender of the Peace. *Trans. and ed. by Alan Gewirth* TB/1310
CHARLES PETIT-DUTAILLIS: The Feudal Monarchy in France and England ° △ TB/1165
HENRI PIRENNE: Early Democracies in the Low Countries TB/1110
STEVEN RUNCIMAN: A History of the Crusades. △ *Vol. I* TB/1143; *Vol. II* TB/1243; *Vol. III* TB/1298

History: Renaissance & Reformation

JACOB BURCKHARDT: The Civilization of the Renaissance in Italy △ Vol. I TB/40; Vol. II TB/41
JOHN CALVIN & JACOPO SADOLETO: A Reformation Debate. *Edited by John C. Olin* TB/1239
G. CONSTANT: The Reformation in England △ TB/314
G. R. ELTON: Reformation Europe, 1517-1559 ** ° △ TB/1270
J. H. HEXTER: More's Utopia: *The Biography of an Idea. New Epilogue by the Author* TB/1195
HAJO HOLBORN: Ulrich von Hutten and the German Reformation TB/1238
JOEL HURSTFIELD, Ed.: The Reformation Crisis △ TB/1267
ULRICH VON HUTTEN et al.: On the Eve of the Reformation. *"Letters of Obscure Men." Introduction by Hajo Holborn* TB/1124
ROBERT LATOUCHE: The Birth of Western Economy TB/1290
J. E. NEALE: The Age of Catherine de Medici ° △ TB/1085
ERWIN PANOFSKY: Studies in Iconology △ TB/1077
J. H. PLUMB: The Italian Renaissance △ TB/1161
A. F. POLLARD: Henry VIII ° △ TB/1249
A. F. POLLARD: Wolsey ° △ TB/1248
A. L. ROWSE: The Expansion of Elizabethan England. ° △ *Illus.* TB/1220
G. M. TREVELYAN: England in the Age of Wycliffe, 1368-1520 ° △ TB/1112
VESPASIANO: Renaissance Princes, Popes, and Prelates: *The Vespasiano Memoirs* TB/1111

History: Modern European

MAX BELOFF: The Age of Absolutism, 1660-1815 △ TB/1062
ASA BRIGGS: The Making of Modern England, 1784-1867: *The Age of Improvement* ° △ TB/1203
CRANE BRINTON: A Decade of Revolution, 1789-1799. * *Illus.* TB/3018
D. W. BROGAN: The Development of Modern France. ° △ Vol. I TB/1184; Vol. II TB/1185
J. BRONOWSKI & BRUCE MAZLISH: The Western Intellectual Tradition: *From Leonardo to Hegel* △ TB/3001
ALAN BULLOCK: Hitler, A Study in Tyranny ° △ TB/1123
E. H. CARR: German-Soviet Relations Between the Two World Wars, 1919-1939 TB/1278
E. H. CARR: International Relations Between the Two World Wars, 1919-1939 ° △ TB/1279
E. H. CARR: The Twenty Years' Crisis, 1919-1939 ° △ TB/1122
GORDON A. CRAIG: Bismarck to Adenauer TB/1171
DENIS DIDEROT: The Encyclopedia: *Selections* TB/1299
FRANKLIN L. FORD: Robe and Sword: *The Regrouping of the French Aristocracy after Louis XIV* TB/1217
RENÉ FUELOEP-MILLER: The Mind and Face of Bolshevism TB/1188
LIONEL KOCHAN: The Struggle for Germany: *1914-45* TB/1304
HANS KOHN, Ed.: The Mind of Modern Russia TB/1065
WALTER LAQUEUR & GEORGE L. MOSSE, Eds.: International Fascism, 1920-1945 ° △ TB/1276
WALTER LAQUEUR & GEORGE L. MOSSE, Eds.: The Left-Wing Intellectuals between the Wars, 1919-1939 ° △ TB/1286
WALTER LAQUEUR & GEORGE L. MOSSE, Eds.: 1914: *The Coming of the First World War* ° △ TB/1306
FRANK E. MANUEL: The Prophets of Paris TB/1218
L. B. NAMIER: Facing East △ TB/1280
L. B. NAMIER: Personalities and Powers △ TB/1186
FRANZ NEUMANN: Behemoth TB/1289
DAVID OGG: Europe of the Ancien Régime, 1715-1783 ** ° △ TB/1271
PENFIELD ROBERTS: The Quest for Security, 1715-1740. * *Illus.* TB/3016
GEORGE RUDÉ: Revolutionary Europe, 1783-1815 ** ° △ TB/1272
LOUIS, DUC DE SAINT-SIMON: Versailles, The Court, and Louis XIV △ TB/1250
A. J. P. TAYLOR: From Napoleon to Lenin: *Historical Essays* ° △ TB/1268
A. J. P. TAYLOR: The Habsburg Monarchy, 1809-1918 ° △ TB/1187
G. M. TREVELYAN: British History in the Nineteenth Century and After: 1782-1919 △ TB/1251
H. R. TREVOR-ROPER: Historical Essays ° △ TB/1269
ELIZABETH WISKEMANN: Europe of the Dictators, 1919-1945 ** ° △ TB/1273

Intellectual History & History of Ideas

ERNST CASSIRER: The Individual and the Cosmos in Renaissance Philosophy △ TB/1097
FRANK E. MANUEL: The Prophets of Paris TB/1218
W. WARREN WAGAR, Ed.: European Intellectual History since Darwin and Marx TB/1297
PHILIP P. WIENER: Evolution and the Founders of Pragmatism. △ *Foreword by John Dewey* TB/1212

Literature, Poetry, The Novel & Criticism

JAMES BOSWELL: The Life of Dr. Johnson & The Journal of a Tour to the Hebrides with Samuel Johnson LL.D.: *Selections* ° △ TB/1254
RICHMOND LATTIMORE: The Poetry of Greek Tragedy △ TB/1257
J. B. LEISHMAN: The Monarch of Wit: *Study of the Poetry of John Donne* ° △ TB/1258
J. B. LEISHMAN: Themes and Variations in Shakespeare's Sonnets ° △ TB/1259
V. DE S. PINTO: Crisis in English Poetry, 1880-1940 ° △ TB/1260
ROBERT PREYER, Ed.: Victorian Literature TB/1302
C. K. STEAD: The New Poetic: *Yeats to Eliot* ° △ TB/1263
BASIL WILLEY: Nineteenth Century Studies: *Coleridge to Matthew Arnold* ° △ TB/1261
BASIL WILLEY: More Nineteenth Century Studies: *A Group of Honest Doubters* ° △ TB/1262
RAYMOND WILLIAMS: Culture and Society, 1780-1950 △ TB/1252
RAYMOND WILLIAMS: The Long Revolution △ TB/1253

Philosophy

G. E. M. ANSCOMBE: An Introduction to Wittgenstein's Tractatus. ° △ *Second edition, Revised* TB/1210
HENRI BERGSON: Time and Free Will ° △ TB/1021
FREDERICK COPLESTON: Medieval Philosophy ° △ TB/376
F. M. CORNFORD: Principium Sapientiae TB/1213
MARVIN FARBER: The Aims of Phenomenology TB/1291
MARVIN FARBER: Phenomenology and Existence TB/1295
PAUL FRIEDLÄNDER: Plato: *An Introduction* △ TB/2017
J. GLENN GRAY: The Warriors: *Reflections on Men in Battle* TB/1294
W. K. C. GUTHRIE: The Greek Philosophers ° △ TB/1008
G. W. F. HEGEL: The Phenomenology of Mind ° △ TB/1303
EDMUND HUSSERL: Phenomenology and the Crisis of Philosophy TB/1170
IMMANUEL KANT: The Doctrine of Virtue TB/110
IMMANUEL KANT: Lectures on Ethics § △ TB/105
QUENTIN LAUER: Phenomenology TB/1169
GABRIEL MARCEL: Being and Having △ TB/310
GEORGE A. MORGAN: What Nietzsche Means TB/1198
MICHAEL POLANYI: Personal Knowledge △ TB/1158
WILLARD VAN ORMAN QUINE: Elementary Logic. *Revised Edition* TB/577
WILLARD VAN ORMAN QUINE: From a Logical Point of View: *Logico-Philosophical Essays* TB/566
BERTRAND RUSSELL et al.: The Philosophy of Bertrand Russell Vol. I TB/1095; Vol. II TB/1096
L. S. STEBBING: A Modern Introduction to Logic △ TB/538
WILHELM WINDELBAND: A History of Philosophy Vol. I TB/38; Vol. II TB/39
LUDWIG WITTGENSTEIN: Blue and Brown Books ° TB/1211

Political Science & Government

KENNETH E. BOULDING: Conflict and Defense TB/3024
CRANE BRINTON: English Political Thought in the Nineteenth Century TB/1071
ROBERT CONQUEST: Power and Policy in the USSR TB/1307
F. L. GANSHOF: Feudalism △ TB/1058
SIDNEY HOOK: Reason, Social Myths and Democracy △ TB/1237
DAN N. JACOBS, Ed.: The New Communist Manifesto & *Related Documents. Third edition, Revised* TB/1078
HANS KOHN: Political Ideologies of the 20th Century TB/1277
ROBERTO MICHELS: First Lectures in Political Sociology. *Edited by Alfred de Grazia* ¶ ° △ TB/1224
BARRINGTON MOORE, JR.: Political Power and Social Theory: *Seven Studies* ¶ TB/1221
BARRINGTON MOORE, JR.: Soviet Politics—The Dilemma of Power ¶ TB/1222
BARRINGTON MOORE, JR.: Terror and Progress—USSR ¶ TB/1266
KARL R. POPPER: The Open Society and Its Enemies △ Vol. I TB/1101; Vol. II TB/1102
BENJAMIN I. SCHWARTZ: Chinese Communism and the Rise of Mao TB/1308
PETER WOLL, Ed.: Public Administration and Policy TB/1284

Psychology

ALFRED ADLER: The Individual Psychology of Alfred Adler △ TB/1154
ARTHUR BURTON & ROBERT E. HARRIS, Editors: Clinical Studies of Personality Vol. I TB/3075; Vol. II TB/3076
HADLEY CANTRIL: Invasion from Mars TB/1282
SIGMUND FREUD: On Creativity and the Unconscious § △ TB/45
C. G. JUNG: Symbols of Transformation △ Vol. I: TB/2009; Vol. II TB/2010
KARL MENNINGER: Theory of Psychoanalytic Technique TB/1144
MUZAFER SHERIF: The Psychology of Social Norms TB/3072

Sociology

JACQUES BARZUN: Race: *A Study in Superstition* TB/1172
BERNARD BERELSON, Ed.: The Behavioral Sciences Today TB/1127
LEWIS A. COSER, Ed.: Political Sociology TB/1293
RICHARD M. JONES, Ed.: Contemporary Educational Psychology TB/1292
R. M. MAC IVER: Social Causation TB/1153
ROBERT K. MERTON, LEONARD BROOM, LEONARD S. COTTRELL, JR., Editors: Sociology Today: *Problems and Prospects* ¶ Vol. I TB/1173; Vol. II TB/1174
ARNOLD ROSE: The Negro in America TB/3048
PHILIP SELZNICK: TVA and the Grass Roots TB/1230
GEORG SIMMEL et al.: Essays on Sociology, Philosophy, and Aesthetics. ¶ *Edited by Kurt H. Wolff* TB/1234
HERBERT SIMON: The Shape of Automation △ TB/1245

RELIGION

Ancient & Classical

HENRI FRANKFORT: Ancient Egyptian Religion TB/77
G. RACHEL LEVY: Religious Conceptions of the Stone Age *and their Influence upon European Thought* △ TB/106
MARTIN P. NILSSON: Greek Folk Religion TB/78
ERWIN ROHDE: Psyche △ Vol. I TB/140; Vol. II TB/141
H. J. ROSE: Religion in Greece and Rome △ TB/55

Biblical Thought & Literature

W. F. ALBRIGHT: The Biblical Period from Abraham to Ezra TB/102
C. K. BARRETT, Ed.: The New Testament Background: *Selected Documents* △ TB/86
C. H. DODD: The Authority of the Bible △ TB/43
GEORGE ADAM SMITH: Historical Geography of the Holy Land TB/138
WALTHER ZIMMERLI: The Law and the Prophets: *A Study of the Meaning of the Old Testament* △ TB/144

The Judaic Tradition

MARTIN BUBER: Eclipse of God △ TB/12
MARTIN BUBER: Hasidism and Modern Man TB/839
MARTIN BUBER: Moses △ TB/837
MARTIN BUBER: Pointing the Way △ TB/103
MARTIN BUBER: The Prophetic Faith TB/73
MARTIN BUBER: Two Types of Faith ° △ TB/75
SOLOMON GRAYZEL: A History of the Contemporary Jews TB/816
JOSHUA TRACHTENBERG: The Devil and the Jews: *The Medieval Conception of the Jew and its Relation to Modern Anti-Semitism* TB/822

Christianity: Origins & Early Development

AUGUSTINE: An Augustine Synthesis △ TB/335
ADOLF DEISSMANN: Paul TB/15
EDWARD GIBBON: The Triumph of Christendom in the Roman Empire § △ *Illus.* TB/46
MAURICE GOGUEL: Jesus and the Origins of Christianity. ° △ Vol. I: TB/65; Vol. II: TB/66
EDGAR J. GOODSPEED: A Life of Jesus TB/1
ROBERT M. GRANT: Gnosticism and Early Christianity △ TB/136
ORIGEN: On First Principles △ TB/311
SULPICIUS SEVERUS et al.: The Western Fathers △ TB/309

Christianity: The Middle Ages and The Reformation

ANSELM OF CANTERBURY: Truth, Freedom and Evil: *Three Philosophical Dialogues* TB/317
JOHN CALVIN & JACOPO SADOLETO: A Reformation Debate. *Edited by John C. Olin* TB/1239
G. CONSTANT: The Reformation in England △ TB/314

Christianity: The Protestant Tradition

KARL BARTH: Dogmatics in Outline △ TB/56
RUDOLF BULTMANN et al.: Translating Theology into the Modern Age TB/252
SOREN KIERKEGAARD: On Authority and Revelation TB/139
SOREN KIERKEGAARD: Crisis in the Life of an Actress *and Other Essays on Drama.* △ *Trans. S. D. Crites* TB/145
SOREN KIERKEGAARD: The Journals ° △ TB/52
SOREN KIERKEGAARD: The Present Age § △ TB/94
SOREN KIERKEGAARD: Purity of Heart △ TB/4
SOREN KIERKEGAARD: Repetition △ TB/117
SOREN KIERKEGAARD: Works of Love △ TB/122
JOHN MACQUARRIE: The Scope of Demythologizing: *Bultmann and his Critics* △ TB/134
JAMES M. ROBINSON et al.: The Bultmann School of Biblical Interpretation: New Directions? TB/251
F. SCHLEIERMACHER: The Christian Faith △ Vol. I TB/108; Vol. II TB/109
PAUL TILLICH: Dynamics of Faith △ TB/42

Christianity: The Roman and Eastern Traditions

DOM CUTHBERT BUTLER: Western Mysticism § ° △ TB/312
A. ROBERT CAPONIGRI, Ed.: Modern Catholic Thinkers △ Vol. I TB/306; Vol. II TB/307
G. P. FEDOTOV: The Russian Religious Mind: *Kievan Christianity, the 10th to the 13th Centuries* TB/370
G. P. FEDOTOV, Ed.: A Treasury of Russian Spirituality TB/303
ÉTIENNE GILSON: The Spirit of Thomism TB/313
DAVID KNOWLES: The English Mystical Tradition TB/302
GABRIEL MARCEL: Being and Having TB/310
GABRIEL MARCEL: Homo Viator TB/397
FRANCIS DE SALES: Introduction to the Devout Life TB/316
GUSTAVE WEIGEL, S. J.: Catholic Theology in Dialogue TB/301

Oriental Religions: Far Eastern, Near Eastern

TOR ANDRAE: Mohammed § △ TB/62
EDWARD CONZE: Buddhism ° △ TB/58
ANANDA COOMARASWAMY: Buddha and the Gospel of Buddhism. △ *Illus.* TB/119
H. G. CREEL: Confucius and the Chinese Way TB/63
FRANKLIN EDGERTON, Trans. & Ed.: The Bhagavad Gita TB/115
SWAMI NIKHILANANDA, Trans. & Ed.: The Upanishads: *A One-Volume Abridgment* △ TB/114

Philosophy of Religion

NICOLAS BERDYAEV: Christian Existentialism △ TB/130
RUDOLF BULTMANN: History and Eschatology ° TB/91
RUDOLF BULTMANN & 5 CRITICS: Kerygma and Myth △ TB/80
MIRCEA ELIADE: The Sacred and the Profane TB/81
LUDWIG FEUERBACH: The Essence of Christianity § TB/11
IMMANUEL KANT: Religion Within the Limits of Reason Alone. § *Intro. by T. M. Greene & J. Silber* TB/67
K. E. KIRK: The Vision of God § △ TB/137
JOHN MACQUARRIE: An Existentialist Theology: *A Comparison of Heidegger and Bultmann* ° △ TB/125
EUGEN ROSENSTOCK-HUESSY: The Christian Future *or the Modern Mind Outrun* TB/143
PIERRE TEILHARD DE CHARDIN: Divine Milieu ° △ TB/384
PIERRE TEILHARD DE CHARDIN: Phenomenon of Man ° △ TB/383
PAUL TILLICH: Morality and Beyond TB/142

NATURAL SCIENCES AND MATHEMATICS

Biological Sciences

CHARLOTTE AUERBACH: Science of Genetics Σ △ TB/568
LUDWIG VON BERTALANFFY: Problems of Life △ TB/521
HAROLD F. BLUM: Time's Arrow and Evolution TB/555
JOHN TYLER BONNER: The Ideas of Biology Σ △ TB/570
O. W. RICHARDS: The Social Insects. △ *Illus.* TB/542
P. M. SHEPPARD: Natural Selection and Heredity △ TB/528
C. H. WADDINGTON: How Animals Develop. △ *Illus.* TB/553
C. H. WADDINGTON: The Nature of Life △ TB/580

Geography

R. E. COKER: The Great and Wide Sea: *An Introduction to Oceanography and Marine Biology. Illus.* TB/551
F. K. HARE: The Restless Atmosphere △ TB/560

History of Science

MARIE BOAS: The Scientific Renaissance, 1450-1630 △ TB/583
O. NEUGEBAUER: The Exact Sciences in Antiquity TB/552
STEPHEN TOULMIN & JUNE GOODFIELD: Architecture of Matter ° △ TB/584
STEPHEN TOULMIN & JUNE GOODFIELD: Discovery of Time ° △ TB/585
LANCELOT LAW WHYTE: Essay on Atomism △ TB/565

Mathematics

E. W. BETH: The Foundations of Mathematics △ TB/581
H. DAVENPORT: The Higher Arithmetic △ TB/526
D. E. LITTLEWOOD: Skeleton Key of Mathematics: *A Simple Account of Complex Algebraic Problems* △ TB/525
GEORGE E. OWEN: Fundamentals of Scientific Mathematics TB/569
WILLARD VAN ORMAN QUINE: Mathematical Logic TB/558
FREDERICK WAISMANN: Introduction to Mathematical Thinking. *Foreword by Karl Menger* TB/511

Philosophy of Science

J. BRONOWSKI: Science and Human Values △ TB/505
ALBERT EINSTEIN et al.: Albert Einstein: Philosopher-Scientist Vol. I TB/502; Vol. II TB/503
JOHN MAYNARD KEYNES: A Treatise on Probability. ° △ *Introduction by N. R. Hanson* TB/557
KARL R. POPPER: Logic of Scientific Discovery △ TB/576
STEPHEN TOULMIN: Foresight and Understanding △ TB/564
G. J. WHITROW: Natural Philosophy of Time ° △ TB/563

Physics and Cosmology

JOHN E. ALLEN: Aerodynamics △ TB/582
STEPHEN TOULMIN & JUNE GOODFIELD: The Fabric of the Heavens: *The Development of Astronomy and Dynamics.* △ *Illus.* TB/579
DAVID BOHM: Causality and Chance in Modern Physics. △ *Foreword by Louis de Broglie* TB/536
P. W. BRIDGMAN: Nature of Thermodynamics TB/537
C. V. DURELL: Readable Relativity △ TB/530
ARTHUR EDDINGTON: Space, Time and Gravitation TB/510
MAX JAMMER: Concepts of Space TB/533